BENTLEY'S

MISCELLANY.

VOL. II.

LONDON:

RICHARD BENTLEY,

NEW BURLINGTON STREET.

1837.

LONDON :
PRINTED BY SAMUEL BENTLEY,
Dorset Street, Fleet Street.

Bentley's Miscellany, Volume 2

Richard Bentley

ADDRESS.

TWELVE months have elapsed since we first took the field, and every successive number of our Miscellany has experienced a warmer reception, and a more extensive circulation, than its predecessor.

In the opening of the new year, and the commencement of our new volume, we hope to make many changes for the better, and none for the worse; and, to show that, while we have one grateful eye to past patronage, we have another wary one to future favours; in short, that, like the heroine of the sweet poem descriptive of the faithlessness and perjury of Mr. John Oakhum, of the Royal Navy, we look two ways at once.

It is our intention to usher in the new year with a very merry greeting, towards the accomplishment of which end we have prevailed upon a long procession of distinguished friends to mount their hobbies on the occasion, in humble imitation of those adventurous and aldermanic spirits who gallantly bestrode their foaming chargers on the memorable ninth of this present month, while

"The stones did rattle underneath,
    As if Cheapside were mad."

These, and a hundred other great designs, preparations, and surprises, are in contemplation, for the fulfilment of all of which we are already bound in two volumes cloth, and have no objection, if it be any additional security to the public, to stand bound in twenty more.

BOZ.

30th November, 1837.

CONTENTS

OF THE

SECOND VOLUME.

Page

CONTENTS.

ILLUSTRATIONS.

BY GEORGE CRUIKSHANK.

BENTLEY'S MISCELLANY.

SONG OF THE MONTH. No. VII.
July, 1837.

BEING A BAPTISMAL CHAUNT FOR THE BIRTH OF OUR SECOND
VOLUME, AS SUNG (IN CHARACTER) BY FATHER PROUT.

(Tune " *The groves of Blarney.*")

" Ille ego qui quondam," &c. &c.—*Æneid.*

I.

In the month of Janus,
When Boz to gain us,
Quite " miscellaneous,"
  Flashed his wit so keen,
One, (Prout they call him,)
In style most solemn,
Led off the volume
  Of his magazine.

II.

Though MAGA, 'mongst her
Bright set of youngsters,
Had many songsters
  For her opening tome;
Yet she would rather
Invite " the Father,"
And an indulgence gather
  From the Pope of Rome.

III.

And, such a beauty
From head to shoe-tie,
Without dispute we
  Found her first boy,
That she determined,
There 's such a charm in 't,
The Father's *sarmint*
  She 'd again employ.

IV.

While other children
Are quite bewilderin',
'Tis joy that fill'd her in
  This bantling; 'cause
What eye but glistens,
And what ear but listens,
When the clargy christens
  A babe of Boz?

V.

I 've got a scruple
That this young pupil
Surprised its parent
  Ere her time was sped;
Else I 'm unwary,
Or, 'tis she 's a fairy,
For in January
  She was brought to bed.

VI.

This infant may be
A six months' baby,
But may his cradle
  Be blest! say I;
And luck defend him!
And joy attend him!
Since we can't mend him,
  Born in July.

VII.

He 's no abortion,
But born to fortune,
And most opportune,
  Though before his time;
Him, Muse, O! nourish,
And make him flourish
Quite Tommy-Moorish
  Both in prose and rhyme!

VIII.

I remember, also,
That this month they call so,
From Roman JULIUS
  The " *Cæsarian* " styled;
Who was no gosling,
But, like this Boz-ling,
From birth a dazzling
  And precocious child!

GOD SAVE THE QUEEN!

OLIVER TWIST;

OR, THE PARISH BOY'S PROGRESS.

BY BOZ.

ILLUSTRATED BY GEORGE CRUIKSHANK.

CHAPTER THE NINTH.

CONTAINING FURTHER PARTICULARS CONCERNING THE PLEASANT OLD
GENTLEMAN, AND HIS HOPEFUL PUPILS.

It was late next morning when Oliver awoke from a sound, long sleep. There was nobody in the room beside, but the old Jew, who was boiling some coffee in a saucepan for breakfast, and whistling softly to himself as he stirred it round and round with an iron spoon. He would stop every now and then to listen when there was the least noise below; and, when he had satisfied himself, he would go on whistling and stirring again, as before.

Although Oliver had roused himself from sleep, he was not thoroughly awake. There is a drowsy, heavy state, between sleeping and waking, when you dream more in five minutes with your eyes half open, and yourself half conscious of everything that is passing around you, than you would in five nights with your eyes fast closed, and your senses wrapt in perfect unconsciousness. At such times, a mortal knows just enough of what his mind is doing to form some glimmering conception of its mighty powers, its bounding from earth and spurning time and space, when freed from the irksome restraint of its corporeal associate.

Oliver was precisely in the condition I have described. He saw the Jew with his half-closed eyes, heard his low whistling, and recognised the sound of the spoon grating against the saucepan's sides; and yet the self-same senses were mentally engaged at the same time, in busy action with almost everybody he had ever known.

When the coffee was done, the Jew drew the saucepan to the hob, and, standing in an irresolute attitude for a few minutes as if he did not well know how to employ himself, turned round and looked at Oliver, and called him by his name. He did not answer, and was to all appearance asleep.

After satisfying himself upon this head, the Jew stepped gently to the door, which he fastened; he then drew forth, as it seemed to Oliver, from some trap in the floor, a small box, which he placed carefully on the table. His eyes glistened as he raised the lid and looked in. Dragging an old chair to the table, he sat down, and took from it a magnificent gold watch, sparkling with diamonds.

George Cruikshank

London Richard Bentley July 1 18

"Aha!" said the Jew, shrugging up his shoulders, and distorting every feature with a hideous grin. "Clever dogs! clever dogs! Staunch to the last! Never told the old parson where they were; never peached upon old Fagin. And why should they? It wouldn't have loosened the knot, or kept the drop up a minute longer. No, no, no! Fine fellows! fine fellows!"

With these, and other muttered reflections of the like nature, the Jew once more deposited the watch in its place of safety. At least half a dozen more were severally drawn forth from the same box, and surveyed with equal pleasure; besides rings, brooches, bracelets, and other articles of jewellery, of such magnificent materials and costly workmanship that Oliver had no idea even of their names.

Having replaced these trinkets, the Jew took out another, so small that it lay in the palm of his hand. There seemed to be some very minute inscription on it, for the Jew laid it flat upon the table, and, shading it with his hand, pored over it long and earnestly. At length he set it down as if despairing of success, and, leaning back in his chair, muttered,

"What a fine thing capital punishment is! Dead men never repent; dead men never bring awkward stories to light. The prospect of the gallows, too, makes them hardy and bold. Ah, it's a fine thing for the trade! Five of them strung up in a row, and none left to play booty or turn white-livered!"

As the Jew uttered these words, his bright dark eyes which had been staring vacantly before him, fell on Oliver's face; the boy's eyes were fixed on his in mute curiosity, and, although the recognition was only for an instant—for the briefest space of time that can possibly be conceived,—it was enough to show the old man that he had been observed. He closed the lid of the box with a loud crash, and, laying his hand on a bread-knife which was on the table, started furiously up. He trembled very much though; for, even in his terror, Oliver could see that the knife quivered in the air.

"What's that?" said the Jew. "What do you watch me for? Why are you awake? What have you seen? Speak out, boy! Quick—quick! for your life!"

"I wasn't able to sleep any longer, sir," replied Oliver, meekly. "I am very sorry if I have disturbed you, sir."

"You were not awake an hour ago?" said the Jew, scowling fiercely on the boy.

"No—no, indeed, sir," replied Oliver.

"Are you sure?" cried the Jew, with a still fiercer look than before, and a threatening attitude.

"Upon my word I was not, sir," replied Oliver, earnestly. "I was not, indeed, sir."

"Tush, tush, my dear!" said the Jew, suddenly resuming his old manner, and playing with the knife a little before he laid it down, as if to induce the belief that he had caught it up in mere sport. "Of course I know that, my dear. I only tried to frighten you. You 're a brave boy. Ha! ha! you 're a brave boy, Oliver!" and the Jew rubbed his hands with a chuckle, but looked uneasily at the box notwithstanding.

"Did you see any of these pretty things, my dear?" said the Jew, laying his hand upon it after a short pause.

"Yes, sir," replied Oliver.

"Ah!" said the Jew, turning rather pale. "They — they 're mine, Oliver; my little property. All I have to live upon in my old age. The folks call me a miser, my dear,—only a miser; that 's all."

Oliver thought the old gentleman must be a decided miser to live in such a dirty place, with so many watches; but, thinking that perhaps his fondness for the Dodger and the other boys cost him a good deal of money, he only cast a deferential look at the Jew, and asked if he might get up.

"Certainly, my dear,—certainly," replied the old gentleman. "Stay. There 's a pitcher of water in the corner by the door. Bring it here, and I 'll give you a basin to wash in, my dear."

Oliver got up, walked across the room, and stooped for one instant to raise the pitcher. When he turned his head, the box was gone.

He had scarcely washed himself and made everything tidy by emptying the basin out of the window, agreeably to the Jew's directions, than the Dodger returned, accompanied by a very sprightly young friend whom Oliver had seen smoking on the previous night, and who was now formally introduced to him as Charley Bates. The four then sat down to breakfast off the coffee and some hot rolls and ham which the Dodger had brought home in the crown of his hat.

"Well," said the Jew, glancing slyly at Oliver, and addressing himself to the Dodger, "I hope you 've been at work this morning, my dears."

"Hard," replied the Dodger.

"As nails," added Charley Bates.

"Good boys, good boys!" said the Jew. "What have *you* got, Dodger?"

"A couple of pocket-books," replied that young gentleman.

"Lined?" inquired the Jew with trembling eagerness.

"Pretty well," replied the Dodger, producing two pocket-books, one green and the other red.

"Not so heavy as they might be," said the Jew, after looking at the insides carefully; "but very neat, and nicely made. Ingenious workman, ain't he, Oliver?"

"Very, indeed, sir," said Oliver. At which Mr. Charles Bates laughed uproariously, very much to the amazement of Oliver, who saw nothing to laugh at, in anything that had passed.

" And what have you got, my dear ?" said Fagin to Charley Bates.

" Wipes," replied Master Bates : at the same time producing four pocket-handkerchiefs.

" Well," said the Jew, inspecting them closely; " they 're very good ones,—very. You haven't marked them well, though, Charley; so the marks shall be picked out with a needle, and we 'll teach Oliver how to do it. Shall us, Oliver, eh ?—Ha! ha! ha!"

" If you please, sir," said Oliver.

" You 'd like to be able to make pocket-handkerchiefs as easy as Charley Bates, wouldn't you, my dear ?" said the Jew.

" Very much indeed, if you 'll teach me, sir," replied Oliver.

Master Bates saw something so exquisitely ludicrous in this reply that he burst into another laugh; which laugh meeting the coffee he was drinking, and carrying it down some wrong channel, very nearly terminated in his premature suffocation.

" He is so jolly green," said Charley when he recovered, as an apology to the company for his unpolite behaviour.

The Dodger said nothing, but he smoothed Oliver's hair down over his eyes, and said he 'd know better by-and-by; upon which the old gentleman, observing Oliver's colour mounting, changed the subject by asking whether there had been much of a crowd at the execution that morning. This made him wonder more and more, for it was plain from the replies of the two boys that they had both been there; and Oliver naturally wondered how they could possibly have found time to be so very industrious.

When the breakfast was cleared away, the merry old gentleman and the two boys played at a very curious and uncommon game, which was performed in this way :—The merry old gentleman, placing a snuff-box in one pocket of his trousers, a note-case in the other, and a watch in his waistcoat-pocket, with a guard-chain round his neck, and sticking a mock diamond pin in his shirt, buttoned his coat tight round him, and, putting his spectacle-case and handkerchief in the pockets, trotted up and down the room with a stick, in imitation of the manner in which old gentlemen walk about the streets every hour in the day. Sometimes he stopped at the fire-place, and sometimes at the door, making belief that he was staring with all his might into shop-windows. At such times he would look constantly round him for fear of thieves, and keep slapping all his pockets in turn, to see that he hadn't lost anything, in such a very funny and natural manner, that Oliver laughed till the tears ran down his face. All this time the two boys followed him closely about, getting out of his sight so nimbly every time he turned round, that it was impossible to follow their motions. At last the Dodger trod upon his toes, or ran upon his boot accidentally, while Charley Bates stumbled up against him behind; and in that one moment they took from him with the most extraordinary rapidity, snuff-box, note-case, watch-guard, chain, shirt-pin, pocket-handkerchief,—even the spectacle-case. If the old gentleman felt a hand in any one of his pockets, he cried out where it was, and then the game began all over again.

When this game had been played a great many times, a couple of young ladies came to see the young gentlemen, one of whom was called Bet and the other Nancy. They wore a good deal of hair, not very neatly turned up behind, and were rather untidy about the shoes and stockings. They were not exactly pretty, perhaps; but they had a great deal of colour in their faces, and looked quite stout and hearty. Being remarkably free and agreeable in their manners, Oliver thought them very nice girls indeed, as there is no doubt they were.

These visiters stopped a long time. Spirits were produced, in consequence of one of the young ladies complaining of a coldness in her inside, and the conversation took a very convivial and improving turn. At length Charley Bates expressed his opinion that it was time to pad the hoof, which it occurred to Oliver must be French for going out; for directly afterwards the Dodger, and Charley, and the two young ladies went away together, having been kindly furnished with money to spend, by the amiable old Jew.

"There, my dear," said Fagin, "that's a pleasant life, isn't it? They have gone out for the day."

"Have they done work, sir?" inquired Oliver.

"Yes," said the Jew; "that is, unless they should unexpectedly come across any when they are out; and they won't neglect it if they do, my dear, depend upon it."

"Make 'em your models, my dear, make 'em your models," said the Jew, tapping the fire-shovel on the hearth to add force to his words; "do everything they bid you, and take their advice in all matters, especially the Dodger's, my dear. He'll be a great man himself, and make you one too, if you take pattern by him. Is my handkerchief hanging out of my pocket, my dear?" said the Jew, stopping short.

"Yes, sir," said Oliver.

"See if you can take it out, without my feeling it, as you saw them do when we were at play this morning."

Oliver held up the bottom of the pocket with one hand as he had seen the Dodger do, and drew the handkerchief lightly out of it with the other.

"Is it gone?" cried the Jew.

"Here it is, sir," said Oliver, showing it in his hand.

"You're a clever boy, my dear," said the playful old gentleman, patting Oliver on the head approvingly; "I never saw a sharper lad. Here's a shilling for you. If you go on in this way, you'll be the greatest man of the time. And now come here, and I'll show you how to take the marks out of the handkerchiefs."

Oliver wondered what picking the old gentleman's pocket in play had to do with his chances of being a great man; but thinking that the Jew, being so much his senior, must know best, followed him quietly to the table, and was soon deeply involved in his new study.

CHAPTER THE TENTH.

OLIVER BECOMES BETTER ACQUAINTED WITH THE CHARACTERS OF HIS NEW ASSOCIATES, AND PURCHASES EXPERIENCE AT A HIGH PRICE. BEING A SHORT BUT VERY IMPORTANT CHAPTER IN THIS HISTORY.

For eight or ten days Oliver remained in the Jew's room, picking the marks out of the pocket-handkerchiefs, (of which a great number were brought home,) and sometimes taking part in the game already described, which the two boys and the Jew played regularly every day. At length he began to languish for the fresh air, and took many occasions of earnestly entreating the old gentleman to allow him to go out to work with his two companions.

Oliver was rendered the more anxious to be actively employed by what he had seen of the stern morality of the old gentleman's character. Whenever the Dodger or Charley Bates came home at night empty-handed, he would expatiate with great vehemence on the misery of idle and lazy habits, and enforce upon them the necessity of an active life by sending them supperless to bed: upon one occasion he even went so far as to knock them both down a flight of stairs; but this was carrying out his virtuous precepts to an unusual extent.

At length one morning Oliver obtained the permission he had so eagerly sought. There had been no handkerchiefs to work upon, for two or three days, and the dinners had been rather meagre. Perhaps these were reasons for the old gentleman's giving his assent; but, whether they were or no, he told Oliver he might go, and placed him under the joint guardianship of Charley Bates and his friend the Dodger.

The three boys sallied out, the Dodger with his coat-sleeves tucked up and his hat cocked as usual, Master Bates sauntering along with his hands in his pockets, and Oliver between them, wondering where they were going, and what branch of manufacture he would be instructed in first.

The pace at which they went was such a very lazy, ill-looking saunter, that Oliver soon began to think his companions were going to deceive the old gentleman, by not going to work at all. The Dodger had a vicious propensity, too, of pulling the caps from the heads of small boys and tossing them down areas; while Charley Bates exhibited some very loose notions concerning the rights of property, by pilfering divers apples and onions from the stalls at the kennel sides, and thrusting them into pockets which were so surprisingly capacious, that they seemed to undermine his whole suit of clothes in every direction. These things looked so bad, that Oliver was on the point of declaring his intention of seeking his way back in the best way he could, when his thoughts were suddenly directed into another channel by a very mysterious change of behaviour on the part of the Dodger.

They were just emerging from a narrow court not far from the open square in Clerkenwell, which is called, by some strange perversion of terms, "The Green," when the Dodger made a sudden stop, and, laying his finger on his lip, drew his companions back again with the greatest caution and circumspection.

" What 's the matter ?" demanded Oliver.

" Hush !" replied the Dodger. " Do you see that old cove at the book-stall ?"

" The old gentleman over the way ?" said Oliver. " Yes, I see him."

" He 'll do," said the Dodger.

" A prime plant," observed Charley Bates.

Oliver looked from one to the other with the greatest surprise, but was not permitted to make any inquiries, for the two boys walked stealthily across the road, and slunk close behind the old gentleman towards whom his attention had been directed. Oliver walked a few paces after them, and, not knowing whether to advance or retire, stood looking on in silent amazement.

The old gentleman was a very respectable-looking personage, with a powdered head and gold spectacles; dressed in a bottle-green coat with a black velvet collar, and white trousers: with a smart bamboo cane under his arm. He had taken up a book from the stall, and there he stood, reading away as hard as if he were in his elbow-chair in his own study. It was very possible that he fancied himself there, indeed; for it was plain, from his utter abstraction, that he saw not the book-stall, nor the street, nor the boys, nor, in short, anything but the book itself, which he was reading straight through, turning over the leaves when he got to the bottom of a page, beginning at the top line of the next one, and going regularly on with the greatest interest and eagerness.

What was Oliver's horror and alarm as he stood a few paces off, looking on with his eye-lids as wide open as they would possibly go, to see the Dodger plunge his hand into this old gentleman's pocket, and draw from thence a handkerchief, which he handed to Charley Bates, and with which they both ran away round the corner at full speed !

In one instant the whole mystery of the handkerchiefs, and the watches, and the jewels, and the Jew, rushed upon the boy's mind. He stood for a moment with the blood tingling so through all his veins from terror, that he felt as if he were in a burning fire; then, confused and frightened, he took to his heels; and, not knowing what he did, made off as fast as he could lay his feet to the ground.

This was all done in a minute's space, and the very instant that Oliver began to run, the old gentleman, putting his hand to his pocket, and missing his handkerchief, turned sharp round. Seeing the boy scudding away at such a rapid pace, he very naturally concluded him to be the depredator, and, shouting "Stop thief!" with all his might, made off after him, book in hand.

But the old gentleman was not the only person who raised the hue and cry. The Dodger and Master Bates, unwilling to attract public attention by running down the open street, had merely retired into the very first doorway round the corner. They no sooner heard the cry, and saw Oliver running, than, guessing exactly how the matter stood, they issued forth with great promptitude, and, shouting "Stop thief!" too, joined in the pursuit like good citizens.

Although Oliver had been brought up by philosophers, he was not theoretically acquainted with their beautiful axiom that self-preservation is the first law of nature. If he had been, perhaps he would have been prepared for this. Not being prepared, however, it alarmed him the more; so away he went like the wind, with the old gentlemen and the two boys roaring and shouting behind him.

"Stop thief! stop thief!" There is a magic in the sound. The tradesman leaves his counter, and the carman his waggon; the butcher throws down his tray, the baker his basket, the milkman his pail, the errand-boy his parcels, the schoolboy his marbles, the paviour his pick-axe, the child his battledore: away they run, pell-mell, helter-skelter, slap-dash, tearing, yelling, and screaming, knocking down the passengers as they turn the corners, rousing up the dogs, and astonishing the fowls; and streets, squares, and courts re-echo with the sound.

"Stop thief! stop thief!" The cry is taken up by a hundred voices, and the crowd accumulate at every turning. Away they fly, splashing through the mud, and rattling along the pavements; up go the windows, out run the people, onward bear the mob: a whole audience desert Punch in the very thickest of the plot, and, joining the rushing throng, swell the shout, and lend fresh vigour to the cry, "Stop thief! stop thief!"

"Stop thief! stop thief!" There is a passion *for hunting something* deeply implanted in the human breast. One wretched, breathless child, panting with exhaustion, terror in his looks, agony in his eye, large drops of perspiration streaming down his face, strains every nerve to make head upon his pursuers; and as they follow on his track, and gain upon him every instant, they hail his decreasing strength with still louder shouts, and whoop and scream with joy "Stop thief!"—Ay, stop him for God's sake, were it only in mercy!

Stopped at last. A clever blow that. He's down upon the pavement, and the crowd eagerly gather round him ; each new comer jostling and struggling with the others to catch a glimpse. "Stand aside!"—" Give him a little air !"—" Nonsense! he don't deserve it."—" Where's the gentleman ?"—" Here he is, coming down the street."—" Make room there for the gentleman !" —" Is this the boy, sir ?"—" Yes."

Oliver lay covered with mud and dust, and bleeding from the mouth, looking wildly round upon the heap of faces that surrounded him, when the old gentleman was officiously dragged and pushed into the circle by the foremost of the pursuers, and made this reply to their anxious inquiries.

" Yes," said the gentleman in a benevolent voice, " I am afraid it is."

" Afraid !" murmured the crowd. " That's a good un."

" Poor fellow !" said the gentleman, " he has hurt himself."

" I did that, sir," said a great lubberly fellow stepping forward ; " and preciously I cut my knuckle agin' his mouth. I stopped him, sir."

The fellow touched his hat with a grin, expecting something for his pains ; but the old gentleman, eyeing him with an expression of disgust, looked anxiously round, as if he contemplated running away himself ; which it is very possible he might have attempted to do, and thus afforded another chase, had not a police officer (who is always the last person to arrive in such cases) at that moment made his way through the crowd, and seized Oliver by the collar. " Come, get up," said the man roughly.

" It wasn't me indeed, sir. Indeed, indeed, it was two other boys," said Oliver, clasping his hands passionately, and looking round : " they are here somewhere."

" Oh no, they ain't," said the officer. He meant this to be ironical ; but it was true besides, for the Dodger and Charley Bates had filed off down the first convenient court they came to. " Come, get up."

" Don't hurt him," said the old gentleman compassionately.

" Oh no, I won't hurt him," replied the officer, tearing his jacket half off his back in proof thereof. " Come, I know you ; it won't do. Will you stand upon your legs, you young devil ?"

Oliver, who could hardly stand, made a shift to raise himself upon his feet, and was at once lugged along the streets by the jacket-collar at a rapid pace. The gentleman walked on with them by the officer's side ; and as many of the crowd as could, got a little a-head, and stared back at Oliver from time to time. The boys shouted in triumph, and on they went.

CHAPTER THE ELEVENTH

TREATS OF MR. FANG THE POLICE MAGISTRATE, AND FURNISHES A SLIGHT SPECIMEN OF HIS MODE OF ADMINISTERING JUSTICE.

THE offence had been committed within the district, and indeed in the immediate neighbourhood of a very notorious metropolitan police-office. The crowd had only the satisfaction of accompanying Oliver through two or three streets, and down a place called Mutton-hill, when he was led beneath a low archway and up a dirty court into this dispensary of summary justice, by the back way. It was a small paved yard into which they turned; and here they encountered a stout man with a bunch of whiskers on his face, and a bunch of keys in his hand.

" What 's the matter now?" said the man carelessly.

" A young fogle-hunter," replied the man who had Oliver in charge.

" Are you the party that 's been robbed, sir?" inquired the man with the keys.

" Yes, I am," replied the old gentleman; " but I am not sure that this boy actually took the handkerchief. I—I 'd rather not press the case."

" Must go before the magistrate now, sir," replied the man. " His worship will be disengaged in half a minute. Now, young gallows."

This was an invitation for Oliver to enter through a door which he unlocked as he spoke, and which led into a small stone cell. Here he was searched, and, nothing been found upon him, locked up.

This cell was in shape and size something like an area cellar, only not so light. It was most intolerably dirty, for it was Monday morning, and it had been tenanted since Saturday night by six drunken people. But this is nothing. In our station-houses, men and women are every night confined on the most trivial *charges*—the word is worth noting—in dungeons, compared with which, those in Newgate, occupied by the most atrocious felons, tried, found guilty, and under sentence of death, are palaces! Let any man who doubts this, compare the two.

The old gentleman looked almost as rueful as Oliver when the key grated in the lock; and turned with a sigh to the book which had been the innocent cause of all this disturbance.

" There is something in that boy's face," said the old gentleman to himself as he walked slowly away, tapping his chin with the cover of the book in a thoughtful manner, " something that touches and interests me. *Can* he be innocent? He looked like— By the bye," exclaimed the old gentleman, halting very abruptly, and staring up into the sky, " God bless my soul! where have I seen something like that look before?"

After musing for some minutes, the old gentleman walked with the same meditative face into a back ante-room opening from the yard; and there, retiring into a corner, called up before his mind's eye a vast amphitheatre of faces over which a dusky curtain had hung for many years. " No," said the old gentleman, shaking his head ; " it must be imagination."

He wandered over them again. He had called them into view, and it was not easy to replace the shroud that had so long concealed them. There were the face of friends and foes, and of many that had been almost strangers, peering intrusively from the crowd ; there were the faces of young and blooming girls that were now old women ; there were others that the grave had changed to ghastly trophies of death, but which the mind, superior to his power, still dressed in their old freshness and beauty, calling back the lustre of the eyes, the brightness of the smile, the beaming of the soul through its mask of clay, and whispering of beauty beyond the tomb, changed but to be heightened, and taken from earth only to be set up as a light to shed a soft and gentle glow upon the path to Heaven.

But the old gentleman could recall no one countenance of which Oliver's features bore a trace ; so he heaved a sigh over the recollections he had awakened ; and being, happily for himself, an absent old gentleman, buried them again in the pages of the musty book.

He was roused by a touch on the shoulder, and a request from the man with the keys to follow him into the office. He closed his book hastily, and was at once ushered into the imposing presence of the renowned Mr. Fang.

The office was a front parlour, with a panneled wall. Mr. Fang sat behind a bar at the upper end ; and on one side the door was a sort of wooden pen in which poor little Oliver was already deposited, trembling very much at the awfulness of the scene.

Mr. Fang was a middle-sized man, with no great quantity of hair ; and what he had, growing on the back and sides of his head. His face was stern, and much flushed. If he were really not in the habit of drinking rather more than was exactly good for him, he might have brought an action against his countenance for libel, and have recovered heavy damages.

The old gentleman bowed respectfully, and, advancing to the magistrate's desk, said, suiting the action to the word, " That is my name and address, sir." He then withdrew a pace or two ; and, with another polite and gentlemanly inclination of the head, waited to be questioned.

Now, it so happened that Mr. Fang was at that moment perusing a leading article in a newspaper of the morning, adverting to some recent decision of his, and commending him, for the three hundred and fiftieth time, to the special and particular notice of the Secretary of State for the Home Department. He was out of temper, and he looked up with an angry scowl.

" Who are you ?" said Mr. Fang.

The old gentleman pointed with some surprise to his card.

"Officer!" said Mr. Fang, tossing the card contemptuously away with the newspaper, "who is this fellow?"

"My name, sir," said the old gentleman, speaking *like* a gentleman, and consequently in strong contrast to Mr. Fang,— "my name, sir, is Brownlow. Permit me to inquire the name of the magistrate who offers a gratuitous and unprovoked insult to a respectable man, under the protection of the bench." Saying this, Mr. Brownlow looked round the office as if in search of some person who would afford him the required information.

"Officer!" said Mr. Fang, throwing the paper on one side, "what's this fellow charged with?"

"He's not charged at all, your worship," replied the officer. "He appears against the boy, your worship."

His worship knew this perfectly well; but it was a good annoyance, and a safe one.

"Appears against the boy, does he?" said Fang, surveying Mr. Brownlow contemptuously from head to foot. "Swear him."

"Before I am sworn I must beg to say one word," said Mr. Brownlow; "and that is, that I never, without actual experience, could have believed——"

"Hold your tongue, sir!" said Mr. Fang peremptorily.

"I will not, sir!" replied the spirited old gentleman.

"Hold your tongue this instant, or I'll have you turned out of the office!" said Mr. Fang. "You're an insolent impertinent fellow. How dare you bully a magistrate!"

"What!" exclaimed the old gentleman, reddening.

"Swear this person!" said Fang to the clerk. "I'll not hear another word. "Swear him!"

Mr. Brownlow's indignation was greatly roused; but, reflecting that he might only injure the boy by giving vent to it, he suppressed his feelings, and submitted to be sworn at once.

"Now," said Fang, "what's the charge against this boy? What have you got to say, sir?"

"I was standing at a book-stall—" Mr. Brownlow began.

"Hold your tongue, sir!" said Mr. Fang. "Policeman!— where's the policeman? Here, swear this man. Now, policeman, what is this?"

The policeman with becoming humility related how he had taken the charge, how he had searched Oliver and found nothing on his person; and how that was all he knew about it.

"Are there any witnesses?" inquired Mr. Fang.

"None, your worship," replied the policeman.

Mr. Fang sat silent for some minutes, and then, turning round to the prosecutor, said, in a towering passion,

"Do you mean to state what your complaint against this boy is, fellow, or do you not? You have been sworn. Now, if you stand there, refusing to give evidence, I'll punish you for disrespect to the bench; I will, by——"

By what, or by whom, nobody knows, for the clerk and jailer coughed very loud just at the right moment, and the former dropped a heavy book on the floor; thus preventing the word from being heard —accidentally, of course.

With many interruptions, and repeated insults, Mr. Brownlow contrived to state his case; observing that, in the surprise of the moment, he had run after the boy because he saw him running away, and expressing his hope that, if the magistrate should believe him, although not actually the thief, to be connected with thieves, he would deal as leniently with him as justice would allow.

"He has been hurt already," said the old gentleman in conclusion. "And I fear," he added, with great energy, looking towards the bar, —"I really fear that he is very ill."

"Oh! yes; I dare say!" said Mr. Fang, with a sneer. "Come; none of your tricks here, you young vagabond; they won't do. What's your name?"

Oliver tried to reply, but his tongue failed him. He was deadly pale, and the whole place seemed turning round and round.

"What's your name, you hardened scoundrel?" thundered Mr. Fang. "Officer, what's his name?"

This was addressed to a bluff old fellow in a striped waistcoat, who was standing by the bar. He bent over Oliver, and repeated the inquiry; but finding him really incapable of understanding the question, and knowing that his not replying would only infuriate the magistrate the more, and add to the severity of his sentence, he hazarded a guess.

"He says his name's Tom White, your worship," said this kind-hearted thief-taker.

"Oh, he won't speak out, won't he?" said Fang. "Very well, very well. Where does he live?"

"Where he can, your worship," replied the officer, again pretending to receive Oliver's answer.

"Has he any parents?" inquired Mr. Fang.

"He says they died in his infancy, your worship," replied the officer, hazarding the usual reply.

At this point of the inquiry Oliver raised his head, and, looking round with imploring eyes, murmured a feeble prayer for a draught of water.

"Stuff and nonsense!" said Mr. Fang; "don't try to make a fool of me."

"I think he really is ill, your worship," remonstrated the officer.

"I know better," said Mr. Fang.

"Take care of him, officer," said the old gentleman, raising his hands instinctively; "he'll fall down."

"Stand away, officer," cried Fang savagely; "let him if he likes."

Oliver availed himself of the kind permission, and fell heavily to the floor in a fainting fit. The men in the office looked at each other, but no one dared to stir.

"I knew he was shamming," said Fang, as if this were incontestable proof of the fact. "Let him lie; he'll soon be tired of that."

"How do you propose to deal with the case, sir?" inquired the clerk in a low voice.

"Summarily," replied Mr. Fang. "He stands committed for three months,—hard labour of course. Clear the office."

The door was opened for this purpose, and a couple of men were preparing to carry the insensible boy to his cell, when an elderly man of decent but poor appearance, clad in an old suit of black, rushed hastily into the office, and advanced to the bench.

"Stop, stop,—don't take him away,—for Heaven's sake stop a moment," cried the new-comer, breathless with haste.

Although the presiding geniuses in such an office as this, exercise a summary and arbitrary power over the liberties, the good name, the character, almost the lives of his Majesty's subjects, especially of the poorer class, and although within such walls enough fantastic tricks are daily played to make the angels weep thick tears of blood, they are closed to the public, save through the medium of the daily press. Mr. Fang was consequently not a little indignant to see an unbidden guest enter in such irreverent disorder.

"What is this? Who is this? Turn this man out. Clear the office," cried Mr. Fang.

"I will speak," cried the man; "I will not be turned out,—I saw it all. I keep the book-stall. I demand to be sworn. I will not be put down. Mr. Fang, you must hear me. You dare not refuse, sir."

The man was right. His manner was bold and determined, and the matter was growing rather too serious to be hushed up.

"Swear the fellow," growled Fang with a very ill grace. "Now, man, what have you got to say?"

"This," said the man: "I saw three boys—two others and the prisoner here—loitering on the opposite side of the way, when this gentleman was reading. The robbery was committed by another boy. I saw it done, and I saw that this boy was perfectly amazed and stupified by it." Having by this time recovered a little breath, the worthy book-stall keeper proceeded to relate in a more coherent manner the exact circumstances of the robbery.

"Why didn't you come here before?" said Fang after a pause.

"I hadn't a soul to mind the shop," replied the man; "everybody that could have helped me had joined in the pursuit. I could get nobody till five minutes ago, and I've run here all the way."

"The prosecutor was reading, was he?" inquired Fang, after another pause.

"Yes," replied the man, "the very book he has got in his hand."

"Oh, that book, eh?" said Fang. "Is it paid for?"

"No, it is not," replied the man, with a smile.

"Dear me, I forgot all about it!" exclaimed the absent old gentleman, innocently.

"A nice person to prefer a charge against a poor boy!" said Fang, with a comical effort to look humane. "I consider, sir, that you have obtained possession of that book under very suspicious and disreputable circumstances, and you may think yourself very fortunate that the owner of the property declines to prosecute. Let this be a lesson to you, my man, or the law will overtake you yet. The boy is discharged. Clear the office!"

"D—me!" cried the old gentleman, bursting out with the rage he had kept down so long, "d—me! I'll——"

"Clear the office!" roared the magistrate. "Officers, do you hear? Clear the office!"

The mandate was obeyed, and the indignant Mr. Brownlow was

conveyed out, with the book in one hand and the bamboo cane in the other, in a perfect phrenzy of rage and defiance.

He reached the yard, and it vanished in a moment. Little Oliver Twist lay on his back on the pavement, with his shirt unbuttoned and his temples bathed with water: his face a deadly white, and a cold tremble convulsing his whole frame.

"Poor boy, poor boy!" said Mr. Brownlow bending over him. "Call a coach, somebody, pray, directly!"

A coach was obtained, and Oliver, having been carefully laid on one seat, the old gentleman got in and sat himself on the other.

"May I accompany you?" said the book-stall keeper looking in.

"Bless me, yes, my dear friend," said Mr. Brownlow quickly. "I forgot you. Dear, dear! I've got this unhappy book still. Jump in. Poor fellow! there's no time to lose."

The book-stall keeper got into the coach, and away they drove.

ELEGIAC STANZAS.

BY MRS. CORNWELL BARON WILSON.

Why mourn we for her, who in Spring's tender bloom,
 And the sweet blush of womanhood, quitted life's sphere?
Why weep we for her? Thro' the gates of the tomb
 She has pass'd to the regions undimm'd by a tear!

To the spirits' far land in the mansions above,
 Unsullied, thus early her soul wing'd its flight;
While she bask'd in the beams of affection and love,
 And knew not the clouds that oft shadow their light!

Fate's hand pluck'd the bud ere it blossom'd to fame,
 No withering canker its leaflets had known;
The ministering angels her fellowship claim,
 And rejoice o'er a spirit as pure as their own!

While she knew but life's purer and tenderer ties,
 The guardian who watches life's path from our birth
Call'd home the bright being Heav'n form'd for the skies
 Ere its bloom had been ting'd by the follies of earth!

Alas! while the light of her young spirit's flame
 Shone a day-star of Hope to illumine us here,
The messenger-seraph too suddenly came,
 And bore his bright charge to her own native sphere!

Yet mourn not for her, who, in Spring's tender bloom,
 Has made life a desert to those left behind;
Like the rose-leaf, tho' wither'd, still yielding perfume,
 In our hearts, ever fragrant, her memory is shrin'd!

FICTIONS OF THE MIDDLE AGES.

BY DELTA.

THE BUTTERFLY BISHOP.

Amongst the numerous grievances complained of, during the reigns of the Anglo-Norman sovereigns, none gave more uneasiness than the inhuman severity of the forest-laws; they disgusted those nobles not in the confidence of the monarch, oppressed the people, and impoverished the country.

The privilege of hunting in the royal forests was confined to the king and his favourites, who spent the greater portion of their time, not engaged in active warfare, in that diversion; many of them pursued wild beasts with greater fury than they did enemies of their country, and became as savage as the very brutes they hunted.

The punishment for hunting or destroying game in royal forests, or other property belonging to the crown, was very severe: the offender was generally put to death; but, if he could afford to pay an enormous mulct to the king, the sentence was commuted either to dismemberment or tedious imprisonment.

The propensity of the dignified clergy to follow secular pastimes, especially that of hunting, is well known: they were ambitious to surpass the laity in the number and splendid livery of their huntsmen, and to excel in making the woods resound with the echo of their bugles; many of them are recorded for their skill in the aristocratic and manly amusement of the chase. Few persons, however, either ecclesiastic or secular, equalled Peter de Roches, Bishop of Winchester, in his fondness for, and prowess in, the chase.

Peter had spent the prime of his life as a soldier,[*] and having rendered King John essential service in such capacity, that monarch conferred upon him the lucrative office of Bishop of Winchester, and he thenceforth became a curer of souls instead of a destroyer of bodies.

Peter's appointment as a bishop afforded him ample time to devote to the fascinating employment of chasing the " full-acorned boar " and stealthy fox: he thought the hunter's shout, the winding notes of the clanging horn, and the joyous bark of the hounds, much sweeter music than the nasal chaunt of the drowsy monks.

It happened one day that Peter, (who was, according to the Chronicle of Lanercost,[†] a proud and worldly man,—as was too often the case with bishops of that period,) with a bugle dangling at his belt, and mounted upon a fiery steed, attended by a vast retinue of men, horses, and hounds, was in hot pursuit of a wary old fox; his courser, —more fleet than the mountain roe, scarce bruising the grass with his iron-shod hoofs,—like Bucephalus of Macedon, took fright at his own shadow, and became unmanageable; nor were all the skill and spur of the rider able to check his impetuous speed: the harder the bishop pulled, the more unruly became his steed; the bridle now suddenly

* Matthew Paris describes him as " *Vir equestris ordinis, et in rebus bellicis eruditus.*"

† The original words are, " *Idem vir vanus et mundanus, ut nimis inolevit nostris pontificibus.*"

snapped in twain, and the bishop was left to the fate that awaited him. Velocipede, for so the horse was called, now seemed exultingly to bound over the deepest ditches, and to clear the highest thorny-twining hedge with the greatest ease : nothing could moderate his foaming rage ; he resembled more the far-famed Pegasus of Medusan blood, than the palfrey of a gentle bishop.   The retinue, and eager hounds, notwithstanding their utmost endeavour to keep pace with their master, were left far behind.

Peter, having no control over his flying barbary, awaited with truly apostolic calmness and gravity the issue of his wondrous ride, seriously expecting every minute a broken neck or leg; or, per-chance, to have his preaching spoilt by the dislocation of a jaw-bone. —Such thoughts will frequently obtrude themselves into the minds of men encompassed with similar difficulties, let their presence of mind be never so great.

After half an hour's ride in such unepiscopal speed, which can only be compared to that of a steam-engine upon the Manchester railroad, Velocipede suddenly stopped before a magnificent castle with frowning battlements and a gloomy moat. The bishop, won-dering at what he saw, was struck dumb with astonishment; for he well knew that so extensive a castle had not hitherto existed in his diocese, nor did he know of any such in England. Velocipede seem-ed also at his wits' end, and commenced frisking and gamboling about ; and, in making a devotional curvet to the castle, threw the gallant, but unprepared bishop, over his head. Peter was either stunned or entranced by the fall,—whether his senses ever returned the reader must determine for himself when he has perused what follows : the bishop, however, always declared that he was never senseless, and that he could preach as well after, as before his fall.

No sooner was the bishop safely located upon the verdant down by the reverential feelings of the awe-struck Velocipede, than the castle's drawbridge fell, and an aged seneschal, of rubicund-tinted face, with at least fifty liveried lackeys in fanciful suits, ran to assist the bishop, and help him to regain his legs.

By the aid of a restorative cordial the bishop was resuscitated, and, upon coming to himself, was welcomed by the seneschal to the castle of Utopia.

The bishop looked aghast.

" My lord bishop," said the seneschal, " the king, our master, has been long expecting you; he is all impatient to embrace you: hasten, my lord, hasten your steps into the castle ; the wines are cooled, the supper is ready; oh, such a supper! my mouth waters at the very smell thereof! Four wild turkeys smoke upon the spit, seven bit-terns, six-and-twenty grey partridges, two-and-thirty red-legged ones, sixteen pheasants, nine woodcocks, nineteen herons, two-and-thirty rooks, twenty ring-doves, sixty leverets, twelve hares, twenty rabbits, and an ocean of Welsh ones, (enough to surfeit all the mice, and kill every apoplectic person in the world,) twenty kids, six roe-bucks, eight he-goats, fifteen sucking wild-boars, a flock of wild-ducks, to say nothing of the sturgeons, pikes, jacks, and other fish, both fresh and saltwater, besides ten tons of the most exquisite native oysters : and then there are flagons, goblets, and mead-cups over-flowing with frothy ale, exhilarating wine, and goodly mead, all longing to empty their contents into our parched and ready stomachs, which are unquenchable asbestos; for we drink lustily, my lord, and eat powdered beef salted at Shrovetide, to season our mouths, and render them rabid for liquid in the same proportion as a rabid dog avoids it."

The seneschal here paused to take breath, for his description of the supper exhausted the wind-trunk of his organ; and the bishop, seizing the opportunity of its being replenished, said,

"Peace, hoary dotard! thou hast mistaken thy man; I am Peter de Roches, Bishop of Winchester, and Protector of England during the king's sojourn abroad."

"You need not tell *me* what I already know," replied the seneschal; "though, it seems, I must again remind *you* that my lord the king awaits your coming within the castle walls, and has prepared a sumptuous supper, with all manner of good cheer, to greet you."

"Supper!" said the bishop in astonishment, "I have not yet dined; besides I never eat supper."

"The devil take your inhuman fashion, then!" replied the seneschal: "in extreme necessity I might forego a dinner, provided I had eaten an overwhelming breakfast; but I would as soon die as go without my supper. To go to bed without supper is a base and aristocratic custom; I say it is an error offensive to nature, and nature's dictates; all fasting is bad save breakfasting. That wicked pope who first invented fasting ought to have been baked alive in the papal kitchen."

To the latter part of the seneschal's speech the bishop mentally assented; but he merely said,

"Go to, thou gorged dullard, and tell thy master to gormandize without me."

"Well, go I suppose I must, if you will not come," returned the seneschal, "for I cannot longer tarry here. Ah, Sir Bishop, did you feel the gnawings of my stomach, you would be glad to throw some food to the hungry mastiff that seems feeding upon my very vitals!"

"Hold thy balderdash!" said the bishop, who had become very irritated, and would have sworn, had it been etiquette to do so in those days, at the effusive and edacious harangue of the seneschal. "Verily, thy hunger and thirst have gotten the better of thy wits! Whence comest thou?"

"From within the pincernary of that castle, where I have been indefatigably filling the goblets," answered the seneschal, smacking his lips. "*Sitio! sitio!* my parched mouth moistens at the thought! Oh! the lachryma Christi, the nectar, the ambrosia, and the true Falernian! Ah! Sir Bishop, some persons drink to quench their thirst, but I drink to prevent it."

"Pshaw!" said the bishop, "the wine that thou hast already drunken hath fuddled thy brains."

"By a gammon of the saltest bacon!" returned the seneschal, "I have more sense of what is good in my little finger than your reverence has in your whole pate, or you would not stand shilly-shambling here whilst so goodly a supper waits within."

The bishop was highly incensed at the seneschal's reflection upon his pate, and would have followed, had he dared, the slashing example of his namesake, and have smitten off the ear of this high-

priest of the pantry; (for he always wore a sword, even in the pulpit,
firmly believing in the efficacy of cold steel, knowing from experience that it would make a deeper and more lasting impression upon
human obduracy than the most eloquent preaching;) but the bishop
was deterred by prudential reflections from such sanguinary vengeance.

How long the confabulation between the bishop and the loquacious
seneschal would have lasted, and to what extent the patience of
the former might have been tried, it would at this remote period
be difficult to determine, especially as the Lanercost Chronicle does
not inform us.   At any rate, it was cut shorter than it would have
been, by the approach of twenty youthful knights, clad in superb
armour, and riding upon horses caparisoned in most costly and gorgeous trappings; they dismounted, and made a low obeisance. The
bishop returned it as lowly as bishops generally do, unless they are
bowing to the premier during the vacancy of an archbishoprick. The
knights advanced; but Peter remained as firm and majestic as the
rock of Gibraltar.

"Sir Bishop," said the chief of the knights, a youth with a most
beautiful and smiling face, "we are come to request your speedy
attendance upon our lord the king, who with any other than yourself
would have been much displeased at your perverse absence, after you
have been bidden by the steward of the household."

The bishop rubbed, shut, and opened his eyes.—"Am I bewitched," thought he to himself, "or do I dream?"

"Neither the one nor the other," said the knight, who perfectly
understood the bishop's cogitations.

"No?   What, then, does all this mean?" inquired the bishop.
"When did my lord the king return from Picardy?"

"Proceed into the castle," replied the knight, "and let him answer
for himself."

"If these people consider this a joke," thought the bishop, "I by
no means think it one.   At all events, come what come may, I will
follow up this strange adventure, and be even with these gentlemen.
I have not a bishop's garment," said he, addressing the seneschal;
"how can I appear before the king, accoutred as I am?"

"Knowing how much you are addicted to hunting," returned the
seneschal, "the king will assuredly receive you in your usual costume."

"Tut, fool!" said the bishop sneeringly; "do you forget, or has
your time been so engrossed with epicurean pursuits, that you have
not learnt how a guest, though bidden, was punished because he attended a supper-party without a proper garment?   Find me a becoming dress, and I will instantly attend his highness' pleasure."

"If you will condescend to follow me," said the youthful knight,
"a sacerdotal dress shall be procured for you."

The bishop, nodding assent, was then conducted in solemn silence
into the wardrobe of the castle, where the obsequious attendants soon
arrayed him in a dress fit for a bishop to sit with the king at supper in.
It was not such unpretending costume as that in which bishops are at
present apparelled; but robes of the tinctured colours of the East,
which were more apt to remind both the wearer and the beholders of
mundane pomps and vanities, than of the humility and simplicity of

Christianity. The alb was of most dazzling white, the dalmatica of gold tissue, the stole was embroidered with precious stones, and the chasuble, of purple velvet wrought with orfraise, was also studded with costly orient gems.

The bishop thus splendidly accoutred was conducted with great state and solemnity into the banqueting-room, one of the most magnificent and spacious of the kind. It excelled everything he had ever before seen: odoriferous and fragrant perfumes, fit for a Peri* to feed on, saluted his nose; his sight was dazzled by splendid and radiant illuminations, the most exquisite music stole upon his ear, and laughter and mirth seemed to be universal; every face (there were many hundreds in the room) was decked with a smile; there wanted but one thing to complete the enchantment of the scene,—the light of woman's laughing eye.

As the bishop entered the hall, five hundred harpers in an instant twanged their harps; and the air resounded with trumpets, clarions, fifes, and other musical instruments, not omitting the hollow drum.

The bishop, being tainted with the superstitious feelings of the age, easily persuaded himself that he was in an enchanted palace; he therefore determined to conform to every custom that prevailed in the assembled company, and by that means he hoped to ingratiate himself with the presiding spirit. When he had reached the centre of the hall, the king (he wore a robe of rich crimson velvet, furred with ermine, over a dalmatica flowered with gold, rubies, emeralds, pearls, and diamonds, and on his head was a splendid crown beyond estimation,) descended from a throne of the purest crystal, and advanced to meet the bishop. As he passed the obsequious nobles, he received their servile adulation with a smile, and, extending his arms, folded the bishop in a royal embrace. The latter surveyed with some awe the brawny shoulders of the king, and regarded with much respect the amber-coloured locks hanging in great profusion down his musculous back. The bishop thought that the aquiline nose, the expansive brow, the large clear azure eye, and the ruddy complexion of his host, about as much resembled those of his own monarch as a terrible-looking bull-dog does a snarling mongrel. But he kept his complimentary thoughts of his host to himself, as he was not at any time of a communicative spirit,—he was a proud, not a vain man,— and he moreover did not know how his compliment might be received.

The king handed the bishop to the upper end of the hall, and placed him at his right hand. No sooner were they seated than twenty trumpeters, in a gallery at the lower end of the room, blew, as the signal for supper to be served up, three such electrifying blasts, that, had the building not been as substantial as beautiful, it must have been shaken.

As the loquacious seneschal, in tempting the bishop to quicken his steps to supper, has put us in possession of many of the various articles provided for this festive entertainment, we shall not weary our reader by recapitulating them; but content ourselves with stating

* The Peris of Persian romance are supposed to feed upon the choicest odours; by which food they overcome their bitterest enemies the Deevs, (with whom they wage incessant war,) whose malignant nature is impatient of fragrance.

that, in addition to the solid fare, there were exquisite and delicate fruits and viands, with wines and liqueurs of the choicest quality and flavour. The supper-service was of the most superb description, frosted silver and burnished gold; the goblets, vases, and wine-cups were of crystal, mounted in gold richly carved. Such a feast the bishop had never seen or tasted; and yet he was, like many of his predecessors and successors too, perfectly familiar with the charms of eating and drinking.

Nothing produces good-fellowship, intimacy, and conviviality more than a good supper. We do not mean the cold, formal, and pompous supper given to a fashionable party of the present day; but such as were peculiar to by-gone days, when the table groaned under hot and solid joints, and the company, with good appetites as provocatives, ate and drank right heartily,—when glee and joy sat merrily upon every face, and the glass went briskly round. Even misanthropes or proud men could not be insensible to such festive scenes; their hearts would necessarily warm as the exhilarating wine washed away their gloomy and proud thoughts.

The bishop soon became familiar with his host, ate, drank, laughed, and was merry; (we will not so scandalise the Bench as to presume that he was drunk, although the Chronicle of Lanercost insinuates as much;) the conversation was brilliant, the wit bright and poignant, and the repartees flashed, and often rebounded upon the discharger.

To put a direct or pointed question at any time is, to say the least of it, ungentlemanly; it very often gives dire offence, is seldom admired or tolerated even by your most intimate acquaintance; and men are seldom guilty of it, unless in their cups, or with a desire of insulting:—how unpalatable must it be to royalty! As we know it was the bishop's desire to keep upon good terms with his host, it is but natural to infer that he would not intentionally insult him by any rude question. If, therefore, any rudeness occurred on the part of the bishop, it is charitable to set it down to inebriation, or perhaps to the bishop's habit of putting questions in the confessional.

To the ineffable surprise of the king, the bishop was so injudicious as to ask his host, in the most direct and pointed manner, who he was, and whence he came there.

No sooner had the bishop attempted to satisfy his prying curiosity by what appeared to him a very natural question, than the hall shook as if Nature were indignant at his presumptuous inquiry; the whole place was filled with an effulgent lambent light so brilliant, that it entirely eclipsed the blaze of the variegated lamps that burned in the hall; a low murmuring wind followed. The king's eyes seemed to flash liquid fire as he answered, "Know me for what I am,—Arthur, formerly lord of the whole monarchy of Britain, son of the mighty Pendragon, and the illustrious founder of the Order of the Round Table."

The bishop, having a firm heart and buxom valour, was far from being daunted, as most men in a similar situation would have been, and he inquired whether the story then current was true, that King Arthur was not dead, but had been carried away by fairies into some pleasant place, where he was to remain for a time, and then return again and reign in as great authority as ever; or whether he died by the sword-wounds he received from the sons of the king of the Picts;

and if so, whether his soul was saved, and come to revisit this sublunary world. The bishop, meditating authorship, asked a thousand
other questions relative to the immortality of the soul; and so subtle
were they, that, had they been put in these days of sciolism and char-
latanry, his fame would have been as brilliant, lasting, and deserved
as that of the noble editor of Paley's Theology.

Whether King Arthur did not choose to satisfy the bishop's curiosity, or whether, judging from the usual depth of the human mind,
he thought the immortality of the soul a subject too deep and mystic
for such moonshine treatises as have been written concerning it, the
Chronicle of Lanercost does not inform us. It merely states, that to all
the bishop's searching questions Arthur only replied, " *Verè expecto mi-
sericordiam Dei magnam.*" He had no sooner uttered those words than
a roar, like the falling of mighty waters such as Niagara's was heard,
and from the incense-altar another blaze of transcendent light issued:
the whole assembly, excepting the bishop, prostrated themselves and
chaunted a hymn, which he, mistaking for a bacchanal-venatical chorus,
heartily joined in. Upon this outrage of public decency, the chaunt
instantly terminated with a crash resembling what is ignorantly called
the falling of a thunderbolt; the altar again smoked, and horrible
and clamorous noises issued therefrom, like the bellowing of buffaloes,
the howling of wolves, the snarling and barking of hounds, the neigh-
ing of horses, the halloo of huntsmen, and the blasts of brazen trumpets, all in heterogeneous mingle. The smoke gradually assumed the
appearance of a host of hunters; one of them, evidently their chief,
fixed his glaring eyes upon the bishop, and frowned awfully. The
bishop did not admire the looks of the hunter-chief, and even winced
a little when he raised his ghastly arm, (as a self-satisfied orator does
when about to enforce some appalling clap-trap sentiment,) and said
in a gruff growl, " I am Nimrod, of hunting fame, and such a hunter
was I as the world had not before, or since, or will ever have again.
Yet was I no monopolizer of game, or murderer of men to preserve it,
as some have unjustly charged me. I loved the chase, and taught my
subjects to love it too; but thou, oh Bishop Peter, hast been a cruel
hunter, and strict preserver of game. The tongues thou hast dilace-
rated, the ears and noses thou hast cut off, and the wretches thou
hast slain, form an awful catalogue of cruelty, and one that will require tears of blood to wash out. Hearken to the lamentations of thy
victims, and the bewailings of the widows and orphans thy cruelty
hath made! Hadst thou not been so peerless and bold a hunter, I
should not have condescended to warn you of the terrible fate you
will experience in the world to come, unless you mend your ways.
Lover and encourager that I was, and interested as I still am in that
manly sport, I would sooner that it were entirely lost to the world
than it should be disgraced by human bloodshed. List, I say, to
the cries of the victims whom thou hast sacrificed at the altar of
Diana, thy divinity!" Loud lamentations were now heard, and a hideous group of dismembered menacing ghosts flitted rapidly before
the bishop's wondering sight. He closed his eyes to avoid their
angry looks; one writer insinuates that he swooned, but we think
that unlikely. Be it, however, as it may, upon his opening his eyes
he neither saw Nimrod, his crew, nor any of the victims of the forest-
laws. They had every one of them disappeared!

King Arthur, like a brave and magnanimous prince, soon forgot and forgave the bishop's want of good breeding in asking impertinent questions; though he severely chid him for having split so many human noses, and dismembered Christians without the slightest remorse, for so trifling an offence as infraction of the forest-laws: and that, too, within the very precinct of Winchester Castle, where the Round Table was preserved. The bishop thought those offences anything but trifling, and that the souls as well as bodies of the offenders merited the severest punishment, instead of commiseration.

King Arthur then denounced the concupiscence of the dignitaries of the church, and their appetite for, and easy digestion of, the good things of the world; and he declared that they regarded nothing but sensual gratification, and wasted their precious lives in banqueting, hawking, and hunting. He entreated the bishop to leave off his hunting habits, and to take unto those that were more episcopal and less sanguinary. He told him that it would add considerably to his mundane happiness, and tend more to his salvation than ten thousand thoughtless repetitions of the " pater noster " and twelve thousand of the " ave Maria." So much did King Arthur say, needless here to be repeated, that the bishop mentally resolved to profit by the king's advice. But it occurred to him that he could not suddenly leave off hunting without assigning a sufficient reason for his determination; and that if he related what had befallen him, his being a bishop would not entitle him to credit, nor protect him from the derision of his sovereign and his courtiers; for who would believe his most solemn asseveration that he had seen Nimrod, and conversed and supped with King Arthur?

King Arthur, perceiving what was agitating the bishop's ideas, determined to assist in fulfilling so righteous a resolve as the bishop was meditating.

" Extend your right hand," said Arthur; the bishop complied. " Shut it," said Arthur; the bishop did as he was told. " Now open it," continued Arthur. The bishop opened his hand, and there flew therefrom an exquisitely beautiful butterfly.

The bishop, notwithstanding all that he had just before seen and heard, now in real good earnest believed himself bewitched, and heartily wished that he had never forsaken the profession of a soldier for that of a bishop, to be subject to miracles; for in those days miracles and visions only occurred to the dignified clergy.

King Arthur, compassionating the bishop's perturbation, said, " Whenever in relating your adventure any one doubts it, you shall afford him sufficient autopsy of its verity by sending, at all seasons of the year, a butterfly from your hand, in memorial of me and of your virtuous resolution."

The bishop cordially thanked King Arthur for his kindness and consideration, and swore by the face at Lucca, (his favourite oath,) that as long as he lived, he would never again sound the bugle, follow hounds, nor punish man, woman, or child for infringing the game-laws; and that he would moreover exert all his influence with King John to relax the inhuman severity of the forest-laws.

No sooner had the bishop made a solemn adjuration to that effect than he felt a stunning blow upon his head, which deprived him of all sensation. When he recovered, he found himself lying where Velocipede had thrown him, and the brute quietly grazing by his side.

The bishop vaulted upon his saddle, spurred his steed, and galloped off as fast as the creature could go. After a ride of about five miles, he found his attendants anxiously seeking him. He related all that had occurred, to their great awe and astonishment; but when they had autoptical evidence of the truth of his narration, by his letting loose a mealy-winged butterfly from his hand, their fear and wonder exceeded all bounds.

The bishop's adventure was soon bruited abroad, and thousands flocked from all parts of England, Scotland, Ireland, and even the Continent, to see the man who had supped with King Arthur, and seen the hunter Nimrod. Many more came to witness a miracle performed a circumstance of rare occurrence to the vulgar in those days, miracles, as we have above observed, being reserved for the private view of bishops and monks. Those pilgrimaging to Winchester always sought and received a blessing from the butterfly hand of the bishop as soon as he was satisfied that a liberal oblation had been made at the high altar of his cathedral.

The frequent repetition of the miracle obtained for Peter the appellation of the BUTTERFLY BISHOP; and the offerings at the high altar so greatly augmented his revenue, that he never once repented of his promise to King Arthur. His time was so occupied in performing the miracle and blessing the people, that he had no time, whatever was his inclination, for hunting.

The Chronicler ends this strange story in the following words "*Quid in hoc anima Arthuri mortalis adhuc docere voluerit, perpendat qui melius conjicere poterit:*"—which, for the benefit of our female readers, may be rendered thus,—"What the still mortal soul of Arthur wished to teach by this, let him consider who can best interpret."

A NEW SONG TO THE OLD TUNE OF "KATE KEARNEY."

O, SAY have you heard of Duvernay?
They tell me she's able to earn a
    Hundred pounds in a night,
    Such crowds she'll delight—
What *danseuse* is like to Duvernay?

If you e'er go to see this Duvernay,
Just notice her when she shall turn a
    Most sweet pirouette,
    And you'll never regret
Forking out to behold this Duvernay.

Would you know where you may see Duvernay?
You must go to Pall-mall, and just turn a
    Little up a wide street,
    When the Opera you'll meet,
And there you'll behold this Duvernay.

Tell me not of Leroux or Taglioni;
One's too stout, and the other's too bony:
    If you see them all three,
    You'll be thinking with me,
Of all dancers the flow'r is Duvernay.   F. G.

City of London Institution,
Aldersgate-street.

WHAT TOM BINKS DID WHEN HE DIDN'T KNOW
WHAT TO DO WITH HIMSELF.

Is it creditable to that very respectable academical abstraction, that indefatigable pioneer to the march of intellect, (which some imagine to be the rogues' march,) the *schoolmaster*, notwithstanding his ubiquity, and his being lately abroad on his travels, that the medical faculty, with all their appliances of pill and book, have not up to this hour been able to devise a remedy for a very common-place disorder, so feelingly enunciated in that touching and eloquent exclamation, "I really don't know what to do with myself!" or to ascertain in what category of diseases incident to humanity it is to be placed? Like hydrophobia, it has baffled the ingenuity of the faculty, who summarily disposed of the evil between two feather-beds; and, though no effectual remedy has been devised for this pet malady, a feather-bed, or an easy-chair, has been found to operate as a sedative. One thing is clear; that, of all the ills that flesh or spirit is heir to, this interesting disorder possesses as respectable a degree of obstinacy and virulency as ever humanity had to cope with.

Talk of being dunned for your own or anybody else's debt; talk of a favourite horse or dog falling sick just as you are ready to mount, and the scent reeking hot on the stubble; of being bored, no matter with what; talk—even if one is put to that—of the devil; and what are all these petty annoyances to that sublime of *blue-devilism* to which a poor devil is reduced, when, in his extremity, he reposes his hands on his "fair round belly," or thrusts them to the very bottom of his breeches' pockets, with not a cross there to keep the devil out, and feelingly exclaims, "I really don't know what to do with myself!" One may double the corner on a dun, or stop his mouth for three months together with a promissory note, though at the end of that period it may be as fructifying as any note of admiration; or, at worst, pay him and be d—d to him, and there's an end. That biped Shank's mare is a very respectable animal, which you may borrow; or any body else's who may be disposed to lend. In case of a *bore*, you may retaliate, and *perforate* in your turn. You may defy the devil, though backed with this world, and his own, and the flesh to boot. But when that *ne plus ultra* of blue-devilism attacks you, what's the remedy? I don't know—do you? but this I know; that it is the most rascally, &c. &c. &c. kind of malady, will be generally admitted.

Your poor devil at the East-end, and your devil-may-care fellow of the West-end, are equally honoured by its visitation; while your happy, active middle-man, who stands aloof from either end, sturdily bids it defiance, and slams the door in its face. Under the influence of this visiter it is that sundry pious pilgrimages are made to the foot of Waterloo or Blackfriars' bridges, to steal out of life through an archway, unless the dear enthusiast is interrupted by a meddling officious waterman, and his senses gently wooed back by the resuscitating apparatus and warm blankets of the Humane Society. Will Sprightly, with four thousand a-year unincumbered, doesn't know what to do with himself, and straightway falls to the agreeable occupation of encumbering it, and, when it will bear no more, he finds he

cannot bear himself, and incontinently flies from one state of suspense to another, and hangs himself; or, should the ruling passion be
strong in death, and he is desirous even then to cut a figure, why, he
cuts his throat; or, the report of a pistol will give you a pretty correct intimation of his whereabouts, and his probable occupation.
" Temporary insanity" is uniformly the verdict of your " crowner's
'quest" on such occasions; even a physician of any repute will honestly state on ordinary occasions, particularly when the patient has
the benefit of his skill and experience in helping him to leave this
wicked world, that he died of such and such a disorder, and will man-
fully state the name of the disorder, and the world gives him credit
for his skill and integrity. Would gentlemen serving upon " crowners'
'quests" imitate this heroic example, instead of recording the foolish
verdict of " temporary insanity," they would say," The deceased *didn't
know what to do with himself!*" This would be intelligible, and the faculty might stumble upon a remedy; but " temporary insanity " is
too transitory, too fugitive to be grappled with, too vague and indefi-
nite in its very name ever to do any good, and the patient is generally
" past all surgery " before one suspects he is attacked with insanity,
be it ever so temporary or evanescent: but in honestly recording
that "he didn't know what to do with himself, *and thereby came by
his death,*" it would be but doing justice to that interesting malady.
Thus it could be easily observed in all its stages, from its incipient
symptoms at the gaming or any other well-garnished table, where it
sometimes takes its rise, through all its phases and evolutions, till the
malady comes to a *head*, and a man blows out his brains. The disease, through each of these changes, might be stayed in its progress,
and society might be benefited by the honesty of the verdict.

Shade of the " mild Abernethy!" how many thousands of thy patients laboured under this disorder! and how often did thy sagacious
and provident spirit turn the halter into a skipping-rope, and, in order
that thy patients should live, insist upon a few mouthfuls the less!

To a feeling very near akin to this, Tom Binks found himself reduced, as, about twelve at noon, he flung himself into an easy-chair,
and sought, from the appliances of its downy cushions, a lenitive for
his wounded spirit. His feet on the fender, the fire gently stirred,
the curtains still undrawn and shutting out the garish sun, his eye
fixed on the glowing landscape formed by the fantastic combination
of the embers in the grate, the corners of his fine mouth drawn down
in hopeless despondency, as if nothing on earth could elevate them,
his hands clasped over his knees, he sat, not knowing what to do with
himself.

The room in which Binks sat was small, but elegant; pictures
of the most costly description covered the walls,—the most exquisite
that owned him or any body else as *master;* gold and silver had done
their work. On the polished surface of the tables were thrown the
most amusing works of the day, the last new novel, the lively magazine, the gay album, the serious review, all exhibiting on the same
board like so many brethren of the *Ravel family*, in the most alluring
and seductive shapes; but they exhibited in vain. With all these
elements of happiness around him, what *could* Binks sigh for? With
easy possessions, he was the most uneasy of human beings. Did he
play, fortune was always in the best humour with him: in the bil-

liard-room the ball bounded from his cue to its destination; in the field his shot was unerring, and the papers regularly chronicled the murder, or the music, of his gun : no man stood better with *ins* and outs; his maiden speech was said to be *shy*, simply because it *was* maiden, but full of promise. With the ladies he was whatever he or they pleased; but now you could " brain him with my lady's fan " as he sits vegetating, or cogitating, on a pile of cushions, his breakfast scarcely touched, and hardly sensible of his shaggy friend that lay couched at his feet, with his snout buried in the hearth-rug, and his bloodshot eye occasionally wandering in search of a regard from his listless master.

At an early age Binks had contrived to run through half the Continent and his fortune together; he had travelled from " Dan to Beersheba," and all was barren ; and, at twenty-three, the gay Binks had serious notions that *this* was not the best of all possible worlds, and that *that* world, commonly known as the other, to distinguish it from this, might hold out a store of enjoyment of higher zest and relish than the common-place realities of this. Whether he should wait for his turn when the passage to it might become quite natural, or force his way *vi et armis*, that is, with a pistol in hand, (for some folks *will* be impatient, and enter in at a breach,) was a matter that sorely perplexed him. Tired of this hum-drum life, which a man of common activity can exhaust of its most stimulating excitements in a few years, was it surprising that he wished for *another ?* But the doubt that it was a better, would sometimes intrude itself, and agitate the very powder in the pan of the pistol that lay before him on the breakfast table. Now that the murder is out, it must be confessed that Binks had a notion of shooting himself.

What heroic resolves he then made ! What a noble contempt for this world he then exhibited as he resolutely eyed the pistol, curiously scanned its silver mounting, saw that the powder was in the pan, looked anxiously around to see that none intruded, or should deprive him of the honour of falling by his own hand : still he hesitated ; he lifted the deadly weapon with one hand, and with the other a volume of Shakspeare, which opened at the play of *Hamlet,* and, by the hasty glance which he threw on it, he perceived that " the Eternal had set his canon 'gainst self-slaughter," and Binks was perplexed. It became now a matter not so much of life and death as of simple calculation; on one side there was a pistol *for,* and on the other a *canon 'gainst* self-slaughter. In this state of indecision, thus sorely beset with adverse arguments, what did Binks do ? Why, he acted somewhat like a sensible man; he yielded to the heavier weight of metal,—the great-gun of Shakspeare carried it ; and he consented to live, drew the charge, lest he should return to it, (for he knew his man,) and made up his mind that Shakspeare was a sensible fellow. Have you ever felt as if your very heart-strings were tugged at by wild horses, when the infernal host of *blues,* marshalled by the devil himself, have taken the field against your peace, and that you don't know what to do with yourself?

" Throw but a stone, the giant dies."

Very good ; but a pebble of such potency is not always at hand, particularly in a drawing-room. Do something, no matter what: go into the open air; there's your window invitingly open, and, provided it is not too far from the ground, 'tis but a step in advance to the shock that may rouse you. Turn financier,—chancellor of your own exchequer; there's your tailor's bill lying on the table, wooing you to analyze its soft items; give it a first reading, and pass it. What a relief, on such occasions, is the presence of any living creature!—your sleek tabby,—no,—that fellow doesn't know what to do with himself neither. Your playful little Italian grey-hound, whose playfulness is the very poetry of motion. And Binks found no relief in these gentle appliances. There he lies, flung upon his ottoman, and dallying with its downy cushions, with his foot of almost feminine symmetry coquetting with his morocco slipper, jerking it off and on according to the intensity of the fit. Ponto stands before him. Noble dog, Ponto! He, too, has his turn at the slipper, and seizes it in his huge mouth, and gambols round the room with it, and now crouches with it before his master, and earnestly looks at him, and those two eyes of his suggest a double-barrelled gun, and this puts a pistol into his head, and there it was at hand, lying on the table, just ready for a charge.

"Mr. Cently," said a servant, half-opening the door; and Binks indolently extended the forefinger of his jewelled hand to his visiter.

"Very glad to see you, Cently; this mortgage, I suppose—"

"Is over due, Mr. Binks,—must redeem, though. I shan't let it out of the family. The sum is large—hard to get—bad times. Fine dog that—bulls and bears are very sulky to-day on 'Change.—Dear me, a murderous-looking pistol that, sir—muzzle to muzzle—then brains against the wall."

"Provided he has them," said Pinks.

"Every man has a little—quality's the thing. I have to meet Scrip in the City at two—no time to lose, sir;" and Binks, who was made aware of the necessity of a visit to the City, to arrange the terms of a loan, put himself under the plastic hands of Bedo, and in a few minutes the pair were rolling towards the City in Cently's carriage, which thundered along, scarcely waiting to take the necessary turns, and narrowly escaped running down several old women of both sexes, till they came to Charing-Cross.

"Money is scarce in these times," said Cently, as a sprinkling of cabs and omnibuses impeded their course; "broad acres are fine things. I mustn't let them go. The sum is large—ten per cent."

All this, and a few other equally interesting particulars, were lost upon the abstract Binks, who was quietly lolling back in the carriage, and exercising his optics and calculating powers on the size, number, and colours of the tom-cats as they sunned themselves on the gutters, or held attic intercourse with one another, between May-fair and Temple-bar.

"You understand me," continued Cently; "let me see; how many thousands? I think it cannot be under fourscore,—great amount that!"

"Not quite so many," said Binks; "I only counted sixty, and I'm correct to a tail; bet you a rump and dozen on it."

"On what, sir?"

"On the cats, Cently."

"Ha! ha! Very facetious, Mr. Binks; but I'm not joking.

"You bore me, Cently. Set me down here. Go, and do the needful; and when all's ready to sign and seal, you'll find me here;" and

Binks alighted from the carriage, and ascended the stairs of the Mansion-house, which was then alive with sounds and sights of gladness: a kind of fancy-fair was being held there for the benefit of some charitable institution, and the *élite* of the North, and wealth of the East and West ends were combined in the holy cause of charity. He entered, and mingled with the gay groups that promenaded the hall, which was converted into a bazaar, where beauty and *bijouterie* lured the careless purchaser,—where a thousand soft things were said and handled, and the angel of charity spread her wings over a scene where streamed and flaunted many a silken banner, and pointed to every little stand. " Happy country !" thought Binks, " that, amid all the anxieties and contentions of commerce and politics, remembers in these noble institutions the cause of the widow and the orphan. This must be the surest mart for beauty when she's found at a stand in the sacred cause of charity. Here the thoughtless forget. themselves, and think of others ; here the merchant is generous, and forgets his change."

" I ain't a-going to be done out of my half-crown that way neither, ma'am," said a burly little personage in top-boots and perspiration to a lovely girl who presided at a stand, and who was trying to lure a supplementary half-crown, the balance of a half-sovereign, which, after much grumbling, he consented to pay for a shaking mandarin. The thorough-bass in which this was uttered roused Binks from his reverie, and, on looking round, he beheld the lovely girl in playful yet earnest contention for the half-crown, which the fat little man finally surrendered to a few persuasive looks, and good-humouredly pocketed his shaking mandarin and his chagrin together, and marched off.

Binks approached, and as she raised her eyes from the gay assortment before her, still animated with the pious contention in which she was engaged, they encountered those of Binks, who was riveted to the spot gazing at the beautiful creature that stood before him. He turned over a few articles, and became at once deeply immersed in the gay little miscellany before him. She would show everything.— Yes,—the articles were of the best description ; and Binks felt those taper fingers, as they tossed them about, as if they were busy with his heart-strings ; and the perverse Binks asked twenty different questions, and got as many answers eloquent and sweet : and then there were looks lustrous and shy, and blushes deep and enchanting ; and she would go on expatiating on the beauty of her *bijouterie,* and he would stand absorbed and drinking in the sweet sound of a voice that was modulated with the sweetest harmony,—and she would help him to a pair of gloves. Binks took several pairs. The first he tried on were very perverse,—too tight ; and the fairest hands in the City would distend them, and she would help to draw them on ; and then their palms would meet, and their fingers seek one another, and the taper finger of the sweet girl and the jewelled hand of Binks would be imprisoned unconsciously for a few seconds in the same glove.

" I shall take the whole," said he, and Julia (for that was her name) was delighted ; and Binks was asking for more, and pulled out, —not his purse, but the disappointed hand that was for seekingit.— The purse was not there.

No doubt it was that very civil gentleman that rubbed against him as he was stepping out of the carriage, and apologised. Here was a grab at heart-strings and purse-strings together. He drew out a box set with brilliants,—it would stand him at a pinch,—and took a small one from the stand, and he would exchange boxes. And this was love,—love at first sight,—which we would match all the world over with any at second sight.

"Oh, love ! no habitant of earth art thou."

Henceforth shalt thou take thy *stand* at a bazaar, and we shall bare our bosom to thy shafts, provided they be tipped with a little charity, and drawn in the holy cause of a benevolent institution! The hours lingered on as if they too had come to a stand, the evening stole on apace, group after group vanished from the bazaar, and Binks and Julia were still in sweet and endearing communion with each other. The evening was chilly, and he would help on her splendid cachmere ; and the loveliest arm in the City leant on Binks as he led her down the steps of the Mansion-house. The evening was fine, and he would see her home ; and both wondered to find themselves at her father's door. And then there was a sweet good-night, and kind looks, and gentle pressings of the hand, and promises to meet again.

"Want a coach, sir ?" said a heavy-coated, slouched-hat brother of the cab to Binks, as he stood wondering at himself, his adventure, and the fairy figure that a smart servant in livery had just closed the door upon.

"Yes—no,—I—I 'll walk, friend,—the night's fine ;" which healthy resolution he was induced to take from certain reminiscences, and his purse, though absent, was thought of with regret.

And Binks trod his perilous way through the "palpable obscure" of the City with buoyant spirits, as if a pinion lifted every limb, notwithstanding a little plebeian pressure from without through Cheapside, as often as he forgot his own side of the way ; and he entered his club the happiest dog that ever moonlight, or its rival luminary gas-light, shone upon, and surrendered himself to the intoxicating influence of the only draught of pure pleasure he ever quaffed.

Julia Deering was the only daughter of a rather comfortable trader, a man well to do in the world,—that is, in the City. Business—business was at once his solace and his pride, and any pursuit or avocation in life of which that bustling noun-substantive was not the principal element, was an abomination in his sight. The West-end, he thought, had no business where it stood. He looked upon it as a huge fungus, the denizens thereof good for nothing ; and lords—no matter of what creation—he looked upon with the most supreme contempt. Julia was his only child, and, next his business, the sole object of his solicitude. She grew into loveliness and womanhood amid the smoke and seclusion of her father's premises ; and, though turned of "quick seventeen," yet he thought that her settlement in the world, like the settlement of an account with an old house in the City, might take place at any time. Any hint to the contrary, whether through the eloquent and suggestive looks of the maiden herself, or the unequivocal assiduity of City beaux, was sure to make the old man peevish.

Julia, with a world of sense, had a spice of romance about her. She loved the West-end, or anything pertaining to it, as much as her father hated it. A noble mirror in her little boudoir, as she toyed and coquetted with her budding beauties before it, frequently hinted that she might be a fine lady; which could only come to pass by her becoming the wife of something like a lord. City beaux were her aversion. They looked at her through *stocks*, and she often wished their necks in them.

Many were the stolen visits to the City which Binks made to see his young betrothed. His suit prospered,—Julia was everything he could wish; but as fathers *will* be in the way on such occasions,—how can they be so hard-hearted?—and as something like his consent was deemed necessary, Binks, through the medium of a friend, had the old man's sentiments sounded on the subject; and a decided refusal, couched in no very flattering terms, was the result. " I cannot disguise from you," said Julia one evening to Pinks, after he had communicated to her the disastrous intelligence, " that there is much to encounter in my father's disposition. He is old and wealthy, with only myself to inherit it; and—would you believe it?—he has the greatest aversion to a man of rank, and thinks superior manners and accomplishments only a cover to heartlessness and deceit; and, what is strange, he has repeatedly said he will never consent to my union with anybody as long as he is in anything like health,—in short, till he is no longer able to protect me himself."

" That is strange indeed!" said Binks, as he hung with the tenderest rapture on the confiding frankness and simplicity of his fair companion; " your father's objections are no less serious than strange."

" Can nothing," inquired Julia despondingly, " be done to get over them?" Had Echo been present, she would have said, " Get over them."

" There can, there can," said Binks with transport; "I have it. So long as your father is in good health, he will never give his consent to your marriage. Now he is old: and suppose he can be persuaded that he *looks* ill,—such things, you know, are done,—and contrive that he shall keep his bed for a few days; and then,—and then, my dear girl, let the affair be again pressed upon him." And Binks met the ingenuous blush and smile of his young betrothed as she acquiesced with an embrace, in which was blended more heartfelt rapture than ever he experienced in the dissipated round of tumultuous and exciting pleasures.

" The times are certainly very bad, Julia," said old Deering to his daughter, as they were at breakfast one morning together; " I never recollect them so bad:" and he helped himself to a large slice of ham.

" They may be bad, pa," said the daughter; " but you mustn't take it so much to heart. Everybody notices how ill you look since the firm of Dobody and Sons went."

The old man suspended a piece of ham, that he had impaled on a fork, midway between his mouth and plate; and, planting his right hand on his thigh, he looked earnestly at the girl.

" What connexion, hussey, has that failure with my looks or my books either? As long as I can keep both free from blotches, I don't care a fig for what the world says. But I do believe, girl, that I am not as well as either of us could wish,—I am fallen off in my appetite. I *could* finish my ham,—three slices,—and a few eggs; but I am a little changed, Julia. Hussey, you 've a sharp eye; and to notice it!"

"Lord! pa," said the insidious Julia, "all your acquaintance notice it. Mr. Coserly was the first to notice it."

"And what did the rascal say?"

"Why, pa, he said nothing; but there was a great deal in *that*. When certain people say little or nothing, they mean a great deal; and when there is a great deal of meaning in what one does not say, why, it 's a very dangerous thing; isn't it, pa?"

"Very true, child, very true. But what can we have for dinner to-day, Julia? I expect an old friend of mine, Mr. Tibbs over the way; a very proper, industrious, well-to-do-in-the-world kind of man is honest Dick Tibbs. He owes me a trifle,—but that is nothing between us. He is none of your West-end chaps,—no lack-silver spend-thrift,—no hair-lipped, hair-brained scamp, with all his fortune on his back, like a pedlar and his wallet.—Another cup of tea, Julia.—As I was saying, honest Dick Tibbs is ——' But what 's the matter with the girl? Why, there 's the tea running out of the urn these last two minutes about the floor. Why, Julia, what *is* the matter? Ah! I see how it is—I thought as much. Ye 're a cunning pair. But not yet a while, Julia; time enough, girl,—time enough. When your dear mother was ——"

"I—I—wo-o-on't be Mrs. Ti-i-bbs for all that, pa," hysterically sobbed Julia; "I won't be married ——".

"That 's a dear love!" whimpered the old man; "don't think of marrying him yet until I 'm——" But I 'm pretty strong yet. I 'll live, so I will, till—ugh!—ugh!—these rheumatics—as long as— Deuce take this old cough!"

"As long as God pleases, pa; as long as God pleases," said Julia; and she slid her arm coaxingly round her father's neck, and wiped away the perspiration that stood like whip-cord upon his brow; and he fell to musing on the girl's words, and left his breakfast unfinished.

In the course of that week, through the industry of his daughter, the old man was plagued wherever he went with condolence and inquiries about his health, which he heard with all the petulance and irritability of a miser upon whose hoards an unexpected demand is to be made. He accordingly dosed himself with physic, gorged himself at his meals, and took such peculiar pains to preserve his health after this fashion as would have deprived any other person of it.

A circumstance at length occurred that bade fair to supersede the necessity of Julia's pious artifice, and to produce ill looks in abundance in the old man. A house with which he was connected failed, and involved him in its ruin. This was a blow that smote the old man to the heart, and he sank under it. Everything was surrendered to the creditors; and his house, with its splendid furniture, was submitted to the hammer of the auctioneer.

On the morning of that day a note was put into Binks' hands; it was from Julia, and to the effect "that as her father's ruin left her no alternative but to share his lot, she could not, under such circumstances, think of involving him in their ruin, and begged he would think no further of the matter."

"Poor girl!" said Binks, as he gazed on the note that told so briefly of so much calamity. What a real *bonâ-fide* misfortune was, crushing and accumulating, and, as it were, breaking the man's heart within him, he had no idea of, except what the pathetic in a novel, or the chapter of accidents in a newspaper, furnished. These things were well enough to read, and to talk about, at a clear fire-side; but for a substantial display of energetic and effective sympathy, by succouring the distressed, it was what he did not think himself capable of. A second time, however, he mastered his indolence, and drove to Julia's house.

What a situation was it in, and what a sight did it present! If there is in this world a scene more harrowing to human feeling than another, 'tis that presented by one's house on the eve of an auction,—a scene of "confusion worse confounded." The tossing about and displacing, by strange hands, of articles that from time and association have become part and parcel of ourselves, linked with a thousand sweet recollections, and the innocent display of which was a source of dearest household pleasure, now parcelled and ticketed out, and catalogued, for the curious and malevolent hands and eyes of strangers! Our dearest and holiest places of privacy intruded upon; our sweet little nooks and haunts, which are, as it were, set apart for the most favoured of our household gods, and where only the footsteps of tenderest love should be heard, now echoing and teeming with strange sounds and sights!

What a sad volume, and in boards too, is a piece of carpeting piled in a corner of a room, revealing the unsightly seams of the naked floor; and "the decent clock," with its hands either broken or pointed to the wrong hour! The bleak and cheerless hearth, every brick of which was an object for the vacant and listless gaze of a pensive abstraction, the scene of sweet gambols and merry gossipings, all are sad mementos of the "base uses" to which the iron hand of necessity will convert objects dear to us from the sweetest household associations.

Elevated in his pulpit, the eloquent Mr. Touchem, the auctioneer, presided; and, seated beside him, the very picture of broken-heartedness, was old Deering, bent, and leaning forward on his gold-headed cane, his eye vacant and listless, looking at every article with the curiosity of a child, speaking not a word, and only betraying his interest in the scene by a sympathetic stamp of his cane on the floor whenever the nervous and grating click of the auctioneer's hammer on his desk announced the sale of some favourite article. There was one lot only which he showed any anxiety to possess, and as the porter handed it round, the old man's countenance gleamed with pleasure as his eye wistfully followed it : it was the representation of a little spaniel worked in worsted, and the joint work of Julia and his deceased wife.

"Rascal!" exclaimed the old man, as the porter somewhat roughly rubbed the dust off it, "be tender of the poor thing. That's Julia's. I—I bid for that; I bid five pounds for that," said the old man, in a voice scarcely articulate with emotion.

"Six pounds," said a voice in the crowd.

"Who bids against me?" muttered old Deering, as he ran his eye over the group whence the voice issued. "It was the work of my poor child's hands, and of her dear departed mother. Another pound for it, Mr. Auctioneer."

The same voice bid against him.

The old man raised himself in his chair, gazed wistfully and imploringly in the direction of the voice, and sank back in sullen resignation in his chair.

"Going for eight pounds—once—twice—the last time!" and the sharp and sudden click of the auctioneer's hammer, as it fell, came with a harsh grating sound on the ear of the old man, as he groaned, and muttered something between a curse and an entreaty.

Old Deering, notwithstanding the utter ruin of his fortune, still continued, from sheer force of habit, to frequent his old haunts; and his drooped and wasted figure, with his well-known *tops* and gold-headed cane, might be seen loitering about the purlieus of the Exchange, inquiring the price of stocks with as much anxiety as ever, and wondering at the ill-manners of some persons who, from his rambling and incoherent expressions, looked upon him as somewhat crazed. He was in truth so.

This was the time for the active benevolence of Binks to show itself; for, except when his indolence stood in the way, he had a heart. He saw Julia, and gave her the most decided assurances of his unaltered attachment, as the old man's malady threatened to become serious. He privately purchased a neat little cottage outside town, and had all the furniture (for he attended the auction, and arranged that every article of it should be bought in,) conveyed to it. He took particular care—for he consulted Julia on the details—that the disposition of the furniture in the new house should, as nearly as circumstances would permit, be exactly the same as in the house in town. Her father's easy-chair, pictures, books, the pianoforte,—for almost every article had been preserved by the management of Binks,—were put into something like their accustomed places; and little Fidelio, the object of contention at the auction, looked quite as brisk as ever, enshrined in his glass-case over the mantelpiece, not a whit the worse for having his jacket dusted. Change of air, and absence from the scene of his former activity, was suggested as the best remedy for the malady of the old man.

To this little cottage Julia and her father drove one day, on pretence of looking for a suitable residence, such as became their altered circumstances. This little cottage struck his fancy, and he expressed a wish to see it. A very agreeable young man showed them over the house. The more he examined it, the more he liked it; every thing in it was so like what he once had.

"Why, Julia, this is your pianoforte! let me hear you play; I'll know it among a thousand;" and Julia played "sweet home" for him,—an air her father always liked. His eye glistened as she played; it reminded him of better days and his old house in the City, and he dropped into his easy-chair. "And Fidelio, the little spaniel! Why, how is this, Julia?—And this gentleman?" and he looked alternately at Binks and Julia. "Ah, hussey! I see how it is; but it's an odd way of coming together."

*   *   *   *   *   *   *

And Binks was happy—happy as the day was long. Julia and he were married. The gay Binks, like another Hercules, gave up his *club* when he married, and was content with his love in a cottage, with no other interruption to his happiness than the occasional pettishness of the old man, who could never well forgive Binks for outbidding him for Fidelio at the auction. And the malady of *not knowing what to do with himself* never afterwards attacked him, now that the odds were two to one against it.

S. Y.

A GENTLEMAN QUITE.

In Bentley's May number I read of a goose,
Whose aim in this life was to be of some use ;
Now *I* always act on the opposite plan,
And endeavour to take the least trouble I can :
I sing at no concert, I dance at no ball,—
I 'm a gentleman quite, and of no use at all !

When invited to dinner, I 'd much rather starve,
Than attempt for some hungry half-dozen to carve ;
And folks do exist, who, when dishes are nice,
Won't scruple to send their plates up to you twice :
All vainly for sauces on me do they call,—
I 'm a gentleman quite, and of no use at all !

If ask'd for some verses an album to fill,
I don't plead want of time, but admit want of skill ;
There 's nothing ungentlemanlike in a dunce,
So I state the plain fact, and save trouble at once ;
For, rather than write, I 'd mend shoes in a stall,—
I 'm a gentleman quite, and of no use at all !

When doom'd to the Opera with ladies to go,
I 'm not quite so green as to play the old beau ;
The fiddlers and dancers are paid to amuse,
And, to stand on their level, is what I don't choose,
When over, for footman or coach I don't bawl,—
I 'm a gentleman quite, and of no use at all !

Of my club in Pall Mall I was very soon cured,
They wanted to make me a sort of a steward ;
Those persons must surely have owed me a grudge,
To wish me to work as an amateur drudge.
A suggestion so horrible made my flesh crawl ;
I 'm a gentleman quite, and of no use at all !

I 've an uncle, or nephew, or kin of some kind,
Who, to sit in St. Stephen's, once felt much inclin'd ;
To his vulgar committee he added my name ;
When my poor valet read it, he redden'd with shame.
With no mob from the hustings will I ever brawl,—
I 'm a gentleman quite, and of no use at all !

But Death 's the great leveller : every one knows
Gentility's essence is graceful repose,
And the grave yields repose that must charm e'en a Turk ;
No labour or toil there, the worm does the work.
When shrouded, and coffin'd, and under a pall,
Man 's a gentleman quite, he 's of no use at all !

J. S.

THE FOSTER-CHILD.

"Ten years to-day! Mercy on us, time does fly indeed! it seems but yesterday. And here she sat, her beautiful fair face all reddened by the heat, as in her childish romps she puffed with might and main the fire in this very grate. Dear heart, how sweet a child it was surely! Well, David, say what folks will, I'm convinced there was a fate about it."

Before I relate how far David coincided in this opinion of his "gude wife," I will mention to whom and to what she alluded, and how I had an opportunity of declaring a similar conviction. Seated, after a kind reception by the master and matron, in their best room in the workhouse of L——, at my request they were proceeding to gratify my curiosity, raised by a picture which hung between the windows. The subject and execution were striking: it had been hit off at one of those luckiest moments for the artist, when, unconsciously, the study presented that inspiration to the task which so rarely occurs in what is termed "a sitting for a likeness." On a three-legged stool, with one foot raised upon the fender, and an old pair of bellows resting on her lap, in the act of blowing the fire,—long clustering locks, the brightest yellow that ever rivalled sunbeams, flowing from a head turned towards her right shoulder, from which a coarse holland pinafore had slipt by the breaking of one of the fastenings,—sat a child, apparently eight or nine years of age, in whose face beamed more beauty, spirit, and intelligence than surely ever were portrayed on canvass. Well might the good dame cry, "Dear heart, how sweet a child it was!" Never before or since have I beheld its equal; and the vivid recollection of the wonder I then felt, will never cease to throw its light upon the page of memory till time turns over the new leaf of existence. What admirable grace! how exquisitely free! she seemed indeed to inhale the breath that panting look bespoke a lack of. What joyous fire in her large blue eyes! and then the parted laughing lips, and small pearl teeth! the attitude how careless, and most natural! all appeared as much to live as if all actual. But, little do I hope, gentle reader, to excite in you as lively an interest for the original, by my weak tints of simple black and white, as the glowing colours of the picture roused in me. I will not attempt it; but at once proceed with the story appertaining to the object of my inquiry, as narrated by the worthy matron of "the house."

"Do you tell the tale, Bessum," said honest David, addressing his spouse, whose name, from Elizabeth and Betsy, had undergone this further proof of the liberties married folks take with one another. "Do you tell the tale, and, if needs be, I can help you on, where you forget any part of it."

"Ah! you're a 'cute fellow, David," said Elizabeth, "you know how to set an easy task as well as any one, 'specially when it's for yourself to go about; but, never mind, I wun't rate 'e for't, for I know 'tis a sad subject for you to deal with."

Bessum was evidently right, for the tear that stood trembling for a moment in the corner of David's eye as she rolled unheeded down his cheek; while the handkerchief that seemed to have been taken from across his knees for the purpose of concealing the simplicity of the tribute his honest heart was paying, was employed, for at least the tenth time that day, to brush the irreverent dust from the picture of his " poor dear child."

I was affected to a degree for which I was unable to account, by the touching sigh poor David heaved as he replaced the handkerchief on his knees, and resigned himself to the pangs my curiosity was about to inflict on him. There was a tender melancholy in the kind creature's face that seemed to mark the lacerated feelings of intense affection. I could have pressed him to my breast in sympathy of his sufferings, for I was already a sharer of his grief before I knew the cause of it. It was at this moment that the dame began her story in the words of my commencement.

" Ten years to-day," said she, " since that picture was painted, sir."

" Ah, my poor dear child!" sighed David; from which ejaculation I inferred that I was about to hear a tale, of which his own daughter was the heroine: but I was soon undeceived by his wife, who thus proceeded:—

" It ben't necessary to go farther back into the dear child's life than to the day on which she was first placed with me to nurse. Who she is has nought to do with what she is, or the story of her life; certain sure it is she was the loveliest babe I ever saw, and I and David were as proud of her as if she were our own, bless her dear heart! How everybody talked about her! and how all the folks did love her too, surely! I can't tell ye, sir, how beautiful she was; and, as she grew, her beauty kept good pace with her years, I promise you. She was nine years old the day the painter came to make a likeness of her for her father. Here she sat in this very room, just as you see her in the picture, sir: she had run in from the garden where she had been at romps with poor George, and was puffing away at the fire with an old pair of bellows which she found among the lumber in the tool-house, when the gentleman, whom she did not notice at first, was arranging his matters for the painting of the picture. It was at the moment that she turned round to see who was in the room, that, as he said, he was so struck with her lovely face he could have taken her likeness if he had not seen her a moment longer; and, sure enough, he was not out much in his reckoning, for scarcely had he taken his pencil in his hand before the little mad-cap bounded out of the room, and ran off to her playmate in the garden. That is a copy of the picture, sir; and if the poor dear child were sitting here as she was on that day, she couldn't look more like herself than that painting does to me."

David was in the very act of again converting his handkerchief into a duster; but, after a momentary struggle, for once in a way he pressed a corner of it to his eyes, and kept his seat.

" Of all those, barring myself and David," continued the dame, " who loved the sweet child,—as, to be sure, everybody did more or less,—none seemed to dote on her so much as the young gentleman who was then our village doctor's assistant, and poor George."

" And, pray, who was poor George?" said I.

" Ah! sir, his sorry story too; but of that anon. He was a gentleman born, sir, dear soul! but, before he was barely out of his teens, study and such like turned his wits, and poor George was placed in our care, an idiot. Oh! how he would watch and wait upon his "young mistress," as he used to call the dear child! and Harri— for so we nicknamed our little Harriet—seemed to look up to him for all her amusements and happiness. Good heart! to see him racing round the garden till he was fairly tired and beat for breath, trundling her in the wheelbarrow, and fancying himself her coachman; and then how he'd follow her wherever she went, as if to protect her; always at a distance when he fancied she didn't wish him with her, but never out of sight. She appeared to be his only care; his poor head seemed filled with nothing but thoughts of her. His friends used to send him trinkets, and money, and baubles, to amuse him; and his greatest pride was to take little Harri into his room, and show her his stores, hang his gilt chains and beads about her neck, seat her in his large arm-chair, and stand behind it as if he were her footman, and play all kinds of pranks to make her laugh; for he seemed pleased when she laughed at him, though he wouldn't bear a smile from anybody else at the same cause. His senses served him at times, and then he would fall into fits of the bitterest melancholy as he sat looking in our sweet child's face, as if reflecting how much he loved her, and how little his wandering mind was able to prove his affection! Ah, poor dear fellow! it's well his sufferings ended when they did, for they would have been terrible indeed if he had lived till now; but all who loved her best, fell off from her either by death or desertion when her day of trouble came."

David's resolution was plainly wavering as to the application of his handkerchief, when Bessum gave it the turn in favour of the picture on perceiving her husband's emotion, by adding,

"As for David and myself, you know, sir, we are nobody; it would be strange indeed if we could ever have turned our backs upon the dear child."

"God forbid!" said David; and little Harri's portrait received the extra polish breathed upon it by a deep sigh, previous to the ordinary one emanating solely from the handkerchief. "God forbid!" repeated David, and Bessum added a hearty amen as she resumed her story.

"As the sweet child grew up," continued she, "she was the talk of all tongues far and near; and, before she was fifteen, sir, gentlefolks came from all parts to see her. A fine time we had of it surely; first one pretence, and then another, kept us answering questions and inquiries about her all day long. As for Dame Beetle, who kept a little shop, and sold gloves, over the way, just facing this window, she made a pretty penny by the beauty of our sweet child, although the old simpleton thought it was the goodness of her gloves that brought her so many gentlemen customers. Why, I have known no fewer than five or six of the neighbouring squires,—ay, and lords too,— so difficult to fit, that they've been standing over the little counter by the hour together; but I warrant not to much purpose, as far as the real object of their visit was concerned. No sooner did horse, or gig, or carriage stop in the village, than dear Mr. George,—that is him that was with the doctor, you know, sir."

"Oh, his name was George too?"

"Yes, that it was, sir; and down here he would run as fast as legs could carry him, and his first question was always, 'David, where is little Harri?' Take her into the garden.'. And here he would sit till the gentlefolks opposite were gone away. If ever one creature did dote upon another, Mr. George loved that sweet child. Ah! would to Heaven he had lived to make her his wife! but it's all fate, and so I suppose it's for the best as it is; though I would have died sooner than things should have fallen out as they have, if that could have prevented it!"

"A thousand times over," responded David, with a fond glance at the picture. "I'd rather never have been born than have lived to weep over the ruin of such heavenly beauty and goodness."

A chill of horror struck upon my heart as I repeated with inquiring emphasis the word that had produced it.

"The ruin!" said I; "impossible!" and as I raised my eyes towards heaven at the thought of such a sacrifice, they caught those of the victim in the picture. I could have wept aloud, so powerful was the influence of the gaze that I encountered. There sat the loveliest creature that the world e'er saw,—an artless, careless child, health, hope, and happiness beaming in her sweet fair face; her lips, although the choicest target for his aim, the foil of Cupid's darts, so pure, so modest was the smile that parted them; her eyes, the beacon-lights of virgin chastity; her joyous look, the Lethe where pale Care could come but to be lost,—it scared off Woe! And were these made for Ruin to write shame upon! Oh, man!—monster!—ingrate fiend!— I was roused from my reverie by the perseverance of the good dame, who thus took up the thread of her discourse, that my exclamation had broken:

"Ah, poor Mr. George! if he had lived, all would have been well. I make bold to say, for certain sure, they would have been man and wife by this time; for though she used to go on finely at 'that doctor,' as the darling girl used to call him, because he was the cause of her being taken into the garden so often, without knowing why,—for all that, she loved him in her heart, poor dear! as well she might; for, as I said before, he fairly doted upon her. And yet, so delicate was his noble mind, he could never as it were talk seriously to her,—that is to say, not to make any kind of love to her, you know, sir. He had known her from a precious babe; and although his whole heart and soul, I do believe, were set upon one day making her his wife, if so be as she should not refuse him of her own free will, still he felt so almost like a father to her, though he was not more than eight or nine years older than she, that he never could bring himself to fairly pay court to her as a lover, you see."

"God bless his noble heart!" said David, as he rested his elbow on his knee, and his chin on the palm of his hand; "he always said he should be drowned: there's fate again, Bessum, sure enough."

"And did he die by drowning?" said I.

"Ay, sir," replied the dame; "and scarce was he dead, as if they only waited for that, than our sweet child's misfortunes began."

"Destiny, indeed!" thought I, as a superstitious feeling seemed to prepare me for the proofs of it.

"She was just sixteen, and that's nearly five years ago, when she lost him who would have been more than all the world to her, as a body may say, and when Lieutenant H—— brought permission from a certain quarter to court her for his wife. Heavy was my poor heart at the thought of parting with the dear child; but more so ten times over, though I couldn't tell why, at the idea of who I was going to part with her to. She, poor darling, was proud of the conceit of being married, and pleased with the gold lace and cocked-hat of the young sailor. I don't believe the thought of love for him ever once entered her head: but that was nothing, for she would have loved any one who behaved kindly to her; and then to be a wife, and her own mistress, and the mistress of a house! Alack-a-day! she little knew what she was doing when she promised her hand where her heart had not gone before, and where none was beating for her. But it was well she made no objection, for it was to be, whether or no; so she was spared at least the pain of being forced against her will. Well, sir, the wedding-day came, and never do I remember such a day as it was. In vain did the bells ring and the sun shine; folks, spite of all, and of themselves too, couldn't be merry: they smiled, and talked, and tried to appear gay; but, to my plain, honest thinking, there was not a light heart in the village. Poor George, to be sure, was dancing with delight, for he saw the preparations, and the fine clothes, and he heard the bells ringing and the neighbours talking, and he understood that all was for and about his lady, as he then called his old playmate; and the idea of so much fuss and bustle on her account made him as proud and happy as if he were to be the sharer of it. Little did he imagine that it was to end in robbing him of the only comfort of his hapless life, poor fellow; and as the bride and bridegroom came from church, where to the very altar he had followed like a guardian saint, his watchful eye faithful in its duty to the last, he picked up here and there a flower that the villagers had strewn, on which she trod, and stuck them in a row in the button-holes of his waistcoat. But when the time came that our dear sweet child was to be torn from our arms, then was a scene I never shall forget. She bade us one by one good-b'ye, as if she didn't dream of being gone from us a day. It fairly seemed as though Providence had deprived her of all thought. But when she came to take her leave of George, she appeared to shrink from bidding him farewell. She took his hand, and with a fluttering smile said, 'George, I am going for a ride,' and she was gone! For full three hours after, George was missing; and when the twilight made us stir to find where he could be, there by the garden-gate he stood, with the old wheelbarrow at his side, his handkerchief spread out upon it, as he was wont to do when he used to wheel his little playmate in it years agone,—there was he waiting till she should come 'to ride.' Poor, poor creature! he had no idea of the journey that she meant, when she told him she was going for a ride. He knew that he had been her coachman many a time and oft, and he thought of no other carriage than that which he had driven. I burst out a-crying at the very sight of him. There he stood, as confident that she was coming as if he had seen her on the threshold of the door with her gypsy hat on her head. Three hours he had waited; and when I saw him, it would have melted a heart of stone to watch his look, and think upon the misery in store for him. The sun had gone down, and there was not a sound to hear, but now and then the melancholy pipe of a robin, or the distant tinkle of a sheep-bell. Everything seemed sorrowing in silence at our loss; and he that would pine most, alone was ignorant of it. I hadn't courage to call him away and tell him his misfortune; but when David brought him in, and told him that his lady had gone for a ride with the 'new footman,' as the poor fellow called the lieutenant, the anguish in his face was more woeful than you can think of, sir. Every day at the same hour he brought the wheelbarrow to the garden-gate, and kept it there till sunset; then, till he went to bed, he'd sit arranging the withered flowers in his waistcoat. He was never obstinate in refusing to do as he was desired; but, unless he had been bidden to eat and drink, no morsel would have passed his lips: he never thought of hunger or of thirst; his little mistress, his old playmate, and, as he thought her, his only friend, alone occupied his mind, that never wandered now. It was fixed upon one object, and on that it dwelt. Ten months he pined and lingered for his loss; and then, more sensible than he had ever been before, poor George, sir, died!"

"And happy for him that he is no more," said I, anticipating the sequel of little Harri's story. "He has gone down to the cold bed, it is true; but his pillow is far smoother than the down that is pressed in vain for quiet and repose by the heartless and unfeeling."

"True, very true, sir," said David, and I was half in doubt whether the handkerchief would be put in requisition again; but it kept its place across the knees of my host, and Bessum continued. "From the day she left us, sir, we saw no more of our dear child for two years; but sad was the tale that reached us in the mean while. Think of her wrongs, sir;—the man who had taken her, to be parted but by death, left her the very next day, after he had robbed scores of honest hearts of the chance of proving the sincerity of their love by a life of cherishing and devotion."

"God forgive him!" said David, "for I never can."

"The gallows pardon him! for I never would," cried I.—"And what became of the deserted wife?"

Bessum, who had for nearly an hour stifled the feelings to which she was all that time hankering to give vent, finding this either too seasonable or powerful an occasion to resist, burst into tears; while David, as a counterpoise to the grief which he had heretofore monopolised, evinced a well-timed symptom of stoicism, by folding up his handkerchief at least three times as small as the usual dimensions which laundresses or common consent have established time out of mind as its proper limit, and then thrusting it into the salt-box pocket of his coat, as being the last place, at that particular crisis, to which, under the influence of his senses, he certainly must have intended its destination.

"I shall make short work of the rest on't, I promise ye, sir," sobbed the tender-hearted foster-mother; "it ben't much use to dwell upon the finish."

"End it at once," said I, impatient of farther melancholy detail.

"Twenty-four hours had not passed, sir, after the heartless fellow had become a husband, before he was aboard ship, and on his way to the Indies. He had completed his bargain; he had married our blessed child, and received his wages for the job. He took her to the house of one of her relations near London, and without telling her whither he was going, or when, if ever, he should return, left

her as I have described. Fancy the sweet soul's sufferings, sir!—
think what she felt when she found herself a widow before she was
fairly a wife! Oh! my heart bleeds when I recollect her wrongs!
Well, sir, she pined and fretted till those with whom she lived would
fain to have got rid of her, I promise you; and it was not long before
they had their wish."

"And did the poor child die of her distress?" said I. "Alas! so
young!"

"Not just then, sir. You'll scarcely think that the worst of her
troubles had yet to come; but so it was, poor dear! As fate would
have it, she was one day met and followed home by a gentleman,
who, she could not help observing, appeared so struck with her, that,
though he did not offer to speak to her, he seemed determined upon
finding where she lived. Every day for more than a week did he watch
the house nearly all day long; and when at last she went out of doors,
he made the best of the opportunity, and began in the most woeful
manner to tell her how much he loved her, and what he was suffering
on her account, and to beg and pray of her not to be angry with him
for what he could not help. Well, sir, he spoke so mild and respectful, and seemed so truly miserable, that the wretched widow couldn't
find it in her heart to speak harshly to him, and so at first she made
no answer at all. He told her that he saw she had something on her
mind that distressed her, and said he felt certain sure he could make
her happy, and that not even her displeasure should make him cease
from the attempt. And, sure enough, to her, poor thing! he seemed
to be as good as his word; for, though she forbade him to approach
her in any way again, still he hovered about the house as much as
ever, and wrote such letters, telling of his misery and anxiety on her
account, that, tired out by the ill-treatment of those to whose tender
mercies she was abandoned, sinking under the pangs of her desertion,
and beset by the arts and entreaties of a fine young man, who seemed
to speak so fairly for her comfort and good, in an evil hour the poor
distracted and deluded creature flew to his arms for that protection
which in vain was pledged her by a husband. I have already told
you that, in my opinion, she never had a thought of any love for the
man she had married. It is not to be wondered at, then, that one,
who at least professed himself to be all that a husband should be,
found no great difficulty or delay in gaining her affections and confidence in return. In short, her young heart, that had never before
known the feeling, was now fixed upon this man with all the fondness
and devotion of a first love. It was no hard matter, therefore, for him
to persuade her to whatever he liked; and the first advice he gave
her for her good, was to take a house in the neighbourhood of one of
the parks, which he made his home, eating, drinking, and riding about
at her expense. Well, sir, for several months this was a life of uninterrupted happiness for our poor Harri. She had quiet or company
as she liked, and the society of him that she loved to madness. The
first sign of interruption to the joys that, alas! are always too dearly
bought at the sacrifice she had made, was the news of the arrival in
England of her husband, and, within two days after that, his appearance at her house. Here was a fine to do, indeed! She was alone
in her drawing-room, and no one else in the house but the two maid-
servants. In vain did she entreat and resist him; by main force he

carried her out of the house; put her into a hackney-coach, without bonnet or shawl; and drove away with her to the house of his mother. That man was born to be her torment and ruin, sir. He had left her when he ought most to have been in her company, and he returned when his desertion had driven her in misery and despair to seek for happiness, in the expectation of which with him he had deceived her; —to disturb the comfort his heartlessness had neglected to afford her. Don't fancy that he loved her, sir. 'Twas no such thing, as I shall soon make clear to you. However, not six hours after she had been taken away, the dear child was home again, and in the arms of the man she would have risked her life for. Here was devotion, sir! She got out of a one-pair of stairs window, by letting herself down with the bed-clothes as far as they would reach, and by jumping the rest; and just as she had been taken from her home, without a bit of out-door covering, off she set, in the cold and wet of a December night, and had to walk for full a mile and a half before she got the coach that carried her home. Did her husband love her, sir? Day after day he rode or walked past the house, and sent letters to her; but never once offered to seek out the man that kept his wife from him. *Can* he have loved her, sir? To leave her in the quiet possession of another, and take himself off again to the Indies! So much for the husband:—and now for the lover, as he called himself. Matters, I don't know what, took him to France, and he was to return to her who was weary of her life in his absence, within a month. He had not been gone a fortnight before she received a letter from him, written in a French prison, where he was confined for debt. That hour she started post for Dover; and in three days they were on their road home together. Little Harri had released the man she adored, and brought him away from his troubles in triumph and joy."

David's handkerchief, notwithstanding the depth into which it had been plunged, and the compactness with which it had been doubled up, was out of his pocket, unfolded, and across his knees in an instant; evincing a conviction in the mind of its proprietor that that part of Bessum's story was approaching to narration which would certainly call for its application in the united capacities to which David was in the habit of appropriating it.

The dame resumed; for I should mention that she had made a preparatory pause, in the interval of which she took occasion to fortify herself for the coming trial with a considerable pinch of Scotch snuff.

"They didn't reach home, sir," said she, "for more than a fortnight; for they stayed a day here, and a day there, to see the sights, and such like; and because she, poor dear! was in no condition for much hurry, though she had forgotten that, when she started, as she did every thing but her devoted love for him she went to rescue. But, when they did arrive, dearly did our sweet child pay for the fault a husband's cruelty had driven her to commit, and bitter was the punishment of Providence: but it was all fate, I'm sure it was; it must have been; for surely her crime did not call for such a dreadful judgment as befell her. Oh, good heart, sir! think of the poor dear after all she had undergone in a journey to a foreign land, where she had never been before, and all alone, too, sir, without a friend to help or to advise her! She had left a house fitted and furnished like a little palace, as a body may say; the homestead of her high-priced, fatal happiness. Think of her reaching what she thought a home, and finding none! She was soon to be a mother, and she had not a bed to lay her down upon! In the short time that she had been away, the servant in whose charge she left her house, by the help and advice of a villain she kept company with, had carried off every thing, under the pretence that she was moving for her mistress! Ah! you may look surprised, sir, and with reason, *but 'tis just as true as you and I sit here.*"

"God's will be done!" sobbed David, as he buried his face in his handkerchief with both his hands. "She's out of harm's way now, Bessum. God's will be done!" and the simple-hearted man wept like a boy. The tears ran so fast down the sorrowful face of the poor dame, that the relief they afforded her enabled her to proceed to the climax of little Harri's misfortunes.

"She didn't rave and take on, sir," said Bessum. "The hand of destiny was on her, and she felt it. As calmly as though nothing had occurred, she bade the coachman drive to a certain hotel; she seemed to reckon but for a moment between what she had lost and what she had regained, and she was satisfied with the account as it stood. All in the world for which she cared was still spared to her,—she had herself preserved him, the author of her dishonour, the cause of her loss; and, the only compensation for it, the father of her child! These were all she prized; and he who was one and all, now sat beside her. With a smile of resignation, confidence, and content, she looked in his face, and said, "What's to be done?"

The eyes upon the canvass seemed to ask *me* for an answer: I felt that I could beg subsistence for such a woman; become a drudge, a slave, or yield my life up for her sake.

"And what was his reply?" cried I.

"Good advice—good advice, sir," sobbed Bessum. "*He asked her if she did not think she had better go to her old nurse!*"

Mute with amazement and disgust, I sank back in my chair.

"What!" cried I, when the power of articulation returned; "was that the good advice?"

"Ay, sir,—ay! that was all the comfort our poor dear got from her *lover*; she asked him for no more. She didn't upbraid him. He had dealt her death-blow, and she followed his advice; she came to her old nurse, sir,—God be praised!—and I and David closed her precious eyes for ever, after they had lingered, in their last dim sight, on the lifeless image of him, whose name, with her forgiveness, and prayer to Heaven for his happiness, were the last words upon her sweet, sweet lips!"

"And if a special hand is not upraised to strew his path of life with tenfold the sharp pangs that he employed to drive his victim to an early grave," cried I, "it can only be that it has already crushed the monster into death."

My heart was faint and sick at the recital I had heard. I returned to my inn; and all that night—for it was in vain that I attempted to sleep—I mused upon this awful dispensation of the wrath of Heaven, and the dread severity with which the wisdom of vindictive Providence had stricken the transgression of poor little Harri!

EUGENIUS.

THE WHITE MAN'S DEVIL-HOUSE.

A FRAGMENT.

BY F. HARRISON RANKIN.

" There is a magic in the craft."

EXOTERICS surmise it to consist in " winks and nods," proverbially of equal inspiration to steeds labouring under the dispensation of *gutta serena.* Mesmer's Animal Magnetism was nothing to the invisible " tractors." Ticklings of the palm have been surmised; talismanic numbers have been hinted at; sounds inaudible have been suggested; together with certain " melodious twangs," awakening pineal sympathy. Mrs. Veal's ghost, from De Foe's autopsy of the apparition, evidently held no less a grade in the scale of shadowy society than that of Master Mason.

John Locke, the philosopher, subsequently one of the fraternity, opined that the art embraced sorcery, alchemy, the transmutation of essences and of metals, together with similar common-place desiderata.

Whatever the nature of the spell, its sway is wide. Affinity of feeling generated by it runs round the world. It may be found in the land of the Chinese, of the Arab, the Red Indian, and the wild Tartar; in the frozen circle, habitat of all seals excepting Solomon's, and in the burning desert,

" Terra domibus negata."

Our story relates to the last pleasant locality.

Upon the windward coast of Africa, in a situation calculated to warm the coolest temperament, stands a European settlement,—a pimple of civilization upon the fiery face of a barbarous continent.

" Once upon a time " a lodge had existed there. Its members had ceased to melt, having gradually melted away; for the constant flux and reflux of white residents, the brief sojourn of many, and the death of an appropriate portion, rapidly vary the population of the little colony. After a lapse of years, however, it was not long since determined that the lodge should be re-opened.

The house formerly used had become ineligible; and, in the true spirit of a mason-soldier, a gallant captain offered to receive his brothers in his own wing of the barracks.

This building was advantageously situated. It crowned the summit of a high conical hill; so that, although the deluges of the rainy season were fast approaching, it could with much facility be closely and effectually tiled. But here, art was still in her swaddling bands; and although, in our accomplished country, bricklayers and plasterers are as " plenty as blackberries," in her colony no tiler could be found.

The name of Solyma,—that prince of architects, and prototype of modern Wrens and Barrys,—his glory, and his power over things seen and unseen, were familiar, especially to the black Mahometan population, to the sojourning Foulah, and the travelled Mandingo; but they possessed neither his skill nor his secret, being as mournfully ignorant of his workmanlike perfections as they are of the name of the mother of Moses. A tiler, however, was indispensable; and here arose a difficulty. What black man, Mahometan or pagan, could be induced to receive instruction; and, regardless of the prophet Mahmoud on the one hand, and, on the other, of Satan,—the principal object of fervid worship amongst the infidels of those hot parts,—to hazard his well-being in this world, and his sombre soul in the next, by tiling the edifice?

Various were the negro gentlemen invited; but few possessed "hearts big enough." No wonder that in the gold-dust country they should prove deficient in the "*æs triplex!*" One refused upon the very admissible ground that the masons had been accustomed to attend service in the colonial church once annually; and that, claiming to himself the same liberty of conscience which he allowed to others, —being by birth, and subsequently by conviction, of that extensive religious "persuasion" called Pagans, and of the particular sect of the said popular church which worships the devil and reverences dead men's teeth,—he must decline compromising his religious principles, and sanctioning by his presence the heterodox tenets of the English colonial chaplain.

A second, however, had forsaken the Heathen modes of his ancestors, and had waxed into a fervent proselyte, under missionary auspices, in all respects save a tough hereditary prejudice in favour of a genteel establishment of eight or ten wives

> "To grind his corn,"

as Mungo Park poetically saith, but

> "To pound his rice,"

as it doubtless ran in the original and vernacular glote, whether Fantee, Mandingo, Cosso, Bullum, or Soosoo. This strange conjugal whim, be it remarked, generally is as unalienable, tenaciously tenable, and adhesive to the negro taste, as "roast pig" was to the palate of the mortal Charles Lamb and the immortal "Elia."

This reclaimed pagan, however, professed that he would rather dine on fried soles, that unclean piscatorial; masticate dog's flesh before it had become putrid; disbelieve in witchcraft; or put away a spouse, however freckled, than adjoin himself unto a society whose *nominal* master indeed might be the Honourable Colonial Secretary, but whose real spiritual president, he well knew, could be no other than Beelzebub the *Bugaboog*, whose ways he had renounced.[*]

The remaining mass of the negro "ton" declined their services on reasons no less satisfactory. They appealed to the yet living reputation of the deceased lodge, which they characterized as *prononcée* to a degree; for the spirit of the building, once redolent of mysteries and fraternity, prolongs a posthumous existence in their imaginings, awful and evitabund. It is desolate, for none will enter it; it is crumbling, for none will repair it; it is shunned as the favourite triclinium of Sathana, Beelzeboub, and Ashtaroth; it is known as

> "THE WHITE MAN'S DEVIL-HOUSE."

As incredulous a negress as ever succumbed to Obeah asserted that, from its vague interior, bells were heard to toll, and chains to clank,

---

[*] It is curious that whilst the Hebrew word Beelzebub means " prince of flies," Bugaboo, in negro language, signifies " the white ant," which is deemed the devil's familiar.

at the lone hour of midnight, twelve,—when the "sun lived in the bush;" and that many a rash eye had been scared away by goblin apparitions and rank sights. With her own orbs, whilst stealthily prying through a window, had she beheld no less a potentate than Satan himself, sucking the blood of a white cock, and feeding a dead man with palaver sauce.

The idea of secret and mysterious associations is not new to the negroes; they have not borrowed it from the white man. A short reference to the nature of such as are familiar to them will throw light upon the awe with which they regarded the old Devil-House of the white man, and declined the privilege of *entrée* at the new one.

Their own hidden fraternities existed in gigantic organisation, and with withering power, long before the diseased and "craw-craw" complexion of European discoverers was known to the natural inheritors of Warren's jet blacking. Evil rites attend them; and bodily mutilation, and the chance of slavery, are united to supernatural horrors. Well aware of this, they naturally imagine similar diabolic mysteries to constitute the "working" of white man's freemasonry; nay, more; recognising the superiority, the mastery of the whites in all things that come under their observation, they take for granted that the same exists in matters which they do not witness, and, if their own orgies are terrific, they suppose that those of the white man must be intensely more so.

Of all men they are most horribly superstitious, and, in consequence, are victims also to superstitious horrors of the first magnitude. The forest, or bush, the air, the streams, the ground, swarm with a surplus population of Satan's imps and witches. Each moment and each step expose the wayfarer to the gripe of some malicious fiend. To evade the unwholesome clutch, the limbs are ornamented with charms and talismans, with dead men's hair and leopards' teeth. To deprecate and conciliate these animavorous specimens of African zoology no pains are spared, and temples named "Devil-Houses" witness the placatory sacrifices to the spirit of evil.

But this will not suffice. It is not enough simply to protect the person. Associations are formed which recognise the necessity of watching over Satan's interests, by visiting with direful vengeance such members of the tribe at large as may have treated his majesty with less respect than his station entitles him to expect. There are liberalists and spiritual republicans even in Africa.

Some writers, in noticing these associations as similar to freemasonry, have fallen into the same error with the black colonists aforesaid, who refused their aid to tile the lodge because they confounded it with their own tremendous and execrable fraternities.

The secret sisterhoods of Africa have their own peculiar charms and peculiar annoyances. The initiated maidens enjoy much respect, and a singular liability to be sold to the slave-factory; and many inducements are held out to the grand-mistress of the order to dispose of her gentle sisters in this manner, since a well-built maiden, warranted of clever action, of unblemished points, and sound lungs, will find bidders at a hundred hard dollars at any respectable bazaar between Senegal and Guinea. "Inshallah!" (God be praised!) as the Mahometan slave-merchant thankfully observed.

The honour, however, compensates for the danger, and they love to entwine the privileged emblem of their order, the ivory circlets, in the hair; an ornament that glads the heart of the simple ebony maid, as feathers and brilliants rejoice that of the blonde or the nut-brown. The initiations, alas! are attended with ungentle mutilation of the person; and the trembling and weeping girl is blindfolded, that she may never know the woman who lacerated her. Gashes, however, on the face, arms, breast, and back, are favourite ornaments; they are the unpretending substitutes for rouge and cosmetics. The society is in a flourishing state, and the worshipful mistress derives a considerable revenue by the sale of refractory maidens. The guilt generally arises in the practice of witchcraft and sorcery;—accomplishments assiduously cultivated by the young ladies of Nigritia.

But, to return to our story. Enough has been said to explain how it happened that ideas of awe rested amongst the black colonists upon "The White Man's Devil-House."

The night was of that deep-toned glory unimagined save by those who have watched the firmament of a tropical sky. No moon was up; but the moon-like planets threw upon the sultry ground shadows of man and horse as they slowly wound round the long mountain path that led from the sea-washed capital at its foot, to the summit of the Barrack Hill. As a higher elevation was gained, the suffocating breath of the low grounds became tempered by the land breeze, that floated down by the channel of the wide river, and flung itself rudely upon the hill side. Yet the still, close atmosphere, and the distant flickering of purple and golden lightning far away to the east over the lands of savage nations, warned against loitering for the chance of a tornado. By ones and twos the little straggling brotherhood alighted at the barrack gates; and there, thousands of miles from Old England and the fire-side of home, men unconnected by birth, by interests, or by office, met, and cordially felt that they were related. Just before entering the chamber whose secrets are bound as by adamant, the eye fell upon a figure sitting in the verandah in the very dignity of overmastering terror. His aspect told that he was following the poet's advice,

" Nimium ne crede colori !"

He was a black man awaiting the ceremony of initiation with much the same intensity of interest that enlivens the criminal at execution. He appeared the living representative of that fear-stricken island tree whose trembling leaves distil a sympathetic dew. He was an old serjeant of the Royal African Corps. Years of discipline had taught him reverence for the tastes of his superiors; and when invited by his officer to tile the lodge, overcome on the one hand by the condescension of the captain, and overwhelmed on the other by misgivings of latent Satanic cajolery, he had plunged into the Rubicon. If his commander had deemed it expedient to form an alliance with so powerful a prince as the prince of darkness, what business had he to do with it? He had fought at Waterloo, and would fight at any time against the devil himself if ordered to the charge; but he had never expected to serve in the same company. However, he sturdily denied flinching from the approaching trial of his courage.

The negro's burnished face smartened up when all was over. Rumour, whose numerous tongues, if well pickled, would pair off with all the boiled turkeys cooked in Christendom on a Christmas-day, and leave plenty to spare, told the tale of wonder in " quarter less no time," how Serjeant B. had become a member of white man's purrah ; how he had sat down to supper with Captain —— on one side, the devil on the other, and the chief judge opposite ; how the serjeant thought he recognised the " old gentleman " as a comrade in the Peninsula ; and how the " old gentleman " politely acknowledged similar remembrances, and took wine with him ; and how they had parted, with mutual hopes and promises of meeting again at some future day, in the hot season, not in " the rains."

The more the woolly-headed men and maidens of his inquisitive acquaintance interrogated the serjeant himself concerning his adventure on that fearful night, the more he would not tell them a word about the matter ; and, to this moment, no mysteries are more mysterious, no secrets more arcane, than those which trouble the black population of the little colony respecting " The White Man's Devil-House."

A LYRIC FOR LOVERS.

Love launch'd a gallant little craft,
   Complete with every rope ;
In golden words was painted aft—
   " The Cupid, Captain Hope."
Pleasure was rated second-mate,
   And Passion made to steer ;
The guns were handed o'er to Fate,
   To Impulse sailing-gear.

Merrily roved the thoughtless crew
   Amidst the billows' strife ;
But soon a sail bore down,—all knew
   'Twas Captain Reason's " Life."
And Pleasure left, though Passion said
   He 'd guard her safe from all harms.
'Twas vain ; for Fate ramm'd home the lead,
   While Love prepared the small-arms.

A storm arose ! The canvass now
   Escaped from Impulse' hand,
While headstrong Passion dash'd the prow
   Swift on a rocky strand.
" All 's lost !" each trembling sailor cried ;
   " Bid Captain Hope adieu !"
But in his life-boat Reason hied
   To save the silly crew.

Impulse the torrents overwhelm,
   But Pleasure 'scaped from wreck ;
Love, making Reason take the helm,
   Chain'd Passion to the deck.
" I thought you were my foe ; but now,"
   Said Love, " we 'll sail together ;
Reason, henceforth through life shalt thou
   My pilot be for ever !"

REMAINS OF HAJJI BABA.

CHAPTER VII.

My great anxiety now was to reach the foot of the English throne as soon as possible; and I consulted my infidel friend upon the safest, easiest, and least public manner of putting my project into execution. I had thought it right to place sufficient confidence in him to inform him that I was an agent of the King of Persia, commissioned to make certain proposals to the King of England; but that it was not my intention to insist upon an *istakbal*, or deputation, upon my entry into the principal city, or to demand either maintenance or lodging at the expense of the nation: in short, I wished to be as little known as possible. He assured me that the most private manner of travelling was a public coach. This rather appeared paradoxical, for how could I be private and public at the same time? but, after certain explanations, I found that he was right; particularly when he assured me that in point of expense the private mode of conveyance cost about seven times more than the public.

Accordingly, the next morning, having, through the interference of my friend, paid what was due to the owner of the caravanserai, I seated myself in the corner of a handsome coach, drawn by four fine horses, which appeared at the door on purpose for my convenience. My friend seated himself by my side, Mahboob was placed on the outside, and we drove off at such a rate, that I neither had time to find out whether the hour was fortunate, or indeed to ascertain which was the direction of Mecca, much less to say my prayers.

We had not proceeded far, when we stopped, and a third person ascended, and took possession of the corner opposite to me. He was a coarse-looking infidel, with a sallow face covered with hair: bushy eyebrows, dirty in appearance, and, as far as I could discover, wishing to look like one of the people, although he might be of the race of the *omrah*. He said nothing upon entrance,—not even the English *Selam alekum*, which I had long learned to be expressed by the words " Good morning, and fine day ;" but there he sat, as if the orifice of his mouth had been closed by a stroke of fate. The cast of his eye as it glanced upon me was not that of hospitality; and I was certain that, had he been an Arab, I should not have heard the sound of his pestle and mortar braying the coffee for me in token of welcome.

I discovered that my friend's name, who had hitherto thrown his shadow over me, was Jān Pûl, words which surprised me, because they are pure Persian, and might be interpreted, " Soul, Money !" Although the new-comer eyed me with little kindness of aspect, yet, when he looked at my friend Jān, there was a slight indication of respect; but still he said nothing.

We had scarcely cleared the town, when the coach again stopped, and we discovered stepping out of a handsome equipage, with servants and men in *kalaats* to help him, an infidel, who, after some delay taken up in providing for his comfort and accommodation, was helped into our conveyance, and he occupied the fourth and last place in it. He was a handsome man, cleanly and handsomely dressed, full of fair forms and politeness; a perfect contrast to his predecessor, and upon whose whole bearing and manners was inscribed, in legible characters, *sahib najib*, or gentleman.

He was as civil to me as his predecessor had been the contrary. Having ascertained that I was a Persian, he welcomed me to his country in a form of words different from those used in Persia; but in so doing, he not only made my heart glad, but made his own face white. He then complimented me upon belonging to a nation whose people willingly obeyed and upheld the authority of their king, and who were satisfied to live under the laws of their ancient monarchy. I had so long been unaccustomed to receive compliments, that, upon hearing this from the sahib najib, I almost thought myself in Persia again, and was about preparing a suitable answer,—one in which I intended at once to uphold the dignity of my sovereign and to exhibit my own individual readiness of wit, — when an uncouth sound proceeded from the unclean infidel, almost the first sign of life which he had given, that made me start, stopped my eloquence, and threw all the sugared words which I had prepared, back into my throat again. As far as I could understand, the purport of this inauspicious noise was to announce to the sahib najib that he had said something in the words he had addressed to me to which he did not agree, for I perceived anger and disgust arise in his countenance, while the looks of "Soul Money," though not much given to change, also became lowering.

"Surely, sir," said the sahib najib, addressing the unclean infidel still with courtesy in his manner,—"surely you will allow, in these unsettled times, that loyalty to one's king, and obedience to established laws, is a subject worthy of compliment."

"I allow nothing," replied the other, looking straight forward, "but what is for the good of the people."

Upon this there arose a discussion so long and so animated, that it lasted almost all the way to the foot of the English throne, and of which I could with difficulty catch the meaning, so new were most of the words used to my ears.

The sahib najib's argument was full of words such as these; the constitution — vested rights—ancient privileges — funded property—established church—landed interest; and although we were driving through a country more prosperous to my eye than even the regions of Mahomet's paradise could be, surrounded by every luxury, and he apparently the lord of wealth and luxury, still he seemed to persist that he was ruined and reduced to beggary, that his country was on the brink of perdition, and that nothing remained for him to do but to sit down for the rest of his days upon the nummud of despair, and to eat the bitter rind of grief.

The rough infidel, on the contrary, argued that constitutional rights, funded property, land, church, laws, and a great many more things, of the import of which I was ignorant, but of which I promised to acquire knowledge, all, he argued, were alone to be turned to the use of the people; and thus I began to have some little idea of what was meant by that People Shah of whom we had heard so much in Persia.

"What!" said the sahib najib, "when you see the constitution in danger, do not you perceive that it will endanger the happiness of the people whose cause you advocate?"

"I do not see that it is in danger," said the other. "If my boat is sinking because we carry too much sail, shall I not trim my sails and inspect my ballast?"

"But by trimming your boat you would throw all your cargo overboard, and thus lose all you have," answered the other.

This part of the conversation I understood, and then I said, "I now understand: when a camel is overladen, and cannot proceed, on account of the weight of his burthen, either the camel will die, or I must lighten his burthen."

"Very good," said the rough man, who now for the first time cast the shadow of his condescension over me. "You are the lord of quick understanding, and see things."

"But," said his well-dressed antagonist, "I neither agree that the boat is badly trimmed, or that the camel is overladen:" then, turning to me, he said, "Surely, sir, you, who have been bred and born a Mussulman, who have let your beard grow according to old-established custom, who have washed your hands and feet in accordance to the precepts of your law,—you would not change all at once, because some new sect in your country were to arise and say, 'Cut off your beard, cease to wash, pray in a new manner, and say to Mahomet, You are a false prophet;' you could not in your conscience do so."

"*Astafarallah!*" said I, blowing over my shoulders at the same time, "am I mad to eat such a profusion of abomination!"

"You are a man of perfection," said he. "I am sure the more you see of my country and get acquainted with its present condition, the more you will agree with me."

I looked towards my friend Jan Pul, who hitherto had not uttered a word, and said, "This sahib says nothing. Perhaps owing to his saying less than we do, he may be the lord of more wisdom than all our heads put together."

"What can I say," said Jan calmly, "when there is much to

be said on both sides? The highest wisdom is to gather experience from the past, and apply it to the necessities of the future."

"Agreed," said the rough man: "we must therefore reform."

"Agreed," said the smooth man: "reform is useless."

I immediately perceived how the matter stood, and, with that penetration for which all Persians are famous, I discovered the true state of the whole country. I saw that the people were divided into two sects, as much opposed to each other as Jews are to true believers; that plain sense had as little chance in the controversy as a sober man may have in the brawls of two drunkards; and that, before things get straight, each of the drunkards must be sobered by breaking their shins in stumbling over a stone, or their heads by carrying them too high.

CHAPTER VIII.

WE continued to drive onwards: the faster we went, the more the infidels argued. I sat in my corner guessing my way through their words, and already making up in my mind the sort of letter which I should write to the Asylum of the Universe upon the state of this extraordinary country, whilst my silent friend, with his hook-stick and close-buttoned coat, shut his eyes and slumbered; only occasionally giving signs of life. At length we arrived at a house which I supposed might be a caravanserai, after the Franc fashion, open to true believers, for, on looking up I saw painted upon a board an elephant with a castle upon its back. I began to think this might be in compliment to me, seeing that elephants are part of the state of Persian monarchs: but I was mistaken, because, instead of taking any notice of me, the sahib najib, on the contrary, did not show his usual civility; but, putting his head out of the window, he asked one of the bystanders, "Is there any news astir?"

"Nothing particular," said an unconcerned infidel; "nothing. The papers say, 'A man threw a stone and has broken the king's head!'"

"There," said the smooth man to the rough, "there, that comes of your reform!"

"I deny that," said the other: "on the contrary, it comes of your no-reform."

"Why, surely," answered the sahib najib, "if you had not taught the people not to respect their king, to despise his nobles, and to laugh at the laws, such an atrocity never would have happened."

"No, indeed, it never would," retorted the other, "if you had made such changes that the people would love their king, respect his nobles, and be satisfied with the laws."

"Then you think stoning your king a right thing to do?" said one.

"Then you allow making him odious," answered the other, "is what ought to be done?"

"Will a stone get up and throw itself?"

"Will a man complain unless he be aggrieved?"

"Hallo! my friend," said the sahib najib to the bystander, "what is said about this atrocious act, eh?"

"Why, some say, 'Poor king!' others say, 'Poor stone!'" answered the bystander in the coolest manner possible.

At this I began truly to have an insight into things, and could not help exclaiming in the bottom of my gullet, "*Allah Allah, il Allah!* There is but one Allah!"

"You understood what that man said?" said Jan Pul to me, with a sigh, and in a low voice.

"*Belli*, yes," said I, "wonderful! The men of this country are lions without saints. Allah! Allah! to throw a stone at the king, and no executioner by, to cut the wretch's head off."

"No, no," said he, "that must be proved; first, whether it was a stone; second, whether it was a man who threw it; and, third, whether it hit the king's head, or some other head."

"*Aman, aman!* Mercy, mercy!" I exclaimed; "let me return to Persia. If so little is said about breaking the king's head, where shall I turn for justice if some one cuts off my ears? Well may the people want reform!"

"I will just prove to you, sir," said the soft infidel, "that this case just proves that we want no reform."

"How!" said I, "break your king's head, and nobody to mend it!"

"That is not the case," said he. "If a people have so much security from the laws, that not even the poorest wretch, even for a crime of such magnitude, can be condemned without proof against him and a full trial, surely they cannot complain: they are all equal in the eye of the law, and more they cannot want." He said this in great exultation, having obtained, as he conceived, a complete triumph over his adversary, and eyed him with appropriate scorn.

The rough man looked as if his head went round and round, and as if he were come to a full stop; but, pulling up the two ends of his shirt,—I suppose to show that he had one,—he said, "If the people have one good law, is that a reason why they should not have more? The great man may get his head broke, —he is rich and mighty, a little salve cures him, and he is as rich and happy as ever; but the poor man who has broken it, save the satisfaction of making a good throw, he remains as poor and miserable as ever."

"Then, sir," said the sahib najib, "you would have what can never be,—you would have perfect equality amongst mankind?"

"Yes, truly," exclaimed the other; "because, if all were equal, there would be no heads broken, and no stones thrown."

This, too, I understood, and said, " What words are these ?" All men cannot be kings, nor can they all be viziers, nor all khans. I, who know nothing of your extraordinary customs, I can understand that. Were I to think of being anything but what I am, might not my neighbour think so too; and if I wished to be him, and he me, why, then the world would soon be upside down, and from one end of the universe to the other there would be nothing but clutching of beards, and cries of justice, and no justice !"

" Whatever you may say," said the rough infidel, " we must have more equality in our country than we have at present, or else the world will turn upside down. The rich must be poorer, and the poor richer."

During this conversation we were in rapid motion, driving through streets lighted up as magnificently as if the Shah himself had ordered a feast of fire-works, and ornamented by shops exhibiting such riches, that not all the wealth brought from Hind by Nadir Shah, or amassed by the Sofi, could compare to it.

" Strange," thought I to myself, " that this people are not satisfied with their lot !" Passing by a splendid shop, resplendent with cutlery, part of my instructions came into my head, and I said to the rough man, " In the name of the Prophet, do you still make penknives and broad-cloth ?"

At this question my companion stared, and said, " Penknives and broad-cloth, did you say ? Why, we have more penknives and broad-cloth than we know what to do with. We have made so much and so many, that the whole world has more of them than it wants ; and the poor creatures, the manufacturers, are starving for want of work. Surely this wants reform."

This was delightful news for me, and I longed to send an immediate courier to the Shah to inform him of the important fact.

" Whose fault is it ?" said the soft man, determined not to be beaten on any ground. " If manufacturers will do too much, whose fault is it but their own ? Unless you make a reform in common sense, surely no other reform is needful."

By this time the coach had stopped, and I found that we had reached our last menzil. The rough man got out first ; but just as he was stepping down, in order to ensure the last word, he exclaimed, " We want reform not only in that, but in everything else,—more particularly in rotten boroughs."

At these two last words, the soft man became evidently angered, his liver turning into blood, whilst his face became red. " Rotten boroughs, indeed ! the country is lost for ever if one borough is disfranchised."

These words were totally new to my ears, and what they meant I knew not ; but I became quite certain that the rough man had hit the smooth man in a sore place. But I was in the

seventh heaven at the end of their controversy. I had never
heard such warmth of argument, not since that famous dispute
at the Medressah, in Ispahan, between two famous Mollahs, the
one a suni, the other a shiah, whether the children of the true
faith, in washing according to the prescribed law, were to let
the water run from the hand to the elbow; or whether from the
elbow to the hand. They argued for three whole moons, and
neither were convinced; and so they remain to this day, each in
his own persuasion.

"How will it be possible," thought I, "to unravel this intricate question? It is plain these English are a nation of madmen. Oh! could they but take one look at my country, where
the will of one man is all in all,—where no man's head is safe
on his shoulders for one moment,—where, if he heaps up riches
in the course of many years, they may be taken from him in
an hour,—where he does not even think for himself, much
less speak,—where man is as withering grass of the field, and
life as the wind blowing over it; could they but know this,
short would be their controversies. They would praise Allah
with gratitude for their condition, be content with their fate,
and drive all wish of change from their thoughts, as threatening
the overthrow of their happiness.

SHAKSPEARE PAPERS.—No. III.

ROMEO.

" Of this unlucky sort our Romeus is one,
For all his hap turns to mishap, and all his mirth to mone."
The Tragicall Historye of Romeus and Juliet.

"NEVER," says Prince Escalus, in the concluding distich of Romeo
and Juliet,

'— was there story of more woe
Than this of Juliet and her Romeo."

It is a story which, in the inartificial shape of a black-letter ballad, powerfully affected the imagination, and awakened the sensibilities, of our ancestors, and in the hands of Shakspeare has become
the love-story of the whole world. Who cares for the loves of Petrarch and Laura, or of Eloisa and Abelard, compared with those of
Romeo and Juliet? The gallantries of Petrarch are conveyed in
models of polished and ornate verse; but, in spite of their elegance,
we feel that they are frosty as the Alps beneath which they were
written. They are only the exercises of genius, not the ebulli-

tions of feeling; and we can easily credit the story that Petrarch
refused a dispensation to marry Laura, lest marriage might spoil his
poetry.   The muse, and not the lady, was his mistress.   In the case
of Abelard there are many associations which are not agreeable; and,
after all, we can hardly help looking upon him as a fitter hero for
Bayle's Dictionary than a romance.   In Romeo and Juliet we have
the poetry of Petrarch without its iciness, and the passion of Eloisa
free from its coarse exhibition.   We have, too, philosophy far more
profound than ever was scattered over the syllogistic pages of Abelard, full of knowledge and acuteness as they undoubtedly are.

But I am not about to consider Romeo merely as a lover, or to use
him as an illustration of Lysander's often-quoted line,

> " The course of true love never did run smooth."

In that course the current has been as rough to others as to Romeo;
who, in spite of all his misfortunes, has wooed and won the lady of
his affections.   That Lysander's line is often true, cannot be questioned; though it is no more than the exaggeration of an annoyed
suitor to say that love has *never* run smoothly.   The reason why it
should be so generally true, is given in " Peveril of the Peak " by Sir
Walter Scott; a man who closely approached to the genius of Shakspeare in depicting character, and who, above all writers of imagination, most nearly resembled him in the possession of keen, shrewd,
every-day common-sense, rendered more remarkable by the contrast
of the romantic, pathetic, and picturesque by which it is in all directions surrounded.

> " This celebrated passage
>
> ['Ah me! for aught that ever I could read,' &c.]

which we have prefixed to this chapter, [chap. xii. vol. i. Peveril of
the Peak,] has, like most observations of the same author, its foundation in real experience.   The period at which love is felt most
strongly is seldom that at which there is much prospect of its being
brought to a happy issue.   In fine, there are few men who do not
look back in secret to some period of their youth at which a sincere
and early affection was repulsed or betrayed, or became abortive
under opposing circumstances.   It is these little passages of secret
history, which leave a tinge of romance in every bosom, scarce permitting us, even in the most busy or the most advanced period of life,
to listen with total indifference to a tale of true love." *

These remarks, the justice of which cannot be questioned, scarcely
apply to the case of Romeo.   In no respect, save that the families
were at variance, was the match between him and Juliet such as not
to afford a prospect of happy issue; and everything indicated the
possibility of making their marriage a ground of reconciliation between their respective houses.   Both are tired of the quarrel.   Lady
Capulet and Lady Montague are introduced in the very first scene of
the play, endeavouring to pacify their husbands; and, when the brawl
is over, Paris laments to Juliet's father that it is a pity persons of

---

* Was Sir Walter thinking of his own case when he wrote this passage?   See
his Life by Lockhart, vol. i. p. 242.   His family used to call Sir Walter *Old Peveril*, from some fancied resemblance of the character.

such honourable reckoning should have lived so long at variance. For Romeo himself old Capulet expresses the highest respect, as being one of the ornaments of the city; and, after the death of Juliet, old Montague, touched by her truth and constancy, proposes to raise to her a statue of gold. With such sentiments and predispositions, the early passion of the Veronese lovers does not come within the canon of Sir Walter Scott; and, as I have said, I do not think that Romeo is designed merely as an exhibition of a man unfortunate in love.

I consider him to be meant as the character of an *unlucky* man,— a man who, with the best views and fairest intentions, is perpetually so unfortunate as to fail in every aspiration, and, while exerting himself to the utmost in their behalf, to involve all whom he holds dearest in misery and ruin. At the commencement of the play an idle quarrel among some low retainers of the rival families produces a general riot, with which he has nothing to do. He is not present from beginning to end; the tumult has been so sudden and unexpected, that his father is obliged to ask

" What set this ancient quarrel new abroach ?"

And yet it is this very quarrel which lays him prostrate in death by his own hand, outside Capulet's monument, before the tragedy concludes. While the fray was going on, he was nursing love-fancies, and endeavouring to persuade himself that his heart was breaking for Rosaline. How afflicting his passion must have been, we see by the conundrums he makes upon it:

" Love is a smoke raised with the fume of sighs ;
Being purged, a fire sparkling in lovers' eyes ;
Being vex'd, a sea nourish'd with lovers' tears.*
What is it else ?—a madness most discreet,
A choking gall, and a preserving sweet."—

And so forth. The sorrows which we can balance in such trim antitheses do not lie very deep. The time is rapidly advancing when his sentences will be less sounding.

" It is my lady ; oh, it is my love !
O that she knew she were !"—

speaks more touchingly the state of his engrossed soul than all the fine metaphors ever vented. The supercilious Spartans in the days of their success prided themselves upon the laconic brevity of their despatches to states in hostility or alliance with them. When they were sinking before the Macedonians, another style was adopted; and Philip observed that he had taught them to lengthen their monosyllables. Real love has had a contrary effect upon Romeo. It has abridged his swelling passages, and brought him to the language of prose. The reason of the alteration is the same in both cases. The brevity of the Spartans was the result of studied affectation. They sought, by the insolence of threats obscurely insinuated in a sort of demi-oracular language, to impose upon others,—perhaps they imposed upon themselves,—an extravagant opinion of their mysterious

* Is there not a line missing?

power. The secret was found out at last, and their anger bubbled over in big words and lengthened sentences. The love of Rosaline is as much affected on the part of Romeo, and it explodes in wire-drawn conceits.

> " When the devout religion of mine eye
>   Maintains such falsehood, then turn tears to fires ;
> And those who often drown'd could never die,
>   Transparent heretics, be burnt for liars.
> One fairer than my love !—the all-seeing sun
> Ne'er saw her match since first the world begun."

It is no wonder that a gentleman who is so clever as to be able to say such extremely fine things, forgets, in the next scene, the devout religion of his eye, without any apprehension of the transparent heretic being burnt for a liar by the transmutation of tears into the flames of an *auto da fe*. He is doomed to discover that love in his case is not a madness most discreet when he defies the stars ; there are then no lines of magnificent declamation.

> "Is it even so? then I defy you, stars !
> Thou knowest my lodging : get me ink and paper,
> And hire post-horses ; I will hence to-night.'

Nothing can be plainer prose than these verses. But how were they delivered ? Balthazar will tell us.

> " Pardon me, sir ; I dare not leave you thus :
> Your looks are pale and wild, and do import
> Some misadventure."

Again, nothing can be more quiet than his final determination :

> " Well, Juliet, I will lie with thee to-night."

It is plain Juliet,—unattended by any romantic epithet of love. There is nothing about " Cupid's arrow," or " Dian's wit ;" no honeyed word escapes his lips,—nor again does any accent of despair. His mind is so made up,—the whole course of the short remainder of his life so unalterably fixed, that it is perfectly useless to think more about it. He has full leisure to reflect without disturbance upon the details of the squalid penury which made him set down the poor apothecary as a fit instrument for what now had become his " need ;" and he offers his proposition of purchasing that soon-speeding gear which is to hurry him out of life, with the same business-like tone as if he were purchasing a pennyworth of sugar-candy. When the apothecary suggests the danger of selling such drugs, Romeo can reflect on the folly of scrupling to sacrifice life when the holder of it is so poor and unfortunate. Gallant and gay of appearance himself, he tells his new-found acquaintance that bareness, famine, oppression, ragged misery, the hollow cheek and the hungry eye, are fitting reasons why death should be desired, not avoided ; and with a cool philosophy assures him that gold is worse poison than the compound which hurries the life-weary taker out of the world. The language of desperation cannot be more dismally determined. What did the apothecary think of his customer as he pocketed the forty ducats? There you go, lad, —there you go, he might have said,—there you go with that in your girdle that, if you had the strength of twenty men, would straight despatch you. Well do I know the use for which you intend it. To-morrow's sun sees not you alive. And you philosophise to me on the necessity of buying food and getting into flesh. You taunt my poverty,—you laugh at my rags,—you bid me defy the law,—you tell me the world is my enemy. It may be so, lad,—it may be so; but less tattered is my garment than your heart,—less harassed by law of one kind or another my pursuit than yours. What ails that lad? I know not, neither do I care. But that he should moralise to me on the hard lot which I experience,—that he, with those looks and those accents, should fancy that I, amid my beggarly account of empty boxes, am less happy than he,—ha! ha! ha!—it is something to make one laugh. Ride your way, boy: I have your forty ducats in my purse, and you my drug in your pocket. And the law! Well! What can the executioner do worse to me in my penury and my age than you have doomed for yourself in your youth and splendour. I carry not my hangman in my saddle as I ride along. And the curses which the rabble may pour upon my dying moments,—what are they to the howling gurgle which, now rising from your heart, is deafening your ears? Adieu, boy,—adieu!—and keep your philosophy for yourself. Ho! ho! ho!

But had any other passion or pursuit occupied Romeo, he would have been equally unlucky as in his love. Ill fortune has marked him for her own. From beginning to end he intends the best; but his interfering is ever for the worst. It is evident that he has not taken any part in the family feud which divides Verona, and his first attachment is to a lady of the antagonist house.* To see that lady,—perhaps to mark that he has had no share in the tumult of the morning,—he goes to a ball given by Capulet, at which the suitor accepted by the family is to be introduced to Juliet as her intended husband. Paris is in every way an eligible match.

"Verona's summer hath not such a flower."

He who has slain him addresses his corse as that of the "noble County Paris," with a kindly remembrance that he was kinsman of a friend slain in Romeo's own cause. Nothing can be more fervent, more honourable, or more delicate than his devoted and considerate wooing. His grief at the loss of Juliet is expressed in few words; but its sincerity is told by his midnight and secret visit to the tomb of her whom living he had honoured, and on whom, when dead, he could not

* Rosaline was niece of Capulet. The list of persons invited to the ball is

"Signior Martino, and his wife and daughters;
County Anselm[o], and his beauteous sisters;
The lady widow of Vetruvio;
Signior Placentio, and his lovely nieces;
Mercutio, and his brother Valentine;
Mine uncle Capulet, his wife and daughters;
My fair niece Rosaline; [and] Livia;
Signior Valentio, and his cousin Tybalt;
Lucio, and the lively Helena."

I have altered *Anselme* to the Italian form *Anselmo*, and in the seventh line inserted *and*. I think I may fairly claim this list as being in verse. It is always printed as prose.

restrain himself from lavishing funereal homage. Secure of the favour
of her father, no serious objection could be anticipated from herself.
When questioned by her mother, she readily promises obedience to
parental wishes, and goes to the ball determined to "look to like, if
looking liking move." Everything glides on in smooth current till the
appearance of him whose presence is deadly. Romeo himself is a
most reluctant visitor. He apprehends that the consequences of the
night's revels will be the vile forfeit of a despised life by an untimely
death, but submits to his destiny. He foresees that it is 'no wit to go,
but consoles himself with the reflection that he " means well in going
to this mask." His intentions, as usual, are good ; and, as usual, their
consequences are ruinous.

He yields to his passion, and marries Juliet. For this hasty act he
has the excuse that the match may put an end to the discord between
the families. Friar Lawrence hopes that

> " this alliance may so happy prove
> To turn your households' rancour into love."

It certainly has that effect in the end of the play, but it is by the sui-
cidal deaths of the flower and hope of both families. Capulet and
Montague tender, in a gloomy peace the hands of friendship, over the
untimely grave of the poor sacrifices to their enmity. Had he met
her elsewhere than in her father's house, he might have succeeded in
a more prosperous love. But there his visit is looked upon by the
professed duellist Tybalt, hot from the encounter of the morning, and
enraged that he was baulked of a victim, as an intrusion and an insult.
The fiery partisan is curbed with much difficulty by his uncle ; and
withdraws, his flesh trembling with wilful choler, determined to wreak
vengeance at the first opportunity on the intruder. It is not long
before the opportunity offers. Vainly does Romeo endeavour to pacify
the bullying swordsman,—vainly does he protest that he loves the
name of Capulet,—vainly does he decline the proffered duel. His
good intentions are again doomed to be frustrated. There stands by his
side as mad-blooded a spirit as Tybalt himself, and Mercutio, all unconscious of the reasons why Romeo refuses to fight, takes up the abandoned quarrel. The star of the unlucky man is ever in the ascendant.
His ill-omened interference slays his friend. Had he kept quiet, the
issue might have been different ; but the power that had the steerage
of his course had destined that the uplifting of his sword was to be
the signal of death to his very friend. And when the dying Mercutio
says, "Why the devil came you between us ? I was hurt under your
arm ;" he can only offer the excuse, which is always true, and always
unavailing, " I thought all for the best." All his visions of reconciliation between the houses are dissipated. How can he now avoid fighting with Tybalt ? His best friend lies dead, slain in his own quarrel,
through his own accursed intermeddling ; and the swaggering victor,
still hot from the slaughter, comes back to triumph over the dead.
Who with the heart and spirit of a man could under such circumstances refrain from exclaiming,

> " Away to heaven, respective lenity !
> And fire-eyed fury be my conduct now."

Vanish gentle breath, calm words, knees humbly bowed !—his weapon in an instant glitters in the blazing sun; and as with a lightning flash,—as rapidly and resistlessly,—before Benvolio can pull his sword from the scabbard, Tybalt, whom his kindred deemed a match for twenty men, is laid by the side of him who but a moment before had been the victim of his blade. What avails the practised science of the duellist, the gentleman of the very first house, of the first and second cause !—how weak is the immortal passado, or the punto reverso, the hay, or all the other learned devices of Vincent Saviola, against the whirlwind rage of a man driven to desperation by all that can rouse fury or stimulate hatred ! He sees the blood of his friend red upon the ground; the accents of gross and unprovoked outrage ring in his ears; the perverse and obstinate insolence of a bravo confident in his skill, and depending upon it to insure him impunity, has marred his hopes ; and the butcher of the silk button has no chance against the demon which he has evoked. " A la stoccata" carries it not away in this encounter ; but Romeo exults not in his death. He stands amazed, and is with difficulty hurried off, exclaiming against the constant fate which perpetually throws him in the way of misfortune. Well, indeed, may Friar Lawrence address him by the title of "thou fearful man !"—as a man whose career through life is calculated to inspire terror. Well may he say to him that

> " Affliction is enamour'd of thy parts,
> And thou art wedded to calamity."

And slight is the attention which Romeo pays to the eloquent arguments by which it is proved that he had every reason to consider himself happy. When the friar assures him that

> " A pack of blessings lights upon thy back,
> Happiness courts thee in her best array,"

the nurse may think it a discourse of learning and good counsel, fit to detain an enraptured auditor all the night. Romeo feels it in his case to be an idle declamation, unworthy of an answer.

The events which occur during his enforced absence, the haste of Paris to be wedded, the zeal of old Capulet in promoting the wishes of his expected son-in-law, the desperate expedient of the sleeping-draught,* the accident which prevented the delivery of the friar's letter, the officious haste of Balthazar to communicate the

---

* Is there not some mistake in the length of time that this sleeping-draught is to occupy, if we consider the text as it now stands to be correct ? Friar Lawrence says to Juliet, when he is recommending the expedient,

> " Take thou this phial, being then in bed,
> And this distilled liquor drink thou off:
> When presently through all thy veins shall run
> A cold and drowsy humour, which shall seize
> Each vital spirit, &c.
> And in this borrow'd likeness of shrunk death
> Thou shalt remain *full two and forty hours,*
> And then awake as from a pleasant sleep."

Juliet retires to bed on Tuesday night, at a somewhat early hour. Her mother says after she departs, " 'Tis now near night." Say it is eleven o'clock: forty-two hours from that hour bring us to five o'clock in the evening of Thursday ;

tidings of Juliet's burial, are all matters out of his control.   But the mode of his death is chosen by himself; and in that he is as unlucky as in everything else.   Utterly loathing life, the manner of his leaving it must be instantaneous.   He stipulates that the poison by which he is to die shall not be slow of effect.   He calls for

> " such soon-speeding gear
> As will disperse itself through all the veins,
> That the life-weary taker may fall dead."

He leaves himself no chance of escape.   Instant death is in his hand ; and, thanking the true apothecary for the quickness of his drugs, he scarcely leaves himself a moment with a kiss to die.   If he had been less in a hurry,—if he had not felt it impossible to delay posting off to Verona for a single night,—if his riding had been less rapid, or his medicine less sudden in its effect, he might have lived. The friar was at hand to release Juliet from her tomb the very instant after the fatal phial had been emptied.   That instant was enough : the unlucky man had effected his purpose just when there was still a chance that things might be amended.   Those who wrote the scene between Romeo and Juliet which is intended to be pathetic, after her awakening and before his death, quite mistake the character of the hero of the play.   I do not blame them for their poetry, which is as good as that of second-rate writers of tragedy in general ; and think them, on the whole, deserving of our commendation for giving us an additional proof how unable clever men upon town are to follow the conceptions of genius.   Shakspeare, if he thought it consistent with the character which he had with so much deliberation framed, could have written a parting scene at least as good as that with which

and yet we find the time of her awakening fixed in profound darkness, and not long before the dawn.   We should allow at least ten hours more, and read,

> " Thou shalt remain full *two and fifty* hours,"—

which would fix her awakening at three o'clock in the morning, a time which has been marked in a former scene as the approach of day.

> " *Cap.* Come, stir, stir, stir !   The second cock has crow'd,—
> The curfew bell hath rung,—'tis three o'clock."

Immediately after he says, " Good faith, 'tis day."   This observation may appear superfluously minute ; but those who take the pains of reading the play critically will find that it is dated throughout with a most exact attention to hours.   We can time almost every event.   Ex. gr.   Juliet dismisses the nurse on her errand to Romeo when the clock struck nine, and complains that she has not returned at twelve.   At twelve she does return, and Juliet immediately proceeds to Friar Lawrence's cell, where she is married without delay.   Romeo parts with his bride at once, and meets his friends while " the day is hot."   Juliet at the same hour addresses her prayer to the fiery-footed steeds of Phœbus, too slowly for her feelings progressing towards the west.   The same exactness is observed in every part of the play.

I may remark, as another instance of Romeo's ill luck, the change of the original wedding-day.   When pressed by Paris, old Capulet says that " Wednesday is too soon,—on Thursday let it be ;" but afterwards, when he imagines that his daughter is inclined to consult his wishes, he fixes it for Wednesday, even though his wife observes that Thursday is time enough.   Had this day not been lost, the letter of Friar Lawrence might still have been forwarded to Mantua to explain what had occurred.

his tragedy has been supplied; but he saw the inconsistency, though his unasked assistants did not. They tell us they did it to consult popular taste. I do not believe them. I am sure that popular taste would approve of a recurrence to the old play in all its parts; but a harlotry play-actor might think it hard upon him to be deprived of a "point," pointless as that point may be.

Haste is made a remarkable characteristic of Romeo,—because it is at once the parent and the child of uniform misfortune. As from the acorn springs the oak, and from the oak the acorn, so does the temperament that inclines to haste predispose to misadventure, and a continuance of misadventure confirms the habit of haste. A man whom his rashness has made continually unlucky, is strengthened in the determination to persevere in his rapid movements by the very feeling that the "run" is against him, and that it is of no use to think. In the case of Romeo, he leaves it all to the steerage of Heaven, *i. e.* to the heady current of his own passions; and he succeeds accordingly. All through the play care is taken to show his impatience. The very first word he speaks indicates that he is anxious for the quick passage of time.

> "*Ben.* Good morrow, cousin.
> *Rom.*   Is the day so young?
> *Ben.* But new struck nine.
> *Rom.*   Ay me, sad hours seem long."

The same impatience marks his speech in the moment of death:

> "O true apothecary,
> Thy drugs are quick!"

From his first words to his last the feeling is the same. The lady of his love, even in the full swell of her awakened affections, cannot avoid remarking that his contract is

> "Too rash, too unadvised, too sudden,
> Too like the lightning, which does cease to be
> Ere one can say, It lightens."

When he urges his marriage on the friar,

> "*Rom.* O let us home: I stand on sudden haste.
> *Friar.* Wisely and slow. They stumble that run fast."

The metaphors put into his mouth are remarkable for their allusions to abrupt and violent haste. He wishes that he may die

> "As violently as hasty powder fired
> Doth hurry from the fatal cannon's womb."

When he thinks that Juliet mentions his name in anger, it is

> "as if that name,
> Shot from the deadly level of a gun,
> Did murder her."

When Lawrence remonstrates with him on his violence, he compares the use to which he puts his wit to

> "Powder in a skilless soldier's flask;"

and tells him that

> "Violent delights have violent ends,
> And in their triumph die; like fire and powder,
> Which, as they kiss, consume."

Lightning, flame, shot, explosion, are the favourite parallels to the conduct and career of Romeo. Swift are his loves; as swift to enter his thought, the mischief which ends them for ever. Rapid have been all the pulsations of his life; as rapid, the determination which decides that they shall beat no more.

A gentleman he was in heart and soul. All his habitual companions love him: Benvolio and Mercutio, who represent the young gentlemen of his house, are ready to peril their lives, and to strain all their energies, serious or gay, in his service. His father is filled with an anxiety on his account so delicate, that he will not venture to interfere with his son's private sorrows, while he desires to discover their source, and if possible to relieve them. The heart of his mother bursts in his calamity; the head of the rival house bestows upon him the warmest panegyrics; the tutor of his youth sacrifices everything to gratify his wishes; his servant, though no man is a hero to his *valet de chambre*, dares not remonstrate with him on his intentions, even when they are avowed to be savage-wild,

> " More fierce, and more inexorable far,
> Than empty tigers or the roaring sea,"—

but with an eager solicitude he breaks his commands by remaining as close as he can venture, to watch over his safety. Kind is he to all. He wins the heart of the romantic Juliet by his tender gallantry: the worldly-minded nurse praises him for being as gentle as a lamb. When it is necessary or natural that the Prince or Lady Montague should speak harshly of him, it is done in his absence. No words of anger or reproach are addressed to his ears save by Tybalt; and from him they are in some sort a compliment, as signifying that the self-chosen prize-fighter of the opposing party deems Romeo the worthiest antagonist of his blade. We find that he fights two blood-stained duels, but both are forced upon him; the first under circumstances impossible of avoidance, the last after the humblest supplications to be excused.

> " O begone !
> By Heaven, I love thee better than myself,
> For I came hither armed against myself.
> Stay not ; begone !—live, and hereafter say
> A madman's mercy bade thee run away."

With all the qualities and emotions which can inspire affection and esteem,—with all the advantages that birth, heaven, and earth could at once confer,—with the most honourable feelings and the kindliest intentions,—he is eminently an unlucky man. The record of his actions in the play before us does not extend to the period of a week; but we feel that there is no dramatic straining to shorten their course. Everything occurs naturally and probably. It was his concluding week; but it tells us all his life. Fortune was against him; and would have been against him, no matter what might have been his pursuit. He was born to win battles, but to lose campaigns. If we desired to moralize with the harsh-minded satirist, who never can be suspected of romance, we should join with him in extracting as a moral from the play

> " Nullum habes numen, si sit prudentia ; sed te
> Nos facimus, Fortuna, deam, cœloque locamus ;"

and attribute the mishaps of Romeo, not to want of fortune, but of prudence. Philosophy and poetry differ not in essentials, and the stern censure of Juvenal is just. But still, when looking on the timeless tomb of Romeo, and contemplating the short and sad career through which he ran, we cannot help recollecting his mourning words over his dying friend, and suggest as an inscription over the monument of the luckless gentleman,

"I THOUGHT ALL FOR THE BEST."

THE PIPER'S PROGRESS.

BY FATHER PROUT.

1.

When I was a boy
  In my father's mud edifice,
Tender and bare
  As a pig in a sty;
Out of the door as I
  Looked with a steady phiz,
Who but Thade Murphy,
  The piper, went by;
Says Thady, "But few play
This music—can *you* play?"
Says I, "I can't tell,
  For I never did try."
So he told me that *he* had a charm
  To make the pipes purtily speak;
Then squeezed a bag under his arm,
  When sweetly they set up a squeak!
    Fa-ra-la la-ra-la loo!

  Och hone!
  How he handled the drone!
    And then the sweet music he blew
  Would have melted the heart of a stone!

2.

"Your pipe," says I, "Thady,
  So neatly comes over me,
Naked I'll wander
  Wherever it blows;
And, if my poor parents
  Should try to recover me,
Sure it won't be
  By describing my clothes.
The music I hear now
Takes hold of my ear now,
And leads me all over
  The world by the nose."
So I follow'd his bagpipe so sweet,
  And I sung, as I leapt like a frog,
"Adieu to my family seat,
  So pleasantly placed in a bog!"
    Fa-ra-la la-ra-la loo!

  Och hone!
  How we handled the drone!
    And then the sweet music we blew
  Would have melted the heart of a stone!

I.

Pater me clauserat
  Domi homunculum;
Grunniens sus erat
  Comes, ut mos:
Transibat tibicen
  Juxta domunculam,
Quando per januam
    Protuli os;
Ille ait impromptu,
  "Hâc tibiâ num tu,
Ut te sine sumptu
    Edoceam, vis?"
Tum pressit amiculam
Sub ulnâ vesiculam
Quæ sonum reddidit
  Vocibus his:
    Fa-ra-la la-ra-la loo!

  Φευ, φευ!
  Modo flens, modo flans,
    Magico ελελευ
  Cor et aurem vel lapidi dans!

II.

Cui ego tum: "Tu sic, ah!
  Me rapis musicâ,
Ut sequar nudulus
    Tibicen, te!
Et si pater, testibus,
  Quærat me, vestibus,
Redibit, ædepol!
    Vacuâ re.
Sic melos quod audio
Me replet gaudio
Ut trahor campos et
  Flumina trans;
Jam linquo rudibus
Hic in paludibus,
Patris tigurium
  Splendidè stans.
    Fa-ra-la la-ra-la loo!

  Dum tibicen, tu,
  Modo flens, modo flans,
    Iteras ελελευ,
  Cor et aurem vel lapidi dans.

F 2

<table>
<tr><td>

3.

Full five years I follow'd him,
  Nothing could sunder us ;
Till he one morning
  Had taken a sup,
And slipt from a bridge
  In a river just under us,
Souse to the bottom
  Just like a blind pup.
He roar'd, and he bawl'd out ;
And I also call'd out,
" Now, Thady, my friend,
  Don't you mean to come up ?" ...
He was dead as a nail in a door ;
  Poor Thady was laid on the shelf.
So I took up his pipes on the shore,
  And now I 've set up for myself.
    Fa-ra-la la-ra-la loo !

Och hone !
Don't I handle the drone,
  And play such sweet music ? I too,
Can't I soften the heart of a stone ?

</td><td>

III.

Ut arte sic magicâ
Egi quinquennium,
Magistro tragica
  Accidit res ;
Bacchi nam numine,
Pontis cacumine
Dum staret, flumine
  Labitur pes !
" E sinu fluctuum,
O puer, duc tuum
(Clamat) didascalum,
  Fer opem nans !" ...
Ast ego renuo ;
Et sumens denuò
Littore tibias
  Sustuli, fans,
    Fa-ra-la la-ra-la loo !

Φευ, φευ !
Modo flens, modo flans,
  Magico ελελευ
Cor et aurem vel lapidi dans !

</td></tr>
</table>

DARBY THE SWIFT;

OR,

THE LONGEST WAY ROUND IS THE SHORTEST WAY HOME.

CHAPTER II.

" Aspettar' e non venire !"

THE Sunday after Darby *lingeringly* started, I began to think it would be just as well to make " assurance doubly sure ;" so I despatched a letter by post to my friend at Bally——, conveying similar instructions and advice to those contained in that entrusted to " *the running footman*" of my establishment. In three days I received a satisfactory answer, so I was at rest upon that point ; but, as to Darby, I was quite at a loss. I turned over and over in my mind the various mishaps that might have befallen him by the way ; but all to no purpose. I called up Eileen, and asked her what she thought about it. Her replies, mixed up, as they were, with her wild immoderate laughter, afforded me nothing beyond a sympathy with her mirth, which certainly was most infective. Reader, I am not a portrait-painter ; but, nevertheless, I will attempt to give you an outline of Eileen. In the first place, she was a poor girl, (else she would not have been *my* servant,) born of honest parents ; but, if fate had placed her in a higher sphere, she had natural accomplishments enough to have graced it,— namely, youth, beauty, and health,—and, beyond these, an intellectual, though uneducated, refinement of thought, when, *by chance*, she was serious ; for gaiety seemed to be an indispensable element of her being. She was eighteen years of age,—well, what do I say?—beautifully formed, had eyes like violets, cheeks like roses, hair, when it was dishevelled (despite Goldsmith's satire), like a weeping willow in a sunset, and—but, hold! I must not go further, lest I be suspected of being enamoured of the original; so I will give up the remaining parts of the picture, and leave them to your imagination!

. The Friday after Darby's setting out I was sitting in my room, very quietly poring over something or other of no importance,—I forget exactly what, but I think it was some speech in the House of Lords,—when a knock at the door agreeably disturbed me from an incipient somnolency, occasioned by a new and unprofitable line of reading.

"Come in!" said I. "Who is it? and what do you want?"

"It's only *me*, sir," said Eileen, laughing, as usual. "There's a crather below that wants to speak to you, sir."

"Who is it?" said I.

"I don't well know, sir," replied she; "but I think he's some relation to poor Darby, that ye sent to Bally—— last Friday afternoon."

"Oh! then send him up; he may account in some way for the extraordinary absence of his relative," said I.

"Sure, an' it's myself, an' no relation at all," shouted Darby from below, indignantly.

"Oh! *widdy-eelish!*" cried Eileen, breaking out into her hearty wild laugh, that was sure to set at defiance anything like gravity!

"Come up, Darby," said I. "I thought we should never have seen you again."

"Troth, an' the same thing came into my head more than oncet, masther. What the divil are ye laughin' at, honey?" said he (entering the room) to Eileen, who still continued her most boisterous mirth.

"Go down stairs, Evelina," said I, "and leave Darby and me alone!"

She did so; but whispered something in his ear as she passed, which made him so furious that I thought he would have knocked her down, had she not adroitly escaped him by shutting the door after her, and holding the handle on the outside so tightly that his efforts to open it and follow her were abandoned in a moment as fruitless.

"What is the meaning of all this?" said I, severely. "Did you mean to strike the girl?"

"Strike the *caileen*, yir honour? Oh, the Lord forbid! but, if I cotch her upon the stairs out o' yir honor's sight, maybe I wudn't give her cherry-lips a *pogue* (yir honor knows what a *pogue* is) that wud drive her sweetheart crazy for a month o' Sundays!"

"Where have you been all this while?" inquired I, not willing to notice his speech.

"Oh then, sure!" said he, in a most mournful tone, "masther, I've had the divil's own time of it, sir, since you were so unfortunate as to part with me, yir honor, on that same journey to Bally—Bally—Bally—bad luck to it! what do they call it?"

"What has happened?" inquired I, anxiously, thinking he might have later news than my post-letter of three days before had conveyed.

"Happened, yir honour! to who?" said Darby, with a wild look of concern. "I hope the family, Christians, bastes, and all, not barrin' the pig that had the measles, are in good health, and well to do as

when I left them. Has the bracket hin taken to standin' upon one
leg yit, sir, since she lost the other through that baste of a bull-dog
belongin' to the parson ?   I 'd lay three of her eggs she 'll never forget the affront he put upon her then !"

"We are all well here," said I; "but give me some account of
what has befallen you on your journey, that delayed you so long."

"Troth, an' I 'll tell ye, masther," replied Darby, " in no time.
Have ye five minutes to spare, sir ?"

"Yes," said I; "let me hear."

"Well then, sir," commenced he, "you may remimber that it was
on a Friday you took lave of me—last Friday of all—Friday was
never a *looky* day by *say* or by land: ye see, I didn't go far afore I
met with a disappointment, for I met a berrin' comin' right *fornenst*
me—what *coud* I do but turn back, in dacency, with it ?—and, after
I 'd *keen'd* about a mile with the mourners, I made bould to ax who
was the body that was makin' a blackberry *ov* himself."

"A blackberry !" interrupted I.

"Yes, yir honor, a blackberry," replied Darby: "do ye know that,
let it shoot never so far, it 's sure to come back as near as it can to
the root of it where it first started; and so arn't we all blackberries ?
As the priest says on Ash-*Wendsday*, "Remember, man, you are but
dust, and into dust you must return." Now, I 've known bigger *dusts*
in their lifetime than they were turned out of afterward, when they
took to studyin' astronamy with

> ' The tops of their toes,
> And the tip of their nose,
> Turn'd up to the roots of the daisies !'

But, whose berrin' should it be, after all, but ould Jemmy Cullen, the
piper's ! Ye know Jemmy Cullen, yir honour ? him that used to play
the organ on the pipes at high-mass durin' Christmas an' Easter. Oh!
he was the boy to lilt at a weddin' or a wake ! but, pace be width 'im
—God rest his sowl ! as I said when I saw the *scragh* put over him
for the first time. Well, ye know, yir honor, that oncet upon the
same road width them I coudn't do more nor less than wet our clay
together ; so, after walkin' the corpse three times round the church-
yard of Glassin-oge— Were ye ever berried there, sir ?—I mane,
wud ye like to be berried there, sir ?"

"Not just yet," said I.

"Oh, the Lord forbid, sir !" cried Darby. "I didn't mane that,
by no manes. God send ye many days, and *prosprous* ones too!
But there 's a taste in chusin' a berrin'-ground as well as there is in a
drawin'-room," said he, looking around him.

"So there may be," said I; "but that is only the whim or notion
of a living man. When he dies, all churchyards are the same to
him ; he then can have no considerations about the matter."

"That 's all very true, sir," replied Darby ; "but would ye like to
be burnt after the breath was out o' ye ?"

"I could have neither liking nor disliking," answered I; "for I
should be an insensible mass of matter."

"But mightn't yir ghost, sir, like to see ye were comfortably provided for ? I mane yir honor's dead body that 's alive an' in good
health now, an' long may it continue so !"

"Oh I never mind," said I; "neither you nor I, Darby, know much about those things; so go on with your story."

"Thank ye, sir!" said Darby, and resumed. "I was sayin', sir, as how we went to wet our clay together at the '*Three Jolly Pigeons*.' Yir honor knows the 'Three Jolly Pigeons,' facing the ould hawthorn o' Goldsmith, in the village of AUBURN hard by here, eh? Sure, an' I 've heer'd as much as how they want to take the merits of the whole place to themselves over in England somewhere, as if it couldn't spake plainly for itself that it was bred and born here in ould Ireland ages ago! Isn't the '*Desarted Village*' a butiful histhory, masther? Lame Kelly, the poet, says, it bates the world for makin' the heart soft. It 's myself that never passes the spot without a tear in my eye, like a widow's pig, as the sayin' is. There 's the ruins of the dacent church on the hill all in butiful repair to this hour, and the parson's house, and the schoolmaster Tom Allen's, and the common, and the pond, width the geese upon it still, as if it was only yistherday, an' the ould hawthorn—bad *look* to their taste that built a stone wall round about it like a *jail!* What did the blessed tree ever do that it should be put in pound in that manner o' way?"

Gentle shade of GOLDSMITH! amongst the many tributes to thy immortal genius, receive kindly the simple but honest homage of poor Darby. He may not be able to appreciate thee in all thy varied splendour of moral and intellectual worth; but he has a heart full of benevolence like thine own, and, although a poor Irish serf, has feeling and fancy enough to reverence the spots thou hast consecrated by the thousand-spelled wand of thy muse!

"Darby," said I, "I promised you something on your return (though you did not come back as soon as I expected); there 's a guinea for you."

"Augh, thin, may the light of Heaven break yir last sleep!" said Darby; "but isn't it too much, masther?"

"You are welcome to it," said I; "go on with your story."

"Thank ye, sir!" replied he. "Whereabouts was I when I left off?"

"Just where you are now," said I.

"Beggin' yir honor's pardon, I think I was at the 'Three Jolly Pigeons.'"

"Be it so," said I, "go on."

"Well, as I was sayin', when we damp'd the grief a trifle at the *sheebeen* width a drop of the rale *stone turf*, I takes up the kish again; but first I put my hand in the straw to see if the *dog-een* was comfortable, and there he was to be sure, warm an' nice as a new-laid egg: so, wishin' the rest of the company every amusement in life, I set out on my travels agen. Just as I was in the doorway, Ned Coffey, the *whisperer*,—ye know Ned Coffey, yir honor, that brakes in the wild *coults* width a charm he 's got? Well, anyhow, if he didn't laugh so as if his mother was a horse; but I never minded him, only went on wonderin' to myself what cud av' made him so humoursome at a berrin'. Well, never mind that, I went on beautifully for a time, as good as an hour an' a half, when, all of a suddent, leppin' a ditch, the hayband I had acrass my breast bruk, and let the *clieve* fall *clane* in the dirty puddle. 'Oh, *hannamandhioul!*' says I, 'what 'll the masther say to this?' The words were scarce past my lips when a *squake* that 'ud av' split the ears of a pitcher came out o' the *clieve*, an' after that a gruntin', such as I never *heer'd* come from mortal man afore, barrin' it was a pig under a gate !"

"What could it have been ?" inquired I, affecting a grave concern ; "it was not my dog Squib, surely ?"

"Who the *nagers* else could it be ?" said Darby. "Only, after crassing myself three times, and turnin' up the basket wid' my *horse*, I found he was bewitched into the shape of a porker, as purty a young pig sure enough, about seven weeks ould, as I'd wish to clap eyes on."

"A pig !" exclaimed I. "Why, he returned home that very night in his own shape."

"Well then, see that, now," said Darby, "thuv', for my own part, I think it was all Ned Coffey's doin' ; but, be that as it may, I was never so frightened in all my born days, for I tuk to my heels, an' was out o' sight in no time, like a *haro !* tho' I hadn't far to go to be that same, for it was pitch-dark ; so, to keep myself company, I began singin'

> ' The first o' my pranks was in little Rathshane,
> Where love, just like whiskey, popp'd into my brain ;
> For Ally Magoolagh, a nate little sowl,
> As tall and as *strate* as a shaverman's pole !'

' Augh ! thin, *was* she ?' says a voice that I cudn't see, tho' 'twas close to my left ear ! ' Who 's there ?' says I. ' Where ?' says it, on th' other side. ' Anywhere,' says I, ' to plaze ye ;' and wid that I fell into a could sweat, for I began to think it was Mihilmas Eve, an' divil a grain of salt I had about me to keep me from harm ! ' Crass o' Christ on us !' says I, ' an' God bless ye !' for I thought it was one of the good people, yir honor ! so I made up my mind to get in*doors* as soon as I could. But that wasn't so aisy as wishin', for there wasn't a village nearer than five miles, nor a cabin by the way-side. At last I spies a light at a distance in the fields aff the road, and away we set, I and my *horse*, full gallup. Oh ! many's the ditch we cleared without seein' ; but still, never a bit did we come nearer to the light ! ' Is it a *Will*,' says I to myself, ' or a *Jack ?*' an' wid that out it goes on a suddent, and laves me up to my chin in a bog. Augh ! then, hadn't I a cruel time of it there ? I was, for all the world, like a *flay* on Father Fogarty's pock-mark'd nose, or a blind horse in a tan-yard,—no sooner out o' one hole than into another ! At last I got upon dry land, and wasn't I thankful for that same ? for I got hoult ov a stone wall that directed me straight on to a gate that was only hasp'd ; so I opened it, an' let myself out upon a *rodeiene*, that I knew by the tracks o' the wheels ; so, turnin' myself round three times for *look*, (and bad *look* it was,) I steps out into a ditch that was handy by the way-side,—for it was acrass the *rodeiene* I went 'stead of lengthways either up or down ; but how could I do betther in the dark ? Well, afther a while floundherin' about like a litther of pups in a bag, I got on my feet agen clane out o' the mud, shiverin' an' shakin' as if I had Jack Nulty's ague 'pon me ! ' Well,' says I to myself, ' it was *looky* I stopp'd to have a drop at the berrin', or I'd av' nothin' to keep the could out o' me now ! It was Providence as well as dacency that put it into my head !"

"If you had not stopped," said I, "you would not have been over-taken by the night, and exposed to such a disagreeable accident!"

"Well, sure, yir honor," replied Darby, "somethin' else might av' happened, an' who knows but it might 'a been worse?—there's no sayin' or accountin' for such things. Well, be that as it may, I be-gan to walk on, feelin' afore me width my *horse* (that never forsook me all the time) whether I was in the right road or not, till at last I comes all ov a suddent into the middle o' the town o' Lanesbro', with *raal* candles (none ov yir *wisps* or *lantherns*) burnin' in every window. Maybe I didn't know where I was then! So, mountin' my horse, sir, strad-legs, away I *canther'd*, blessin' my stars that I got on my jour-ney so well and so far, width only a wettin' in the bog-holes an' ditches, and a scratch or two on my hands an' cheeks, that I made nothin' ov. 'Where will we put up for the night,' says I to my horse; but yir honor knows the *crathur* cudn't answer me: so I tuk my own advice, an' went sthraight to 'The Cat and Bagpipes.' 'Will I get a lodgin' here the night?' says I to the lan'lady.—'Who are ye?' says she.—'Who am I!' I says; 'I'm yir honor's servant, on a mission,' says I, mentionin' yir name, masther.—'Can ye pay for a bed?' says she.—'Can money do it?' says I.—'To be sure,' says she.—'Then, look here,' says I; an' wid that I show'd her four and six-pence—for I only spent sixpence at the berrin'.—'Go into the kitchen,' says she, 'an' I'll see what I can do for ye.'—'Thank ye, ma'am,' says I. So I goes my ways into the kitchen, and sits down by the hob. That was very agreeable for a time; but, when I dried myself, an' wanted to go to bed after a drop or two, how d'ye think they sarved me? only sure, yir honor, by putting me in bed with a *furrener*,—nothin' more nor less than a *black*, savin' yir presence,—for it was the *fair* night o' the town, and beds were scarce, an' not to be had for love or money; so I was *oblidged* to sleep double, plaze ye, sir, in a two-bedded room. They tould me he was only a *sweep*; but he turned out to be a *raal* black, to my sorrow!"

"In what way?" inquired I.

"Oh! in many ways, sir," replied Darby. "First and forenenst, he prevented me takin' my natural rest afore midnight; for I took a Bible oath on a child's catechism that I wouldn't enther the room where he was afore the *good people* were gone to roost; for who knows what they might have made of me? Lord bless ye! they'd av' turn'd every hair o' my head into pump-handles, if they liked, afore morn! so I thought it best to sit up a while, an' kick up a bit ov a dance in the kitchen width Katheen the maid, an' two or three other *spreesans* that were inclined for the fun; an' fine sport we had, to be sure, to the tune of '*The Hare in the Corn*,' and '*Roger de Cuvverly*,' —did ye ever trip it to '*Roger de Cuvverly*,' yir honor? Oh! it's an illigant cure for the gout!"

"I never dance," said I.

"An' more's the sorrow!" said Darby, "for ye've a fine pair o' legs o' yir own, an' it's a pity that a lame piper shudn't be the better o' them some night or other!"

"We'll see about that," said I; "holiday-time is coming."

"Thank ye, and long life to yir honor! Will ye give us the barn, sir, for a hop width the girls a-comin' Christmas?"

"Yes," said I, "and a barrel of ale into the bargain.'

"Oh! then won't that be illigant?" said Darby, cutting an anti-cipatory caper on the carpet. "An' won't yir honor dance yirself, sir?"

"I have said already that I never dance," replied I. "Go on."

"Yes, sir, immediately," said he, and continued. "Well, after a bit we had a game o' blindman's buff, an', to be sure, *raal* fun it was while it lasted, and that was till we got into the little hours; an' many's the trick we play'd one another, till myself felt the miller throwin' dust in my eyes; so, givin' Katheen the wink that I was goin' aff slily, I tould her to call me early in the morn, an' left the party to themselves. I soon tuk aff me, an' was asleep in no time; but in less than half an hour I had a most wonderful *drame*. I thought I was the first paycock that ever wore a tail in Paradise; an' maybe I wasn't proud o' myself, sated in the tree of knowledge, width Adam an' Eve, *ketchin'* flies width their mouth open, lookin' at me for wonder. 'Arrah! *cushlah!*' says Adam to his wife; 'isn't it a *butiful* sight?'—'Troth, an' it is,' says she; 'avick! I hope he won't fly away, for I'd like to make a pet ov 'im. I'll just step in-*doors* for the blundherbuss!' When I came to this part o' my *drame*, the blood o' me ran could, an' I couldn't think what was the mat-ther width me, barrin' it was the night-*mare*; but it was no such thing, for I turned on th' other side, and thought then I was a race-*horse* on the Curragh of Kildare, an' yir honor clappin' spurs into me within twenty yards of the winnin' post! Well, that was better than t'other; but, as I was draming in this fashion, I began to think they'd never call me at all, when Katheen, yir honor,—the purty little girl, sir, that kept me up so late the night afore, dancin' with her in the back-kitchen,—gave a *puck* at the door with her fist, that sent in one of the panels, and dumb-foundered quite an ould clock on the back of it, that was pointin' width its two hands to some hour last year. 'Who the divil's that?' says I.—'It's only me,' says she, with a voice like a spaking-trumpet, or a chorus of ganders. (I think the crather had a could upon her.) 'Arrah! d'ye never mane to lave off sleepin'?'—'What o'clock is it, alanna!' says I.—'Oh! the same hour it was this time yisterday, I suppose,' says she, 'for the clock is *down*.'—'Faith! it is,' says I, nate and clane upon the *flooer*; but never mind that, the sun's *up!*'—'Ay,' says Katheen, 'this two hours or more.'—'And so wud I,' says I, 'if I had as far to travel in the day as he has!'—'Augh!' said Katheen, 'you lazy *puckaun*, did ye never hear that the early bird *ketches* the worm?'—'Troth, an' I did,' says I, 'putting on my shirt; 'but what an *ummadhaun* the worm must be to get up afore him.' — 'An' over an' above,' says Katheen, 'the man that was on the road betimes in the mornin' found a purse.'—'Ay!' says I, 'but the poor divil that lost it was there first.'—'Oh, the *divil* be width ye! stop there till ye're stiff av ye like,' said Katheen, and run down stairs afore I could say Jack Robison. Well, then, yir honor, I was soon drest an' up; so, as I'd *ped* my way *the night*, I had *nawthin'* to do but pass clane through the kitchen in the mornin', an' take to the road agen, when I saw Katheen a-lightin' the fire. I just stepped towards her for a kiss *a-dhurrus*, when she cried murther in Irish, loud enough to waken the whole house; so I thought I'd have nothin' more to do width her this time, and went my ways paceably. It was a fine mornin', barrin' the mist, that wudn't let ye see a yard afore ye at a time, an', to be sure, I *kep* it up at a fine rate 'till I *r*ached the town of Kilcronan. But, what d'ye think happened me there, yir honor ?"

" I 'm sure I cannot say," said I.

" Well, then, I 'll tell ye, sir. As I was passin' by a pawnbroker's that was settin' out his goods for sale, what did I see but a lookin'-glass starin' me in the face, an' a blackamoor's head in the middle of it. Well, I look'd, and look'd, and look'd agen, but divil a bit was it like me ; so, turnin' 'pon my heel, ' Bad look to them !' says I, ' they 've woke the *wrong man ;*' for yir honor remimbers that I slept width a *furrener* the night afore, and left orders to be called early ; so I had nothin' for it but run back agen as hard as I could lay foot to ground for twelve honest miles ; and lucky sure it was that the fog was so thick as ye could cut it with a knife, or I 'd av' 'ad the divil's own time of it on the way. But, as it happened, I met nobody that knew me, 'cept blind M'Diarmot the sign-painther."

" Sign-painter !" exclaimed I. " I thought you said he was blind."

" Augh ! sure it was afore he lost his eye-sight," said Darby, " that he was the most illigant sign-painther in the county. Didn't he paint *The Pig and Thrush* for Mat Sleven ; an' *The Three Blacks,* that ye 'd take for two twins, they 're so like one anuther ; and *The Red Herrin'* for Pat Gaveny in the market, that look'd so *salt* it made yir mouth wather to that degree, that ye cudn't help, passin' by, goin' in to have a drop. Oh ! it brought powers of custom anyhow !"

" How did he lose his eyes ?" inquired I.

" He didn't lose them at all, sir," replied Darby, " only the sight o' *one* o' them, (for he never had th' other,) an' that was all through Molly, *the Lump,* that advised him, (bad win' to her !) to use *crame* when he had a could upon his intellects after the *typus ;* so he mis-tuk a pot o' white lead for the same, one evenin' that he had a drop too much, and fairly painted himself blind ; for from that hour to this he can't see a hole in a forty-fut laddher. And more 's the pity, for he had plenty o' *drawin'* about the counthry to do ; an' now his dog has got into the *line* ov it for him, the crathur ! Well, anyhow, knowin' he was a jidge o' colours, I ax'd him to feel my face, an' tell me what was the matther width it ; so he puts his hand upon me, an' may I never die, masther, if it didn't turn as black as a crow as soon as he drew it acrass my cheek ! ' Well,' says I, ' this bates cock-fightin' !' But I soon found out the trick they played me ; for M'Diarmot, when he smelt his hand, said there was *sut* and goose-*grase* upon it. So ye see, yir honor, the truth was, they blackened my face in the kitchen afore they put me to sleep with the black, that I mightn't know which was myself in the mornin'. May they live till the ind o' the world, that the divil may have a race after them, say I, for that same !"

THE DUEL.

I was educated, said a French gentleman whom I met in quarantine, at Poitiers, though Lusignan is my native town.

Poitiers is well known to the antiquary as having possessed a Roman amphitheatre, of which, however, when I was at that university, only a vault, supposed to have been a cage for the wild beasts, remained. This cage, from the solidity of the masonry, and the enormous size of the blocks, seemed indestructible, but was not so; for when I last visited Poitiers, and asked for the key of the cavern, I found that it no longer existed, and that on the site had been constructed the inn of the "Trois Pelerins."

It is a stone's throw from the Salle d'Armes, a place with which I had been better acquainted than with the schools. To revive my ancient recollection, I entered the *salle*, and found there an inhabitant of the town whom I had known at college. He proposed that we should dine together at the "Trois Pelerins;" and, after drinking as good a bottle of wine as it afforded, he related to me what a few days before, in the very room where we were sitting, had happened at a dinner of the collegians. It was ordered for twelve; but, one of the party having invited a friend, the number swelled to thirteen.

It is said that superstition supplies the place of religion; I have observed this to be the case with the most sceptical of my acquaintance: and thus this number thirteen occasioned some remarks, and the stranger was looked upon with no very favourable eye, and considered as a supernumerary, who brought with him ill luck.

One of the set at last summoned resolution enough to say,

"I do not dine thirteen."

"Nor I," said another.

"Nor I," was repeated on all sides.

The guest, naturally embarrassed at this rudeness, got up, and was about to retire, when Alfonse, to whom he came as an *umbra*, proposed an ingenious expedient for doing away with the evil augury, and said,

"There is one way of annulling the proverb that threatens death in the course of the year to one of a party of thirteen; that way is, to decide which of us shall fight a duel this evening, or to-morrow morning."

"Done!" cried all the students at a breath.

"Shall it be among ourselves?" said one of them.

"No," replied the author of the proposition; "for then two of us would have to fight, whereas it ought to be the thirteenth."

"Right," said all the young men.

"Then let it be with one of the officers of the garrison."

"Be it so," said Alfonse; "we will make a pool, as usual, at the *café*, all thirteen of us; and——"

"The first out," said the student.

"No," interrupted Alfonse, "that would be a bad omen; it shall be the winner."

"Agreed!" replied all, and they sate down to table with as much gaiety and *insouciance* as if nothing had been said.

The stranger, just as the soup was being put on the table, got up, and with a magisterial tone of voice addressed the assembly. "Gentlemen," said he, "I feel suddenly inspired with a sublime idea. We are about to eat and drink in the ruins of Roman greatness (alluding to the amphitheatre). Let us imitate that people in every thing that is great. Nothing could be more splendid than the games of the gladiators which were celebrated over the tombs of the mighty dead, —nothing more sumptuous than the festivals held at their funerals. This is probably also a funereal fête; with this difference, that it is held before, and not after death. Let Poitiers therefore rival Rome in her magnificence; let this *cena* be in honour of the mighty remains over which we are sitting; let it be *morituro*,—sacred to him who is about to perish."

"Bravo!" exclaimed the guests one and all; "a splendid idea, by Jove!—a splendid *cena* be it!"

"Open the windows!" cried Alfonse. The windows were opened. As soon as the soup was served, smash went all the plates into the yard, and shivered against the pavement. So, during the rest of dinner, every plate as fast as it was cleared, every bottle as soon as emptied, followed their fellows. One might perceive, by the practised dexterity of this feat, that it was not the first time they had played the same game.

During the first course nothing particular occurred to disturb their harmony; but it so happened that the *rôti*, which is, as you know, in France always served last, was burnt. Then there arose a general burst of indignation.

"Send the cook!" exclaimed they all to the waiters.

"Order up the cook! Here, cook! cook!" was the universal cry. But the *chef* was not forthcoming.

Alfonse, the president, then said, "Must I go myself and fetch him?"

This menace had its effect: the *pauvre chef*, pale as death, and all cotton cap in hand, crawled into the room. He was greeted with deafening shouts.

"Come here!" said Alfonse. "Do you take us for the officers? What do you mean by serving us in this manner,—eh?"

The man of the spit stammered out an apology. Alfonse looked at him askance.

"If I served you right," said he, "I should make you eat this detestable *rôti* of yours; but, as it is the first time of happening, my chastisement shall be a paternal one. Hold out your cotton cap."

The *chef* obeyed, and Alfonse turned out of a dish into it an enormous clouted cream (*omelet soufflé*), and said,

"Come, now, on with the cap, and see you don't first spill a drop."

He was forced to comply; and the unhappy Ude (*udus*), his face and white jacket streaming with the contents of the *plat*, was followed out of the room with hisses and bursts of laughter.

Thus went on the dinner, and with it a concert of broken plates, dishes, glasses, and bottles, accompanied by noises of all sorts, which rose to *fortissimo* as the wine, of which they drank to excess, got into their heads.

The dessert, which succeeded the second course, was ended by what they called a salad. This salad was thus mixed. They turned up the four corners of the table-cloth, and rolled therein all the fragments that were left. At this juncture the waiters disappeared, conjecturing shrewdly that, if they stayed any longer, the feast might be too grand for them. In short, when all that remained of the dessert was bundled well up, the collegians got on the table, and, at the risk of cutting their feet with the fragments of the crockery, and the splinters of the glass, danced thereon, till everything was pounded, smashed, and broken. Then the table-cloth, with all it contained, (the salad,) was thrown out of the window; after it the table, then the chairs, then the rest of the furniture, and, when there was nothing more to destroy, the frenzied youths thought they could do no better than throw themselves out; and all the thirteen "followed the leader," Alfonse, and jumped from the first floor into the court.

There is a saying, that over drunkards watches an especial Providence. But there are, it seems, two; for the students, on this occasion, found one of their own, which doubtless befriended them in this mad leap. Certain it is that none of the party met with the slightest accident, and, gloriously drunk, they rushed out into the street, after the most remarkable orgie that had taken place for some time at Poitiers.

They made a brilliant *entrée* into the *café*,—a general place of rendezvous for the students and officers when they were not at daggers drawn.

Two of the latter were playing at billiards when they entered. But Alfonse, without waiting till the game was ended, asked, or rather demanded, in an authoritative tone, that the table should be given up for a single pool to the thirteen.

Thinking that the object was, as usual, to decide who should pay for the dinner, or the *demi-tasse et chasse*, the players did not seem inclined to comply with this requisition; but when they learnt that a more momentous affair, a duel, was on foot, they hastened to lay down their cues. A duel! everything must yield to that!

There were but few military men present, for that very day there was a *soirée* at the general-commandant's of the garrison; and those few consisted of veterans, who preferred passing the evening at the *café* to putting on silk-stockings and shoes, or of *chenapans*, who in the regiment went by the name of *crans*, or *bourreaux des cranes*. The old *grognards*, however, did not quit the room. The *chenapans* interchanged glances with each other; and one or two of the sub-lieutenants, who had come to take their *demi-tasse* before they went to the ball, also remained. They had all more or less formed a shrewd guess of what was to happen; and, for the honour of the service, waited for the quarrel to break out.

In our schools and garrisons at Paris we are totally unacquainted with that *esprit de corps* which engages a whole regiment, and an entire body of young men, in a duel, when two only are concerned; nor can we form a notion how slight a thing a duel is considered, when it is the custom to decide all questions sword in hand. Habit is all in all; and people soon learn to think no more of fighting than going to breakfast.

It becomes a general endemic; and a person who, lost in the

world of Paris, where he is unknown, might hesitate about demanding satisfaction for an insult however gross, would, in that atmosphere, be ready any day, or hour of the day, to call a man out for merely looking at him.

The pool was begun. Never did a party, when a large sum of money depended on the issue of the game, play with more care and caution than those thirteen to decide which of them was to fight. By degrees the players lost their three lives, and the number was at last reduced to two; these two were the stranger guest and Alfonse. The lookers-on watched anxiously every stroke. Those balls, that as they rolled carried with them the fate of a man, were followed by earnest looks. The officers came nearer and nearer, and ranged themselves round the billiard. They were not a little interested to know whether they, or rather one of them,—which they knew not,—was to enter the lists with a freshman, no doubt unpractised in fencing, or with the most adroit and terrible duellist of the university.

The chances were against them. The stranger lost.

A singular excitement was occasioned by the disappearance of the last ball in the pocket. Some faces grew pale; but no one stirred from the spot where he had been standing as a spectator. Alfonse looked steadily round him, and made two or three times the circuit of the room, as though he were in search, but in vain, of some one worth quarrelling with. At last he perceived a sort of sub-lieutenant, originally drum-major and *maître-d'armes*, and who boasted of having killed his thirty pequins, sitting quietly in a corner. Alfonse walked straight up to him, and, saluting him with a politeness that electrified the company, said, in his cool way,

"Monsieur, I am exceedingly distressed at the situation in which I find myself placed; but my honour is concerned, and you will allow me to engage yours."

Without further preliminaries, he gave him a severe hit in the face.

The officer, who little expected so abrupt and unanswerable a mode of provocation, sprang like a madman from his chair; and had not Alfonse, with the activity and nimbleness of a cat, leaped with one bound on the table, the ex-drum-major would probably have strangled him on the spot.

He was quickly at the aggressor's heels, when his own comrades stopped him of their own accord, saying,

"Come, come! no child's play or boxing! the thing is too serious! *C'est un combat à la mort!*"

"Where shall I find you to-morrow?" said one of the officers, addressing Alfonse.

"Fix your ground," was the reply.

"No to-morrows!" said the officer who had received the blow; "this instant!"

"This instant be it, if you please," replied Alfonso with the utmost indifference.

"I shall not sleep to-night till that blow is avenged!" said the other, foaming with rage,

"I, too, want to unnumb my hand. I have hurt my knuckles against your cheek-bones," said Alfonse.

"Where would they fight at such a time of night as this?" observed some of the officers.

" In the garden behind the *café*," cried the ancient *maître d'armes* ; " a sword in one hand, and a billiard-lamp in the other."

" But," said Alfonse, " I am tired. I know your style of fighting men, *Crane* ; you want to make me break ground, and drive me step by step round the garden. Don't think it, my lad. Besides, the lamp may go out. But, if you have no objection, the billiard-table will be a good arena. We shall be well lighted, and there will be no means of drawing back a foot.

" Be it so," said the other.

The doors were closed, and they laid hands on the waiters and the proprietor of the *café*, who were going to the police. The swords were then brought. The two adversaries cast lots for them, and then pulled off their coats and waistcoats, and unbuttoned their shirts, to show that they had nothing under.

Both then took their swords.

The officer wrapt round his hand a handkerchief, leaving both ends dangling. Alfonse neglected this practice, the object of which was to distract the attention of the adversary by the perpetual flutter of their two white points, thus to turn away his attention from the sword. But Alfonse had a manner of fighting of his own, and cared little for these petty proceedings. He never looked at the steel ; but, fixing his eye on that of his antagonist, anticipated every motion that he made.

The two wrestlers, or gladiators I might say, got on the table together, and, according to the terms or conditions agreed on between the students and the officers, rested their swords on the toes of their boots. A traveller from a commercial house who happened to be present, and could have no interest in the scene other than what its novelty excited, was fixed on to clap his hands three times, and at the third the swords were upraised in the air, and the two combatants came to guard.

A terrible silence reigned through the room, and for some seconds it was only broken by the clashing of the steel ; for both parties, as they skirmished, were well aware that a single *faux pas* was death. The slightest stepping back, shrinking of the body, or leaping on one side, must inevitably prove fatal.

The officer was a head and shoulders taller than Alfonse, and looked as though he could crush him ; but he little heeded this advantage, if advantage it was, for he by degrees lowered his body till he was right under the sword of his foe, and almost bent himself down upon the bed of the table. No other change in his attitude then took place.

All at once the officer, taking this posture for the effect of fear, made a furious lunge, which was parried with the greatest *sang froid* and skill, and Alfonse allowed the officer to return to his ground without attempting to return it. His adversary was deceived by this sort of timid defence, and, become more adventurous, attacked him again with increased fury,—so much so, that, thrown off his guard, his left foot quitted the cushion of the table, against which it had been fixed. Then it was that Alfonse made a rapid lunge at the officer's face. He endeavoured to regain the ground he had lost, to resume his position. The student would not give him time, and charged with impetuosity his disconcerted enemy, who could only avoid his thrusts by keeping his body bent backwards. Alfonse forced him to the edge of the table, when his foot tripped, and at that moment drove the sword up to the hilt in his heart.

The unhappy officer cried out "Hit! hit!" Then he raised himself to his full height, and fell backwards from the top of the table to the floor.

Awful was the sound that the weight of that body made upon the boards of the room! There was mixed up with it a feeling—a dread lest the dead man should hurt himself in falling. Never did I see, for I was present, so dreadful a contest! Never did I experience anything so frightful as the silence of those two men,—as the flashing of their swords by the light of the lamps,—as the fall of the vanquished, who, disappearing behind the table, seemed at once to have been engulfed in a tomb that opened from behind to receive him!

THE MONK OF RAVENNE.

THE Monk of Ravenne was daring and great,
He had risk'd his life for the Church's estate;
He was loved by all who the Virgin love,
And the Pope and he were hand and glove;
Not a deed was done by friars or men,
But *that* deed was known to the Monk of Ravenne.

The Monk of Ravenne on his death-bed lay,
His eyes were closed to the light of day,
His ears drank in the fathers' prayers,
And his soul shook off its earthly cares;
Many a tongue and many a pen
Moved in praise of the Monk of Ravenne.

The Monk of Ravenne in the tomb was placed,
With noble and fair the chapel was graced,
The requiem rose with the organ's swell,
And an hundred voices peal'd his knell;
The lightning flash'd, and up started agen *
The ghastly form of the Monk of Ravenne.

"Fools!" cried the monk, "do you pray for *me*,
Who have plunder'd you all, of every degree?
I have blasted your fame, I have mock'd at your shrine,
And now do I suffer this doom of mine,
' Deserted of heaven, detested of men,
Lost, body and soul, is the Monk of Ravenne!'"

CLEIAUBUID.

* *Vide* Chaucer, &c.

A MARINE'S COURTSHIP.

BY MICHAEL BURKE HONAN.

WITH AN ILLUSTRATION BY GEORGE CRUIKSHANK.

I HAVE the honour to be one of that class of amphibious animals called in his Majesty's service *sea-soldiers;* that is to say, I have the honour to hold a commission in the noble, ancient, and most jolly body of the Royal Marines. I am by profession, therefore, as well as by nature, a miscellaneous individual; and circumstances have more than once thrown me into situations where the desire to support the credit of the cloth, added to my own stock of cheerful impudence, have carried me through, in spite of difficulties which would have appalled another man. I had the misfortune to be employed on board one of the ships of the inner squadron in the Douro during the siege of Oporto. I do not say misfortune out of any disrespect to the commodore, or to the captain under whose command I was immediately placed, or to my brother officers, for a more generous, convivial set of fellows could not be got together; but I speak of the place, and of the people, and of the few opportunities which were afforded me of showing off a handsome uniform, and, I must say, rather a well-made person, which it inclosed. Besides, I was kept on hard duty; and though there were some pretty women who appeared on Sunday during the cessations of the usual shower of shells from the Miguelite camp, yet there were so many competitors for their smiles, that I really could not take the trouble of making myself as amiable as I otherwise should, and, as I flatter myself, I could. Don Pedro the emperor, who now sleeps with his fathers, and whose heart is deposited in the cathedral of Oporto, was then without the society of his imperial and beautiful wife; and, whether it was to set a good example to his court, or to prevent his mind from dwelling on the absence of his true love, he was one of the most active of my rivals, and I protest there was not a pretty face in the whole town that he had not the pleasure of paying his addresses to. The Marquis of Loule, his brother-in-law, also separated from that most lovely and most generous of Portuguese princesses who now sits nightly at Lisbon, smiling on all the world from her box at the French theatre in the *Rua dos Condes,* was regularly employed in the same operations; and I never took a sly peep at a pair of dark and bewitching eyes that I did not find the emperor or the marquis also reconnoitring. The marquis is one of the handsomest men in Europe, but with the most vacant expression possible. He wins every heart at first sight, but he loses his conquests as fast as he makes them. Women may be caught by glare; and a man of high rank, an Adonis in face and person, must tell: but I'll be hanged if the dear creatures are such fools as we think them; and the marquis's wife first, and every other flame of his after, have dismissed him, on finding that his good looks and brains were not measured by the same scale. Then there was the Count Villa Flor, and several other martial grandees; not to speak of the generals and colonels of regiments, and the well-built and well-whiskered officers of the British and French Legion, and the captains and first lieutenants of our squadron. I run over this list just to show what diffi-

Geo Cruikshank

London. Richard Bentley, July, 1, 1837.

culties I had to contend with; and that, if I did not turn the head of the whole town, there was a numerous list of operative love-makers who shared the market with me.

About this time the senior captain of the squadron determined to establish a signal-station to communicate with the ships of his Britannic Majesty outside the bar; and, no fitting place being found on the Pedroite side of the river, an application was made to General San Martha, who commanded for the Miguelites, for permission to erect a post on the left bank, which permission was most liberally granted. A party was instantly set to work, and in the course of a few days a flag-staff was hoisted; and a large house and court-yard given for the accommodation of the officer and men who were to work it. As luck would have it, I was selected for this service, in company with a wild lieutenant of the fleet, and we soon established ourselves in a comfortable quarter, having the permission to rove about among the Miguelite grounds where we pleased, and to cross as usual to Oporto, when leave of absence was to be procured.

We had not been long established at this fort, when the batteries which the Miguelites had established at the mouth of the river began to do their work in good earnest, and so effectually to close the bar, that not only was the usual supply of provisions cut off, but strong fears were entertained that the city would be reduced by famine to capitulate. There was an abundance of salt fish, or *bacalhao*, and a superfluity of port wine; but even the best fare will tire on repetition, and you may be assured that salt fish for breakfast, dinner, and supper was not very acceptable to the officers or the men. Our commodore, with the foresight that distinguishes a British officer, had provided for the coming difficulty; and had arranged with the Miguelite general for an abundant supply of fresh provisions, meat, poultry, and vegetables, for all the ships' crews, on the distinct understanding that no part of it was to be passed over to the besieged city. The squadron therefore lived in abundance, while the garrison was half starved; and as we passed through the streets with our shining red faces and sleek sides, puffed out by the good cheer our commodore had provided, we formed a strong contrast to the lean and shrivelled soldiers of glory, who were starving in honour of the charter. The private families of the town also began to suffer, and the beauty of many of the most admired, sensibly to diminish; salt fish and port wine did not in combination make a healthy chyle: and I could observe that the Oporto ladies, more carefully than before, wrapped their long dark cloaks about them, to hide the ravages which short commons was making in the plumpness of their persons.

It was at this moment that I conceived and executed the bold plan which forms the subject of this paper, and from which all learned communities may be informed that, for originality of thought and ability in the execution, no adventurer can compare to a British marine.

The most beautiful maiden at Oporto was a Spanish girl called Carolina. She was the daughter of the alcade of Ponte Vedra in Galicia, who had fled some time before, from the retributive justice of the law, which he himself had so long administered; he had died months before the present period, leaving Carolina exposed to all the privations of a besieged town, and to the temptations of a profligate

and military court. I never saw a more lovely creature: her eyes
were as dark as night, and her cheeks glowed with a warmth unknown in the cold complexions of the north. Her person was
faultless; her feet and her hands were small: one could span her
waist; and she walked with that combination of majesty and grace
which a Spanish woman can alone assume. Poor Carolina was as
good as she was beautiful; and though the emperor, and his hopeful brother-in-law, and all the gay cavaliers of the camp, were ready to throw
themselves at her feet, she behaved with a discretion which won her
the good opinion of the whole army, not to speak of the fleet, where
such remarkable virtue could be fully estimated. I among the rest
of the inflammable multitude had been struck with the magic charms
of the angelic Carolina, and devoted every moment of the occasional
leave of absence which I procured, to promenading up and down before her window, in the hope of catching a glance of her beautiful
eyes, and of attracting her regard to my own beloved person. I was
as much in love with her as a marine could be, and my hopeless passion became so well known that it was a standing joke at the mess-
table, and our wicked wag of a commodore, who I fancied was a little
caught himself, never failed to inquire if I had taken my usual walk,
and met with the same good fortune.

You can easily imagine my delight when I heard that a scarcity
was making such rapid progress in the city, and when I found that
even the emperor's table was limited to the ordinary rations of *bacalhao*, black bread, and port wine. I will own that my heart
leaped for joy when I ascertained from an emissary employed to
watch the house of Carolina that she too was experiencing the pangs
of want, and that with her scanty means she was unable to procure
the common necessaries for her sustenance. Our ships were abundantly supplied, as I have before informed you; and the little signal-
station which I occupied was the abode of plenty. The Miguelites
faithfully performed their engagement; and day after day the regular
supplies of beef, poultry, vegetables, and fruit came in. The commodore of course respected the contract that he had entered into; and
though the emperor made several advances to his favour, and though
he was openly solicited on his behalf by various officers of the staff,
he refused to allow a pound of meat to be passed into the city. Several of the British residents represented their claims in a formal
manner for his protection; but he did his duty like a man, and he
resolutely determined not to break the engagement he had entered
into with the general of Don Miguel, or compromise the safety of his
own crews by giving way to his good-nature. The value of a leg of
fowl may therefore be estimated; and it immediately occurred to me
that I could soften the obdurate heart of the beautiful Spaniard by
secretly conveying to her some portion of the stock which was appro-
priated to our own table.

I therefore set about purloining a capital *gallina*; and when I had
secured it, in defiance of the jealous watch of the steward, I crammed it into my pocket, and, asking leave to go on shore, started
about the close of day to try whether hunger, which breaks through
stone walls, would open the oak door of the charming Carolina. I
soon found myself in the well-known quarter, and before the house
that contained my love; and, after reconnoitring for an instant to

see that the emperor or his staff were not in the way, ran up to the first landing, where she lived, and pulled the little bell-string which hung at the door. In an instant I heard the pretty feet tapping along the passage, and the soft voice of Carolina herself exclaiming "*Quien es ?*" Who is there? "It is I, a British officer, and a friend of yours," I replied; "I want particularly to speak to you."

"Sir," said Carolina, "I have not the honour of your acquaintance."

"It is true, señorita; but I come to serve you, and my good intentions will excuse the absence of ceremony."

"Sir, I must wish you a good day: I cannot accept a service from strangers; I have not asked you for any."

"Stay, beautiful Carolina," I exclaimed; "I adore you."

"Sir, I have the honour to wish you good evening."

"Stay, angelic vision: I am an officer of Marines."

"What have I to do with the Marines?"

"I come to devote myself to you."

"Sir,—really sir, you carry the joke too far; I must dispense with your unseasonable visit. I have again the honour to wish you good evening."

Carolina was about to close the little slide of the door through which this brief conversation had been carried on, when, growing desperate with vexation, I held the slide open with one hand, while with the other I pulled the fowl from my pocket, and held it dangling before her face. Oh! if you had seen her look!—her eyes were fixed as Hamlet's when he sees his father's ghost, her mouth opened, and two little rivulets of water ran down at each side as when an alderman gets the first odour of a well-kept haunch.

"Señorita," said I, eager to take advantage of the favourable impression the vision of the fowl had made on my beloved; "this bird is a proof of the warm interest which I take in your welfare. I have heard that you were suffering from the severe affliction that has fallen on this city; and, though I risk my character and the safety of his Britannic Majesty's fleet by bringing into Oporto any part of the provision allotted for the crews, I could not resist the impulse of stealing this bird, which I now have the honour to lay at your feet."

The señorita answered not: pride on the one hand, and hunger on the other, were struggling. The physical want prevailed over the moral feeling. "Señor," said she, "I will accept the fowl, and cannot but feel obliged by the interest you have taken in my welfare. Good night, señor; it is getting late: I am certain you are anxious to return to your ship." With these words she shut the little slide of the door, and I remained in the passage, gaping with astonishment, confounded with delight, and wondering at the new recipe I had invented for making love. I waited for some time, hoping that the little wicket would be again opened; but Carolina, I presume, was too much occupied with the present I had made her to think of returning to bid me a second farewell; and I descended the staircase, charmed beyond expression with the result of my stratagem.

I kept, of course, my recipe for making love a profound secret; but I did not venture to put it again into operation for two or three days. I made, however, the accustomed regular survey of the street in which Carolina resided, and watched with much interest for the reception given to my rivals. I cannot express the delight with which I witnessed them all, one after the other, refused admittance to her house. " She is picking the bones of the fowl," thought I; " that is a much better employment than listening to their stupid declarations. I must take care to keep my mistress in good humour, and to improve the favourable opinion she has already formed of me." I therefore watched my opportunity; secured a duck out of the next basket of poultry, and hastened on the wings of love to lay my treasure at her feet. No sooner did my trembling hand pull the bell-cord, and my eager voice announce my name, than I heard her gentle step in the passage, and soon the little slide of the door was opened, and I felt my heart leap to my mouth as I beheld her beautiful eye beaming on me with undisguised satisfaction. To ensure my welcome, and to save the dear creature from the pangs of expectation, I produced the duck, swinging it to and fro before the wicket, as a nurse does a pretty toy that she offers to the longing wishes of the child. Carolina smiled her sweetest smile; and, when I pushed in the prize, she returned me thanks in so endearing a manner that I lost all command of my reason, and poured out upon the staircase a volume of protestations of eternal love which might have served for the whole ship's company. From that hour my affair was done. Carolina could not resist the voice of truth, and the tender proofs of esteem which I alone had the power to offer. She refused to admit me then, but promised to consult her aunt on the propriety of receiving my visits; and that, if the discreet matron permitted it, she would be too happy in my acquaintance. I entreated the dear girl not to delay my happiness, and I fixed the following Thursday for the formidable interview with the aunt.

I lay the whole of the next night awake, thinking over the present which would be most acceptable to the old lady. I finally resolved to purloin a small leg of lamb, which I observed hung up in the steward's pantry; and, in order to make room for it in my pocket, I cut a great hole in the bottom, so that the handle of the leg would hang down, while the thicker part prevented it from slipping through. *Armed* with my leg, I asked leave to go to Oporto, and received with joy the accustomed friendly nod. I soon landed at the arsenal, and mounted the long hill which led into the town, holding myself as straight as possible, so that the exuberance of my pocket should not be perceived. Unfortunately for me, a score of hungry dogs, which infest all Portuguese towns, were holding a council of war at the quay when I stept on shore; and one of them, getting scent of the end of the leg of mutton which hung through the hole in my pocket, gave a hint to the rest of the contraband which was going on, and I soon had the whole train after me, sniffing at my tail, and making snaps at the tempting morsel. I would have stooped to pick up a stone, which is the only way of frightening a Portuguese street dog; but I was afraid to disarrange the perpendicular, recollecting that, as I bent down, the end of the leg of lamb would be visible. I therefore bore the annoyance as well as I could, kicking out behind from time to time when my friends were most troublesome.

Carolina and her aunt were at the window, probably expecting my arrival, and enduring the grumbling recollections of an ill-digested dinner of *bacalhao*, in the hope of a more wholesome supper being pro-

vided for them through my care; but when they saw me turn the
corner of the street, and at least two dozen dogs smelling and sniffing
at my skirts, they both burst out into an uncontrollable fit of laughter, and roared and roared again in a paroxysm of mirth. A crowd
of dandies were passing at the moment, watching the window
of Carolina, each hoping to be the favoured man; but when they
heard the sudden burst of merriment which proceeded from her window, they looked round naturally for the cause, and they soon joined
in the same chorus at my expense, on seeing me parade, with all the
gravity of a drum-major, at the head of a legion of filthy curs.

To make my situation worse, I dared not enter the house of Carolina; her character would be compromised by a visit in presence of
so many admirers: and I had the additional mortification of being
obliged to pass her door, and to walk a considerable distance until I
escaped the impertinence of the sneering puppies, though I could
not shake off the annoyance of those that followed at my heels. How
gladly would I have drawn my sword, and challenged the whole party! how cheerfully would I have drawn the leg of lamb from my
pocket, and stuffed it in the mouth of each impertinent dandy! but not
only was my own honour at stake, but that of the British fleet, and I
bore all in the king's name, and for the credit of the service. I have
been in many a hot engagement, but I never suffered more than I
did that day. At length, after doubling through two or three by-
streets, I got rid of my impudent macaroni, and traced my way back
again to the house of my beloved. She, with the old lady, were
watching me from the window; but, grown wiser by experience, and
probably afraid of losing a good supper, they did not laugh again with
the same violence. I observed, however, the wicked smile with which
my fair one retired to receive me at the door, and the suppressed
titter with which the maiden aunt pulled her head from the window.

The cursed dogs followed me up stairs, and it was with considerable difficulty I could prevent the most insolent from forcing their way
with me into the presence of my mistress; but, after I got in, I heard
them growling and barking on the stairs. The neighbours wondered what the deuce was the matter with the curs, or why they had
come from their usual haunts to that unfrequented quarter.

The señorita presented me in due form to her aunt.

"Allow me," said she, " to introduce to you, dear aunt, this gallant English cavalier, Señor *Gallina*,—I beg pardon, Señor Marinero,
—and permit me to present to you, señor, my respected aunt, Donna
Francisca Azanares."

I made a low bow, but said nothing, seeing that my mistress
thought more of the fowl than of me; such is the way of the world,
and those who will win women must endure to have their pride occasionally mortified. The old lady, however, covered me with compliments; she was delighted to make my acquaintance; her niece
had told her what an amiable and gentlemanlike young man I was.
I could observe, while the aunt was hard at work overloading me
with compliments, that Carolina was taking a sly peep at the bulk of
my pockets, and wondering what kind of commodity it was that produced so misplaced a swelling on so well-formed a young man as I
flatter myself no one can deny I am; but, just at this moment,
the bevy of hungry curs at the door set up such a howl in concert,

that my angel was fain to cram her handkerchief into her mouth to conceal her laughing, and I thought the old dame would go into a fit, so violent was her merriment. Finding the case going thus hard against me, I determined to strike a bold stroke for conquest; so, slipping out my penknife, I slit up the pocket where the treasure lay, and down fell the leg of lamb in all its natural beauty on the floor. I thought the aunt would have fainted with delight, such an unexpected vision of glory dazzled her understanding and her sight. The *bouquet* of the meat was, I suppose, conveyed through the keyhole to the canine multitude that still lined the stairs, and another universal howl proclaimed their despair that it was beyond their reach.

I soon took my leave, to the delight of Carolina and her aunt. I think I showed considerable tact in so doing; well knowing that a slice off the leg of lamb would be more acceptable to both than all the professions of admiration which I was prepared to make. I ventured on two or three civil things, but I could see my beloved's eyes fixed upon the handle of the leg; and it was evident the aunt was carrying on an internal debate whether it should be boiled, broiled, roasted, or stewed, or served up, according to the fashion of the province, with a mass of garlic. The dogs were waiting for me in the passage, and they eagerly followed me as I went down stairs; even the smell of my pocket had its attraction for them, but they dropped off one by one when they found the reality was gone. One old savoury rogue alone persecuted me to the river side; and though I pelted him with stones, and kicked him when I could, he still hung on my rear with his tongue out, licking the shreds which dangled from my torn pocket.

The next day, when I went on board ship to make the usual report to the captain, I found that a court of inquiry was going on into the disappearance of the very leg of lamb which I had feloniously purloined. The steward had reported the accident to the purveyor of the mess, and he had called a council of war, who thought fit to make an official report to the skipper; so that the readers will readily imagine the agony of my feelings when I was asked to join the board, and to assist in the investigation. Fortunately for me, one of the aides-de-camp of the emperor had that morning come on board to request of the captain some provision for the imperial table, protesting that Don Pedro and his staff had nothing better than salt fish for rations; which request the captain was compelled, by a strict sense of duty, to refuse; and everybody set it down as certain, the instant the circumstance was brought to mind, that it was the aide-de-camp who stole the lamb. He had come wrapped up in his cloak, which was a circumstance fatal to his character; and it was agreed by the whole conclave that the gentleman with the gold-laced hat and large cloak had been the thief. I blushed up to the eyes at the consciousness of my guilt, and the dishonourable part I was playing in allowing an innocent person to be wronged for my misdeed; but I recollected that the young man was one of the party who ridiculed me the day before in the presence of Carolina, and wounded vanity made me disregard the twitchings of conscience.

In order to avoid suspicion, I lay quiet for a day or two, and allowed Carolina and her aunt to feel the value of such an acquaintance as I was, under existing circumstances. While engaged with the captain on some official duty, the following morning, in his cabin, a young officer was introduced who solicited an immediate audience. The young man appeared buried in grief, and every now and then applied a handkerchief to his eyes, to wipe off the unbidden tears which mocked the sword which hung at his side. His profound sorrow and gentlemanlike appearance interested the good heart of our excellent captain; he begged him to be seated, and wished to know what service he could render him. The young man could with difficulty master his emotion, and the only words that were heard from him were, "My aunt !—my aunt !"

"Pray, sir, be composed;" said the captain, a little tired of the display.

"I will, sir," replied the young man, giving a great gulp, as if to swallow his misery, and applying his handkerchief to wipe off the tears from both his swimming eyes. "Oh! sir," he continued, "my poor aunt, she who reared me from a child, when I was left an unprotected orphan, and has placed me in the station which I now hold, is at the point of death, and the doctors all agree that nothing but *caldo di gallina* (fowl broth) can save her life. You know the state which we are in at Oporto, and that not a fowl is to be had if one offered a thousand milreas for it; I come to you, as a man and a Christian, to beg you will give me one single chicken from your larder."

"It is impossible," said the captain; "you know the convention we have made with Santa Martha."

"I know all that," resumed the young man; "but you must admit, my dear captain, that the convention is directed against the troops of Don Pedro, and the inhabitants at large who support him; but surely an old woman at the point of death was not contemplated by the treaty, and I entreat you to save the life of this most deserving and venerable of aunts." With these words the young officer again took out his handkerchief, and gave way to a flood of tears that would have moved the strictest disciplinarian that ever commanded a ship.

It was not to be wondered at that the soft heart of our benevolent skipper was affected. He took the young man by the hand, and said, "My dear fellow, I can do nothing for you; I have signed a convention, and I cannot break it, were it to save the emperor's life: but go you to my steward, and if you can manage to extract a fowl from what he has prepared for my table, you may do so; but take care, I am not to know anything about it."

I fancied the young fellow smiled in the midst of his grief at the mention of the emperor; but he dried up his tears in double quick time, and soon made his way to the steward's room, where I suppose he contrived to settle his affair to his satisfaction. He called on the following day to return his grateful thanks; but the captain would not hear a word. I observed, however, that he went down to the steward's cabin, and took a hasty leave as he went over the ship's side on his return. He scarcely failed to pay us a daily visit, and made us all take a strong interest in him and the recovery of this favourite aunt to whom he was so devotedly attached.

This aunt, we found out afterwards, was the emperor; and so reduced was the imperial table for a short time, that Don Pedro must have starved, or lived on *bacalhao*, if this stratagem had not been adopted. The young fellow acted his part in a consummate manner, and I am told he boasts to this day of the trick he played the British squadron in the Douro. The captain, I am also told, gave him a little of his mind, having met him last year near the Admiralty, dressed out in fine feathers, and swelling with the importance of new-born greatness. "How is your aunt, you d— lying Portuguese?" said the skipper. "If I ever catch you on board my ship, I'll give you a rope's end, you dog!"

The more you beat one of the class of which this hero was a specimen, the more he likes it. So our Pedroite friend shrugged up his shoulders, and vanished in double quick time, the captain vociferating after him, "How is your aunt, you lubber?"

Afraid of the consequences in case a discovery should take place, I kept quiet for nearly a week together, until a little note, written in a cramped hand, was brought for me to the signal-station, from which I found by the confession of the aunt that Carolina was in despair at not seeing me again, and that she was very ill from a salt-fish diet. I was conscience-stricken at the consequences of my neglect, and determined not to lose a moment in carrying provisions to my starving beauty; so, running to a basket that had just been brought in from the Miguelite market to be passed on board the commodore, I seized a turkey-poult, feathers and all, and thrust it into the same coat-pocket which had been enlarged to hold the leg of lamb. I asked and received leave to go on shore, and pushed as fast as four oars could impel me to the usual landing-place near the old nunnery. I saw some of the idle dogs basking in the sun, but did not heed their presence, so filled was I with the idea of my Carolina; and, jumping out of the boat, I ran along the quay, totally unconscious of the sneers that my presence excited. At last, when I got to the open rope-walk where the market is usually held, the number of my canine assailants became increased; and one of them, bolder than the rest, making a sudden snap at the head of the young turkey, which hung down through the fatal hole in my pocket, dragged its long neck to view, and exposed my shame to the assembled multitude. A crowd immediately gathered round me, and a score of other dogs began to contest the prize with him that held the head of the turkey in his mouth. I was in despair, and drew my sword to rid me of the cursed assailants; when, on the instant, as if to overwhelm me with disgrace, the captain of the ship to which I belonged forced his way through the crowd, and, laying his hand on my arm, told me to consider myself under arrest.

The turkey-poult had by this time been torn from my pocket by the perseverance of my tormentors. It was pulled from one to the other on the ground; while the hungry citizens endeavoured to save its mangled remains, and a running fight was kept up between them and the dogs, which under other circumstances would have been highly amusing. My heart was heavy, and I was incapable of enjoying the most palpable joke. I walked slowly to the quay side, threw myself into the first boat that offered, went on board my ship, gave up my sword to the senior officer; was placed under a formal arrest, and told to prepare myself for a court of inquiry. I must say that I felt more for poor Carolina than I did for myself; and I could not

help expressing my anxiety on her account to one of the brother
officers who came to condole with me on my situation. The false
friend, I was told afterwards, profited by the hint; and, instead of committing himself as I did, he hired a little cottage at the Miguelite
side of the river, under cover of the guns of the fleet, where he placed
Carolina and her aunt, and soon taught them to forget me. The
worst of the affair was, that General Santa Martha sent in a formal
complaint to the consul and the commodore of the squadron, and
threatened to stop the usual supply of provisions for the ships' use.
A long correspondence took place on the subject, which may be found
now in the records of the Foreign Office. I am glad to say, for the
credit of the service, that the affair was hushed up in the end, and
the Miguelites consented to give the required number of rations. I
was made the victim of that arrangement, and was glad to retire from
the service on half-pay, to escape being ignominiously dismissed by a
court-martial. I now live a miserable example of the doctrine of
expediency. I entertain a horror of young turkeys and of dogs, and
would be gladly informed of some land where neither of those odious
creatures are to be met with.

FAMILY STORIES.—No. VI.—MRS. BOTHERBY'S STORY.

THE LEECH OF FOLKESTONE.

READER, were you ever bewitched? I do not mean by a "white
wench's black eye," or by love-potions imbibed from a ruby lip; but,
were you ever really and *bonâ fide* bewitched, in the true Matthew
Hopkins sense of the word? Did you ever, for instance, find yourself
from head to heel one vast complication of cramps? or burst out into
sudorific exudation like a cold thaw, with the thermometer at zero?
Were your eyes ever turned upside down, exhibiting nothing but
their whites? Did you ever vomit a paper of crooked pins? or expec-
torate Whitechapel needles? These are genuine and undoubted
marks of possession; and if you never experienced any of them,—why,
" happy man be his dole!"

Yet such things have been; yea, we are assured, on no mean
authority, still are.

The world, according to the best geographers, is divided into Europe, Asia, Africa, America, and Romney Marsh. In this last-
named and fifth quarter of the globe, a witch may still be occasionally discovered in favourable, *i. e.* stormy, seasons, weathering Dunge-
ness Point in an egg-shell, or careering on her broomstick over
Dymchurch wall. A cow may yet be sometimes seen galloping like
mad, with tail erect, and an old pair of breeches on her horns, an unerring guide to the door of the crone whose magic arts have drained
her udder. I do not, however, remember to have heard that any
conjuror has, of late, been detected in the district.

Not many miles removed from the verge of this recondite region, stands a collection of houses, which its maligners call a fishing-town, and its well-wishers a Watering-place. A limb of one of the Cinque Ports, it has (or lately had) a corporation of its own, and has been thought considerable enough to give a second title to a noble family. Rome stood on seven hills; Folkestone seems to have been built upon seventy. Its streets, lanes, and alleys,—fanciful distinctions without much real difference—are agreeable enough to persons who do not mind running up and down stairs; and the only inconvenience at all felt by such of its inhabitants as are not asthmatic, is when some heedless urchin tumbles down a chimney, or an impertinent passenger peeps into a garret window. At the eastern extremity of the town, on the sea-beach, and scarcely above high-water mark, stood, in the good old times, a row of houses then denominated "Frog-hole;" modern refinement subsequently euphonized the name into "East-street:" but what's in a name? the encroachments of Ocean have long since levelled all in one common ruin. Here, in the early part of the seventeenth century, flourished, in somewhat doubtful reputation, but comparative opulence, a compounder of medicines, one Master Erasmus Buckthorne; the effluvia of whose drugs from within, mingling agreeably with the "ancient and fish-like smells" from without, wafted a delicious perfume throughout the neighbourhood. At seven of the clock in the morning when Mrs. Botherby's narrative commences, a stout Suffolk punch, about thirteen hands and a half in height, was slowly led up and down before the door of the pharmacopolist by a lean and withered lad, whose appearance warranted an opinion, pretty generally expressed, that his master found him as useful in experimentalizing as in household drudgery, and that, for every pound avoirdupoise of solid meat, he swallowed at the least two pounds troy-weight of chemicals and galenicals. As the town clock struck the quarter, Master Buckthorne emerged from his laboratory, and, putting the key carefully into his pocket, mounted the sure-footed cob aforesaid, and proceeded up and down the acclivities and declivities of the town with the gravity due to his station and profession. When he reached the open country, his pace was increased to a sedate canter, which, in somewhat more than half an hour, brought "the horse and his rider" in front of a handsome and substantial mansion, the numerous gable-ends and bayed windows of which bespoke the owner a man of worship, and one well to do in the world.

"How now, Hodge Gardener?" quoth the leech, scarcely drawing bit; for Punch seemed to be aware that he had reached his destination, and paused of his own accord; "how now, man? How fares thine employer, worthy Master Marsh? How hath he done? How hath he slept? My potion hath done its office? Ha!"

"Alack! ill at ease, worthy sir,—ill at ease," returned the hind; "his honour is up and stirring; but he hath rested none, and complaineth that the same gnawing pain devoureth, as it were, his very vitals: in sooth he is ill at ease."

"Morrow, doctor!" interrupted a voice from a casement opening on the lawn. "Good morrow! I have looked for, longed for, thy coming this hour and more; enter at once; the pasty and tankard are impatient for thine attack!"

"Marry, Heaven forbid that I should baulk their fancy!" quoth the leech *sotto voce*, as, abandoning the bridle to honest Hodge, he dismounted, and followed a buxom-looking handmaiden into the breakfast parlour.

There, at the head of his well-furnished board, sat Master Thomas Marsh, of Marshton-Hall, a Yeoman well respected in his degree; one of that sturdy and sterling class which, taking rank immediately below the Esquire, (a title in its origin purely military,) occupied, in the wealthier counties, the position in society now filled by the Country Gentleman. He was one of those of whom the proverb ran:

> " A Knight of Cales,
>   A Gentleman of Wales,
>   And a Laird of the North Countree ;
> · A Yeoman of Kent,
>   With his yearly rent,
>   Will buy them out all three !"

A cold sirloin, big enough to frighten a Frenchman, filled the place of honour, counter-checked by a game-pie of no stinted dimensions; while a silver flagon of " humming-bub," *viz.* ale strong enough to blow a man's beaver off, smiled opposite in treacherous amenity. The sideboard groaned beneath sundry massive cups and waiters of the purest silver; while the huge skull of a fallow-deer, with its branching horns, frowned majestically above. All spoke of affluence, of comfort,—all save the master, whose restless eye and feverish look hinted but too plainly the severest mental or bodily disorder. By the side of the proprietor of the mansion sat his consort, a lady now past the bloom of youth, yet still retaining many of its charms. The clear olive of her complexion, and " the darkness of her Andalusian eye," at once betrayed her foreign origin; in fact, her " lord and master," as husbands were even then, by a legal fiction, denominated, had taken her to his bosom in a foreign country. The cadet of his family, Master Thomas Marsh, had early in life been engaged in commerce. In the pursuit of his vocation he had visited Antwerp, Hamburg, and most of the Hanse Towns; and had already formed a tender connexion with the orphan offspring of one of old Alva's officers, when the unexpected deaths of one immediate and two presumptive heirs placed him next in succession to the family acres. He married, and brought home his bride; who, by the decease of the venerable possessor, heart-broken at the loss of his elder children, became eventually lady of Marshton-Hall. It has been said that she was beautiful, yet was her beauty of a character that operates on the fancy more than the affections; she was one to be admired rather than loved. The proud curl of her lip, the firmness of her tread, her arched brow, and stately carriage, showed the decision, not to say haughtiness of her soul; while her glances, whether lightening with anger, or melting in extreme softness, betrayed the existence of passions as intense in kind as opposite in quality. She rose as Erasmus entered the parlour, and, bestowing on him a look fraught with meaning, quitted the room, leaving him in unconstrained communication with his patient.

" 'Fore George, Master Buckthorne !" exclaimed the latter, as the leech drew near, " I will no more of your pharmacy ;—burn, burn—gnaw, gnaw,—I had as lief the foul fiend were in my gizzard as one of your drugs. Tell me, in the devil's name, what is the matter with me !"

Thus conjured, the practitioner paused, and even turned somewhat pale. There was a perceptible faltering in his voice as, evading the question, he asked, " What say your other physicians ?"

" Doctor Phiz says it is wind,—Doctor Fuz says it is water,—and Doctor Buz says it is something between wind and water."

" They are all of them wrong," said Erasmus Buckthorne.

" Truly, I think so," returned the patient. " They are manifest asses; but you, good leech, you are a horse of another colour. The world talks loudly of your learning, your skill, and cunning in arts the most abstruse; nay, sooth to say, some look coldly on you therefore, and stickle not to aver that you are cater-cousin with Beelzebub himself."

" It is ever the fate of science," murmured the professor, " to be maligned by the ignorant and superstitious. But a truce with such folly; let me examine your palate."

Master Marsh thrust out a tongue long, clear, and red as beet-root. " There is nothing wrong there," said the leech. " Your wrist :—no ; the pulse is firm and regular, the skin cool and temperate. Sir, there is nothing the matter with you !"

" Nothing the matter with me, Sir Potecary ?" But I tell you there is the matter with me,—much the matter with me. Why is it that something seems ever gnawing at my heart-strings ? Whence this pain in the region of the liver ? Why is it that I sleep not o' nights, rest not o' days ? Why ——"

" You are fidgety, Master Marsh," said the doctor.

Master Marsh's brow grew dark; he half rose from his seat, supported himself by both hands on the arms of his elbow-chair, and in accents of mingled anger and astonishment repeated the word '' Fidgety !"

" Ay, fidgety," returned the doctor calmly. " Tut, man, there is nought ails thee save thine own overweening fancies. Take less of food, more air, put aside thy flagon, call for thy horse ; be boot and saddle the word ! Why,—hast thou not youth ?"——

" I have," said the patient.

" Wealth, and a fair domain ?"

" Granted," quoth Marsh cheerily.

" And a fair wife ?"

" Yea," was the response, but in a tone something less satisfied.

" Then arouse thee, man, shake off this fantasy, betake thyself to thy lawful occasions, use thy good hap, follow thy pleasures, and think no more of these fancied ailments."

" But I tell you, master mine, these ailments are not fancied. I lose my rest, I loathe my food, my doublet sits loosely on me,—these racking pains. My wife, too,—when I meet her gaze, the cold sweat stands on my forehead, and I could almost think ——" Marsh paused abruptly, mused a while, then added, looking steadily at his visitor, " These things are not right ; they pass the common, Master Erasmus Buckthorne."

A slight shade crossed the brow of the leech, but its passage was momentary; his features softened to a smile, in which pity seemed slightly blended with contempt. " Have done with such follies, Master Marsh. You are well, an you would but think so. Ride, I say, hunt, shoot, do anything,—disperse these melancholic humours, and become yourself again."

"Well, I will do your bidding," said Marsh thoughtfully. "It may be so; and yet,—but I will do your bidding. Master Cobbe of Brenzet writes me that he hath a score or two of fat ewes to be sold a pennyworth; I had thought to have sent Ralph Looker, but I will essay to go myself. Ho, there!—saddle me the brown mare, and bid Ralph be ready to attend me on the gelding."

An expression of pain contracted the features of Master Marsh as he rose and slowly quitted the apartment to prepare for his journey; while the leech, having bidden him farewell, vanished through an opposite door, and betook himself to the private boudoir of the fair mistress of Marshton, muttering as he went a quotation from a then newly-published play,

"Not poppy, nor mandragora,
Nor all the drowsy syrups of the world,
Shall ever medicine thee to that sweet sleep
Which thou own'st yesterday."

* * * * *

Of what passed at this interview between the Folkestone doctor and the fair Spaniard, Mrs. Botherby declares she could never obtain any satisfactory elucidation. Not that tradition is silent on the subject,—quite the contrary; it is the abundance, not paucity, of the materials she supplies, and the consequent embarrassment of selection, that make the difficulty. Some have averred that the leech, whose character, as has been before hinted, was more than threadbare, employed his time in teaching her the mode of administering certain noxious compounds, the unconscious partaker whereof would pine and die so slowly and gradually as to defy suspicion. Others there were who affirmed that Lucifer himself was then and there raised *in propriá personá*, with all his terrible attributes of horn and hoof. In support of this assertion, they adduce the testimony of the aforesaid buxom housemaid, who protested that the Hall smelt that evening like a manufactory of matches. All, however, seem to agree that the confabulation, whether human or infernal, was conducted with profound secrecy, and protracted to a considerable length; that its object, as far as could be divined, meant anything but good to the head of the family; that the lady, moreover, was heartily tired of her husband; and that, in the event of his removal by disease or casualty, Master Erasmus Buckthorne, albeit a great philosophist, would have had no violent objection to throw physic to the dogs, and exchange his laboratory for the estate of Marshton, its live stock included. Some, too, have inferred that to him did Madam Isabel seriously incline; while others have thought, induced perhaps by subsequent events, that she was merely using him for her purposes; that one José, a tall, bright-eyed, hook-nosed stripling from her native land, was a personage not unlikely to put a spoke in the doctor's wheel; and that, should such a chance arise, the Sage, wise as he was, would, after all, run no slight risk of being "bamboozled."

Master José was a youth well-favoured and comely to look upon. His office was that of page to the dame; an office which, after long remaining in abeyance, has been of late years revived, as may well be seen in the persons of sundry smart hobbledehoys, now constantly to be met with on staircases and in boudoirs, clad, for the most part, in garments fitted tightly to the shape, the lower moiety adorned with a broad stripe of crimson or silver lace, and the upper with what the

first Wit of our times describes as " a favourable eruption of buttons."
The precise duties of this employment have never, as far as we have
heard, been accurately defined.   The perfuming a handkerchief, the
combing a lap-dog, and the occasional presentation of a sippet-shaped
billet doux, are, and always have been, among them ; but these a young
gentleman standing five foot ten, and aged nineteen " last grass,"
might well be supposed to have outgrown.   José, however, kept his
place, perhaps because he was not fit for any other.   To the conference between his mistress and the physician he had not been admitted ; his post was to keep watch and ward in the ante-room ; and,
when the interview was concluded, he attended the lady and her
visitor as far as the court-yard, where he held, with all due respect, the
stirrup for the latter, as he once more resumed his position on the
back of Punch.

Who is it that says " little pitchers have large ears ?"   Some deep
metaphysician of the potteries, who might have added that they have
also quick eyes, and sometimes silent tongues.   There was a little
metaphorical piece of crockery of this class, who, screened by a huge
elbow-chair, had sat a quiet and unobserved spectator of the whole
proceedings between her mamma and Master Erasmus Buckthorne.
This was Miss Marian Marsh, a rosy-cheeked, laughter-loving imp of
some six years old ; but one who could be mute as a mouse when the
fit was on her.   A handsome and highly-polished cabinet of the darkest
ebony occupied a recess at one end of the apartment ; this had long
been a great subject of speculation to little Miss.   Her curiosity,
however, had always been repelled ; nor had all her coaxing ever won
her an inspection of the thousand and one pretty things which its
recesses no doubt contained.   On this occasion it was unlocked, and
Marian was about to rush forward in eager anticipation of a peep at
its interior, when, child as she was, the reflection struck her that she
would stand a better chance of carrying her point by remaining *per-
due*.   Fortune for once favoured her : she crouched closer than before, and saw her mother take something from one of the drawers,
which she handed over to the leech.   Strange mutterings followed,
and words whose sound was foreign to her youthful ears.   Had she
been older, their import, perhaps, might have been equally unknown.
—After a while there was a pause ; and then the lady, as in answer to
a requisition from the gentleman, placed in his hand a something
which she took from her toilette.   The transaction, whatever its nature, seemed now to be complete, and the article was carefully replaced in the drawer from which it had been taken.   A long and apparently interesting conversation then took place between the parties,
carried on in a low tone.   At its termination, Mistress Marsh and
Master Erasmus Buckthorne quitted the boudoir together.   But the
cabinet !—ay, that was left unfastened ; the folding-doors still remained
invitingly expanded, the bunch of keys dangling from the lock.   In
an instant the spoiled child was in a chair ; the drawer so recently
closed yielded at once to her hand, and her hurried researches were
rewarded by the prettiest little waxen doll imaginable.   It was a first-
rate prize, and Miss lost no time in appropriating it to herself.   Long
before Madam Marsh had returned to her *Sanctum*, Marian was
seated under a laurestinus in the garden, nursing her new baby with
the most affectionate solicitude.

    *   *   *   *   *

"Susan, look here; see what a nasty scratch I have got upon my hand," said the young lady, when routed out at length from her hiding-place to her noontide meal.

"Yes, Miss, this is always the way with you! mend, mend, mend, —nothing but mend! Scrambling about among the bushes, and tearing your clothes to rags. What with you, and with madam's farthingales and kirtles, a poor bower-maiden has a fine time of it!"

"But I have not torn my clothes, Susan, and it was not the bushes; it was the doll: only see what a great ugly pin I have pulled out of it! and look, here is another!" As she spoke, Marian drew forth one of those extended pieces of black pointed wire, with which, in the days of toupees and pompoons, our foremothers were wont to secure their fly-caps and head-gear from the impertinent assaults of Zephyrus and the "Little Breezes."

"And pray, Miss, where did you get this pretty doll, as you call it?" asked Susan, turning over the puppet, and viewing it with a scrutinizing eye.

"Mamma gave it me," said the child.—This was a fib!

"Indeed!" quoth the girl thoughtfully; and then, in half soliloquy, and a lower key, "Well! I wish I may die if it doesn't look like my master!—But come to your dinner, miss. Hark! the *bell is striking One!*"

Meanwhile, Master Thomas Marsh, and his man Ralph, were threading the devious paths, then, as now, most pseudonymously dignified with the name of roads, that wound between Marshton-Hall and the frontier of Romney Marsh. Their progress was comparatively slow; for, though the brown mare was as good a roadster as man might back, and the gelding no mean nag of his hands, yet the tracks, rarely traversed save by the rude wains of the day, miry in the "bottoms," and covered with loose and rolling stones on the higher grounds, rendered barely passable the perpetual alternation of hill and valley.

The master rode on in pain, and the man in listlessness; although the intercourse between two individuals so situated was much less restrained in those days than might suit the refinement of a later age, little passed approximating to conversation beyond an occasional and half-stifled groan from the one, or a vacant whistle from the other. An hour's riding had brought them among the woods of Acryse; and they were about to descend one of those green and leafy lanes, rendered by matted and over-arching branches alike impervious to shower or sunbeam, when a sudden and violent spasm seized on Master Marsh, and nearly caused him to fall from his horse. With some difficulty he succeeded in dismounting, and seating himself by the road side. Here he remained for a full half-hour in great apparent agony; the cold sweat rolled in large round drops adown his clammy forehead, a universal shivering palsied every limb, his eye-balls appeared to be starting from their sockets, and to his attached, though dull and heavy serving-man, he seemed as one struggling in the pangs of impending dissolution. His groans rose thick and frequent; and the alarmed Ralph was hesitating between his disinclination to leave him, and his desire to procure such assistance as one of the few cottages, rarely sprinkled in that wild country, might afford, when, after a long-drawn sigh, his master's features as suddenly relaxed: he declared him-

self better, the pang had passed away, and, to use his own expression, he "felt as if a knife had been drawn from out his very heart." With Ralph's assistance, after a while, he again reached his saddle; and, though still ill at ease from a deep-seated and gnawing pain, which ceased not, as he averred, to torment him, the violence of the paroxysm was spent, and it returned no more.

Master and man pursued their way with increased speed, as, emerging from the wooded defiles, they at length neared the coast; then, leaving the romantic castle of Saltwood, with its neighbouring town of Hithe, a little on their left, they proceeded along the ancient paved causeway, and, crossing the old Roman road, or Watling, plunged again into the woods that stretched between Lympne and Ostenhanger.

The sun rode high in the heavens, and its meridian blaze was powerfully felt by man and horse, when, again quitting their leafy covert, the travellers debouched on the open plain of Aldington Frith, a wide tract of unenclosed country stretching down to the very borders of "the Marsh" itself. Here it was, in the neighbouring chapelry, the site of which may yet be traced by the curious antiquary, that Elizabeth Barton, the "Holy Maid of Kent," had, something less than a hundred years previous to the period of our narrative, commenced that series of supernatural pranks which eventually procured for her head an unenvied elevation upon London Bridge; and, though the parish had since enjoyed the benefit of the incumbency of Master Erasmus's illustrious and enlightened Namesake, yet, truth to tell, some of the old leaven was even yet supposed to be at work. The place had, in fact, an ill name; and, though Popish miracles had ceased to electrify its denizens, spells and charms, operating by a no less wondrous agency, were said to have taken their place. Warlocks, and other unholy subjects of Satan, were reported to make its wild recesses their favourite rendezvous, and that to an extent which eventually attracted the notice of no less a personage than the sagacious Matthew Hopkins himself, Witchfinder-General to the British government.

A great portion of the Frith, or Fright, as the name was then, and is still, pronounced, had formerly been a Chace, with rights of Freewarren, &c. appertaining to the Archbishops of the Province. Since the Reformation, however, it had been disparked; and when Master Thomas Marsh, and his man Ralph, entered upon its confines, the open greensward exhibited a lively scene, sufficiently explanatory of certain sounds that had already reached their ears while yet within the sylvan screen which concealed their origin.

It was Fair-day: booths, stalls, and all the rude *paraphernalia* of an assembly that then met as much for the purposes of traffic as festivity, were scattered irregularly over the turf; pedlars, with their packs; horse-croupers, pig-merchants, itinerant vendors of crockery and cutlery, wandered promiscuously among the mingled groups, exposing their several wares and commodities, and soliciting custom. On one side was the gaudy riband, making its mute appeal to rustic gallantry; on the other the delicious brandy-ball and alluring lollipop, compounded after the most approved receipt in the "True Gentlewoman's Garland," and "raising the waters" in the mouth of many an expectant urchin.

Nor were rural sports wanting to those whom pleasure, rather than business, had drawn from their humble homes. Here was the tall and slippery pole, glittering in its grease, and crowned with the ample cheese, that mocked the hopes of the discomfited climber. There the fugitive pippin, swimming in water not of the purest, and bobbing from the expanded lips of the juvenile Tantalus. In this quarter the ear was pierced by squeaks from some beleaguered porker, whisking his well-soaped tail from the grasp of one already in fancy his captor. In that, the eye rested, with undisguised delight, upon the grimaces of grinning candidates for the honours of the horse-collar. All was fun, frolic, courtship, junketing, and jollity.

Maid Marian, indeed, with her lieges, Robin Hood, Scarlet, and Little John, was wanting; Friar Tuck was absent; even the Hobbyhorse had disappeared: but the agile Morrice-dancers yet were there, and jingled their bells merrily among stalls well stored with gingerbread, tops, whips, whistles, and all those noisy instruments of domestic torture in which scenes like these are even now so fertile. —Had I a foe whom I held at deadliest feud, I would entice his child to a Fair, and buy him a Whistle and a Penny-trumpet!

In one corner of the green, a little apart, from the thickest of the throng, stood a small square stage, nearly level with the chins of the spectators, whose repeated bursts of laughter seemed to intimate the presence of something more than usually amusing. The platform was divided into two unequal portions; the smaller of which, surrounded by curtains of a coarse canvass, veiled from the eyes of the profane the *penetralia* of this moveable temple of Esculapius, for such it was. Within its interior, and secure from vulgar curiosity, the Quack-salver had hitherto kept himself ensconced; occupied, no doubt, in the preparation and arrangement of that wonderful *panacea* which was hereafter to shed the blessings of health among the admiring crowd. Meanwhile his attendant Jack-pudding was busily employed on the *proscenium*, doing his best to attract attention by a practical facetiousness which took wonderfully with the spectators, interspersing it with the melodious notes of a huge cow's horn. The fellow's costume varied but little in character from that in which the late—(alas! that we should have to write the word!)—the late Mr. Joseph Grimaldi was accustomed to present himself before " a generous and enlightened public:" the principal difference consisted in this, that the upper garment was a long white tunic of a coarse linen, surmounted by a caricature of the ruff then fast falling into disuse, and was secured from the throat downwards by a single row of broad white metal buttons. His legs were cased in loose wide trousers of the same material; while his sleeves, prolonged to a most disproportionate extent, descended far below the fingers, and acted as flappers in the summersets and caracoles with which he diversified and enlivened his antics. Consummate impudence, not altogether unmixed with a certain sly humour, sparkled in his eye through the chalk and ochre with which his features were plentifully bedaubed; and especially displayed itself in a succession of jokes, the coarseness of which did not seem to detract from their merit in the eyes of his applauding audience.

He was in the midst of a long and animated harangue explanatory of his master's high pretensions; he had informed his gaping auditors that the latter was the seventh son of a seventh son, and of course, as they very well knew, an Unborn Doctor; that to this happy accident of birth he added the advantage of most extensive travel; that in his search after science he had not only perambulated the whole of this world, but had trespassed on the boundaries of the next; that the depths of Ocean and the bowels of the Earth were alike familiar to him; that besides salves and cataplasms of sovereign virtue, by combining sundry mosses, gathered many thousand fathom below the surface of the sea, with certain unknown drugs found in an undiscovered island, and boiling the whole in the lava of Vesuvius, he had succeeded in producing his celebrated balsam of Crackapanoko, the never-failing remedy for all human disorders, and which, a proper trial allowed, would go near to reanimate the dead. "Draw near!" continued the worthy, "draw near, my masters! and you, my good mistresses, draw near, every one of you! Fear not high and haughty carriage; though greater than King or Kaiser, yet is the mighty Aldrovando milder than mother's milk; flint to the proud, to the humble he is as melting wax; he asks not your disorders, he sees them himself at a glance—nay, without a glance; he tells your ailments with his eyes shut! Draw near! draw near! the more incurable the better! List to the illustrious Doctor Aldrovando, first Physician to Prester John, Leech to the Grand Llama, and Hakim in Ordinary to Mustapha Muley Bey!"

"Hath your master ever a charm for the toothache, an't please you?" asked an elderly countryman, whose swollen cheek bespoke his interest in the question.

"A charm!—a thousand, and every one of them infallible. Toothache, quotha! I had hoped you had come with every bone in your body fractured or out of joint. A toothache!—propound a tester, master o' mine,—we ask not more for such trifles: do my bidding, and thy jaws, even with the word, shall cease to trouble thee!"

The clown, fumbling a while in a deep leathern purse, at length produced a sixpence, which he tendered to the jester. "Now to thy master, and bring me the charm forthwith."

"Nay, honest man; to disturb the mighty Aldrovando on such slight occasion were pity of my life: areed my counsel aright, and I will warrant thee for the nonce. Hie thee home, friend; infuse this powder in cold spring-water, fill thy mouth with the mixture, and sit upon thy fire till it boils!"

"Out on thee for a pestilent knave!" cried the cozened countryman; but the roar of merriment around bespoke the by-standers well pleased with the jape put upon him. He retired, venting his spleen in audible murmurs; and the mountebank, finding the feelings of the mob enlisted on his side, waxed more impudent every instant, filling up the intervals between his fooleries with sundry capers and contortions, and discordant notes from the cow's horn.

"Draw near! draw near, my masters! Here have ye a remedy for every evil under the sun, moral, physical, natural, and supernatural! Hath any man a termagant wife?—here is that will tame her presently! Hath any one a smoky chimney?—here is an incontinent cure!"

To the first infliction no man ventured to plead guilty, though there were those standing by who thought their neighbours might have profited withal. For the last-named recipe started forth at least a dozen candidates. With the greatest imaginable gravity, Pierrot, having pocketed their groats, delivered to each a small packet curiously folded and closely sealed, containing, as he averred, directions which, if truly observed, would preclude any chimney from smoking for a whole year. They whose curiosity led them to dive into the mystery, found that a sprig of mountain ash culled by moonlight was the charm recommended, coupled, however, with the proviso that no fire should be lighted on the hearth during the interval.

The frequent bursts of merriment proceeding from this quarter at length attracted the attention of Master Marsh, whose line of road necessarily brought him near this end of the fair; he drew bit in front of the stage just as its noisy occupant, having laid aside his formidable horn, was drawing still more largely on the amazement of "the public" by a feat of especial wonder,—he was eating fire! Curiosity mingled with astonishment was at its height; and feelings not unallied to alarm were beginning to manifest themselves among the softer sex especially, as they gazed on the flames that issued from the mouth of the living volcano. All eyes indeed were fixed upon the fire-eater with an intentness that left no room for observing another worthy who had now emerged upon the scene. This was, however, no less a personage than the *Deus ex machinâ*,—the illustrious Aldrovando himself. Short in stature and spare in form, the sage had somewhat increased the former by a steeple-crowned hat adorned with a cock's feather; while the thick shoulder padding of a quilted doublet, surmounted by a falling band, added a little to his personal importance in point of breadth. His habit was composed throughout of black serge, relieved with scarlet slashes in the sleeves and trunks; red was the feather in his hat, red were the roses in his shoes, which rejoiced, moreover, in a pair of red heels. The lining of a short cloak of faded velvet, that hung transversely over his left shoulder, was also red. Indeed, from all that we could ever see or hear, this agreeable alternation of red and black appears to be the mixture of colours most approved at the court of Beelzebub, and the one most generally adopted by his friends and favourites. His features were sharp and shrewd, and a fire sparkled in his keen grey eye much at variance with the wrinkles that ran their irregular furrows above his prominent and bushy brows. He had advanced slowly from behind his screen while the attention of the multitude was absorbed by the pyrotechnics of Mr. Merryman, and, stationing himself at the extreme corner of the stage, stood quietly leaning on a crutch-handled walking-staff of blackest ebony, his glance steadily fixed on the face of Marsh, from whose countenance the amusement he had insensibly begun to derive had not succeeded in removing all traces of bodily pain. For a while the latter was unobservant of the inquisitorial survey with which he was regarded; the eyes of the parties, however, at length met. The brown mare had a fine shoulder; she stood pretty near sixteen hands. Marsh himself, though slightly bowed by ill health and the "coming autumn" of life, was full six feet in height. His elevation giving him an unobstructed view over the heads of the pedestrians, he had naturally fallen into the rear of the assembly, which brought him close to the diminutive Doctor, with whose face, despite the red heels, his own was about upon a level.

"And what makes Master Marsh here?—what sees he in the mummeries of a miserable buffoon to divert him when his life is in jeopardy?" said a shrill cracked voice that sounded as in his very ear. It was the Doctor who spoke.

"Knowest thou me, friend?" said Marsh, scanning with awakened interest the figure of his questioner : " I call thee not to mind ; and yet—stay, where have we met ?"

" It skills not to declare," was the answer ; " suffice it we *have* met,—in other climes, perchance,—and now meet happily again,—happily at least for thee."

" Why truly the trick of thy countenance reminds me of somewhat I have seen before, where or when I know not ; but what wouldst thou with me ?"

" Nay, rather what wouldst thou here, Thomas Marsh ? What wouldst thou on the Frith of Aldington ?—is it a score or two of paltry sheep ? or is it something *nearer to thy heart ?*"

Marsh started as the last words were pronounced with more than common significance : a pang shot through him at the moment, and the vinegar aspect of the *Charlatan* seemed to relax into a smile half compassionate, half sardonic.

" Grammercy," quoth Marsh, after a long-drawn breath, " what knowest thou of me, fellow, or of my concerns ? What knowest thou——"

" This know I, Master Thomas Marsh," said the stranger gravely, " that thy life is even now perilled : evil practices are against thee ; but no matter, thou art quit for the nonce — other hands than mine have saved thee ! Thy pains are over. Hark ! *the clock strikes One !*" As he spoke, a single toll from the bell-tower of Bilsington came, wafted by the western breeze, over the thick-set and lofty oaks which intervened between the Frith and what had been once a priory. Dr. Aldrovando turned as the sound came floating on the wind, and was moving, as if half in anger, towards the other side of the stage, where the mountebank, his fires extinct, was now disgorging to the admiring crowd yard after yard of gaudy-coloured riband.

" Stay ! Nay, prithee, stay !" cried Marsh eagerly, " I was wrong ; in faith I was. A change, and that a sudden and most marvellous, hath come over me ; I am free ; I breathe again ; I feel as though a load of years had been removed ; and—is it possible ?—hast thou done this ?"

" Thomas Marsh !" said the doctor, pausing, and turning for the moment on his heel, " I have *not ;* I repeat, that other and more innocent hands than mine have done this deed. Nevertheless, heed my counsel well ! Thou art parlously encompassed ; I, and I only, have the means of relieving thee. Follow thy courses ; pursue thy journey ; but, as thou valuest life, and more than life, be at the foot of yonder woody knoll what time the rising moon throws her first beam upon the bare and blighted summit that towers above its trees."

He crossed abruptly to the opposite quarter of the scaffolding, and was in an instant deeply engaged in listening to those whom the cow's horn had attracted, and in prescribing for their real or fancied ailments. Vain were all Marsh's efforts again to attract his notice ; it was evident that he studiously avoided him ; and when, after an hour or more spent in useless endeavour, he saw the object of his anxiety seclude himself once more within his canvass screen, he rode slowly and thoughtfully off the field.—What should he do ? Was the man a mere quack ? an impostor ? His name thus obtained ! —that might be easily done. But then, his secret griefs ; the doctor's knowledge of them ; their cure : for he felt that his pains were gone, his healthful feelings restored ! True ; Aldrovando, if that were his name, had disclaimed all co-operation in his recovery: but he knew or, he announced it. Nay, more; he had hinted that he was yet in jeopardy; that practices—and the chord sounded strangely in unison with one that had before vibrated within him—that practices were in operation against his life! It was enough! He would keep tryst with the Conjuror, if conjuror he were; and, at least, ascertain who and what he was, and how he had become acquainted with his own person and secret afflictions.

When the late Mr. Pitt was determined to keep out Buonaparte, and prevent his gaining a settlement in the county of Kent, among other ingenious devices adopted for that purpose, he caused to be constructed what was then, and has ever since been, conventionally termed a "Military canal." This is a not very practicable ditch, some thirty feet wide, and nearly nine feet deep—in the middle, extending from the town and port of Hithe to within a mile of the town and port of Rye, a distance of about twenty miles; and forming, as it were, the cord of a bow, the area of which constitutes that remote fifth quarter of the globe spoken of by travellers. Trivial objections to the plan were made at the time by cavillers; and an old gentleman of the neighbourhood, who proposed, as a cheap substitute, to put up his own cocked-hat upon a pole, was deservedly pooh-pooh'd down; in fact, the job, though rather an expensive one, was found to answer remarkably well. The French managed, indeed, to scramble over the Rhine, and the Rhone, and other insignificant currents; but they never did, or could, pass Mr. Pitt's "Military canal." At no great distance from the centre of this cord rises abruptly a sort of woody promontory, in shape almost conical, its sides covered with thick underwood; above which is seen a bare and brown summit rising like an Alp in miniature. The "defence of the nation" not being then in existence, Master Thomas Marsh met with no obstruction in reaching this place of appointment long before the time prescribed.

So much, indeed, was his mind occupied by his adventure and extraordinary cure, that his original design had been abandoned, and Master Cobbe remained unvisited. A rude hostel in the neighbourhood furnished entertainment for man and horse; and here, a full hour before the rising of the moon, he left Ralph and the other beasts, proceeding to his rendezvous on foot and alone.

"You are punctual, Master Marsh," squeaked the shrill voice of the Doctor, issuing from the thicket as the first silvery gleam trembled on the aspens above. "'Tis well; now follow me, and in silence."

The first part of the command Marsh hesitated not to obey; the second was more difficult of observance.

"Who and what are you? Whither are you leading me?" burst not unnaturally from his lips; but all question was at once cut short by the peremptory tones of his guide.

"Hush! I say; your finger on your lip; there be hawks abroad: follow me, and that silently and quickly." The little man turned as he spoke, and led the way through a scarcely perceptible path, or track, which wound among the underwood. The lapse of a few minutes brought them to the door of a low building so hidden by the surrounding trees that few would have suspected its existence. It was a cottage of rather extraordinary dimensions, but consisting of only one floor. No smoke rose from its solitary chimney; no cheering ray streamed from its single window, which was, however, secured by a shutter of such thickness as to preclude the possibility of any stray beam issuing from within. The exact size of the building it was in that uncertain light difficult to distinguish, a portion of it seeming buried in the wood behind. The door gave way on the application of a key, and Marsh followed his conductor resolutely but cautiously along a narrow passage feebly lighted by a small taper that winked and twinkled at its farther extremity. The Doctor, as he approached, raised it from the ground, and, opening an adjoining door, ushered his guest into the room beyond. It was a large and oddly-furnished apartment, insufficiently lighted by an iron lamp that hung from the roof, and scarcely illumined the walls and angles, which seemed to be composed of some dark-coloured wood. On one side, however, Master Marsh could discover an article bearing strong resemblance to a coffin; on the other was a large oval mirror in an ebony frame, and in the midst of the floor was described in red chalk a double circle, about six feet in diameter, its inner verge inscribed with sundry hieroglyphics, agreeably relieved at intervals with an alternation of skulls and cross-bones. In the very centre was deposited one skull of such surpassing size and thickness as would have filled the soul of a Spurzheim or De Ville with wonderment. A large book, a naked sword, an hour-glass, a chafing-dish, and a black cat, completed the list of moveables; with the exception of a couple of tapers which stood on each side the mirror, and which the strange gentleman now proceeded to light from the one in his hand. As they flared up with what Marsh thought a most unnatural brilliancy, he perceived, reflected in the glass behind, a dial suspended over the coffin-like article already mentioned: the hand was fast verging towards the hour of nine. The eyes of the little Doctor seemed rivetted on the horologe.

"Now strip thee, Master Marsh, and that quickly: untruss, I say! discard thy boots, doff doublet and hose, and place thyself incontinent in yonder bath." The visitor cast his eyes again upon the formidable-looking article, and perceived that it was nearly filled with water. A cold bath, at such an hour and under such auspices, was anything but inviting: he hesitated, and turned his eyes alternately on the Doctor and the Black Cat.

"Trifle not the time, man, an you be wise," said the former: "Passion of my heart! let but yon minute-hand reach the hour, and, thou not immersed, thy life were not worth a pin's fee!"

The Black Cat gave vent to a single Mew,—a most unnatural sound for a mouser,—it seemed as it were mewed through a cow's horn!

"Quick, Master Marsh! uncase, or you perish!" repeated his strange host, throwing as he spoke a handful of some dingy-looking powders into the brasier. "Behold, the attack is begun!" A thick cloud rose from the embers; a cold shivering shook the astonished Yeoman: sharp pricking pains penetrated his ankles and the palms of his hands, and, as the smoke cleared away, he distinctly saw and recognised in the mirror the boudoir of Marshton Hall. The doors of the well-known ebony cabinet were closed; but, fixed against them, and standing out in strong relief from the contrast afforded by the sable background, was a waxen image—of himself! It appeared to be secured and sustained in an upright posture by large black pins driven through the feet and palms, the latter of which were extended in a cruciform position. To the right and left stood his wife and José; in the middle, with his back towards him, was a figure which he had no difficulty in recognising as that of the Leech of Folkestone. It had just succeeded in fastening the dexter hand of the image, and was now in the act of drawing a broad and keen-edged sabre from its sheath. The Black Cat mewed again. "Haste, or you die!" said the Doctor. Marsh looked at the dial; it wanted but four minutes of nine: he felt that the crisis of his fate was come. Off went his heavy boots; doublet to the right, galligaskins to the left; never was man more swiftly disrobed: in two minutes, to use an Indian expression, "he was all face!" in another, he was on his back, and up to his chin, in a bath which smelt strongly as of brim-stone and garlick.

"Heed well the clock!" cried the Conjuror: "with the first stroke of Nine plunge thy head beneath the water; suffer not a hair above the surface: plunge deeply, or you are lost!"

The little man had seated himself in the centre of the circle upon the large skull, elevating his legs at an angle of forty-five degrees. In this position he spun round with a velocity to be equalled only by that of a tee-totum, the red roses on his insteps seeming to describe a circle of fire. The best buckskins that ever mounted at Melton had soon yielded to such rotatory friction; but he spun on, the Cat mewed, bats and obscene birds fluttered over head, Erasmus was seen to raise his weapon, the clock struck!—and Marsh, who had "ducked" at the instant, popped up his head again, spitting and sputtering, half choked with the infernal mixture, which had insinuated itself into his mouth, and ears, and nose. All disgust at his nauseous dip was, however, at once removed, when, casting his eyes on the glass, he saw the consternation of the party whose persons it exhibited. Erasmus had evidently made his blow and failed; the figure was un-mutilated; the hilt remained in the hand of the striker, while the shivered blade lay in shining fragments on the floor.

The Conjuror ceased his spinning, and brought himself to an an-chor; the Black Cat purred,—its purring seemed strangely mixed with the self-satisfied chuckle of a human being. Where had Marsh heard something like it before?

He was rising from his unsavoury couch, when a motion from the little man checked him. "Rest where you are, Thomas Marsh; so far all goes well, but the danger is not yet over!" He looked again, and perceived that the shadowy triumvirate were in deep and eager consultation; the fragments of the shattered weapon appeared to un-dergo a close scrutiny. The result was clearly unsatisfactory; the lips of the parties moved rapidly, and much gesticulation might be observed, but no sound fell upon the ear. The hand of the dial had nearly reached the quarter: at once the parties separated; and Buck-thorne stood again before the figure, his hand armed with a long and sharp-pointed *misericorde*, a dagger little in use of late, but such as, a century before, often performed the part of a modern oyster-knife, in tickling the osteology of a dismounted cavalier through the shelly de-fences of his plate-armour. Again he raised his arm. "Duck!" roared the Doctor, spinning away upon his cephalic pivot: the Black Cat cocked his tail, and seemed to mew the word "Duck!" Down went Master Marsh's head; but one of his hands had unluckily been resting on the edge of the bath: he drew it hastily in, but not altogether scathless; the stump of a rusty nail, projecting from the margin of the bath, had caught and slightly grazed it. The pain was more acute than is usually produced by such trivial accident; and Marsh, on once more raising his head, beheld the dagger of the leech sticking in the little finger of the wax figure, which it had seemingly nailed to the cabinet door.

" By my truly, a scape o' the narrowest!" quoth the Conjuror : " the next course, dive you not the readier, there is no more life in you than in a pickled herring. What! courage, Master Marsh; but be heedful : an they miss again, let them bide the issue!" He drew his hand athwart his brow as he spoke, and dashed off the perspiration, which the violence of his exercise had drawn from every pore. Black Tom sprang upon the edge of the bath, and stared full in the face of the bather : his sea-green eyes were lambent with unholy fire, but their marvellous obliquity of vision was not to be mistaken,—the very countenance, too!—Could it be?—the features were feline, but their expression that of the Jack-Pudding? Was the Mountebank a Cat, or the Cat a Mountebank?—it was all a mystery; and Heaven knows how long Marsh might have continued staring at Grimalkin, had not his attention been again called by Aldrovando to the magic mirror. Great dissatisfaction, not to say dismay, seemed to pervade the conspirators; Dame Isabel was closely inspecting the figure's wounded hand, while José was aiding the pharmacopolist to charge a huge petronel with powder and bullets. The load was a heavy one; but Erasmus seemed determined this time to make sure of his object. Somewhat of trepidation might be observed in his manner as he rammed down the balls, and his withered cheek appeared to have acquired an increase of paleness; but amazement rather than fear was the prevailing symptom, and his countenance betrayed no jot of irresolution. As the clock was about to chime half-past nine, he planted himself with a firm foot in front of the image, waved his unoccupied hand with a cautionary gesture to his companions, and, as they hastily retired on either side, brought the muzzle of his weapon within half a foot of his mark. As the shadowy form was about to draw the trigger, Marsh again plunged his head beneath the surface ; and the sound of an explosion, as of fire-arms, mingled with the rush of water that poured into his ears. His immersion was but momentary, yet did he feel as though half suffocated : he sprang from the bath, and, as his eye fell on the mirror, he saw, or thought he saw, the Leech of Folkestone lying dead on the floor of his wife's boudoir, his head shattered to pieces, and his hand still grasping the stock of a bursten petronel. He saw no more ; his head swam, his senses reeled, the whole room was turning round, and, as he fell to the ground, the last impressions to which he was conscious were the chucklings of a hoarse laughter and the mewings of a Tom Cat.

Master Marsh was found the next morning by his bewildered serving-man, stretched before the door of the humble hostel at which he sojourned. His clothes were somewhat torn and much bemired; and deeply did honest Ralph marvel that one so staid and grave as Marsh of Marston should thus have played the roisterer, missing perchance a profitable bargain for the drunken orgies of midnight wassail, or the endearments of some rustic light-o'-love. Tenfold was his astonishment increased when, after retracing in silence their journey of the preceding day, the Hall, on their arrival about noon, was found in a state of uttermost confusion. No wife stood there to greet with the smile of bland affection her returning spouse; no page to hold his stirrup, or receive his gloves, his hat, and riding-rod. The doors were open, the rooms in most admired disorder; men and maidens peeping, hurrying hither and thither, and popping in and out, like rabbits in a warren. The lady of the mansion was nowhere to be found.

José, too, had disappeared: the latter had been last seen riding furiously towards Folkestone early in the preceding afternoon; to a question from Hodge Gardener he had hastily answered, that he bore a missive of moment from his mistress. The lean apprentice of Erasmus Buckthorne declared that the page had summoned his master in haste about six of the clock, and that they had rode forth together, as he very believed, on their way back to the Hall, where he had supposed Master Buckthorne's services to be suddenly required on some pressing emergency. Since that time he had seen nought of either of them: the grey cob, however, had returned late at night, masterless, with his girths loose, and the saddle turned upside down.

Nor was Master Erasmus Buckthorne ever seen again. Strict search was made through the neighbourhood, but without success; and it was at length presumed that he must, for reasons which nobody could divine, have absconded with José and his faithless mistress. The latter had carried off with her the strong box, divers articles of valuable plate, and jewels of price. Her boudoir appeared to have been completely ransacked; the cabinet and drawers stood open, and empty; the very carpet, a luxury then newly introduced into England, was gone. Marsh, however, could trace no vestige of the visionary scene which he affirmed to have been last night presented to his eyes. Much did the neighbours marvel at his story: some thought him mad; others, that he was merely indulging in that privilege to which, as a traveller, he had a right indefeasible. Trusty Ralph said nothing, but shrugged his shoulders; and, falling into the rear, imitated the action of raising the wine-cup to his lips. An opinion, indeed, soon prevailed, that Master Thomas Marsh had gotten, in common parlance, exceedingly drunk on the preceding evening, and dreamt all that he had so circumstantially related. This belief acquired additional credit when they whom curiosity induced to visit the woody knoll of Aldington Mount declared that they could find no building such as that described; nor any cottage near, save one, indeed, a low-roofed hovel, once a house of public entertainment, but now half in ruins. The "Old Cat and Fiddle"— so was the tenement called—had been long uninhabited; yet still exhibited the remains of a broken sign, on which the keen observer might decypher something like a rude portrait of the animal from which it derived its name. It was also supposed still to afford an occasional asylum to the smugglers of the coast, but no trace of any visit from sage or mountebank could be detected; nor was the wise Aldrovando, whom many remembered to have seen at the fair, ever found again on all that country-side. Of the runaways nothing was ever certainly known. A boat, the property of an old fisherman who plied his trade on the outskirts of the town, had been seen to quit the bay that night; and there were those who declared that she had more hands on board than Carden and his son, her usual complement;

but, as a gale came on, and the frail bark was eventually found keel upwards on the Goodwin Sands, it was presumed that she had struck on that fatal quicksand in the dark, and that all on board had perished.

Little Marian, whom her profligate mother had abandoned, grew up to be a fine girl, and a handsome. She became, moreover, heiress to Marshton Hall, and brought the estate into the Ingoldsby family by her marriage with one of its scions.

It is a little singular that, on pulling down the old Hall in my grandfather's time, a human skeleton was discovered among the rubbish, under what particular part of the building I could never with any accuracy ascertain; but it was found enveloped in a tattered cloth, that seemed to have been once a carpet, and which fell to pieces almost immediately on being exposed to the air. The bones were perfect, but those of one hand were wanting; and the skull, perhaps from the labourer's pick-axe, had received considerable injury.

The portrait of the fair Marian hangs yet in the Gallery of Tappington; and near it is another, of a young man in the prime of life, whom Mrs. Botherby pronounces her father. It exhibits a mild and rather melancholy countenance, with a high forehead, and the picked beard and moustaches of the seventeenth century. The signet-finger of the left hand is gone, and appears, on close inspection, to have been painted out by some later artist; possibly in compliment to the tradition, which, *teste Botherby*, records that of Mr. Marsh to have gangrened, and to have undergone amputation at the knuckle-joint. If really the resemblance of the gentleman alluded to, it must have been taken at some period antecedent to his marriage. There is neither date nor painter's name; but, a little above the head, on the dexter side of the picture, is an escutcheon, bearing Quarterly, Gules and Argent; in the first quarter, a horse's head of the second; beneath it are the words "*Ætatis suæ*, 26." On the opposite side is the following marks which Mr. Simpkinson declares to be that of a Merchant of the Staple; and pretends to discover in the anagram comprised in it all the characters which compose the name of THOMAS MARSH, of MARSHTON.

THOMAS INGOLDSBY.

SONG OF THE MONTH. No. VIII.

August, 1837.

I.

Of all the months in the twelve that fly
So lightly on, and noiselessly by,
There is not one who can show so fair
As this, with its soft and balmy air.
The light graceful corn waves to and fro,
Tinging the earth with its richest glow;
The forest trees in their state and might
Proclaim that Summer is at his height.

II.

Of all the months in the twelve that speed
So quickly by, with so little heed
From man, of the years that swiftly pass
As an infant's breath from a polished glass,
There is not one whose fading away
Bears such a lesson to mortal clay,
Warning us sternly, when in our prime,
To look for the withering winter time.

III.

I stood by a young girl's grave last night,
Beautiful, innocent, pure, and bright,
Who, in the bloom of her summer's pride,
And all its loveliness, drooped and died.
Since the sweetest flow'rs are soonest dust,
As truest metal is quick to rust,
Look for a change in that time of year,
When Nature's works at their best appear.

OLIVER TWIST;

OR, THE PARISH BOY'S PROGRESS.

BY BOZ.

ILLUSTRATED BY GEORGE CRUIKSHANK.

CHAPTER THE TWELFTH.

IN WHICH OLIVER IS TAKEN BETTER CARE OF, THAN HE EVER WAS BEFORE. WITH SOME PARTICULARS CONCERNING A CERTAIN PICTURE.

THE coach rattled away down Mount Pleasant and up Ex-mouth-street,—over nearly the same ground as that which Oliver had traversed when he first entered London in company with the Dodger,—and, turning a different way when it reached the Angel at Islington, stopped at length before a neat house in a quiet shady street near Pentonville. Here a bed was prepared without loss of time, in which Mr. Brownlow saw his young charge carefully and comfortably deposited; and here he was tended with a kindness and solicitude which knew no bounds.

But for many days Oliver remained insensible to all the good-ness of his new friends; the sun rose and sunk, and rose and sunk again, and many times after that, and still the boy lay stretched upon his uneasy bed, dwindling away beneath the dry and wasting heat of fever,—that heat which, like the subtle acid that gnaws into the very heart of hardest iron, burns only to corrode and to destroy. The worm does not his work more surely on the dead body, than does this slow, creeping fire upon the living frame.

Weak, and thin, and pallid, he awoke at last from what seemed to have been a long and troubled dream. Feebly rais-ing himself in the bed, with his head resting on his trembling arm, he looked anxiously round.

"What room is this?—where have I been brought to?" said Oliver. "This is not the place I went to sleep in."

He uttered these words in a feeble voice, being very faint and weak; but they were overheard at once, for the curtain at the bed's head was hastily drawn back, and a motherly old lady, very neatly and precisely dressed, rose as she undrew it, from an arm-chair close by, in which she had been sitting at needle-work.

"Hush, my dear," said the old lady softly. "You must be very quiet, or you will be ill again, and you have been very bad,—as bad as bad could be, pretty nigh. Lie down again, there's a dear." With these words the old lady very gently placed Oliver's head upon the pillow, and, smoothing back his hair from his forehead, looked so kindly and lovingly in his

George Cruikshank

face, that he could not help placing his little withered hand upon her's and drawing it round his neck.

" Save us !" said the old lady, with tears in her eyes, " what a grateful little dear it is. Pretty creetur, what would his mother feel if she had sat by him as I have, and could see him now !"

" Perhaps she does see me," whispered Oliver, folding his hands together ; " perhaps she has sat by me, ma'am. I almost feel as if she had."

" That was the fever, my dear," said the old lady mildly.

" I suppose it was," replied Oliver thoughtfully, " because Heaven is a long way off, and they are too happy there, to come down to the bedside of a poor boy. But if she knew I was ill, she must have pitied me even there, for she was very ill herself before she died. She can't know anything about me though," added Oliver after a moment's silence, " for if she had seen me beat, it would have made her sorrowful ; and her face has always looked sweet and happy when I have dreamt of her."

The old lady made no reply to this, but wiping her eyes first, and her spectacles, which lay on the counterpane, afterwards, as if they were part and parcel of those features, brought some cool stuff for Oliver to drink, and then, patting him on the cheek, told him he must lie very quiet, or he would be ill again.

So Oliver kept very still, partly because he was anxious to obey the kind old lady in all things, and partly, to tell the truth, because he was completely exhausted with what he had already said. He soon fell into a gentle doze, from which he was awakened by the light of a candle, which, being brought near the bed, showed him a gentleman, with a very large and loud-ticking gold watch in his hand, who felt his pulse, and said he was a great deal better.

" You *are* a great deal better, are you not, my dear ?" said the gentleman.

" Yes, thank you, sir," replied Oliver.

" Yes, I know you are," said the gentleman : " you 're hungry too, an't you ?"

" No, sir," answered Oliver.

" Hem !" said the gentleman. " No, I know you 're not. He is not hungry, Mrs. Bedwin," said the gentleman, looking very wise.

The old lady made a respectful inclination of the head, which seemed to say that she thought the doctor was a very clever man. The doctor appeared very much of the same opinion himself.

" You feel sleepy, don't you, my dear ?" said the doctor.

" No, sir," replied Oliver.

" No," said the doctor with a very shrewd and satisfied look. " You 're not sleepy. Nor thirsty, are you ?"

" Yes, sir, rather thirsty," answered Oliver.

"Just as I expected, Mrs. Bedwin," said the doctor. "It's very natural that he should be thirsty—perfectly natural. You may give him a little tea, ma'am, and some dry toast without any butter. Don't keep him too warm, ma'am; but be careful that you don't let him be too cold; will you have the goodness?"

The old lady dropped a curtsey; and the doctor, after tasting the cool stuff, and expressing a qualified approval thereof, hurried away: his boots creaking in a very important and wealthy manner as he went down stairs.

Oliver dozed off again soon after this, and when he awoke it was nearly twelve o'clock. The old lady tenderly bade him good-night shortly afterwards, and left him in charge of a fat old woman who had just come, bringing with her in a little bundle a small Prayer Book and a large nightcap. Putting the latter on her head, and the former on the table, the old woman, after telling Oliver that she had come to sit up with him, drew her chair close to the fire and went off into a series of short naps, chequered at frequent intervals with sundry tumblings forward and divers moans and chokings, which, however, had no worse effect than causing her to rub her nose very hard, and then fall asleep again.

And thus the night crept slowly on. Oliver lay awake for some time, counting the little circles of light which the reflection of the rushlight-shade threw upon the ceiling, or tracing with his languid eyes the intricate pattern of the paper on the wall. The darkness and deep stillness of the room were very solemn; and as they brought into the boy's mind the thought that death had been hovering there for many days and nights, and might yet fill it with the gloom and dread of his awful presence, he turned his face upon the pillow and fervently prayed to Heaven.

Gradually he fell into that deep tranquil sleep which ease from recent suffering alone imparts; that calm and peaceful rest which it is pain to wake from. Who, if this were death, would be roused again to all the struggles and turmoils of life, —to all its cares for the present, its anxieties for the future, and, more than all, its weary recollections of the past!

It had been bright day for hours when Oliver opened his eyes; and when he did so, he felt cheerful and happy. The crisis of the disease was safely past, and he belonged to the world again.

In three days' time he was able to sit in an easy-chair well propped up with pillows; and, as he was still too weak to walk, Mrs. Bedwin had him carried down stairs into the little housekeeper's room, which belonged to her, where, having sat him up by the fireside, the good old lady sat herself down too, and, being in a state of considerable delight at seeing him so much better, forthwith began to cry most violently.

"Never mind me, my dear," said the old lady; "I'm only

having a regular good cry. There, it's all over now, and I'm quite comfortable."

" You're very, very kind to me, ma'am," said Oliver.

" Well, never you mind that, my dear," said the old lady; "that's got nothing to do with your broth, and it's full time you had it, for the doctor says Mr. Brownlow may come in to see you this morning, and we must get up our best looks, because the better we look, the more he'll be pleased." And with this, the old lady applied herself to warming up in a little saucepan a basin full of broth strong enough to furnish an ample dinner, when reduced to the regulation strength, for three hundred and fifty paupers, at the very lowest computation.

" Are you fond of pictures, dear?" inquired the old lady, seeing that Oliver had fixed his eyes most intently on a portrait which hung against the wall just opposite his chair.

" I don't quite know, ma'am," said Oliver, without taking his eyes from the canvass; " I have seen so few that I hardly know. What a beautiful mild face that lady's is!"

" Ah," said the old lady, " painters always make ladies out prettier than they are, or they wouldn't get any custom, child. The man that invented the machine for taking likenesses might have known *that* would never succeed; it's a deal too honest,— a deal," said the old lady, laughing very heartily at her own acuteness.

" Is—is that a likeness, ma'am?" said Oliver.

" Yes," said the old lady, looking up for a moment from the broth; " that's a portrait."

" Whose, ma'am?" asked Oliver eagerly.

" Why, really, my dear, I don't know," answered the old lady in a good-humoured manner. " It's not a likeness of anybody that you or I know, I expect. It seems to strike your fancy, dear."

" It is so very pretty : so very beautiful," replied Oliver.

" Why, sure you're not afraid of it?" said the old lady, observing in great surprise the look of awe with which the child regarded the painting.

" Oh no, no," returned Oliver quickly; " but the eyes look so sorrowful, and where I sit they seem fixed upon me. It makes my heart beat," added Oliver in a low voice, " as if it was alive, and wanted to speak to me, but couldn't."

" Lord save us!" exclaimed the old lady, starting; " don't talk in that way, child. You're weak and nervous after your illness. Let me wheel your chair round to the other side, and then you won't see it. There," said the old lady, suiting the action to the word; " you don't see it now, at all events."

Oliver *did* see it in his mind's eye as distinctly as if he had not altered his position, but he thought it better not to worry the kind old lady; so he smiled gently when she looked at him, and Mrs. Bedwin, satisfied that he felt more comfortable, salted

and broke bits of toasted bread into the broth with all the
bustle befitting so solemn a preparation. Oliver got through it
with extraordinary expedition, and had scarcely swallowed the
last spoonful when there came a soft tap at the door. "Come
in," said the old lady; and in walked Mr. Brownlow.

Now, the old gentleman came in as brisk as need be; but he
had no sooner raised his spectacles on his forehead, and thrust
his hands behind the skirts of his dressing-gown to take a good
long look at Oliver, than his countenance underwent a very
great variety of odd contortions. Oliver looked very worn and
shadowy from sickness, and made an ineffectual attempt to stand
up, out of respect to his benefactor, which terminated in his
sinking back into the chair again; and the fact is, if the truth
must be told, that Mr. Brownlow's heart being large enough
for any six ordinary old gentlemen of humane disposition, forced
a supply of tears into his eyes by some hydraulic process which
we are not sufficiently philosophical to be in a condition to
explain.

"Poor boy, poor boy!" said Mr. Brownlow clearing his
throat. "I'm rather hoarse this morning, Mrs. Bedwin; I'm
afraid I have caught cold."

"I hope not, sir," said Mrs. Bedwin. "Everything you
have had has been well aired, sir."

"I don't know, Bedwin,—I don't know," said Mr. Brownlow;
"I rather think I had a damp napkin at dinner-time yesterday:
but never mind that. How do you feel, my dear?"

"Very happy, sir," replied Oliver, "and very grateful indeed, sir, for your goodness to me."

"Good boy," said Mr. Brownlow stoutly. "Have you given
him any nourishment, Bedwin?—any slops, eh?"

"He has just had a basin of beautiful strong broth, sir," replied Mrs. Bedwin, drawing herself up slightly, and laying a
strong emphasis on the last word, to intimate that between
slops, and broth well compounded, there existed no affinity or
connexion whatsoever.

"Ugh!" said Mr. Brownlow, with a slight shudder; "a
couple of glasses of port wine would have done him a great
deal more good,—wouldn't they, Tom White,—eh?"

"My name is Oliver, sir," replied the little invalid with a
look of great astonishment.

"Oliver!" said Mr. Brownlow; "Oliver what? Oliver
White,—eh?"

"No, sir, Twist,—Oliver Twist."

"Queer name," said the old gentleman. "What made you
tell the magistrate your name was White?"

"I never told him so, sir," returned Oliver in amazement.

This sounded so like a falsehood, that the old gentleman
looked somewhat sternly in Oliver's face. It was impossible to
doubt him; there was truth in every one of its thin and
sharpened lineaments.

"Some mistake," said Mr. Brownlow. But, although his motive for looking steadily at Oliver no longer existed, the old idea of the resemblance between his features and some familiar face came upon him so strongly that he could not withdraw his gaze.

"I hope you are not angry with me, sir," said Oliver, raising his eyes beseechingly.

"No, no," replied the old gentleman.—"Gracious God, what's this! Bedwin, look, look there!"

As he spoke, he pointed hastily to the picture above Oliver's head, and then to the boy's face. There was its living copy,— the eyes, the head, the mouth; every feature was the same. The expression was for the instant so precisely alike, that the minutest line seemed copied with an accuracy which was perfectly unearthly.

Oliver knew not the cause of this sudden exclamation, for he was not strong enough to bear the start it gave him, and he fainted away.

CHAPTER THE THIRTEENTH

REVERTS TO THE MERRY OLD GENTLEMAN AND HIS YOUTHFUL FRIENDS, THROUGH WHOM A NEW ACQUAINTANCE IS INTRODUCED TO THE INTELLIGENT READER, AND CONNECTED WITH WHOM VARIOUS PLEASANT MATTERS ARE RELATED APPERTAINING TO THIS HISTORY.

WHEN the Dodger and his accomplished friend Master Bates joined in the hue and cry which was raised at Oliver's heels, in consequence of their executing an illegal conveyance of Mr. Brownlow's personal property, as hath been already described with great perspicuity in a foregoing chapter, they were actuated, as we therein took occasion to observe, by a very laudable and becoming regard for themselves: and forasmuch as the freedom of the subject and the liberty of the individual are among the first and proudest boasts of a true-hearted Englishman, so I need hardly beg the reader to observe that this action must tend to exalt them in the opinion of all public and patriotic men, in almost as great a degree as this strong proof of their anxiety for their own preservation and safety goes to corroborate and confirm the little code of laws which certain profound and sound-judging philosophers have laid down as the mainsprings of all Madam Nature's deeds and actions; the said philosophers very wisely reducing the good lady's proceedings to matters of maxim and theory, and, by a very neat and pretty compliment to her exalted wisdom and understanding, putting entirely out of sight any considerations of heart, or generous impulse and feeling, as matters totally beneath a female who is acknowledged by universal admission to be so far beyond the numerous little foibles and weaknesses of her sex.

If I wanted any further proof of the strictly philosophical

nature of the conduct of these young gentlemen in their very
delicate predicament, I should at once find it in the fact (also
recorded in a foregoing part of this narrative) of their quitting
the pursuit when the general attention was fixed upon Oliver,
and making immediately for their home by the shortest possible
cut; for although I do not mean to assert that it is the practice
of renowned and learned sages at all to shorten the road to any
great conclusion, their course indeed being rather to lengthen
the distance by various circumlocutions and discursive stagger-
ings, like those in which drunken men under the pressure of a
too mighty flow of ideas are prone to indulge, still I do mean to
say, and do say distinctly, that it is the invariable practice of all
mighty philosophers, in carrying out their theories, to evince great
wisdom and foresight in providing against every possible contin-
gency which can be supposed at all likely to affect themselves.
Thus, to do a great right, you may do a little wrong, and you
may take any means which the end to be attained will justify;
the amount of the right or the amount of the wrong, or indeed
the distinction between the two, being left entirely to the philosopher concerned: to be settled and determined by his clear,
comprehensive, and impartial view of his own particular case.

It was not until the two boys had scoured with great rapidity through a most intricate maze of narrow streets and courts,
that they ventured to halt by common consent beneath a low
and dark archway. Having remained silent here, just long
enough to recover breath to speak, Master Bates uttered an exclamation of amusement and delight, and, bursting into an uncontrollable fit of laughter, flung himself upon a door-step, and
rolled thereon in a transport of mirth.

" What 's the matter ?" inquired the Dodger.

" Ha ! ha ! ha !" roared Charley Bates.

" Hold your noise," remonstrated the Dodger, looking cautiously round. " Do you want to be grabbed, stupid ?"

" I can't help it," said Charley, " I can't help it. To see
him splitting away at that pace, and cutting round the corners,
and knocking up against the posts, and starting on again as if
he was made of iron as well as them, and me with the wipe in my
pocket, singing out arter him—oh, my eye !" The vivid imagination of Master Bates presented the scene before him in too
strong colours. As he arrived at this apostrophe, he again
rolled upon the door-step and laughed louder than before.

" What 'll Fagin say ?" inquired the Dodger, taking advantage of the next interval of breathlessness on the part of his
friend to propound the question.

" What !" repeated Charley Bates.

" Ah, what ?" said the Dodger.

" Why, what should he say ?" inquired Charley, stopping
rather suddenly in his merriment, for the Dodger's manner was
impressive; " what should he say ?"

Mr. Dawkins whistled for a couple of minutes, and then, taking off his hat, scratched his head and nodded thrice.

" What do you mean ?" said Charley.

" Toor rul lol loo, gammon and spinnage, the frog he wouldn't, and high cockolorum," said the Dodger with a slight sneer on his intellectual countenance.

This was explanatory, but not satisfactory. Mr. Bates felt it so, and again said, " What do you mean ?"

The Dodger made no reply, but putting his hat on again, and gathering the skirts of his long-tailed coat under his arms, thrust his tongue into his cheek, slapped the bridge of his nose some half-dozen times in a familiar but expressive manner, and then, turning on his heel, slunk down the court. Mr. Bates followed, with a thoughtful countenance.

The noise of footsteps on the creaking stairs a few minutes after the occurrence of this conversation roused the merry old gentleman as he sat over the fire with a saveloy and a small loaf in his left hand, a pocket-knife in his right, and a pewter pot on the trivet. There was a rascally smile on his white face as he turned round, and, looking sharply out from under his thick red eyebrows, bent his ear towards the door and listened intently.

" Why, how's this ?" muttered the Jew, changing countenance; " only two of 'em ! Where's the third ? They can't have got into trouble. Hark !"

The footsteps approached nearer; they reached the landing, the door was slowly opened, and the Dodger and Charley Bates entered and closed it behind them.

" Where's Oliver, you young hounds ?" said the furious Jew, rising with a menacing look : " where's the boy ?"

The young thieves eyed their preceptor as if they were alarmed at his violence, and looked uneasily at each other, but made no reply.

" What's become of the boy ?" said the Jew, seizing the Dodger tightly by the collar, and threatening him with horrid imprecations. " Speak out, or I'll throttle you !"

Mr. Fagin looked so very much in earnest, that Charley Bates, who deemed it prudent in all cases to be on the safe side, and conceived it by no means improbable that it might be his turn to be throttled second, dropped upon his knees, and raised a loud, well-sustained, and continuous roar, something between an insane bull and a speaking-trumpet.

" Will you speak ?" thundered the Jew, shaking the Dodger so much that his keeping in the big coat at all seemed perfectly miraculous.

" Why, the traps have got him, and that's all about it," said the Dodger sullenly. " Come, let go o' me, will yer !" and, swinging himself at one jerk clean out of the big coat, which he left in the Jew's hands, the Dodger snatched up the toasting-fork and made a pass at the merry old gentleman's waistcoat, which, if it had taken effect, would have let a little more merriment out than could have been easily replaced in a month or two.

The Jew stepped back in this emergency with more agility than could have been anticipated in a man of his apparent decrepitude, and, seizing up the pot, prepared to hurl it at his assailant's head. But Charley Bates at this moment calling his attention by a perfectly terrific howl, he suddenly altered its destination, and flung it full at that young gentleman.

"Why, what the blazes is in the wind now!" growled a deep voice. "Who pitched that 'ere at me? It's well it's the beer and not the pot as hit me, or I'd have settled somebody. I might have know'd as nobody but an infernal rich, plundering, thundering old Jew could afford to throw away any drink but water, and not that, unless he done the River company every quarter. Wot's it all about, Fagin. D—me if my neckankecher an't lined with beer. Come in, you sneaking warmint; wot are you stopping outside for, as if you was ashamed of your master. Come in!"

The man who growled out these words was a stoutly-built fellow of about five-and-forty, in a black velveteen coat, very soiled drab breeches, lace-up half-boots, and grey cotton stockings, which enclosed a very bulky pair of legs, with large swelling calves,—the kind of legs which in such costume always look in an unfinished and incomplete state without a set of fetters to garnish them. He had a brown hat on his head, and a dirty belcher handkerchief round his neck, with the long frayed ends of which, he smeared the beer from his face as he spoke; disclosing when he had done so, a broad heavy countenance with a beard of three days' growth, and two scowling eyes, one of which displayed various parti-coloured symptoms of having been recently damaged by a blow.

"Come in, d'ye hear?" growled this engaging-looking ruffian. A white shaggy dog, with his face scratched and torn in twenty different places, skulked into the room.

"Why didn't you come in afore?" said the man. "You're getting too proud to own me afore company, are you. Lie down!"

This command was accompanied with a kick which sent the animal to the other end of the room. He appeared well used to it, however; for he coiled himself up in a corner very quietly without uttering a sound, and, winking his very ill-looking eyes about twenty times in a minute, appeared to occupy himself in taking a survey of the apartment.

"What are you up to? Ill-treating the boys, you covetous, avaricious, in-sa-ti-a-ble old fence?" said the man, seating himself deliberately. "I wonder they don't murder you; *I* would if I was them. If I'd been your 'prentice I'd have done it long ago; and— no, I couldn't have sold you arterwards, though; for you 're fit for nothing but keeping as a curiosity of ugliness in a glass bottle, and I suppose they don't blow them large enough."

"Hush! hush! Mr. Sikes," said the Jew, trembling; "don't speak so loud."

"None of your mistering," replied the ruffian; "you always mean mischief when you come that. You know my name: out with it. I shan't disgrace it when the time comes."

"Well, well, then, Bill Sikes," said the Jew with abject humility. "You seem out of humour, Bill."

"Perhaps I am," replied Sikes. "I should think *you* were rather out of sorts too, unless you mean as little harm when you throw pewter pots about, as you do when you blab and——"

"Are you mad?" said the Jew, catching the man by the sleeve, and pointing towards the boys.

Mr. Sikes contented himself with tying an imaginary knot under his left ear, and jerking his head over on the right shoulder; a piece of dumb show which the Jew appeared to understand perfectly. He then in cant terms, with which his whole conversation was plentifully besprinkled, but which would be quite unintelligible if they were recorded here, demanded a glass of liquor.

"And mind you don't poison it," said Mr. Sikes, laying his hat upon the table.

This was said in jest; but if the speaker could have seen the evil leer with which the Jew bit his pale lip as he turned round to the cupboard, he might have thought the caution not wholly unnecessary, or the wish, at all events, to improve upon the distiller's ingenuity not very far from the old gentleman's merry heart.

After swallowing two or three glassfuls of spirits, Mr. Sikes condescended to take some notice of the young gentlemen; which gracious act led to a conversation in which the cause and manner of Oliver's capture were circumstantially detailed, with such alterations and improvements on the truth as to the Dodger appeared most advisable under the circumstances.

"I'm afraid," said the Jew, "that he may say something which will get us into trouble."

"That's very likely," returned Sikes with a malicious grin. "You 're blowed upon, Fagin."

"And I'm afraid, you see," added the Jew, speaking as if he had not noticed the interruption, and regarding the other closely as he did so,—"I 'm afraid that, if the game was up with us, it might be up with a good many more; and that it would come out rather worse for you than it would for me, my dear."

The man started, and turned fiercely round upon the Jew; but the old gentleman's shoulders were shrugged up to his ears, and his eyes were vacantly staring on the opposite wall.

There was a long pause. Every member of the respectable

coterie appeared plunged in his own reflections, not excepting
the dog, who by a certain malicious licking of his lips seemed
to be meditating an attack upon the legs of the first gentleman
or lady he might encounter in the street when he went out.

"Somebody must find out what's been done at the office,"
said Mr. Sikes in a much lower tone than he had taken since he
came in.

The Jew nodded assent.

" If he hasn't peached, and is committed, there's no fear till
he comes out again," said Mr. Sikes, "and then he must be
taken care on.   You must get hold of him, somehow."

Again the Jew nodded.

The prudence of this line of action, indeed, was obvious ; but
unfortunately there was one very strong objection to its being
adopted ; and this was, that the Dodger, and Charley Bates,
and Fagin, and Mr. William Sikes, happened one and all to
entertain a most violent and deeply-rooted antipathy to going
near a police-office on any ground or pretext whatever.

How long they might have sat and looked at each other in
a state of uncertainty not the most pleasant of its kind, it is
difficult to say.   It is not necessary to make any guesses on
the subject, however ; for the sudden entrance of the two young
ladies whom Oliver had seen on a former occasion caused the
conversation to flow afresh.

" The very thing !" said the Jew.   " Bet will go ; won't you,
my dear ?"

" Wheres ?" inquired the young lady.

" Only just up to the office, my dear," said the Jew coaxingly.

It is due to the young lady to say that she did not positively
affirm that she would not, but that she merely expressed an
emphatic and earnest desire to be " jiggered " if she would ; a
polite and delicate evasion of the request, which' shows the
young lady to have been possessed of that natural good-breed-
ing that cannot bear to inflict upon a fellow-creature the pain
of a direct and pointed refusal.

The Jew's countenance fell, and he turned to the other
young lady, who was gaily, not to say gorgeously attired, in a
red gown, green boots, and yellow curl-papers.

" Nancy, my   dear," said the Jew in   a soothing manner,
" what do *you* say ?"

" That it won't do ; so it's no use a trying it on, Fagin,"
replied Nancy.

" What do you mean by that ?" said Mr. Sikes, looking up in
a surly manner.

" What I say, Bill," replied the lady collectedly.

" Why, you're just the very person for it," reasoned Mr.
Sikes : " nobody about here, knows anything of you."

" And as I don't want 'em to, neither," replied Miss Nancy

in the same composed manner, "it's rayther more no than yes with me, Bill."

"She'll go, Fagin," said Sikes.

"No, she won't, Fagin," bawled Nancy.

"Yes she will, Fagin," said Sikes.

And Mr. Sikes was right. By dint of alternate threats, promises, and bribes, the engaging female in question was ultimately prevailed upon to undertake the commission. She was not indeed withheld by the same considerations as her agreeable friend, for, having very recently removed into the neighbourhood of Field-lane from the remote but genteel suburb of Ratcliffe, she was not under the same apprehension of being recognised by any of her numerous acquaintance.

Accordingly, with a clean white apron tied over the red gown, and the yellow curl-papers tucked up under a straw bonnet,—both articles of dress being provided from the Jew's inexhaustible stock,—Miss Nancy prepared to issue forth on her errand.

"Stop a minute, my dear," said the Jew, producing a little covered basket. "Carry that in one hand; it looks more respectable, my dear."

"Give her a door-key to carry in her t'other one, Fagin," said Sikes; "it looks real and genivine like."

"Yes, yes, my dear, so it does," said the Jew, hanging a large street-door key on the fore-finger of the young lady's right hand. "There; very good,—very good indeed, my dear," said the Jew, rubbing his hands.

"Oh, my brother! my poor, dear, sweet, innocent little brother!" exclaimed Miss Nancy, bursting into tears, and wringing the little basket and the street-door key in an agony of distress. "What has become of him!—where have they taken him to! Oh, do have pity, and tell me what's been done with the dear boy, gentlemen; do, gentlemen, if you please, gentlemen."

Having uttered these words in a most lamentable and heart-broken tone, to the immeasurable delight of her hearers, Miss Nancy paused, winked to the company, nodded smilingly round, and disappeared.

"Ah! she's a clever girl, my dears," said the Jew, turning to his young friends, and shaking his head gravely, as if in mute admonition to them to follow the bright example they had just beheld.

"She's a honor to her sex," said Mr. Sikes, filling his glass, and smiting the table with his enormous fist. "Here's her health, and wishing they was all like her!"

While these and many other encomiums were being passed on the accomplished Miss Nancy, that young lady made the best of her way to the police-office; whither, notwithstanding a little natural timidity consequent upon walking through the streets alone and unprotected, she arrived in perfect safety shortly afterwards.

Entering by the back way, she tapped softly with the key
at one of the cell-doors and listened. There was no sound
within, so she coughed and listened again. Still there was no
reply, so she spoke.

"Nolly, dear?" murmured Nancy in a gentle voice;—"Nolly?"

There was nobody inside but a miserable shoeless criminal,
who had been taken up for playing the flute, and who—the
offence against society having been clearly proved—had been
very properly committed by Mr. Fang to the House of Correction for one month, with the appropriate and amusing remark that since he had got so much breath to spare, it would
be much more wholesomely expended on the treadmill than in
a musical instrument. He made no answer, being occupied
in mentally bewailing the loss of the flute, which had been con-
fiscated for the use of the county; so Miss Nancy passed on
to the next cell, and knocked there.

"Well," cried a faint and feeble voice.

"Is there a little boy here?" inquired Miss Nancy with a
preliminary sob.

"No," replied the voice; "God forbid!"

This was a vagrant of sixty-five, who was going to prison
for *not* playing the flute, or, in other words, for begging in the
streets, and doing nothing for his livelihood. In the next
cell was another man, who was going to the same prison for
hawking tin saucepans without a licence, thereby doing something for his living in defiance of the Stamp-office.

But as neither of these criminals answered to the name of
Oliver, or knew anything about him, Miss Nancy made straight
up to the bluff officer in the striped waistcoat, and with the
most piteous wailings and lamentations, rendered more piteous
by a prompt and efficient use of the street-door key and the
little basket, demanded her own dear brother.

"I haven't got him, my dear," said the old man.

"Where is he?" screamed Miss Nancy in a distracted
manner.

"Why, the gentleman's got him," replied the officer.

"What gentleman? Oh, gracious heavins! what gentleman?" exclaimed Miss Nancy.

In reply to this incoherent questioning, the old man informed the deeply affected sister that Oliver had been taken ill
in the office, and discharged in consequence of a witness having
proved the robbery to have been committed by another boy
not in custody; and that the prosecutor had carried him away
in an insensible condition to his own residence, of and concerning which all the informant knew was, that it was somewhere at
Pentonville, he having heard that word mentioned in the directions to the coachman.

In a dreadful state of doubt and uncertainty the agonised
young woman staggered to the gate, and then,—exchanging her

faltering gait for a good swift steady run, returned by the most devious and complicated route she could think of, to the domicile of the Jew.

Mr. Bill Sikes no sooner heard the account of the expedition delivered, than he very hastily called up the white dog, and, putting on his hat, expeditiously departed, without devoting any time to the formality of wishing the company good-morning.

"We must know where he is, my dears; he must be found," said the Jew, greatly excited. "Charley, do nothing but skulk about, till you bring home some news of him. Nancy, my dear, I must have him found : I trust to you, my dear,—to you and the Artful for every thing. Stay, stay," added the Jew, unlocking a drawer with a shaking hand; "there's money, my dears. I shall shut up this shop to-night: you 'll know where to find me. Don't stop here a minute,—not an instant, my dears !"

With these words he pushed them from the room, and carefully double-locking and barring the door behind them, drew from its place of concealment the box which he had unintentionally disclosed to Oliver, and hastily proceeded to dispose the watches and jewellery beneath his clothing.

A rap at the door startled him in this occupation. "Who 's there ?" he cried in a shrill tone of alarm.

"Me !" replied the voice of the Dodger through the keyhole.

"What now ?" cried the Jew impatiently.

"Is he to be kidnapped to the other ken, Nancy says ?" inquired the Dodger cautiously.

"Yes," replied the Jew, "wherever she lays hands on him. Find him, find him out, that's all ; and I shall know what to do next, never fear."

The boy murmured a reply of intelligence, and hurried down stairs after his companions.

"He has not peached so far," said the Jew as he pursued his occupation. "If he means to blab us among his new friends, we may stop his windpipe yet."

WHAT THOUGH WE WERE RIVALS OF YORE.

A ROMANCE. BY HAYNES BAYLY.

I.

" WHAT though we were rivals of yore,
    It seems you the victor have proved,
Henceforth we are rivals no more,
    For I must forget I have loved.
You tell me you wed her to-day,
    I thank you for telling the worst;
Adieu then! to horse, and away!—
    But, hold!—let us drink her health first!

II.

"Alas! I confess I was wrong
    To cope with so charming a knight;
Excelling in dance, and in song,
    Well-dress'd, *debonnaire*, and polite!
So, putting all envy aside,
    I take a new flask from the shelf;
Another full glass to the bride,
    And now a full glass to yourself.

III.

" You 'll drink a full bumper to me,
    So well I have borne my defeat?
To the nymphs who the bridemaids will be,
    And to each of the friends you will meet.
You are weary?—one glass to renew;
    You are dozing?—one glass to restore;
You are sleeping?—proud rival, adieu!
    Excuse me for locking the door."

IV.

There 's a fee in the hand of the priest!
    There's a kiss on the cheek of the bride!
And the guest she expected the least
    Is He who now sits by her side!
Oh, well may the loiterer fail,
    His love is the grape of the Rhine;
And the spirit most sure to prevail
    Was never the spirit of wine.

LOVE IN THE CITY.

In the prefatory observations I thought advisable to make when placing "Love in the City" before the world, I stated that my chief aim was the restoration of the drama to its pristine purity by avoiding those unnatural and superhuman agencies which modern writers have so extensively indulged in. Opposing myself thus, to innovation, I have ventured on one of the boldest changes in dramatic arrangement, by postponing the performance of the overture until the commencement of the second act. Having thus admitted my offending, I trust that, when the reasons which induced it are explained and understood, I shall have justified this daring step, and obtained a verdict of public acquittal.

Is there a frequenter of our theatres on a first night whose musical sensibilities have not been lacerated by the noise and tumult incidental to a crowded house? Let him achieve by desperate exertion a favourable place in the undress circle,—suppose the theatre crammed to the pigeon-holes, the orchestra already tuned, and every eye bent upon the leader, awaiting his premonitory tap;—then, when the nervous system should be quiescent, the ear open to receive delicious sounds, the heart ready to expand itself into harmonious ecstacy,—at that very moment of rapturous expectation has not his tranquillity been annihiláted by

> " Some giggling daughter of the queen of love"

pinching him in the ribs to acquaint him that he is " sitting on her boa !" While, from that " *refugium peccatorum*," the shilling gallery, infernal cries of " Down in the front !" " Music !" " Curse your pedigree !" " Hats off !" " How 's your mother ?" drown even the double-drums, and render the overture inaudible from the opening crash to the close.

To remedy this nuisance,—to allow the excited feelings of an over-crowded house to subside sufficiently to enable the audience, by presenting them with the first act, to judge how far the music of the overture is adapted to the business of the stage,—these considerations have induced me thus to postpone its performance, and with what success the public will best decide.

Another, and a more agreeable duty, now devolves upon me,—to express my ardent thanks to all and every to whom this drama is in any way indebted for its brilliant and unparalleled success. To Messrs. Flight and Robson ; the commanding officers of the Foot and Fusileer Guards; the King of the Two Sicilies; the Hereditary Prince of Coolavin; and his serene highness the Duke of Darmstadt, I am eternally grateful. To the performers, male and female, the composers, the orchestra at large, scene-painters and scene-shifters, prompters and property-men, box-keepers and check-takers, sentries and police, I present my heartfelt acknowledgements. And to the most crowded and fashionable audience that ever graced a metropolitan theatre, I shall only say, that the rapturous and reiterated plaudits bestowed upon this drama shall never fade from the recollection of their most devoted, very humble, too fortunate, and ever grateful servant,

THE AUTHOR.

July 1, 1837.

LOVE IN THE CITY;

OR, ALL'S WELL THAT ENDS WELL.

A MELODRAMATIC EXTRAVAGANZA.

ACT II.

Grand Overture,— composed jointly by Spohr, Haynes Bayly, Newkom, and Rossini, and performed by the largest orchestra ever collected in a European theatre, assisted by the Duke of Darmstadt's brass band, and the entire drums of the Foot and Fusileer Guards.

In the course of the overture the following novelties will be introduced.

A duet upon the *double-drums* with *one stick only,* by Mons. TAMBOURETTE, Member of the Legion of Honour, K. T. S., and drum-major to the *King of the Two Sicilies.*

Planxty Mac Swain, and *"What have you got in your jug?"* with brilliant variations for the *Irish pipes,* by *Kalkbrenner,*—Mr. PATRICK HALLIGAN, Minstrel in ordinary to the Prince of Coolavin.

A capriccio on the *German flute,* by a *distinguished amateur,* who has lost four fingers and a thumb.

A grand fantasia (Henry Hertz) on *one piano by eight performers.*
Director, Sir GEORGE SMART.
Conductor, on *The Apollonicon,*—lent to the lessee for that night only,—Mr. PURKIS.
Leader, Mr. T. COOKE.

The overture having been twice encored, bell rings, and curtain draws up.

ACT II.—SCENE I.

A public-house, "Black Horse," in the Borough. A tap-room. *Mags* and *Poppleton* discovered drinking "heavy wet." *Mags* rather fresh, and *Poppleton* evidently the worse of liquor. *Mags,* after a long pull, deposits the pot upon the table.

Pop.—Now for your news, Mags.
Mags.   I told you, worthy Pop,
That Stubs and Smith put keepers on the shop.
Pop.—And how's our missus?
Mags.   Why, hearty, when last seen
With a Life-Guardsman, crossing Turnham-green.
Pop.—And honest Snags?
Mags (*with emotion*).   Ah! would that epithet were true,
Or I could keep the sad details from you!
Snags is not *honest!*

(*Poppleton buttons his coat, and puts himself into a boxing attitude.*)

He has robb'd the till,
And lost the money, betting at a mill!

(*Noise without. Door opens. Enter Young Clipclose hastily.*)

Mr. C.—What, Mags and Pop! the coves I wish'd to see
Above all others.   Curse my pedigree!

AIR—*Mr. Clipclose.*—(" I 've been roaming.")

I 've been nabb'd, sirs,—I 've been nabb'd, sirs,—
  And bundled off direct to jail,
By the villains when they grabb'd, sirs,
  And now I 'm out upon stag-bail.

(*Mr. C. seizes the pewter in his right hand.*)

Mr. C.—Is this good stout?
Mags (*feelingly*).   My honest master, quaff!
You 'll find it strengthening, real half-and-half.

AIR—*Poppleton.*—(" Here we go up, up, up.")

Come, Bob, take a sup, sup, sup!
  Let the liquor your stiff neck slide down, boy;
There 's nothing like keeping steam up,
  When a man 's at the worst, and done brown, boy.

(*Clipclose starts, looks anxiously at Mags.*)

Mr. C.—How 's all at home,—I mean on Ludgate-hill,—
And have you heard the winner of the mill?
Mags (*with considerable hesitation*).—We all, alas! for Fortune's
    frowns seem fix'd on.
Poor Jerry Scout is bundled off to Brixton;
The shop 's done up; and, for your lady wife,
I fear she 's joined the Guards, yclept " The Life;"
On other things, barring the fight, I 'm barren,
And Owen Swift was beat by Barney Aaron.

(*Clipclose staggers across the room, and catches at the chimney-piece.*)

Mr. C.—My wife levanted, and the shop done up!
Mags, hand the quart; I need another sup.
Othello like, Bob's occupation 's done;
For I back'd Owen freely two to one.
Like Antony at Actium, this fell day
Strips me of all, shop, cash, and lady gay.
Would I had nerve to take myself away!
Pop. (*aside.*)—I 'll watch him close. Although his looks are placid,
He 'll take a dose, I fear, of prussic acid.

(*Enter Pot-boy.*)

Pot-boy.—Is there a gent call'd Mr. Clipclose here?
Mr. C.—I am that wretched man!   (*Slaps his forehead.*)
Pot-boy.   Who pays the beer?
Pop.—I.
Pot-boy.—Here 's a note.   (*To Mr. C.*) Lord, but the man looks
    queer!
  (*Mr. Clipclose reads it; jumps up, and whistles " Bobbing Joan."*)

QUARTETTO.

Mags.

Master, are you mad?

Mr. C.

No; but I'm distracted.

Pot-boy.

Times are wery bad,

Pop.

And I in grief abstracted.

Mags.

Odds! he'll take his life!

Mr. C. (kissing the billet.)

Sweet note! thou'rt balm and manna!

Mags to Pop. (who is reading it over Mr. C.'s shoulder.)

Is it from his wife?

Pop. (slaps his thigh.)

No! from Miss Juliana!"

Clipclose, when he reads it, rushes out; *Mags* after him. *Poppleton* attempts to follow, but is detained by pot-boy. He forks out tanner, and disappears. SOLO — *Apollonicon.* Hurried music descriptive of three cabs: *Clipclose* in 793, at a rapid pace; *Mags,* 1659; *Poppleton* 1847, pursuing. Scene closes.

SCENE II.

Thompson and Fearon's, Holborn; gin-palace at full work; company less select than numerous, and ladies and gentlemen taking " some'ut short" at the counter. Enter, in full uniform, Captain Connor; O'Toole and Blowhard in shell jackets. They call for a flash of lightning, touch glasses affectionately, and bolt the ruin. The captain stumps down for all.

GLEE—*Connor, O'Toole, and Blowhard.*

Capt.

Gin cures love, my boys, and gin cures the colic;

O'T.

Gin fits a man for fight, or fits him for a frolic;

Blow.

Come, we'll have another go, then hey for any rollic!

Trio.

Come, we'll have another go, and hey then for a rollic!

Blow.—Lass! (*to an attendant, whom he chucks under the chin,*)
        some more jacky! Connor, do you still
Bend at the shrine of her on Ludgate-hill?
    O'T. (contemptuously).—Zounds! a cit's helpmate. That would
        never do.
One of us Guards, and one of taste like you.
    Capt.—Faith, honest Blowhard, and you, my pal, O'Toole,
Tho' fond of flirting, yet your friend's no fool!
Think ye that I could live upon my pay,
And keep four wives on three and six a day?

No. Let me have a monied mistress still,
My El Dorado be a tradesman's till.
Love fed by flimsies, is the love that thrives,
And let the mercers keep the Guardsman's wives.

    O'T.—I see how matters stand, my trump; enough.
    Blow. (*to O'T.*)—He's wide awake, Tim. (*To the Capt.*) Con.
      you're up to snuff!
    Capt.—Come, one more round of jacky, and we part,—
I, to the peerless lady of my heart
In Stamford-street;—to Knightsbridge barrack you;
And mind don't split that I was out at Kew.

    (*They take each another johnny, shake hands, and separate. The
      scene closes.*)

SCENE III.

    A drawing-room; doors in the flat; one opening into Miss Juliana
Smashaway's boudoir, and the other to her bed-chamber. She is discovered standing at the window in a pensive attitude. She sighs heavily,
and rubs her temples with " eau de Cologne."

    Miss S.—He comes not—half-past four! Ah, fickle Connor!
Is this thy plighted faith, and thrice-pledged honour?
Was it for this, I waived a grocer's hand,
And twice refused a counter in the Strand,
Sent back an offer from a Tenth Hussar,
And without warning left Soho bazaar,
Rejected Griskin, that rich man of mutton;
Shy'd Lincoln Stanhope, and cut Manners Sutton?

               (*Sudden noise. Voices without.*)

    1st voice.—Fare's sixteen-pence, and with one bob I'm shamm'd!
Fork out the four-pence!
    2nd voice.   First I'd see you d—d!

    (*Door opens. Clipclose rushes in, and embraces Miss Smashaway.*)

    Miss S. (*with considerable spirit.*)—Unhand me, fellow! Whence
      this bold intrusion?
I think I'll faint, I feel in such confusion.

        DUET—*Clipclose and Miss S.*—(" Pray Goody.")

                Mr. C.

    Oh, come, Juliana, lay aside your anger and surprise;
      One trifling kiss you'll scarcely miss, you know.
    I saw a ready pardon seal'd already in your eyes,
      Else, 'pon my soul! I scarce had ventur'd so.

                Miss S.

      True, sir; but you, sir,
      Should recollect what's due, sir,
      To one so young and innocent

                Mr. C.

      As pretty Missus Ju—.
    Oh, come, Miss S. do lay aside your anger and surprise;
      A trifling kiss you'll scarcely miss, you know.
    I saw a ready pardon seal'd already in your eyes,
      Else, 'pon my soul! I had not ventur'd so.

(*Cab stops suddenly at the door. Miss S. looks out alarmed. Loud knocking. Alarum.*)

Miss S.—Lost—lost for ever!

Mr. C.   Pray, madam, what's the matter?

Miss S.—Heard ye no broadsword on the pavement clatter?

Mr. C.—A broadsword! Zounds! My teeth begin to chatter!

Miss S.—Where shall I hide him?—(*Opens the chamber door.*)—In, sir, or you're dead.

Mr. C.—Can nothing save me?

Miss S.   Creep beneath the bed.

                              (*Door opens. Mags peeps in.*)

Mags.—She's quite alone.   Oh, happy Matthew Mags!

(*Maid-servant enters.*)

Maid.—A chap's below who says he's Samuel Snags.

Mags.—I'm a done man; for that 'ere cove will blow me.

Miss S.—Follow me in, and I will safely stow ye.

(*Enter Snags.*)

Snags.—Divine Miss Smashaway, I humbly kneel
To plead a passion you can never feel;
A smile will save, a frown as surely kill,
One who for you has robb'd his master's till.

Miss S.—Well, after that the man deserves some pity.—
Knocking again! and here comes my maid Kitty.

(*Enter Maid.*)

Maid.—One Mr. Poppleton.

Miss S.   Was ever one so courted?

Snags.—All's up with me; for life I'll be transported!
Ma'am, could you save a lover?

Miss S.   Let me see.
Oh, yes; the bed will surely cover three.

            (*Puts Snags into bed-chamber. Enter Poppleton.*)

Pop.—Where is my charmer?

(*Enter Maid, hastily.*)

Maid (*to Pop.*)   Sir, you're dead as mutton;
The Captain's come.   Your life's not worth a button.

Pop.—Where shall I hide?

Miss S. (*to the Maid.*)   Put him with t' other three;
They're the same firm, " Clipclose and company."

(*A heavy footstep is heard, and a sword strikes against the stairs. Enter the Captain, whistling " Darby Kelly."*)

Miss S. (*flies into his arms.*)—My own loved Guardsman, and my fancy beau.
Oh, Terence Connor!   (*Kissing him.*)

Capt. (*embracing her.*)—Sweet Juliana, O!

Miss S.—Why did you dally, dearest; tell me all?
Were you on guard?

Capt.   Yes, sweetest, at Whitehall.

Miss S.—Ah, you false man,—(*taps his cheek playfully,*)—I 'll
watch you close.

> (*Somebody sneezes within.*)

Capt.   What 's that?

Miss S.—Nothing, dear Terence, but the landlord's cat.

> (*Somebody coughs twice.*)

Capt.—A cough!—another! Do cats cough so, my fair?
Ha! her cheeks redden! Tell me who is there?
That guilty look! Zounds! If my fears be true,
He 'll curse the hour he dared to visit you!

> (*Draws his sword, and rushes into the bed-chamber. Miss S.
> faints. Voices within.*)

Capt.—A man!—my eyes! another!—and another!
A fourth one still!

Snags.   I 'm dead with fright!

Pop.   I smother!

> (*Capt. drives them before him into the drawing-room.*)

Capt. (*in a frenzy.*)—Why, hell and Tommy! the maid whom I
adore
To prove untrue, and play me false with four!
But all shall die!

> (*Captain Connor cuts No. 6. with his sword, while Clipclose and
> company fall upon their knees.*)

Mags.   Oh, Lord! I 'm dead already!

Capt.—Prepare for death!

Snags and Pop.   Indeed, sir, we an't ready.

Mr. C.—Probably, sir, affection for my wife
Might plead my pardon, and reprieve my life.

> (*Enter, hastily, Mrs. Clipclose and Annette.*)

Mrs. C.—Why, what 's all this? What do my eyes discover?
An errant husband, and a truant lover!
(*Aside to Mr. C.*)—Was it for this I gave my faith to you?
(*Aside to Capt. C.*)—Was it for this I drove you out to Kew,
Paid cab and lunch, brown stout, and ruin blue?

> (*Capt. C. drops the point of his sword, and evinces great contrition
> for attempting the lives of the company, when enter an elderly
> pieman with a juvenile dealer in "all-hots," attended by two
> policemen. Pieman identifies Miss Smashaway.*)

Pieman.—That 'ere flash madam hit me in the withers.

All-hot (*pointing to Mr. Clipclose*).—And that cove knock'd my
kitchen-range to shivers!

Mr. C. (*to Policeman.*)—Let me explain, sir.

Miss S.   Pray, sir, let me speak.

Policeman.—Silence! and keep your gammon for the beak.

> (*A rumbling noise heard underneath, attended by a disagreeable
> vapour.*)

Policeman.—Zounds! what is this? it smothers me almost.
Is it the gas-pipe?

Capt. C.   No, dash my wig! a ghost!

(Slow music.   Apparition of Old Clipclose rises through the stage, dressed in a white shirt, and scarlet nightcap.)

ROUNDELAY—*Ghost and Company.*

("Good morrow to you, Madam Joan.")

Ghost.

All in the family way,
          Whack-fal-li, fal-la-di-day !
Are you met here to take tea ?
          Whack-fal-li, &c.
Or is it love-making you 're come ?
          Tol-de-re-lol, &c.
Or to keep clear away from a bum ?
          Whack-fal-li, &c.

Miss S.

Oh, no, sir ! we 're going to jail,
          Whack-fal-li, &c.
Unless, Mister Ghost, you 'll go bail,
          Whack-fal-li, &c.

Policeman.

A spectre, Miss S. will not do,
          Whack-fal-li, &c.

(To the Ghost.)

Where the blazes ! should we look for you ?
          Whack-fal-li, &c.

(Enter Capt. C's four wives.)

1st Wife.

Ah, Terry, you traitor, you 're there !
          Whack-fal-li, &c.

2nd Wife.

As usual, deceiving the fair !
          Whack-fal-li, &c.

3rd Wife.

You 'll pay dear enough for your pranks !
          Whack-fal-li, &c.

4th Wife.

You 're broke, and reduced to the ranks !
          Whack-fal-li, &c.

(Capt. C. seems thunderstruck, grinds his teeth passionately, then strikes his forehead, and sings.

AIR—*Capt. C.*—(" The night before Larey was stretch'd.")

Capt. C.

By St. Patrick, I 'm done for, at last !
     From a captain come down to a private.
Terry Connor, your glory is past ;
     A very nice pass to arrive at !

(To the Ghost.)

I say, you old rum-looking swell,
     I would deem it a favour, and civil,
In spite of your sulphur'ous smell,
     To take me down stairs to the devil,
          And get me a troop in his guards.

Ghost (to the Capt.)—Shut your potato-trap! we still refuse—
The corps 's so moral—Life-Guardsmen and Blues.
4th Wife.—Cheer up, my Connor; 'twas in jest I spoke,
When I affirm'd my best beloved was broke.
 Ghost (addressing the company).—Ladies and Gemmen, give the
  ghost a hearance,
As this, his first, must be his last appearance.
(*To Mr. and Mrs. Clipclose*)—Bent upon wedlock, and an heir, to vex
 ye,
If toasted cheese had not brought apoplexy,
I died asleep, and left my hard-won riches;
Search the left pocket of my dark drab breeches;
Open the safe, and there you 'll find my will;
Deal for cash only and stick to Ludgate-hill;
Watch the apprentices, and lock the till;
And quit the turf, the finish, and the mill;
Turn a new leaf, and leave off former sins;
Pay the pieman, and mend young " All-hot's " tins.
 Mr. C. (doubtfully.)—Did you die rich, dad?
 Ghost.   Rich as any Jew;
And half a plum, son Bob, devolves on you.
 Mrs. C.—What a dear ghost, to die when he was wanted!
Will you forgive me?
 Ghost.   Ma'am, your pardon 's granted.
My time 's but short; but still, before I go,
With Miss Juliana I would sport a toe.
 Miss S.—With all my heart. What would your ghostship order?
 Ghost.—Tell them to play, " Blue bonnets o'er the border."

> *Apollonicon* strikes up the country-dance. *Ghost* leads off with *Miss Smashaway*; the *Captain* follows with *Mrs. Clipclose*; *Clipclose, Mags, Snags,* and *Poppleton* each choose one of the *Captain's Wives*; the *Police* dance with the *Ladies' Maids*; and the *Pieman* with " *All-hot.* " Twice down the middle, poussette, and form hands round. At the end of the dance, the *Ghost* vanishes, and the remainder of the *dramatis personæ* take hands, and advance to the stage-lights.

GRAND FINALE—(" There's nae luck about the house.")

> Dad 's away, and we may play,
> Nor dread Old Grumpy's frown;
> Well may we say, " thrice happy day
> When Square-toes toddled down!"
>   There 's now luck about the house,
>   There 's now luck to a';
>   There 's now luck about the house
>   Since grumpy dad 's awa!

(*Curtain falls amid tremendous applause, and a call for the author.*)

CRITICAL REMARKS BY AN M.P.

" I AM not in the habit of frequenting the theatres, nor indeed any public house, except the House of Commons; neither do I pretend to be particularly conversant with the drama: but, by general consent, this play has been declared not inferior to the happiest effort of the bard of Avon, as player-people call William Shakspeare. I have not seen it represented; for, the free list being suspended, prudence would not permit me to attend. Had half-price been taken, I think I should have gone to the two-shilling gallery; but this question is irrelevant.

"The author deserves well of his country. Indeed, his is a double claim; and the debt consequently due by the public would amount to a large *tottle*. No doubt the restoration of the drama is a matter of some importance; but surely the diminution of drumsticks is one of infinitely greater consideration!

"I perceive by the playbills,—one of which I was enabled to obtain *gratis*,—that a gentleman called Tambourette performs upon two drums with a single stick. Now, I call the public attention to this important discovery; and, in these times of retrenchment and reform, the introduction of this system into our military establishment should be at once insisted on. The saving would be immense. Assuming that there are one hundred and three battalions of foot, and, on an average, twelve drums to each regiment,—a shameful waste of public money, by-the-bye, one drum and fife being quite sufficient for each corps, as they only alarm an enemy in war-time, and, in peace, destroy the utility of servant-maids by seducing them eternally to the windows. Well, even permitting this extravagant number to remain; by adopting Mr. Tambourette's system of performance, one thousand two hundred and thirty-six drumsticks would be saved to the country. Now, averaging the cost of the smaller-sized drumstick at sixpence, and the larger at one shilling, a reduction in the army estimates might be effected of *one thousand one hundred and thirty-three small* and *one hundred and three large ones;* making a *tottle* to the credit of the nation of 33*l.* 9*s.* 6*d.*!!!

"If the author will furnish me with the necessary information to enable me to frame a bill, I will move for a return of the drummers attached at present to the army: specifying their respective names, weights, heights, and ages, and take the earliest opportunity of bringing the matter before parliament.

"J. H.

       "July 1, 1837.

"P. S. If one thousand two hundred and thirty-six drumsticks be dispensed with, it follows that a similar number of drummers' hands will then remain unoccupied. Might not a *one-handed fife* be introduced, or a pandean pipe substituted, and fifers totally abolished? I see no reason why the same man should not play the drum and fife together. This, indeed, would be a reduction worthy a reformed parliament, and a tremendous saving to the public purse.

"J. H."

THREE NOTCHES FROM THE DEVIL'S TAIL;

OR,

THE MAN IN THE SPANISH CLOAK.

A TALE OF "ST. LUKE'S."

I HAD often met with him before in my travels, and had been much struck with the peculiar acumen of his remarks whenever we entered into conversation. His observations were witty, pungent, and sarcastic; but replete with knowledge of men and things. He seemed to despise book-knowledge of every kind, and argued that it only tended to mislead. "I have good reason to be satisfied on this point," he said to me one day at Vienna. "History is not to be relied on; a fact is told a hundred different ways; the actions of men are misrepresented, their motives more so; and as for travels, and descriptions of countries, manners, customs, &c. I have found out that they are the most absurd things in the world,—mere fables and fairy tales. Never waste your time on such trash!"

I again met this gentleman in Paris; it was at a *salon d'écarté;* and he amused me much by informing me of the names and circumstances of the most distinguished persons present. Whether English, French, or Germans, he knew something of the private history of each, some ridiculous adventure or silly *contre-tems*. I marvelled how he could have collected so great a store, such as it was, of anecdote and information; how he carried it all in remembrance; and, still more, at the perfect *sang-froid* with which he detailed these things under the very noses of the persons concerned, who would, had they heard them, no doubt have made as many holes in his body with " penetrating lead" as there are in a cullender.

To avoid getting into any scrape myself, I invited this *well-informed* gentleman to spend an evening with me at my hotel, where, over a bottle of claret, we might discuss some of those amusing matters, more, at least, to my own ease. Before we separated, I pointed out a certain Englishman to him, who was playing high, and did not notice us; I asked him "If he knew anything respecting that gentleman?" I had my private reasons for asking this question, unnecessary now to mention, and was pleased to find my colloquial friend knew, as they say, "all about him;" so we parted, with a promise on his side that on the following evening he would visit me, and give me every particular.

He came punctually to appointment, but I could not prevail on him to put off his large Spanish cloak, what they call technically " *an all-rounder ;*" he complained of cold, said he had been accustomed to *a warm climate*, and sat down just opposite to me, when, without hesitation, in a sort of business-like way, he entered at once into the details I most wished to know respecting the young Englishman we had left at the *salon d'écarté ;* and left no doubt on my mind, from some circumstances I already knew respecting him, that the account was most veracious. I fell into a fit of musing in consequence of his narration, which he did not interrupt by a single remark; but, fixing his eyes upon me, seemed to be amusing himself with watching the progress of my thoughts.

"It will never do!" said I, forgetting I was not alone; "he is not worthy of her."

I stopped, and the stranger rose, gave me a peculiar significant look, and was retiring, but I would not permit it; and, apologising for my abstraction, insisted that he should finish the bottle with me: so he sat down again, and we tried to converse as before, but it would not do.

There we sat, facing each other, and both nearly silent; and now it was that I remembered I had never once seen this stranger without this same Spanish cloak,—a very handsome one it is true, richly embroidered, and decorated with Genoese velvet, and a superb clasp and chain of the purest gold and finest workmanship. I pondered on this circumstance, as I recollected that even in Italy and the Ionian islands, where I had before met him by some extraordinary chance, as well as at Constantinople and at Athens, he had always been enveloped in this same most magnificent mantle. At last I thought of the fable of the man, the sun, and the wind; so concluded that he wore this Spanish cloak to guard him equally from heat and cold, to exclude the sun's rays and the winter's winds; or, perhaps, I argued, he wears it to conceal the seedy appearance of his inner garments, or sundry deficiencies of linen, &c. "Things will wear out, and linen will lose its snowy whiteness, but what the devil have I to do with the matter? Let him wear his cloak, and sleep in it too, if it please him; why should I trouble my head about it?

"You are returning to England soon, sir," said, at length, the cloaked stranger (but I am certain that I had not intimated such intention to him); "I am proceeding there myself on some pressing business, and will do myself the honour of there renewing our acquaintance."

I paused and hesitated ere I replied to this proposition. It is one thing to invite an agreeable stranger to drink a bottle of claret with you at an hotel in Paris, and another to bring him to the sanctuary of your home, to the fireside of an Englishman, to the board of your ancestors, to suffer him to gaze freely on the faces of your sisters, and to pay his court at his ease to every other female relative beneath the paternal roof!

The stranger saw my embarrassment, and seemed to penetrate the cause. He gave me a smile of most inexplicable expression as he said,

"Your late father, Sir George F——, and myself, were old acquaintances. We spent some months together at Rome, and met with a few adventures there, which I dare say have never reached the ears of his son."

This was said in his usual sarcastic way; but I could not endure that he should allude in the slightest manner of disrespect to my deceased father; so I answered, with much reserve, and some sign of displeasure, "That I did not wish to pry into the youthful follies of so near a relative; at the same time I thought it odd I never should have heard my father mention that he had formed any particular intimacy with any one at Rome, but, on the contrary, had even been given to understand that all his recollections of the Eternal City were rather of an *unpleasing* nature."

" Did he never mention to you the baths of Caracalla?" demanded my strange guest; " but it matters little, for the son of Sir George F—— merits every attention from me *on his own account*, as well as for the sake of *another*——" He did not finish the sentence; but, folding his cloak more closely round him, he made me a profound bow, something between an Eastern salaam and the bow of a dancing-master, and politely took his leave.

For two or three days I thought much of this extraordinary man; but after that time I became so deeply interested in a Platonic *liaison* with Madame de R——, the beautiful wife of a Parisian banker, that I forgot him altogether. I had to read, as well as to write, sentimental *billets-doux* sometimes twice a day, for so often they passed between my fair Platonist and myself. I had to select all her books, her flowers, and to choose her ribbons. I know not how it might have ended, for affairs began to wear a very critical aspect; but I was summoned to England by an express. My beloved mother was dangerously ill. I tore myself away, disregardful of the tears that gathered in the brightest pair of eyes in the world, and travelled post-haste to Calais.

Scarcely had I put my foot on the deck of the vessel ere I perceived my acquaintance of the Spanish cloak. There he was, walking up and down the deck, — tall, erect, gentlemanly; there was his magnificent cloak, without a wrinkle or a spot, the gloss still on it. I sat still, and watched him, not without a sensation of annoyance, as I was not at all in the humour just then to enter into conversation. I was uneasy respecting the life of an only parent, and I had just parted with one of the prettiest women in France, at the moment, too, when we both wished Platonism in the same place its founder was, dead and buried; but I might have saved myself the trouble of being annoyed, for the stranger did not seem to recognise me, nor wish to speak to any one. His carriage was lofty and reserved; his eye was proud, and sought to *overlook* the rest of the passengers as unworthy of its notice; and so marked was his avoidance of myself, that I began to feel piqued, and to imagine that my own personal appearance, if not our former knowledge of each other, might have gained for me the honour of his notice. Never before did I see so imperious an eye, or so magnificent a cloak!

The passage was a very boisterous one; and all the passengers, both male and female, began to show evident signs enough that the human animal was never intended by Nature to ride upon the ocean's billows. Strange sounds were heard from the very depths of human stomachs, as if in response to the roaring of the winds and the dashing of the waves! I began to sympathise most sincerely with the unhappy sufferers; for such sights and sounds are sure to affect the feelings of those who both see and hear. In short, I began to look grave, and become squeamish. I saw nothing but livid lips and blue cheeks around me,—a perfect pandæmonium of wretchedness; yet there walked the stately man in the cloak, perfectly unmoved in countenance and stomach. I perceived he had lighted a cigar, which glowed of a bright red colour, and threw a glow over his handsome features.

I grew still worse, and my disorder was coming to its climax, when the eye of the stranger for the first time condescended to notice me, and he bowed ceremoniously, with a smile which seemed to say, " I wish you joy, young man, of your sea-sickness !" I turned from him, and sincerely wished him in the same condition as myself and the other victims of the wrath of Neptune. He advanced towards me.

" You look ill, sir !" he exclaimed. " Take the advice of an old sailor ; only try one of my cigars ; *they are not of common use ;* one or two whiffs will drive away your nausea. I never knew them fail."

Now I loathe smoking at all times ; it is a vulgar and idle amusement, fit only, as a modern writer says, for " the swell-mob ;" but at this moment the thought of it was execrable. I could have hurled the stranger, when he offered me one of his cigars already ignited, into the sea.

" I never smoke, sir," said I, pettishly, " and I always get as far away as I can from those who do. May I thank you to go a little to the windward ?"

" My dear sir, do not be obstinate," said the pertinacious stranger ; " we have many hours before we shall touch the shore, for you see both wind and tide are against us. I assure you the remedy is always efficacious ;" and he handed me a lighted cigar, immediately under my nose.

I snatched at the burning preparation, and flung it overboard, with an exclamation of no gentle kind ; it dropped into the boiling waves, making a noise like a hissing red-hot iron, as it is put by the smith into the water of the stone cistern.

" It is not of the slightest consequence," said my tormentor, affecting to believe I had dropped the cigar by accident, " I have plenty more in my case ;" and with the most provoking coolness he lighted another from his own, and presented it to me. I was puzzled what to do, for the courtesy of this man was extreme. I was exceedingly sick, and wished to get rid of him ; for who likes to have a witness during the time of Nature's distress ? I therefore accepted his cigar, and turned from him, with a very equivocal bow of acknowledgement.

There was something of a very refreshing nature in the smell of this extraordinary-looking cigar, which was burning steadily in my hand. I resolved to try its boasted efficacy ; and accordingly put it to my lips, and inhaled its fragrance. In a moment I was well, more than well ; for a delicious languor seized me. After that, my nerves were braced, invigorated ; I felt as a hunter does after a long day's sport, hungry almost to famine, and I descended to the saloon, and called lustily to the steward to bring me a cold fowl, a plate of ham, and a bottle of porter. No more nausea, no more livid lips and blue cheeks. All of a sudden I became eloquent, poetical, and brimful of the tender passion. I wished to console some of my fair companions who were languishing around me, and offered my cigar to all who would accept it. Had it not been for an occasional thought of my mother's illness, which would intrude upon me whether I wished it or not, what folly and entanglement might I have got into with a pretty milliner on board, just returned from Paris, with fashions in her head, and French levity in her heart !

I ought to have acknowledged my obligation to the stranger for his remedy; but I had conceived so insuperable a dislike to him, that I could not account for it, and my only wish was to escape from his society at Dover, as I feared he would offer to accompany me to London, and I could hardly refuse him after the service he had rendered me. I therefore lingered below some few minutes when we arrived, and looked cautiously around me when I ascended the companion-ladder; but the stranger was gone. I saw no trace of his august person then, or his superb Spanish cloak.

I hastened on with four horses to —— Square, and met my weeping sisters. My mother still breathed; but that was all. The physicians could not comprehend her malady, but agreed to call it a general debility, an exhaustion of the vital energies, without any particular complaint. She was extremely weak, but knew me instantly, and smiled her welcome as I knelt and kissed her hand.

My mother was only of the middle age, which made it more strange that physical weakness should thus overpower her. I inquired at what time she was first seized; and on reference to my note-book, found out that her first appearance of illness was at the *precise hour* when the stranger in the Spanish cloak was sitting with me at my hotel, and talking to me of my father. Well! what of that? it was a mere chance!

It is no use disguising it. I am naturally superstitious. We can no more help the frailties of our minds than the blemishes of our features. As I sat by my declining mother's side, I pondered again and again on this mysterious stranger. I recollected how he had cured me of my sickness in a moment; how wonderfully he knew the private history of every individual; and I ended by believing that there was something of a supernatural agency about him. "Perhaps," thought I, starting up suddenly, and speaking aloud, "perhaps this wonderful cigar of his might recover my beloved mother." I searched every pocket, hoping that a remnant of it might have remained: but, no; it had been whiffed away by the ladies in the cabin, and I had not a vestige left.

When once an idea seizes hold on the mind, it scarcely ever lets go its hold. I began to consider myself mad, yet could not prevent myself from going out I knew not whither, to make inquiries for the cloaked stranger, and request him to give me another of his marvellous cigars. As I passed Louisa and Emily, my sisters, and ——, now no more, they were alarmed by the wildness of my looks, and endeavoured to arrest my progress.

"I go to seek a remedy for my mother," exclaimed I, breaking from them, and I darted from the house.

I made inquiries at all the principal hotels and club-houses for the stranger in the magnificent cloak. The waiters at the Oriental, the Travellers, and the Albion, had all seen him, but knew not his address or name. I sought him in the parks, at the exhibitions; but could not find him. At length I thought of the British Museum, but *why* I did so appears to me most mysterious; I drove instantly thither, and ran through all the rooms with the most searching gaze. In George the Fourth's splendid library there, seated at his ease by special permission from Sir Henry Ellis, I beheld the man I sought, with a large folio volume of Eastern learning spread open before him.

I felt ashamed to address him; for, had I not been most uncourteous, most repulsive to him? and now I wanted another favour. I stood before the table at which he sat, and watched his countenance as he seemed engrossed with his Oriental literature; but it was only for a moment, for he raised his eyes by some sudden impulse, and fixed them straight upon me.

The stranger acknowledged me not even by a bow or a look of recognition. I knew not what to say to him, yet the case was urgent.

"Pardon me, sir," I stammered out, "I fear I interrupt you; but——"

"Proceed, sir," said the stranger, coldly. "I am always ready to listen to the son of Sir George F——, for I owe to the father some obligation."

"You possess the power of allaying the most tormenting sickness by some mysterious drug or preparation," I said, hesitating as I spoke: "that was no common cigar. Have you other remedies?"

"A thousand," replied the stranger. "Pray go on."

"My mother lies dangerously ill; can you restore her?"

"May I behold the patient?" demanded the stranger, and an inexpressible glance flashed from his brilliant eyes.

What made me tremble at this natural request? for such it might have been deemed, since every medical man has free liberty to inquire into the symptoms of the case before he prescribes.

Fixedly did his eyes rest on mine; they seemed as if turned to stone, for they moved not in the slightest degree.

"I will *describe* my mother's case to you, sir," I said, evasively.

He made me no answer; but, casting down his eyes, he calmly resumed his reading, and I walked up and down the spacious apartment, in which there were not above a dozen other persons, in a state of mind resembling a chaos, occasionally glancing with angry eyes at the reading stranger, who seemed perfectly composed, and unconscious of my presence.

"What a fool am I!" said I, mentally; "what *harm* can this man do my dying mother? but, then, *she* may see him—this being that resembles a demi-god—and *she* too of so peculiar a mind, so enamoured of all that is great and wonderful; so romantic, too! Wretch that I am! is my beloved mother's life to be sacrificed—at least the chance of saving her—to a wild and jealous fantasy? No!" and I walked up again to the table.

The stranger was rising as I approached him, had closed his book, and returned it to the librarian. He would have passed me, but I laid my hand upon his arm.

"Most extraordinary being!" said I, "*come*, I conjure you, and save my mother!"

He entered my carriage without saying a word, and silently followed me to the apartment of my languishing parent, who was dozing in a sort of lethargic stupor, that appeared to be the precursor of death. My two sisters stood gazing on her pale features, and —— was holding her thin white hand in one of hers, and bathing it with her tears.

The stranger took my mother's hand from hers, and—I cannot be mistaken, for I watched every movement—some strong agitation, some convulsive spasm, passed over his countenance as he looked upon that face which never had its equal yet on earth; but, whatever was his emotion, he soon mastered it, and desired that a silver plate and lamp might be brought to him.

From a small crystal box the stranger took out a brown preparation, and, breaking it in two, placed them on the silver plate; then with a slip of paper lighted from the lamp he ignited the substance so placed, which sent up a pale blue flame, and a most intoxicating odour. He desired that my mother should be raised in bed, even to a sitting posture, when he placed the blazing plate immediately beneath her nostrils, and some portion of the actual flame entered and curled about her face. My sisters shrieked, but —— spake not a word, and I waited the result with agonised impatience.

"She revives! she revives!" exclaimed the latter, "and my blessed aunt will live!"

It was true. Years have gone by, and *my mother is still alive.* Never has she had an hour's illness from that hour. Was I grateful to the stranger for saving a life so prized? No. In my heart I loathed him at the very time he was heaping benefits upon me. And why? I detected a look of wonder, and admiration, and gratitude, and a smile of ineffable beauty directed towards him by one who——

Disguising as well as I was able the hatred that swelled within my heart, I offered to place on the finger of this mysterious visitant a ring of great value, that belonged once to my father. He started as he saw it, and, pressing a secret spring in it that I knew not of, restored it to me.

"It was a present from myself to him at Rome," he said, and his voice faltered, "for a signal benefit conferred. Behold! there is my own miniature!"

And it was so. Most exquisitely painted was there concealed, a minute resemblance of himself. I now perceived, and I cursed him in my heart for it, that —— retained the ring, after having expressed her astonishment at the fidelity of the likeness. I rudely snatched it from her hand, and threw the ring from me.

"Theodore," said my mother, "give me that ring. I know full well who it was presented that ring to him who is now no more. Marquis! I must speak to you alone, but not now. Come hither to-morrow. Now, I beseech you, retire!"

How dreadful is it to bear about with us the seeds of insanity. I have felt them shoot and grow within me from my childhood. The fibres had twined about my very being. *I knew* that madness must some time or other scorch my brain; I was full of delusions; I could behold nothing clear with my mental vision. I once heard a learned physician say to my father, "Take care of him, sir. Excitement may drive that boy mad. Do not let him study too much; and, above all, I trust he will never meet with disappointment in any affair of the heart."

Have I met with such? Let me not think about it, or——*And yet I am not mad now.*

From this time I became gloomy and morose, and always worse whenever this accursed man in the Spanish cloak came to the house, which now was very often. He charmed all but myself. I hated the sound of his voice. My sisters would come and try to soothe me into sociability and calmness. I repelled them with harshness and severity; and even when my gentle cousin tried each soft persuasive art to lead me to his presence, I taunted her in the cruellest manner with her hypocrisy, as I chose to call her blandishments, and bade her " go to the fascinating marquis, and heap her witcheries on him." Nothing could exceed the patience of this devoted being, her sweetness of temper, her angelic forbearance, but my own ferocity and hellish brutality; yet how did I love her, even when I bitterly reviled her! Once, when I observed that ring upon her finger, which my mother had permitted her to wear,—that ring, bearing the portrait of *that man*,—I absolutely spurned her from my presence, and wonder now that I did not murder her.

Cloud after cloud obscured the light of reason in my brain, and it was deemed advisable by those who loved me still, notwithstanding my growing malady, to have some one with me night and day, lest I should lay violent hands upon myself, as if a life like mine were worth the caring for.

An intelligent young man, one of my tenants, accepted this painful task, and he performed it with gentleness and fidelity. He soon perceived that I grew more furious when the voice or the name of the Marquis —— met my ears. He mentioned this circumstance to my mother, and from that time the marquis was not permitted to enter the house. I heard of this at first with incredulity, then with complacency. By degrees I grew calmer. I was afterwards shown a letter from the cloaked stranger, dated Rome; and it confirmed their assertions. I once more enjoyed the society of my family, and basked in the smiles of my beloved cousin. She was all kindness, all attention; and I began to flatter myself that the ardent love I had borne her from my very boyhood was returned. It was her reserve that before drove me from my country.

To my great astonishment and delight, that young Englishman who had interested me so much in the *salon d'écarté* at Paris, was formally refused by her who was dearer to me than life. He was of ancient family, and of great possessions; I knew he loved her, and feared he would gain her: but on my saying one day, as if by accident, in her presence, " that I feared S—— gamed high, and consequently was not worthy of the regard of any woman of discretion," she gave me a smile of ineffable sweetness, and told me, " It was of little consequence to her his frailties or his virtues; for she had long determined to give him a refusal, and, in fact, had done so before he went to Paris."

I considered the *manner* of my cousin, more than her mere words, as encouragement to myself, and with all the ardour of my nature declared to her my passion. These were her words in reply: " Theodore, I pretend not to misunderstand you; and, if it be any comfort to you, believe that I most tenderly return your affection. But, oh, my beloved cousin! think how you have been afflicted,—and then ask yourself whether I ought to listen to your proposals? whether you ought to marry? Theodore, I solemnly promise you that, for your sake, never will I wed another; but, oh! ask me not to become your wife whilst you are subject to such a fearful malady."

In vain I represented to her that my late mental affliction had been caused wholly by my fear of losing her, as I believed that detested foreigner was exactly the man to charm her, and thus I considered her lost to me for ever.

"This, dear Theodore," she answered, "is one of your delusions. You had no cause why you should form such a preposterous notion, —a man old enough to be my father, and ——"

"That is true," said I, "there is disparity of years ; but, then, what a splendid being !"

"Yes," she replied coldly, "he wears a most magnificent cloak."

"Not always, sure ?" I asked inquiringly, for I had never entered the room where he was, since he had cured my mother. "Did he not remove it when he dined and drank tea with you so often, and stayed so late, that I could have torn him to pieces for it ?"

"Softly, my beloved cousin," said the sweet girl, placing her soft hand before my lips ; "why are you so excited now when talking of this stranger ? *Your* mother, Theodore, has been restored by him ; and for that service what do we not all owe him ?"

"Was it for this," I said, "from gratitude alone, you wore that ring ?"

"Yes, from gratitude only. Are you now satisfied ?"

"Blessings on you, dearest, for your kindness !" I continued. "But say, did you ever see him without that cloak ?"

"Never, Theodore, never. It was always too hot or too cold ; or he was poorly, or some excuse or other. We never could persuade him to take off that cloak."

I fell into a long reverie after this ; nor could I blame her for her decision. I knew myself that my brain was not steady, and consequently I had no right to marry, to entail on my innocent offspring such a calamity. But then this inexplicable stranger ;—perhaps he had the power to cure me,—he had already performed almost a miracle ; if he could but settle my head, my beloved cousin would become mine, and I should be free from those fears that were constantly besetting me of becoming incurably mad.

Nothing would now do but my immediately setting out for Rome to seek the stranger with the large Spanish cloak. My mother did not think it advisable that I should go alone ; so it was determined that she, with Louisa and Emily, accompanied by our sweet relative, should bear me company to Italy, and thither we accordingly went. We lingered not on our progress to look at curiosities, or paintings, or prospects. We journeyed as fast as four horses could carry us, and arrived quite safe at imperial Rome.

I was sorry to learn that the Marquis —— was now at Naples ; and, after settling my family in an elegant villa a few miles from modern Rome, I set off in quest of the man for whom I had an antipathy, powerful, incurable ; and for what purpose? To request his aid, mysterious, perhaps sinful, to cure me of a disorder, of which the consciousness was part of its calamity. The raving madman, at least, is saved from *knowing* his own misery.

I had not been an hour at Naples, attended by my favourite servant, the young man who once acted to me as my keeper, when I saw from the window of my hotel the cloaked stranger pass with a lady on his arm. But I hesitated not,—I might lose him for ever ; so I ran into the street, and hastily accosted him.

What I said to him I know not, for my words were wild and ambiguous; but he promised that he would dine with me the following day, although his manners were even more reserved than when I spoke to him at the Museum.

Our instincts ought ever to be attended to; the brute creation follow nothing else, and *they* commit no sin. The first time I saw this stranger, he was looking at an inscription at Athens, and I felt a secret desire to get from his presence; but he entangled me with his talk, his knowledge of everything around, his high bearing, his intelligent eyes, and his superb Spanish cloak.

Again we were seated at the same table, and I again requested him to remove his mantle.

" Not yet," he said significantly; " but after the cloth is removed I will, if you still wish it, take off this upper clothing."

Oh how sarcastically were these words pronounced! My heart beat violently; I could not eat, and became abstracted and melancholy; not a word was said respecting my request to him, nor did he ask me why I sought him. He ate in silence, and seemed to have forgotten he was not alone.

When the table was cleared, the stranger coolly took a book from under his cloak, and began to read; whilst I, pondering on all I had ever known of him, began to feel the most burning desire to see this man once *without* his cloak, and was determined to do my utmost to effect it.

" The cloth *is* now removed, signor," said I, " and you promised *then* you would take off that everlasting garment."

" It displeases you, then?" retorted my companion. " *Is it not unsafe to penetrate below the exterior of all things?* Is not the surface ever the most safe? Is not the *outer* clothing of nature ever the most beautiful to the eye? What deformity dwells in mines, in caverns, at the bottom of the ocean! Nature wears a cloak as beautiful as mine: do you wish also to strip off her covering as well as mine?"

" At this moment, signor," said I gloomily, " I was not thinking of Nature at all, but of the strangeness of your ever wearing that cloak."

" Was it for this you came from England, Sir Theodore?" inquired the marquis, " and sought me at Naples? The knowledge, I should deem, could never compensate you for the loss of your cousin's society so many days."

" It was not for this I sought you, noble marquis," I replied, piqued at his irony; " but, when a man ever wears a cloak, it must be for some purpose."

" Granted," slowly said my companion; " I have such purpose."

" Which you promised to unfold!" I exclaimed, with pertinacity. " Is it still your pleasure so to do?"

" *It is necessary first that we should have no intruders,*" he answered, with a tone that froze me to the heart. Oh, how cutting, how sarcastic did it sound in my ears!

" No person will enter this apartment save my faithful servant, Hubert; therefore——"

" I promised to enlighten the master, and not the servant. If you insist on this strange request, the door must be securely locked; there must be no chance of interruption."

" Oh, what a fuss," I thought, " about a mantle! Why, *he* must be mad too! How can he cure me of an evil he has himself?: Lock the door, forsooth, because he takes off his cloak! But I must humour him, I suppose, or he will find an excuse for breach of promise." As I thought this, I walked to the door, locked it, and, placing the key upon the table, merely said, " Now, signor, your promise?"

" Would it not be prudent, young gentleman," he observed, laying his finger on my sleeve, " that you should speak of your request,— that one that brought you hither, and which I should conceive of more importance than the satisfying an idle curiosity,—would it not be wiser of you to mention this previously to my taking off my cloak."

" Oh, what importance he attaches to so trifling a thing!" thought I; " but, after all, the man is right; I had better attend to the most essential, nor was I wise to couple two requests together."

" Signor Marquis," said I, " have you any cure for insanity?"

" *I cured your father,*" was the answer, " and this your mother knows. He in return did *me* a service; he presented me with—this excellent cloak."

I was more puzzled than ever; I had never before *heard* that my poor father had unsettled reason, but many circumstances made me now believe it. I fancied too that my youngest sister gave indications of the same disorder; she was growing melancholy and reserved. " Oh, heavens!" thought I, " there will be more work for this man to do; I had better invite him at once to England, and make him physician in ordinary to our family."

" I have an engagement at nine," said the stranger; " have you any other inquiries to make?"

" But, if you *cured* my father, Signor Marquis," I observed, " how is it that I have inherited the disease? Should not the *cure* have eradicated it for ever from him and his posterity?"

" Is it not enough that I prevented the display of such a malady during his life? that I drove away the cloud that obscured his day, so that the sun of reason shone brightly on him until his death? What had I to do with future generations? with a race of men then unborn? *I performed my contract,* and he was satisfied. Shall the son be more difficult to please than the father?"

I interrupted him, " Oh, mysterious man! canst thou not cure the *root* of this disease? stop its fatal progress? prevent the seed from partaking of the nature of the plant?"

" Young man!" solemnly returned the marquis, " was not thy first progenitor, the man who resided in Paradise, *mad*—essentially mad? and has not his disease been carried on, in spite of all physicians, down, down to the present hour? It is woven into man's very nature; the warp and woof of which he is composed. I can check its open manifestation in a single individual; but the evil will only be dammed up during his time, to give it an increased impetus and power to those who follow him. Art thou not an instance of this fact? Hast thou not been madder than thy father?"

I groaned aloud. I remembered my own wild delusions, my sudden bursts of passion. I even began to think that madness ruled me at that very hour; that all I saw and heard was the coinage of a distempered brain.

At length I said, dejectedly, unknowing that I spoke aloud, " Then I must never marry; my children will become worse than myself. Farewell then——"

"Or rather," interrupted the cloaked stranger, "farewell to human marriages altogether, if those who marry must be free from madness. Why, 'tis the very sign they are so, their wishing to rivet fetters on themselves; but, no matter. What have I to do with all the freaks and frenzied institutions of such a set of driveling idiots?"

"Art thou not a man?"

"Thou shalt judge for thyself, thou insect of an hour!" and he unclasped his cloak, and stood erect before me. Coiled around him like a large boa-constrictor, reaching to his very throat,—— But I sicken as I write! The remembrance of that moment, how shall it be effaced? Time deadens thousands of recollections, but has never weakened the impression made upon me at that appalling moment!

The immense mass that wound its lengthy fibres round him, like a cable of a ship, now became sensibly animated by life! I beheld it move, and writhe, and unfold itself! I heard its extremity drop upon the floor! I saw it extend itself, and creep along! More—more still descended; fewer coils were round him! He turned himself to facilitate its descent; and, when the enormous whole encircled him, still undulating on the ground, that being looked towards me with one of those smiles, that Satan might be supposed to use.

"Behold!" said he, pointing to the dark undulation on the floor, "*behold the reason why I wear a cloak!*"

Insensibility closed up my senses. I could behold no more. When I recovered, I was alone. The stranger had departed, leaving the door ajar; but he had written on a slip of paper, and placed it just before me, these words:

"The remedy I bestowed upon the father, for *his* sake I will give unto the son. *Three notches of the devil's tail* will perfectly restore you; but it must be cut off by the hand of *the purest person that you know on earth. It will grow again!!*"

*   *   *   *   *   *   *

I hastily caught up this paper on hearing the step of my attendant, and placed it in my bosom. I think he saw the action, for he looked mournfully on me, and shook his head. I told him I was ready to set off instantly for Rome: his simple answer was,

"I wish we had remained there!"

"And *why*, Hubert?"

"You are pale as a sheeted corpse, and the boards of the floor are *singed*, yet there has been no fire in the room!"

I looked where he pointed; and, in a serpentine form, I beheld the traces of that enormous tail I had seen fall from the body of the cloaked stranger, coiled round him as an immense serpent twines itself around a tree. I shuddered at the sight. I felt my brain working; yet I wrestled with the spirit of darkness within. I tried to persuade myself that I had been overtaken only by a dream; that my whole acquaintance with the pretended marquis was nothing but an illusion, a vision of the imagination, an optic delusion, an hallucination of an excited state of mind; but it would not do. There were the dark and calcined marks, which it was my duty to account for to my host, who cared very little how they were occasioned, so as he received an ample sum to have the boards removed, and others in their place.

Our accounts were soon arranged, and I returned to my anxious family; but my disorder was increasing hourly. The wildest imaginations haunted and perplexed me. My beloved mother looked at me with tears swimming in her eyes. My eldest sister strove, by a hundred stratagems, to dispel the gloom that arose amongst us all. Emily sat, absorbed in her own melancholy thoughts, a fellow-sufferer, I fancied, with myself. My lovely, innocent, affectionate cousin held my fevered hand in one of hers, and imploringly asked me to be tranquil; said she would sing to me if I would try to sleep. I felt the gentle charm, and gave myself up to it. I laid myself upon the sofa; and she, whose name I cannot utter, sitting on a low stool by my side, sought to soothe me with her voice.

THE SONG OF ——.

" Come from Heaven, soft balmy Sleep,
Since thou art an angel there !
Come, and watch around him keep—
Watch that I with thee will share.

Strew thy poppies o'er his head,
Calm the fever of his mind ;
All thy healing virtues shed,
That he may composure find !"

"Oh, God !" I cried, jumping up; " and must I never call this angel mine ? Better to die at once, or lose all consciousness of what a wretch I am !"

"Hush, my dearest cousin ! I have invoked an angel from the skies to visit you ; drive her not away by ill-timed violence ; here, let me hold your hand ;" and she began again to murmur in a low tone,

" Strew thy poppies o'er his head,
Calm the fever of his mind."

and so I fell asleep.

When I awoke, my gentle cousin, (more constant than my heavenly visitant, Sleep,) was still seated by my side ; all the rest were gone ; candles burned on the table—it was midnight ; I had slept for hours, she yet retained my hand. I looked at her, and burst into tears.

"We are alone, Theodore," said my beloved; " tell me, I beseech you, what is labouring on your mind. You have spoken strange things during your sleep. You have declared that I had the power to restore you ; can I do this ? Theodore, be candid ! Were it to cost my life, I would gladly lay it down to be of benefit to you."

I could not answer her ; but I clasped my arms round that pure, angelic form, and wept like an infant on her bosom.

"Can I do you service, Theodore ? You deny not what your lips murmured in sleep."

" You can restore my reason, for you are the purest person that I know on earth."

"By what means ? But, alas ! you are wandering still ; this is one of your delusions ! Would that it were in my power to heal thy mind, my dearest cousin."

" In this, my heart's treasure, I am at least perfectly sane. *You have the power to cure me.*"

"Tell me the means."

I related to —— the whole of my adventures at Naples. I hid nothing from her excepting that our children might be infected with the same disease. Many reasons prevented my naming this. She was too delicate for me to allude to such a circumstance; I was willing to run all hazards of my posterity inheriting so dreadful a disease. My father had done as I intended to do; and the remedy was as open to *my* offspring as to myself, for had not the cloaked stranger told me that "the tail would grow again"? Even without such growth, had it not notches enough for a whole line of my posterity, supposing them all in want of such a restorative.

There was a pause of a full minute ere she spoke; her cheek was blanched, and her hand trembled in mine.

"Theodore, I know not what to think, whether from madness or from sanity comes your wondrous tale; but I will go through it, come what may. I will see this being; and, should he be indeed the author of all evil, out of evil shall come good, for I have courage, for your dear sake, to take from him the horrid remedy; but speak not of it, even to your mother or your sisters. Ah, poor Emily! she too may need such help! I will procure enough for her also."

Every thing was arranged. I was in that state that all I demanded was granted to me, for they feared to oppose my wishes. I entered the travelling carriage with my beautiful betrothed.

We had no attendants. We drove to the same hotel in which I had been before. We were shown into the same room; but the marks upon the floor were gone, — new boards were there. We ordered dinner *for three;* and I went out in search of the cloaked stranger.

It may seem strange that those who seek the devil, should seek in vain; but what is so perverse as the Origin of Evil?

Towards the close of day I however brought him in, as lofty, proud-looking, and handsome as ever; his features bore the stamp of angelic beauty; but, alas! the expression was — *the fallen angel.* He saluted with much politeness, nay, even kindness, my lovely friend; and we entered at once upon the business.

When he heard *who* was to perform the operation, he absolutely turned pale, and made a thousand objections. Some other person might be found; but I, fool that I was! overruled them all, and insisted on it, that she was the purest person that I knew on earth.

He then endeavoured to intimidate her; but she was resolute, though her lip quivered. We had a long argument about it, and most subtle was his reasoning. Yet he seemed as if he had no power absolutely to refuse. Reluctantly he drew from a secret pocket in his cloak a small steel hatchet, with many figures inscribed upon it. She received it at his hands; but I observed a fixedness in her beautiful eyes, and a rigidity about her mouth, that I did not like; still she grasped the shining instrument, and hesitated not. But, when his cloak fell off, oh, what a look of horror did those dear eyes assume!

Slowly descended the voluminous appendage; its extreme end fell on the chair on which he had been sitting. She flew like lightning thither, raised the glittering tool, marked the precise spot, and severed at a blow "three notches of the devil's tail!"

"Take—take your remedy, dear Theodore!" she whispered, "for I cannot touch it."

I stooped, and took the severed quivering part, *but could not hold it for its heat;* so thrust it into my coat-pock; I then turned to congratulate my deliverer, *but she was a lifeless corpse at my feet;* and the stranger had vanished, I knew not and I cared not whither.

How often have I called on madness, or on death, to take from me the memory of her loss! Neither would come! I have had no return of my malady, but I have experienced anguish fourfold! The only benefit derived has been that my sister Emily has been totally cured by the specific that was so dearly purchased, for it proved efficacious in both cases.

Perchance it may prove useful for the future members of our family, should they be infected with this hereditary complaint; for myself, I shall never need it for my offspring, my affections are buried in the grave; but I have bequeathed it to my beloved sisters—with my hopes, more than my belief, that it may prove effective,—
" the three notches of the devil's tail !"

TRANSLATION FROM UHLAND.

THE SERENADE.

WHAT soft low strains are these I hear
    That come my dreams between?
Oh! mother, look! who may it be
    That plays so late at e'en?

"I hear no sound, I see no form;
    Oh! rest in slumber mild:
They'll bring no music to thee now,
    My poor, my sickly child!"

It is not music of the earth
    That makes my heart so light;
The angels call me with their songs,
    Oh! mother dear, good night!

THE PORTRAIT GALLERY.—No. III.

MY friend was proceeding to relate many curious anecdotes of SIR RUBY RATBOROUGH, when a row of several portraits of persons I had seen abroad struck me. The librarian informed me that they were those of the Cannon family, who had long resided on the Continent; and I immediately recognised a most eccentric set of people, met so often, and at various places, with such a rapidity of locomotion, that many fancied they were gifted with ubiquity. The portraits, my conductor informed me, were taken at Florence; and their history might serve as a hint to artists. The painter had, unfortunately, commenced with the handsomest of the girls; and, having somewhat flattered the likeness, of course the family were delighted with his performance: but, when the older and the uglier Cannons came to sit, no flattery could render their portraits tolerable to them. The consequence was, that they were considered as bad resemblances, and left on the painter's hand; the more favoured young ones, of course, not being allowed by their indignant elders to take theirs away. I had heard so much of this family that I requested my friend to postpone our review of the political character, to give me some account of these wandering emigrants; and he gratified my curiosity by putting into my hands the following MS. containing a sketch of their adventures at home and abroad, drawn out by Quintilian Quaint.

THE CANNON FAMILY.

WHO has not seen the Cannons in their Continental excursions? or, to use Mrs. Cannon's malapropic expression, their *incontinental* tours? Whoever has strolled, or lounged, or lurked in a French *promenade*, a Spanish *alameda*, or an Italian *corso*, has fallen upon some branch of the family; nay, more properly, on two or three of them; for, if a body perchance hits upon one individual of that numerous race, he is sure to be rebounded on a brother or a sister, illustrating their name by making what is called a *canon* in billiard-room parlance.

So very *répandu* is this moving train of curious ordnance, and the young ladies have been so walked about, and stalked about, and dragged about in pick-nicks, *déjeuners champêtres*, gipsy-parties, marooning-parties, through woods and forests, hills and dales, brushwood and underwood, that the witty Lady A—— called them *the field-pieces.*

What took this family from their delightful box at Muckford, in Shropshire, to visit France, and Italy, and Germany; to paddle in the Seine, dabble in the Arno, and stroll with the rabble along the Rhine? Surely it must have been love of the fine arts, or the cultivation of foreign tongues, with the ladies; or pursuits of political economy, statistics, or the study of men and manners, with the gentlemen. Not in the least degree. The only paintings the fair part of the family admired were their own lovely faces. All foreign tongues were as foreign to them as Sanscrit. The only pursuit of polity that occupied Messrs. Cannons', senior and juniors, was where to find cheap wines and parsimonious amusements; their statistics, a census of the geese and turkeys, turbots and mullets, brought to market; and their study of the "varying shore o' the world" was, congregating with their countrymen, who, like themselves, disported their nonentity in gambling-houses and *restaurans.*

What was it then that induced the Cannons to quit their delightful box in Shropshire? Simply because Lord Wittington and his family had purchased the estate of Myrtle-Grove, near unto Wick-Hall, —the name given by Mr. Cannon to his aforesaid delightful box. Now the motives that induced Mr. Commodus Cannon to bestow upon this box the euphonious appellation of *Wick-Hall,* arose from a natural association of ideas and a proper sense of gratitude; for, be it known, that Mr. Commodus Cannon had once been a tallow-chandler of great renown in the ward of Candlewick, in which business he had realised a large fortune; therefore, without much perplexity of the various ramifications of the brain, its circumvolutions and ventricles, it may be conjectured why his rural residence was denominated, despite all the arguments of the ladies, *Wick-Hall.*

The next question that arose in the curious and impertinent minds of those who must know the causation of all causes, was, how did it come to pass that the arrival of the Earl of Wittington at Myrtle-Grove should have induced, in a manner direct or indirect, the family of an ex-tallow-chandler to migrate from a comfortable residence; to have left Muckford and their Penates, their well-trimmed lawns, their well-stocked gardens, their orchards and their paddocks, their dairy, and their brew-house, and their wash-house, and their ice-house, and their hot-house, their cosey fire-side and their snug bed-rooms, to wander about the world, and dwell in cold and dreary, or in broiling and stewing lodgings; drink sour *ordinaire* wine instead of port, sherry, gooseberry, and nut-brown October; be cheated and laughed at by foreign servants, instead of being attended by worthy, homely, and honest domestics; and become the ridicule of strangers, instead of being respected and liked by their neighbours? How did it come to pass that the Earl of Wittington's arrival should have driven the Cannons away from their Eden? The reader who cannot guess it at once,—who gives it up, like a hard riddle or a puzzling conundrum,— must be stultified, unread, unsophisticated, never have subscribed to a circulating library. However, as dulness of intellect is more a misfortune than a fault, we shall kindly condescend to inform him.

Myrtle-Grove had long been untenanted. Mr. Cannon was the wealthiest resident in or near the village; therefore was *Wick-Hall* called "the squire's mansion." Now, stupid, do you take?

Everybody has read Joe Miller. Now it may be recollected that, in that valuable vade-mecum of *very delightful* and *charming fellows,* there is recorded the strange vanity of an ugly scholar in the College of Navarre, who maintained most strenuously and syllogistically,—nay, would have met any modern Crichton with a thesis on the subject to show and prove, that he was the greatest man in the world; and he argued that Europe being the finest part of the creation, France the most delightful country in Europe, Paris the most splendid city in France, the College of Navarre the most enlightened and precious establishment in Paris, his room unquestionably the best chamber in the college, and he most undoubtedly the greatest ornament in his room, *ergo,* he was the greatest man in the world.

In the same train of ratiocination did the Cannons come to the conclusion that they were the magnates, the top-sawyers, the leaders of fashion of the village of Muckford. They patronised the Rev. Mr. Muzzle, the curate, whose meek back was suited to the burthen of a wife and eight little ones on fifty pounds a year; Mr. Hiccup, M. R. C. S., who, to the duties of his profession in the attendance of man and beast, added the pursuits of rat and mole-catcher, perfumer, stationer, and tobacconist; and Mr. Sniffnettle, the attorney, solicitor, conveyancer, proctor, appraiser, auctioneer, poet-laureat and parish-clerk. A *hop* at Wick-Hall was anticipated with as much delight by all the young and old ladies as the opening of Almacks; a game at loo or twopenny long-whist offered all the attractions of Crockford's; and the Sunday visits after church were as distinguished for figure and fashion as a St. James's drawing-room on a birth-day.

This high patrician stand in society unfortunately made the Cannons proud,—some say haughty, supercilious, and arrogant. It might have been so; such is the nature of frail mortality, for, alas!

> " Pride has no other glass
> To show itself but pride; for supple knees
> Feed arrogance !"

and Mr. Muzzle, and Dr. Hiccup, and Mr. Sniffnettle, had their *vertebræ* and their articulations so greased, and oiled, and anti-attritioned, that they would bob, and bend, and curl, and coil like a tom-cat's tail, whenever they visited the mansion.

And strange dreams, and visions, and fantasies would be brewing in the brains of Mr. Cannon, both when sleeping and awake. He was wealthy; the Cannons had a dragon rampant for their crest, and *Crepo* for their motto,—a motto that was traced to the discovery of a bronze figure of the Egyptian god Crepitus in the tomb of one of his noble ancestors. To this proud circumstance the family also owed the Christian-name of " Commodus," which the elder Cannon always bore,—Commodus being of Gallic origin. Sometimes Mr. Commodus Cannon thought that he might purchase a peerage by paying some damages incurred by indiscreet influential personages; sometimes he fancied that he might be created a baronet upon a mortgage, or a marriage of one of the Miss Cannons to some broken-down nobleman.

But, alas! how transient are the visions of glory! of worldly greatness! Greatness—that gaudy torment of our soul!

> "The wise man's fetter, and the rage of fools!"

Lord Wittington arrived, and the Countess of Wittington, and the Ladies Desdemona Catson, and Arabella Catson, and Celestina Catson, and Euripida Catson, and the Hon. Tom Catson, and the Hon. Brindle Catson, with their aunt, Lady Tabby Catson; and all Muckford was in a state of commotion, of effervescence, of ebullition, boiling over with hope and fear. A comet wagging its tail over their steeple, —an eclipse, which would have set all the Muckfordians smoking bits of glass, and picking up fragments of broken bottles for astronomical observations,—could not have occasioned such a stir as the arrival of four travelling carriages, with dickeys and rumbles crowded with ladies' women, and gentlemen's gentlemen, rattling away with four post-horses to Myrtle-Grove.

And now were speculations busily at work. The minds of Ma-

homet and Confucius, of Galileo and Copernicus, of Locke and Bacon, were idle when compared to the brains of the Muckfordians.
What was the point in question? Was it the increase of business
and of profit that would accrue from the consumption of these wealthy
visitors?—No. Was it the advantages that might be derived from their
parliamentary connexions and ministerial interest?—No. Was it the
hopes that their residence might induce other rich families to in-
habit the neighbourhood?—No—no—no! If the reader cannot guess,
he must have lived at the antipodes, or in a desert, or never lived
in life. The question was, "I wonder if his lordship and her lady-
ship will visit Wick-Hall?" No treaty of alliance, of commerce, of
peace—no protocol that ever issued from the most perfect cerebral
organ in Downing-street—was ever weighed with more momentous
disquietude than this question, "I wonder if his lordship and her lady-
ship will visit Wick-Hall?"

"I should think not," observed Mrs. Curate Muzzle; "the Wittingtons are great folks, and the Cannons were chandlers!"

"Tallow-chandlers, my dear madam," remarked Mrs. Doctor Hiccup.

"Had they even been wax-chandlers," added Mrs. Sniffnettle.

"Or corn-chandlers," replied Mrs. Hiccup.

"But a tallow-chandler," exclaimed Mr. Sniffnettle, who, as we
have seen, was the laureat of Muckford, "as Gay says,

'Whether black, or lighter dies are worn,
The chandler's basket, on his shoulders borne,
With tallow spots thy coat.'"

This appropriate quotation not only drew forth a loud laugh of approbation, but illumined the minds of the party as brightly as two
pounds of fours might have enlightened Mr. Hiccup's back-shop parlour on a long-whist and welsh-rabbit night.

"I'm sure I wish them no harm," remarked Mrs. Muzzle, with a
benevolent smile; "but pride is a sad failing, which deserves to be
brought down."

"Oh, the deuce mend them!" rejoined Mrs. Sniffnettle; "if they're
brought to their proper bearings a peg or two."

"Because they had a little dirty cash—the Lord knows how they
made it!—they were as pert as a pear-monger's horse!" exclaimed
Mr. Hiccup.

"Pride comes first, shame comes after," added Mr. Sniffnettle.

"The priest forgets that he was a clerk," professionally observed
Mrs. Muzzle.

"I could put up with pride, now," said Mr. Hiccup, "from the
Wittingtons."

"Ay!" replied the poet, quoting Byron,

'The vile are only vain, the great are proud.'"

"Exactly!" observed Mrs. Hiccup, who, like most persons doting
upon poesy, did not understand what she most admired.

Is it not strange that none of these ladies or gentlemen ever said
"I wonder if *we* shall be invited to Myrtle-Grove?"

Whoever expected or fancied that on such an occasion such a
thought could have entered any well-disposed and educated mind
must be an ass. Who cares, if they are at the foot of the ladder, if

those who are climbing up are properly rolled down? There is no need of crying " Heads below !" the grovellers will all get out of the way, and let the tumblers roll in the mire to their hearts' content. I mean the hearts' content of the lookers-on.

Now, while this most important point was discussed by the chief authorities of Muckford, a question of still greater importance was agitated at Wick-Hall.

" I wonder if we ought to call first upon the Wittingtons, or wait until they call upon us ?" said Mrs. Cannon, after dinner.

Mr. Commodus Cannon halted a glassful of port that was marching towards his mouth, and kept it suspended in air like Mahomet's tomb.

Miss Molly Cannon delayed the cracking of a nut she had just introduced between two ivory grinders.

Miss Biddy Cannon kept her hand under a roasted chestnut napkin, unconscious of its temperature, without withdrawing it.

Miss Lucy Cannon cut into an orange she was carefully peeling with a steel knife; a circumstance that would have produced a galvanic thrill under other circumstances.

Miss Kitty Cannon filled a bumper of cherry brandy instead of "just the least drop in the world."

Mr. Cannon, junior, drove a toothpick in his gums instead of his teeth.

George Cannon started, and trod on the cat's tail.

Cornelius Cannon (commonly called Colcannon, having had an Irish godfather,) made a horrible mistake, by drinking out of his finger-glass instead of his tumbler.

Peter Cannon used his damask napkin instead of a pocket-handkerchief; and Oliver Cannon, who had been lolling and rocking his chair, rolled off his centre of gravity.

A dead silence followed the important question. The ghost of Chesterfield ought in mercy to have burst from his cerements to have answered it. Mr. Cannon first ventured to give an opinion—a judicious opinion.

" Why, as to the matter of that," he said, scratching his brown wig,—which was, by-the-bye, an action which might have been called manual tautology, since it was a scratch already,—"as to the matter of that, it is clear that, if we are to be acquainted with his lordship, they must call upon us, or we must call upon them."

Now, it is a matter worthy of consideration, that, in difficult and knotty points, perspicuity of language seldom or ever elucidates the business. Nothing could be more clear, more lucid, nay, more pellucid, than Mr. Commodus Cannon's remark,—more self-evident, more conclusive,—yet it only tended to make darkness visible. Mrs. Cannon, who possessed greater powers of eloquence, was therefore imperiously called upon for a rejoinder.

" If you could think, Mr. Cannon, of waiting until my Lord What-do-you-call-him thinks proper to *honour* us with a call, you are a mean-spirited, petty-minded fellow. I'd have you to know we are every inch as good as they are."

" To be sure we are !" replied all the Cannons in one simultaneous and spontaneous roar, one well-fired volley of approbation without a straggling shot,—all but Mr. Cannon senior, who remained as still as a target.

"We owe nothing to nobody," added the speaker; "and can hold up our heads as high as anybody that ever wore one."

This reloaded the Cannons, and another fire of coincidence was let off.

"If your nobility give themselves airs with us, let me tell you, Mr. Cannon, just look at your crest and your motto, and show them that you can let fly at them hollow."

All applauded except Mr. Cornelius Cannon, who was a good Latin scholar.

"For my part I wouldn't give a brass farthing—no, that's what I wouldn't—to know them, as it's ten to one they will be shortly wanting to borrow money from us; but, as we are neighbours, and we are longer resident at Muckford, it's our business to leave our cards with them, more especially as there's no *quality* whatever in this here neighbourhood but ourselves."

There was no necessity of putting this proposition to the vote; it was carried by *nem. diss.* acclamations, and the visit fixed upon that day week.

Now, strange to say, by one of those singular anomalies in the human mind that puzzle metaphysicians, psychologists, materialists, and immaterialists, although this acquaintance with the family of Myrtle-Grove was not, to use Mrs. Cannon's expression, "worth a brass farthing," everything in the house, from the furniture to the young ladies, was turned topsy-turvy for a week. There was nothing but dusting, and polishing, and furbishing, and scrubbing, and rubbing, and bees'-waxing, and varnishing, and tweezing, and plucking, and puffing, and blowing at all ends; and swearing, and cursing, and shouting from the top of the stairs to come up, and bellowing from the foot of the stairs to come down; and souls, and eyes, and blood, and bones were sent the Lord knows where by the impatient gentlemen, while the ladies, who were too well bred to pronounce the vulgar name of the infernal regions, only wished every servant in the house a visit to the monarch of that grilling kingdom every hour of the day; and every horse, and every ass, nay, the very colts and fillies, shod and unshod, broken or unbroken, were sent to and fro from Wick-Hall to the neighbouring town, like buckets up and down a well, for silks, and ribands, and bobbins, and laces, and caps, and bonnets, and feathers, furs, and furbelows, and rouge-pots, and cold cream, and antique oil, and pomatum, and washes, and lotions, Circassian and Georgian, that were ever employed since the days of Jezebel to scrub out freckles and wrinkles, fill up pits and creases, pucker relaxed fibres and relax puckerings, eradicate warts, pimples, blossoms, excrescences, efflorescences, and effluences; with collyria for red eyes, and ointments for crusty eye-lids, liniments for gummy ankles, with odoriferous and balsamic tooth-powders, and gargles; with stores of swan and goose down for gigots, and rear-admirals, and polissons, and bussels; not to mention the means of throwing out various forms that distinguish the *beau idéal* of the undulating line from the rigid severity of the straight line and the acute angle; while all the wigs, tops, toupets, fronts, tresses, plaits, curls, ringlets, black, brown, auburn, fair, and foxy, were put into requisition.

It was not only physical brushing up that was resorted to; the mind received a proper frizzing; and Debrett's Peerage and Joe

Miller, the Racing-calendar and the Court-guide, were studied during every leisure moment; while all the scandal-registering Sunday papers were devoured with avidity.

Various were the accidents that arose in this confusion. Biddy Cannon broke a blood-vessel in straining her voice to D alt. in practising a fashionable Italian song. A pet cat of the same (who had been trodden on by George Cannon) was well nigh scalded to death by the overboiling of a pipkin of oil of cucumber for Lucy Cannon's sunburns; and Kitty Cannon caught a desperate sore-throat in trying to catch a hint of a fashionable walking-dress one rainy morning that the Ladies Catsons were riding out, peeping at them under a heavy shower from behind a holly hedge. Poor Kitty Cannon was in a most piteous plight from having made a trifling mistake in the use of some medicines sent her by Mr. Hiccup; for, in a very great hurry to try on an invisible corset, she rubbed her throat with some palma Christi oil, and swallowed a hartshorn liniment that had been intended for external use. In her burning agonies she of course kept the whole house in hot water, for everybody was so busy that nobody could attend upon the poor sufferer; who, unable to call out, and having torn up her bell by the roots, was only able to attract attention to her wants by throwing every thing she could lay hands on about the room, more especially water-jugs, basins, physic bottles, and every vessel within her reach. Mrs. Cannon swore she was an unnatural child; and her sisters accused her of being ill-natured and jealous when she disturbed them in their important occupations. In short, the Tower of Babel, or the Commons on an Irish question, were nothing to Wick-Hall, in-doors and out-of-doors, where the young Cannons were grooming, and docking, and trimming, and figging their horses.

Mr. Commodus Cannon was the wisest of the party; he smoked his pipe, muddled over a bowl of punch, and only ordered his scratch wig to be *curled tight*, with the not unfrequent vulgar wish that the whole family might be *blown* to the same exiguous dimensions. He was ambitious, but he did not like to be *bothered* with any schemes but his own.

The day, the great day, big with the fate of the Cannons, was drawing nigh, and impatiently looked for, as a circumstance had taken place which gave the Wick-Hall family much to think of and inwardly digest.

Lady Tabby Catson, his lordship's aunt, was subject to nightmare and sleep-walking when in bed, and liable to fearful hysterics when out of it. Her case was altogether most distressing, since, according to her account, she could not lie on either side, was in agony when on her back, and distracted in any other position. A physician was called in, but, as he could only pay occasional visits, Mr. Hiccup was in constant attendance; and as the Ladies Catsons were well supplied with novels, and were of a most amiable disposition, Hiccup carried various new publications to his daughters, who immediately ran to show them to the Miss Cannons, calling the ladies by their Christian names with singular impertinence,—such a book having been lent by the beautiful Lady Arabella,—such a review by the lovely Lady Celestina. Moreover, Lady Tabby Catson, during the intermissions of her ailments, had fits of devotion that took her like stitches in the side, when Mr. Muzzle was instantly sent for in one of the carriages. Thus were the curate and the surgeon in constant attendance, and many little acts of kindness shown to them by the family, such as presents of fruits and flowers, all of which passed under the windows of Wick-Hall like the fearful regal apparitions to Macbeth; and, what was still more offensive, the favoured families, even the attorney, Sniffnettle, began to grow rigid in their vertebræ though in the heat of summer, walking past the Cannons with a mere nod of recognition, and preserving an insulting perpendicularity.

There was no time to lose in recovering their lost ground, and the day for commencing a campaign that would terminate in the utter discomfiture of these vulgar intruders was fast approaching. But, alas for human and mortal hopes! one hour,—nay, one half-hour,— one quarter,—the time of reading a letter on foolscap paper, on letter paper, on note paper, only a few lines written in an intelligible un-author-like hand, that required neither time nor spectacles, a hand that could be read running,—and all the airy fabric of the Cannons' visions was dissolved.

It was on a Friday morning, the day previous to the intended visit, —one of those unlucky days in the calendar of human disappointments, the fifth day of the month, which, according to Hesiod, is inevitably calamitous; a day that gave birth to Pluto and the Eumenides; a day when the earth brought forth the monster Typhon, and those vile giants who dared the Father of the gods,—on this day did Mr. Commodus Cannon draw on his stockings the wrong side, the eldest Miss Cannon—I know not why or wherefore—took a morning walk among the nettles, and her sister Biddy spilled salt at breakfast, forgetting to propitiate the angry heavens by casting some over her left shoulder. A thundering rap at the hall-door made the whole family jump, start, and stare. A footman in the Wittington livery was at the door! he delivered a letter! Oh! how all the young hearts did beat and leap! and how the old fount of circulation of Mrs. Cannon did palpitate, as in days of yore! Scarcely had the door been closed, when the whole family, with the exception of Mr. Cannon, who was buttering toast, rushed like a torrent, or a cataract, or any thing else you like, to secure the missive, anxious as they were to ascertain its contents. Much time was lost in scrambling for possession of the letter, snatched alternately from hand to hand without any regard to filial duty or the rights of primogeniture. At last the letter, be-buttered, be-honeyed, be-marmaladed, and be-egged, fell into the possession of Miss Cannon. But oh! horror! instead of the broad armorial seal of the noble earl, the note was wafered!—ay, gentle reader, wafered!—moreover, the wafer, still damp, had been broken, and bent, and divided, exhibiting evident marks of having been moistened by an abundant secretion of the salivary glands! Oh, fie, my Lord W.!

Philosophers and naturalists tell us there is a method in roasting eggs; now there is a method in closing letters, which has lately been adopted by a nobleman whom I have the honour to know, which may be considered a wrinkle in politeness. To his superiors, such as emperors, kings, popes, and newspaper editors, his lordship writes on coloured, perfumed, ornamented, and gilt-edged satin paper, and he closes his epistle with his armorials, six of which usually consume a stick of odoriferous wax. To his equals, though they are but few, he writes on paper somewhat inferior, with a smaller seal. To his titled inferiors, plain note paper, with a crest and motto. To his untitled correspondents, half a sheet of letter paper (it must be cut in an uneven and ragged manner), with a fancy seal, that his noble blazon may not be polluted by vulgar eyes. To people in business, cits, snobs, a wafer — but still a wafer — gently dipped in water. But to solicitors, postulants, petitioners, and humble applicants, he actually spits in their faces in the same manner as the Earl of Wittington spat in the crimson phiz of all the Cannons. But the offence did not rest there. MR. CANNON was on the superscription ! ay, a plain MR.! a *Mr.* that could only be washed out in blood ! a *Mr.* that would even make a respectable tailor jump from his shopboard, and grasp his goose with proper indignation.

"Lord Wittington, wishing to become the purchaser of Mr. Cannon's paddock under Breakneck-Cliff, part of his domain, is willing to treat with him, and will direct his steward to call upon him. His lordship has been led to understand that Mr. Cannon's young men have been in the practice of shooting on his grounds; now his lordship wishes it to be distinctly understood that his keepers have received instructions to proceed with all the severity of the laws against trespassers."

Mrs. Cannon of course fell into fits; Commodus Cannon cast his scratch *jasey* into the fire; some of the young ladies rushed out of the room; others, in whom no rush had been left, drooped in or on various supporting parts of the furniture. The *young men*, as his lordship had dared to call Mr. Cannon's promising and amiable sons, bore the insult with all the calm dignity of men wantonly offended; they only bit their lips, turned pale and red, clenched their fists, and paced about the room at the rate of fourteen miles per hour, while the words " young men " were muttered and murmured in deadly indignation.

" I 'll be d—d if the fellow ever gets my paddock ! sooner see him, and all his seed, breed, and generation, tumbling off Breakneck-Cliff !"

The allocution of Leonidas to his Spartan heroes at the Thermopylæ could not have been more spirit-stirring than this short and pithy speech of Commodus Cannon; even Mrs. Cannon, forgetting, in a moment of just indignation, that female discretion that ought to characterise a lady's language, could not help supporting the vote by an amendment, exclaiming, " Ay, and doubly d——d too !"

"And, moreover," added Mr. Cannon, "I 'll be blown if I don't stick my paddock chokefull of buck-wheat, and not leave the fellow a pheasant or a partridge,—that 's what I will !"

It is difficult to say what dire plans of destruction and desolation might not have been suggested in the family council, had not another rap at the door, louder, if possible, and more authoritative than the footman's, interrupted the discussion. All and every one ran to the windows. Mr. Carrydot, Lord Wittington's steward, was at the entrance of Wick-Hall, and desired a private interview with Mr. Cannon.

Mrs. Cannon reluctantly swept out of the room, followed by all the young ladies and the *young men.*

Mr. Carrydot was a smart, dapper, little man, with a bald head, ferret eyes, aquiline nose tipped with purple, and with a prying countenance that would have picked out flaws in Magna Charta or the

Bill of Rights. His costume sable ; but coat, waistcoat, and unavoidables to match, were all of a different black, more or less rusty and shining; his coat-sleeves, or rather cuffs, were short, and allowed his dirty wristbands to be seen puckered up above his ·hairy and meagre hands, and bony, long, crooked-fingers, with hooked nails in half mourning. How comes it that the coat-sleeves of certain petty attorneys and apothecaries are generally too short, save and excepting when they have donned their Sabbath and visiting raiment ? It surely must arise from the usual practice of extending the arms beyond the limits of their restrictions whenever a body is going to perform some dirty business, possibly and probably that the said dirty business may not·stain the cloth they wear, since a cloth may be respectable although the wearer may be as spotted as a panther. Mr. Carrydot walked, or rather stalked in ; and, without·a bow or a preamble, seated himself, without being asked to take a seat.

Cannon looked an encyclopedia of indignation.

" His lordship has directed me to call upon you, Mr. Cannon, regarding the approaching county election. You can command several votes, sir ?"

" Of course, sir," replied Mr. Cannon, with a proper emphasis and conciseness.

" You are aware, sir, that his lordship intends to put up Mr. Elfin Eelback, of Stoop-Lodge ?"

" Well, sir ! what 's that to me ? What do I care for his lordship's candidate ?"

Bravo, Cannon ! Mrs. Cannon would have inflicted a kiss had she been present.

Mr. Carrydot's eyes glared with indignation, and beamed with *ousters* and *ejectments*, as he repeated the words, " What 's that to you, sir !"

" Ay !" replied Cannon, giving the table a liberal thump. " What the devil is it to me ?"

" Why, his lordship desires that you will vote for Mr. Eelback."

" Then tell his lordship that I 'd sooner see Mr. Eelback skinned alive !"

Cannon was furious. Carrydot was calm, nay, he smiled ; for the fury of Cannon spoke volumes of prospective *foreclosures*, and *distresses*, and *rescous*, and *replevin*, and *denial* ; more especially as Cannon seemed to be a *good man*, with a silver urn and tea-pot·on the table, and every appearance of wealth and independence about the goods and chattels on the premises. " You seem to forget, sir," he quietly replied, " that you only hold Wick-Hall upon a lease, and that your interest in the lease expires next Michaelmas."

This was a thunderbolt to Cannon, who had laid out upwards of three thousand pounds on Wick-Hall.

" What, sir, if I refuse to vote for this Eelback ?"

"You must turn out, sir, *nolens volens* ; so sayeth the law !"

" But justice, sir ?"

" So sayeth the law. Every man has a right to do what he likes with his own, Mr. Cannon."

" What ! whatever my political opinions may be ?"

" You must poll for his lordship's candidate."

" This is infamous, oppressive, tyrannical !"

" Perhaps you may think so. Your politics, as you say, may differ from those of his lordship, but his lordship must be in the right.

Primò, he is lord of the manor; *secundò*, his property in the county is very considerable; and, *ergo*, he has a better right to know what is good for the people than a mere tenant."

"But, sir, he has no right—"

"Once more, sir, every one has a right to do what he likes with his own."

"Then, let me tell you, sir," replied Mr. Cannon, in a paroxysm of rage, "that there cudgel is my own, and suppose I knocked you down with it? This here foot is my own, and suppose I kicked you out of my house, Mr. Thingembob?"

"In that case," replied Carrydot, with a tranquillity which would have made Job himself smash all his crockery,—"In that case, sir, if you made use of that *there* cudgel, as you call it, the law would soon make you *cut your stick;* and if you did make the aforesaid use of that *there* foot, unless you took *leg-bail*, you should pay dearly for the experiment."

So saying, Mr. Carrydot took an enormous pinch of snuff, clapped on his broad beaver with forensic dignity, pulled up his coat-sleeves still higher with a twisting thrust of the hand, ready for anything—as the Irish say—from pitch-and-toss to manslaughter, and bidding Cannon, in a vulgar language unbecoming a solicitor, to prepare "to tip his rags a gallop by roast-goose time," which in the dignified metaphorical phraseology of the bar meaneth Michaelmas, he left Commodus Cannon to his deep reflections.

He was roused from this apathetic state by the entrance of Mrs. Cannon. "Well, sir?" said she, in an anxious tone. "Well, sir?"

"Mrs. Cannon, I regret it, but we *must* have a revolution in this here slavish, this here degraded country!"

"Lord-a-mercy! what has happened?" replied his affrighted lady.

"It is not what has happened, madam," replied the regenerated free-born Briton; "it is what shall happen. By gums!—(he was already beginning to be somewhat puritanical and sanctified; the day before, nay, a few moments previous to Carrydot's entrance, he would have sworn by G—, like any duke or marquis,)—by gums! this here proud big-wig aristocracy must be brought down; nothing can save poor England but the abolition of this insolent peerage, these hereditary law-makers from father to son. I say, no peers! no bishops! no lords! a yearly parliament! universal sufferance!—(it is presumed he meant suffrage,)—vote by ballot! Throw up your pew, Mrs. Cannon! kick the tax-gatherer down stairs! I 'll kick the fat gold-laced beadle myself! and tell Parson Muzzle that he 's a humbug and a leech!"

Mrs. Cannon, and all the Cannons, great-guns and small-arms, were terrified, and fancied the worthy man was out of his senses. She proposed to send for Mr. Hiccup.

"Hiccup be d—d! Do you think, woman, that Hiccup would condescend to come to you and me were we kicking in fits, dying with the pip, or had swallowed a mutton-chop the wrong way? Hiccup is with his lordship, with the Most noble, the Right honourable the Earl of Wittington, the Right honourable the Lady Tabby Catson! If their noble fingers ached, 'twould be in the Gazette, so it would. If they got a surfeit from cramming turtle down their noble throats, it would be in the papers! Hiccup! the rascal! the Tory pill-gilder! wouldn't give a commoner, an independent citizen, or an honest pauper, second-hand physic if a lord wanted him! No, not to save a fellow Christian's life!"

All this was inexplicable to the open-mouthed and alarmed family, when a sudden burst of tears followed this violent paroxysm; and the Cannon circle, drawing round their chief with becoming uneasiness, were soon made *au fait* to the full extent of the fresh indignities offered their name and fame.

What was to be done? To remain at Wick-Hall after such an insult would have been the height of degradation; to keep possession of it at the expense of conscience by voting for Mr. Eelback, an abnegation of a freeman's independence. All was doubt; and the thoughts of the Cannon family were, to use the words of Otway,

> " Like birds, that, frighted from their rest,
> Around the place where all was hush'd before,
> Flutter, and hardly flutter, and hardly settle anywhere,"

when another nerve-upsetting rapping at the hall once more interrupted the busy circle. Mr. and Mrs. Grits were announced.

"Who is Mr. Grits?" exclaimed Mrs. Cannon.

The question was answered by Mrs. Grits in person; and in her, to her utter horror, Mrs. Cannon recognised the daughter of Mr. Suet, a carcase butcher, who had lived near them when Mr. C. was in the tallow line.

To see her at Muckford appeared to Mrs. Cannon as wonderful as though she had beheld the spirits of all the bullocks Mr. Suet had ever slaughtered scampering about Smithfield. The ex-Miss Suet explained matters. She had married Mr. Grits, a grocer, who had failed thrice, once a bankrupt, and twice an insolvent, by which means he had realised a tolerable independence; yet, for appearance sake, he preferred improving his condition with the means of others, and had travelled abroad as a *maître d'hôtel*, with the Wittingtons.

At another time,—nay, a few hours before their visit,—the Grits would not have been received; now, in the distressed state of the family, they were welcomed with cordiality.

But the mind sickens at the object of their visit,—to advise Mr. Cannon to accede to his lordship's proposals, and not irritate a powerful enemy by an idle show of independence!!—But to think of a reconciliation brought about by a butcher's daughter and a butler!— No, no, thrice no;—the breach was immeasurably widened. Mr. Cannon stuttered and stammered all the insults that had been heaped upon him. Mrs. Grits plainly saw that no pacification could be expected; and, although she expressed the utmost regret, she was inwardly delighted, as it did not exactly suit her views that she should be known to be a butcher's daughter. She, therefore, seizing both Mrs. Cannon's trembling hands in the kindest manner, attempted to console and advise her.

"I can readily imagine, my dear friend, how much this overbearing conduct of my lord should have annoyed you. Oh! he is as proud as Lucifer when he goes to open his parliament! It is such men, my dear, that make me abhor this horrible England."

"Ay, horrible England!" repeated Mr. Cannon with ferocity.

"I have lived too long in that dear delicious France, that *belle France*, to exist, or rather vegetate, in this abominable country."

This word, "*France*," acted like a magic spell; it seemed a password, a *Shibboleth*, an *open sesame* to regions of delight.

" Ay, France is the country ! only ask Mr. Grits."

" Oh, there's nothing like it !" responded Mr. Grits, a jolly red-faced fellow, with an enormous abdomen, rendered more *salient* by a flapped white waistcoat.

" And such society, oh ! such an opening for young people, oh ! No one asks who and what you are, only have the caraways ! Lord bless me ! there was Mrs. Triplet, the pawnbroker of Islington's wife, married her daughter Peg to a French count ; and Mr. Rumstuff, the tailor in the Minories, married his daughter to a general,—ay, a real general ; and then, such living, and such society, and such amuse--ments ! *Gardes du corps* with such nice moustaches, and *pâtés de truffes*, and *omelettes soufflées*, and *bals champêtres* at Tivoli, and *glasses* at Tortoni's, and *poulets à la crapaudine*, and *salmis de lièvre*, and then, the masked-balls at the opera, oh ! and *des œufs à la neige*, and *des œufs au miroir !* How many ways have the French of cooking eggs, Mr. G. ?"

" Three hundred and forty-three, Mrs. G."

" Only think of that ! I make Mr. G. live upon eggs *à la coque, à la tripe.* And then meat at fourpence per pound !"

" Fivepence halfpenny for prime joints, if you please, Mrs. G." add-ed Mr. G.

" And such poultry ! such capons ! You have no capons in Eng-land, my dear. Bless us, they don't know what's what ! and so many delicious ways of cooking them, *chapon à la barbare, chapon à la Veluti, chapon au parfait amour ;* and then, the Hussars, and the Lancers, and the horse and foot dragoons. Oh ! women there may do whatever they like ! and girls may string lovers like a *brochette of ortolans !*"

In short, Mrs. Grits gave such a flattering account of France, its pleasures, its cookery, and its economy, that it was decided that to France the family should go. Mr. Cannon said he was too old to learn to *parlez-vous*, but the ladies procured grammars and dic-tionaries, to brush up their boarding-school education ; and in ten days the whole family were packed up in three travelling carriages, and set out for Dover ; their only domestics, Sam Surly, a Yorkshire coachman, and Sukey Simper, a Kentish maid, whom we shall again find on the road.

Such is the ingratitude of mankind that all Muckford was de-lighted with their departure. " *Hurrah ! All the Cannons are gone off !*" exclaimed Mr. Sniffnettle.

Lady Tabby Catson died soon after, leaving a handsome legacy to Mr. Hiccup, the surgeon. Muzzle got a living, and resided at Wick-Hall, the name of which he changed into *Cushion-Lodge*, al-luding, no doubt, to the *otium* he enjoyed. Sniffnettle was made under-steward of Lord Wittington's estate ; and Mr. Grits opened an inn at the sign of the *Mitre*, opposite *Cushion-Lodge*, and, as the Rev. Mr. Muzzle had been appointed tutor to the youngest of the honour-able Catsons, whenever he saw the sign bearing the episcopal diadem swinging in the wind, despite all humility, a warrantable ambition would often lead him to an association of ideas in which a crosier acted as a favourite crotchet ; nay, in his sleep sometimes Queen Mab would tickle his nose until he dreamt of bishopricks, *congés d'élire*, and visitation dinners, and then he would suddenly awake and terrify Mrs. Muzzle, roaring out " Nolo Episcopari !"

A CHAPTER ON LAUGHING.

"And Laughter holding both his sides."—MILTON.

IF you were to ask a learned physician to explain to you the peculiar sensation termed laughter, it is more than likely he would astonish you with an amazing profundity of erudition, ending in the sage conclusion that he knows nothing more about the matter than that it is a very natural emotion of the senses, generally originating with a good joke, and not unfrequently terminating in a fit of indigestion. If he happened to be (as there are many) a priggish quack, it is not unlikely he would add as a sequel, that it was a most injurious and unmannerly indulgence, particularly favouring a determination of blood to the head, and decidedly calculated to injure the fine nerves of the facial organ! If, on the contrary, he should be a good, honest follower of Galen, he would not fail to pronounce it the most fearful enemy to his profession, as being altogether incompatible with physic and the blues, and, by way of illustration, he might go so far as to read a chapter of Tom Hood's best, in order to prove the strength of his position.

Laughter—good, hearty, cheerful-hearted laughter—is the echo of a happy spirit, the attribute of a cloudless mind. Life without it were without hope, for it is the exuberance of hope. It is an emotion possessed by man alone,—the happy light that relieves the dark picture of life.

We laugh most, when we are young; the thoughts are then free and unfettered, there is nothing to bind their fierce impulse, and we sport with the passions with the bold daring of ignorance. Smiles and tears, it has been observed, follow each other like gloom and sunshine; so the childish note of mirth treads on the heels of sorrow. It was but yesterday we noticed a little urchin writhing apparently in the agony of anguish; he had been punished for some trivial delinquency, and his little spirit resented it most gloriously. How the young dog roared! His little chest heaved up and down; and every blue vein on his pure forehead was apparent,—bursting with passion. Anon, a conciliatory word was addressed to him by the offended *gouvernante;* a smile passed over the boy's face; his little eyes, sparkling through a cloud of tears, were thrown upwards; a short struggle between pride and some other powerful feeling ensued; and then there burst forth such a peal of laughter, so clear, so full, so round, it would have touched the heart of a stoic!

Our natural passions and emotions become subdued, or altogether changed, as we enter the world. The laugh of the schoolboy is checked by the frown of the master. He is acquiring wisdom, and wisdom (ye Gods, how dearly bought!) is incompatible with laughter. But still, at times, when loosened from his shackles, the pining student will burst forth as in days gone by: but he has no longer the cue and action for passion he then had; the cares of the world have already mingled themselves in his cup, and his young spirit is drooping beneath their influence. The laughter of boyhood is a merry carol; but the first rich blush has already passed away. The boy enters the world, full of the gay buoyancy of youth. He looks upon those he meets as the playmates of other hours. But Experience teaches him her lessons; the natural feelings of his heart are checked; he may laugh and talk as formerly, but the spell, the dreams that cast such a halo round his young days, are dissipated and broken.

There are fifty different classes of laughers. There is your smooth-faced politic laugher, your laugher by rule. These beings are generally found within the precincts of a court, at the heels of some great man, to whose conduct they shape their passions as a model. Does his lordship say a *bon mot*, it is caught up and grinned at in every possible manner till, the powers of grimace expended, his lordship is pleased to change the subject, and strike a different chord. And it is not astonishing. Who would refuse to laugh for a pension of two hundred a year? Common gratitude demands it.

There is, then, your habitual laugher, men who laugh by habit, without rhyme or reason. They are generally stout, piggy-faced gentlemen, who eat hearty suppers, and patronise free-and-easys. They will meet you with a grin on their countenance, which, before you have said three sentences, will resolve itself into a simper, and terminate finally in a stentorian laugh. These men may truly be said to go through life laughing; but habit has blunted the finer edges of their sympathies, and their mirth is but the unmeaning effusion of a weak spirit. These personages generally go off in fits of apoplexy, brought on by excessive laughter on a full stomach!

There is, then, your discontented cynical laugher, who makes a mask of mirth to conceal the venom of his mind. It is a dead fraud that ought not to be pardoned. Speak to one of these men of happiness, virtue, &c. he meets you with a sneer, or a bottle-imp kind of chuckle; talk to him of any felicitous circumstance, he checks you with a sardonic grin, that freezes your best intentions. He is a type of the death's head the Egyptians placed at their feasts to check exuberant gaiety.

There is, then, your fashionable simperer, your laugher *à-la-mode*, your inward digester of small jokes and tittle-tattle. *He* never laughs, —it is a vulgar habit; the only wonder is, that he eats. People, he will tell you, should overcome these vulgar propensities; they are abominable. A young man of this class is generally consumptive, his lungs have no play, he is always weak and narrow-chested; he vegetates till fifty, and then goes off, overcome with a puff of *eau de rose*, or *millefleur*, he has encountered accidentally from the pocket-handkerchief of a cheesemonger's wife!

Last of all, there is your real, good, honest laugher; the man who has a heart to feel and sympathize with the joys and sorrows of others; who has gone through life superior to its follies, and has learnt to gather wisdom even from laughter. Such are the men who do honour to society, who have learnt to be temperate in prosperity, patient in adversity; and, who, having gathered experience from years, are content to drink the cup of life mingled as it is, to enjoy calmly the sweeter portion, and laugh at the bitter.

There is a strange affinity in our passions. The heart will frequently reply to the saddest intelligence by a burst of the most unruly laughter, the effigy of mirth. It seems as though the passion, like a rude torrent, were too strong to pursue its ordinary course; but, breaking forth from the narrow channel that confined it, rushed forth in one broad impetuous stream. It is the voice of anguish that has chosen a different garb; and would cheat the sympathies. But we have ourselves been demonstrating the truth of our last proposition; for we have been writing on laughter till we have grown sad. But what says the old song?

> " To-night we 'll merry, merry be,
> To-morrow we 'll be sober."

So sadness, after all, is but joy deferred.

A MUSTER CHAUNT

FOR THE MEMBERS OF THE TEMPERANCE SOCIETIES.

Wine! wine! fill up
The sparkling cup
With champagne hissing to the brim ;
For wit, and joy, and rapture, swim
In bumpers. The grape's blood is mine ;
I 'll steep my heart in it till it shine
With the warm flush
The purple blush
Of wine!

Wine! wine! the frown
Of Care we 'll drown
In deep libations to the God
Who planted first on Nysa's sod
The branches of the illustrious vine.
Bacchus, we worship at thy shrine !
In Pleasure's bowers
Swift fly the Hours
Whose wings are wash'd with wine !

Wine! wine! the brow
Is mantling now ;
The eye is flashing with " the flow
Of soul," the cheek has caught its glow ;
The lips are breathing words divine,
While wreaths of song around them twine
In glorious lays,
Chaunting the praise
Of racy wine !

Wine! wine! fill up
And quaff the cup
To lovely woman ! Drink again
To all bold festive souls who drain
The crystal bowl, and wear the sign
Of bacchanals. Hurrah ! we 're there,
Thou soul of joy !
Immortal boy !
God of immortal wine !

REMAINS OF HAJJI BABA.

CHAPTER IX.

I ALIGHTED with my friend at the caravanserai where the coach had stopped, and there he advised me to put up for the night, promising to come on the following morning to assist me in procuring a lodging.

"But first tell me," said I, "who are the two persons who were so violently opposed to each other."

"The fair man," said he, "is one of our *omrahs* or lords; the other is one of the middle ranks, who has made himself conspicuous by advocating the cause of the people. Our whole country is principally divided into two factions, holding their opinions. There is also a moderate set who do not partake of their violence, but unfortunately their voice is not sufficiently heard. But we will talk more upon these matters again," said he, and then left me

The next day he came, and without much difficulty succeeded in settling me in a lodging, where I found everything prepared to receive me, as well as if the Shah's chief tent-pitcher had preceded me to give the requisite orders. The English habits, which I had acquired when here before in the days of our embassy, returned as fast as I recognised the objects which before had been familiar to my sight, but which had been much obliterated by my absence in Persia. I again sat upon chairs instead of my heels; again I ate with knives and forks instead of my fingers; and once more I found myself called upon to walk about upon my own legs with the activity of a Franc, instead of making use of a horse to take me daily to attend the Shah's selam, or to sit at the Royal Gate in attendance upon the Grand Vizier.

I had always a memory for localities; places which I had once seen I scarcely ever forgot; thus I was at no loss to find my way about the city. Of the language I remembered enough to make myself understood; and so far I felt independent, and needed not the attendance of a *mehmander*. I thanked my friend Jan for all his kindness; and assured him, whenever I was in any difficulty, or whenever I required information upon matters relating to his country, I would not fail to call upon him.

The lodgings in which I had taken up my abode were situated in a large house that looked upon a garden inclosed by iron spikes. It was a better sort of caravanserai, greatly resorted to by people of all nations; Francs, from different parts of Frangistan, who spoke each their different language, and adapted themselves as well as they could to the manners of the English. I was visited by the landlord, a well-looking, well-spoken man, and his wife, an elderly lady, who, having come once to see, as the English frequently say, that I was comfortable, did not again trouble me by their presence. I occupied two rooms; one to sit in and receive my guests, the other to sleep in. My servant, Mahboob, slept in another room close to mine.

My first care was to walk out to take a survey of the city, in order to discover those symptoms of ruin and poverty which I had so frequently been assured were spreading over England, and marking her downfall. I soon found myself in a street, of whose magnificence I had no recollection. It seemed composed of entirely new houses. The shops, which were opened on each side, were so brilliant, and seemed to be so overflowing with merchandise and riches of all sorts, that my senses seemed to have escaped from my head as I looked on in astonishment; and ever and anon I found myself standing with my finger in my mouth, exclaiming, " Bah! bah! bah!" "Is this decay?" thought I. "Can this people be really on the brink of ruin? There must be something more in this than I can understand." The street was positively more thronged with men and women than even one of the most crowded bazars of Ispahan. I saw more carriages, more horses, more carts, and more stir, than I recollected to have seen when here before. Every one seemed busy, and bustled along, as if all depended upon their haste. Whence they were coming, whither going, who could say? Were they all thinking of ruin, or were they bent upon happiness? I was longing to stop and ask each person what had happened, so very uncommon was this state of things compared with what I had been accustomed to witness in my own country, or even in the European countries through which I had travelled. I continued to walk through this astonishing street, thinking I should never come to the end of it, when I reached a magnificent opening, where, to my still greater astonishment, I discovered an unbounded prospect of dazzling white palaces, standing amidst gardens and fields, and looking like the habitations of the blessed in the seventh heaven promised to us by the Prophet. " Can this be decay?" again I exclaimed. " These people must have a different way of going to ruin, to the one which I have been accustomed to contemplate. In my country ruin speaks for itself. At Ispahan we see whole districts of broken walls which once were houses, tottering mosques, deserted baths, and untenanted caravanserais. But here, in the short space of twelve years, here is a new creation; unbounded prosperity seems here to speak for itself; and, if this be a country of paupers, what are we to call riches?"

As I was turning my steps homewards, I was struck all at once with the conviction that I was near the spot (a spot which had never left my imagination) where, enamoured as I then was of the moonfaced Bessy, I proposed marriage to that heart-enslaver. I looked about me, and recognised the very portal where, under a mutual umbrella,—as it poured with rain,—I

told her of my love. I recollected that, not very far off, in this
same street, lived her father, and mother, and family; and I determined forthwith to seek them out, and to renew my acquaintance. I paced along the street, looking upon every house with
uplifted eyes, in the hope of discovering some sign by which I
might recognise it; but the buildings were all so hopelessly
alike that I began to despair of hitting upon the right knocker.
It came to my mind that a lion's head held the knocker, because
I had compared it in former days to the face of the mamma Hogg
herself; but, upon inspecting the knockers, they all had lions'
heads. What was to be done? "I will try what Fate will
do for me," thought I. So, judging that I was somewhere near
the spot, I boldly walked up to a door, and gave a knock
which, I remembered to have been told, indicated a man of
consequence, and, as it turned out, I was not mistaken. The
door was opened, not by a well-dressed servant, as it used to be,
but by an old woman, who was so surprised at seeing my
strange figure that she would have shut it in my face had I not
quickly exclaimed,

"Is Mr. Hogg at home?"

"Mr. Hogg!" she exclaimed, in an astonished voice. "Mr.
Hogg has been dead ever so long. Can't you see by the hatch-
ment?" Upon which she pointed to a painting fixed upon the
outside of the house, which explained to me, what I had never
known before, that, when an Englishman dies, it is the custom
to make a painting, as I supposed, explanatory of the history of
his life; for, afterwards, in contemplating the said performance,
I remarked a boar's head at the top, whilst certain little swine
seemed to be scattered about, evidently indicating the name and
origin of the family.

"But Mrs. Hogg is not dead too?" said I; "where is she,
and Mrs. Figsby?"

"La! sir; you're the Persian prince, I declare," said the
old woman, "of whom we all talk so much about." Upon
which, she immediately undertook to give me a history of the
family since I had left England. The father Hogg, it seems,
had died not many months ago of apoplexy; his widow was
living in a neighbouring street, in a small house, with her eldest
daughter, who was still unmarried. Mrs. Figsby (alas! my
own Bessy!) occupied a handsome house nearly opposite to
the one at the door of which I now stood, and which the old
woman pointed out to me; the youngest daughter had married,
and lived in the country.

Leaving the old woman, I immediately crossed the street,
and knocked at the Figsby gate, not without a certain palpita-
tion of the heart. It was opened by a brilliantly-dressed servant
in a gaudy *kalaat*, with a thick paste of white dust upon his
head, and a bunch of ropes as thick as tent-ropes at his shoulder. Two others stood in the hall.

"Is Mrs. Figsby at home, by the blessing of the Prophet?" said I.

He said "Yes," with hesitation, eyeing me well from head to foot; and, delivering me over to the keeping of another man without a *kalaat*, I was walked up stairs. When we came to the head of the stairs, he stopped, and asked,

"Who shall I say?"

"Mirza Hajji Baba," I answered, recollecting well the whole ceremonial.

Upon which he opened the door, and exclaimed aloud, as well as I could understand, "Mister Hatchababy,"—or some such name.

"Mister who?" exclaimed a female within, whom, when I entered, I immediately recognised to be my former love, the moon-faced Bessy. But, oh! how different from the lovely Bessy I had known her! Instead of that light cypress-waisted figure which had charmed me so much, she was now grown into a woman fat enough to be a Turk's wife. Her cheeks were rounded into coarse cushions, behind which reposed her almost secluded eyes. The beautiful throat of former days was scolloped into graduated ridges; and those arms, which formerly were lovely by themselves, were now so bound over with broad belts of golden bracelets, that they looked like the well-fitted hoops of a wine-cask. The hair, which flowed in ringlets over her brow and down her cheeks, was now confined to two lumps of curls, which were placed in a dense cluster on either side of her forehead; and her whole person, which formerly gave her the appearance of a Peri, now exhibited a surface agreeable only to the silk-mercer and the milliner who were called upon to clothe it.

A faint blush threw itself out over her forehead when she perceived me, and she immediately came forward with her hand extended, and welcomed me back to her country with great sincerity. She expressed all sorts of surprises at seeing me, particularly as I had never been announced in the public newspapers; assured me that Mr. Figsby, who was not at home, would be delighted to see me; sent for her children, and exhibited a vast number to me of all sizes, boys and girls; and repeated to me what I had just heard from the old woman, the circumstances in which her family were placed.

I expressed my satisfaction at seeing her so richly circumstanced in the world, and that she should have made a marriage with a man who seemed to be a favourite of Fortune, and whose luck appeared to be ever on the rise. At this she sighed, and her features assumed a saddened expression.

"'Twas true," she said, "that Figsby could not complain, and that, as long as it lasted, it was all very well. But, prince!" she exclaimed, "this is not the country you once knew it to be! Things are sadly altered! The people have got a reform, 'tis true; and Figsby is rejoiced, and hopes to be returned for Marylebone, and, who knows whether he may not sit in the cabinet one of these days? But the aristocracy they won't be quiet, do what you will, and they will drive us on to a revolution at last, and oblige us to put them down, and divide all their property amongst us; and, you know, that will be sad work, particularly if Figsby should be made a lord before it takes place."

All this was new language to me, and brought to my mind the conversation which I had heard in the coach. "What news is this?" thought I, "that women should thus talk the language of viziers, and mix themselves in the business of state!"

"I thought that Figsby Sahib was a grocer," said I, to his much-altered wife.

"A grocer, indeed!" said she, with considerable angry emphasis. "He is a West-India merchant! A grocer, indeed!"

"How long is it," said I, "since he has left his private business for public life?"

"Don't you know," said she, "the changes which have taken place since you were here last? Rotten boroughs and nomination boroughs have been abolished. Schedule A. and schedule B. have been all the fashion of late; we talk of nothing else; and there are to be members for Marylebone, and Figsby is canvassing as hard as he can; and I am sure, prince, if you can help him with a vote, you will."

"A vote!" said I, "what does that mean?"

"It means," she answered, with some hesitation, "that you wish Figsby may become a member of parliament, and sit in the house, and make speeches, and give franks, and all that."

"If it is only to wish your husband may be all you desire," said I, "in the name of the Imams you shall have my vote, and welcome."

"That's right!" said Bessy; "that's right! that's being an old friend in truth. I knew that you would be on the right side, and stick up for the people."

"But who is the people? is he a new Shah, or what?"

"Oh, the people!" said she; "the people! they are the sovereign people! They are all the men and women you see walking about; they want their rights—their rights—that's all!"

"All the men and women walking about!" exclaimed I. "What news is this? They have got a king already. What do they want more?"

"They have, 'tis true," said she; "but what is that without their rights?"

"I don't know what you mean about their rights," said I; "but we have a Shah, and I know that if any Persian wanted anything more, and talked about his rights, all that he would get for his pains would be the *felek*—a good bastinado on the soles of his feet; that's what he would get."

"Oh, la!" said Mrs. Figsby, "that may do for Persians, but

it won't do for Englishmen. They must be fairly represented; and, if such men as Figsby are not elected, it is a great shame, and the country will go to rack and ruin.

At this stage of our conversation a knocking at the door was heard, and soon after entered the moonfaced Bessy's husband. I immediately recognised my former rival, but great changes had taken place in his person also. In former days he was happy to be allowed to take the lowermost place in the *mejlis* or assembly; now he walked in with an air of consequence and protection. He came into the room with a noise and bustle; his boots creaked most independently; he was all over chains; and seemed strangled from the tightness of his clothes. He soon got over his surprise at seeing me; and, before he had done shaking my hand, he exclaimed,

"All is going as it ought to be! I have been at the meeting. I made such a speech, Bessy, you would have been quite charmed. There is no doubt of my coming in. We shall beat the Tories hollow."

"That is charming!" said his overjoyed wife. "Then you will be an M. P., and who knows what else! And here is the prince," said she, "who is ready to give you his vote."

"That's right!" said the entranced grocer. "That's very kind of him! But stop! let me see; are you a ten-pound householder? is your name stuck up against the church-door? and have you paid your shilling?"

"*Allah! Allah!*" I exclaimed. "What do I know of all this? I am nothing but a Persian Mirza. I am ignorant of your ten-pounds, your church-doors, and your shillings. Do leave off this child's play, and let us talk of other things."

"Other things!" cried one.

"Child's play!" exclaimed the other.

"It is the only thing now thought of," said the man.

"It is of the greatest consequence to the state, and to Marylebone, that Figsby should be elected!" vociferated the lady.

I found that I had put my unlucky leg foremost on this occasion, and so I thought of making my retreat; but, before I did so, after having observed a look of recognition between husband and wife, Mr. Figsby stept up to me, and said,

"We shall have a few of my political friends to dine with me in a few days; I hope, prince, that we may be honoured with your company?"

I said, "*Inshallah!* please Allah!" and then returned to my home.

CHAPTER X.

I RETURNED to my lodging full of thought. What with the conversations I had heard in the coach, what with the strange sayings of Mrs. Figsby and her husband, I began to have my eyes a little more opened than they were before. I considered that, notwithstanding the flourishing exterior of things, and the general appearances of prosperity which had struck my eyes, there might be truth in the rumours which had been so current in Persia, that England was declining fast in greatness, and was on the brink of ruin. I had occasionally seen madmen in my own country, from whose brain all sense had fled when their minds were bent upon a particular subject, but who still upon others were rational, and acted like sane men. " May not that be the case here?" thought I ; "and, if all the nation has run mad by one common consent upon this desire of change, they may have sapped the foundation of their real happiness and prosperity, although they still build fine houses and exhibit resplendent shops."

I determined, in conformity to my instructions from the asylum of the universe, to present my letters to the English vizier ; to have a conversation with him, and then to settle whether I should deliver the fortunate letter, of which I was the bearer, from the king of kings to the King of England. Accordingly, I proceeded to a certain dark and obscure street, where, on former occasions, I recollected the sovereign had ordered his vizier to receive the ambassadors and ministers of foreign powers, and there to transact their business, and, sure enough, I found things just as I had left them ; thus far there had been no reform. I found no parade of guards, executioners, officers, or heralds ; but one little man seated in a great leather chair, and through his interference I was introduced into a dark room, without a single word of welcome being said, not even " Good morning," and " Fine day ;" and there I was left until the vizier could speak to me.

I waited what appeared to me a long time,—quite long enough to consider, if this was an English palace, what must be an English prison ! At length another infidel invited me to follow him, and, after having been paraded through a few rooms, I found myself in the presence of one whom I first took for the vizier, but who I soon found was only his deputy. He was very kind and civil, and asked my business in courteous language ; upon which I told him that I was just arrived from the foot of the Persian throne, and was the bearer of a letter to the English vizier, as well as to his royal master. He seemed pleased at this information ; but he asked me a question which made the wind fly out of my head.

" Pray, sir," said he, "do you bring us any letter from our minister in Persia ? I do not think that we have been apprised of your mission."

Upon this I stroked down my beard, and, searching in the depths of my wit for a ready answer, I answered that I was despatched from the imperial stirrup as a courier, and not as a minister. " I have no letter but this ;" upon which I drew from my breast the grand vizier's letter, which I delivered into his hand. He was at a loss whilst he unrolled it, for he evidently did not know the top from the bottom; and all communication must have ceased between us, had I not possessed the translation, which I had prudently caused to be made at Tabriz by one of my own countrymen who had received his education in England.

This, the vizier's deputy read over very attentively; and, as he read, I observed certain smiles break out on his features, from which I augured favourably. He then desired me to wait, whilst he took up the papers, and left the room to lay them before his chief, saying not a word of his own opinion upon their contents.

He soon returned, and, asking me to follow, he led the way into an adjacent room, where I found the English vizier in person. The appearance and manners of this personage were full of charm; and, although a man in his high office had usually the power of awing me into fear and diffidence of myself, still I felt no other sensations than what were agreeable when he addressed me.

"I have been reading strange things in this letter," said the vizier. "I am informed that my country is on the brink of ruin, and that his majesty the Shah, apprehending disaster might accrue to my own sovereign, has been pleased to offer him an asylum at his gate."

"That is, in truth, the object of my mission," said I. "You have spoken right."

"But how," said the vizier, "has this information travelled to Persia? It is new to me, as it is, I believe, to every member of his majesty's government."

"How do I know?" I answered, with some little confusion; for, in truth, I began to feel that I had come upon a fool's errand, and was about to swallow much abomination. "Our news in Persia is not printed every day upon paper as it is here, but comes to us as it may please the will of Allah! The asylum of the universe, upon whom be blessings! who knows all, and does all for the good of his subjects, was convinced of the fact; the same was confirmed by all strangers arriving at his imperial gate; and it was announced by the English minister himself that a great change was about to take place in his country; that old counsels, which had been followed since the recollection of the most ancient greybeards of the country, were about to be abolished and replaced by new; and that a certain thing, called People, whether man or beast we never could discover, was on the point of obtaining supremacy, and despoiling your reverend monarch, for whom the king of kings entertains the highest friendship, of his ancient hereditary throne."

"Your news," observed the vizier, "was partly right, and partly false. That a change has taken place in the government of this country," said he, "is true; and our minister's words are confirmed. A change has taken place; but change does not argue total destruction."

Recollecting that I was here at the fountain-head of information, and that the vizier's words were words to be repeated to the king of kings, I inquired, "As I am less than the least, may it please you to inform your slave what is this change?"

"The principal change has been in giving the people a better means than they had before of making their wishes known through their representatives. You know, of course," said he, " what our ' parliament' means ?"

"Yes," said I. "I believe I am right in saying that a representative means a man who is supposed to be a concentrated essence of the thousands and tens of thousands of those who choose him; and that he cries out 'black' or 'white' as the fit seizes him. A collection of such men means a parliament."

"You have a tolerable notion of what I mean," said the vizier, smiling. "Now, certain of these representatives could only cry out 'black' or 'white' as it choosed to please, not themselves, but certain khans or omrahs of our country, who sent them instead of the people. That is the principal change we have made."

"I understand—I understand!" I exclaimed, as if a new light had opened upon me. "The omrahs, therefore, are displeased, and cry out 'Ruin !' and the people are overjoyed, and cry out, 'We are sovereigns ;' and both are wrong."

The vizier seemed greatly amused with my great discovery, and then entered into certain long explanations concerning the various topics which I had heard discussed between the smooth and rough infidels whom I had met in the coach, and which only tended to obscure the great conclusion to which I had come by the light of my own wit. I allowed him to talk, and he seemed pleased to do so, as if he were defending himself from imputations, and of which, in truth, I understood not one word. However, he seemed amazingly struck, when, in rising to go, I said,

"It is plain, then, that some great mistake has been committed somewhere ; otherwise, why should this great country be so terribly torn from one end of it to the other by animosities, which seem to have led it to the brink of anarchy ?"

"No great change," said he, "can take place without producing a great shock of interests and opinions, and consequently animosities."

"And that is just what a good and wise government ought to avoid," said I. " Our Shah is called *Zil Allah*, the Shadow of the Almighty ; and, according to the saying of one of our ancient sages, the acts of a king ought to follow the same course perceivable in the dispensations of Providence, and in the laws by which God, the great and good, directs the fates of his creatures.

All changes in government ought to be as gradual as changes in the seasons. If a great change takes place without a previous preparation of the people's minds, and an almost imperceptible one in their habits, of course the sudden transition will produce a shock so violent, that the mischief may perhaps be without remedy. If, during the heats of summer, the Almighty were to give this globe a sudden accelerated turn, and throw us at once into the snows of winter, the effects might almost produce sudden death upon one half of his creatures; but he allows the intervening autumn gradually to blend the two extremes, and thus produces a healthy action in the operations of nature."

He did not seem so much struck by the wisdom of this speech as I was, and I was about leaving him, when I recollected the letter with which I was charged from the *Shah-en-Shah*, the king of kings, and asked when I should deliver it. He paused a little in thought, and then said,

"Perhaps it may be as well that we hear something from our minister in Persia before you deliver your letter." Upon which, seeing that my countenance was turned upside down, he said, with great kindness of manner, "There will be no harm done if you deliver it immediately. The King of England is ready to receive the application of every one, from the peasant in the field to the greatest potentate."

MY UNCLE.

A FRAGMENT.

> He kept a store,
> A place of refuge to which all might fly
> In the dark hour of bleak adversity,
> When sunshine friends, like summer birds, had flown.
> He was misfortune's shield,—a goodly man!
> In fact, so kind a soul could scarce be found;
> For he would lend to any graceless wight
> A sum of money, and would never ask
> His bond or bill, or even say " Be sure
> To pay me this again next week, or so."
> *He never craved a debtor in his life!*
>   *   *   *   *   *   *
>
> Around his house, in many a goodly pile,
> All sorts of wares were ranged in order nice,
> Shoes, hats, great-coats, and gowns, with many pairs
> Of certain parts of dress (not pantaloons),
> Which, it is said, some married females wear.
>   Above his door
> Invitingly were hung three golden balls,
> As if to say, " Who pennyless would go ?"
> Here is a banking-house, whence every man
> Who has an article to leave behind,
> May draw for cash, nor fear his cheque unpaid.
>
> Ah me! full many an ungrateful wight
> In this same store, without a sigh or tear,
> Parted his *bosom friend*, altho' he knew
> That friend must dwell among the *unredeemed*.

WHY THE WIND BLOWS ROUND ST. PAUL'S.

BY JOYCE JOCUND.

WHOEVER has walked round St. Paul's church-yard must have had good evidence of the wind being always boisterous there, on the most balmy day of spring, in summer's more sultry hour, in autumn's bracing time, or in winter's chilling air; all tides and every season bear strong testimony that the wind is ever blowing there, not in those gentle gales that love to play and wanton round other edifices, but in such rude, boisterous burstings, that the traveller is fain to look to his footing, and put up with a *blow* which is neither to be parried nor returned. I cannot fix the precise date, but it was during the last century, that a bit of a breeze was kicked up in the higher circles among the Winds; and, from the strife that ensued, more serious consequences seemed to threaten than were at first apprehended. Whether the East was intent on going westward, or the North determined on veering to the south, is of trifling import. From words the disputants nearly came to blows, and the weathercocks were sadly put to their shifts during all the changes that occurred: those who consulted them found how little attention was paid to the cardinal points, which from time immemorial had been considered their cardinal virtues; in short, it was impossible to tell which way the wind lay. Nothing was to be heard among them but wranglings, wailings, and contentions.

"As for you," roared old Boreas, addressing a mild-looking individual personifying the South wind, "a poor, soft, effeminate creature, only fit to breathe o'er a bed of violets, what, in the name of all that's trifling, can you possibly presume to know?"

"I may not be so bluff as you, nor so excellent a bully," replied the other; "yet I flatter myself that I am equally esteemed by mankind."

"Doubtless! by old maids, invalids, and anglers."

"And I prefer their welcome to the maledictions so lavishly heaped upon you, by the aged, the gouty, and the suffering," was the rejoinder.

"Fie! fie!" lisped the West wind, an exquisite of the most exclusive order. "If you persist, I shall positively arraign you at the bar of good breeding and fashion."

"Which I believe is not situated on *my* side Temple-bar," exclaimed the East, in a tone that reminded one of the equinox.

"Your intimacy with the bar is confined to the Old Bailey," chirruped his opponent, who commenced,

> "Cease rude Boreas, blustering railer:
> List ye."

At this personal attack the North looked particularly black, and the East BLEW with increased violence.

"How the puppy squalls!" said the latter, in reference to the singing.

" Rather more melodious than your howling," replied the tormentor ; for the West wind is occasionally pretty sharp when its powers are exerted.

With this slight specimen you may suppose that the Winds began to get very high ; ill-natured replies followed angry remarks ; while the East wind distributed his usual cutting retorts with unsparing profusion. In short, the only subject on which they appeared agreed was to perform " The Storm," *ad libitum*, with hail and rain accompaniments. There is an old adage, " as busy as the Devil in a high wind :" how busy that may be, let others determine ; but truly his Satanic Majesty was never more occupied than on this memorable occasion, for he seemed to have possessed the contending parties with an implacable spirit of opposition, and contrived to divide his influence so impartially that each played the very devil with the other. When the uproar had sufficiently subsided to permit observation, it was clearly apparent that the North, as was his wont, rather sided with the East, and the South as plainly inclined to the West ; so, after amusing himself with their differences, the crafty instigator of the feud proposed that the affair should be permitted to blow over, and, by way of cooling themselves, that the four Winds should accompany him on a stroll through London streets, towards the City ; where he promised them plenty of adventures, with many sights worthy their attention. After a few more gusts of passion exhibited by the North and East, venting their spite upon their more peaceful opponents, the party set forth on their ramble, with somethinglike outward decency of demeanour, although opposition and dissatisfaction were rankling in their hearts. Their cicerone pointed to a plot of ground in Hyde Park.

" Here," said he, " will be erected an imperishable monument to that greatest of modern heroes, the victor of a hundred fights. In every land shall his matchless deeds be known, and his fame proclaimed by——"

" The four Winds !" exclaimed they all.

" Yonder will be his town-residence," resumed their guide, " the scarcely less than princely mansion of the nation's idol ; yet, so evanescent is popularity, and so great is the distinction between civil matters and military, that coming years will display his windows barricaded against the assaults of that people whose opinions are as changeable as the——"

" What?" said his hearers in a breath, ready to take offence should he indulge in any *personal* allusion.

" As changeable as—as the weather."

" Oh !" exclaimed the East, with a significant whistle, that sounded very like the blast of a war-trumpet.

They walked some distance without further remark, until reaching Pall-Mall.

" This," said the Devil, directing their attention to a range of buildings on the right, " this will ere long disappear. Of yon regal habitation, the scene of revelry and delight, not a vestige will remain ; vast local improvements will be completed, magnificent residences erected ; and here a lofty column shall be raised, on whose ' tall pillar, pointing to the skies,' will be placed the statue of a princely commander——"

"Who will doubtless be *highly indebted* to the people," observed the North, in his most unpleasant manner.

" And what may be that heavy-looking temple opposite?" inquired the East, pointing to the Opera-house.

" That is celebrated as the resort of beauty, rank, wealth, and fashion."

Here the West wind nodded his assent, as if perfectly cognisant of affairs so particularly appertaining to *his* quarter of the metropolis.

" Where the aristocracy of this kingdom assemble to lavish their wealth and favours on foreign *artistes*, as they are called, while native industry and talent are neglected and unrequited. But my sentimentality outruns my prudence ; *I* patronise the Opera, notwithstanding," said the Devil.

" And I," said the West.

Continuing their perambulation, they reached the present site of Waterloo-bridge.

" A splendid structure," observed their conductor, " will here span that mighty stream, on whose waves float a thousand argosies freighted with riches from every distant land. Speculation will soon furnish means sufficient for the enterprise, and——"

" The profits?" inquired old Boreas, too far *north* to lose sight of the main chance.

" Will be shared among the subscribers."

" By what rule?"

" *Short* division," was the answer.

" This building on the right is Somerset House, where the Royal Academy holds its annual exhibition of British artists, at which persons pay a shilling to view their own portraits that have cost most exorbitant sums, if painted by popular professors of the art."

" A noble institution," said the South, in simplicity of soul, " and most encouraging to rising talent."

" Very," was the devilish dry reply.

" And where young exhibitors have fine opportunities afforded them to profit by the experience, skill, and fostering care of their superiors."

" Exactly," said the Devil, with a malicious smile. " In the arrangement and distribution of the pictures the committee show an intimate knowledge of ' light and shade,' which is particularly instructive to others. They appropriate all the ' light ' to their own pictures, and the ' shade ' to their neighbours'. Yonder dirty-looking gate is Temple-bar, where in the olden time traitors' heads stood in goodly row, as plentiful as the portraits in the Exhibition, only that the ' bodies' never came to own them. But"—and here the Devil sighed like a furnace—" innovation and improvement have destroyed all venerable customs."

So, venting his regrets, they journeyed down Fleet-street, when the attention of the gentle South was attracted to the large gloomy edifice which is so prominent in that locality.

" Ah!" said their guide, " that is the Fleet."

" Where?" said the East, springing up at the idea of stiff breezes and swelling sails ; " I see no ships."

" Yet there is no lack of *craft*, I promise you," replied the Devil. " One of the considerate laws of this realm declares that a debtor shall pay in person what he is deficient in pocket : a sapient method to man his Majesty's *fleet*, and as pretty a piece of legislation as *I* would propose."

Turning from the prison and its solid-looking brickwork, the first glimpse of St. Paul's met their astonished gaze. The strangers were enraptured at that mighty monument of man's power and perseverance. After surveying the exterior, the Winds expressed an eagerness to view the inside of the cathedral ; but their importunities were negatived by their companion, who intimated in strong terms his repugnance to such a proposition. "Besides," he observed, "which of you will pay the twopences demanded for admission? By-the-bye, do me the favour to wait here a few moments. Some most intimate and particular friends are now assembled at the Chapter Coffeehouse."

"Do not let us detain you unwillingly," growled the North.

"We are much indebted for your care and guidance," murmured the South.

"I feel more at home in my own quarter of the town," said the East; "let me prove no hindrance."

"But promise me to remain,—rely upon my speedy return," said the Devil.

"Agreed!" roared the North, who seemed to think the spot a good place to make himself heard.

"Then I depend upon your awaiting my coming. For the present, farewell!"

"*Au revoir!*" lisped the West, as the arch deceiver disappeared down one of the narrow avenues which abound in that locality.

Well, the poor Winds went whistling up and down, looking at the shops, watching the crowd, and amusing themselves as best they could under such disagreeable circumstances. They made several rounds of the church, the hands of the clock made several rounds of the dial, yet the absent one appeared not; and their patience was nearly exhausted, when the South modestly offered to sing them a song, if indeed such feeble powers could lighten the time and lessen their suspense, and then breathed the following words to a soft plaintive *air :*

SONG OF THE SOUTH.

I.

I love to roam where the spice-groves send
   Their mingled sweets o'er the fragrant air,
Where orange-blossoms their bright buds lend
   To weave a wreath for the blushing fair ;
And I waft each shining tress aside
That shades the brow of the blooming bride.

II.

I love to roam at the sunset hour,
   To breathe farewell to the parting day,
And kiss the dew from each star-lit flower,
   That ever weeps as light fades away.
Oh! I woo them all with my softest sighs,
And gently whisper,—that Love never dies !

"Enough! enough!" grumbled the East; "I cannot waste my time in such frivolities.   Where is the fellow who brought us here?"

"Ay!" said the North, "does he fancy we have nothing better to occupy us than attending his pleasure, dancing attendance?"

And thereat the watchers became mighty impatient.   At length the North declared that he had business of great importance that night upon the coast.

"What fools we were to pledge ourselves!   My engagements are imperative,—go I must!" roared he with vehemence.

"And I," added the East, with similar violence.

"I have made an appointment in Bond-street," muttered the West, mentioning the fashionable lounge of that period; "moreover, the Countess of B—— expects me at her party.   I am irrevocably bound to the countess, and would not disappoint the sweet creature for worlds."

"I cannot remain alone in this gloomy place," sighed the South.

"Listen!" said the North, puffing himself up to an unusual pomposity, even for him; "I have a plan to remedy the dilemma.   I go,— that is settled.   You three can easily find an excuse for my absence."

"And mine," cried the East.   "Two are very good company,— three damp conversation."

"As I have nothing particular to communicate, I shall follow your example," said the West, looking significantly at the East.

"I was assured the puppy would oppose me," grunted the latter; "'tis his constant practice."

Thus affairs appeared in tolerable train for a repetition of the former bickering, when it was at last decided, but not without much turbulent and acrimonious feeling, that each should wait in turn, and give timely notice to the others of the truant's arrival; and with this understanding they separated, leaving one on guard.   It is hardly necessary to state that the Devil never reappeared.   He always leaves his votaries in the lurch; and on this occasion his boon companions at the Chapter gave him such good cheer, that he forgot the poor winds, who have ever since been alternately looking, but in vain, for his arrival.   To their honour be it told, that they each and every one performed his promise of remaining for a stated period, neither excepting the boisterous North, the cutting East, the fashionable West, nor the gentle South.   Their various watchings may be easily distinguished by their respective degrees of violence in the neighbourhood; and to this very hour is one of them to be heard either roaring, blowing, moaning, or sighing for their emancipation.   And this accounts for the fact of their constant presence, and shows why "THE WIND BLOWS ROUND ST. PAUL'S."

The tradition inculcates a moral.   Had the four Winds pursued the "path of duty," this trial had been spared them; but they listened to the tempter. Let all profit by their example: Men, as well as Winds, should " KEEP WITHIN COMPASS."

RATHER HARD TO TAKE.

An artist—'tis not fair to tell his name;
   But one whom Fortune, in her freakish tricks,
   Saluted with less smiles than kicks,
More to the painter's honour, and her shame,—
Was one day deep engaged on his *chef d'œuvre*,
(A painting worthy of the Louvre,)
Dives and Lazarus the theme,—
The subject was his earliest boyish dream!
And, with an eye to colour, breadth, and tone,
   He painted, skilfully as he was able,
   The good things on the rich man's table,—
Wishing they were, no doubt, upon his own;
When suddenly his hostess—best of creatures!—
Made visible her features,
And to this world our artist did awaken:
   "A gentleman," she said, "from the next street,
   Had sent a special message in a heat,
Wanting a likeness taken."
The artist, with a calmness oft the effect
Of tidings which we don't expect,
Wip'd all his brushes carefully and clean,
Button'd his coat—a coat which once had been,—
Put on his hat, and with uncommon stress
On the address,
Went forth, revolving in his nob
How his kind hostess, when he'd got the job,—
Even before they paid him for his skill,—
Would let him add a little to the bill.

He found a family of six or seven,
   All grown-up people, seated in a row;
There might be seen upon each face a leaven
   Of recent, and of decent woe,
But that the artist, whose chief cares
Were fix'd upon his own affairs,
Gazed, with a business eye, to be acquainted
Which of the seven wanted to be painted.

But a young lady soon our artist greeted,
Saying, in words of gentlest music, "Ah!—
Pray, Mr. Thingo'me, be seated,—
We want a likeness of our grandpapa."

Such chances Fortune seldom deigns to bring:
The very thing!
How he should like
To emulate Vandyke!
Or, rather—still more glorious ambition—
To paint the head like Titian,
A fine old head, with silver sprinkled:
A face all seam'd and wrinkled:—
The painter's heart 'gan inwardly rejoice;
   But, as he pondered on that "fine old head,"
Another utter'd, in a mournful voice,
   "But, sir, he's dead!"

The artist was perplex'd—the case was alter'd :
  Distrust, stirr'd up by doubt, his bosom warps ;
"God bless my soul!" he falter'd ;
  "But, surely, you can let me see the corpse ?
An artist but requires a hint :
There are the features—give the cheeks a tint—
Paint in the eyes—and, though the task 's a hard 'un,
  You 'll find the thing, I 'll swear,
As like as he can,—no, I beg your pardon,—
  As like as he *could* stare !"

"Alas ! alas !" the eldest sister sigh'd,
And then she sobb'd and cried,
So that 'twas long ere she again could speak,—
"We buried him last week !"

The painter heaved a groan : "But, surely, madam,
  You have a likeness of the dear deceased ;
  Some youthful face, whose age might be increased ?"
"No, no,—we haven't, sir, no more than Adam ;
  Not in the least !"

This was the strangest thing that e'er occurr'd ;—
  "You 'll pardon me," the baffled painter cried ;
"But, really, I must say, upon my word,
  You might have sent for me before he died."
And then he turn'd to the surviving tribe,—
"Can you describe
But a few items, features, shape, and hue ?
I 'll warrant, I 'll still paint the likeness true !"

"Why, yes, we could do that," said one : "let 's see ;
He had a rather longish nose, like me."
"No," said a second ; " there you 're wrong,
His nose was not so very long."
"Well, well," pursued the first ; "his eyes
Were rather smaller than the common size."
"How ?" cried a third, "how ?—not at all ;
Not small—not small !"
"Well, then, an oval face, extremely fine."
"Yes," said the eldest son, "like mine."
The painter gazed upon him in despair,—
The fellow's face was square !

"I have it," cried another, and arose ;
"But wait a moment, sir," and out she goes.
With curiosity the artist burn'd—
"What was she gone for ?" but she soon return'd.
"I knew from what *they* said, to expect to gain
A likeness of grandpa was quite in vain ;
But, not upon that point to dwell,
I have got something here will do as well
As though alive he for his portrait sat !"
  So, saying, with a curtsey low,
She from behind, with much parade and show,
  Presented an old hat !

                                    C. W.

NIGHTS AT SEA;

Or, Sketches of Naval Life during the War.

BY THE OLD SAILOR.

No. IV.

> " Impute it not a crime
> To me, or my swift passage, that I slide
> O'er sixteen years."   *   *   *
>
> " There's some ill planet reigns;
> I must be patient till the heavens look
> With an aspect more favourable."
>
> SHAKSPEARE.

THERE glides the dashing Spankaway over the smooth surface of the ocean, whilst, close in her wake, moves the vanquished Hippolito. The damages have been repaired so as to be scarcely perceptible; the shot-holes have been well plugged and secured; and the two frigates appear more like consorts on a cruise than enemies so recently engaged in deadly strife. The breeze is a royal breeze; and gallantly the beautiful ships are splitting the yielding waters, whilst the watches are employed in necessary duties. Near the taffrail of the Spankaway stand two prominent figures, both remarkably fine-looking men, who might be taken for brother officers but for the difference in their uniforms. The one on the larboard hand has his head erect, his chest thrown forward, his left hand thrust into his waistcoat, and his right foot in advance planted firmly on the deck; he is indulging in high-wrought and proud feelings as he silently gazes on the prize; his voice is not heard, but there is a speaking meaning in his look as he contemplates the red cross of St. George upon a white field floating majestically above the tricolour, whilst his own untarnished ensign waves singly at his peak. The individual on the starboard hand has a cast of melancholy on his countenance; his head is depressed, his arms are folded on his breast; and, though sensible that he has done his duty, and defended his command as long as his crew rendered it tenable, yet he knows that he was not well supported by his fellow-citizens, among whom equality is the order of the day; and he is suffering from a sense of deep humiliation at the degraded condition in which he is placed. These are the captains of the two frigates,—the victor and the vanquished.

Upon the quarter-deck of the Hippolito is Mr. Seymour, hurrying to and fro, issuing his orders, and rendering the prize as effective as possible. There is a laughing glee upon his features that plainly evidences the pleasure he cherishes in his heart; he looks around with exultation as he anticipates the moment when he himself shall have such a desirable command. One step he makes sure of; a few hours more may perform fresh wonders; and his mind, with all the vividness of a seaman's hope, is making a hop, skip, and a jump progress to certain conclusions favourable to promotion. The fact is, Seymour had been long neglected; he was an excellent officer, and a brave man; had fought in several actions, been severely wounded on more than one occasion; but the coveted distinction had been withheld because he was not a first lieutenant. Now, however, he made sure of it; and he already began to feel the weight of the epaulette on the left shoulder, with an ardent determination to do something that would transfer it to the right shoulder.

But whither are the frigates steering? their heads are not on the compass-point for a friendly port, but directly the reverse. Night is coming on; they are running into the gulf of Genoa. There are the Hieres, a little open on the larboard bow, just rising from the sea. South-west should carry them to Gibraltar, and there are they going away north-east.

"Your undertaking is rather hazardous, my lord," said Citizen Captain Begaud; "there are ships of the line in the immediate neighbourhood, and the English fleet may have again resumed its station."

"If the latter is the case," replied Lord Eustace, "I can run no hazard; for Lord Nelson will have a bright eye upon the enemy. On the other hand, the enterprise is worth a little risk; and, though I despise the fellows who gave me the information, yet it is my duty, as well as according with my inclination, to make the most of it."

"*Vous avez raison, milord,*" rejoined the Frenchman; "*mais—*" he paused: "*sacré!* the rascal who told you merits the guillotine; he is a disgrace to the *grande nation.*"

"Well, I'm blow'd if I can make any thing o' this here!" exclaimed old Savage, the boatswain, to his subordinate, Jack Sheavehole, as they stood upon the forecastle; "it beats my larning out and out. Here we captures a French frigate, and has all the prisoners in limbo, when, instead of seeing her into a place of safety, why here we goes happy-go-lucky right down into the bight of Ginoar, slap into the enemy's teeth."

"Is that why you calls it a bite, Mr. Savage?" asked Jemmy Ducks, touching his hat with all due respect.

"Calls what a bite, you egg-sucker?" responded the boatswain somewhat roughly, at the presumption of the inquirer in addressing an officer of his distinction so freely. "Calls what a bite?"

"Going into the enemy's teeth, sir!" answered the humble poulterer, again touching his straw covering.

"Did you ever hear such an hignoramus, Jack?" said the boatswain to his veteran mate, in a tone of extreme contempt.

"Why, for the matter o' that, not often, sir," answered the individual addressed, "thof it is but nat'ral for him;" and, seeing that the boatswain was twiddling his rattan with his fingers, as a prelude to castigation, he turned to the poulterer, and, giving him a friendly shove, exclaimed, "Away out o' that, Jemmy; there 's the cow's babby bleating for you;" and off he went.

"The sarvice is going to ——, Jack!" said Mr. Savage; "the captain arn't half strict enough with them there 'long-shore lubbers, as pay no more respect to an officer than they do to a timber-head! and, in the regard o' that, his lordship himself too often speaks to 'em as if they had flesh and blood like his own, when, Lord love you! they arn't got never no such thing. And where his lordship is bound to now, puzzles my calculations. I say, Muster Blueblazes," to the gunner, who approached them, "what 's all this here about?"

"Flannel cartridges," replied the gunner, passing on in a hurry, and calling to his several mates to descend to the magazine.

"Flannel devils!" retorted old Savage. "That's all the answer I gets for my pains! Pray, Muster Nugent, may I presume to ax you if you can just deligthning my mind as to what cruise we 're going on in this course, seeing as it takes us slap down into the bight of the bay?"

"Gulf, Mr. Savage,—not bay," replied the junior lieutenant, "the gulf of Genoa, named after a celebrated city that formerly monopolised the commerce of the world. Christopher Columbus was a Genoese. Did you never read about Christopher Columbus?"

"Can't say as I have, sir," returned the impatient boatswain ; "are we bound in chase of him, sir?"

"In chase of whom? Columbus?" responded the lieutenant, laughing; "why, he 's been dead nearly two hundred years. No, no, Mr. Savage ; we 're going——"

"Mr. Nugent !" shouted Lord Eustace from the quarter-deck; and, to the great vexation of the boatswain, who was on the *qui-vive* to ascertain where they were bound, the young officer instantly responded, and went aft.

"That 's just the way I 'm al'ays sarved," said Savage petulantly, and applying his rattan to the shoulders of a poor unfortunate lad who passed him without touching the locks that hung clustering on his forehead,—for hat or cap he had none. "Here 's a pretty know-nothing! Do you forget, sir, that an officer 's an officer, sir? and it 's customary, sir, to pay proper respect, sir, to your superiors, sir, your betters, sir, you scape-grace, lubberly blackguard, sir ;" and down came the stick at every "sir." The boy made the best of his way across the forecastle ; but was again stopped by the boatswain. "Come back here, you wagabone. Don't you know, sir, that it 's a great mark of disrespect, sir, to run away when an officer 's starting you, sir? There, go along, you useless lumber! pretty regulations we shall have by and by, when such hard bargains as you fall aboard the King's biscuit! We 're all going to the devil together, Jack!" and he turned to look over the bows.

"If we are going to the devil," muttered Jack to the captain of the forecastle, "I hopes he 'll sarve out his infarnal favours as the Lords of the Admiralty shares the prize-money,—three parts among the officers."

Lovely is a Mediterranean twilight in those balmy months that breathe the odorous incense of exulting Nature in all its richest perfumes! then is the hour for contemplation! it is then the mind ranges over its best affections ; and hearts, though oceans divide them, hold a mysterious communing with each other.

> "Deeper, oh twilight, let thy shades increase
> Till every feeling, every pulse, is peace."

It is the poet alone that can describe its influences, for the art of the painter is baffled; he cannot produce the deepening tints as the web of darkness appears to be progressively weaving over the face of the heavens.

"I love this season," said Lord Eustace to his captive, as they still stood side by side abaft ; "there is a holy tranquillity about it that calms every turbulent passion, and soothes the heart in its sorrow."

"*C'est vrai, milord,*" returned the Frenchman, mournfully enough for one of his country ; "and yon star there," pointing to Algol in Medusa's head, "has ever been to me the star of my destiny. Three days since I quitted Toulon; that orb at night was dim, and a heavy foreboding rested on my spirit; on the following night its brightness, even its dimensions, had decreased, and then I knew the doom of my honour was at hand."

"Whatever presentiment you might have had," said Lord Eustace, "rest satisfied your honour remains untarnished. You fought your ship well, and be assured my account of the action shall do you ample justice. But I should like to know why you consider that particular star as connected with your fortunes."

"You shall be gratified then," responded the Frenchman, "if you have no objections to a tale of horror."

"None, none,—not in the least!" answered the noble captain; "the hour, the quiet, the dubious light, it is just the time for such a thing. Pray favour me, and I will gaze on the Gorgon, and listen with profound attention."

"We are both of us young, my lord," commenced the Frenchman; "I am but six-and-twenty, and you——"

"One year your junior, Monsieur Capitaine," uttered his lordship; "but I fancy I have seen more active service than you?"

"Afloat, 'tis probable, my lord," rejoined Begaud. "I was not at first destined for the marine: my early career was in the army of the North, when your Duke of York, deserted by the allied powers, (who received your money whilst they negotiated with the Directory,) retreated before our victorious troops. But I am forestalling my narrative,—heaving ahead of my reckoning, I think you'd call it. I am by birth a native of Paris, and the night of my entering the world was one of wailing, lamentation, and death. It was that on which three thousand persons were killed and wounded during a grand exhibition of fire-works, displayed in honour of the marriage of the Dauphin to the Archduchess Antoinetta Maria. Thus was I ushered into existence amidst shrieks and groans; and neither of my parents ever beheld their child. My father perished in the streets; the circumstance was indiscreetly announced to my mother; it brought on premature labour, and the living infant was taken from a corpse. What could be expected of such an introduction into life? I had an uncle residing upon the vine-clad hills that rise near the banks of the Garonne, a few leagues from Bordeaux, and there I passed my boyhood; but he was an austere man, and, having a large family of his own, I was looked upon as an incumbrance, and the only individual who appeared to commiserate my fate was an aged woman who lived in a cottage upon the estate, and was looked upon as a sibyl of no mean pretensions. She it was who first taught me to look upon yon star, and watch its capricious changes, so as to connect them with the occurrences of my life; and she it was who read my future fate on the tablets of inspiration. And who was this female? Twenty years before she had been the favourite of fortune, enjoying the luxuries of the capital, yet with an unblemished reputation. She had an only child,—a daughter, resplendent in her opening beauty of girlhood,— a type of that loveliness with which we characterise the angels. She was seen in the garden of the Tuileries by that depraved debauchee, the Fifteenth Louis; his agents secretly forced her to the Parc aux Cerfs; and the distracted mother, ascertaining the lost condition of her child, spoke publicly and loudly of the cruel grievance. But there was a Bastile then, monsieur," added he, with bitter emphasis, "engines of torture and iron cages to silence babblers; and thither was the parent sent by order of that monarch, who held the daughter in his unchaste embraces. That fellow was a wretch, my lord. It was he, and such as he, that deluged France with blood. The measure of their iniquity ran over. But the Bourbons were ever an accursed race. The property of the mother was seized upon by the emissaries of the police; and when a few years afterwards, she was released from her imprisonment, it was to find herself a homeless outcast, and her daughter,—the beauteous child of her soul's affections,—the inmate of a madhouse. Kings should be the protectors, the benefactors of their subjects; not their bane, their curse, the agents of their torture. Monsieur, that woman was my relative, and early did she stamp upon my young heart that hatred to royalty which remains unconquerably the same to this very hour. Yes, here it is," and he pressed his hand with energetic firmness over the seat of life; "here, —here it is, and, like a memorial carved on the bark of a sapling, it has become enlarged with my growth, and deeper indented with my years. It is my fate, monsieur,—it is my fate.

"The days of my boyhood passed on in mental misery. I felt for the injuries that had been heaped upon my only friend; I yielded to her instructions to be prepared against the hour of vengeance, when retributive justice should sweep tyranny from the throne; I nursed the hope in the secret recesses of my breast; I cherished it in my heart's core; it was the subject of my nightly dreams and waking thoughts; and, whilst other lads sought amusement in boyish pastimes, the demon of revenge led me into solitary nooks, where I hoarded up my ardent desire to redress the wrongs of Madame T——. Such, monsieur, was Jacques Begaud in his thirteenth year, when, tired of a vegetative life, I quitted my uncle's house, which, though it had been a place of shelter, had never been a home to me, and travelled on foot to Toulon. My small stock of money was soon expended; but yet I wanted for nothing. A piece of bread and a little fruit, with some wine, no one denied me; and, monsieur, I felt the sweets of liberty. Why I went to Toulon I do not know, for Paris was my aim; and Madame T—— had prophesied,—there was something terrible in her denunciations,—she had prophesied desolation and destruction to the house of the Bourbons; and as rumours were spreading of disunion at court, so did she eagerly feed upon them, and urge me to redress her wrongs. It is true the debauchee was in his grave; but then there was his grandson, the celebration of whose marriage had made me an orphan even before my birth; and, boy as I was, with a mind care-worn and cankered, I even looked upon *that* event as a legitimate cause of hatred."

"But the star, the star!" exclaimed Lord Eustace; "I am anxious to learn in what manner you considered yourself influenced by the star."

"Madame T—— made it the source of her divination," returned Citizen Begaud. "She would sit and silently gaze upon it for hours; and at my departure she bade me observe it on the first day of every month. If in full splendour, my career for the time would be prosperous; if shorn of its glory, I was then to expect adversity. I strictly followed her directions, and my fortunes were as varied as the brightness of yon orb. At Toulon I was much struck with the naval yard and arsenal; and in the former I laboured for several months in the humble occupation of an oakum-picker, gaining not only sufficient to keep life within me, but even with my scanty pittance I contrived to save a small sum, with which I traversed Corsica, and from thence embarked for Sicily, where I narrowly escaped one of those dreadful visitations which swallowed up so many thousands in its vortex. At Messina, where I obtained temporary employ, one great source of delight to me was standing on the rocky shore and viewing the fearful commotion of the waters, as they rushed through the straits. To witness this spectacle I have walked miles; and the roaring and tumbling of the billows excited in my heart feelings of joyous pleasure. I had frequently observed a youth of my own age similarly engaged. He stood with his arms behind him looking down upon the troubled ocean, as if he wished to penetrate its hidden depths, and search for undiscovered mysteries; he seemed to view it as a monster with which he longed to cope, but was coolly calculating the most appropriate method of effecting his purpose. His dress was rather superior to mine, and he affected a dignity which did not suit my companionable qualities. We never spoke; but whilst I hurled the largest stones that I could lift into the boiling foam, and saw them, heavy as they were, thrown floating on the surface by the bubbling fury of the swelling billows, he looked calmly on, disdaining to move a muscle of his countenance, though his brilliant eyes were lighted up, and seemed to flash with intense delight. Sometimes I made approaches to familiarity, but he cautiously repulsed all attempts at acquaintance; and at length I forbore. Monsieur has been to Messina?"

Lord Eustace bowed acquiescence.

"It is a beautiful place, and I loved to look at the white buildings thrown out in strong relief by the dark green forests behind them. My evenings, when my occupation would admit, were passed upon the Marina, watching the setting sun. One day I had walked to my usual spot for witnessing the contest of the currents; and, as I had frequently done before, I stripped, and plunged into the wave at a place where the eddies had hollowed out an artificial bay. I loved to breast the surge, to dash aside the threatening breaker, or dive beneath its power. My limbs were strong and pliant; I was fearless in an element that is seldom, if ever, conquered. The afternoon was sultry; there was an oppressive heat, that seemed to steam from both land and water, for the atmosphere above was clear and shining. My star had shone but dimly the night before, portending danger; yet I knew not from what quarter to expect it. After bathing, I dressed, and seated myself upon a rock, enjoying the scene, when, on turning my head, I beheld the youth I have mentioned at no great distance from me, standing on the extreme angle of low rock that jutted into the sea. He looked more serious and sedate than ever; there was a cast of melancholy on his features, and he seemed to be involved in intensity of thought. Suddenly a darkness overspread us, a heavy gloom arose; it was the work of a moment; I felt my earth-embedded seat lifted up, and oscillating to and fro. I saw huge pieces of solid rock rent from their mountain fastnesses, and hurled, crashing and thundering, into the torrent that roared and raged with unusual fury below. I beheld a wall of water rushing through the strait, and, calling to mind the dimness of my star, I knew the hour of trial was come: but I was too elevated to fear that mass of liquid element that swept every thing before it, though the strife that was apparently go-

ing on within the very bowels of the earth left me but small prospect
of escape. The awful phenomenon at first paralysed my faculties, and
I forgot the pale youth for the moment; but, on looking again towards
him, there he stood, still gazing on the deep, whilst the heavy shocks
of the earthquake were opening graves for his fellow-creatures. Onward rushed the perpendicular wave, and in an instant he was swept
from his position into the maddened vortex of the hissing foam. I
saw the catastrophe, monsieur, and for a second or two my spirit exulted in his overthrow; 'But he has parents,' thought I, 'they will
moan his loss; and yet I cannot save him if I would.' The youth
had disappeared beneath the mighty swell that inundated all the adjacent shore; but again he arose upon the surface, and was borne rapidly along past the spot where I was stationed. I had no home, no
parents, no one who cared for the destitute outcast, not a creature in
existence whose heart beat with affection for the child of misery; if
I perished, I perished, and there would be none to weep for me.
Without hesitation I sprang into that hissing foam, and was instantly
thrown half body out again by the turbulence of the underset, as it
forced itself to the surface. I struck out steadily and strongly with
my arms and feet, but could preserve very little command as the impetuous waters rolled me over and over; but still I neared the object
of my solicitude, who kept afloat, and at length I was by his side.
Yet what could I do to aid him in his peril? "Lift your head well
up!' exclaimed I; 'strike out boldly with the current. I will not leave
you.' He gave me one look; it was full of calm pride. I saw he
was getting weak and required help, yet he disdained to ask for it.
Mon Dieu! but that was a struggle for existence! and momentarily
was strength failing in that youth, whilst I felt my own gradually
grow less. 'Dive!—dive!' shouted I, as I beheld that gigantic wave
returning, in all its terrible vengeance, to meet us; 'dive for your
life!' But he was nearly insensible to my call. I seized him by the
shoulder, forced him under as far as possible, and the enormous bil-
low passed above our heads. Once more the light of Heaven was
on us,—once more we could see the blue expanse as if resting like a
canopy on the summits of the mountains, and the eddy had whirled
us to the entrance of an inlet, where the water was comparatively
tranquil. 'Save yourself,' said my companion, 'I will do my best to
follow. Save yourself, my friend.' I know not how it was, but the
appellation, 'my friend,' seemed to instil fresh vigour into me. 'I
will not abandon you,' shouted I; 'and, if you can fetch the cove, we
are both saved.'—'It is impossible,' answered he; 'run no further
hazard on my account.' His head was drooping, nature was nearly
exhausted; he swam deep, and I became sensible that, unless by some
desperate impulse, I could not save him. I swam close to him, gave
him one end of my neckerchief, and told him to grip it tight; the
other end I fixed between my teeth, and boldly tried for the inlet. A
wave assisted my endeavours; the swell bore me onward, but it was
towards a point where the sea was breaking fearfully high, and the
passage to the inlet was extremely narrow. My companion complied
with my injunctions; yet I could not forbear shuddering when I
looked at the craggy barrier that seemed to foretell our fate. We
neared the rocks, and, had the swell been rolling in, must have been
dashed to pieces; but, just as we approached, the wave was receding;

it carried us into the inlet stream. Hope cheered me on a few strokes more: the water was undulating, but smooth; but that youth, that pale youth, had disappeared. Still he could not be far distant. I turned, and dived; long practice had rendered me perfectly familiar with the art. I saw him sinking,—almost helpless; he was near the bottom. I went down after him even lower, and, taking renewed impetus from striking my feet against the ground, I bore him once more to the surface. The land was only a few yards distant, but his weight overpowered me. I struggled hard to gain the shore. Despair began to take possession of my mind; it rendered me desperate. A few feet was all that divided us from safety, when a dizziness came over me, my brain whirled, the waters were over my mouth; I thought of the dimness of my star, and believed my minutes were numbered. Another rally from the heart produced another effort; my hands were on the rocks. I grappled them, but my fingers could not retain their clutch; I slipped away: the water was deep even there, and death seemed certain. Oh, God! how dreadful was that moment of suspense! The burthen, which I still sustained, was inanimate, and I was about to loose my hold of him, when another gigantic wave swept in; it lifted me on to the flat that I had been striving for; it receded, and left us on hard ground: the ocean had lost its prey. I stripped my young companion, chafed his limbs; his heart still beat, and in about half an hour he evinced signs of returning consciousness. That moment was to me one of the happiest of my existence. In another hour he was perfectly restored, though weak; and, leaning on my arm, we proceeded towards the town. But where was Messina? that beautiful Messina that we had quitted so recently? A mass of ruins! A scene of indescribable confusion and dismay! The inhabitants had thronged to the mountains for a place of refuge; and, as we entered the deserted streets, a death-like stillness prevailed, broken only by the deep groan or the shrill shriek of those who yet remained alive with shattered frames and broken limbs, unable to escape. Houses were levelled with the ground. Here yawned a hideous chasm that had buried its living victims; there lay huge masses of stone with crushed and mutilated bodies beneath them,—the dead and the dying. Oh! my lord, it was a fearful spectacle, and my spirit drank in all its horrors. We sought the humble residence in which I had found an asylum; no vestige of it remained. We looked for the more noble mansion in which my companion had taken up his abode; it was a chaos. Food there was plenty, Faro wine in abundance; and we amply refreshed ourselves, whilst I own my heart swelled with pride at the thought that we were the masters in this once noble city. My companion expressed his gratitude for the services I had rendered him; but he did it proudly. He said he was going to France; and my heart yearned to revisit my native land. I remembered Madame T——, and the solemn pledge I had given her: I longed to see Paris,—that Paris of which I had heard so much; and I earnestly brooded on the schemes which were to level royalty to the dust. You will say I was but a boy. True! But what instruction was to others, deadly revenge was to me; it had been my lesson conned at every season, my sole education,—and my teacher fully competent to superintend her pupil.

"But Messina!—there it lay prostrate with the dust; churches thrown down, and the sacred vestments scattered; public buildings in wreck, hotels and palazzos as if they had never been. We were standing in the square, when another shock tumbled the fragments hither and thither, mingling them in greater confusion. My companion was for hastening up the eminences to see who had escaped: I preferred remaining, as all places were alike to me; besides, I was poor, wretchedly poor, and there was the prospect of gold to be obtained. The pale youth did not tell me his name, nor did I think to ask it: he gave me a small silver medal that he had worn round his neck by way of remembrance, and I presented him with a flat piece of whalebone on which in my idle hours I had rudely carved my name. We parted, and in a short time my hazardous enterprise was richly recompensed. I found what I coveted, gold! I filled my slender pockets, and yet there was gold; I dug a hole and buried my treasure, but still wealth almost unbounded lay scattered in the streets. I hastened to the harbour; wrecks and dead bodies were everywhere floating. A boat was drifting near the quay, and, having secured her, I hastened back to the place where my riches were concealed. But the marauders had entered the town, and I feared that they would plunder me; so I returned to the boat and shoved off from the shore, and there I lay in her bottom as she drove into the bay, dreading detection, and fearing to lose my ill-acquired wealth. I had been contented with a little when only a few copper coins had been my fortune; but, now I was possessed of gold, I coveted that which I had left behind. A brigantine that was making her escape from the devastation picked me up. I offered the captain gold to give me a passage to whatever place he might be going. My dress and appearance bespoke poverty,—the glittering coin betrayed me: I was stripped of every ducat, thrust into the boat again, and cast adrift upon a tempestuous night. The only valuable I retained was the medal which I slung round my neck next to my skin.

"Dark and dreary was the tumultuous ocean as my little vessel floated at the mercy of the wind and sea; the gale howled fearfully over me, the waves rolled angrily beneath me; no star illumined the vault of heaven; but there was a glowing brilliancy of sparkling lustres on the waters, as if the caverns of the deep had sent forth their gems to supply the defection of the starry host. The billows threw up their haughty heads crested with feathery foam, and the spray saturated my clothes through and through: but the weather was warm to a child of the North; and thus I continued for many long lonely hours, till daylight once again appeared. And such a daylight! The storm had passed away,—the gorgeous splendour of the sun as he arose from the horizon was worth all the pain I had endured only to witness; but his cheering rays came as kindly to my heart as they were welcome to my person. It was like the smiling face of a friend to gladden the spirit in adversity. I was at no great distance from the shore; yet so beautiful was the scene, that, but for hunger, I should have been contented to have remained gazing on the spectacle. The cravings of nature, however, were powerful; I paddled to the rocks, landed, and hurried back to that remnant of a town I had been so eager to quit. I found no difficulty in appeasing my appetite: the inhabitants were returning in groups to weep over their shattered dwellings, and, as they looked mournfully on each other, most of them were uttering lamentations for a relative or a friend. Piece by piece I was enabled to change my dress, and make a more creditable appearance; and this, too, without being over scrupulous as to the appropriation. I was unknown to every one, for nobody remembered the poor child of labour. I made inquiry after my companion of the former day, but could gain no intelligence of him; and thus I wandered amongst the dust and ashes of ruins, an observer unheeded and uncared for.

"But I well remembered the spot where I had hidden my treasure, and, when the shades of evening shrouded the surrounding objects in their gloom, I went stealthily towards it. No language can adequately describe the perturbation of my mind; hope and fear, anticipations of good and evil, the pleasures of anxious expectation, and the dread of bitter disappointment, alternately held their influence over me. I had not a marvedi in the world; but, if the place of concealment was untouched, I was the possessor of wealth beyond my most sanguine wants for years. I beheld the stone which I had rolled over the excavation, at once to hide and to direct; its position was unchanged. I gazed earnestly around,—I listened for a sound; but all was solitary and silent. In ecstasy I rolled away the obstruction, thrust in my arm, and, whilst my fingers clutched the golden heaps, my breast was on the earth, and I could hear the beatings of my heart. Thus I lay for some time indulging in delicious dreams of future enjoyment, not unmingled, however, with those contemplations which had become harmonised with every action of my existence. At various intervals I removed my gold to a place of greater security, and soon after availed myself of an opportunity of returning to Toulon with the captain who had first of all landed me in Corsica. Oh, what anxious moments did I pass lest another discovery should deprive me of my store! I did not dare to close my eyes in sleep, lest my person or my small matter of luggage should be searched. I no longer threw myself heedlessly down in any spot to court repose. Suspicion and distrust poisoned the very source of pleasure; I looked upon all men as my enemies, because I could confide in none. But I reached Toulon unmolested, and without loss of time I hastened to the cottage of Madame T——, vain-glorious of my achievement——"

"Which, to my mind, looks most d——ly like thieving, monsieur," said Lord Eustace warmly.

"My lord, I am sensible of the wrong I perpetrated," responded Citizen Begaud; "but you seem to forget I was a boy, steeped in poverty to the very lips, bound by a solemn pledge to a certain purpose, through influences that had actuated me from my earliest remembrances. I looked upon the gold as a means to further my views. I had no guide for my youth, and my star——"

"Was, it seems, anything but an honourable one," added Lord Eustace, interrupting him. "Yet, monsieur, I own your narrative has interested me; and, under the hope that there is something of a redeeming quality yet to come, I earnestly request the favour of its continuation."

The Frenchman bowed, and darkness hid both the frown on his brow and the flush of anger on his cheek.

"Madame T—— had left the neighbourhood of Bordeaux, and gone to Paris. Thither I followed; but all my efforts were unavailing to discover her habitation. The internal state of the city was that of dissatisfaction with the ruling powers; plots and conspiracies were hatched, quarrels fomented, and the seeds of discord were rapidly swelling to burst the earth that covered them, and spread into a tree of monstrous growth. The *intriguantes* industriously circulated reports of the queen and the nobility, that were eagerly swallowed by the lower orders, to increase and justify their hostility to the great. At first I kept aloof from any decided course, and for two years was a silent observer of all that was passing around me. I lived frugally, so as neither to excite envy nor create suspicion; and I saw with inexpressible satisfaction that the machinery was putting together that would, when brought into full operation, decide the fate of the Bourbons. I was almost daily in the vicinity of the palaces, and frequently, whilst gazing on the beauty of the queen, my purposes were shaken. Numerous opportunities offered to deprive the sovereign of his life; but I disdained to become an assassin. Besides, it was not Louis alone whose downfal I had been taught to consider an act of justice. It was the whole of the privileged orders, of which he was the head and chief; and a blow at him would have aroused the aristocrats to a sense of impending danger.

"Such was the position of my own and public affairs when I had attained my seventeenth year. But I had not passed the intermediate time in indolence. I went to school, I studied hard, became an expert swordsman, and tolerably proficient in the branches of general education: I perused the works of authors both dead and living; I tested their writings by a careful examination of men and manners. But I had yet much to learn. One day I made an excursion on horseback to Fontainbleau; the royal family were at the palace, and there was a young female in the suite of her majesty— Why should I withhold the fact? Monsieur, my soul was captivated by that angelic girl. I was not aware that she had ever noticed or even seen me so as to recall my features to remembrance; I had made no show of my attachment beyond that silent adoration of the heart which the countenance is but too apt to reveal. She it was who drew me towards Fontainbleau, under the hope of obtaining a casual glance. I was wandering in the forest, nursing the secret thoughts of her who controlled my actions: evening came on, and darkness surprised me in one of the most retired parts. I was too well inured to privations to heed the occurrence. The night was serene and warm, and I prepared to pass it beneath the branches of some venerable tree; in fact, I was sitting down for the purpose of repose, when a shouting and the report of fire-arms at no great distance aroused me to energy. The direction of the parties was well defined: they might be friends or foes, honest men or thieves; to me it was a matter of indifference, for in either case I should find a guide out of the wood. Without a moment's hesitation I dashed through the tangled briers, and on a nearer approach ascertained that a deadly conflict was going on. A few minutes brought me to the scene of action; it was upon the main road which I had missed, and the opening between the trees admitted sufficient light to show two of the combatants stretched upon the ground. There were still two to two engaged with swords; but one of them fell soon after my arrival, and the survivor turned to assist his fellow against the only opponent left. Whilst they were upon an equality I did not care to interfere, especially as I knew not which was the injured party; but the odds decided me at once, and, snatching up a sword, I placed myself in attitude by the side of the solitary. My antagonist was a skilful swordsman; but I had time to observe that the individual whom I befriended was richly dressed, and by no means a master of his weapon, whilst the person opposed to him was greatly his inferior. I got close to him, parried a thrust from my own immediate *engagé*, and returned by a side sleight upon his comrade, who received it in his breast, and, staggering backwards with great violence, pulled the sword from my hand and left me at the mercy of the other. His pass was sure; but, dexterously evading it, the weapon only went through the fleshy part of my arm, and the force with which it was given brought it up to the hilt. We grappled together. I was young and vigorous, but he possessed all the muscular strength and power of manhood. I felt his grip upon my throat; we fell heavily together upon the earth. He retained his superiority above me; and strangulation was rapidly going on, when suddenly his hold relaxed, he sprang from me, rolled over and over, and then stretched himself stiffly out a lifeless corpse. The sword of the disengaged had passed through his heart. I was not long in recovering sensibility, and on raising my head saw that we were all down, wounded and bleeding. The gentleman in rich attire was seated with his back against a tree, wiping the perspiration from his forehead, and, on seeing me move, he exclaimed, 'Whoever you are, take my best thanks. If you live, I will prove my sense of the obligation by more than words; if you die, carry the gratitude of a nation with you before your maker. But how is it? are you seriously or mortally hurt? *Mon Dieu!* this has been no boy's pastime, anyhow.' I assured him my injuries were not severe; and, to prove the truth of my assertion, I got up, went towards him, and tendered my assistance. '*Grace à Dieu!*' said he, 'I have only a few scratches. But we must not remain here: the rascals have driven off with the carriage to plunder it; they will return directly to help their comrades. Are all my fellows dead?' I felt the breasts of each to ascertain if there was any throbbing of the heart. One of the servants and two of the robbers were yet living, though desperately wounded, and I reported to that effect. 'We can expect nothing from them,' said he, 'and therefore must trust to our own resources. You know the passages of the forest?' '*Non, monsieur,*' returned I. 'My acquaintance with the forest has been only that of a few hours. I am a stranger here, and was about to pass the night between the trees when I heard the report of fire-arms.'—'Ah! they shot my coachman,' said he, 'the villains; and my carriage has the edicts in it for the royal sign-manual, with other matters. Bah! there would be a pretty prize for the robbers did the rogues know their worth.' This was uttered to himself, and apparently not designed for me to hear. 'May I inquire the name and rank of the noble who so opportunely saved my life?' asked I.—'All in good time, young man; you should never listen to state secrets. Saved your life, eh? You have been to court and have learned to flatter. Abandon it, young man: flattery is bad enough in old age, but detestable from youth. I need no such incitements to remembrance. Help me rise.' I obeyed. 'And now,' continued he, 'we must find our way to the palace.'

"My heart leaped with joy at the thought: I should see, I should be near the young Countess de M——. Ever prone to extravagance, the most preposterous hopes and prospects filled my mind: I laughed outright. 'Are you mad?' inquired my companion. 'In what can you find cause for mirth?'—'The heart knoweth its own bitterness,' returned I, 'and a stranger intermeddleth not with its joy.'—'True, true,' responded he. 'But come, let us strive to find our way.' He put his arm within mine, and silently we traced the road for about two miles, when we came to one of the lodges that formed a residence for a keeper, and here we obtained horses and a guide, and in less than half an hour we were within the walls of that venerable building the palace of Fontainbleau. My companion had gained a ready admittance; his word of command was almost electric, and at first I thought it was the Duke of Orleans, but that his visit to the royal family would be deemed an insult. At all events I was consigned to the care of an officer of the household, and I had no cause to complain of my treatment. After the lapse of an hour, an attendant summoned me to wait upon the individual I had so timely rescued. My dress, from being torn by the brambles, certainly was not much suited for the ostentatious gaiety of a court at a period when extravagant profusion was considered as essential to the prosperity of the nation; nor had it lost anything by the struggle on the ground with the bandit. Still I obeyed without hesitation; and, after passing through several gorgeous apartments, an officer with a white wand arrested our further progress. He then tapped gently at an inner door; there was the tinkling of a bell, the portal flew back, and within was a resplendent blaze of light that dazzled and confounded me. I was reassured, however, by the voice of my companion, who uttered in a low voice, 'Enter, young man;' and obeying, I found myself in the presence of the king and queen. Louis was seated at a table covered with toys, and the young prince was on his knee. Marie Antoinette was watching with the eye of maternal affection the playful delight of her child; and, much as I had imbibed an undeviating hatred to royalty, I could not behold the spectacle unmoved. Near her majesty stood the young Countess de M——, and the fascination of her beauteous eye enchained my faculties. In a few minutes the queen and her suite retired, and my companion questioned me in the presence of the monarch relative to my station in life, the cause of my being in the forest, and on several other topics, all which I answered as best suited my own purposes. Louis spake kindly to me, but his very kindness filled my heart with bitter feelings; and when, turning to my companion of the forest, he said, 'Monsieur Calonne, we must find some fitting service for this youth,' I could have stabbed him through and through. This, then, was Monsieur Calonne, the head of the ministry,—he who had dared to propose a tax upon the privileged orders, and had assembled the Notables to shame them into compliance with his scheme; this was the man who had plunged the finances of the country into confusion and ruin, for the purpose of bringing down the pride of the nobles and the clergy, who had raised him to his elevated exaltation. His place was one of danger and distrust: he aimed a severe blow at the privileged orders, without conciliating the people; for, though the latter applauded the equalizing system, yet they despised the minister who, by his reckless profusion, was involving them in ruin. That night I retired——"

"Sail, ho!" was shouted from the forecastle, and Lord Eustace immediately started from his attitude of deep attention.

"Whereabouts is she?" demanded the officer of the watch, his voice reverberating amongst the sails, and the most profound stillness reigning fore and aft.

"Broad away on the starboard bow, sir," replied the look-out; and Lord Eustace, being furnished with his night-glass, walked forward to examine the stranger, leaving the recital of Citizen Captain Begaud to be finished at another opportunity.

SONG OF THE OLD BELL.

In an old village, amid older hills,
That close around their verdant walls to guard
Its tottering age from wintry winds, I dwell
Lonely, and still, save when the clamorous rooks
Or my own fickle changes wound the ear
Of Silence in my tower!   ANON.

For full five hundred years I 've swung
  In my old grey turret high,
And many a different theme I 've sung
  As the time went stealing by!
I 've peal'd the chaunt of a wedding morn;
  Ere night I have sadly toll'd,
To say that the bride was coming, love-lorn,
  To sleep in the church-yard mould!
        Ding-dong,
                My careless song;
          Merry and sad,
                But neither long!

For full five hundred years I 've swung
  In my ancient turret high,
And many a different theme I 've sung
  As the time went stealing by!
I 've swell'd the joy of a country's pride
  For a victory far off won,
Then changed to grief for the brave that died
  Ere my mirth had well begun!
        Ding-dong,
                My careless song;
          Merry or sad,
                But neither long!

For full five hundred years I 've swung
  In my breezy turret high,
And many a different theme I 've sung
  As the time went stealing by!
I have chimed the dirge of a nation's grief
  On the death of a dear-loved king,
Then merrily rung for the next young chief;
  As told, I can weep or sing!
        Ding-dong,
                My careless song;
          Merry or sad,
                But neither long!

For full five hundred years I 've swung
  In my crumbling turret high;
'Tis time my own death-song were sung,
  And with truth before I die!
I never could love the themes they gave
  My tyrannized tongue to tell:
One moment for cradle, the next for grave—
  They 've worn out the old church bell!
        Ding-dong,
                My changeful song;
          Farewell now,
                And farewell long!   W.

George Cruikshank

Midnight Mishaps

MIDNIGHT MISHAPS.

BY EDWARD MAYHEW.

WITH AN ILLUSTRATION BY GEORGE CRUIKSHANK.

OH the rural suburbs of London!—the filthy suburbs!—where nothing is green but the water, nothing natural but the dirt,—where the trees are clipt into poles, and the hedges grow behind palings,—where " no thoroughfare" forbids you to walk in one place, and the dust prevents you from walking in another,—the filthy suburbs!

It was these delightful precincts of peace and " *caution*," retirement and " *handsome rewards*," that Mr. Jacob Tweasle honoured with his decided preference. This gentleman had inhabited a small shop at the foot of Snow-hill for more than forty years, retailing tobacco to the tradesmen, and cigars to the apprentices; and, having by supplying other people's boxes gradually filled his own, he, now in his sixtieth year, declined the manufacture of weeds for the cultivation of exotics.

An " Italian villa," beautifully situated in a back lane near Hornsey, was pointed out to the tobacconist by a house-agent as particularly " snug and retired." Before the ostentatious white front of this " enviable residence" were exactly twenty square yards of lawn, " delightfully wooded" by a solitary laburnum, which was approached over a highly " ornamental Chinese bridge," crossing " a convenient stream of water." The interior of the building it was "impossible for the most fastidious to object to;" the rooms were so low, and the windows so small, that the happy occupant always imagined himself a hundred miles from the metropolis; the prospect, too, from the upper stories " revelled in all the luxuries of the picturesque;" the dome of St. Paul's lent magnificence to the distance, while the foreground was enlivened by a brick-field.

Mr. Tweasle saw, approved, yet doubted. He did not know what to say to it. There was, he acknowledged, everything that heart of man could desire; the garden was walled in, and the steel-traps and cabbages might be taken as fixtures; nevertheless he reached the bridge without having made up his mind. There he paused, and gazed in anxious meditation upon the black and heavy liquid that stagnated beneath. " Can one fish here ?" suddenly asked the tobacconist, at the same time leaning over and disturbing the " convenient stream of water" with his cane.

" *I* never do myself," replied the agent, in such a manner as to imply that other people frequently did; for Tweasle instantly inquired,

" What do they catch?"

The agent was puzzled. Was the Londoner really ignorant, or was this a design to test the truth of all his former assertions? It was a case which required extreme caution. " I am no angler myself,—I have no time for that delightful recreation; but—I should think—that eels—eels—probably—eels—might ——"

" Stewed eels make a nice supper," interrupted Tweasle with gluttonous simplicity. " Fish arn't to be got fresh in London."

" Fish ought to be eaten the moment it is taken from the water," cried the agent with decision.

" My boy 's got a fishing-rod," said Tweasle ; and he took the Italian villa on a repairing lease.

The announcement of this event created a " sensation " at the foot
of Snow-hill; the Rubicon was past; the business *was* to be disposed
of ; and, that no time might be lost, Mr. Tweasle, without taking off
his gloves, began to scribble an advertisement, while Mrs. Tweasle
waddled into the shop and insulted a customer.

All was confusion. To fly from the paternal protection of the
Lord Mayor, and emigrate off the stones, was no casual event to him
who had hitherto proudly exulted in the freedom of the city. Much
was necessary to reconcile the mind to so bold a measure. The lady
undertook to pack up everything that could be got in London, and
purchase everything that could not be got in the country. The gentleman, acting as a man should, wholly neglected the domestic. He
gave his attention to the noble arts of agriculture and self-defence,
botanical theories, treatises, and directories. Horticultural implements, instruments, and improvements, swords and pistols, guns and
blunderbusses, detonating crackers for the shutters, and alarums for
the bedrooms, he spared neither trouble nor expense to procure.

" Now, Hanney, dear," said Tweasle to his wife, surveying the weapons which had just been sent home, " I thinks here 's everything a
contented mind could desire : the thieves will know better than to
come where we are."

But the timid woman's ideas of defence were concentrated in a
flannel gown and a rattle ; she looked more terrified than assured :—
fire-arms and accidents were, in her mind, synonymous ; and her only
answer was an urgent entreaty that " those nasty things might be
always so locked up that *nobody could* get at them."

In due time everything that the family thought they could possibly
want was procured ; and when, to render the whole complete, Master
Charles, only son and heir, was commissioned to procure live stock
from St. Giles's, the boy returned with almond tumblers for pigeon-
pies, and bantam-cocks for poultry.

" New-laid eggs for breakfast!" chuckled his papa.

All being at length ready for starting on the following day, and as
the house was dismantled even to the junction of the bed-posts, the
family determined to pass their last evening in London, whispering
soft adieus to their more intimate acquaintance. At first Tweasle
conducted himself with becoming hypocrisy. He lamented his separation from the " friends of his youth," and ate cake and drank wine
with imposing solemnity ; but, as the ceremony was repeated, he
committed himself by an occasional smile, and at last slipped out
something about " poor devils, who were smoked to death like red
herrings." Mrs. Tweasle was shocked, and hurried her husband
away ; who, however, warmed into truth, would not acknowledge his
error or go to bed, but insisted on saying good-b'ye to his old friend
Gingham. They found the Ginghams preparing for supper ; and, on
company arriving, the servant was whispered " to bring up the beef,"
which Tweasle overhearing, he turned to the hostess, and exultingly
cried,

" Come and see us in the country, and I 'll give you stewed eels
and chicken for supper."

"I'm very sorry we've nothing *better* than cold beef to offer *you*, sir," replied the lady with a look; "but I can send out."

"Not for the world!" shouted Mrs. Tweasle, who was rejoiced when a request to be seated relieved her from reiterating her conciliatory wishes that no one would mind her good man, who during supper would converse on no other subject than the pleasures of new-laid eggs and the country, till, having finished one glass of gin and water, he undertook to explain to his friend how it was that *he* also could leave off business like a squire. Nor was this personal investigation of private family affairs rendered less unpleasant by the indelicate egotism which induced the exhibitor to illustrate his friend's faults by his own virtues; till, though repeatedly requested to "drop it," Tweasle wound up his harangue by calling his host a fool.

"You're a fool, Gingham. You might ha' been as well off as I am at the present moment, if you hadn't lived at such a rate, like a fool."

The lady of the house instantly arose, and left the room in company with her daughters, telling Mr. Tweasle "*they* were going to bed;" and Mr. Gingham leant over the table to inform his guest, "he had no wish to quarrel."

Of the rest of that evening Tweasle the next day retained a very confused recollection. He thought some one pushed him about in a passage, and remembered his wife's assisting him to put on his great-coat in the middle of the street.

At the appointed hour, the glass-coach which was to convey the family from London stopped at the foot of Snow-hill. Mr. Tweasle was the first to jump in; the person to whom the business had been advantageously disposed of, gave his hand to Mrs. Tweasle, and then turned to say farewell to her husband.

"All I've got in this blessed world I made in that shop," said Tweasle, anxious to give his successor a high opinion of the bargain, and leave a good name behind him. "The many—many—happy—peaceful days I've seen in it!—I can't expect to see them again!—On a Saturday and on a Monday I've often been fit to drop behind my own counter, quite worn out with customers. I'm afraid I've done a rash thing; but I've this consolation, I've left the business in good hands."

"Come, don't look dull, Tweasle," cried his wife, who was imposed on by her husband's pathetics: "cheer up! You know trade ain't what it was, and I'm sure the two last years must have been a 'losing game.'"

It is impossible to say whether he who had bought or he who had sold the business looked most appalled by this untimely truth. However, Tweasle was the first to recover himself: he took his victim affectionately by the hand, and, leaning forward, whispered in propitiatory confidential accents, "Always put a little white pepper in Alderman Heavyside's Welsh, or he'll think you've adulterated it."

But the successor was hurt past such slender consolation. With lofty integrity he spurned the advice of his deceiver; for, jerking his hand away, and looking Tweasle sternly in the face, he said, "Sir, I shall do my duty!" and he strutted into the shop; whereupon the coach began to move.

Disposed by this little incident to sadness, its late occupant looked at the house till his eyes watered. He was no longer a "public man;" his opinion of the weather was now of no importance; he might henceforth loiter over his dinner undisturbed by any thought of the shop! Feelings such as these could not be suppressed, and Tweasle was about to apostrophise, when his gentle partner startled him by exclaiming,

"Thank our stars, we're off at last!" and, catching a glimpse of the house as the coach turned into Hatton-garden, she added, "there's the last of it, I hope; I never wish to set eyes on the hole again!"

"Don't be ungrateful," said Tweasle, chidingly. "That roof has sheltered me near forty years."

"Well, it was a nuisance to live in it,—no place to dry a rag in but the servant's bed-room."

"And Martha made you give her rum and water, mother, or else she *would* catch cold," added the son.

"Stop there!—stop there!—stop!" a voice was heard to cry.

"That can't be for us," observed Mrs. Tweasle.

As if in the spirit of matrimonial contradiction, her husband the next moment exclaimed, "By George! it is though!"

It proved to be a debtor, who had journeyed to London in consequence of some information which had been afforded him by an attorney. Three hundred and odd pounds were in his pocket ready for disbursement, if Mr. Tweasle would accompany him to an inn in the Borough, and there go through the account. This was vexatious. The *fear* of losing the money had long disturbed the late tobacconist's mental monotony, and now the *certainty* of its payment absolutely angered him. He turned to his lady, and said to her in a voice of positive wrath,

"Hanney, I shall go. Don't you wait for me, do you hear? I shall walk probably in the evening down to Hornsey,—when I've given a receipt for the money. Now, sir, I'm at your service. Will you show the way?"

"Please to remember a poor fellow who wants works," said a florid muscular mendicant, thrusting his huge hand close to the late tobacconist's face.—"The fellow must have overheard the arrangement," thought Tweasle; and an undefined feeling of alarm took the roses from his cheeks. As he hastily threw the man a few pence, he delivered some very profound remarks upon the Vagrant Act.

"Hanney, dear," cried he in a loud voice, while the beggar was stooping for the money, "don't make yourself uneasy, but set the steel-traps. I have pistols,—mind that, love,—I have pistols!" for, afraid to acknowledge his own terror, he found relief in supposing that others were more timid than himself.

Leaving his wife, Tweasle walked to the inn, where he remained till all the items of a long bill had been discussed, when the clock announced the hour of nine, and then the debtor insisted on being asked to supper, so that it was fairly half-past ten before Tweasle left the Borough.

So long as the lights of London illumined his way, he proceeded in comparative composure, only occasionally feeling at his coat-pockets to assure himself that the pistols were safe; but when the unaided darkness announced that he had quitted the extremest outskirts of the metropolis, Mr. Tweasle paused, and audibly informed himself that "he was not afraid:" on receiving which information, he buttoned his coat closer, slapped his hat firmer on his cranium, frowned, and shook his head; and, endeavouring to act bravery, took a pistol in either hand as he marched onward with every symptom of excessive alarm.

He had not more than two miles farther to proceed, when the distant notes of St. Paul's cathedral announced the hour of midnight. At this time Tweasle was creeping along a lane rendered gloomy by high and parallel hedges, which inclosed fruitful pastures, and prevented grazing cattle from being impounded; at a little distance from him, behind one of these "leafy screens," stood a "pensive brother," —a fine he-ass, which had retired thither to nibble the tender shoots of the mellifluous hawthorn.

As the last vibration died away, he stumbled into a cart-rut. On recovering his perpendicular, panting from the unnecessary exertion he had used, the poor traveller stared around him, and endeavoured to survey the place whereon he was standing. It was a gloomy spot,— one unrelieved mass of shade, in which the clouded heavens seemed to harmonize; everything was in awful repose,—the night was cold, but not a zephyr was abroad. Painfully oppressed by the utter loneliness of his position, a sense of extreme lassitude gradually crept over Tweasle,—he closed his eyes, and shuddered violently; he could have wept, but the fear of being afraid made him suppress the desire.

"This is a dreadful place!" he said aloud, with much gravity; "just such a spot as a murder might be committed in. I'm very glad I'm armed."

Scarcely had he uttered the words, when the donkey thrust forward his "pensive nose," and shook the hedge by pulling at a switch of more than common luxuriance. "I'll sell my life dearly!" was Tweasle's first sensation,—it could hardly be called idea, it was too confused,—as, preparing for attack, he instinctively clapped one hand upon his money, while with the other he presented a pistol towards the spot whence the noise proceeded. Not being, as he expected, immediately assaulted, he by a violent exertion of his mental powers so far mastered his bodily alarm as to gulp first and then breathe. He listened,—all was still. "They didn't know I was armed," thought Tweasle; "it was lucky I showed them my determination:" and, in something bordering upon confidence in the effects of his own courage, he ventured to whisper "Who's there?" when, receiving no answer, he increased his demand to "Who's there, *I say?*" in a somewhat louder voice. He was anxiously waiting the result of this boldness on his part when the animal, probably attracted by the sound, slowly moved towards the spot where Tweasle was standing. "Ah! come — d—n — don't — now — I — I'm armed, you know!" screamed the traveller, running about and wildly striking right and left with the pistol, confident that the action this time had positively commenced; but after some interval, becoming gradually convinced that he remained unhurt, he was quite satisfied that nothing but the extraordinary courage he had displayed could have saved him from this second desperate attempt upon his life; and, somewhat anxious to support the first dawn of his heroism, he said, or rather stammered,

in a voice not always distinct, " Now—now,—whoever you are,—
don't go too far, because it's no pleasure to me to shoot you ;—but I
will, if you do:—so, in the King's name, who are you?—I *must* fire if
you won't speak!"

The last appeal was made more in the tone of entreaty than command, for Tweasle beheld a black mass thrust itself against the
hedge, evidently inspecting him. A rush of confused ideas, a tumult
of strange suspicions and surmises, a " *regular row* " of contending
emotions, deprived him of all self-control ; and, if the pistol had not
just at that moment accidentally exploded, he had probably fallen to
the ground. As it was, the noise revived him ; and, taking advantage
of the circumstance, with a ready conceit he cried out " *There !*" for
he had seen the object disappear, and heard a faint cry as of one in
agony,—whereon he walked from the place with every appearance of
impertinent composure.

But this simulation did not long continue. As he became more
conscious, he grew more agitated: he had probably shot a robber.
For this he felt no remorse, and was persuading himself he would
repeat the act, when he discovered that he had lost his pistols. This
discovery gave him a fearful shock,—he was unarmed! Now came
another dread.—Was the miscreant he had killed alone? or had he
companions ? Did not robbers usually congregate in bands ; and might
he not be pursued? But Tweasle was adopting the very best mode of
avoiding such a danger, as, long before he asked himself the question,
his walk had quickened into a sort of hand-gallop, which this fresh
terror increased to the wild speed of utter despair. Without slacken-
ing his pace, the affrighted man had nearly reached his home, when a
sharp blow across the shins brought him to the ground, and, looking
up, Tweasle perceived the mendicant of the afternoon, and two other
suspicious-looking fellows standing over him. He could not speak ;
but, turning his face downwards, stretched himself upon the earth.

" *Are you going to sleep there ?*" inquired the beggar with a kick
that was violently anti-soporific ; and, seeing that Tweasle naturally
writhed under the infliction, the fellow vociferated, " Come, that
didn't hurt you. It's no use shamming here."

" I shan't wait about, all night for him," cried a diminutive gentleman disguised in a coalheaver's hat worn jockey-fashion, who, seizing
Tweasle by the collar, lifted him from the ground, and giving him a
shake that was sufficient to render any human nerves unsteady for
eternity, asked the tottering man in a voice of angry expostulation,
" Why the devil he couldn't stand still ?"

Too terrified to offer the slightest opposition, the unhappy Tweasle
endeavoured to obey, which spirit of accommodation was repaid by
the most scrupulous attentions. With a delicate dexterity that
scarcely acquainted the owner of the abstraction, everything that his
pockets contained was removed without unnecessary delay ; and
Tweasle was beginning to hope that the robbers would be content
with their booty, when one of the fellows, anxious to have his clothes
also, told him in the slang phraseology to undress, by shouting,

" Come, skin yourself."

" Skin *myself !*" cried Tweasle, understanding the words literally,
and bounding from the place in horror of what appeared to him a
refinement on even fictitious barbarity. " Skin *myself !*—You can't

mean it. I couldn't do it, if you 'd give me the world.—It 's impossible !—Oh, heavens !"

" No flash,—it won't do,—you 'll undress," said the taller of the three with a calmness that thrilled his auditor.

" Oh! good gentlemen," continued Tweasle, wishing to touch their hearts by saying something pathetic, " do consider I 'm a married man !—think of my poor wife !—think of my poor wife !"

" Carry her that 'ere with my compliments," cried the beggar, dashing his fist into Tweasle's face ; an act which was received by the rest as an excellent joke.

" It will do you no good to ill-use a fellow-creature," replied Tweasle distinctly, as though the blow had refreshed him. " Don't think I shall resist ; take what you please ; only, as you are a man—in human form—in this world and in the next ——"

" Sugar me ! You 're just agoing it nicely !" interrupted the mendicant. " I 'm blowed if ve pads don't teach more vartey than a bench of bishops. Never in all my born life *borrowed on a friend* that the beggar didn't funk pious and grunt gospel."

" But it is a natural impossibility for any man to skin himself."

" We 'll do it for you, if you don't begin."

" Oh my heart ! No!—Think of something else ;—I 'm willing to do anything but that."

" Stow that ! Skin yourself,—shake them rags off your ugly pig of a body ;—undress, and be d—d to you !"

Mr. Tweasle, who from this last speech gathered enough to remove his more horrible misgivings, delicately hinted at the inappropriateness of the place for such a purpose, the coolness of the night, the dislike he had to spectators at his toilet, and other things objectionable, but without effect : his opposition only confirmed the robbers' resolution, till a smart blow on the left cheek showed that they were inclined to silence, if they could not convince him.

Reluctantly the old man began to unrobe, parting with his garments one by one, and begging as a favour he might be allowed to retain only his waistcoat, on the worthlessness of which he expatiated till he convinced the plunderers it was of more value than its outside promised, as proved to be the case, notes to the amount of several hundreds being found pinned to the lining. They made many mock apologies for depriving him of this ; sarcastically complimenting him for his modesty, which easily parted with other coverings, but blushed to expose his bosom : then, kicking him till he fell to the earth, there they left him..

Mrs. Tweasle reached the Italian villa as it was getting dusk, and the family sat up till midnight expecting Mr. Tweasle's arrival. As the hours advanced, the lady became alarmed, and sent Charles with a tumbler of rum and water into the kitchen, who, on his return, announced that Martha had declined the kitchen chair in favour of John's knee. " Never mind," cried the lady, made considerate by her fears ; " such things are thought nothing of in the country." Whereupon she proceeded, with a strange concatenation of ideas, to state her opinion of second marriages ; lamented that widows' caps were so difficult to get up ; drank a little more rum and water ; endeavoured to divert her mind with the Newgate Calendar, but could not enjoy it for thinking how cruel it was of Mr. Tweasle not to come home earlier, and openly protested against sleeping alone in a strange house ; then took upon herself, in Mr. Tweasle's absence, to read prayers and lock up for the night. The signal for retiring being given, each took a candlestick; but, before they separated, the mistress entreated all of them to be very watchful in their sleep for fear of robbers, as she was certain Mr. Tweasle would not be home that night, and did not know what his absence might bring about.

The subject being once started, every one tarried to relate some tale of midnight assassination ; and all of them selected a strange un- inhabited dwelling as the scene of their agitating incidents. The straw and half-opened packages which strewed the apartment gave the place where they were congregated a cheerless aspect; and they were excited to a degree of listening silence, and staring inquisitively at one another, while John recounted how a lady of high respectabi- lity chanced to be sitting by herself in the kitchen of a dilapidated mansion about two hours after midnight, and looking thoughtfully, not knowing what ailed her, at a round hole where a knot in the wainscot had been thrust out, when she saw the large dark sparkling eye of a most ferocious assassin peeping at her through the opening.

Just as John had reached this point of painful interest, the heavy foot of a man was heard to pass hastily over the bridge, and the next moment the front-door was violently shaken. The two females in- stantly pinioned John by clinging round him with all the tenacity of terror, while at the same time they were loud in their demands for that protection which, had they needed it, he was by them effectually disabled from affording ; while Master Tweasle, seizing the rattle, and aiding its noise with his voice, in no small degree increased the family distraction ; above which, however, was plainly heard some one with- out, using his best endeavours to force the entrance. Whoever that some one was, he appeared wholly unmindful of secrecy ; which pal- pable contempt of caution, and open disregard of whatever resistance the inhabitants might be able to make, greatly increased their fear of the villain's intentions. At each shock the door sustained, shrieks were uttered by the women, accompanied by a very spirited move- ment by the boy upon the rattle ; and the interval between these assaults Mrs. Tweasle employed in murmuring prayers and com- plaints to Heaven and John for the protection of her life and property.

At last the assailant appeared to get exhausted ; his attempts gra- dually became weaker and less frequent. Emboldened by this, the family ventured to the first-floor window, whence they could plainly see what all agreed was a countryman in a white smock-frock pacing to and fro in front of the house in all the bitterest rage of excessive disappointment.

"Oh, the wretch!" cried Mrs. Tweasle. " What a good door that is ! I make no doubt he knew the furniture was not unpacked ; and, if he could only have got in, he would have carried it all off before morning : he must have known Mr. Tweasle was not at home. Oh dear me !"

Soon after she had spoken, the man seemed to have conquered his vexation, and, approaching the door, he gave a very decent double knock ; but, not receiving an answer, he knocked again somewhat louder, and then with all his former violence frequently returned, making actions as if he were vowing vengeance against the family, or calling imprecations down upon their heads for their resistance : but of what he said nothing could be heard, for this conduct so terrified the women that they screamed and shrieked, and Master Tweasle, as before, accompanied them on the rattle.

At length the robber, as if despairing of entrance, was seen to retire, but it was only to change the point of assault ; they watched the villain move towards the back of the house ; saw him, with a lofty courage that disdained at broken bottles, scale the garden-wall ; and to their extreme delight, just as they were certain the *back*-door would not hold out, beheld him approach the jessamine bower where John had on the previous evening set one of the man-traps—and there he stayed.

A council of war was now held, which would have lasted till morning had it not been interrupted by Master Charles's firing a blunderbuss out of the window, thus bravely endeavouring to bring down the robber at a long shot ; and he would have repeated his aim till he had hit his object, who might be distinctly seen making various strange contortions near the jessamine bower, had not his mother forbidden him. The boy, vexed by the check he received, mistook his ill-humour for bravery, and pettishly volunteered to advance to the thief, if John would accompany him on the expedition ; but Mrs. Tweasle asked in surprise, " Was she to be left alone at the mercy of Heaven, without protection ?" and John, with strong moral courage preferring duty to honour, rejected the proposal.

" Well, then," said the lad, " come along, Martha."

" Oh !—*me ?*" cried the girl : " oh, Master Charles !" for the boy, when he requested her company, only thought that the exchange of a woman for a man was a vast sacrifice on his part ; he never once considered how the substitution might affect the party it principally concerned.

Thus abandoned, he had stayed within, had not his mother insisted that he should not stir out : filial obedience supplied the place of resolution ; he unbolted the back-door, and in a state of obstinate alarm issued into the garden.

Advancing cautiously, and by a most circuitous way, the boy approached the jessamine bower, and there discovered *his father* writhing and moaning, with one leg fast in a trap, which, according to his own orders, had been set for the protection of the cabbages.

" Oh ! my dear boy, don't fire any more. It's me, Charles ! let me out of this—I'm dying !"

" Why, if it isn't you, father !—only wait a bit——"

" *Wait !*—don't talk nonsense !" cried Tweasle, looking at his unfortunate leg, which was held in the trap, and feeling his condition aggravated by the supposition that it was one of choice.

" Yes, I'll fetch mother."

" Hang your mother !—let me out of this !" ejaculated the poor man, who was no ways desirous of continuing his agony that it might be made a kind of domestic exhibition of ; but, deaf to his parent's entreaties, the boy ran away, quite full of his discovery. On the steps he met the maid-servant, whom he rebuked with much coarseness for appearing alarmed, and presently returned, marching like a conqueror at the head of a triumph.

All were much surprised at beholding Mr. Tweasle in such a

situation, unrobed and wounded, shivering from cold and terror, and deprived of all self-command by exhaustion and a man-trap. Mrs. Tweasle was quite overpowered by the sight: her feelings rather claimed pity than bestowed it; for while John was removing the steel trap from his master's legs, she kept moaning, and entreating her husband *only* to consider how his conduct had pained *her*. The poor maid-servant displayed great goodness of heart; she tenderly bound her master's naked legs, gently lifted him into the chair that was brought to convey him into the house, and appeared quite to overcome the natural delicacy of her sex in the praiseworthy endeavour to render a fellow-creature every possible assistance; while John and Master Tweasle seemed more inclined to converse on what had happened than to mingle in what was taking place, repeatedly putting questions which the sufferer was incapable of answering, as to wherefore he did that, or why he did not do this.

Tweasle's injuries were rather painful than dangerous: in a few days he was convalescent, and was beginning to grow valiant in his descriptions of his midnight mishaps, when the following hand-bill was submitted to his notice.

" Whereas a valuable male donkey, the property of Stephen Hedges, was on the night of the 6th of May last maliciously shot at and killed by some person or persons unknown; this is to give notice, that whoever will render such information as shall lead to the conviction of the offender or offenders, shall receive Five Pounds reward."

For some time after reading this, Tweasle appeared full of thought, when he surprised his family by a sudden resolution to send Stephen Hedges five pounds; nor could any remonstrance on the part of his wife change his charitable purpose. No one could account for this: in pence the late tobacconist had always been a pattern of benevolence; but to give *pounds* was not in the ordinary scale of his charity. None could assign a reason for so boundless a beneficence, more than they could comprehend why Tweasle should, whenever the subject was mentioned, expatiate with so much feeling on " What the poor ass must have suffered !"

TRANSLATION FROM UHLAND.

THE DREAM.

In a garden fair were roaming
  Two lovers hand in hand;
Two pale and shadowy creatures,
  They sat in that flowery land.

On the lips they kiss'd each other,
  On the cheeks so full and smooth;
They were lock'd in close embracings,
  They were blithe with the flush of youth.

Two bells were tolling sadly,—
  The dream has pass'd away;
She in the narrow cloister,
  He in a dungeon lay.

FAMILY STORIES, No. VII.

PATTY MORGAN THE MILKMAID'S STORY.

"LOOK AT THE CLOCK!"

FYTTE I.

"Look at the Clock!" quoth Winifred Pryce,
  As she open'd the door to her husband's knock,
Then paus'd to give him a piece of advice,
  "You nasty Warmint, look at the Clock!
      Is this the way, you
      Wretch, every day you
Treat her who vow'd to love and obey you?
      Out all night!
      Me in a fright;
Staggering home as it 's just getting light!
You intoxified brute! you insensible block!
Look at the Clock!—Do.—Look at the Clock!"

Winifred Pryce was tidy and clean,
Her gown was a flower'd one, her petticoat green,
Her buckles were bright as her milking cans,
And her hat was a beaver, and made like a man's;
Her little red eyes were deep set in their socket-holes,
Her gown-tail was turn'd up, and tuck'd through the pocket-holes:
      A face like a ferret
      Betoken'd her spirit:
To conclude, Mrs. Pryce was not over young,
Had very short legs, and a very long tongue.

      Now David Pryce
      Had one darling vice;
Remarkably partial to anything nice,
Nought that was good to him came amiss,
Whether to eat, or to drink, or to kiss!
      Especially ale—
      If it was not too stale
I really believe he 'd have emptied a pail;
      Not that in Wales
      They talk of their Ales;
To pronounce the word they make use of might trouble you,
Being spelt with a C, two Rs, and a W.

      That particular day,
      As I 've heard people say,
Mr. David Pryce had been soaking his clay,
And amusing himself with his pipe and cheroots,
The whole afternoon at the Goat in Boots,
      With a couple more soakers,
      Thoroughbred smokers,
Both, like himself, prime singers and jokers;
And, long after day had drawn to a close,
And the rest of the world was wrapp'd in repose,
They were roaring out "Shenkin!" and "Ar hydd y nos;"
While David himself, to a Sassenach tune,
Sang, "We 've drunk down the Sun, boys! let 's drink down the Moon!
      What have we with day to do?
      Mrs. Winifred Pryce, 'twas made for you!"

At length, when they couldn't well drink any more,
Old "Goat-in-Boots" shew'd them the door;
  And then came that knock,
  And the sensible shock
David felt when his wife cried, "Look at the Clock
For the hands stood as crooked as crooked might be,
The long at the Twelve, and the short at the Three!

This self-same Clock had long been a bone
Of contention between this Darby and Joan;
And often among their pother and rout,
When this otherwise amiable couple fell out,
  Pryce would drop a cool hint,
  With an ominous squint
At its case, of an "Uncle" of his, who'd a "Spout."
  That horrid word "Spout"
  No sooner came out,
Than Winifred Pryce would turn her about,
  And with scorn on her lip,
  And a hand on each hip,
"Spout" herself till her nose grew red at the tip,
  "You thundering willain,
  I know you'd be killing
Your wife,—ay, a dozen of wives,—for a shilling!
  You may do what you please,
  You may sell my chemise,
(Mrs. P. was too well-bred to mention her stock,)
But I never will part with my Grandmother's Clock!"

Mrs. Pryce's tongue ran long and ran fast;
But patience is apt to wear out at last,
And David Pryce in temper was quick,
So he stretch'd out his hand, and caught hold of a stick;
Perhaps in its use he might mean to be lenient,
But walking just then wasn't very convenient,
  So he threw it, instead,
  Direct at her head.
  It knock'd off her hat;
  Down she fell flat;
Her case, perhaps, was not much mended by that;
But, whatever it was,—whether rage and pain
Produc'd apoplexy, or burst a vein,
Or her tumble induc'd a concussion of brain,
I can't say for certain,—but *this* I can,
When, sober'd by fright, to assist her he ran,
Mrs. Winifred Pryce was as dead as Queen Anne!

  The fearful catastrophe
  Named in my last strophe
As adding to grim Death's exploits such a vast trophy,
Soon made a great noise; and the shocking fatality
Like wild-fire ran over the whole Principality.
And then came Mr. Ap Thomas, the Coroner,
With his jury to sit, some dozen or more, on her.
  Mr. Pryce, to commence
  His "ingenious defence,"
Made a "pow'rful appeal" to the jury's "good sense,"
  "The world he must defy
  Ever to justify
Any presumption of "Malice Prepense;"
  The unlucky lick
  From the end of the stick
He "deplored," he was "apt to be rather too quick;"

But, really, her prating
Was so aggravating:
Some trifling correction was just what he meant; all
The rest, he assured them, was " quite accidental !"

Then he called Mr. Jones,
Who deposed to her tones,
And her gestures, and hints about "breaking his bones."
While Mr. Ap Morgan, and Mr. Ap Rhys
Declared the Deceased
Had styled him "a Beast,"
And swore they had witness'd, with grief and surprise,
The allusions she made to his limbs and his eyes.

The jury, in fine, having sat on the body
The whole day, discussing the case, and gin-toddy,
Return'd about half-past eleven at night
The following verdict, " We find, *Sarve her right !*"

FYTTE II.

Mr. Pryce, Mrs. Winifred Pryce being dead,
Felt lonely, and moped; and one evening he said
He would marry Miss Davis at once in her stead.

Not far from his dwelling,
From the vale proudly swelling,
Rose a mountain; its name you'll excuse me from telling,
For the vowels made use of in Welsh are so few
That the A and the E, the I, O, and the U,
Have really but little or nothing to do ;
And the duty, of course, falls the heavier by far
On the L, and the H, and the N, and the R.
Its first syllable, " PEN,"
Is pronounceable;—then
Come two L Ls, and two H Hs, two F Fs, and an N ;
About half a score Rs, and some Ws follow,
Beating all my best efforts at euphony hollow:
But we shan't have to mention it often, so when
We do, with your leave, we'll curtail it to " PEN."

Well,—the moon shone bright
Upon " PEN " that night,
When Pryce, being quit of his fuss and his fright,
Was scaling its side
With that sort of stride
A man puts out when walking in search of a bride.
Mounting higher and higher,
He began to perspire,
Till, finding his legs were beginning to tire,
And feeling opprest
By a pain in his chest,
He paus'd, and turn'd round to take breath, and to rest;
A walk all up hill is apt, as we know,
To make one, however robust, puff and blow,
So he stopped, and look'd down on the valley below.

O'er fell, and o'er fen,
Over mountain and glen,
All bright in the moonshine, his eye rov'd, and then
All the Patriot rose in his soul, and he thought
Of Wales, and her glories, and all he'd been taught

Of her Heroes of old,
So brave and so bold,—
Of her Bards with long beards, and harps mounted in gold;
Of King Edward the First,
Of mem'ry accurst;
And the scandalous manner in which he behaved,
Killing Poets by dozens,
With their uncles and cousins,
Of whom not one in fifty had ever been shaved.
Of the Court Ball, at which, by a lucky mishap,
Owen Tudor fell into Queen Katherine's lap;
And how Mr. Tudor
Successfully woo'd her,
Till the Dowager put on a new wedding ring,
And so made him Father-in-law to the King.

He thought upon Arthur, and Merlin of yore,
On Gryffyth ap Conan, and Owen Glendour;
On Pendragon, and Heaven knows how many more.
He thought of all this, as he gazed, in a trice,
And on all things, in short, but the late Mrs. Pryce;
When a lumbering noise from behind made him start,
And sent the blood back in full tide 'to his heart,
Which went pit-a-pat
As he cried out, "What's that?—
That very queer sound?
Does it come from the ground?
Or the air,—from above, or below, or around?
It is not like Talking,
It is not like Walking,
It's not like the clattering of pot or of pan,
Or the tramp of a horse,—or the tread of a man,—
Or the hum of a crowd,—or the shouting of boys,—
It's really a deuced odd sort of a noise!
Not unlike a Cart's,—but that can't be; for when
Could "all the King's horses and all the King's men,"
With Old Nick for a waggoner, drive one up "Pen?"

Pryce, usually brimful of valour when drunk,
Now experienced what schoolboys denominate "funk."
In vain he look'd back
On the whole of the track
He had traversed; a thick cloud, uncommonly black,
At this moment obscured the broad disc of the moon,
And did not seem likely to pass away soon;
While clearer and clearer,
'Twas plain to the hearer,
Be the noise what it might, it drew nearer and nearer,
And sounded, as Pryce to this moment declares,
Very much "like a Coffin a-walking up stairs."

Mr. Pryce had begun
To "make up" for a run,
As in such a companion he saw no great fun,
When a single bright ray
Shone out on the way
He had pass'd, and he saw with no little dismay
Coming after him, bounding o'er crag and o'er rock,
The deceased Mrs. Winifred's "Grandmother's Clock!!"
'Twas so!—it had certainly moved from its place,
And come, lumbering on thus, to hold him in chase;
'Twas the very same Head, and the very same Case,
And nothing was alter'd at all but the Face!

In that he perceived, with no little surprise,
The two little winder-holes turn'd into eyes
    Blazing with ire,
    Like two coals of fire;
And the " Name of the Maker " was changed to a Lip,
And the Hands to a Nose with a very red tip.
No!—he could not mistake it,—'twas SHE to the life !
The identical Face of his dear defunct Wife ! !

    One glance was enough,
    Completely " *Quant. Suff.*"
As the doctors write down when they send you their " stuff,"—
Like a Weather-cock whirl'd by a vehement puff,
    David turn'd himself round ;
    Ten feet of ground
He clear'd, in his start, at the very first bound !

I 've seen people run at West-End Fair for cheeses,
I 've seen Ladies run at Bow Fair for chemises,
At Greenwich Fair twenty men run for a hat,
And one from a Bailiff much faster than that ;
At foot-ball I 've seen lads run after the bladder,
I 've seen Irish Bricklayers run up a ladder,
I 've seen little boys run away from a cane,
And I 've seen, (that is, *read of*,) good running in Spain ;
    But I never did read
    Of, or witness, such speed
As David exerted that evening.—Indeed
All I ever have heard of boys, women, or men,
Falls far short of Pryce, as he ran over " PEN !"

    He reaches its brow,—
    He has past it, and now
Having once gain'd the summit, and managed to cross it, he
Rolls down the side with uncommon velocity ;
    But, run as he will,
    Or roll down the hill,
That bugbear behind him is after him still !
And close at his heels, not at all to his liking,
The terrible Clock keeps on ticking and striking,
    Till, exhausted and sore,
    He can't run any more,
But falls as he reaches Miss Davis's door,
And screams when they rush out, alarm'd at his knock,
" Oh ! Look at the Clock !—Do.—Look at the Clock ! !"

Miss Davis look'd up, Miss Davis look'd down,
She saw nothing there to alarm her ;—a frown
    Came o'er her white forehead,
    She said " It was horrid
A man should come knocking at that time of night,
And give her Mamma and herself such a fright ;
    To squall and to bawl
    About nothing at all—"
She begg'd " he 'd not think of repeating his call,
    His late wife's disaster
    By no means had past her,"
She 'd " have him to know she was meat for his Master !"
Then, regardless alike of his love and his woes,
She turn'd on her heel as she turn'd up her nose.

Poor David in vain
Implored to remain,
He " dared not," he said, " cross the mountain again."
Why the fair was obdurate
None knows,—to be sure, it
Was said she was setting her cap at the Curate ;—
Be that as it may, it is certain the sole hole
Pryce could find to creep into that night was the Coal-hole !
In that shady retreat,
With nothing to eat,
And with very bruis'd limbs, and with very sore feet,
All night close he kept ;
I can't say he slept ;
But he sigh'd, and he sobb'd, and he groan'd, and he wept,
Lamenting his sins
And his two broken shins,
Bewailing his fate with contortions and grins,
And her he once thought a complete *Rara Avis*,
Consigning to Satan,—viz. cruel Miss Davis !

Mr. David has since had a " serious call,"
He never drinks ale, wine, or spirits, at all,
And they say he is going to Exeter Hall
To make a grand speech,
And to preach, and to teach
People that " they can't brew their malt-liquor too small !"
That an ancient Welsh Poet, one PYNDAR AP TUDOR,
Was right in proclaiming " ARISTON MEN UDOR !"
Which means " The pure Element
Is for the belly meant !"
And that *Gin*'s but a *Snare* of Old Nick the deluder !

And " still on each evening when pleasure fills up,"
At the old Goat-in-Boots, with metheglin, each cup,
Mr. Pryce, if he 's there,
Will get into " the Chair,"
And make all his *quondam* associates stare
By calling aloud to the landlady's daughter,
" Patty ! bring a cigar, and a glass of Spring Water !"
The dial he constantly watches ; and when
The long hand 's at the " XII," and the short at the " X,"
He gets on his legs,
Drains his glass to the dregs,
Takes his hat and great-coat off their several pegs,
With his President's hammer bestows his last knock,
And says solemnly,—" Gentlemen !
        " LOOK AT THE CLOCK ! ! !"

THOMAS INGOLDSBY.

Tappington Everard, July 24.

SONG OF THE MONTH. No. IX.
September, 1837.

THE DOUBLE BARREL.

BY FATHER PROUT.

Duo quisque Alpina coruscat
Gæsa manu.—*Æneid. lib. 8.*
Παν πραγμα δυας εχιι λαϐας.—*Epictetus.*

SEPTEMBER the first on the moorland hath burst,
    And already with jocund carol
Each NIMROD of NOUSE hurries off to the grouse,
    And has shouldered his DOUBLE BARREL;
For well doth he ken, as he hies through the glen,
    That scanty will be *his* laurel
        Who hath not
        On the spot
    (Should he miss a first shot)
Some resource in a DOUBLE BARREL.

'Twas the Goddess of Sport, in her woodland court,
    DIANA, first taught this moral,
Which the Goddess of Love soon adopted, and strove
    To improve on the " double barrel."
Hence her CUPID, we know, put two strings to his bow;
    And she laughs, when two lovers quarrel,
        At the lot
        Of the sot
    Who, to soothe him, han't got
The resource of a DOUBLE BARREL.

Nay, the hint was too good to lie hid in the wood,
    Or to lurk in two lips of coral;
Hence the God of the Grape (who his betters would ape)
    Knows the use of a DOUBLE BARREL.
His escutcheon he decks with a double XX,
    And his blithe *October* carol
        Follows up
        With the sup
    Of a flowing ale-cup
September's DOUBLE BARREL.

Water-grass-hill, Kal. VII^{bre}.

GENIUS; OR, THE DOG'S-MEAT DOG.

BEING A SECOND "TAILED SONNET," IN THE ITALIAN MANNER.*

BY EGERTON WEBBE.

" Hal, thou hast the most unsavoury similes."—*Falstaff.*

SINCE Genius hath the immortal faculty
    Of bringing grist to other people's mills,
    While for itself no office it fulfils,
And cannot choose but starve amazingly,

* For the former specimen, as well as some critical account of the comic sonnets of the Italians, see the April number of *Bentley's Miscellany.*

Methinks 'tis very like the dog's-meat dog,
 That 'twixt Black Friars and White sometimes I've seen,—
 Afflicted quadruped, jejune and lean,
Whom none do feed, but all do burn to flog.

For why? He draws the dog's-meat cart, you see,—
 Himself a dog. All dogs his coming hail,
 Long dogs and short, and dogs of various tail,
Yea truly, every sort of dogs that be.
Where'er he cometh him his cousins greet,
Yet not for love, but only for the meat,—
  In Little Tower Street,
Or opposite the pump on Fish-street Hill,
Or where the Green Man is the Green Man still,
  Or where you will :—
It is not he, but, ah! it is the cart
With which his cousins are so loth to part ;
  (That's nature, bless your heart!)
And you'll observe his neck is almost stiff
With turning round to try and get a sniff,
  As now and then a whiff,
Charged from behind, a transient savour throws,
That curls with hope the corners of his nose,
  Then all too quickly goes,
And leaves him buried in conjectures dark,
Developed in a sort of muffled bark.
  For I need scarce remark
That that sagacious dog hath often guess'd
There's something going on of interest
  Behind him, not confest ;
And I have seen him whisk with sudden start
Entirely round, as he would face the cart,
  Which could he by no art,
Because of cunning mechanism. Lord!
But how a proper notion to afford ?
  How possibly record,
With any sort of mental satisfaction,
The look of anguish—the immense distraction—
  Pictured in face and action,
When, whisking round, he hath discovered there
Five dogs,—all jolly dogs—besides a pair
  Of cats, most debonair,
In high assembly met, sublimely lunching,
Best horse's flesh in breathless silence munching,
  While he, poor beast! is crunching
His unavailing teeth ?—You must be sensible
'Tis aggravating—cruel—indefensible—
  Incomprehensible.
And to his grave I do believe he'll go,
Sad dog's-meat dog, nor ever know
  Whence all those riches flow
Which seem to spring about him where he is,
Finding their way to every mouth but his.—
  I know such similes
By some are censured as not being savoury ;
But still it's better than to talk of " knavery,"
  And " wretched authors' slavery,"
With other words of ominous import.
I much prefer a figure of this sort.
  And so, to cut it short,
(For I abhor all poor rhetoric fuss,)
Ask what the devil I mean—I answer thus,
  THAT DOG'S A GENIUS.

George Cruikshank

OLIVER TWIST;

OR, THE PARISH BOY'S PROGRESS.

BY BOZ.

ILLUSTRATED BY GEORGE CRUIKSHANK.

CHAPTER THE FOURTEENTH.

COMPRISING FURTHER PARTICULARS OF OLIVER'S STAY AT MR. BROWNLOW'S, WITH THE REMARKABLE PREDICTION WHICH ONE MR. GRIMWIG UTTERED CONCERNING HIM, WHEN HE WENT OUT ON AN ERRAND.

OLIVER soon recovered from the fainting-fit into which Mr. Brownlow's abrupt exclamation had thrown him; and the subject of the picture was carefully avoided, both by the old gentleman and Mrs. Bedwin, in the conversation that ensued, which indeed bore no reference to Oliver's history or prospects, but was confined to such topics as might amuse without exciting him. He was still too weak to get up to breakfast; but, when he came down into the housekeeper's room next day, his first act was to cast an eager glance at the wall, in the hope of again looking on the face of the beautiful lady. His expectations were disappointed, however, for the picture had been removed.

"Ah!" said the housekeeper, watching the direction of Oliver's eyes. "It is gone, you see."

"I see it is, ma'am," replied Oliver, with a sigh. "Why have they taken it away?"

"It has been taken down, child, because Mr. Brownlow said, that, as it seemed to worry you, perhaps it might prevent your getting well, you know," rejoined the old lady.

"Oh, no, indeed it didn't worry me, ma'am," said Oliver. "I liked to see it; I quite loved it."

"Well, well!" said the old lady, good-humouredly; "you get well as fast as ever you can, dear, and it shall be hung up again. There, I promise you that; now let us talk about something else."

This was all the information Oliver could obtain about the picture at that time, and as the old lady had been so kind to him in his illness, he endeavoured to think no more of the subject just then; so listened attentively to a great many stories she told him about an amiable and handsome daughter of hers, who was married to an amiable and handsome man, and lived in the country; and a son, who was clerk to a merchant in the West Indies, and who was also such a good young man, and wrote such dutiful letters home four times a year, that it brought the tears into her eyes to talk about them. When the old lady had expatiated a long time on the excellences of her children, and the merits of her kind good husband besides, who had been dead and gone, poor dear soul! just six-and-twenty years, it was time to have tea; and after tea she began to teach Oliver cribbage, which he learnt as quickly as she could teach, and at which game they played, with great interest and gravity, until it was time for the invalid to have some warm wine and water, with a slice of dry toast, and to go cosily to bed.

They were happy days those of Oliver's recovery. Everything was so quiet, and neat, and orderly, everybody so kind and gentle, that after the noise and turbulence in the midst of which he had always lived, it seemed like heaven itself. He was no sooner strong enough to put his clothes on properly, than Mr. Brownlow caused a complete new suit, and a new cap, and a new pair of shoes, to be provided for him. As Oliver was told that he might do what he liked with the old clothes, he gave them to a servant who had been very kind to him, and asked her to sell them to a Jew, and keep the money for herself. This she very readily did; and, as Oliver looked out of the parlour window, and saw the Jew roll them up in his bag and walk away, he felt quite delighted to think that they were safely gone, and that there was now no possible danger of his ever being able to wear them again. They were sad rags, to tell the truth; and Oliver had never had a new suit before.

One evening, about a week after the affair of the picture, as Oliver was sitting talking to Mrs. Bedwin, there came a message down from Mr. Brownlow, that if Oliver Twist felt pretty well, he should like to see him in his study, and talk to him a little while.

"Bless us, and save us! wash your hands, and let me part your hair nicely for you, child," said Mrs. Bedwin. "Dear heart alive! if we had known he would have asked for you, we would have put you a clean collar on, and made you as smart as sixpence."

Oliver did as the old lady bade him, and, although she lamented grievously meanwhile that there was not even time to crimp the little frill that bordered his shirt-collar, he looked so delicate and handsome, despite that important personal advantage, that she went so far as to say, looking at him with great complacency from head to foot, that she really didn't think it would have been possible on the longest notice to have made much difference in him for the better.

Thus encouraged, Oliver tapped at the study door, and, on Mr. Brownlow calling to him to come in, found himself in a little back room, quite full of books, with a window looking into some pleasant little gardens. There was a table drawn up before the window, at which Mr. Brownlow was seated reading. When he saw Oliver, he pushed the book away from him, and told him to come near the table and sit down. Oliver complied, marvelling where the people could be found to read such a great number of books as seemed to be written to make the world wiser,—which is still a marvel to more experienced people than Oliver Twist every day of their lives.

"There are a good many books, are there not, my boy?" said Mr. Brownlow, observing the curiosity with which Oliver surveyed the shelves that reached from the floor to the ceiling.

" A great number, sir," replied Oliver; " I never saw so many."

" You shall read them if you behave well," said the old gentleman kindly; " and you will like that, better than looking at the outsides,—that is, in some cases, because there *are* books of which the backs and covers are by far the best parts."

" I suppose they are those heavy ones, sir," said Oliver, pointing to some large quartos with a good deal of gilding about the binding.

" Not those," said the old gentleman, patting Oliver on the head, and smiling as he did so; " but other equally heavy ones, though of a much smaller size. How should you like to grow up a clever man, and write books, eh?"

" I think I would rather read them, sir," replied Oliver.

" What! wouldn't you like to be a book-writer?" said the old gentleman.

Oliver considered a little while, and at last said he should think it would be a much better thing to be a bookseller; upon which the old gentleman laughed heartily, and declared he had said a very good thing, which Oliver felt glad to have done, though he by no means knew what it was.

" Well, well," said the old gentleman, composing his features, "don't be afraid; we won't make an author of you, while there's an honest trade to be learnt, or brick-making to turn to."

" Thank you, sir," said Oliver; and at the earnest manner of his reply the old gentleman laughed again, and said something about a curious instinct, which Oliver, not understanding, paid no very great attention to.

" Now," said Mr. Brownlow, speaking if possible in a kinder, but at the same time in a much more serious manner than Oliver had ever heard him speak in yet, " I want you to pay great attention, my boy, to what I am going to say. I shall talk to you without any reserve, because I am sure you are as well able to understand me as many older persons would be."

" Oh, don't tell me you are going to send me away, sir, pray!" exclaimed Oliver, alarmed by the serious tone of the old gentleman's commencement; " don't turn me out of doors to wander in the streets again. Let me stay here and be a servant. Don't send me back to the wretched place I came from. Have mercy upon a poor boy, sir; do!"

" My dear child," said the old gentleman, moved by the warmth of Oliver's sudden appeal, " you need not be afraid of my deserting you, unless you give me cause."

" I never, never will, sir," interposed Oliver.

" I hope not," rejoined the old gentleman; " I do not think you ever will. I have been deceived before, in the objects whom I have endeavoured to benefit; but I feel strongly disposed to trust you, nevertheless, and more strongly interested in your behalf than I can well account for, even to myself. The persons on whom I have bestowed my dearest love lie deep in their graves; but, although the happiness and delight of my life lie

buried there too, I have not made a coffin of my heart, and
sealed it up for ever on my best affections.   Deep affliction has
only made them stronger ; it ought, I think, for it should refine
our nature."

As the old gentleman said this in a low voice, more to himself than to his companion, and remained silent for a short time
afterwards, Oliver sat quite still, almost afraid to breathe.

" Well, well," said the old gentleman at length in a more
cheerful voice, " I only say this, because you have a young
heart ; and knowing that I have suffered great pain and sorrow, you will be more careful, perhaps, not to wound me again.
You say you are an orphan, without a friend in the world ; and
all the inquiries I have been able to make confirm the statement.
Let me hear your story ; where you came from, who brought
you up, and how you got into the company in which I found
you.   Speak the truth ; and if I find you have committed no
crime, you will never be friendless while I live."

Oliver's sobs quite checked his utterance for some minutes ;
and just when he was on the point of beginning to relate how
he had been brought up at the farm, and carried to the workhouse by Mr. Bumble, a peculiarly impatient little double-
knock was heard at the street-door, and the servant, running
up stairs, announced Mr. Grimwig.

" Is he coming up ?" inquired Mr. Brownlow.

" Yes, sir," replied the servant.   " He asked if there were
any muffins in the house, and, when I told him yes, he said he
had come to tea."

Mr. Brownlow smiled, and, turning to Oliver, said Mr. Grimwig was an old friend of his, and he must not mind his being a
little rough in his manners, for he was a worthy creature at
bottom, as he had reason to know.

" Shall I go down stairs, sir ?" inquired Oliver.

" No," replied Mr. Brownlow ; " I would rather you stopped
here."

At this moment there walked into the room, supporting himself by a thick stick, a stout old gentleman, rather lame in one
leg, who was dressed in a blue coat, striped waistcoat, nankeen
breeches and gaiters, and a broad-brimmed white hat, with the
sides turned up with green.   A very small-plaited shirt-frill
stuck out from his waistcoat, and a very long steel watch-chain,
with nothing but a key at the end, dangled loosely below it.
The ends of his white neckerchief were twisted into a ball about
the size of an orange ;—the variety of shapes into which his
countenance was twisted defy description.   He had a manner
of screwing his head round on one side when he spoke, and
looking out of the corners of his eyes at the same time, which
irresistibly reminded the beholder of a parrot.   In this attitude
he fixed himself the moment he made his appearance ; and, holding out a small piece of orange-peel at arm's length, exclaimed
in a growling, discontented voice,

" Look here! do you see this? Isn't it a most wonderful
and extraordinary thing that I can't call at a man's house but I
find a piece of this cursed poor-surgeon's-friend on the staircase?
I 've been lamed with orange-peel once, and I know orange-peel
will be my death at last. It will, sir; orange-peel will be my
death, or I 'll be content to eat my own head, sir!" This was
the handsome offer with which Mr. Grimwig backed and confirmed nearly every assertion he made; and it was the more
singular in his case, because, even admitting, for the sake of
argument, the possibility of scientific improvements being ever
brought to that pass which will enable a gentleman to eat his
own head in the event of his being so disposed, Mr. Grimwig's
head was such a particularly large one, that the most sanguine
man alive could hardly entertain a hope of being able to get
through it at a sitting, to put entirely out of the question a
very thick coating of powder.

" I 'll eat my head, sir," repeated Mr. Grimwig, striking his
stick upon the ground. " Hallo! what 's that?" he added,
looking at Oliver, and retreating a pace or two.

" This is young Oliver Twist, whom we were speaking
about," said Mr. Brownlow.

Oliver bowed.

" You don't mean to say that 's the boy that had the fever, I
hope?" said Mr. Grimwig, recoiling a little further. " Wait a
minute, don't speak: stop—" continued Mr. Grimwig abruptly,
losing all dread of the fever in his triumph at the discovery;
" that 's the boy that had the orange! If that 's not the boy,
sir, that had the orange, and threw this bit of peel upon the
staircase, I 'll eat my head and his too."

" No, no, he has not had one," said Mr. Brownlow, laughing.
" Come, put down your hat, and speak to my young friend."

" I feel strongly on this subject, sir," said the irritable old gentleman, drawing off his gloves. " There 's always more or less
orange-peel on the pavement in our street, and I *know* it 's put
there by the surgeon's boy at the corner. A young woman
stumbled over a bit last night, and fell against my garden-rail-
ings; directly she got up I saw her look towards his infernal
red lamp with the pantomime-light. ' Don't go to him,' I called out of the window, ' he 's an assassin,—a man-trap!' So
he is. If he is not——" Here the irascible old gentleman
gave a great knock on the ground with his stick, which was always understood by his friends to imply the customary offer
whenever it was not expressed in words. Then, still keeping his
stick in his hand, he sat down, and, opening a double eye-glass
which he wore attached to a broad black riband, took a view of
Oliver, who, seeing that he was the object of inspection, coloured, and bowed again.

" That 's the boy, is it?" said Mr. Grimwig, at length.

" That is the boy," replied Mr. Brownlow, nodding good-
humouredly to Oliver.

" How are you, boy ?" said Mr. Grimwig.

"A great deal better, thank you, sir," replied Oliver.

Mr. Brownlow, seeming to apprehend that his singular friend was about to say something disagreeable, asked Oliver to step down stairs, and tell Mrs. Bedwin they were ready for tea, which, as he did not half like the visitor's manner, he was very happy to do.

" He is a nice-looking boy, is he not ?" inquired Mr. Brownlow.

"I don't know," replied Grimwig, pettishly.

"Don't know ?"

" No, I don't know. I never see any difference in boys. I only know two sorts of boys,—mealy boys, and beef-faced boys."

" And which is Oliver ?"

" Mealy. I know a friend who's got a beef-faced boy; a fine boy they call him, with a round head, and red cheeks, and glaring eyes; a horrid boy, with a body and limbs that appear to be swelling out of the seams of his blue clothes—with the voice of a pilot, and the appetite of a wolf. I know him, the wretch !"

" Come," said Mr. Brownlow, " these are not the characteristics of young Oliver Twist; so he needn't excite your wrath."

"They are not," replied Grimwig. " He may have worse."

Here Mr. Brownlow coughed impatiently, which appeared to afford Mr. Grimwig the most exquisite delight.

" He may have worse, I say," repeated Mr. Grimwig. " Where does he come from ? Who is he ? What is he ? He has had a fever—what of that ? Fevers are not peculiar to good people, are they ? Bad people have fevers sometimes, haven't they, eh ? I knew a man that was hung in Jamaica for murdering his master; he had had a fever six times; he wasn't recommended to mercy on that account. Pooh ! nonsense !"

Now, the fact was, that, in the inmost recesses of his own heart, Mr. Grimwig was strongly disposed to admit that Oliver's appearance and manner were unusually prepossessing, but he had a strong appetite for contradiction, sharpened on this occasion by the finding of the orange-peel; and inwardly determining that no man should dictate to him whether a boy was well-looking or not, he had resolved from the first to oppose his friend. When Mr. Brownlow admitted that on no one point of inquiry could he yet return any satisfactory answer, and that he had postponed any investigation into Oliver's previous history until he thought the boy was strong enough to bear it, Mr. Grimwig chuckled maliciously, and demanded, with a sneer, whether the housekeeper was in the habit of counting the plate at night; because, if she didn't find a table-spoon or two missing some sunshiny morning, why, he would be content to ——, et cetera.

All this Mr. Brownlow, although himself somewhat of an impetuous gentleman, knowing his friend's peculiarities, bore with great good humour; and as Mr. Grimwig, at tea, was graciously pleased to express his entire approval of the muffins, matters went on very smoothly, and Oliver, who made one of the party, began to feel more at his ease than he had yet done in the fierce old gentleman's presence.

"And when are you going to hear a full, true, and particular account of the life and adventures of Oliver Twist?" asked Grimwig of Mr. Brownlow, at the conclusion of the meal: looking sideways at Oliver as he resumed the subject.

"To-morrow morning," replied Mr. Brownlow. "I would rather he was alone with me at the time. Come up to me to-morrow morning at ten o'clock, my dear."

"Yes, sir," replied Oliver. He answered with some hesitation, because he was confused by Mr. Grimwig's looking so hard at him.

"I'll tell you what," whispered that gentleman to Mr. Brownlow; "he won't come up to you to-morrow morning. I saw him hesitate. He is deceiving you, my dear friend."

"I'll swear he is not," replied Mr. Brownlow, warmly.

"If he is not," said Mr. Grimwig, "I'll ——" and down went the stick.

"I'll answer for that boy's truth with my life," said Mr. Brownlow, knocking the table.

"And I for his falsehood with my head," rejoined Mr. Grimwig, knocking the table also.

"We shall see," said Mr. Brownlow, checking his rising passion.

"We will," replied Mr. Grimwig, with a provoking smile; "we will."

As fate would have it, Mrs. Bedwin chanced to bring in at this moment a small parcel of books which Mr. Brownlow had that morning purchased of the identical bookstall-keeper who has already figured in this history; which having laid on the table, she prepared to leave the room.

"Stop the boy, Mrs. Bedwin," said Mr. Brownlow; "there is something to go back."

"He has gone, sir," replied Mrs. Bedwin.

"Call after him," said Mr. Brownlow; it's particular. He's a poor man, and they are not paid for. There are some books to be taken back, too."

The street-door was opened. Oliver ran one way, and the girl another, and Mrs. Bedwin stood on the step and screamed for the boy; but there was no boy in sight, and both Oliver and the girl returned in a breathless state to report that there were no tidings of him.

"Dear me, I am very sorry for that," exclaimed Mr. Brownlow; "I particularly wished those books to be returned to-night."

"Send Oliver with them," said Mr. Grimwig, with an ironical smile; "he will be sure to deliver them safely, you know."

"Yes; do let me take them, if you please, sir," said Oliver; "I'll run all the way, sir."

The old gentleman was just going to say that Oliver should not go out on any account, when a most malicious cough from Mr. Grimwig determined him that he should, and by his prompt discharge of the commission prove to him the injustice of his suspicions, on this head at least, at once.

"You *shall* go, my dear," said the old gentleman. "The books are on a chair by my table. Fetch them down."

Oliver, delighted to be of use, brought down the books under his arm in a great bustle, and waited, cap in hand, to hear what message he was to take.

"You are to say," said Mr. Brownlow, glancing steadily at Grimwig,—"you are to say that you have brought those books back, and that you have come to pay the four pound ten I owe him. This is a five-pound note, so you will have to bring me back ten shillings change."

"I won't be ten minutes, sir," replied Oliver, eagerly; and, having buttoned up the bank-note in his jacket pocket, and placed the books carefully under his arm, he made a respectful bow, and left the room. Mrs. Bedwin followed him to the street-door, giving him many directions about the nearest way, and the name of the bookseller, and the name of the street, all of which Oliver said he clearly understood; and, having super-added many injunctions to be sure and not take cold, the careful old lady at length permitted him to depart.

"Bless his sweet face!" said the old lady, looking after him. "I can't bear, somehow, to let him go out of my sight."

At this moment Oliver looked gaily round, and nodded before he turned the corner. The old lady smilingly returned his salutation, and, closing the door, went back to her own room.

"Let me see; he'll be back in twenty minutes, at the longest," said Mr. Brownlow, pulling out his watch, and placing it on the table. "It will be dark by that time."

"Oh! you really expect him to come back, do you?" inquired Mr. Grimwig.

"Don't you?" asked Mr. Brownlow, smiling.

The spirit of contradiction was strong in Mr. Grimwig's breast at the moment, and it was rendered stronger by his friend's confident smile.

"No," he said, smiting the table with his fist, "I do not. The boy has got a new suit of clothes on his back, a set of valuable books under his arm, and a five-pound note in his pocket; he'll join his old friends the thieves, and laugh at you. If ever that boy returns to this house, sir, I'll eat my head."

With these words he drew his chair closer to the table, and there the two friends sat in silent expectation, with the watch between them. It is worthy of remark, as illustrating the importance we attach to our own judgments, and the pride with which we put forth our most rash and hasty conclusions, that, although Mr. Grimwig was not a bad-hearted man, and would have been unfeignedly sorry to see his respected friend duped and deceived, he really did most earnestly and strongly hope at that moment that Oliver Twist might not come back. Of such contradictions is human nature made up!

It grew so dark that the figures on the dial were scarcely discernible; but there the two old gentlemen continued to sit in silence, with the watch between them.

CHAPTER THE FIFTEENTH.

SHEWING HOW VERY FOND OF OLIVER TWIST, THE MERRY OLD JEW AND MISS NANCY WERE.

IF it did not come strictly within the scope and bearing of my long-considered intentions and plans regarding this prose epic (for such I mean it to be,) to leave the two old gentlemen sitting with the watch between them long after it grew too dark to see it, and both doubting Oliver's return, the one in triumph, and the other in sorrow, I might take occasion to entertain the reader with many wise reflections on the obvious impolicy of ever attempting to do good to our fellow-creatures where there is no hope of earthly reward; or rather on the strict policy of betraying some slight degree of charity or sympathy in one particularly unpromising case, and then abandoning such weaknesses for ever. I am aware that, in advising even this slight dereliction from the paths of prudence and worldliness, I lay myself open to the censure of many excellent and respectable persons, who have long walked therein; but I venture to contend, nevertheless, that the advantages of the proceeding are manifold and lasting. As thus : if the object selected should happen most unexpectedly to turn out well, and to thrive and amend upon the assistance you have afforded him, he will, in pure gratitude and fulness of heart, laud your goodness to the skies; your character will be thus established, and you will pass through the world as a most estimable person, who does a vast deal of good in secret, not one-twentieth part of which will ever see the light. If, on the contrary, his bad character become notorious, and his profligacy a by-word, you place yourself in the excellent position of having attempted to bestow relief most disinterestedly; of having become misanthropical in consequence of the treachery of its object; and of having made a rash and solemn vow, (which no one regrets more than yourself,) never to help or relieve any man, woman, or child again, lest you should be similarly deceived. I know a great number of persons in both situations at this moment, and I can safely assert that they are the most generally respected and esteemed of any in the whole circle of my acquaintance.

But, as Mr. Brownlow was not one of these; as he obstinately persevered in doing good for its own sake, and the gratification of heart it yielded him; as no failure dispirited him, and no ingratitude in individual cases tempted him to wreak his vengeance on the whole human race, I shall not enter into any such digression in this place : and, if this be not a sufficient reason for

this determination, I have a better, and, indeed, a wholly unanswerable one, already stated; which is, that it forms no
part of my original intention so to do.

In the obscure parlour of a low public-house, situate in the
filthiest part of Little Saffron-Hill,—a dark and gloomy den;
where a flaring gas-light burnt all day in the winter-time, and
where no ray of sun ever shone in the summer,—there sat,
brooding over a little pewter measure and a small glass, strongly impregnated with the smell of liquor, a man in a velveteen
coat, drab shorts, half-boots, and stockings, whom, even by that
dim light, no experienced agent of police would have hesitated
for one instant to recognise as Mr. William Sikes. At his feet
sat a white-coated, red-eyed dog, who occupied himself alternately in winking at his master with both eyes at the same time,
and in licking a large, fresh cut on one side of his mouth,
which appeared to be the result of some recent conflict.

"Keep quiet, you warmint! keep quiet!" said Mr. Sikes,
suddenly breaking silence. Whether his meditations were so
intense as to be disturbed by the dog's winking, or whether his
feelings were so wrought upon by his reflections that they required
all the relief derivable from kicking an unoffending animal to
allay them, is matter for argument and consideration. Whatever was the cause, the effect was a kick and a curse bestowed
upon the dog simultaneously.

Dogs are not generally apt to revenge injuries inflicted upon
them by their masters; but Mr. Sikes's dog, having faults of
temper in common with his owner, and labouring perhaps, at this
moment, under a powerful sense of injury, made no more ado
but at once fixed his teeth in one of the half-boots, and, having
given it a good hearty shake, retired, growling, under a form:
thereby just escaping the pewter measure which Mr. Sikes levelled at his head.

"You would, would you?" said Sikes, seizing the poker in
one hand, and deliberately opening with the other a large clasp-
knife, which he drew from his pocket. "Come here, you born
devil! Come here! D'ye hear?"

The dog no doubt heard, because Mr. Sikes spoke in the very
harshest key of a very harsh voice; but, appearing to entertain
some unaccountable objection to having his throat cut, he remained where he was, and growled more fiercely than before, at
the same time grasping the end of the poker between his teeth,
and biting at it like a wild beast.

This resistance only infuriated Mr. Sikes the more; so, dropping upon his knees, he began to assail the animal most furiously. The dog jumped from right to left, and from left to
right, snapping, growling, and barking; the man thrust and
swore, and struck and blasphemed; and the struggle was reaching a most critical point for one or other, when, the door suddenly opening, the dog darted out, leaving Bill Sikes with the
poker and the clasp-knife in his hands.

There must always be two parties to a quarrel, says the old adage; and Mr. Sikes, being disappointed of the dog's presence, at once transferred the quarrel to the new-comer.

"What the devil do you come in between me and my dog for?" said Sikes with a fierce gesture.

"I didn't know, my dear, I didn't know," replied Fagin humbly—for the Jew was the new-comer.

"Didn't know, you white-livered thief!" growled Sikes. "Couldn't you hear the noise?"

"Not a sound of it, as I'm a living man, Bill," replied the Jew.

"Oh no, you hear nothing, you don't," retorted Sikes with a fierce sneer, "sneaking in and out, so as nobody hears how you come or go. I wish you had been the dog, Fagin, half a minute ago."

"Why?" inquired the Jew with a forced smile.

"'Cause the government, as cares for the lives of such men as you, as haven't half the pluck of curs, lets a man kill his dog how he likes," replied Sikes, shutting the knife up with a very expressive look; "that's why."

The Jew rubbed his hands, and, sitting down at the table, affected to laugh at the pleasantry of his friend,—obviously very ill at his ease, however.

"Grin away," said Sikes, replacing the poker, and surveying him with savage contempt; "grin away. You'll never have the laugh at me, though, unless it's behind a nightcap. I've got the upper hand over you, Fagin; and, d— me, I'll keep it. There. If I go, you go; so take care of me."

"Well, well, my dear," said the Jew, "I know all that; we —we—have a mutual interest, Bill,—a mutual interest."

"Humph!" said Sikes, as if he thought the interest lay rather more on the Jew's side than on his. "Well, what have you got to say to me?"

"It's all passed safe through the melting-pot," replied Fagin, "and this is your share. It's rather more than it ought to be, my dear; but as I know you'll do me a good turn another time, and——"

"'Stow that gammon," interposed the robber impatiently. "Where is it? Hand over!"

"Yes, yes, Bill; give me time, give me time," replied the Jew soothingly. "Here it is—all safe." As he spoke, he drew forth an old cotton handkerchief from his breast, and, untying a large knot in one corner, produced a small brown-paper packet, which Sikes snatching from him, hastily opened, and proceeded to count the sovereigns it contained.

"This is all, is it?" inquired Sikes.

"All," replied the Jew.

"You haven't opened the parcel and swallowed one or two as you come along, have you?" inquired Sikes suspiciously.

" Don't put on a injured look at the question ; you 've done it
many a time.   Jerk the tinkler."

These words, in plain English, conveyed an injunction to
ring the bell.   It was answered by another Jew, younger
than Fagin, but nearly as vile and repulsive in appearance.

Bill Sikes merely pointed to the empty measure, and the Jew,
perfectly understanding the hint, retired to fill it, previously
exchanging a remarkable look with Fagin, who raised his eyes
for an instant as if in expectation of it, and shook his head in
reply so slightly that the action would have been almost imperceptible to a third person.   It was lost upon Sikes, who was
stooping at the moment to tie the boot-lace which the dog had
torn.   Possibly if he had observed the brief interchange of signals, he might have thought that it boded no good to him.

" Is anybody here, Barney ?" inquired Fagin, speaking—now
that Sikes was looking on—without raising his eyes from the
ground.

" Dot a shoul," replied Barney, whose words, whether they
came from the heart or not, made their way through the nose.

" Nobody ?" inquired Fagin in a tone of surprise, which perhaps might mean that Barney was at liberty to tell the truth.

" Dobody but Biss Dadsy," replied Barney.

" Miss Nancy !" exclaimed Sikes.   " Where ?   Strike me
blind, if I don't honor that 'ere girl for her native talents."

" She 's bid havid a plate of boiled beef id the bar," replied
Barney.

" Send her here," said Sikes, pouring out a glass of liquor ;
" send her here."

Barney looked timidly at Fagin, as if for permission ; the
Jew remaining silent, and not lifting his eyes from the ground,
he retired, and presently returned ushering in Miss Nancy,
who was decorated with the bonnet, apron, basket, and street-
door key complete.

" You are on the scent, are you, Nancy ?" inquired Sikes,
proffering the glass.

" Yes, I am, Bill," replied the young lady, disposing of its
contents ; " and tired enough of it I am, too.   The young
brat 's been ill and confined to the crib ; and——"

" Ah, Nancy, dear !" said Fagin, looking up.

Now, whether a peculiar contraction of the Jew's red eyebrows, and a half-closing of his deeply-set eyes, warned Miss
Nancy that she was disposed to be too communicative, is not a
matter of much importance.   The fact is all we need care for
here ; and the fact is, that she suddenly checked herself, and,
with several gracious smiles upon Mr. Sikes, turned the conversation to other matters.   In about ten minutes' time, Mr. Fagin
was seized with a fit of coughing, upon which Miss Nancy
pulled her shawl over her shoulders, and declared it was time to
go.   Mr. Sikes, finding that he was walking a short part of her
way himself, expressed his intention of accompanying her : and

they went away together, followed at a little distance by the dog, who slunk out of a back-yard as soon as his master was out of sight.

The Jew thrust his head out of the room door when Sikes had left it, looked after him as he walked up the dark passage, shook his clenched fist, muttered a deep curse, and then with a horrible grin reseated himself at the table, where he was soon deeply absorbed in the interesting pages of the Hue and Cry.

Meanwhile Oliver Twist, little dreaming that he was within so very short a distance of the merry old gentleman, was on his way to the bookstall. When he got into Clerkenwell he accidentally turned down a by-street which was not exactly in his way; but not discovering his mistake till he had got halfway down it, and knowing it must lead in the right direction, he did not think it worth while to turn back, and so marched on as quickly as he could, with the books under his arm.

He was walking along, thinking how happy and contented he ought to feel, and how much he would give for only one look at poor little Dick, who, starved and beaten, might be lying dead at that very moment, when he was startled by a young woman screaming out very loud, "Oh, my dear brother!" and he had hardly looked up to see what the matter was, when he was stopped by having a pair of arms thrown tight round his neck.

"Don't!" cried Oliver struggling. "Let go of me. Who is it? What are you stopping me for?"

The only reply to this, was a great number of loud lamentations from the young woman who had embraced him, and who had got a little basket and a street-door key in her hand.

"Oh my gracious!" said the young woman, "I 've found him! Oh, Oliver! Oliver! Oh, you naughty boy, to make me suffer such distress on your account! Come home, dear, come. Oh, I 've found him. Thank gracious goodness heavins, I 've found him!" With these incoherent exclamations the young woman burst into another fit of crying, and got so dreadfully hysterical, that a couple of women who came up at the moment asked a butcher's boy, with a shiny head of hair anointed with suet, who was also looking on, whether he didn't think he had better run for the doctor. To which the butcher's boy, who appeared of a lounging, not to say indolent disposition, replied that he thought not.

"Oh, no, no, never mind," said the young woman, grasping Oliver's hand; "I 'm better now. Come home directly, you cruel boy, come."

"What 's the matter, ma'am?" inquired one of the women.

"Oh, ma'am," replied the young woman, "he ran away near a month ago from his parents, who are hard-working and respectable people, and joined a set of thieves and bad characters, and almost broke his mother's heart."

"Young wretch!" said one woman.

"Go home, do, you little brute," said the other.

"I'm not," replied Oliver, greatly alarmed. "I don't know her. I haven't got any sister, or father and mother either. I'm an orphan; I live at Pentonville."

"Oh, only hear him, how he braves it out!" cried the young woman.

"Why, it's Nancy!" exclaimed Oliver, who now saw her face for the first time, and started back in irrepressible astonishment.

"You see he knows me," cried Nancy, appealing to the bystanders. "He can't help himself. Make him come home, there's good people, or he'll kill his dear mother and father, and break my heart!"

"What the devil's this?" said a man, bursting out of a beershop, with a white dog at his heels; "young Oliver! Come home to your poor mother, you young dog! come home directly."

"I don't belong to them. I don't know them. Help! help!" cried Oliver, struggling in the man's powerful grasp.

"Help!" repeated the man. "Yes; I'll help you, you young rascal! What books are these? You've been a stealing 'em, have you? Give 'em here!" With these words the man tore the volumes from his grasp, and struck him violently on the head.

"That's right!" cried a looker-on, from a garret window. "That's the only way of bringing him to his senses!"

"To be sure," cried a sleepy-faced carpenter, casting an approving look at the garret-window.

"It'll do him good!" said the two women.

"And he shall have it, too!" rejoined the man, administering another blow, and seizing Oliver by the collar. "Come on, you young villain! Here, Bull's-eye, mind him, boy! mind him!"

Weak with recent illness, stupified by the blows and the suddenness of the attack, terrified by the fierce growling of the dog and the brutality of the man, and overpowered by the conviction of the bystanders that he was really the hardened little wretch he was described to be, what could one poor child do? Darkness had set in; it was a low neighbourhood; no help was near; resistance was useless. In another moment he was dragged into a labyrinth of dark, narrow courts, and forced along them at a pace which rendered the few cries he dared to give utterance to, wholly unintelligible. It was of little moment, indeed, whether they were intelligible or not, for there was nobody to care for them had they been ever so plain.

    *   *   *   *   *

The gas-lamps were lighted; Mrs. Bedwin was waiting anxiously at the open door; the servant had run up the street twenty times, to see if there were any traces of Oliver; and still the two old gentlemen sat perseveringly in the dark parlour, with the watch between them.

THE POISONERS OF THE SEVENTEENTH CENTURY.

BY GEORGE HOGARTH.

THERE are few things in the history of mankind more extraordinary than the frightful extent to which the crime of secret poisoning was carried, in several countries of Europe, during a large portion of the seventeenth century. It appears to have taken its rise in Italy, where it prevailed to a degree that is almost incredible. The instrument chiefly used in its perpetration was a liquid called *aqua tofanu*, from the name of Tofania, its inventor, a woman who has acquired an infamous celebrity. According to the account of Hoffmann, the famous physician, this woman confessed that she had used this liquid in poisoning above six hundred persons; and Gmelin says that more people were destroyed by it than by the plague, which had raged for some time before it came into use. This crime also prevailed, though for a shorter time and to a smaller extent, in France; and was far from being unknown in England. We intend to give our readers such information as we have collected on this curious subject; and though the most regular way might be to begin with the Signora Tofania herself, and the diffusion of her practices in her own country, we prefer giving at present the history of the most eminent of her followers, the Marchioness de Brinvillier, whose atrocities created so much excitement in France in the time of Louis the Fourteenth, as we shall thus be enabled at once to place the matter in its most striking light. We have consulted, we believe, most of the French works in which there are any particulars respecting this lady; and our readers may take the following as a faithful account of her life.

Marie-Marguerite d'Aubray was the daughter of M. d'Aubray, a gentleman who held a considerable judicial office in Paris. In 1651 she married the Marquis de Brinvillier. The match was a suitable one, both in respect to station and property. The marquis had estates of thirty thousand livres a-year; and his wife, who had two brothers and a sister, brought him a fortune of two hundred thousand livres, with the prospect of a considerable share of her father's inheritance. The marchioness enjoyed the gifts of nature as well as of fortune. Her figure was not remarkably handsome, but her face was round and pretty, with a serene and quiet expression; and she had an air of innocence, simplicity, and good-nature which gained the confidence of everybody who had any intercourse with her.

The Marquis de Brinvillier was colonel of a regiment of foot. While on service, he had contracted an' intimacy with a gentleman of the name of St. Croix, a captain of cavalry. There was some mystery about this man's birth. It was known that he was from Montauban. Some thought him an illegitimate scion of a noble house; others said he belonged to a respectable family; but all agreed that he was totally destitute of the gifts of fortune.

The part which this personage acted in the occurrences of which we are about to give a sketch, makes it worth while to repeat the description of him contained in some of the memoirs of the time. His

countenance was handsome and intelligent; he was remarkably courteous and obliging, and entered into any benevolent or pious proposal
with the same alacrity with which he agreed to commit a crime.
He was vindictive, susceptible of love, and jealous to madness. His
extravagance was unbounded, and, being unsupported by any regular
income, led him into every sort of wickedness. Some years before
his death, he assumed an appearance of devotion, and it is said even
wrote some tracts on religious subjects.

The Marquis de Brinvillier was much addicted to pleasure. St.
Croix got into his good graces, and was introduced into his house.
At first he was only the husband's friend, but presently he became the
wife's lover; and their attachment became mutual. The dissipation
of the marquis's life prevented him from observing his wife's conduct,
so that the pair carried on a guilty commerce without any suspicion
on his part. His affairs became so disordered, that his wife succeeded, on this ground, in obtaining a separation, and after this paid
no respect to decency or concealment in her connexion with her
paramour. Scandalous, however, as her conduct was, it made no
impression on the mind of the marquis, whose apathy induced the
marchioness's father, M. d'Aubray, to use his paternal authority. He
obtained a *lettre de cachet* against St. Croix, who was arrested one day
when he was in a carriage with the marchioness, and carried to the
Bastile, where he remained for a year.

Absence, far from abating the marchioness's passion, only inflamed
it; and the constraint to which she found it necessary to subject herself in order to prevent a second separation, inflamed it still more.
She conducted herself, however, with such apparent propriety, that
she regained her father's favour, and even his confidence. St. Croix
availed himself of the power which love had given him over his mistress to root out every good principle or feeling from her mind.
Under his horrid lessons she became a monster, whose atrocities, we
hope and believe, have hardly ever been paralleled. He resolved to
take a dreadful revenge on the family of D'Aubray, and at the same
time to get his whole property into the possession of the marchioness, that they might spend it together in guilty pleasures.

While St. Croix was in the Bastile, he had formed an acquaintance
with an Italian of the name of Exili, to whom he communicated his
views. Exili excited him to vengeance, and taught him the way to
obtain it with impunity. Poisoning may be called, *par excellence*, an
Italian art. With many fine qualities, vindictiveness and subtlety
must be acknowledged to be strong features in the character of that
people; and hence their early superiority in this art of taking the
most deadly, and at the same time the safest, revenge on their enemies. It appears, accordingly, (as we have already said,) that it was
from the Italians that the poisoners of other countries derived their
skill. They acquired the art of composing poisons so disguised in
their appearance and subtle in their effects, that they baffled the penetration and art of the physicians of that age. Some were slow,
and consumed the vitals of the victim by almost imperceptible degrees; others were sudden and violent in their action; but few of
them left any traces of their real nature, for the symptoms they produced were generally so equivocal, that they might be ascribed to
many ordinary diseases. St. Croix greedily devoured the instruc-

tions of his fellow-prisoner, and left the Bastile prepared to exercise his infernal art.

His first object of vengeance was M. d'Aubray himself; and he soon found means to persuade the daughter to become the agent in the destruction of her father. The old gentleman had a house in the country, where he used to spend his vacations. All his fondness for his daughter, whom he now believed to have been " more sinned against than sinning," had returned; and she, on her part, behaved to him with an appearance of affectionate duty. She anxiously attended to his every comfort; and, as his health had suffered from the fatigues of his office, she employed herself in superintending the preparation of nice and nourishing broths, which she gave him herself with every appearance of tender care. It is needless to say that these aliments contained some articles of Italian cookery; and the wretch, as she sat by his bed-side, witnessing his sufferings and listening to his groans, shed abundance of crocodile tears, while she eagerly administered to him remedies calculated to insure the accomplishment of her object. But neither the agonies of the poor old man, nor his touching expressions of love and gratitude to the fiend at his side, could turn her for a moment from her fell purpose. He was carried back to Paris, where in a few days he sunk under the effects of the poison.

No suspicion was entertained of the cause of his death; the idea of such a crime could not even have entered into the imagination of any one. No external symptoms appeared, and the expedient of opening the body was never thought of. The friends of the family were desirous only of pitying and comforting them; and the inconsolable daughter, who had tended her father with such filial piety, had the largest share of sympathy. She returned as soon as possible to the arms of her paramour, and made up for the restraint imposed on her during her father's life by spending the money she had inherited by his death in undisguised profligacy.

It afterwards appeared that this abandoned woman had made sure of the efficacy of her drugs by a variety of experiments, not only upon animals, but on human beings. She was in the habit of distributing to the poor poisoned biscuits, prepared by herself, the effect of which she found means to learn without committing herself. But this was not enough: she desired to be an eye-witness of the progress and symptoms of the effects produced by the poison; and for this purpose made the experiment on Françoise Roussel, her maid, to whom she gave, by way of treat, a plate of gooseberries and a slice of ham. The poor girl was very ill, but recovered; and this was a lesson to St. Croix to make his doses stronger.

Madame de Sevigné, in one of her letters, written at a time when the public attention was engrossed by this strange affair, says, " La Brinvillier used to poison pigeon-pies, which caused the death of many people whom she had no intention of destroying. The Chevalier du Guet was at one of these pretty dinners, and died of it two or three years ago. When in prison, she asked if he was dead, and was told he was not. ' His life must be very tough, then,' said she. M. de la Rochefoucauld declares that this is perfectly true."

M. d'Aubray's inheritance was not so beneficial to his infamous daughter as she had expected. The best part of his property went to his son, M. d'Aubray, who succeeded to his father's office, and another brother a counsellor. It was necessary, therefore, to put them out of the way also; and this task St. Croix, thinking his accomplice had done enough for his purposes, took upon himself.

He had a villain at his devotion of the name of La Chaussée. This man had been in his service, and he knew him to be a fit agent in any atrocity. The marchioness got La Chaussée a place as servant to the counsellor, who lived with his brother the magistrate, taking great care to conceal from them that he had ever been in the service of St. Croix. La Chaussée's employers promised him a hundred pistoles and an annuity for life if he succeeded in causing the death of the magistrate, who was their first object of attack. His anxiety to do his business promptly made him fail in his first attempt. He gave the magistrate a glass of poisoned wine and water; but the dose was too strong: and no sooner had the magistrate put his lips to the glass, than he cried, " Ah, you scoundrel, what is this you have given me?—do you want to poison me?" He showed the liquid to his secretary, who, having examined it in a spoon, said it was bitter, and had a smell of vitriol. La Chaussée did not lose countenance, but, without any appearance of confusion, took the glass and poured out the liquor, saying that the younger M. d'Aubray's valet had taken some medicine in this glass, which had produced the bitter taste. He got off with a reprimand for his carelessness, and the matter was no more thought of.

This narrow escape from a discovery did not deter the murderers from prosecuting their design; but they took more effectual measures for its success, not caring though they should sacrifice by the same blow a number of people with whom they had no concern.

In the beginning of April 1670, the magistrate went to pass the Easter holidays at his house in the country. His brother the counsellor was of the party, and was attended by La Chaussée. One day at dinner there was a giblet-pie. Seven persons who eat of it became very ill, while those who had not partaken of it suffered no uneasiness. The two brothers were among the former, and had violent fits of vomiting. They returned to Paris a few days afterwards, having the appearance of persons who had undergone a long and violent illness.

St. Croix availed himself of this state of things to make sure of the fruit of his crimes. He obtained from the marchioness two promissory deeds, one for thirty thousand livres in his own name, and another for twenty-five thousand livres in the name of Martin, one of his familiars. The sum at first sight appears a small one, amounting only to about two thousand three hundred pounds sterling; but the immense difference in the value of money since the seventeenth century must be taken into account. Such, however, at all events, was the price paid by this demon for the death of her two brothers.

Meanwhile the elder D'Aubray became worse and worse; he could take no sustenance, and vomited incessantly. The three last days of his life he felt a fire in his stomach, which seemed to be consuming its very substance. At length he expired on the 17th of June 1670. On being opened, his stomach and *duodenum* were black, and falling to pieces, as if they had been put on a large fire; and the liver was burnt up and gangrened. It was evident that he had been poisoned : but on whom could suspicion fall ?—there was no clue whatever to, guide it. The marchioness had gone to the country. St. Croix wrote her that the magistrate was dead, and that, from his brother's situation, he must soon follow. It so turned out. The unfortunate counsellor died, after having lingered three months in excruciating torments ; and he was so far from suspecting La Chaussée of any hand in his death, that he left him a legacy of three hundred livres, which was paid.

These three murders were still insufficient. There was yet a sister who kept from the marchioness the half of the successions which she wished to gain by the death of her father and brothers. The sister's life was repeatedly attempted in the same way ; but the shocking occurrences in her family had made her suspicious, and her precautions preserved her.

The poor Marquis de Brinvillier was intended by his fury of a wife for her next victim. "Madame de Brinvillier," says Madame de Sevigné in another of her letters, "wanted to marry St. Croix, and for that purpose poisoned her husband repeatedly. But St. Croix, who had no desire to have a wife as wicked as himself, gave the poor man antidotes ; so that, having been tossed backward and forward in this way, sometimes poisoned, and sometimes *un*poisoned, (*désempoisonné*), he has, after all, got off with his life."

Though everybody was convinced that the father and his two sons had been poisoned, yet nothing but very vague suspicions were entertained as to the perpetrators of the crime. Nobody thought of St. Croix as having had anything to do with it. He had for a long time ceased, to all appearance, to have any connexion with Madame de Brinvillier ; and La Chaussée, the immediate agent, had played his part so well, that he was never suspected.

At last the horrible mystery was discovered. St. Croix continued to practise the art which had been so useful to him ; and, as the poisons he made were so subtle as to be fatal even by respiration, he used to intercept their exhalations while compounding them by a glass mask over his face. One day the mask by accident dropped off, and he fell dead on the spot ; "a death," says the French writer who mentions this occurrence, "much too good for a monster who had inflicted it by long and agonizing pangs on so many valuable citizens."[*] Having no relations that were known, his repositories

---

[*] This incident has suggested to Sir Walter Scott the catastrophe of the diabolical Alasco, in *Kenilworth :*

"The old woman assured Varney that Alasco had scarce eaten or drunk since her master's departure, living perpetually shut up in the laboratory, and talking as if the world's continuance depended on what he was doing there.

" 'I will teach him that the world hath other claims on him,' said Varney, seizing a light and going in search of the alchemist. He returned, after a considerable absence, very pale, but yet with his habitual sneer on his cheek and nostril. 'Our friend,' he said, 'has exhaled.'

" 'How! what mean you ?' said Foster ; 'run away—fled with my forty pounds, that should have been multiplied a thousand fold ? I will have Hue and Cry !'

" 'I will tell thee a surer way,' said Varney.

" 'How ! which way ?' exclaimed Foster. ' I will have back my forty pounds —I deemed them as surely a thousand pounds multiplied—I will have back my in-put at the least.' " 'Go

were sealed up by the public authorities. When they were opened and examined, the first thing which was found was a casket, in which was a paper in the following terms :

" I earnestly request those into whose hands this casket may fall, to deliver it into the hands of Madame la Marquise de Brinvillier, residing in the Rue Neuve St. Paul, seeing that all that it contains concerns and belongs to her only, and that it can be of no use to any person in the world except herself; and, in case of her being dead before me, to burn it, and all that it contains, without opening or meddling with anything.   And should any one contravene these my intentions on this subject, which are just and reasonable, I lay the consequences on their head, both in this world and the next ; protesting that this is my last will.   Done at Paris this 25th May, after- . noon, 1672.   (Signed) De Sainte Croix."

The casket contained a number of parcels carefully sealed up, and some phials containing liquids.   The parcels were found to contain a variety of drugs, which, having been submitted to the examination of physicians, were found to be most subtle and deadly poisons.   This was ascertained by many experiments made upon pigeons, dogs, cats, and other animals, all which were detailed in a formal report made on the subject.   It is stated in that report that no traces of the action of the poison, either external or internal, appeared on the bodies of the animals which had perished by it, and that it was impossible to detect its existence by any chemical tests.   It would appear, therefore, that St. Croix had by his studies greatly increased in skill since the deaths of the D'Aubray family.   The poisons administered to them were of a comparatively coarse and ordinary kind ; they burnt up the stomach and bowels, produced horrid torment, and left unequivocal marks of their operation when any suspicion caused these marks to be sought for.   But, with the skill subsequently acquired, this hateful pair might have destroyed thousands of their fellow-creatures with absolute impunity.   It is impossible to suppose that St. Croix could have been constantly engaged, for a long series of years, in the composition of these secret instruments of death without making use of them ; and there is no saying to what extent his work of destruction may have been carried.

The same casket contained ample evidence of the marchioness's share in these transactions.   There were a number of letters from her to St. Croix, and the deed of promise which she had executed in his favour for thirty thousand livres.

When the marchioness heard that St. Croix was dead, and that his repositories had been sealed up, she showed the utmost anxiety to get possession of the casket.   At ten o'clock at night she came to the house of the commissary who had affixed and taken off the seals, and

" ' Go hang thyself, then, and sue Alasco in the devil's court of Chancery, for thither he has carried the cause.'

" ' How !—what dost thou mean ?—is he dead ?'

" ' Ay, truly is he,' said Varney, ' and properly swollen already in the face and body.   He had been mixing some of his devil's medicines, and the glass mask, which he used constantly, had fallen from his face, so that the subtle poison entered the brain and did its work.'

" ' Sancta Maria !' said Foster; ' I mean, God in his mercy preserve us from covetousness and deadly sin !'"

desired to speak with him. Being told by his clerk that he was asleep, she said she had come to inquire about a casket which belonged to her, and which she wished to get back, and would return next day. When she came back, she was told that the casket could not be given up to her. Thinking it high time, therefore, to take care of herself, she went off during the following night, and took refuge in Liege; leaving, however, a power to an attorney to appear for her and contest the validity of the promise she had given to St. Croix. La Chaussée, too, had the impudence to put in a claim to certain sums of money, which, as he pretended, belonged to him, and which were deposited, in places which he mentioned, in St. Croix's study. This proved that La Chaussée was acquainted with the localities of a place into which it was to be presumed that St. Croix admitted none but his confidants and confederates; and La Chaussée was arrested on suspicion, which was greatly strengthened by the confusion he betrayed when informed of the discoveries made at the removal of the seals.

A judicial inquiry was now set on foot, and many witnesses examined. Among others, Anne Huet, an apothecary's daughter, who was a sort of servant of the marchioness, deposed, that one day, when the marchioness was intoxicated, she had the imprudence to show the witness a little box which she took out of a casket, and which, she said, contained the means of getting rid of her enemies, and acquiring good inheritances. Mademoiselle Huet saw that the box contained sublimate of mercury in powder and in paste. Afterwards, when the fumes of the wine had evaporated, the witness told the marchioness what she had said. "Oh," she said, "I was talking nonsense;" but at the same time she earnestly begged her not to repeat what she had heard. The marchioness (this witness added) was in the habit, when anything chagrined her, to say she would poison herself. She said there were many ways of getting rid of people when they stood in one's way,—a bowl of broth was as good as a pistol-bullet. The girl added, that she had often seen La Chaussée with Madame de Brinvillier, who chatted familiarly with him; and that she had heard the marchioness say, "He is a good lad, and has been very serviceable to me." Mademoiselle Villeray, another witness, declared that she had seen La Chaussée on a very familiar footing with Madame de Brinvillier; that she had seen them alone together since the death of the magistrate; that, two days after the death of the counsellor, she made La Chaussée hide himself behind the bed-curtains when the magistrate's secretary came to see her. La Chaussée himself, on his examination, admitted this fact. Other persons related that La Chaussée, when he was asked how his master was during his illness, used to say, "Oh, he lingers on, the ——!" adding a coarse epithet; "he gives us a deal of trouble. I wonder when he will kick the bucket."

On the 4th of March 1673, the court of La Tournelle pronounced a sentence, whereby La Chaussée was convicted of having poisoned the magistrate and the counsellor, and condemned to be broke alive upon the wheel, after having been put to the question ordinary and extraordinary, to discover his accomplices; and the Marchioness de Brinvillier was condemned, by default, to be beheaded. Under the torture, La Chaussée confessed his crimes, and gave a full account of all the transactions we have related, in so far as he was connected with them. He was executed in the Place de Grève, according to his sentence.

Desgrais, an officer of the Marechaussée, was sent to Liege to arrest the marchioness. He was provided with an escort, and a letter from the king to the municipality of that city, requesting that the criminal might be delivered up. Desgrais was permitted to arrest her and carry her to France.

She had retired to a convent, a sanctuary in which Desgrais durst not attempt to seize her; he therefore had recourse to stratagem. Disguising himself in an ecclesiastical habit, he paid her a visit, pretending that, being a Frenchman, he could not think of passing through Liege without seeing a lady so celebrated for her beauty and misfortunes. He even went so far as to play the gallant, and his amorous advances were as well received as he could desire. He persuaded the lady to take a walk with him; but they had no sooner got into the fields than the lover transformed himself into a police-officer. He arrested the lady, and put her into the hands of his followers, whom he had placed in ambush near the spot; and then, having obtained an order from the authorities to that effect, he made a search in her apartment. Under her bed he found a casket, which she vehemently insisted on having returned to her, but without effect. She then tried to bribe one of the officer's men, who pretended to listen to her, and betrayed her. During her retreat she had carried on an intrigue with a person of the name of Theria. To him she wrote a letter, (which she intrusted to her confidant,) beseeching him to come with all haste and rescue her from the hands of Desgrais. In a second letter she told him that the escort consisted only of eight persons, who could easily be beaten by five. In a third, she wrote to " her dear Theria," that if he could not deliver her by open force, he might at least kill two out of the four horses of the carriage in which she was, and thus, at least, get possession of the casket, and throw it into the fire; otherwise she was lost. Though Theria, of course, received none of his *chère amie*'s letters, yet he went of his own accord to Maestricht, through which she was to pass, and tried to corrupt the officers by an offer of a thousand pistoles, if they would let her escape; but they were immovable. All her resources being thus exhausted, she attempted to kill herself by swallowing a pin; but it was taken from her by one of her guards.

Among the proofs against her, that which alarmed her the most was a written confession containing a narrative of her life, kept by her in the casket which she made such desperate efforts to recover. No wonder she was now horrified at what she had thus committed to paper. In the first article she declared herself an incendiary, confessing that she had set fire to a house. Madame Sevigné, speaking of this paper, says, " Madame de Brinvillier tells us, in her confession, that she was debauched at seven years old, and has led an abandoned life ever since; that she poisoned her father, her brothers, and one of her children; nay, that she poisoned herself, to try the effect of an antidote. Medea herself did not do so much. She has acknowledged this confession to be of her writing,—a great blunder; but she says she was in a high fever when she wrote it,—that it is mere frenzy,— a piece of extravagance which no one can read seriously." In a sub-

sequent letter, Madame de Sevigné adds, " Nothing is talked of but
the sayings and doings of Madame de Brinvillier. She says in her
confession that she has murdered her father;—she was afraid, no
doubt, that she might forget to accuse herself of it. The peccadilloes
which she is afraid of forgetting are admirable !"

The proceedings of her trial are fully reported in the *Causes Célé-
bres.* She found an able advocate in the person of M. Nivelle, whose
pleading in her behalf is exceedingly learned and ingenious. He
laboured hard to get rid of the confession ; maintaining that this paper
was of the same nature as a confession made under the seal of secrecy to a priest ; and cited a number of precedents to show that circumstances thus brought to light cannot be used in a criminal prosecution. Her confused, evasive, and contradictory answers to the
questions put to her on her interrogatory by the court,—a very objectionable step, by the way, of French criminal procedure,—were considered as filling up the measure of evidence against her; though, in
this case, it was sufficiently ample without the aid either of her confession or examinations before the judges. The *corpus delicti* (in the
language of the law) was certain. The deaths of her two brothers by
poison were proved by the evidence of several medical persons ; and
the testimony of other witnesses established the commission of these
crimes by St. Croix and her, through the instrumentality of La
Chaussée.

At length, by a sentence of the supreme criminal court of Paris, on
the 16th of July 1676, Madame de Brinvillier was convicted of the
murder of her father and her two brothers, and of having attempted
the life of her sister, and condemned to make the *amende honorable*
before the door of the principal church of Paris, whither she was to
be drawn in a hurdle, with her feet bare, a rope about her neck, and
carrying a burning torch in her hands ; from thence to be taken to
the Place de Grève, her head severed from her body on a scaffold,
her body burnt, and her ashes thrown to the wind ; after having been,
in the first place, put to the question ordinary and extraordinary, to
discover her accomplices.

Though she had denied her crimes as long as she had any hope of
escape, she confessed everything after condemnation. During the
latter days of her life, she was the sole object of public curiosity. An
immense multitude assembled to see her execution, and every window on her way to the Place de Grève was crowded with spectators.
Lebrun, the celebrated painter, placed himself in a convenient situation for observing her, in order, probably, to make a study for his
" Passions." Among the spectators were many ladies of distinction,
to some of whom, who had got very near her, she said, looking them
firmly in the face, and with a sarcastic smile, " A very pretty sight
you are come to see !"

Madame de Sevigné gives an account of this execution the day it
took place, in a tone of levity which is not a little offensive, and unbecoming a lady of her unquestionable elegance and refinement.
" Well !" she says, " it is all over, and La Brinvillier is in the air.
Her poor little body was thrown into a large fire, and her ashes scattered to the winds ; so that we breathe her, and there is no saying
but this communication of particles may produce among us some poisoning propensities which may surprise us. She was condemned yes-

terday. This morning her sentence was read to her, and she was shown the rack; but she said there was no occasion for it, for she would tell everything. Accordingly she continued till four o'clock giving a history of her life, which is even more frightful than people supposed. She poisoned her father ten times successively before she could accomplish her object; then her brothers; and her revelations were full of love affairs and pieces of scandal. She asked to speak with the procureur-général, and was an hour with him; but the subject of their conversation is not known. At six o'clock she was taken in her shift, and with a rope round her neck, to Nôtre Dame, to make the *amende honorable.* She was then replaced in the hurdle, in which I saw her drawn backwards, with a confessor on one side and the hangman on the other. It really made me shudder. Those who saw the execution say she ascended the scaffold with a great deal of courage. Never was such a crowd seen, nor such excitement and curiosity in Paris." In another letter the fair writer says, " A word more about La Brinvillier. She died as she lived, that is boldly. When she went into the place where she was to undergo the question, and saw three buckets of water, ' They surely are going to drown me,' she said; ' for they can't imagine that I am going to drink all this.' She heard her sentence with great composure. When the reading was nearly finished, she desired it to be repeated, saying, ' The hurdle struck me at first, and prevented my attending to the rest.' On her way to execution she asked her confessor to get the executioner placed before her, ' that I may not see that scoundrel Desgrais,' she said, ' who caught me.' Her confessor reproved her for this sentiment, and she said, ' Ah, my God! I beg your pardon. Let me continue, then, to enjoy this agreeable sight.' - She ascended the scaffold alone and barefooted, and was nearly a quarter of an hour in being trimmed and adjusted for the block by the executioner; a piece of great cruelty which was loudly murmured against. Next day persons were seeking for her bones, for there was a belief among the people that she was a saint. She had two confessors, she said; one of whom enjoined her to tell everything, and the other said it was not necessary. She laughed at this difference of opinion, and said, ' Very well, I am at liberty to do as I please.' She did not please to say anything about her accomplices. Penautier will come out whiter than snow. The public is by no means satisfied."

This Penautier was a man of wealth and station, holding the office of treasurer of the province of Languedoc and of the clergy. He was discovered to have been intimately connected with St. Croix and Madame de Brinvillier, and strongly suspected of having been a participator in their crimes. He was accused by the widow of M. de Saint Laurent, receiver-general of the clergy, of having employed St. Croix to poison her husband, in order to obtain his place, and of having accomplished this object by means of a valet whom St. Croix had got into her husband's service. Penautier was put in prison; but Madame de Sevigné says that the investigation was stifled by the influence of powerful protectors, among whom were the Archbishop of Paris and the celebrated Colbert. In one of her letters she says, " Penautier is fortunate; never was a man so well protected. He will get out of this business, but without being justified in the eyes of the world. Extraordinary things have transpired in the course of this investigation; but they cannot be mentioned." He was released, resumed the exercise of his offices, and lived in his former splendour. The first people had no objection to enjoy his luxurious table; but his charactér with the public was irrecoverably gone. Cardinal de Bonzy, who had to pay some annuities with which his archbishopric of Narbonne was burdened, survived all the annuitants, and said that, thanks to his star! he had buried them. Madame de Sevigné, seeing him one day in his carriage with Penautier, said to a friend, "There goes the Archbishop of Narbonne with *his star!*"

The Marquis of Brinvillier is never mentioned in the course of the proceedings in this extraordinary case, and there are no traces of his subsequent life. Madame de Sevigné says that he petitioned for the life of his *chère moitié*. Wretched as he must have been, he is the less entitled to sympathy because his own dissolute character contributed to bring his misfortunes upon himself. He probably spent his latter days in the deepest retirement, hiding himself from the world, as the bearer of a name indissolubly associated with crime and infamy.

(*This paper will be followed, in our next number, by another on the same subject.*)

SERENADE TO FRANCESCA.

" Quei trasporti soavi
Ch'io provai nell' amore nascente !"

I.

UNDER your casement, lady dear!
A voice, that has slumber'd for many a year,
Is waking to know if the same heart-vow
That bound us erewhile doth bind us now.
 Waken! my early—only love!
 And be to my bosom its still sweet dove!

II.

Under your casement, lady bright!
The bird that you charm'd with your beauty's light
Is singing again to his one loved flower,
As often he sang in a happier hour!
 Waken! my early—only love!
 And be to my bosom its gentle dove!

III.

Under your casement, lady fair!
The heart that you often have vow'd to share
Is beating to know if it still remain,
A prisoner of heaven, in your dear chain!
 Waken! my early—only love!
 And be to my bosom its first sweet dove!

W.

THE NARRATIVE OF JOHN WARD GIBSON.

CHAPTER I.

As I do not intend that any human being shall read this narrative until after my decease, I feel no desire to suppress or to falsify any occurrence or event of my life, which I may at the moment deem of sufficient importance to communicate. I am aware how common a feeling, even amongst those who have committed the most atrocious crimes, this dread of entailing obloquy upon their memories is; but I cannot say that I participate in it. Perhaps I wish to offer some atonement to society for my many and grievous misdeeds; and, it may be, the disclosures I am about to make will be considered an insufficient expiation. I cannot help this, now. There is One from whom no secrets are hid, by whom I am already judged.

I regret that I did not execute this wretched task long ago. Should I live to complete it, I shall hold out longer than I expect; for I was never ready at my pen, and words sometimes will not come at my bidding. Besides, so many years have elapsed since the chief events I am about to relate took place, that even *they* no longer come before me with that distinctness which they did formerly. They do not torture me now, as of old times. The caustic has almost burnt them out of my soul. I will, however, give a plain, and, as nearly as I am able, a faithful statement. I will offer no palliation of my offences, which I do not from my soul believe should be extended to me.

I was born on the 23rd of October 1787. My father was a watch-case maker, and resided in a street in the parish of Clerkenwell. I went a few months ago to look at the house, but it was taken down; indeed, the neighbourhood had undergone an entire change. I, too, was somewhat altered since then. I wondered at the time which of the two was the more so.

My earliest recollection recalls two rooms on a second floor, meanly furnished; my father, a tall, dark man, with a harsh unpleasing voice; and my mother, the same gentle, quiet being whom I afterwards knew her.

My father was a man who could, and sometimes did, earn what people in his station of life call a great deal of money; and yet he was constantly in debt, and frequently without the means of subsistence. The cause of this, I need hardly say, was his addiction to drinking. Naturally of a violent and brutal temper, intoxication inflamed his evil passions to a pitch—not of madness, for he had not that excuse—but of frenzy. It is well known that gentleness and forbearance do not allay, but stimulate a nature like this; and scenes of violence and unmanly outrage are almost the sole reminiscences of my childhood. Perhaps, the circumstance of my having been a sufferer in one of these ebullitions, served to impress them more strongly upon my mind.

One evening I had been permitted to sit up to supper. My father had recently made promises of amendment, and had given an earnest of his intention by keeping tolerably sober during three entire days; and upon this festive occasion,—for it was the anniversary of my mother's marriage,—he had engaged to come home the instant he quitted his work. He returned, however, about one o'clock in the morning, and in his accustomed state. The very preparations for his comfort, which he saw upon the table, served as fuel to his savage and intractable passions. It was in vain that my mother endeavoured to soothe and to pacify him. He seized a stool on which I was accustomed to sit, and levelled a blow at her. She either evaded it, or the aim was not rightly directed, for the stool descended upon my head, and fractured my skull.

The doctor said it was a miracle that I recovered; and indeed it was many months before I did so. The unfeeling repulse I experienced from my father when, on the first occasion of my leaving my bed, I tottered towards him, I can never forget. It is impossible to describe the mingled terror and hatred which entered my bosom at that moment, and which never departed from it. It may appear incredible to some that a child so young could conceive so intense a loathing against its own parent. It is true, nevertheless; and, as I grew, it strengthened.

I will not dwell upon this wretched period of my life; for even to me, at this moment, and after all that I have done and suffered, the memory of that time is wretchedness.

One night, about two years afterwards, my father was brought home on a shutter by 'two watchmen. He had fallen into the New River on his return from a public-house in the vicinity of Sadler's Wells Theatre, and was dragged out just in time to preserve for the present a worthless and degraded life. A violent cold supervened, which settled upon his lungs; and, in about a month, the doctor informed my mother that her husband was in a rapid decline. The six months that ensued were miserable enough. My mother was out all day, toiling for the means of subsistence for a man who was not only ungrateful for her attentions, but who repelled them with the coarsest abuse.

I was glad when he died, nor am I ashamed to avow it; and I almost felt contempt for my mother when the poor creature threw herself upon the body in a paroxysm of grief, calling it by those endearing names which indicated a love he had neither requited nor deserved. Had I been so blest as to have met with one to love me as that woman loved my father, I had been a different, and a better, and, perhaps, a good man!

"Will you not kiss your poor father, John, and see him for the last time?" said my mother on the morning of the funeral, as she took me by the hand.

No; I would not. I was no hypocrite then. It is true I was terrified at the sight of death, but that was not the cause. The manner in which he had repulsed me nearly three years before, had never for a moment departed from my mind. There was not a day on which I did not brood upon it. I have often since recalled it, and with bitterness. I remember it now.

My mother had but one relation in the world,—an uncle, possessed of considerable property, who resided near Luton, in Bedfordshire. She applied to him for some small assistance to enable her to pay the funeral expenses of her husband. Mr. Adams—for that was her uncle's name—sent her two guineas, accompanied by a request that she would never apply to, or trouble him again. There was, however, one person who stept forward in this extremity,—Mr. Ward, a tradesman, with whom my mother had formerly lived as a servant, but who had now retired from business. He offered my mother an asylum in his house. She was to be his housekeeper; and he promised to take care of, and one day to provide for, me. It was not long before we were comfortably settled in a small private house in Coppice-row, where, for the first time in my life, I was permitted to ascertain that existence was not altogether made up of sorrow.

The old gentleman even conceived a strong liking, it may be called an affection, for me. He had stood godfather to me at my birth; and I believe, had I been his own son, he could not have treated me with more tenderness. He sent me to school, and was delighted at the progress I made, or appeared to make, which he protested was scarcely less than wonderful; a notion which the tutor was, of course, not slow to encourage and confirm. He predicted that I should inevitably make a bright man, and become a worthy member of society; the highest distinction, in the old gentleman's opinion, at which any human being could arrive. Alas! woe to the child of whom favourable predictions are hazarded! There never yet, I think, was an instance in which they were not falsified.

We had been residing with Mr. Ward about three years, when a slight incident occurred which has impressed itself so strongly upon my memory that I cannot forbear relating it. Mr. Ward had sent me with a message into the City, where, in consequence of the person being from home, I was detained several hours. When I returned, it appeared that Mr. Ward had gone out shortly after me, and had not mentioned the circumstance of his having despatched me into the City. I found my mother in a state of violent agitation. She inquired where I had been, and I told her.

"I can hardly believe you, John," she said; "are you sure you are telling me the truth?"

I was silent. She repeated the question. I would not answer; and she bestowed upon me a sound beating.

I bore my punishment with dogged sullenness, and retired into the back kitchen; in a corner of which I sat down, and, with my head between my hands, began to brood over the treatment I had received. Gradually there crept into my heart the same feeling I remembered to have conceived against my father,—a feeling of bitter malignity revived by a fresh object. I endeavoured to quell it, to subdue it, but I could not. I recalled all my mother's former kindness to me, her present affection for me; and I reminded myself that this was the first time she had ever raised her hand against me. This thought only nourished the feeling, till the aching of my brain caused it to subside into moody stupefaction.

I became calmer in about an hour, and arose, and went into the front kitchen. My mother was seated at the window, employed at her needle; and, as she raised her eyes, I perceived they were red with weeping. I walked slowly towards her, and stood by her side.

"Mother!" I said, in a low and tremulous voice.

"Well, John; I hope you are a good boy now?"

" Mother !" I repeated, ." you don't know how you have hurt me."

" I am sorry I struck you so hard, child ; I did not mean to do it ;" and she averted her head.

" Not that—not that !" I cried passionately, beating my bosom with my clenched hands. " It 's here, mother—here. I told you the truth, and you would not believe me."

" Mr. Ward has returned now," said my mother ; " I will go ask him ;" and she arose.

I caught her by the gown. " Oh, mother !" I said, " this is the second time you would not believe me. You shall not go to Mr. Ward yet !" and I drew her into the seat. " Say first that you are sorry for it—only a word. Oh, do say it !"

As I looked up, I saw the tears gathering in her eyes. I fell upon my knees, and hid my face in her lap. " No, no ; don't say anything now to me—don't—don't !" A spasm rose from my chest into my throat, and I fell senseless at her feet.

My mother afterwards told me that it was the day of the year on which my father died, and she feared from my lengthened stay that I had come to harm. Dear, good woman ! Oh ! that I might hope to see her once more, even though it were but for one moment,—for we shall not meet in heaven !

It was a cruel blow that deprived us of our kind protector ! Mr. Ward died suddenly, and without a will ; and my mother and I were left entirely unprovided with means. The old gentleman had often declared his intention of leaving my mother enough to render her comfortable during the remainder of her days, and had expressed his determination of setting me on in the world immediately I became of a proper age. It could hardly be expected that the heir-at-law would have fulfilled these intentions, even had he been cognisant of them. He was a low attorney, living somewhere in the neighbourhood of Drury-lane ; and when he attended the funeral, and during the hour or two he remained in the house after it, it was quite clear that he had no wish to retain anything that belonged to his late relative except his property, and his valuable and available effects. He however paid my mother a month's wages in advance, presented me a dollar to commence the world with, shook hands with us, and wished us well.

It was not long before my mother obtained a situation as servant in a small respectable family in King-street, Holborn ; and, as I was now nearly eleven years of age, it was deemed by her friends high time that I should begin to get my own living. Such small influence, therefore, as my mother could command, was set on foot in my behalf ; and I at length got a place as errand-boy to a picture-dealer in Wardour-street, Oxford-street. The duties required of me in this situation, if not of a valuable description, were, at least, various. I went with messages, I attended sales, I kept the shop, I cleaned the knives and shoes, and, indeed, performed all those services which it is the province of boys to render, some of which are often created because there happens to be boys to do them.

This routine was, for a time, irksome. When I recalled the happy days I had spent under the roof of Mr. Ward, and the hopes and expectations he had excited within me of a more prosperous commencement of life,—hopes which his death had so suddenly destroyed,—it is not surprising that I should have felt a degree of discontent of my condition, for which I had no other cause. As I sat by the kitchen fire of an evening when my day's work was done, I often pictured to myself the old man lying where we had left him in the churchyard, mouldering insensibly away, unconscious of rain, or wind, or sunshine, or the coming of night, or the approach of day, wrapped in a shroud which would outlast its wearer, and silently waiting for oblivion. These thoughts became less frequent as time wore on; but I have never been able to dissociate the idea of death from these hideous conditions of mortality.

My master, Mr. Bromley, when I first entered his service, was a man of about the middle age, and of rather grave and formal manners. He had not a bad heart; but I have since discovered that what appeared to my boyish fancy a hard and cold selfishness was but the exterior of those narrow prejudices which too many of that class, if not of all classes, indulge, or rather inherit. He felt that a distance ought to be preserved between himself and his servant; and what he thought he ought to do, he always did; so that I had been with him a considerable period before he even addressed a word to me which business did not constrain him to utter.

He had a daughter, a girl about eighteen years of age. What a human being was Louisa Bromley! She was no beauty; but she had a face whose sweetness was never surpassed. I saw something like it afterwards in the faces of some of Raffaele's angels. The broad and serene forehead, the widely-parted eyebrow, the inexplicable mouth, the soul that pervaded the whole countenance! I can never forget that face; and, when I call it back to memory now, I admire it the more because, to use the modern jargon, there was no *intellect* in it. There was no thought, no meditation or premeditation; but there was nature, and it was good-nature.

Her gentleness and kindness soon won upon me. To be kind to me was at all times the way to win me, and the only way. I cannot express the happiness I felt at receiving and obeying any command from her. A smile, or the common courtesy of thanks from her lips, repaid me a hundred-fold for the performance of the most menial office.

I had now been with Mr. Bromley about four years. I employed my leisure, of which I had a great deal, in reading. All the books I could contrive to borrow, or that fell in my way, I devoured greedily. Nor did I confine myself exclusively to one branch of reading,—I cannot call it study. But my chief delight was to peruse the lives of the great masters of painting, to make myself acquainted with the history and the comparative merits of their several performances, and to endeavour to ascertain how many and what specimens existed in this country. I had, also, a natural taste for painting, and sometimes surprised my master by the remarks I ventured to make upon productions he might happen to purchase, or which had been consigned to him for sale.

Meanwhile, I was permitted to go out in the afternoon of each alternate Sunday. Upon these occasions I invariably went to see my mother. How well can I remember the gloomy underground kitchen in which I always found her, with her Bible before her on a small round table! With what pleased attention did she listen to me when

I descanted on the one subject upon which I constantly dwelt,—the determination I felt, as soon as I had saved money enough, and could see a little more clearly into my future prospects, to take her from service, that she might come and live with me! This was, in truth, the one absorbing thought—it might almost be termed the one passion—of my existence at that time. I had no other hope, no other feeling, than that of making her latter years a compensation for the misery she must have endured during my father's life.

One Sunday when I called, as usual, an old woman answered the door. She speedily satisfied my inquiries after my mother. She had been very ill for some days, and was compelled to keep her bed. My heart sank within me. I had seen her frequently in former years disfigured by her husband's brutality; I had seen her in pain, in anguish, which she strove to conceal; but I had never known her to be confined to her room. When I saw her now, young as I was, and unaccustomed to the sight of disease, I involuntarily shrunk back with horror. She was asleep. I watched her for a few minutes, and then stole softly from the room, and returned to my master's house.

He was gone to church with his daughter. I followed thither, and waited under the portico till they came forth. I quickly singled them out from the concourse issuing from the church-doors. I drew my master aside, and besought him to spare me for a few days, that I might go and attend my mother, who was very ill.

"Is she dying?" he inquired.

I started. "No, not dying. Oh, no!"

"Well, John, I can't spare you: we are very busy now, you know."

And what was that to me? It is only on occasions like these, that the value of one's services is recognised. I thought of this at the time. I turned, in perplexity, to Louisa Bromley. She understood the silent appeal, and interceded for me. I loved her for that; I could have fallen down at her feet, and kissed them for it. She prevailed upon the old man to let me go.

The people of the house at which my mother was a servant were kind, and even friendly. They permitted me to remain with her.

I never left her side for more than half an hour at a time. She grew worse rapidly, but I would not believe it. My mother, however, was fully aware of her situation. She told me frequently, with a smile, which I could not bear to see upon her face, it was so unlike joy, but it was to comfort me,—she told me that she knew she was about to die, and she endeavoured to impress upon me those simple maxims of conduct for my future life which she had herself derived from her parents. She must not die—must not; and I heard with impatience, and heedlessly, the advice she endeavoured to bestow upon me.

She died. The old nurse told me she was dead. It could not be, —she was asleep. My mother had told me not an hour before, that she felt much better, and wanted a little sleep; and at that moment her hand was clasped in mine. The lady of the house took me gently by the arm, and, leading me into an adjoining room, began to talk to me in a strain, I suppose, usually adopted upon such occasions,—for I knew not what she said to me.

In about two hours I was permitted to see my mother again.

There was a change—a frightful change! The nurse, I remember, said something about her looking like one asleep. I burst into a loud laugh. Asleep! that blank, passive, impenetrable face like sleep—petrified sleep! I enjoined them to leave me, and they let me have my own way; for, boy as I was, they were frightened at me.

I took my mother's hand, and wrung it violently. I implored her to speak to me once more, to repeat that she still loved me, to tell me that she forgave all my faults, all my omissions, all my sins towards her. And then I knew she *was* dead, and fell down upon my knees to pray; but I could not. Something told me that I ought not—something whispered that I ought rather to —— ; but I was struck senseless upon the floor.

The mistress of my mother, who was a good and worthy woman, offered to pay her funeral expenses ; but I would not permit it. Not a farthing would I receive from her ; out of my own savings I buried her.

If I could have wept—but I never could weep—when this calamity befell me, I think that impious thought would never have entered my brain. That thought was, that the Almighty was unjust to deprive me of the only being in the world who loved me, who understood me, who knew that I had a heart, and that, when it was hurt and outraged, my head was not safe—not to be trusted. That thought remained with me for years.

CHAPTER II.

FIVE years elapsed. The grief occasioned by my mother's death having in some measure subsided, my thoughts became concentrated upon myself with an intensity scarcely to be conceived. A new passion took possession of my soul: I would distinguish myself, if possible, and present to the world another instance of friendless poverty overcoming and defying the obstacles and impediments to its career. With this view constantly before me, I read even more diligently than heretofore. I made myself a proficient in the principles of mathematics ; I acquired some knowledge of mechanical science ; but, above all, I took every opportunity of improving my taste in the fine arts. This last accomplishment was soon of infinite service to me ; many gentlemen who frequented our shop were pleased to take much notice of me ; my master was frequently rallied upon having a servant who knew infinitely more of his business than himself ; and my opinion on one or two remarkable occasions was taken in preference to that of my employer.

Mr. Bromley naturally and excusably might have conceived no slight envy of my acquirements ; but he was not envious. Shall I be far wrong when I venture to say, that few men are so, where pecuniary interest points out the impolicy of their encouraging that feeling ? Be this as it may, he treated me with great kindness; and I was grateful for it, really and strongly so. I had been long since absolved from the performance of those menial duties which had been required of me when I first entered his service ; my wages were increased to an extent which justified me in calling them by the more respectable term, salary; I was permitted to live out of the house ;

and in all respects the apparent difference and distance between my master and myself were sensibly diminished.

During this period of five years I never received one unkind word or look from Louisa Bromley: and the affection I bore towards this young woman, which was the affection a brother might have felt, caused me to strive by every means at my command to advance the fortunes of her father. And, indeed, the old man had become so attached to me,—partly, and I doubt not unconsciously, because my talents were of value to him,—that I should not have had the heart, even had my inclinations prompted me, to desert him. It is certain that I might have improved my own position by doing so.

At this time Frederick Steiner became acquainted with Mr. Bromley. He was a young man about thirty years of age, of German descent, and possessed of some property. The manners of Steiner were plausible, he was apparently candid, his address indicated frankness and entire absence of guile, and he was handsome; yet I never liked the man. It is commonly supposed that women are gifted with the power of detecting the worst points of the characters of men at the first glance. This gift is withheld when they first behold the man they are disposed to love. This, at any rate, was the case with Louisa Bromley.

Not to dwell upon this part of my narrative, in a few months Bromley's daughter was married to Steiner, who was taken into partnership.

I must confess I was deeply mortified at this. I myself had conceived hopes of one day becoming Bromley's partner; and my anxiety for the happiness of his daughter led me to doubt whether she had not made a choice which she might have occasion afterwards to deplore. However, things went on smoothly for a time. Steiner was civil, nay, even friendly to me; and the affection he evinced towards his little boy, who was born about a year after the marriage, displayed him in so amiable a light, that I almost began to like the man.

It was not very long, however, before Steiner and I came to understand each other more perfectly. He was possessed with an overweening conceit of his taste in pictures, and I on my part obstinately adhered to my own opinion, whenever I was called upon to pronounce one. This led to frequent differences, which commonly ended in a dispute, which Bromley was in most cases called upon to decide. The old man, doubtless, felt the awkwardness of his position; but, as his interest was inseparable from a right view of the question at issue, he commonly decided with me.

Upon these occasions Steiner vented his mortification in sneers at my youth, and ironical compliments to me upon my cleverness and extraordinary genius; for both of which requisites, as he was signally deficient in them, he especially hated me. I could have repaid his hatred with interest, for I kept it by me in my own bosom, and it accumulated daily.

I know not how it happened that the child wound itself round my heart, but it was so. It seemed as though there were a necessity that, in proportion as I detested Steiner, I must love his child. But the boy, from the earliest moment he could take notice of anything, or could recognise anybody, had attached himself to me; and I loved

T 2

him, perhaps for that cause, with a passionate fondness which I can scarcely imagine to be the feeling even of a parent towards his child.

If I were not slow by nature to detect the first indications of incipient estrangement, I think I should have perceived in less than two years after Steiner had been taken into partnership by Mr. Bromley, a growing reserve, an uneasy constraint in the manners of the latter, and a studied, an almost formal civility on the part of his daughter. I now think there must have been something of the kind, although it was not at the time apparent to me. I am certain, at all events, there was less cordiality, less friendship, in the deportment of Mrs. Steiner towards me : a circumstance which I remember to have considered the result of her altered situation. The terms of almost social equality, however, were no longer observed.

One Mr. Taylor, a very extensive picture-dealer, who lived in the Haymarket, made several overtures to me about this time. He had heard many gentlemen of acknowledged taste speak of me in the highest terms ; and, in truth, I was now pretty generally recognised throughout the trade as one of the best judges of pictures in London. I had more than one interview, of his own seeking, with this gentleman. He made me a most flattering and advantageous offer : he would have engaged my services for a certain number of years, and at the expiration of the period he would have bound himself to take me into partnership. I had received many similar offers before, although none that could be for a moment compared, on the score of emolument and stability, with this. I rejected those for the sake of Bromley : I rejected this for my own.

Shall I be weak enough to confess it ? The respect I bore the old man even now ; my affection for his daughter, my love for the child, went some part of the way towards a reason for declining Taylor's proposal ; but it did not go all the way. I hated Steiner so intensely, so mortally, and he supplied me daily with such additional cause of hatred, that I felt a species of excitement, of delight, in renewing from time to time my altercations with him : a delight which was considerably increased by the fact that he was quite incapable of competing with me in argument. There was another reason, which added a zest, if anything could do so, to the exquisite pleasure I derived from tormenting him,—the belief I entertained that Bromley and himself dared not part with me : they knew my value too well. Bromley, at least, I was well aware, was conscious enough of that.

I had been attending one day a sale of pictures, the property of a certain nobleman whose collection, thirty years ago, was the admiration of connoisseurs. Mr. —— (I need not give his name, but he is still living,) had employed me to bid for several amongst the collection ; and had requested my opinion of a few, the merit of which, although strongly insisted upon, he was disposed to doubt. When I returned in the evening, I saw Steiner in the shop waiting for me, and —for hate is quick at these matters, quicker even than love—I knew that he meditated a quarrel. I was not mistaken. He looked rather pale, and his lip quivered slightly.

" And so," said he, " you have been holding several conversations with Mr. Taylor lately ; haven't you, Mr. Gibson ?"

" Who told you that I had been holding conversations with him ?"

"No matter: you have done so. Pray, may I ask the tenour of them?"

"Mr. Taylor wished to engage my services," I replied, "and I declined to leave Mr. Bromley."

"That's not very likely," said Steiner with a sneer.

Steiner was right there; it was not very likely. He might with justice consider me a fool for not having embraced the offer.

"I suppose," pursued Steiner in the same tone, "Mr. —— would follow you to your new situation. You would select his pictures for him as usual, doubtless."

"Doubtless I should," said I with a cool smile that enraged him. "Mr. —— would follow *me* certainly, and many others would follow *him*, Mr. Steiner."

"I'll tell you what it is," cried Steiner, and a flush overspread his face; "Taylor has been using you for his own purposes. You have been endeavouring to undermine our connexion, and have been serving him at the same time that you have taken our wages."

It was not a difficult matter at any time to move me to anger. I approached him, and with a glance of supreme scorn replied, "It is false!—nay, I don't fear you—it's a lie,—an infamous lie!"

Steiner was a very powerful man, and in the prime of manhood; I was young, and my limbs were not yet fixed,—not set. He struck me a violent blow on the face. I resisted as well as I was able; but what can weakness do against strength, even though it have justice on its side? He seized me by the cravat, and, forcing his knuckles against my throat, dealt me with the other hand a violent blow on the temple, and felled me to the earth. O that I had never risen from it! It had been better.

When I came to my senses, for the blow had for a while stunned me, I arose slowly, and with difficulty. Steiner was still standing over me in malignant triumph, and I could see in the expression of his eyes the gratified conviction he felt of having repaid the long score of ancient grudges in which he was indebted to me. His wife was clinging to his arm, and as I looked into her face I perceived terror in it, certainly; but there was no sympathy,—nay, that is not the word,—I could not have borne that; there was no sorrow, no interest, no concern about me. My heart sickened at this. Bromley was there also. He appeared slightly perplexed; and, misconceiving the meaning of my glance, said coldly, but hurriedly, "You brought it entirely upon yourself, Mr. Gibson."

I turned away, and walked to the other end of the shop for my hat. I had put it on, and was about leaving them. As I moved towards the door, I was nearly throwing down the little boy, who had followed me, and was now clinging to the skirt of my coat, uttering in imperfect accents my name. I looked down. The little thing wanted to come to me to kiss me. Sweet innocent! there was one yet in the world to love me. I would have taken the child in my arms; but Mrs. Steiner exclaimed abruptly, "Come away, Fred,—do; I insist upon it, sir." From that time, and for a long time, I hated the woman for it.

I retreated to my lodging, and slunk to my own room with a sense of abasement, of degradation, of infamy, I had never felt before. Mrs.

Matthews, the woman of the house, who had answered the door to me, and had perceived my agitation, followed me up stairs. She inquired the cause, and was greatly shocked at the frightful contusion upon my temple. I told her all, for my heart was nigh bursting, and would be relieved. She hastened down stairs for an embrocation, which the good woman had always by her, and, returning with it, began to bathe my forehead.

"Wouldn't I trounce the villain for it," she said, as she continued to apply the lotion.

"What did you say, Mrs. Matthews?" and I suddenly looked up.

"Why, that I'd have the rascal punished,—that's what I said. Hanging's too good for such a villain."

The kind creature—I was a favourite of hers—talked a great deal more to the same effect, and at last left me to procure a bottle of rum, which, much to her surprise, for I was no drinker, I requested her to fetch me.

How exquisite it was,—what a luxury to be left alone all to myself! Punished!—the woman had said truly,—he must be punished. They, too, must not escape. The ingratitude of the old man,—his insolence of ingratitude was almost as bad as the conduct of Steiner. After what I had done for him!—an old servant who had indeed served him!—who had refused a certainty, a respectable station in society, perhaps a fortune, for his sake! And he must escape,—he must go unpunished,—he must revel in the consciousness of the impunity of his insult? *No.* I swore that deeply; and, lest it should be possible that I could falter, or perhaps renounce my intention, I confirmed that oath with another, which I shudder to think of, and must not here set down.

I emptied the bottle of rum, but I was not drunk. When I went to bed I was as sober as I am at this moment. I did not go to bed to sleep. My senses were in a strange ferment. The roof of my head seemed to open and shut, and I fancied I could hear the seething of my brain below. I presently fell into a kind of stupor.

It was past midnight when I recovered from this swoon, and I started from the bed to my feet. Something had been whispering in my ear, and I listened for a moment in hideous expectation that the words—for I did hear words—would be repeated; but all was silent. I struck a light, and after a time became more composed. Even the furniture of the room was company to me. Before morning I had shaped my plan of revenge, and it was in accordance with the words that had been spoken to me. Oh, my God! what weak creatures we are! This fantasy possessed, pervaded me; it did not grow,—it did not increase from day to day,—it came, and it overcame me.

I returned the next morning to Bromley's house, and requested to see Steiner. I apologised to him for the words I had used on the previous day, and requested to be permitted to remain in my situation, if Mr. Bromley would consent to it, until I could turn myself round; and I hoped, in the mean time, that what had taken place would be overlooked and forgotten. Steiner received me with a kind of civil arrogance, and went to confer with his partner. They presently returned together, and my request, after an admonitory lecture, rather confusedly delivered, from Bromley, was acceded to;

Steiner warning me at the same time to conduct myself with more humility for the future, under pain of similar punishment.

I did do so, and for six months nothing could exceed the attention I paid to business, the zeal I evinced upon every occasion, the forbearance I exercised under every provocation. And I had need of forbearance. Bromley had been entirely perverted by his son-in-law; and the kind old man of former years was changed into a morose and almost brutal blackguard—to me,—only to me. Mrs. Steiner had likewise suffered the influence of her husband to undermine, and for the time to destroy her better feelings; and she treated me upon all occasions, not merely with marked coldness, but with positive insult. I need hardly say that Steiner enjoyed almost to satiety the advantage he had gained over me. Even the very servants of the house took the cue from their superiors, and looked upon me with contempt and disdain. The little boy alone, who had received express commands never to speak to me, sometimes found his way into the shop, and as he clung round my neck, and bestowed unasked kisses upon my cheek, my hatred of the rest swelled in my bosom almost to bursting.

The persecution I endured thus long was intense torment to me; the reader, whoever he may be, will probably think so. He will be mistaken. It was a source of inconceivable, of exquisite pleasure. It was a justification to me; it almost made the delay of my vengeance appear sinful.

It was now the 22nd of December 1808. I cannot refrain from recording the date. Steiner had been during the last six weeks at Antwerp, and was expected to return in a day or two. He had purchased at a sale in that city a great quantity of pictures, which had just arrived, and were now in the shop. They were severally of no great value, but the purchase had brought Bromley's account at the banker's to a very low ebb. Mrs. Steiner and the child were going to spend the Christmas holidays with some relatives residing at Canterbury. She passed through the shop silently and without even noticing me, and hurried the boy along lest he should wish—and he did make an effort to do so—to take his farewell of me. It was evening at the time, and Bromley was in his back parlour. I was busy in the shop that evening; it was business of my own, which I transacted secretly. Having completed it, I did what was rather unusual with me; I opened the door of the parlour, and bade Bromley good night.

All that evening I hovered about the neighbourhood. I had not resolution to go from it. Now that the time was come when I should be enabled, in all human probability, to fulfil, to glut my vengeance, my heart failed me. The feeling which had supported me during the last six months, which had been more necessary to my soul than daily sustenance to my body, had deserted me then, but that by a powerful effort I contrived to retain it. While I deplored having returned to Bromley's employment, and the abject apology I had made to Steiner, that very step and its consequences made it impossible for me to recede. It must be. It was my fate to do it, and it was their's that it should be done.

What trivial incidents cling to the memory sometimes, when they are linked by association to greater events! I was, I remember standing at the door of a small chandler's shop in Dean-street, almost lost to myself, and to all that was passing about me.

The woman of the house tapped me on the shoulder.

"Will you be so good," she said, "as to move on; you are preventing my customers from entering the shop."

"My good woman," I said, "I hope there is no harm in my standing here?"

"Not much harm," replied the woman, good-humouredly. "I hope you have been doing nothing worse to-day?"

I started, and gazed at the woman earnestly. She smiled.

"Why, bless the man! you look quite flurried. I haven't offended you, I hope?"

"No, no!" I muttered hastily, and moved away. The agony I endured for the next hour I cannot describe.

I passed Bromley's house several times from the hour of nine till half-past. All was silent, all still. What if my design should not take effect! I almost hoped that it would not; and yet the boy who cleaned out the shop must inevitably discover it in the morning. I trembled at the contemplation of that, and my limbs were overspread with a clammy dew. It was too late to make a pretext of business in the shop at that time of night. Bromley was at home, and might, nay would, suspect me. I resolved to be on the premises the first thing in the morning, and retired in a state of mind to which no subsequent occurrence of my life was ever capable of reducing me.

It was about half-past eleven o'clock, or nearer to twelve, that the landlord of the Green Man, in Oxford-street, entered the parlour where I was sitting, gazing listlessly upon two men who were playing a game at dominos.

"There is a dreadful fire," said he, "somewhere on the other side of the street;—in Berwick or Wardour-street, I think."

I sprang to my feet, and rushed out of the house, and, turning into Hanway-yard, ran down Tottenham-court road, crossed the fields, (they are now built upon,) and never stopped till I reached Pancras Church.

As I leaned against the wall of the churchyard some men came along.

"Don't you see the fire, master?" said one, as they passed me.

Then, for the first time, I did see the fire, tingeing the clouds with a lurid and dusky red, and at intervals casting a shower of broken flame into the air, which expanded itself in wide-spreading scintillations.

God of Heaven! what had I done? Why was I here? I lived in the neighbourhood of Bromley's house, and they would be sending for me. The landlord, too, would afterwards remember having seen me in his parlour, and informing me of the fire in the neighbourhood, and I should be discovered. These thoughts were the duration of a moment, but they decided me. I ran back again in a frenzy of remorse and terror, and in a few minutes was in Wardour-street.

The tumult and confusion were at their height. The noise of the engines, the outcries of the firemen, the uproar of the crowd, faintly shadowed forth the tumult in my mind at that moment. I made my way through the dense mass in advance of me, and at length reached the house.

Bromley had just issued from it, and was wringing his hands, and stamping his naked feet upon the pavement. He recognised me, and seized me wildly by the arms.

"Oh! my good God! Gibson," said he, "my child!"

"What child—what child?" cried I, eagerly.

"Mine—mine! and the infant! they are in there!"

"They are gone out of town; don't you remember?" I thought the sudden fright had deprived him of his senses.

"No, no, no! they were too late! the coach was gone!"

With a loud scream I dashed the old man from me, and flew to the door, which was open. I made my way through the stifling smoke that seemed almost to block up the passage, and sprang up stairs. The bed-room door was locked. With a violent effort I wrenched off the lock, and rushed into the room.

All was darkness; but presently a huge tongue of flame swept through the doorway, and, running up the wall, expanded upon the ceiling; and then I saw a figure in white darting about the room with angular dodgings like a terrified bird in a cage.

"Where is the child?" I exclaimed, in a voice of frenzy.

Mrs. Steiner knew me, and ran towards me, clasping me with both arms. She shook her head wildly, and pointed she knew not where.

"Here, Gibson,—here," cried the child, who had recognised my voice.

I threw off my coat immediately, and, seizing the boy, wrapt him closely in it.

"This way, madam,—this way; at once, for Heaven's sake!" and I dragged her to the landing.

There was hell about me then! The flames, the smoke, the fire, the howlings; it was a living hell! But there was a shriek at that moment! Mrs. Steiner had left my side. Gracious Heavens! she had been precipitated below! A sickness came upon me then,—a sensation of being turned sharply round by some invisible power; and, with the child tightly clasped in my arms, I was thrown violently forward into the flames, that seemed howling and yearning to devour me.

MASCALBRUNI.

I HAVE frequently observed that there are some people who haunt you in all parts of the world, and to whom you have a sort of secret antipathy, yet who, by an attraction in spite of repulsion, are continually crossing your path, as though they were sent as emissaries to link themselves with your destiny, or on the watch mysteriously to bring it about. One person in particular, whose name I do not even know, if he has one, I have met fifty times in as many different places, and we each say to ourselves, " 'Tis he!—what, again!" So with a personage too well known at home and abroad, of whom, by a curious concatenation of circumstances, I am enabled to become the biographer.

Geronymo Mascalbruni was the son of a pauper belonging to a village whose name I forget, in the marshes of Ancona. He had begged his way when a boy to Rome, and supported himself for some time there, by attending at the doors of the courts of justice, and running on errands for the advocates or the suitors. His intelligence and adroitness did not escape the observation of one of the attorneys, who, wanting a lad of all work, took Mascalbruni into his service, and taught him to read and write; finding him useful in his office, and having no children of his own, he at length adopted him, *in formâ pauperis*, and gave him a small share in his business. This man of the law did not bear the most exemplary of characters, and perhaps it was in order to conceal some nefarious practices to which Mascalbruni was privy that he made the clerk his associate. Perhaps also he discovered in his character a hardihood, combined with cunning and chicanery, that made him a ready instrument for his purposes, and thus enabled him, like Teucer, to fight behind the shield of another. Under this worthy master—a worthy disciple—Mascalbruni continued for some years; till at length, tired of confinement to the desk, and having the taste early acquired for a roving and profligate life revived, he, during his old benefactor's confinement to his bed with a rheumatic attack, administered to him a dose of poison instead of medicine, and having robbed him of all the money and plate that was portable, and of certain *coupons*, and *bons* in the Neapolitan and other funds, standing in his name, he decamped, and reached Florence in safety.

Every one has heard of the laxity of the Roman police. The impunity of offenders, even when their crimes are established by incontestable proof, is notorious. The relations of the lawyer, contrary to all their expectations, (for he had never recognised them,) had come into their inheritance, and little regarded the means, having attained the end. They perhaps, also, from having had no admission into the house during the old miser's life, were ignorant of the strength of his coffers; and the disappearance of the murderer, who, by a will which they discovered and burnt, had been made his sole heir, was by them deemed too fortunate a circumstance; so that they neither inquired into the manner of his death, nor had any *post mortem* examination of the body. They gave their respectable relative a splendid funeral, erected to his memory a tomb in one of the rival churches that front the Piazza del Popolo, in which his many virtues were not forgotten, and established an annual mass for his *povera anima*, that no doubt saved him

> "From many a peck of purgatorial coals."

Having quietly inurned the master, let us follow the man. The sum which he carried with him is not exactly known, but it must have been considerable. His stay in the Tuscan state was short, and we find him with his ill-gotten wealth in "that common sewer of London and of Rome," Paris. He was then about twenty years of age, had a good person, talents, an insinuating address, and a sufficient knowledge of the world, at least of the worst part of mankind, to avoid sinking in that quagmire, which has swallowed up so many of the thoughtless and inexperienced who have trusted to its flattering surface. In fact, Nature seemed to have gifted him with the elements of an accomplished sharper, and he seconded her attributes by all the resources of art. He took an apartment in the Rue Neuve de Luxembourg, that street so admirably situated between the Boulevards and the Gardens of the Tuileries, and had engraven on his cards, "Il Marchese Mascalbruni." He was attached to his name: it was a good, sonorous, well-sounding name; and the addition of Marchese dovetailed well, and seemed as though it had always, or ought always, to have belonged to it.

But before he made his *entrée* in the world of Paris, he was aware that he had much to learn; and, with the tact and nice sense of observation and *disinvoltura nel maneggiar* peculiar to his nature, he soon set about accomplishing himself in the externals of a gentleman. With this view he passed several hours a day in the *salle d'armes*, where he made himself a first-rate fencer; and became so dexterous *au tir*, that he could at the extremity of the gallery hit the bull's-eye of the target at almost every other shot.

Pushkin himself was not more dexterous; and, like him, our hero in the course of his career signalised himself by several rencontres which proved fatal to his antagonists, into the details of but one of which I shall enter. He heard that nothing gives a young man greater *éclat* at starting into society than a duel. Among those who frequented the *salle* was an old officer who had served in the campaigns of Napoleon, one of the *reliquiæ Danaum*, the few survivors of Moscow; for those who did not perish on the road, mostly fell victims to the congelations and fatigues of that memorable retreat. Mascalbruni, now a match for the *maître d'armes*, frequently exercised with this old *grognard*, who had the character of being a *crane*, if not a *bourreau des cranes ;** and one day, before a numerous *gallerie*, having struck the foil out of his hand, the fencer so far forgot himself, in the shame and vexation of defeat by a youngster, as to pick up the weapon and strike the Italian a blow on the shoulders with the flat part of the foil, if it be not an Irishism so to call it. Those who saw Mascalbruni at that moment would not have forgotten the traits of his countenance. His eyes flashed with a sombre fire; his Moorish complexion assumed a darker hue, as the blood rushed from his heart to his brain in an almost suffocating tide; his breath came forth in long and audible expirations; his features were convulsed

* Military terms for a professed duellist, and a duellist-killer.

with the rage of a demoniac. I only describe what Horace Verney, who was present, faithfully sketched from memory after the scene. Mascalbruni, tearing off the button of his foil, vociferated, putting himself in position, "*A la mort, à la mort!*" The lookers-on were panic-stricken; but the silence was interrupted by the clinking of the steel. The aggressor soon lay stretched in the agonies of death.

Though he had now taken his first degree, Mascalbruni's education was not yet complete. He had made himself master of French, so as to speak it almost without any of the accent of a foreigner; and having a magnificent voice, he added to it all the science that one of his own countrymen could supply, and became in the end a finished musician and vocalist.

Such was the course of his studies; and now, with all the *préstige* of his singular *affaire* to give him *éclat*, the Marchese Mascalbruni made his *début*. By way of recreation, he had frequently gone into the gambling-houses of the Palais Royal, and had been much struck with these words, almost obliterated, on the walls of one of them, "*Tutus veni, tutus abi.*" Mascalbruni was determined to profit by the advice, and to confirm its truth by one solitary exception—to come and depart in safety, or rather a winner.

Mascalbruni invented a theory of his own, that has since been practised by several of the *habitués* of the hells, particularly by a man denominated, in the *maisons de jeu*, L'Avocat. He won such enormous sums of the bank, that, on his return to his lodgings one night, he was assassinated, not without suspicion that he fell by the hands of some kind bravo of the company. *Chi lo sa?* But to revert to Mascalbruni.

Impares numeri are said to be fortunate: strange to say, the number three is the most so. Three was a mystic number. The triangle was sacred to the Hindoos and Egyptians. There were three Graces, three Furies, three Fates. He played a martingale of one, three, seven, fifteen, &c. on triple numbers, *i. e.* after three of a colour, either red or black, had come up, and not till then, he played, and opposed its going a fourth; thus rendering it necessary that there should be twelve or thirteen successive *coups* of four, *et sequentia*, without the intervention of a three. The gain, it is true, could not be great, for he began with a five-franc piece: but it seemed sure; and so he found it, making a daily profit of three or four louis in as many hours.

I have gone into this dry subject to show the character of the man, and his imperturbable *sang-froid*. He did not, however, confine himself to *rouge et noir*, but soon learned all the niceties of that scientific game *écarté*. In addition to *sauter le coup*, which he practised with an invisible dexterity, he used to file the ends of the fingers of his right hand, so that he could feel the court-cards, which, having a thicker coat of paint, are thus made easily sensible to the touch; and would extract from each pack one or two, the knowledge of whose non-existence was no slight advantage in discarding. He did not long wait for associates in his art. There was formed at that time a club in the Rue Richelieu on the principle of some of the English clubs, it being entirely managed by a committee. Of this he became a member, and afterwards got an introduction at the *salon*. Most of the English at Paris joined this

circle ; and it was broken up in consequence of the discovery of manœuvres and sleights of hand such as I have described, but not until
Mascalbruni had contrived to bear away a more than equal share of
the plunder. The English, of course, were the great sufferers.

He now turned his face towards the Channel, and opened the campaign in London on a much more extensive scale. He took up his
quarters at Higginbottom's hotel in the same year that young Napoleon came to England, and only left it when it was given up to
that lamented and accomplished prince. It is not generally known
that he ever visited England. His sojourn in the capital was kept
a profound secret. The master of the hotel and all his servants
took an oath of secrecy ; and Prince Esterhazy and the members
of the Austrian embassy were not likely to betray it. The prince
passed a week with George the Fourth at the Cottage at Windsor,
and afterwards assisted at a concert at the Hanover Square rooms,
himself leading a concert on the piano. This by the bye. Mascalbruni on that occasion attracted all eyes, and fascinated all ears, and
was greeted after a solo with the loudest plaudits. He had now become the fashion, and, having forged a letter from one of the cardi-
nals at Rome to a patroness of Almacks, obtained the *entrée*, and
made one of the three hundred that compose the world of London.
You know, however, in this world that there is another world—orb
within orb—an *imperium in imperio*—the Exclusives. It is difficult
to define what the qualifications for an exclusive are : it is not rank,
connexion, talents, virtues, grace, elegance, accomplishments. No.
But I shall not attempt to explain the inexplicable. Certain it is,
however, that our hero was admitted into the *coteries* of this caste,
as distinct—as much separated by a line of demarcation drawn round
them from the rest—as the Rajhpoot is from the Raiot, who sprang,
one from the head, the other from the heels of Brahma.

It was on the daughter of one of these extra-exclusives that Mascalbruni cast his eye. He flew at high game. The Honourable Miss
M. was the belle of the season. I remember seeing her the year
before at a fancy ball. A quadrille had been got up, for which were
selected twelve of the most beautiful girls to represent the twelve
Seasons. Louisa was May, and excelled the rest, (I do not speak of
the present year,) as much as that season of flowers does the other
months. It was an ' incarnation of May !'—a metaphor of Spring,
and Youth, and Morning !—a rose-bud just opening its young leaves,
that brings the swiftest thought of beauty, though words cannot embody it :—a sylph borne by a breath, a zephyr, as in the celebrated
Hebe of John of Bologna, may make intelligible the lightness of her
step,—the ethereal grace of her form. She was a nymph of Canova,
without her affectation. Hers was the poetry of motion,—

> " It was the soul, which from so fair a frame
>   Look'd forth, and told us 'twas from heaven it came,"—

that would have been the despair of sculpture or poetry. I have
never seen but one who might compare with her, and she was engulfed that same year in the waters of the inexorable Tiber,—Rosa
Bathurst.*

* Singularly enough, when her body was discovered near the Ponte Rotto,
she was untouched by the fish, as though they even ventured not to deface her
celestial purity. She looked like a marble form that slept.

Louisa M. was the only daughter of an Irish bishop. His see was one of the most valuable in the sister island ; and some idea may be formed of his accumulated wealth, by the circumstance of his having received thirty thousand pounds in one year by fines on the renewal of leases. He had one son, then on a Continental tour with his tutor ; but having no entailed estates, and his fortune consisting of ready money, Louisa was probably one of the *meilleures parties* in the three kingdoms.

There was at that time a mania for foreign alliances. The grand tour, which almost every family of distinction had taken, introduced a rage for Continental customs and manners, which had in some degree superseded our own.

A spring in Paris, and winter in Italy, left behind them regrets in the minds of old and young, but especially the latter, who longed to return to those scenes that had captivated their senses and seduced their young imaginations. No language was spoken at the opera but French or Italian,—no topics of conversation excited so much interest as those which had formed the charm of their residence abroad,—and the fair daughters of England drew comparisons unfavourable to fox-hunting squires and insipid young nobles, when they thought of the accomplished and fascinating foreigners from whom, in the first dawn of life, when all their impressions were new and vivid, they had received such flattering homage.

The mother of Louisa, still young, had not been insensible to pre-possessions ; and had a *liaison* at Rome, where she was unaccompanied by her husband, the effects of which she had not altogether eradicated.

It is said that the road to the daughter's affections is through the heart of the mother. Certainly in Italy *cavalier-servente*ism gene-rally has this termination ; and, though it is not yet openly established in England, there are very many women in high life who have some secret adorer, some favourite friend, to keep alive the flame which too often lies smothered in the ashes of matrimony. I do not mean that this attachment is frequently carried to criminal lengths ; nor am I ready to give much credence to the vain boastings of those foreigners who, when they return to their own country, amuse their idle hours, and idler friends, with a detailed account of their *bonnes fortunes* in London.

I shall not prostitute my narrative, had I the data for so doing, by tracing step by step the well-organised scheme by which Mascal-bruni contrived to ingratiate himself with both the mother and the daughter. He was young, handsome, and accomplished ; an inimitable dancer, a perfect musician. His dress, his stud, and cabriolet were in the best taste, and he passed for a man of large fortune.

It may be asked how he supported this establishment ? By play. Play, in men whose means are ample, if considered a vice, is thought a very venial one. He got admission into several clubs,—Crockford's among the rest :—his games were *écarté* and whist ; games at which he was without a match. Cool, cautious, and calculating, he lost with perfect nonchalance, and won with the greatest seeming indifference.

There was a French *vicomte*, with whom he seemed to have no par-ticular acquaintance, but who was in reality his ally and confederate, and who had accompanied him to England expressly that they might play into each other's hands. He belonged to one of the oldest families, and had one of those historical names that are a *passe par-tout*. I had seen him at the *soirées* of Paris, and he was in the habit at the *écarté* table, if he had come without money, which was not unfrequently the case, of claiming, when the division took place at the end of the game, two napoleons; pretending that at its commencement he had bet one on the winner. I need say no more.

He had signalised himself in several rencontres. I have him before me now, as he used to appear in the Tuileries' gardens, with his narrow hat, his thin face, and spare figure,—so spare, that sideways one might as well have fired at the edge of a knife. To this man Mascalbruni frequently pretended to have lost large sums, and it is now well known that they divided the profits of their gains during the season. No one certainly suspected either of unfair practices, though their uniform success might have opened the eyes of the blindest. The Marchioness of S.'s card-parties and those of Lady E. were a rich harvest, as well as the private routs and *soirées* to which they obtained easy admission. Lady M. was well aware that Mascalbruni had a *penchant* for play; but it seemed to occupy so little of his thoughts or intrench on his time, that it gave her no serious alarm.

I have not yet told you, however, as I ought to have done, that he was a favoured suitor.

The bishop, who, by nature of his office, was seldom in town, was a cypher in the family, and little thought of interfering with his lady in the choice of a son-in-law.

But the season now drew to a close, and Mascalbruni received an invitation to pass the summer at the episcopal palace in the Emerald Isle. He had succeeded in gaining the affections, the irrevocable affections of Louisa. Yes,—she loved him,

"Loved him with all the intenseness of first love!"

Time seemed to her to crawl with tortoise steps when he was absent, —but how seldom was that the case! They sang together those duets of Rossini that are steeped in passion. How well did his deep and mellow voice marry itself with her contralto! They rode together, not often in the parks, but through those shady and almost unfrequented lanes of which there are so many in the environs of the metropolis; they waltzed together; they danced the mazourka together,—that dance which is almost exclusively confined to foreigners, from the difficulty of its steps, and the grace required in its mazes.

They passed hours together alone,—they read together those scenes of Metastasio, so musical in words, so easily retained in the memory. But why do I dwell on these details? When I look on this picture and on that, I am almost forced to renounce the opinion that kindred spirits can alone love; for what sympathy of soul could exist between beings so dissimilar, so little made for each other? Poor Louisa!

Mascalbruni accompanied them to Ireland. That summer was a continual fête. It was settled that the wedding was to take place on their return to town the ensuing season.

In the mean time the intended marriage had been long announced in the Morning Post, and was declared in due form to the son at Naples. Louisa, who was her brother's constant correspondent, in the openness of her heart did not conceal from him that passion, no longer, indeed, a secret. Her letters teemed with effusions of her admiration for the talents, the accomplishments, and the virtues, for such they seemed, of her intended—her *promesso sposo*, and the proud delight that a very few months would seal their union.

William, who had now had some experience of the Italians, and who had looked forward to his sister's marrying one of his college friends, an Irishman with large estates in their immediate neighbourhood, could not help expressing his disappointment, though it was urged with delicacy, at this foreign connexion. He wrote also to the bishop, and, after obtaining from him all the necessary particulars as to the Marchese Mascalbruni,—through what channel he became acquainted with them, by what letter got introduced to Lady ——, lost no time in proceeding to Rome, though the mountains were then infested by brigands, and the Pontine marshes, for it was the month of September, breathed malaria.

Our consul was then at Città Vecchia, but willingly consented to accompany Mr. M. to Rome, in order to aid in the investigation. He was intimate with Cardinal ——, and they immediately proceeded to his palace. They found from him that he had never heard the name of Mascalbruni; that there was no *marchese* in the pontifical states so called; and he unhesitatingly declared the letter to be a forgery, and its writer an impostor.

They then applied to the police, who, after some days' inquiry, discovered that a person answering the description given had quitted Rome a few years before, and had been a clerk in the office of a *notario*.

No farther evidence was necessary to convict Mascalbruni of being a swindler; and, not trusting to a letter's safe arrival, Mr. M. travelled night and day till he reached the palace at ——.

It is not difficult to imagine the scene that ensued,—the indignation of the father, the vexation and self-reproaches of the mother, or the heart-rending emotions of the unfortunate girl.

Mascalbruni at first, with great effrontery, endeavoured to brave the storm; contended that Louisa was bound to him by the most sacred ties, the most solemn engagements; that his she should be,—or, if not his, that she should never be another's; denounced them as her murderers; and ended with threats of vengeance,—vengeance that, alas! he too well accomplished.

It is not very well known what now became of Mascalbruni; but there is reason to believe that he lay *perdu* somewhere in the neighbourhood, watching like a vulture over the prey from which he had been driven, the corpse of what was once Louisa.

A suspicious-looking person was frequently seen at night-fall prowling about the environs of the palace; and Miss M.'s *femme de chambre*, with whom he is said to have carried on an intrigue, was observed by the servants in animated conversation with a stranger in the garb of a peasant among the shrubberies and pleasure grounds.

It was through her medium that Mascalbruni gained intelligence of all that was passing in the palace.

The shock which Louisa had sustained was so sudden, so severe, that, acting on a frame naturally delicate, it brought on a brain fever. Her ravings were so dreadful, and so extraordinary; and so revolting was the language in which she at times clothed them, that even her mother—and no other was allowed to attend her—could scarcely stay by her couch. How perfect a knowledge of human nature has Shakspeare displayed in depicting the madness of the shamelessly-wronged and innocent Ophelia!—The fragments of those songs to which her broken accents gave utterance, especially that which ends with

> " Who, in a maid, yet out a maid,
>   Did ne'er return again,"

may suggest an idea of the wanderings of the poor sufferer's heated imagination.

For some weeks her life hung on a thread; but the affectionate cares and sympathy of a mother, and a sense of the unworthiness of the object of her regard, at last brought back the dawn of reason; and her recovery, though slow, was sufficiently sure to banish all anxiety.

The afflictions as well as the affections of woman are, if I may judge by my own experience, less profoundly acute than those of our own sex. Whether this be owing to constitution or education, or that the superior delicacy and fineness of the nervous system makes them more easily susceptible of new impressions to efface the old, I leave it to the physiologist or the psychologist to explain. The river that is the most ruffled at the surface is seldom the deepest. Thus with Miss M. Her passion, like

> " A little brook, swoln by the melted snow,
>   That overflows its banks, pour'd in her heart
>   A scanty stream, and soon was dry again."*

In the course of three months the image of Mascalbruni, if not effaced from her mind, scarcely awakened a regret; and, save that at times a paleness overspread her cheek, rapidly chased by a blush, be it of virgin innocence or shame, no one could ever have discovered in her person or bearing any traces of the past.

At this time a paragraph appeared in the Court Journal of the day, nearly in these words:

" Strange rumours are afloat in the Sister Island respecting a certain Italian *marchese*, who figured at the clubs and about town during the last season. Revelations of an extraordinary nature, that hastened the return of the Honourable Mr. M. from the Continent, have led to a rupture of the marriage of the belle of the season, which we are authorised to say is definitively broken off."

It was a telegraph that the field was open for new candidates; but no one on this side the water answered it. Louisa M. was no longer the same,—the *préstige* was fled,—the bloom of the peach was gone.

Scarcely had four months elapsed, however, when fresh preparations were made for her marriage, and a day fixed for the nuptials.

The hour came; and behold, in the conventional language used on such occasions, the happy pair, Lady M. the bride-maids, and a numerous party of friends assembled in the chapel of the palace. The bishop officiated.

The ceremony had already commenced, and the rite was on the point of being ratified by that mystical type of union—the ring—when a figure burst through the crowd collected about the doors; a figure more like a spectre than a man.

So great a change had taken place in him, from the wild and savage life that he had been leading among the mountains, the pri-

---

* Faust.

vations he had endured, and the neglect of his person, that no one
would have recognised him for the observed of all observers, the
once elegant and handsome Mascalbruni. His hair, matted like the
mane of a wild beast, streamed over his face and bare neck. His
cheek was fallen, his eyes sunken in their sockets; yet in them burned,
as in two dark caves, a fierce and sombre fire. His lips were tremulous and convulsed with passion; his whole appearance, in short, exhibited the same diabolical rage and thirst of vengeance that had
electrified the *salle d'armes* in his memorable conflict. He advanced straight to the altar with long and hurried steps, and, tearing
aside the hands of the couple, the ring fell over the communion rails
to the ground. So profound was the silence, so great the consternation and surprise the sight of this apparition created in the minds
of all, that the sound of the ring, as it struck and rolled along the
vaulted pavement, was audibly heard. It was an omen of evil augury,—a warning voice as from the grave, to tell of the death of promised joys—of hopes destroyed—of happiness for ever crushed. He
stood wildly waving his arms for a moment between the pair, looking
as though they had been transformed into stone, more like two statues kneeling at a tomb than at the altar. Then he folded his arms;
gazed with a triumphant and ghastly smile at the bride; said, or
rather muttered, " Mine she is !" then, turning to the bridegroom,
with a sneer of scorn and mockery he howled, " Mine she has been ;
now wed her !"

With these laconic words he turned on his heel, and regained
without interruption the portal by which he had entered. So suddenly had all this passed, so paralysed and panic-stricken were the
spectators and audience of this scene, that they could scarcely believe it to be other than a dream, till they saw the bride extended
without sense or motion on the steps. Thus was she borne, the service being unconcluded, to her chamber. The ceremony was privately completed the ensuing day.

No domestic felicity attended this ill-fated union. It was poisoned by doubts and suspicions, and embittered by the memory of
Mascalbruni's words. " Mine she has been" continually rang in the
husband's ears; and on the anniversary of that eventful day, after a
lingering illness of many months, a martyr to disappointment and
chagrin, she sunk into an untimely grave.

The next we hear of Mascalbruni was his being at Cheltenham.
There he frequented the rooms under very different auspices, and
had to compete with another order of players than those he had been
in the habit of duping. He was narrowly watched, and detected in
the act of pocketing a queen from an *écarté* pack. The consequence
was his expulsion from the club with ignominy. His name was pla-
carded, and his fame, or rather infamy, noised with a winged speed
all over the United Kingdom.

It was no longer a place for him. In the course of the ensuing
week the following announcement was made in a well-known and
widely-circulated weekly paper. It was headed—

" *An Italian black sheep.*

" We hope in a short time to present our readers with the exploits
of a new Count Fathom, a *soi-disant* marchese, better known than

trusted, the two first syllables of whose name more than rhyme with
rascal. And as it is our duty to un-*mask all* such, we shall confine
ourselves at present to saying that he has been weighed at a fashionable watering-place in Gloucestershire, and found wanting, or
rather practising certain sleights of hand for which the charlatans of
his own country are notorious. He had better sing small here !"

Mascalbruni took the vulgar hint. His funds were nearly exhausted, and with but a few louis in his pocket he embarked at
Dover, and once more repaired to Paris.

His prospects were widely different from those with which he had
left it. To play the game I have described at *rouge et noir,* requires
a capital. Every respectable house was closed against him. He
now disguised his appearance, so that his former acquaintance should
not be able to recognise him, and frequented the lowest hells—those
cloacæ, the resort of all the *vilains* and *chenapans,* the lowest dregs
of the metropolis. By what practices this *mauvais sujet* contrived
to support life here for some years is best known to the police,
where his name stands chronicled pretty legibly; it is probable that
he passed much of that time in one of the prisons, or on the roads.

Eighteen months had now elapsed, and the Honourable Mr. M.
with his bride, to whom he had been a short time married, took an
apartment in the Rue d'Artois. A man in a cloak—an *embocado,*—
which means one who enwraps his face in his mantle so that only
his eyes are visible,—was observed from the windows often passing
and repassing the hotel. The novelty of the costume attracted the
attention of Mrs. M.; and the blackness of his eyes, and their peculiarly gloomy expression, made her take him for a Spaniard. She
more than once pointed him out to her husband, and said one day,
" Look, William, there stands that man again. He answers your description of a bandit, and makes me shudder to look at him."

" Don't be alarmed, dear," replied Mr. M. smilingly ; "we are not
at Terracina. It will be time enough to be frightened then."

The recollection of Mascalbruni had been almost effaced from his
mind; but, had he met him face to face, it is not unlikely that he
would have remembered the villain who had destroyed the hopes of
his family, and marred their happiness for ever.

For some time he never went out at night unaccompanied by his
wife, and always in a carriage. But a day came when he happened
to dine without her in the Rue St. Honoré. The weather being
fine, and the party a late one, he sent away his cabriolet, and after
midnight proceeded to walk home. Paris was at that time very
badly lighted; the *reverberées* at a vast distance apart, suspended between the houses, giving a very dim and feeble ray. Few persons
—there being then no *trottoirs*—were walking at that hour ; and it so
happened that not a soul was stirring the whole length of the street.
But, within a few yards of his own door, the figure I have described
rushed from under the shadow of a *porte cochère,* and plunged a
dagger in his heart. He fell without a groan, and lay there till the
patrol passed, when he was conveyed, cold and lifeless, to the arms
of his bride, who was anxiously awaiting his return. Her agony I
shall not make the attempt to depict : there are some sorrows that
defy description.

Notwithstanding the boasted excellence of the Parisian police, the author of this crime, who I need not say was Mascalbruni, remained undiscovered.

Strange as it may appear, I am enabled to connect two more links in the chain of this ruffian's history, and thus, as it were, to become his biographer. Having been in town at the period when he was in the zenith of his glory, and being slightly acquainted with the family whom, like a pestilence, it was his lot to destroy and blight, I was well acquainted with his person, and he with mine; indeed, once seen, it was not easy to mistake his.

After two winters at Naples, I travelled, by the way of Ravenna and Rimini, to Venice. The carnival was drawing to a close, and, on quitting a *soirée* at Madame Benzon's, I repaired to the Ridotta. The place was crowded to excess with that mercurial population, who during this saturnalia, particularly its last nights, mingle·in one orgie, and seem to endeavour, by a kind of intoxication of the senses, and general licentiousness, to drown the memory of the destitution and wretchedness to which the iron despotism of the Austrian has reduced them. The scene had a sort of magnetic attraction in it.

I had neither mask nor domino, but it is considered rather *distingué* for men to appear without them; and, as I had no love-affair to carry on, it was no bad means of obtaining one, had I been so inclined.

Among the other groups, I observed two persons who went intriguing round the *salle*, appearing to know the secrets of many of their acquaintances, whom it seemed their delight to torment and persecute, and whom, notwithstanding their masks, they had detected by the voice, which, however attempted to be disguised, betrays more than the eyes, or even the mouth, though it is the great seat of expression. The pair wore fancy dresses. The domino of the man was of Persian or Turkish manufacture, a rich silk with a purple ground, in which were inwoven palm-leaves of gold, The costume of the lady, who seemed of a portly figure, not the most symmetrical, was a rich Venetian brocade, such as we see in the gorgeous pictures of Paul Veronese, and much in use during the dogal times of the republic. As they passed me, I heard the lady say, looking at me, "That is a foreigner." "*Si signora, è Inglese,*" was the reply; "*lo conosco.*" Who this could be who knew me,—me, almost a stranger at Venice, I was curious to discover. By the slow and drawling accent peculiar to the Romans, I felt satisfied he was one, and fancied that I had heard that voice before,—that it was not altogether unfamiliar to me.

I was desirous of unravelling the secret, for such it was, as the man did not address me; and I remained at the Ridotta much later than I should otherwise have done, in order to find out my unknown acquaintance. I therefore kept my eye on the couple, hoping that accident might favour my wish.

On the last nights of the carnival it is common to sup at the Ridotta, and I at length watched the *incognito* into a box with his *inamorata*, where he took off his mask, and whom should I discover under it but the identical hero of romance, the villain Mascalbruni.

· He was an acquaintance who might well shun *my* recognition, and I was not anxious he should see I had attracted *his* observation. As I was returning to my hotel on the Grand Canal, I asked the gondolier if he knew one Signor Mascalbruni. These boatmen are a kind of Figaros, and, like the agents of the Austrian police, are acquainted with the names and address of almost every resident in Venice, especially of those who frequent the public places. The man, however, did not know *my friend* by that name,—perhaps he had changed it. But when I described his costume, he said that the signor was the *cavalier servente* of a Russian princess, who had taken for a year one of the largest palaces in Venice. "*Il signor,*" he added, "*canta come un angelo.*"

The idea of coupling an angel and Mascalbruni together amused me. "An angel of darkness!" I was near replying; but thought it best to be silent.

I had no wish to encounter Mascalbruni a second time. I went the next day to Fusina, and thence to Milan; indeed I had made all the preparations for my departure, nothing being more dull than the *Carême* at Venice.

Two years after this adventure, I was travelling in the Grisons, after having made a tour of the *petits cantons,* with my knapsack on my back, and a map of Switzerland in my pocket, to serve the place of a guide,—a description of persons to whom I have almost as great an objection as to cicerones, preferring rather to miss seeing what I should like to see, than to be told what I ought to like to see; not that it has fallen to the lot of many guides, or travellers either, to be present at a spectacle such as I am going to describe. I had been pacing nine good leagues; and that I saw it was merely accidental, for if *it* had not come in my way, *I* should not have gone out of mine to witness it.

Coire, the capital of the Grisons, my place of destination for the night, had just appeared, when I observed a great crowd collecting together immediately in front, but at some distance off, the peasants running in all directions from the neighbouring hills, like so many radii to meet in a centre.

One of these crossed me; and, on inquiring of him the occasion of all this haste and bustle, I learned that an execution was about to take place. My informant added with some pride that the criminal was not a Swiss, but an Italian. He seemed perfectly acquainted with all the particulars of the event that had transpired, for he had been present at the trial; and, as we walked along the road together, in his *patois,*—bad German, and worse French, with here and there a sprinkling of Italian,—he related to me in his own way what I will endeavour to translate.

"An Englishman of about twenty years of age was travelling, as you may be, on foot, about seven weeks ago, in this canton, having lately crossed the St. Gothard from Bellinzona. He was accompanied by a courier, whom he had picked up at Milan. They halted for some days in our town, waiting for the young gentleman's remittances from Genoa, where his letters of credit were addressed. On their arrival at Coire they had a guide; but the Italian persuaded his master, who seemed much attached to him, to discharge Pierre, on the pretence that he was thoroughly acquainted with the country, and spoke the language, which indeed he did. He was a dark brigand-looking fellow, with a particularly bad expression of countenance, and a gloomy look about his eyes; and, for my part, I am surprised that the young man should have ventured to trust himself in his company, for I should not like to meet his fellow on the road by myself even in the day-time. Well: the Englishman's money, a good round sum,—they say, two hundred napoleons d'or,—was paid him by an order on our bankers; and then they set out, but not as before.

"They had only been two days in company, when the villainous Italian, who either did not know the road over the mountains, or had purposely gone out of the way, thought it a good opportunity of perpetrating an act, no doubt long planned, which was neither more nor less than despatching his master. It was a solitary place, and a fit one for a deed of blood. A narrow path had been worn in the side of a precipice, which yawned to the depth of several hundred feet over a torrent that rushed, as though impatient of being confined, foaming and boiling through a narrow chasm opened for itself through the rocks. I could show you the spot, for I know it well, having a right of *commune* on the mountains; and have often driven my cows, after the melting of the snows, up the pass, to feed on the herbage that, mixed with heath and rhododendrons, forms a thick carpet under foot. It is a pasture that makes excellent cheese.

"But, solitary as the place looks, the Italian did not know that there are several *chalets*, mine among the rest, in the Alp; and herdsmen. As for me, I happened to be down in the plain, or I might have been an eye-witness of much of what I am about to describe. I was saying that the spot seemed to suit his purpose; and his impatience to ease his master of his gold was such, that, happily for the ends of justice, he could not wait till night-fall, or none but (and here he pointed to the sky) He above might have been privy to the crime. It was, however, mid-day. Into the deep-worn pass I have mentioned runs a rivulet, which, sparkling on the green bank, had made for itself a little basin. The day was hot and sultry; and the young gentleman, tempted, it would seem, by the gentle murmur of the water as it fell rippling over the turf, and its crystal brightness, stooped down to drink. The Italian watched this opportunity, sprung upon him like a tiger, and plunged a dagger, which he always carried concealed about him, into the Englishman's back. Fortunately, however, the point hit upon the belt in which he carried his money, perhaps on the napoleons; for, before the assassin could give him a second blow, he sprang up and screamed for help, calling 'Murder, murder!'

"Three of the herdsmen whom I have mentioned heard the cries, and came running towards the direction whence they proceeded, when they discovered two men struggling with each other; but, before they could reach them, one had fallen, and the other was in the act of rifling him, in order afterwards to hurl him down the precipice into the bed of the river. So intent was he on the former of these occupations, that he did not perceive my countrymen till they seized him. He made much resistance; but his dagger was not within his reach. They bound his hands, and, together with the lifeless corpse of his master, transported him to Coire, where, not to enter into the trial, he was condemned to death.

"But he has been now some weeks in prison, in consequence of our not being able to procure a *bourreau*; and we have been forced to send for one to Bellinzona, no Grison being willing to perform the office. 'He arrived last night; and how do you think, sir? According to our laws, he is to be executed with a sword that has not been used for forty years,—no murder having been committed in the canton during all that period,—though no sword could be applied to better purpose than it will in a few moments."

Whilst he was thus speaking, we reached the dense circle already formed. On seeing a stranger approach, they made room for me; and curiosity to witness this mode of execution, the remnant of barbarous times, as well as to see the Italian, induced me to enter the Place de Grève.

At the first glance I recognised Mascalbruni. He was stripped of his shirt, and on his knees; by his side was a Jesuit to whom he had just made his confession; and over him, on an elevation from the ground by means of a large stone, stood the *prevôt*, with a sword of prodigious length and antique shape, and covered with the rust of ages, pendent in his hands.

The lower part of Mascalbruni's face was fallen, whilst all above the mouth was drawn upward as from some powerful convulsion. The eyes, that used to bear the semblance of living coals, had in them a concentrated and sullen gloom. The cold and damp of the cell, and the scantiness of his diet, which consisted of bread and·water, had worn his cheek to the bone, and given it the sallowness of one in the black stage of cholera. His face was covered with a thick beard, every hair of which stood distinct from its fellows; and his matted locks, thickly sprinkled with grey, trailed over his ghastly features and neck in wild disorder. His shoulders down to the waist were, as I said, bare; and they and his arms displayed anatomically a muscular strength that might have served as a model for a gladiator. Over all was thrown an air of utter prostration moral and physical, —the desolation of despair.

A few yards to the right, the priest, with his eyes uplifted to heaven, seemed absorbed in prayer; and between them the *bourreau*, who might have superseded Tristan in his office, and been a dangerous rival in the good graces of Louis the Eleventh. He called to mind a figure of Rubens',—not the one who is turning round in the Descent of the Cross at Antwerp, and saying to the thief, writhing in horrible contortions after he has wrenched his lacerated foot from the nail, " *Sacre, chien*,"—but a soldier in another of his pictures in the Gallery at Brussels (the representation of some martyrdom,) who has just torn off the ear of the saint with a pair of red-hot pincers, and is eyeing it with a savage complacency.

It was, in short, exactly such a group, with its pyramidical form and startling contrasts of colour and expression, as the great Flemish painter could have desired.

A dead silence, which the natural horror, the novelty of the scene created, prevailed among the assembled crowd; and it spoke well for the morality and good feeling of the simple peasantry, that not a woman was present on the occasion.

The hand of the swordsman was raised, and the stroke fell on the neck of the culprit; but, horrible to say,—what was it then to witness?—though given with no common vigour, so blunt was the instrument, that, instead of severing the head, it only inflicted a gash which divided the tendons of the neck, and the undecapitated body fell doubled up, whilst only a few *gouts* of blood issued from the wound.

The tortured wretch's groans and exclamations found an echo in all bosoms; and it was not till after two more sabre strokes that the head lay apart, and rolled upwards in the dust. I then saw what I have heard described of Charlotte Cordé, after she had been guillotined;—the muscles of the face were convulsed as if with sensibility, and the eyes glared with horrid meaning, as though the soul yet lingered there. Even the executioner could scarcely meet their scowl without shuddering.

It was the first and last spectacle of this kind at which I mean ever to be present; and I should not have awaited its awful termination, could I have penetrated through the living wall that was a barrier to my exit.

You may now guess from whom I obtained many of the details contained in this memoir of Mascalbruni. It was from the confessor, who had endeavoured, but in vain, to give him spiritual consolation in the dungeon and at the block. The Jesuit and myself had mutual revelations to make to each other, connecting the present with the past, and which have enabled me to weave the dark tissue of his life's thread into one piece. I repeat the last words of the good old man at our final interview,—" May God have mercy on his soul !"

F. MEDWIN.

SMOKE.

" A trifle light as air."

Swift sang a broomstick, and with matchless lore
Rehearsed the contents of a housemaid's drawer;
Great Burns's genius shone sublime in lice;
Old Homer epicised on frogs and mice ;
And, leaping from his swift Pindaric car,
Great Byron eulogised the light cigar ;
Pope for a moment left the critic's chair,
And sang the breezy fan that cools the fair ;
And he whose harp to loftiest notes was strung,
E'en Mantua's Swan, the homely salad sung ;
Colossal Johnson, famed for dictionary,
A sprig of myrtle ; Cowper, a canary,
Nor scorn'd the humble snail ; and Goldsmith's lyre
A haunch of venison nobly did inspire ;—
Of such light themes the loftiest lyres have spoke,
And my small shell shall sound the praise of smoke.

Essence sublime ! serenely curling vapour !
Fierce from a steam-boat, gentle from a taper,—
Daughter of fire, descendant of the sun,
Breath of the peaceful pipe and murderous gun,—
How gloriously thou roll'st from chimneys high,
To seek companion clouds amidst the sky !

Thrice welcome art thou to the traveller's sight,
And his heart hails thee with sincere delight;
As soft thou sail'st amid the ethereal blue,
Visions of supper float before his view !
Emblem of peace in council, when profound
The sacred calumet goes slowly round !
Breath of the war, thou canopiest the fight,
And veil'st the bloody field in murky night !
Precursor of the cannon's deadly shot,
And soft adorner of the peasant's cot ;
With Etna's roaring flames dost thou arise,
And from the altar's top perfume the skies !
  I see thee now
  To the breezes bow,
Thy spiral columns lightly bending
  In gentle whirls
  And graceful curls,
Thy soft grey form with the azure blending.
When Nature's tears in dewy showers descend,
Close to the earth thine aerial form doth bend ;
  But when in light
  And beauty bright,
With radiant smile she gladdens all,
  And the sun's soft beam
  On thy shadowy stream
Does in a ray of glory fall,
  Thou risest high
  'Mid the deep blue sky,
Like a silver shaft from a fairy hall !

When from the light cigar thy sweet perfume
In od'rous cloudlets hovers round the room,
Inspired by Fancy's castle-building power,
Thy fragile form cheers many a lonely hour.
O'er every wave thy misty flag is seen
Careering lightly over billows green ;
And when, 'mid creaming foam and sparkling spray,
Celestial Venus rose upon the day,
Thy vapoury wreath the goddess did enshroud,
And wrapt her beauties in a milk-white cloud.
'Twas thou, majestic ! led the way before
Retreating Israel from th' Egyptian shore ;
From out thy sable cloud, 'mid lightning's flash,
The trumpet's clangour and the thunder's crash,
From Sinai's mount the law divine was given,
Thy veil conceal'd the Majesty of Heaven !
When sun, and moon, and heaven's bright hosts expire,
And the great globe decays in flames of fire,
Then shalt thou rise, thy banner be unfurl'd
Above the smouldering ruins of the world !

SNODGRASS.

SOME PASSAGES IN THE LIFE OF
A DISAPPOINTED MAN.

WITH AN ILLUSTRATION BY GEORGE CRUIKSHANK.

ARE you a sympathetic reader? If not, I pray you to pass over the few pages which constitute this article, and indulge your risible propensity with the happier effusions of the laughing philosophers of this Miscellany. I have no cachinnatory ambition, and would have my leaves well watered, not with the sunny drops of joy, but with the camomilical outpourings of sorrow.

Concluding that my request is granted, I will now proceed, sympathetic reader, to narrate a few passages of my "strange, eventful history."

I am a disappointed man,—nay, I was even a disappointed baby; for it was calculated that the parental anticipations of my forebears would have been realised on the 1st of May 1792, whereas, by some contradictory vagary of Dame Nature, I entered this valley of tears on the 1st of April! This ought to have been considered prognosticatory of my future disappointments, and the law of Sparta should have been rigidly enforced; for what are crooked limbs to a crooked destiny?

It was the intention of my father (whose name was Jacob Wise) to have had me christened after my maternal uncle, Theodosius Otter, Esq.; but, having selected a stuttering godfather, I was unfortunately baptized as "The-odd-dose-us Oth-er Wise." Nor was this the only disappointment which attended me on this occasion, for the pew-opener having received instructions to clean the copper coal-scuttle in the vestry-room, the basin which contained the vitriol necessary for that purpose was by some means or other placed in the font; and to this day I have more the appearance of a tattooed Indian than a Christian Englishman.

My babyhood was composed of a series of disappointments. My hair was to have been, in the words of the monthly nurse, "the most beautifulest horburn," but sprouted forth a splendid specimen of that vegetable dye called carroty. I was to have been "as straight as an arrow;" but a cup of tea having been spilled over me as I lay in the servant's lap before the kitchen fire, I became so dreadfully warped that I am now a sort of demi-parenthesis, or, as a malicious punster once called me, "a perfect bow."

I had the measles very mildly, as it was affirmed, for the whole virulence of the disorder displayed itself in one enormous pustule on the tip of my nose. This luminary so excited my infant wonder, that my eyes (really fine for green) were continually riveted to the *spot*, and have never forgotten it, for one or other of them is invariably engaged in searching for the lost treasure.

I was not in convulsions above a dozen times during teething; but no sooner had I completed my chaplet of pearls, than the striking-weight of a Dutch clock which overhung my cradle dropped into my mouth, and convinced me of the extreme simplicity of dental surgery.

My "going alone" was the source of an infinitude of anxieties to my excellent mamma, who was so magnificently proportioned that it

George Cruikshank

A Disappointed Man

was many months before I could make the circuit of her full-flounced printed calico wrapper without resting. Poor mamma! she lost her life from a singular mistake. The house in which we lived had taken fire, and two good-natured neighbours threw Mrs. Wise out of the window instead of a feather-bed. She alighted on the head of Captain S——, who was then considered the *softest* man in the three kingdoms, and received little injury by the ejectment; but her feelings were so lacerated by the mistake, that she refused all food, and lived entirely by suction, till she died *from* it.

I will pass over my school-days, merely observing *en passant* that

> " Each day some unlucky disaster
> Placed me in the vocative case with my master,"

a squabby, tyrannical, double-jointed pedagogue. He was nicknamed *Cane-and-Able*, and I can testify to the justness of the nomenclature. At college the same *mis*-fortune attended me. There was ever an under-current of disappointment, which rendered all my exertions nugatory. If I was by accident " full of the god," I could never knock down any one but a proctor. If I determined on keeping close in my rooms, the wind immediately changed to N.E. by N. at which point my chimneys smoked like a community of Ya-Mynheers. My maternal uncle, Theodosius Otter, Esq. had signified that my expectations from him must be regulated entirely by my academical distinctions, and I was " pluck'd for my little-go." This occurred three months before the old booby's death. My legacy consisted of a presentation to the Gooseborough free school.

The time at length arrived for me to fall in love. I experienced the first symptom of this epidemic at a bombazine ball in the city of Norwich. Selina Smithers was the name of my fair enslaver: she was about nineteen, fair as Russia tallow, tall, and somewhat slender. Indeed her condition is perhaps better described by " the slightest possible approximation to lanky." During one short quadrille she told me of all her tastes, hopes, experience, family connexions, (including a brother at sea,) expectations 'probable and possible, and of two thousand seven hundred and forty-five pounds, fourteen shillings, and sixpence, standing in her own name in the three and a half per cents.

With the last *chassez* I was a victim. At the close of the ball I handed Selina and her mamma into a green fly, and found the next morning that I had a violent cold in my head, and a violent heat in my heart.

As I flourished the brass knocker of Mrs. Smithers' door on the following day, the clock of St. Andrew's church struck two; and chimed a quarter past, as a girl strongly resembling a kidney-potato, red and dirty, gave me ingress into a room with green blinds, seven horsehair-bottomed chairs, a round mahogany table, four oil-paintings (subjects and masters unknown), two fire-screens of yellow calico fluted, and a very shabby square piano. On the music-rest was the song, " We met,—'twas in a crowd." Singular coincidence,—*we* met in a crowd!

The door opened, and Selina bounded into the room like a young fawn. Our eyes met, and then simultaneously sought the carpet. I know not what object her pale blue orbs encountered; but mine fell on the half-picked head of a red herring! " Can it be possible," thought I, " that Selina— Pshaw ! her brother has returned from sea ;" and to his account I placed the body of the vulgar fish. I took her hand, and gracefully led her to a chair, and then seated myself beside her. Our conversation grew animated,—confiding. She recapitulated the amount of her three and a half per cents, and in the most considerate manner inquired into *my* pecuniary situation. I was then possessed of seven thousand pounds ; for my father, during the three last years of his life, had been twice burned out, and once sold up, and was thus enabled to leave me independent. She could not conceal her delight at my prosperous situation,—generous creature ! Possessing affluence herself, she rejoiced at the well-doing of others. Day after day passed in this delightful manner, until I ventured to solicit her to become my wife. Judge of my ecstasy when, bending her swan-like neck until her fair cheek rested on the velvet collar of my mulberry surtout, she whispered almost inaudibly,

" How can you ask me such a question ?"

" How can I ask you such a question ? Because—because it is necessary to my happiness. Oh ! name the happy hour when Hymen's chain—that chain which has but one link—shall bind you to me for ever !"

She paused a moment, and then faltered out,

" To-morrow week."

I fell upon my knees. Selina did the same ; for, in my joy at her compliance, I had forgotten that one chair was supporting us both.

Oh, what a busy day was that which followed ! I entered Skelton's (the tailor's) shop with the journeymen. I ordered three complete suits !

As the rolls were taken into Quillit's parlour, I was shown into the office. The worthy lawyer thrice scalded his throat in his anxiety to comply with my repeated requests to " see him immediately." He came at last. A few brief sentences explained the nature of my business, and he hastened to accompany me to Selina. I was so excited by the novelty of my situation, that I fell over the maid who was cleaning the step of the door, and narrowly escaped dragging Quillit after. Had he fallen, I shudder at the contemplation of the probable result ; for he was a man well to do in the world, and enjoyed a rotundity of figure unrivalled in the good city of Norwich. His black waistcoat might have served for a bill of fare to an eating-house, for it exhibited samples of all Mrs. Glass's choicest preparations.

Away we went, realising the poet's description of Ajax and Camilla :

> " When Ajax strives some rock's vast weight to throw,
> The line too labours, and the words move slow :
> Not so when swift Camilla scours the plain,
> Flies o'er the unbending corn, and skims along the main."

We resembled Reason and Hope, or one of Pickford's barges and a towing-horse.

The little brass knocker was again in my hand, the kidney-potato was again at the door, and I led in the perspiring lawyer, but looked in vain for that expression of admiration which I fondly anticipated would have illumined his little grey eyes at the sight of my Venusian Selina.

" This is Mr. Quillit," said I.

" Indeed ?" replied Selina.

" We have come, mum," said Quillit, " to arrange a very necessary preliminary to the delicate ceremony which my friend Wise has informed me will take place on this day week."

Selina blushed. Her mother (bless me ! I 've quite overlooked her !) screwed up her face into an expression between laughing and crying ; and I—I pushed one hand through my hair, and the other into my breeches pocket.

" Mum," continued Quillit, " our business this morning is to make the arrangements for your marriage-settlement ; and my friend Wise wishes to know what part of your two thousand——"

" Seven hundred and forty-five pounds, fourteen shillings, and sixpence," said I *sotto voce*.

" —You wish settled upon yourself."

" Oh, nothing,—I require nothing !" exclaimed Selina.

" Hur—!" said I, half rising from my chair in ecstasy at her disinterestedness.

" Hem !" coughed Quillit, and took out his toothpick.

" Nothing !" I at length ejaculated. " No, Selina ; you shall not be subject to the accidents of fortune. Mr. Quillit, put down two thousand pounds." And so he did.

The day before my intended nuptials I had paid my customary visit to Selina, and it was arranged that the *settlement* should be executed (what a happy union of terms !) that night. I had left but a few minutes when I missed my handkerchief. I returned for it. The kidney-potato shot out of the house as I turned the corner of the street. I found the door ajar, and, not considering any ceremony necessary, I walked into the parlour. I had put my handkerchief into the left pocket of my coat when I was somewhat startled by a burst of very boisterous male and female merriment. I paused. A child's treble was then heard, and in a moment after *a child—a live child* entered the room crying most piteously. It ceased on beholding me ; and when its astonishment had subsided, it sobbed out,

" I want mamma !"

" Mamma ?" said I. " And who 's mamma ?"

My query was answered from the first floor.

" Come to mamma, dear !" shouted—Selina !

I don't know what the sensations of a humming-top in full spin may be, but I should imagine they are very similar to those which I experienced at this particular moment. When I recovered, I was stretched on the hearth-rug with my head in the coal-scuttle, surrounded by my Selina, her mother, the maid, and I suppose her " brother at sea."

" What is the matter, love ?" said— You know whom I mean,—I can't write her name again.

" Nothing, madam," I replied, " nothing ; only I anticipated being married to-morrow,—but I shall be disappointed."

The ensuing week I received notice of action for a breach of promise of marriage ; the ensuing term the cause was tried before an intelligent jury ; and the ensuing day Quillit handed me a bill for seven hundred and sixty-two pounds, one shilling, and eightpence, being the amount of damages and costs in Smithers *versus* Wise. I paid Quillit, sold my house and furniture at Norwich, and took up my abode at Bumbleby, in Lancashire, resolving to be as love-proof as

Miss Martineau, which resolution I have religiously observed to this day.

I was, however, involved in one other tender affair, by proxy, which produced me more serious annoyances than even my own.

I became acquainted with a merry good-looking fellow, of the name of Thomas Styles, who had come from somewhere, and was related to somebody, but no one recollected the who or the where. In the same town lived an old gentleman, who rejoiced in the singular name of Smith. He was blessed with one daughter and a wife. The latter did not reside with him, having taken up her permanent residence in a small octagonal stone building in the dissenters' burial ground. Styles, by one of those accidents common in novels, but very occasional in real life, had become acquainted with Miss Smith. They had gone through those comparative states of feeling,—acquaintance, friendship, love; and, when I was introduced to him, he was just in want of a good fellow to help him into matrimony. I was just the boy; my expensive experience, my good-nature, my leisure,—in short, there was nothing wanting to fit me for this confidential character. Now, be it known that old Smith had very strong parliamentary predilections, and one of his *sine quâ nons* was, that his son-in-law should be M. P. for somewhere,—Puddle-dock would do,—but an M. P. he must be. Politics were of no consequence; but he must have a decided opinion that the Bumbleby railway would be most beneficial, if carried through a swampy piece of ground which Smith had recently purchased. Styles was of the same opinion; but then he was only a member of the "Bull's-eye Bowmen," and Mr. Snuffmore's sixpenny whist club. I had made myself particularly uncomfortable one afternoon, in Styles' summer-house, with three glasses of brandy and water and four mild havannas, when old Smith rushed in to announce the gratifying intelligence that Mr. Topple, the member for our place, had fallen into the crater of Mount Vesuvius, and that nothing had been heard from him since, but a solitary interjection, in consequence of which there was a vacancy in the representation. The writ had been issued, and so had an address from Mr. Wiseman, a gentleman possessing every virtue under the sun, save and except a due sense of the advantages of Smith's swamp to the railway. This was conclusive. Smith made a speech, which, being for interest and not for fame, was short and emphatic.

"Tom, you must contest this election, or never darken my doors again."

"My dear, sir," said Tom, "nothing would give me greater pleasure; but——"

"I'll do all that. I'll form a committee *instanter*," replied Smith; leave all to me. Capital hand at an address—pith, nothing but pith. Ever see my letter in support of the erection of a pound for stray cattle?—pithy and conclusive:—'Inhabitants of Bumbleby, twenty shillings make a pound.' The motion was carried."

"One moment," said Tom. "It will appear so presumptuous on my part, unless a deputation waited on me."

"Certainly,—better, by all means,—I'll form one directly," said Smith.

"In the mean time, issue a placard to prevent the electors making promises, and——"

"I will," said Smith. And so he did ; for in an hour afterwards there was not a dead wall in Bumbleby but was papered from one end to the other.

"Other Wise," said Styles, as Smith waddled up the garden, "this won't do for me. I couldn't make a speech of ten consecutive lines, if the revenues of the Duchy of Cornwall were depending upon it."

"Pooh !" replied I, rolling my head about in that peculiar style which an over-indulgence in bibicals will induce.

"It's a fact," replied Tom. "Now, my dear fellow, you can serve me and your country at the same time. Smith would be equally gratified at your return for Bumbleby ; your opinions are the same as my own ; and your abilities require no panegyric from me."

Whether it was the suddenness of the probable glory, or the effect of the tobacco and brandy and water, I sat speechless. Silence gives consent, says an old adage, and so did the town of Bumbleby the next morning, for every quarter cried out "Other Wise for ever !" It was too late to retract ; and accordingly I was nominated, seconded, and unanimously elected by a show of hands. A poll was demanded ; and, after a short contest of two days, it was announced in very large letters, and still larger figures,

> Wiseman, ... 786
> Other Wise, . . .   92
> Majority, . . —694

I was satisfied, and so was my party. During the preparation for this unfortunate contest I had allowed Styles to draw *ad libitum* upon my banker. His friendship knew no bounds ; his liberality was as boundless ; and so chagrined was he at the defeat I had experienced, that he left the next morning without an adieu. I must confess that I was rather disappointed at his sudden retreat, and considerably more so on finding that his exertions in my behalf had reduced my income from four hundred pounds to forty pounds per annum. For the first time I doubted his friendship. Subsequent inquiries convinced me he was a scoundrel, and I commenced an immediate pursuit of him, and an action at law.

Some three months afterwards, I was sauntering about the streets in the neighbourhood of St. James's Square, when I encountered Styles. His surprise was as great as mine, but not so enduring ; for, advancing towards me with all the coolness of the 1st of December, he exclaimed,

"Other Wise, how are you ? I dare say you thought my sudden departure odd ; I did myself ; but I couldn't help it. I'm sorry to hear how much your contest has distressed you. I was the cause. Give me your check for fifty pounds, and here's a bill for five hundred, due to-morrow."

Suiting the action to the word, he handed me an acceptance for that amount inclosed in a dirty piece of paper. All this was so rapidly said and done, that before I was aware of it I had given him a draft on Drummond, shaken hands with him, and was mechanically discussing a mutton-chop and a bottle of sherry, which I had unconsciously ordered in the delirium which succeeded Styles' unheard-of generosity.

I went the next day to Messrs. Podge and Co. in Lombard-street, with my promise-to-pay—Eldorado in my pocket. I entered the counting-house, presented my bill, and fully expected to have received either bank-notes or gold in exchange. I waited a few minutes, and was then ushered into a back-room, and politely requested to account for this money promissory document.

"From whom did you receive this bill?" said a gentleman with a powdered head and an immense watch-chain.

"From Mr. Styles."

"Where does he live?"

"I don't know exactly; but I hope there is nothing irregular."

"You can step in, Banks," said the powdered head; and a stout well-fed man, in a blue coat, with the City arms on the button, *did* step in, and very unceremoniously proceeded to inspect the contents of my various pockets. "Conclusive!" said the powdered head, as he minutely examined a small piece of crumpled paper which had occupied one of the pockets of my small-clothes.

I was handed into a hackney-coach, and then into the Mansion-house, where I was informed that I was to live rent-free for the next week in his Majesty's jail of Newgate. The bill was a forgery!

The day of trial approached. I walked into the dock with *mens conscia recti* depicted on my countenance. I knew I was innocent of any felonious intention or knowledge; and was certainly very much *disappointed* at being found guilty upon the silent evidence of the little piece of crumpled paper, which was covered with pen and ink experiments on the signature of John Allgold and Co. whose name occupied the centre of Styles' bill. The recorder (in a very impressive manner, I must allow, for his white handkerchief was waving about the whole time) passed sentence of death upon me, and I was ordered to be taken from thence, and on the Monday following to be hung by the neck till I was dead. A pleasant termination, truly!

I was led, stupified by the result of my trial, back to the prison. When I regained the use of my faculties, my awful situation became horridly apparent. There was I, an innocent and injured man, condemned to suffer the extreme penalty of the law. For endeavouring to gain possession of my own, I was about to become a spectacle for the fish-fags and costermongers of London,—to have my name handed down to posterity by that undying trumpeter of evil-doers, Mr. Catnach, of the Seven-dials, who alternately delights the public with "three yards long of every new song, and all for a penny," and "the last dying speech and confession" of those who, dreading to be bed-ridden, and possessing an unconquerable aversion to doctors' stuff and virtue, have danced upon nothing, and died with their shoes on. "How often," thought I, "have I seen a withered hag kneeling at the rails of an area, exciting the sympathies and curiosity of servants of all-work, and greasy melting cooks, by the recital of atrocities that the hand of man never executed. 'Here's a full, true, and 'tickler account of a horrid murder, which was performed in the New-cut, Lambeth, on the body of a baked-'tater manufacturer, who was savagely and inhumanly murdered by that ferocious and hard-hearted villain, Benjamin Burker;—here you have the account how, arter putting a poor man's plaister, composed of pitch and bird-lime, over the unhappy *indivigual's mouf* until the breath was out on his body, he shoved him into the oven, and lived seven days and nights on baked taters and the manyfacterers.' Thus might I be misrepresented. The thought was madness !"

The morning at length arrived for my execution ; but, oh ! the horrors of the night that preceded it ! Young, and in the full enjoyment of life, the morrow was to bring me death ! In a little week, the hand which I then gazed on, would be a banquet for the red worm of the grave. Even the mother who watched the cradle of my infancy would have turned loathingly away from the corrupted mass ; the earth which covered me would be thought unhallowed, and my name would become symbolical with crime. But even this, was nothing to the contemplation of the scene I had still to enact. To be led forth " the observed of all observers," who would look on me with an eye, not of pity, but of morbid curiosity,—to [hang quivering in the air,—and to feel, while consciousness remained, that each shuddering of struggling nature was imparting a savage delight to those who could be the willing witnesses of the sacrifice of a fellow-creature ! My brain sickened with its agony, and I fell into a stupor which my jailor called sleep. I was pinioned, and led forth to die. Life had now no charm for me, —I was beyond the reach of hope, and death was a desired blessing. The hangman's hands were about my neck,—the blood curdled in my veins as I felt the deadly embrace of the cord. I longed for the signal of departure ; but I was again disappointed. I was reprieved,— for I awoke, and found that the bill and all its frightful consequences were but the result of having eaten a hearty supper of pork-chops very much underdone ! So I was once again a disappointed man, though, on this occasion, I must own, most agreeably so.

THE PROFESSOR.—A TALE.

BY GOLIAH GAHAGAN.

" Why, then, the world's mine oyster."

CHAPTER I.

I HAVE often remarked that, among other ornaments and curiosities, Hackney contains more ladies' schools than are to be found in almost any other village, or indeed city, in Europe. In every green rustic lane, to every tall old-fashioned house there is an iron gate, an ensign of blue and gold, and a large brass plate, proclaiming that a ladies' seminary is established upon the premises. On one of these plates is written —(or rather was, — for the pathetic occurrence which I have to relate took place many years ago)—on one of these plates, I say, was engraven the following inscription :

BULGARIA HOUSE.

Seminary for Young Ladies from three to twenty.

BY THE MISSES PIDGE.

(Please wipe your shoes.)

The Misses Pidge took a limited number of young ladies, (as limited, in fact, or as large as the public chose,) and instructed them in those branches of elegant and useful learning which make the British female so superior to all other shes. The younger ones learned the principles of back-stitch, cross-stitch, bob-stitch, Doctor Watts's hymns, and " In my cottage near a wood." The elder pupils diverged at once from stitching and samplers: they played like Thalberg, and pirouetted like Taglioni; they learned geography, geology, mythology, entomology, modern history, and simple equations (Miss Z. Pidge); they obtained a complete knowledge of the French, German, and Italian tongues, not including English, taught by Miss Pidge; Poo-nah painting and tambour (Miss E. Pidge); Brice's questions and elocution (Miss F. Pidge); and, to crown all, dancing and gymnastics (which had a very flourishing look in the Pidge prospectus, and were printed in German text,)—DANCING and GYMNASTICS, we say, by Professor DANDOLO. The names of other professors and assistants followed in modester type.

Although the signor's name was decidedly foreign, so English was his appearance, and so entirely did he disguise his accent, that it was impossible to tell of what place he was a native, if not of London, and of the very heart of it; for he had caught completely the peculiarities which distinguish the so-called cockney part of the City, and oblite-rated his h's and doubled his v's, as if he had been for all his life in the neighbourhood of Bow-bells. Signor Dandolo was a stout gentle-man of five feet nine, with amazing expanse of mouth, chest, and whiskers, which latter were of a red hue.

I cannot tell how this individual first received an introduction to the academy of the Misses Pidge, and established himself there. Rumours say that Miss Zela Pidge at a Hackney ball first met him, and thus the intimacy arose; but, since the circumstances took place which I am about to relate, that young lady declares that *she* was not the person who brought him to Bulgaria House,—nothing but the infa-tuation and entreaties of Mrs. Alderman Grampus could ever have in-duced her to receive him. The reader will gather from this, that Dan-dolo's after-conduct at Miss Pidge's was not satisfactory,—nor was it; and may every mistress of such an establishment remember that con-fidence can be sometimes misplaced; that friendship is frequently but another name for villany.

But to our story. The stalwart and active Dandolo delighted for some time the young ladies at Miss Pidge's by the agility which he displayed in the dance, as well as the strength and manliness of his form, as exhibited in the new amusement which he taught. In a very short time, Miss Binx, a stout young lady of seventeen, who had never until his appearance walked half a mile without puffing like an apoplectic Lord Mayor, could dance the cachouca, swarm up a pole with the agility of a cat, and hold out a chair for three minutes with-out winking. Miss Jacobs could very nearly climb through a ladder (Jacob's ladder he profanely called it); and Miss Bole ring such changes upon the dumb-bells as might have been heard at Edmonton, if the bells could have spoken. But the most promising pupil of Professor Dandolo, as indeed the fairest young creature in the esta-blishment of Bulgaria House, was Miss Adeliza Grampus, daughter of the alderman whose name we have mentioned. The pride of her mother, the idol of her opulent father, Adeliza Grampus was in her nineteenth year. Eyes have often been described; but it would re-quire bluer ink than ours to depict the orbs of Adeliza; the snow when it first falls in Cheapside is not whiter than her neck,—when it has been for some days upon the ground, trampled by dustmen and jarvies, trodden down by sweeps and gentlemen going to business, not blacker than her hair. Slim as the Monument on Fish-street-hill, her form was slender and tall: but it is needless to recapitulate her charms, and difficult indeed to describe them. Let the reader think of his first love, and fancy Adeliza. Dandolo, who was employed to instruct her, saw her, and fancied her too, as many a fellow of his inflammable temperament would have done in his place.

There are few situations in life which can be so improved by an enterprising mind as that of a dancing-master,—I mean in a tender or amatory point of view. The dancing-master has over the back, the hands, the feet and shoulders of his pupils an absolute command; and, being by nature endowed with so much authority, can speedily spread his sway from the limbs to the rest of the body, and to the mind inclusive. *"Toes a little more out, Miss Adeliza,"* cries he with the tenderest air in the world; "back a *little* more straight," and he gently seizes her hand, he raises it considerably above the level of her ear, he places the tips of his left-hand fingers gently upon the young lady's spine, and in this seducing attitude gazes tenderly into her eyes! I say that no woman at any age can stand this attitude and this look, especially when darted from such eyes as those of Dandolo. On the two first occasions when the adventurer attempted this audacious manœuvre, his victim blushed only and trembled; on the third she dropped her full eyelids and turned ghastly pale. "A glass of water," cried Adeliza, "or I faint." The dancing-master hastened eagerly away to procure the desired beverage, and, as he put it to her lips, whispered thrillingly in her ear, "Thine, thine for ever, Adeliza!"

Miss Grampus sank back in the arms of Miss Binx, but not before her raptured lover saw her eyes turning towards the ceiling, and her clammy lips whispering the name of "Dandolo."

When Madame Schroeder, in the opera of Fidelio, cries, "Nichts, nichts, mein Florestan," it is as nothing compared to the tenderness with which Miss Grampus uttered that soft name.

"Dandolo!" would she repeat to her confidante, Miss Binx; "the name was beautiful and glorious in the olden days; five hundred years since, a myriad of voices shouted it in Venice, when one who bore it came forward to wed the sea—the Doge's bride! the blue Adriatic! the boundless and eternal main! The frightened Turk shrunk palsied at the sound; it was louder than the loudest of the cannon, or the stormy screaming of the tempest! Dandolo! how many brave hearts beat to hear that name! how many bright swords flashed forth at that resistless war-cry! Oh, Binx," would Adeliza continue, fondly pressing the arm of that young lady, "is it not passing strange that one of that mighty ducal race should have lived to this day, and lived to love *me!* But I, too," Adeliza would add archly, "am, as you know, a daughter of the sea."

The fact was, that the father of Miss Adeliza Grampus was a shell-fishmonger, which induced the young lady to describe herself as a daughter of Ocean. She received her romantic name from her mother after reading Miss Swipes's celebrated novel of Toby of Warsaw, and had been fed from her youth upwards with so much similar literary ware, that her little mind had gone distracted. Her father had

x 2

sent her from home at fifteen, because she had fallen in love with the young man who opened natives in the shop, and had vowed to slay herself with the oyster-knife. At Miss Pidge's her sentiment had not deserted her; she knew all Miss Landon by heart, had a lock of Mr. Thomas Moore's hair or wig, and read more novels and poetry than ever. And thus the red-haired dancing-master became in her eyes a Venetian nobleman, with whom it was her pride and pleasure to fall in love.

Being a parlour-boarder at Miss Pidge's seminary, (a privilege which was acquired by paying five annual guineas extra,) Miss Grampus was permitted certain liberties which were not accorded to scholars of the ordinary description. She and Miss Binx occasionally strolled into the village by themselves; they visited the library unattended; they went upon little messages for the Misses Pidge; they walked to church alone, either before or after the long row of young virgins who streamed out on every Sabbath day from between the filigree iron railings of Bulgaria House. It is my painful duty to state that on several of these exclusive walks they were followed, or met, by the insidious and attentive teacher of gymnastics.

Soon Miss Binx would lag behind, and—shall I own it?—would make up for the lost society of her female friend by the company of a man, a friend of the professor, mysterious and agreeable as himself. May the mistresses of all the establishments for young ladies in this kingdom, or queendom rather, peruse this, and reflect how dangerous it is for young ladies of any age,—ay, even for parlour-boarders—to go out alone! In the present instance Miss Grampus enjoyed a more than ordinary liberty, it is true: when the elder Misses Pidge would remonstrate, Miss Zela would anxiously yield to her request; and why?—the reason may be gathered from the following conversation which passed between the infatuated girl and the wily _maître de danse_.

"How, Roderick," would Adeliza say, "how, in the days of our first acquaintance, did it chance that you always addressed yourself to that odious Zela Pidge, and never deigned to breathe a syllable to me?"

"My lips didn't speak to you, Addly," (for to such a pitch of familiarity had they arrived,) "but my heyes did."

Adeliza was not astonished by the peculiarity of his pronunciation, for, to say truth, it was that commonly adopted in her native home and circle. "And mine," said she tenderly, "they followed when yours were not fixed upon them, for _then_ I dared not look upwards. And though all on account of Miss Pidge you could not hear the accents of my voice, you might have heard the beatings of my heart!"

"I did, I did," gasped Roderick; "I eard them haudibly. I never spoke to you then, for I feared to waken that foul friend sispicion. I wished to henter your seminary, to be continually near you, to make you love me; therefore I wooed the easy and foolish Miss Pidge, therefore I took upon me the disguise of—ha! ha!—of a dancing-master." (And the young man's countenance assumed a grim and demoniac smile.) "Yes; I degraded my name and my birthright,—I wore these ignoble trappings, and all for the love of thee, my Adeliza!" Here Signor Dandolo would have knelt down, but the road was muddy; and, his trousers being of nankeen, his gallant purpose was frustrated.

But the story must out, for the conversation above narrated has betrayed to the intelligent reader a considerable part of it. The fact is, as we have said, that Miss Zela Pidge, dancing at the Hackney assembly, was introduced to this man; that he had no profession,— no means even of subsistence; that he saw enough of this lady to be aware that he could make her useful to his purpose; and he who had been, we believe it in our conscience, no better than a travelling mountebank or harlequin, appeared at Bulgaria House in the character of a professor of gymnastics. The governess in the first instance entertained for him just such a *penchant* as the pupil afterwards felt; the latter discovered the weakness of her mistress, and hence arose Miss Pidge's indulgence, and Miss Grampus's fatal passion.

"Mysterious being!" continued Adeliza, resuming the conversation which has been broken by the above explanatory hints, "how did I learn to love thee? Who art thou?—what dire fate has brought thee hither in this lowly guise to win the heart of Adeliza?"

"Hadeliza," cried he, "you say well; *I am not what I seem.* I cannot tell thee what I am; a tale of horror, of crime, forbids the dreadful confession. But dark as I am, and wretched, nay, wicked and desperate, I love thee, Hadeliza,—love thee with the rapturous devotion of purer days: the tenderness of happier times! I am sad now and fallen, lady; suffice it that I once was happy, ay, respectable."

Adeliza's cheek grew deadly pale, her step faltered, and she would have fallen to the ground, had she not been restrained by the strong arm of her lover. "I know not," said she, as she clung timidly to his neck,

> "I know not, I hask not, if guilt's in that art,
> I know that I love thee, whatever thou hart."

"*Gilt* in my heart," said Dandolo, "gilt in the heart of Roderick? No, never!" and he drew her towards him, and on her bonnet, her veil, her gloves, nay, on her very cheeks, he imprinted a thousand maddening kisses. "But say, my sweet one," continued he, "who art *thou?* I know you as yet, only by your lovely baptismal name, and your other name of Grampus."

Adeliza looked down and blushed. "My parents are lowly," she said.

"But how then came you at such a seminary?" said he; "twenty pound a quarter, extras and washing not included."

"They are humble, but wealthy."

"Ha! who is your father?"

"An alderman of yon metropolis."

"An alderman! and what is his profession?"

"I blush to tell; he is—*an oystermonger.*"

"AN OYSTERMONGER!" screamed Roderick in the largest capitals. "Ha! ha! ha! this is too much!" and he dropped Adeliza's hand, and never spoke to her during the rest of her walk. They moved moodily on for some time, Miss Binx and the other young man marching astonished in the rear. At length they came within sight of the seminary. "Here is Bulgaria House," cried the maiden steadily; "Roderick, we must part!" The effort was too much for her: she flung herself hysterically into his arms.

But, oh, horror! a scream was heard from Miss Binx, who was seen scuttling at double-quick time towards the school-house. Her

young man had bolted completely; and close at the side of the lovely
though imprudent couple, stood the angry—and justly angry—Miss
Zela Pidge!

"Oh, Ferdinand," said she, "is it thus you deceive me? Did I
bring you to Bulgaria House for this?—did I give you money to buy
clothes for this, that you should go by false names, and make love
to that saucy, slammerkin, sentimental Miss Grampus? Ferdinand,
Ferdinand," cried she, "is this true,—can I credit my eyes?"

"D— your eyes!" said the signor angrily as he darted at her a
withering look, and retired down the street. His curses might be
heard long after he had passed. He never appeared more at Bulgaria House, for he received his dismissal the next day.

That night all the front windows of the Miss Pidges' seminary
were smashed to shivers.   *   *   *

On the following Thursday *two* places were taken in the coach to
town. On the back seat sate the usher, on the front the wasted and
miserable Adeliza Grampus.   *   *   *

CHAPTER II.

BUT the matter did not end here. Miss Grampus's departure elicited from her a disclosure of several circumstances which, we must
say, in no degree increased the reputation of Miss Zela Pidge. The
discoveries which she made were so awkward, the tale of crime and
licentiousness revealed by her so deeply injurious to the character of
the establishment, that the pupils emigrated from it in scores. Miss
Binx retired to her friends at Wandsworth, Miss Jacobs to her relations in Houndsditch, and other young ladies not mentioned in this
history to other and more moral schools; so that absolutely, at the
end of a single half year, such had been the scandal of the story, the
Misses Pidge were left with only two pupils,—Miss Dibble, the ar-
ticled young lady, and Miss Bole, the grocer's daughter, who came in
exchange for tea, candles, and other requisites supplied to the establishment by her father.

"I knew it, I knew it!" cried Zela passionately, as she trod the
echoing and melancholy school-room; "he told me that none ever
prospered who loved him,—that every flower was blighted upon which
he shone! Ferdinand, Ferdinand! you have caused ruin there"
(pointing to the empty cupboards and forms); "but what is that to
the blacker ruin *here!*" and the poor creature slapped her heart, and
the big tears rolled down her chin, and so into her tucker.

A very, very few weeks after this, the plate of Bulgaria House was
removed for ever. That mansion is now designated "Moscow Hall,
by Mr. Swishtail and assistants:"—the bankrupt and fugitive Misses
Pidge have fled, Heaven knows whither! for the steamers to Boulogne cost more than five shillings in those days.

Alderman Grampus, as may be imagined, did not receive his daughter with any extraordinary degree of courtesy. "He was as grumpy,"
Mrs. G. remarked, "on the occasion as a sow with the measles."—
But had he not reason? A lovely daughter who had neglected her
education, forgotten her morals for the second time, and fallen almost
a prey to villains! Miss Grampus for some months was kept in close
confinement, nor ever suffered to stir, except occasionally to Bunhill-
row for air, and to church for devotion. Still, though she knew him

to be false,—though she knew that under a different, perhaps a prettier name, he had offered the same vows to another,—she could not but think of Roderick.

That *Professor* (as well—too well—he may be called!) knew too well her father's name and reputation to experience any difficulty in finding his abode. It was, as every City man knows, in Cheapside ; and thither Dandolo constantly bent his steps : but though he marched unceasingly about the mansion, he never (mysteriously) would pass it. He watched Adeliza walking, he followed her to church ; and many and many a time as she jostled out at the gate of the Artillery-ground, or the beadle-flanked portal of Bow, a tender hand would meet hers, an active foot would press upon hers, a billet discreetly delivered was as adroitly seized, to hide in the recesses of her pocket-handkerchief, or to nestle in the fragrance of her bosom ! Love ! Love ! how ingenious thou art ! thou canst make a ladder of a silken thread, or a weapon of a straw ; thou peerest like sunlight into a dungeon ; thou scalest, like forlorn hope, a castle wall ; the keep is taken !—the foeman has fled !—the banner of love floats triumphantly over the corpses of the slain ! *

Thus, though denied the comfort of personal intercourse, Adeliza and her lover maintained a frequent and tender correspondence. Nine times at least in a week, she by bribing her maid-servant, managed to convey letters to the Professor, to which he at rarer intervals, though with equal warmth, replied.

" Why," said the young lady in the course of this correspondence, " why, when I cast my eyes upon my Roderick, do I see him so wofully changed in outward guise ? He wears not the dress which formerly adorned him. Is he poor ?—is he in disguise ?—do debts oppress him, or traitors track him for his blood ? Oh that my arms might shield him !—Oh that my purse might aid him ! It is the fondest wish of   " ADELIZA G.

" P.S.—Aware of your fondness for shell-fish, Susan will leave a barrel of oysters at the Swan with Two Necks, directed to you, as per desire.   " AD. G.

" P.S.—Are you partial to kippered salmon ? The girl brings three pounds of it wrapped in a silken handkerchief. 'Tis marked with the hair of   " ADELIZA.

" P.S.—I break open my note to say that you will find in it a small pot of anchovy paste : may it prove acceptable. Heigho ! I would that I could accompany it.   " A. G."

It may be imagined, from the text of this note, that Adeliza had profited not a little by the perusal of Mrs. Swipes's novels; and it also gives a pretty clear notion of the condition of her lover. When that gentleman was a professor at Bulgaria House, his costume had strictly accorded with his pretensions. He wore a black German coat loaded with frogs and silk trimming, a white broad-brimmed beaver, hessians, and nankeen tights. His costume at present was singularly changed for the worse : a rough brown frock-coat dangled down to the calves of his brawny legs, where likewise ended a pair of greasy shepherd's-plaid trousers ; a dubious red waistcoat, a blue or bird's-

---

* We cannot explain this last passage ; but it is so beautiful, that the reader will pardon the omission of sense, which the author certainly could have put in if he liked.

eye neckerchief, and bluchers, (or half-boots,) remarkable for thickness and for mud, completed his attire. But he looked superior to his fortune; he wore his grey hat very much on one ear; he incessantly tugged at his smoky shirt-collar, and walked jingling the halfpence (when he had any) in his pocket. He was, in fact, no better than an adventurer, and the innocent Adeliza was his prey.

Though the Professor read the first part of this letter with hope and pleasure, it may be supposed that the three postscripts were still more welcome to him,—in fact, he literally did what is often done in novels, he *devoured* them; and Adeliza, on receiving a note from him the next day, after she had eagerly broken the seal, and with panting bosom and flashing eye glanced over the contents,—Adeliza, we say, was not altogether pleased when she read the following:

"Your goodness, dearest, passes belief; but never did poor fellow need it more than your miserable, faithful Roderick. Yes! I *am* poor,—I *am* tracked by hell-hounds,—I *am* changed in looks, and dress, and happiness,—in all but love for thee!

"Hear my tale! I come of a noble Italian family,—the noblest, ay, in Venice. We were free once, and rich, and happy; but the Prussian autograph has planted his banner on our towers,—the talents of his haughty heagle have seized our wealth, and consigned most of our race to dungeons. I am not a prisoner, only an exile. A mother, a bed-ridden grandmother, and five darling sisters, escaped with me from Venice, and now share my poverty and my home. But I have wrestled with misfortune in vain; I have struggled with want, till want has overcome me. Adeliza, I WANT BREAD!

"The kippered salmon was very good, the anchovies admirable. But, oh, my love! how thirsty they make those who have no means of slaking thirst! My poor grandmother lies delirious in her bed, and cries in vain for drink. Alas! our water is cut off; I have none to give her. The oysters was capital. Bless thee, bless thee! angel of bounty! Have you any more sich, and a few srimps? My sisters are *very* fond of them.

"Half-a-crown would oblige. But thou art too good to me already, and I blush to ask thee for more.   "Adieu, Adeliza,
                              "the wretched but faithful
                                        "RODERICK FERDINAND,
"Bell-yard, June —."   "(38th Count of Dandolo.)

A shade of dissatisfaction, we say, clouded Adeliza's fair features as she perused this note; and yet there was nothing in it which the tenderest lover might not write. But the shrimps, the half-crown, the horrid picture of squalid poverty presented by the count, sickened her young heart; the innate delicacy of the woman revolted at the thought of all this misery.

But better thoughts succeeded: her breast heaved as she read and re-read the singular passage concerning the Prussian autograph, who had planted his standard at Venice. "I knew it!" she cried, "I knew it!—he is of noble race! O Roderick, I will perish, but I will help thee!"

Alas! she was not well enough acquainted with history to perceive that the Prussian autograph had nothing to do with Venice, and had forgotten altogether that she herself had coined the story which this adventurer returned to her.

But a difficulty presented itself to Adeliza's mind. Her lover asked for money,—where was she to find it? The next day the till of the shop was empty, and a weeping apprentice dragged before the Lord Mayor. It is true that no signs of the money were found upon him; it is true that he protested his innocence; but he was dismissed the alderman's service, and passed a month at Bridewell, because Adeliza Grampus had a needy lover!

"Dearest," she wrote, "will three-and-twenty and sevenpence suffice? 'Tis all I have: take it, and with it the fondest wishes of your Adeliza.

"A sudden thought! Our apprentice is dismissed. My father dines abroad; I shall be in the retail establishment all the night, *alone*.   "A. G."

No sooner had the Professor received this note than his mind was made up. "I will see her," he said; "I will enter that accursed shop." He did, and *to his ruin*.   *   *   *

That night Mrs. Grampus and her daughter took possession of the bar or counter, in the place which Adeliza called the retail establishment, and which is commonly denominated the shop. Mrs. Grampus herself operated with the oyster-knife, and served the Milton morsels to the customers. Age had not diminished her skill, nor had wealth rendered her too proud to resume at need a profession which she had followed in early days. Adeliza flew gracefully to and fro with the rolls, the vinegar bottle with perforated cork, and the little pats of butter. A little boy ran backwards and forwards to the Blue Lion over the way, for the pots of porter, or for the brandy and water, which some gentlemen take after the play.

Midnight arrived. Miss Grampus was looking through the window, and contrasting the gleaming gas which shone upon the ruby lobsters, with the calm moon which lightened up the Poultry, and threw a halo round the Royal Exchange. She was lost in maiden meditation, when her eye fell upon a pane of glass in her own window: squeezed against this, flat and white, was the nose of a man! —that man was Roderick Dandolo! He seemed to be gazing at the lobsters more intensely than at Adeliza; he had his hands in his pockets, and was whistling Jim Crow.*

Miss Grampus felt sick with joy; she staggered to the counter, and almost fainted. The Professor concluded his melody, and entered at once into the shop. He pretended to have no knowledge of Miss Grampus, but *aborded* the two ladies with easy elegance and irresistible good-humour.

"Good evening, ma'am," said he, bowing profoundly to the *elder* lady. "What a precious hot evening, *to* be sure!—hot, ma'am, and hungry, as they say. I could not resist them lobsters, 'specially when I saw the lady behind 'em."

At this gallant speech Mrs. Grampus blushed, or looked as if she would blush, and said,

"Law, sir!"

"Law, indeed, ma'am," playfully continued the Professor; "you're a precious deal better than law,—you're *divinity*, ma'am; and this, I presume, is your sister?"

---

* I know this is an anachronism; but I only mean that he was performing one of the popular melodies of the time.—G. G.

He pointed to Adeliza as he spoke, who, pale and mute, stood fainting against a heap of ginger-beer bottles. The old lady was quite won by this stale compliment.

"My daughter, sir," she said. "Addly, lay a cloth for the gentleman. Do you take hoysters, sir, hor lobsters? Both is very fine."

"Why, ma'am," said he, "to say truth, I have come forty miles since dinner, and don't care if I have a little of both. I'll begin, if you please, with that there, (Lord bless its claws, they're as red as your lips!) and we'll astonish a few of the natives afterwards, *by* your leavè."

Mrs. Grampus was delighted with the manners and the appetite of the stranger. She proceeded forthwith to bisect the lobster, while the Professor in a *dégagé* manner, his cane over his shoulder, and a cheerful whistle upon his lips, entered the little parlour, and took possession of a box and a table.

He was no sooner seated than, from a scuffle, a giggle, and a smack, Mrs. Grampus was induced to suspect that something went wrong in the oyster-room.

"Hadeliza!" cried she; and that young woman returned blushing now like a rose, who had been as pale before as a lily.

Mrs. G. herself took in the lobster, bidding her daughter sternly to stay in the shop. She approached the stranger with an angry air, and laid the lobster before him.

"For shame, sir!" said she solemnly; but all of a sudden she began to giggle like her daughter, and her speech ended with an "*Have done now!*"

We were not behind the curtain, and cannot of course say what took place; but it is evident that the Professor was a general lover of the sex.

Mrs. Grampus returned to the shop, rubbing her lips with her fat arms, and restored to perfect good-humour. The little errand-boy was despatched over the way for a bottle of Guinness and a glass of brandy and water.

"HOT WITH!" shouted a manly voice from the eating-room, and Adeliza was pained to think that in her presence her lover could eat so well.

He ate indeed as if he had never eaten before: here is the bill as written by Mrs. Grampus herself.

"Two lobsters at **3s. 6d.**	.	:	7s. 0d.
Sallit	.	.	1 3
2 Bottils Doubling Stott	.	.	2 4
11 Doz. Best natifs	.	.	7 4
14 Pads of Botter	.	.	1 2
4 Glasses B & W. .	.	.	4 0
Bredd (love & ¼)	.	.	1 2
Brakitch of tumler .	.	.	1 6
			————
"To Samuel Grampus,			1 5 9

"At the Mermaid in Cheapside.

"Shell-fish in all varieties. N.B. a great saving in taking a quantity."

"A saving in *taking a quantity*," said the stranger archly. "Why, ma'am, you ought to let me off *very cheap*;" and the Professor, the pot-boy, Adeliza, and her mamma, grinned equally at this pleasantry.

" However, never mind the pay, missis," continued he; "we an't agoing to quarrel about *that*. Hadd another glass of brandy and water to the bill, and bring it me, when it shall be as I am now."

"Law, sir," simpered Mrs. Grampus, "how's that?"

" *Reseated*, ma'am, to be sure," replied he as he sank back upon the table. The old lady went laughing away, pleased with her merry and facetious customer; the little boy picked up the oyster-shells, of which a mighty pyramid was formed at the Professor's feet.

"Here, Sammy," cried out shrill Mrs. Grampus from the shop, " go over to the Blue Lion and get the gentleman his glass: but no, you are better where you are, pickin' up them shells. Go you, Hade-liza; it is but across the way."

Adeliza went with a very bad grace; she had hoped to exchange at least a few words with him her soul adored; and her mother's jealousy prevented the completion of her wish.

She had scarcely gone, when Mr. Grampus entered from his dinner-party. But, though fond of pleasure, he was equally faithful to business: without a word, he hung up his brass-buttoned coat, put on his hairy cap, and stuck his sleeves through his apron.

As Mrs. Grampus was tying it, (an office which this faithful lady regularly performed,) he asked her what business had occurred during his absence.

"Not so bad," said she; "two pound ten to-night, besides one pound eight to receive;" and she handed Mr. Grampus the bill.

"How many are there on 'em?" said that gentleman smiling, as his eye gladly glanced over the items of the account.

"Why, that's the best of all: how many do you think?"

" If four did it," said Mr. Grampus, " they wouldn't have done badly neither."

" What do you think of *one*?" cried Mrs. G. laughing, " and he an't done yet. Haddy is gone to fetch him another glass of brandy and water."

Mr. Grampus looked very much alarmed. "Only one, and you say he an't paid?"

" No," said the lady.

Mr. Grampus seized the bill, and rushed wildly into the dining-room: the little boy was picking up the oyster-shells still, there were so many of them; the Professor was seated on the table, laughing as if drunk, and picking his teeth with his fork.

Grampus, shaking in every joint, held out the bill: a horrid thought crossed him; he had seen that face before!

The Professor kicked sneeringly into the air the idle piece of paper, and swung his legs recklessly to and fro.

" What a flat you are," shouted he in a voice of thunder, " to think I 'm a goin' to pay! Pay! I never pay—I 'M DANDO!"

The people in the other boxes crowded forward to see the celebrated stranger; the little boy grinned as he dropped two hundred and forty-four oyster-shells, and Mr. Grampus rushed madly into his front shop, shrieking for a watchman.

As he ran, he stumbled over something on the floor,—a woman and a glass of brandy and water lay there extended. Like Tarquinia reversed, Elijah Grampus was trampling over the lifeless body of Adeliza.

Why enlarge upon the miserable theme? The confiding girl,

in returning with the grog from the Blue Lion, had arrived at the shop only in time to hear the fatal name of DANDO. She saw him, tipsy and triumphant, bestriding the festal table, and yelling with horrid laughter! The truth flashed upon her—she fell!

Lost to worldly cares in contemplating the sorrows of their idolized child, her parents forgot all else beside. Mrs. G. held the vinegar-cruet to her nostrils; her husband brought the soda-water fountain to play upon her; it restored her to life, but not to sense. When Adeliza Grampus rose from that trance she was a MANIAC!

But what became of *the deceiver?* The gormandizing ruffian, the lying renegade, the fiend in human shape, escaped in the midst of this scene of desolation. He walked unconcerned through the shop, his hat cocked on one side as before, swaggering as before, whistling as before: far in the moonlight might you see his figure; long, long in the night-silence rang his demoniac melody of Jim Crow!

*   *   *

When Samuel the boy cleaned out the shop in the morning, and made the inventory of the goods, a silver fork, a plated ditto, a dish, and a pewter pot were found to be wanting. Ingenuity will not be long in guessing the name of *the thief.*

Gentles, my tale is told. If it may have deterred one soul from vice, my end is fully answered: if it may have taught to school-mistresses carefulness, to pupils circumspection, to youth the folly of sickly sentiment, the pain of bitter deception; to manhood the crime, the *meanness* of gluttony, the vice which it occasions, and the wicked passions it fosters; if these, or any of these, have been taught by the above tale, Goliah Gahagan seeks for no other reward.

NOTE. Please send the proceeds as requested per letter; the bearer being directed not to give up the manuscript without.

BIDDY TIBS, WHO CARED FOR NOBODY.

" MARRY in thy youth!" This golden truth is writ in one of the " gates," or articles of the " Sadder." We know not if the eyes of Jacob Tibs ever opened upon this questionable axiom; or whether the consciousness of his own weakness was the load-star which lighted him, " poor darkened traveller," to the *blessed state.* Be it as it might, Jacob, though no longer in youth, and in spite of my Uncle Toby's showing that " love is below a man,"—Jacob took unto himself a wife, —an unquestionable *better half,* seeing his share was so small in the economy of domestic life. But at how high a standard Jacob *ought* to have placed his happiness,—and marriage is with some supposed to be a good,—he held it a plague, a sickness long in killing! Jacob, as we have before stated, married, and from that seed his crops of evil sprung! *The apple of his eye,* like that of the East, was ashes to his taste. Alas! that Jacob ever married!

Biddy Tibs, " *who cared for nobody,*" was, at the time we write, a small withered piece of stale old age. In her husband's days,—and they a bountiful Providence, or rather rope, had shortened; not that he was hanged, for Jacob was a modest-minded man!—she made up in temper what she lacked in size; which temper, in the opinion of many, was the personal property of the devil! And as the most difficult conquest of Mahomet was that of his wife, so it proved with Jacob, who vainly hoped that, " as with time and patience the leaf of the mulberry-tree becomes satin," so might his wife's temper from sour turn to sweet! How little did Jacob appreciate the constancy of woman!

Jacob Tibs was part owner of a Liverpool West India trader, and of which he was nominally the captain. But Mrs. T., in this as in all other instances, was the great " captain's captain:" her lungs—and never had a speaking-trumpet such lungs—were hurricane-proof! and the title of " boatswain" was not improperly a sobriquet of this fair cheapener of sugar, with which the vessel was ostensibly freighted, though upon occasions she had more slaves than her husband on board; so that, what with natural and human produce, Jacob climbed a golden ladder. Tired with a " life of storms," he changed his vessel for a house, the sea for a quiet town, and might have rested his old age in peace; but, alas for Jacob! he was married!

Argus is reported to have slept,—can we wonder that Mrs. Tibs's two eyes for once lost their vigilance, and left her husband the master of himself, and one day—for that she passed a short distance off; and Jacob resolved that this drop of comfort should prove a well; and in truth it *did*, as will be shown. Old Jacob had friends, as who has not that has anything to give?—and this day—the only one he could look forward to with a smile since he had been " blessed "—he determined should prove a golden one; and, spite of the servant-girl's warnings of " How missus would wop him!" Jacob held a levee, —some dozen sons of Eve, whose mouths sucked brandy like a sponge,—good old souls of a good old age, whose modest wants 'bacca and brandy could supply.

Jacob held his levee! but as he boasted no privy purse, no stocking with a foot of guineas, and no brandy but a bottle two-thirds full, left by strange accident in the cupboard, what was to be done? For the first time in his life Jacob was surprised into an act of rebellion; and with a death-doing hammer in one hand, and a screwdriver in the other, did Jacob invade the—to him—sanctity of the cellar. The lock was wrenched, lights were stuck in empty bottles, and Jacob, who in his young-going days had swilled it with the best, soon verified the sentiment of Le Sage, that " a reformed drunkard should never be left in a cellar." Now, whether joy or brandy had to answer for the sin, we know not; but, certain it is, Jacob got drunk, and measured his length — he was a tall man — upon the ground. Friends should be our brothers in affliction; *his* were true ones, and at happy intervals of time they sank beside him, completely overcome,—showing how little was their pride, how great their fellowship!

How long they might have continued in this undeniable state of bliss would be an useless guess, for the last of Jacob's friends—and he was no sudden faller-off—had scarcely deposited himself upon the ground in happy indifference for his clothes, when the cracked-bell voice of Mrs. Tibs, who had unexpectedly returned, roused the maid into a consciousness that missus had come home! Domestic contentions are at no time an interesting theme; and as most of our readers—we allude to the married portion—have doubtless experienced them in real life, romance would fall far short of the truth; the single we advise to marry, and experience will teach them what we here pass over. When Jacob's better half beheld her bottles empty, her casks upturned, and her husband, for the first time since he had enjoyed that felicity, deaf to the music of her voice, a bucket of water from the well refreshed Jacob to a truth he would willingly have slept in ignorance of,—that the wife of his bosom was alive, and he started as a thief would at an opening door. She seized him by the collar, and, showering the first-fruits of her passion upon him who could so well appreciate it, the "boatswain" rose within her, and, after bestowing sundry terms of approbation upon his boon companions, she turned them out of the house, as the vulgar saying hath it, "with their tails between their legs." Jacob would have slunk away, but Fortune willed it otherwise. His "rib" shouted the word of command, "Tack, you lubber, and be —— to you!" Jacob recognised the voice,—how could he have mistaken it?—and waited for orders. Now it so fell out, as Mrs. Tibs ran for the bucket of water, her cap, in the press of business, caught by a twig, dropped into the well, and eighteen-pence had been that day expended in decoration. With the assistance of Nanny the maid, Jacob was to be wound down in the bucket; and, spite of his appeals to the contrary, with one foot in the tub, and both hands on the rope, he was lowered, and half soused in water, until he reached the ribbon treasure of his wife's head. The cap clutched in one hand, he was raised dripping by the windlass. Each twist brought him nearer to the top, when, sorrowful to relate, the rope gave way, and Jacob dropped like lead into the well; a hollow splash was heard in the water, and Mrs. Tibs stood by in speechless agony. At length her grief found vent, and, pitching her voice to its shrillest note, she cried, "Oh, my cap!"

Alas for Jacob! his head struck with swingeing force against the bricks, where to this day the impression may be seen: he fell stunned into the water, and before aid could be obtained, which Mrs. Tibs did in less than two hours and a half, Jacob was dead!

Now, though Jacob was dead, he was not buried. A good wife is a jewel to her husband: what must she be to his mortal remains? Biddy's affection was too great to allow any but herself to be his undertaker, and she contracted with a jobbing carpenter for a wooden shell. Jacob never loved luxuries, and the pride of cloth covered not his outside, gilt nails syllabled not his virtues. Four ploughmen were hired at a shilling a-head—half-a-crown they had the uncharity to ask—to be his bearers, and Jacob was lowered to what he had been for years a stranger to—a house of peace!   *   *   *

In the city of C——, famous for its antiquities, its cathedral, and its hop-grounds, is a terrace, commanding an extensive view of a cattle-market and the road beyond; along which road, one sunny afternoon, a gentleman, or, for fear of mistakes, we will simply call him an officer, rode on a piebald horse. Passing along, a certain window on the terrace attracted his attention, and the officer on the piebald horse kissed his hand to its fair occupant. Now, it so happened that Miss Lauretta Birdseye was seated at the very next window, in the very next house to that on which the officer had bestowed his atten-

tions; and no sooner was the kiss blown, than slam went the window!
A glazier who was passing felt himself a richer man by at least
three and sixpence. No sooner was the window closed, than —
curtains are always in the way—they were drawn aside, and a face
was glued to the glass, all eyes and wire ringlets. Another kiss from
the officer on the piebald horse. The lady nodded her head, and was
thinking of blushing; but as blushes, like hedge-side roses, are vulgar,
and glass *so* thick, her prudence whispered her not to be wasteful.
As the rider passed, the window was once more opened, and her
head thrust out, to see what to her was indeed a sight,—a man, as she
thought, looking at her,—when what should she behold at the next
window but Laura Dyke, "that impudent slut," as she said, looking
after the men!" Her modesty was scandalized, and once more the
window descended with a crash!

The following morning Miss Lauretta Birdseye knocked a gentle
knock at the dwelling of Mrs. Tibs, her next-door neighbour. The
door was opened by Laura, who filled the double capacity of drudge
and niece to her loving aunt Biddy Tibs. Since the demise of the late
lamented Jacob, she had led a life of widowhood, no man being found
rash enough to venture where Jacob had trod before. Years had passed, and Biddy Tibs was old and withered, and her skin, like parchment,
hung dry and shrivelled! The fire of her youth was gone, but the embers still remained: what her tongue had lost in might it had gained
in bitterness; she stabbed a reputation at each word, and mixed her
gall in every household hive! Such was Biddy Tibs; and, though
possessed of no mean wealth, her avarice clung like birdlime to her.
Biddy had a brother, an honest tradesman: his wife died young,
and his children, for he had two, a boy and a girl, were unto him gold
and jewels! Biddy held up her hands, and called it a tempting of
Providence. Long sickness and misfortunes—for brother Dick had
friends—and serving others, placed him in a debtors' prison! Without means, and lacking food, Dick asked his sister's aid,—a score of
pounds to make him a man again. Biddy with thousands saw him
want on;—saw him, sick and feeble, die, a prisoner for a friend's
debt, and his children without a roof but heaven! Now, whether
Biddy's conscience smote her,—and it was speculated by some that
she possessed that luxury,—we know not; but, a few weeks after, her
servant-girl, for some or for no fault, had been turned out of doors
in the middle of the night; and, as her place must be supplied, pity
came to Biddy's aid, and her niece, an interesting girl of some sixteen years, was sent for. The boy, Teg, less fortunate, was left to
starve; but he was a shrewd youth, fourteen, and had a squint eye,
a sign of a kind of cunning, and, if a jest may be pardoned, Teg always
looked round the corner. Laura luxuriated in the waggon; Teg, less
fortunate, trudged behind, begging as he went his food. But charity
dwells not on the highway, and Teg's food was mostly unasked; a
turnip diet and a hedge-side bed ended not a youth who was never
born to be choked by indigestion.

Mrs. Tibs took in the girl, for she must have a drudge; Teg had
a penny given him, and the door shut in his face. Teg cried first,
then got in a passion, and, like most people in a pet, quarrelled with
his bread and butter; for he flung the penny through one of the parlour windows, when, as ill luck would have it, it missed the head of

his loving aunt, and ended the days of a cracked tea-cup. Alas! that charity should bring evil upon the giver! for, taking the window and cup into consideration, Biddy's charity cost her shillings, when she had only intended to bestow a penny.

Teg spat upon her threshold, and went, no one cared or knew whither.   *   *   *   *

Laura was now eighteen, and opened the door to Miss Lauretta Birdseye, who looked daggers of indignation,—for Laura was a pretty girl,—and asked if Mrs. Tibs were at home. Laura's meek answer was, "Yes, Miss Birdseye; will you walk in?" Lauretta did, and sat in the parlour *tête-à-tête* with Mrs. Tibs.

Mrs. Tibs was to the city of C—— what Ariadne's thread was to Theseus,—the leading-string in all amours, all stolen meetings, all clandestine marriages. Numberless were the wives and husbands, maids and bachelors, who through her means had held communion sweet with objects of their choice. Messages and letters were her peculiar province; in fact, Biddy Tibs was a post-office in her own person; and these praiseworthy efforts she exercised not altogether from mercenary motives, though, to do her justice, her pride never stood in the way where money was offered: but she loved mischief as a cat loves milk, and would cheat for nothing, rather than not cheat at all. Now, as the officer on the piebald horse had kissed his hand, as Lauretta thought, to her, she could not rest until she had consulted old Tibby, for so she was called. *There* at all events she should know all about the officer, and there, no doubt, the officer would inquire after her; and, seated opposite old Tibby, the conversation began.

"Do you know, Mrs. Tibs," commenced Lauretta, "I am horrorfied to think what the girls about here are come to; for *my* part, you know, I hate the men!"

"I know you do," chimed in Biddy; "your mother tells everybody so: but them gals about here have no shame!"

"None!" and Lauretta rose with her subject. "As for those Greyham's girls, I declare a man can't walk for them; and those Miss Highwaters, they are no better than they should be, I know. Look how they dress! and we all know what they have to live upon. And those Miss Cartriges, with their thick ankles, waddling up and down, and looking after the men: for *my* part, I never walk without mother's with me, for those nasty fellows do look at one so."

Here an indistinct "Hem!" escaped Biddy.

"But I never look at them again, like the girls about here! never!"

Biddy looked at her from under her grey eyes, but said nothing.

"Men," continued Miss B. "are such impudent fellows, especially military men; and, would you think it? an officer on a piebald horse actually kissed his hand to me yesterday afternoon!"

Old Tibby looked up with a face full of wonder and infidelity.

"Who would have thought it!" ejaculated Lauretta.

Biddy shook her head as she added, "Who, indeed!"

"But I let him know I wasn't one of those sort of people, for I shut the window in his face, and I saw him kiss his hand again."

"What! after you had shut the window?" and Biddy looked a note of interrogation in each eye.

"Oh—I—I saw him through the curtains."

"Ah!" was Tibby's echo. "And—well, I couldn't imagine who it could be for."

"Who what was for?" inquired Miss B.

"A letter."

"A letter!" and Lauretta's voice fluttered.

"Yes," said Tibby; "but, knowing how much *you hated* the men, I never thought of you." Saying which, the old woman fumbled in her pocket, and, taking a three-cornered note from a whole phalanx of others, read the inscription,—"To Laura."

"People will call me Laura," said Lauretta, as she seized upon the note, broke the seal, and read as follows:—"Sweet Laura,—When I saw you at the window, and kissed my hand,"—twice, Mrs. Tibs,—"need I say how I wished your rosy lips were near me; but, before many hours, I trust I shall whisper in your ear the love I feel for my pretty little angel." Lauretta held her breath till she was red in the face in a vain endeavour to look celestial. The letter continued:—"And if my sweet Laura will meet me on the 'Mount,' this evening, I will fly with her from the misery she now suffers, to love and happiness. Should you not be there, I shall return to the barracks, and put an immediate end to the existence of your devoted,

"AUGUSTUS GREEN HORN, Royal Rifle Corps."

Miss Birdseye felt twenty years younger at the intelligence,—for a man must be in earnest when he threatens to kill himself,—and, with a true tragedy uplifting of the hands, she exclaimed,

"Mrs. Tibs, I wouldn't have a man's death at my door for a world! No, Augustus——" Further exclamation was cut short by a sort of titter outside the parlour-door. Now none knew better than Lauretta Birdseye how well a keyhole afforded sight and sound; and, throwing the door suddenly open, she burst into the passage. A hurried footstep on the stair convinced her of what she knew from experience to be a fact, that by the time the door is opened the listener gets out of sight.

After sundry comments upon the meanness of listening, Lauretta informed Mrs. Tibs, who sat like a cat watching a mouse, of her Christian determination to save human life by sacrificing herself, all loth as she was, to the officer of the piebald horse!

"It was the first time in her life," as she said, "a man had ever made an appointment with her,"—who shall question the truth?— and her delicacy yielded to her philanthropy!

Lauretta determined to go,—and, what is more, without her mother.   *   *   *   *   *

The "Mount" alluded to in Augustus Green Horn's letter is a hill planted round with winding hedges; and the lawn on which it stands forms the principal promenade of all the little gentry, all the small-consequence people, their pride stuck like a nosegay in their button-holes, who look in looks of hot-bed consequence the dignity the tradesman bows to.

It was a dark evening, and the cathedral clock struck nine as Lauretta Birdseye passed through the gates of the broad walk. Her horror may be imagined when she saw servant-maids and others,—who had nothing but their character to live upon, stealing in and out the trees in loving paces with—Lauretta shut her eyes—the fellows! 'Prentice boys were here whispering golden precepts in the ears of willing maids, who, as servant-maids are not supposed to blush, cried "La!" Lauretta hurried across the green,—doubtless to escape such infamy,—to the foot of the "Mount;" a man and some "impudent hussy" were coming down the way she was to go up,—and, or her eyes deceived her, no less a hussy than Laura Dyke! who, she shuddered to think, had picked up a new man. Lauretta heard—or fancied she heard—a titter as they passed; and the man—he looked very like an officer—laughed outright. Lauretta bridled in the full virginity of three-and-thirty, and walked up the opposite side! How long she walked up and down, this side and that side, from the top to the bottom, and sate "like Patience" on one of the seats at the top, we will not here describe. Suffice it, after waiting two hours and three-quarters, a boy, who brought the candles, laid hold of her in the dark, and, spite of her exertions to the contrary,—Lauretta was strong and bony,—ravished a kiss! Whether the boy's taste was not matured, or what, we know not, but he did not offer to repeat his rashness; and Lauretta, who held kissing a vice, after telling him "what a rude boy he was," and "hoping he would not do it again," walked very slowly down the "Mount," waited ten minutes at the bottom, and then, with a heavy heart went home to bed, strengthened in the truth that men have no taste, and women no shame!

To her gentle summons on the next morning, Biddy herself opened the door. Lauretta looked, and so did Biddy as she cried, "What you! then where 's that devil's niece of mine? the jade 's been out all night, and——"

"With some of the fellows, take my word for it. Mrs. Tibs, the age we live in is a disgrace to our sex—look at *me!*"

"Well, if I do," half screamed the old woman, "I do more than the men do. And haven't you been carried off after all? Oh! oh!" and Biddy wheezed and chuckled like an old grey ape.

"Ma'm!" and Lauretta looked a vestal, "I am not aware, ma'm, what you mean."

"What! not of the officer on the piebald horse?" Biddy's countenance changed, and she turned white with passion as she added, "And that beggar's slut of mine, I 'll teach her to cross me!" But, as her eye rested upon Lauretta, her face changed again, and pursed into a thousand wrinkles as she chuckled, "How long did you wait? Oh! oh!" and she gloated on the wincing countenance of her next-door neighbour.

"Mrs. Tibs!" and Lauretta spoke with the conscious dignity of a Cleopatra; "I have had a strange thought about Laura, and I am afraid we have made a little mistake."

"Mistake!" and Biddy's eyes opened like an owl's.

"Yes; for, after the officer kissed his hand, I opened the window, and there I saw that good-for-nothing girl of yours looking after him, and he *might* have blown his filthy kisses to her; and last night,—I won't be certain,—but I think I saw her coming down the 'Mount' with a man, and he looked very like my dear Augus——"

The countenance of Biddy fell, and her skin became lead as she gasped, "Bat that I was not to see it; that letter was for her after all!"

"Instead of *me!*" and Lauretta waxed wrathful as she added, "She heard us read it through the key-hole. I thought I heard a titter."

Let us not mistake the passion of Biddy Tibs; it was not the ruin of her niece grieved her,—no! she could get another servant from the workhouse; but she had fattened on the idea that, Lucretia as Lauretta was, she had at length stumbled on a Tarquin!—it was wine and oil to her heart. But, to find herself cozened, to have hatched the wrong egg!—her fury knew no bounds. She raved, and—we trust, for the first time in her life—uttered curses, and in so wild a scream that neighbours came running to her assistance; when, lashed by her own temper, the amiable Biddy Tibs fell down in a swoon, having burst a blood-vessel, and was carried to bed.

Miss Birdseye took the opportunity of informing a room-full of attentive listeners, "that the shameless hussy, Laura Dyke, had gone off with a man!" and so great was her horror, that, upon the butcher-boy's bringing the meat, she wouldn't suffer him to come into the passage, but kept the door ajar, for fear, as she said, "the fellow should look at her!"

The sick lion was a baby to Biddy Tibs, and, though *she* "cared for nobody," everybody cared for her—last will and testament. Her wealth had been looked upon by the telescopic eyes of an attentive few, who brought her—as "trifles show respect"—trifles of the least ambitious nature; and now, when Biddy was ill, and not likely to last above a day or two, their consideration knew no bounds. One would bring her—they were so cooling—some currants, on a cabbage leaf; another, a pot of jam; a third, an invitation,—if she *could* go, it would do her so much good. Biddy was not expected to live the day. But—oh, the ingratitude of this old creature!—ill as she was, her grey eyes looked like glass upon them, and twinkled with a cunning light; and in the course of the day she promised, in no less than six different quarters, the house she lived in, and a legacy beside. How good are they who wait upon the sick! but, though sick, Biddy, as the saying is, was "hard to die," and the doctor was justly surprised, who, after giving her over the preceding night, found her alive the next morning; and, notwithstanding she had three doctors, in the space of a few weeks, as her friends justly lamented, Biddy had cheated the devil, and, what was of still more consequence, themselves of currants and jam.

In due course of time Mrs. Tibs was restored to health; and not only left the city of C——, but her loving friends, who looked their last of Biddy Tibs, "who cared for nobody." *   *   *

We have now to trace the history of Teg Dyke, who, we before said, was a shrewd boy, and, like most shrewd children taught by bad example, he became of the bad the worst. Driven from his aunt's door, without shelter and without food, Teg turned his steps where chance directed, and, "with Providence for his guide," before nightfall was some miles on the London road. Begging or stealing his way, as accident and his necessity compelled, the poor lad found himself sore-footed, hungry, hopeless, in the outskirts of London, which then, even more than now, was a huge nursery for crime,—a living chess-board, and circumstance the player! Teg was ragged, and none would employ him; begging was so unprofitable there was no living by it. Without food for two whole days Teg grew desperate, and, tempted by the smell, stole from the door of a cook-shop a plateful of savoury tit-bits,—the third lost that morning; and, in the act of tasting, Teg was detected, seized, and, by a merciful magistrate sent to the House of Correction. Teg, himself no sinner, was here shut round by sin. Teg stole a meal, urged by the crying wants of hunger, and he was here mated with those who held theft a principle; and, like a bur, he clung to vice, since honesty had cast him down: and, to say truth, Teg found more fellowship in a jail, more communion, than in the outer world; for here they took delight in teaching what they knew without a premium. Where else could Teg have learnt a trade so cheaply? "The cove was quick and willing," and, respecting nothing else,—they must have been rogues,—respected genius! Genius lies hid in corners; and Teg who, had his aunt not thrust him from her door, might have become merely an honest man, sent to jail for stealing what none would give him,—food,—became, with a little practice, an accomplished thief!

Who shall say Biddy was to blame for shutting her door on so much depravity? Again, was not her wisdom shown in her behaviour to her niece? Should she have treated her with the least appearance of kindness, who, driven like a dog, had the wickedness to stain her threshold with ingratitude? Had she bestowed a sign of goodness upon her, she had then deserved it. But, no; she had treated her niece like a beast of burthen, and how had she returned her affection? Biddy trembled as she thought of it!

Laura's ingratitude must have risen like a ghost upon her sleepless eye! What must have been her self-accusation when, deserted by the Honourable Augustus Green Horn, she found herself not only a mother, but a beggar, halting in the streets, and with a pale and stricken countenance suing for bread? Then, indeed, must her aunt's loving-kindness have come in sweet dreams of the past, and whispered love and gentleness! But Laura had a callous mind, and, strange to say, never once felt her deprivation, or she would have sunk beneath it, as an outcast from society, her freshness gone; her beauty, like an autumn's leaf, seared, and cast forth unto the winds; her heart bruised, and her hopes destroyed, she crawled at midnight through the worst streets of London's worst quarter, the scoff of many, the despised of all, the debauched victim of any, her child a cripple from its birth, and in the malignity of a fever dead! And yet Laura, midst all these evils, wept hot tears; but, what proved she must have been dead to feeling, she never once thought of the motherly kindness of Biddy Tibs.   *   *   *

Some years had passed since Biddy turned her back upon the city of C——, and left a name blushing with its good deeds behind her. She now lived in a small town in the neighbourhood of the metropolis, where her riches formed the subject of many an alehouse gossip. But, as old age fell upon her, the vice of gold came with it, and she lived in a crazy wooden house, without the fellowship of a breathing thing, and for the best of reasons. No cat could live upon her fare, and hope to be alive at the end of the month,—no dog was ever seen to stop at a bone Biddy threw away; her charity never descended to her garden, nor did the sparrows,—they knew it would be a waste of time;—and thus she lived without kin and without kind, no servant being so little a feeder as to live upon abuse. And it was noted as a peculiar fact, that, the older she grew, the more evil grew her tongue. Characters fell like grass before her.

Young or old, weak or strong, all felt her lash! And upon one occasion she made such inroads upon the chastity of two maiden ladies, sisters, and worthy to be so of the far-famed Irish giant, that, under pretence of tea and scandal, Biddy could not resist the temptation; she was induced to pay them a visit. A stream ran through these maiden sisters' grounds; and lifting Biddy in their arms,—a mere shuttlecock to two such battledores,—she was gently dropt into the water, where she enjoyed, what she had been for years a stranger to, a comfortable wash. So runs the story; and Biddy, vowing vengeance and the law, which last she obtained, for Biddy was rich, added so much by her daily tales to their reputations, that in the end she remained sole mistress of the field,—the maiden ladies leaving Biddy and the town behind them.

It was a cold November night, the wind howled, and the rain beat against the windows as Biddy Tibs sat in her room; the night was without moon or stars, and the sky looked black as the old woman peered through the window into the garden, and the fields at the back of her house; the rain fell in streams, and the wind moaned like a human voice. For an instant she saw, or thought she saw, a light shoot across the garden. She looked, and looked, and—she closed the shutters, and sat closer to the fire; and, rocking herself over it in her chair, mumbled, "Blind eyes that I have!—how should a light get there? I could see in the dark once like a cat; but now—" and the old woman rocked over the fire, with her head bent double to the grate. A rushlight with a long snuff burnt on the table, and the room looked shadowy and full of forms.

'Twas midnight; but still Biddy sat within her chair, and rocked, and rocked, and looking at the fire, as cinder after cinder blackened in the grate, she muttered, and spoke as to herself, "They're none of my getting,—none of my flesh! Didn't I feed, clothe her?—she ran away from my roof, and let her want. A night like this will break her spirit, and teach her what it is to be without one—'twill——" She paused suddenly, and bent her ear as in the act of listening; her grey eyes gazed round the room as she said, "It sounded like a door creaking, or a bolt;" and again she listened. The candle burnt dimly on the table, and the embers grew darker and darker as Biddy spread her hands to catch their warmth, and muttered, "At night, one is full of fancies; it's only the wind;" and, communing with herself, she added, "I've paid them back their own, and given them lies for lies, and they hate me for it: but they fear me, too,—that's one comfort,—for they know I'm rich. Rich—ha! ha! there's a sly cupboard there," and she pointed to a recess in the wall, where a concealed door stood half ajar; "there's a nest holds more eggs than they think for; and if I had liked—but the boy is none of mine—the boy—" A draught of air as from an opened door made her look round. She sat frozen to her chair as the figure of a man darkened in the room; a second, masked like his fellow, stood in the shadow of the door; and Biddy, with a fixed stare, looked like a corpse, blue-lipped and hollow-eyed. Her chair shook under her, and her voice came not, though her mouth opened, and her throat worked as if to scream! The man moved a step; it was electric! Biddy started to her feet, and with a hollow voice cried "Murder!" The ruffian with a curse darted at her throat, and, in a hissing whisper between his teeth, cried, "Quiet, you hag, or I'll settle you!" Biddy, old and feeble as she was, fastened with both hands upon his, and struggled in his grip. The mask fell from his face, and with starting eyes she looked at what seemed to scorch them, uttered a choking scream, and— Let us draw the curtain.

The next morning speculation was busy that at so late an hour the shutters of Mrs. Tibs's house remained unopened; she was an early riser, and now 'twas noon: their knocking obtaining no answer, the door was forced; and in the back room they found Biddy Tibs upon the ground, dead, with a handkerchief knotted round her throat. The small cupboard in the recess was thrown wide open, and her drawers forced; and it was soon spread over the town that Biddy Tibs was murdered!

A few weeks had passed, and anxious and expectant thousands were seen moving in a huge mass on the road to Tyburn. A man was to be hanged! And, as the people have so little recreation, of course the roads were thronged with delighted crowds, all hastening to the "gallows-tree." Women yelled their execrations at the head of the pale and shaking culprit, for he had murdered one of their own sex; and clapped and shouted as the cart drew from under his clinging feet. Men, "as it was only for a woman," "thought hanging too bad," and merely hooted, groaned, and hissed. Indeed, so popular was the excitement, that ladies—*real* ones, for they paid guineas for a sight on a waggon,—waved their handkerchief, and wondered such wretches were suffered to exist.

As the last struggle of the swinging corpse left him stiff and dead, a half-clothed and haggard woman asked, in a hoarse and shaking voice, the name of the murderer.

"What, that 'ere?" was the reply, and a finger pointed to the stripling figure of the hanging man; "he as murdered his aunt? —why Slashing Bill, *alias* Teg Dyke."

A scream—a wild and shrieking scream rang through the air, and Laura dropt senseless.

The bulk of Mrs. Tibs's property came to her niece, but disease had left her scarce a shadow of herself. Her eyes looked leaden! Want, sorrow, and dissipation had writ their blight upon her, and, at the end of six months,—an apothecary having been frequent in his visits,—poor Laura was no more!

How different had been the fate of Biddy Tibs had she lent her brother Dick the score of pounds! Teg would have been an honest tradesman like himself, Laura a tradesman's wife, Biddy had lived for years, and the pillow of her death-bed been smoothed by the hands of loving friends. But, as it was, her brother died from want; Biddy fell, strangled by her nephew's hand. He had been seen in a taproom, where the wealth of the old woman who lived at the wooden house was talked of; part was traced to him; his companion confessed; and Teg died a felon's death; Laura, from the effects of want and dissipation!

Biddy's property was the subject of a law-suit between two of her distant relations, which, to the best of our knowledge, remains unsettled to this day!

In a village churchyard in the neighbourhood of London the grass grows rank about a tombstone which is still pointed at as the grave of "*Biddy Tibs, who cared for nobody!*"

H. HOLL.

THE REGATTA.—No. I.

RUN ACROSS CHANNEL.

ONCE more upon the dark blue water! It is noon,—the sun shines gloriously; the sea, undulated by a slight swell from the Atlantic, falls gently on the beach, or breaks upon the beetling precipice which forms the headland of Rathmore. The wind has almost " sighed itself to rest," and, coming across the sparkling surface of the ocean in partial eddies, ruffles it for a moment and passes on. Fainter and fainter still,—nothing but an occasional cat's-paw is visible, far as the helmsman's eye can range. The cutter has no longer steerage way; the folds of the ample mainsail flap heavily as the yacht rolls in the run of the tide, which, setting rapidly to the eastward, drifts the unmanageable vessel along a chain of rocky islands, severed by some tremendous convulsion from the main, to which they had been originally united.

A more magnificent and a more varied scene than that visible from the yacht's deck could not be imagined. A-beam lay the grey ruins of Dunluce, lighted up by a flood of sunshine; the shores of Portrush, with its scattered bathing-houses, and the highlands of Donegal at the extreme distance, appeared astern. On the left was an expanse of ocean, boundless, waveless, beautiful: the sea-gull was idly resting on the surface, the puffin and the cormorant diving and appearing continually; while a league off a man-of-war brig, covered to the very trucks with useless canvass, lay as if she rode at anchor. Beyond the motionless vessel, the Scottish coast was clearly defined; the bold outline of the shores of Isla presented itself: and, half lost in the haze, the cone of Jura showed yet more faintly. On the starboard bow the Giant's Causeway rose from the water, and with a glass you could trace its unequal surface of basaltic columns; while right ahead Bengore and Rathlin completed this mighty panorama.

Nor was the cutter from which this scene was viewed an object void of interest. She was a vessel of some seventy tons, displaying that beauty of build and equipment for which modern yachts are so remarkable. The low black hull was symmetry itself, while the taunt spars and topmast displayed a cloud of sail, which at a short distance would appear to require a bark of double the size to carry. Above deck everything was simple and ship-shape; below, space had been accurately considered, and not an inch was lost. Nothing could surpass the conveniency of the cabins, or the elegance with which the fittings and furniture were designed.

Four hours passed,—not a breath of wind stirred: a deader calm I never witnessed. We drifted past the Causeway, and, leaving the dangerous rock of Carrickbannon between us and the flying bridge of Carrick-a-rede, found ourselves at five o'clock rolling in the sound of Rathlin, with Churchbay and Ballycastle on either beam.

There is not in calm or storm a nastier piece of water than that which divides the island from the main. Its currents are most rapid; and, from the peculiar inequality of the bottom, in calms there is a

heavy and sickening roll, and in storms a cross and dangerous sea.
Without a leading wind, or plenty of it, a vessel finds it difficult to
stem the current; and, in making the attempt with a light breeze, a
man is regularly hung up until a change of tide enables him to slip
through.

Judging from the outline of Rathlin, this island must have been
originally disparted from the main; and the whole bottom of the
sound evinces volcanic action. Nothing can be more broken and
irregular than the under surface. At one cast the lead rests at
ten, and at the next it reaches thirty fathoms. Beneath, all seems
rifted rocks and endless caverns, and easily accounts for the short
and bubbling sea that flows above. Everything considered, the
loss of life occasioned by the passage of this sound is trifling. For
weeks together all communication with the main land is frequently
totally interrupted; and, until the weather moderates, the hardiest
islander will not dare to venture out. But as the sea seldom gives
up its dead, and the furious under-currents sweep them far from the
place where they perished, many a stranger has here met his doom,
and his fate remained a mystery for ever.

Still the calm continued, the tide was nearly done, and we had the
comfortable alternative of anchoring in Churchbay or drifting back
" to the place from whence we came." It would have vexed a saint,
had there been one on board. Calculating on a speedy and certain
passage, we had postponed our departure until the last hour. On
Monday the regatta would commence; and we should have been in
the Clyde the day before. A breeze for half an hour would have
carried us clear of the tides, and liberated us from this infernal sound;
and every man on board had whistled for it in vain. Dinner was
announced, and, wearied with rolling and flapping, we briskly obeyed
the summons. I paused with my foot within the companion: the
master's eye was turned to the brig outside us; mine followed in the
same direction.

" It's coming—phew!" and he gave a low and lengthened whistle,
as if the tardy breeze required encouragement to bring it on. The
light duck in the brig's royals fluttered for a moment, and then blew
gently out; the top-gallant sails filled; presently the lower canvass
told that the wind had reached it. The vessel has steerage way again;
the breeze steals on, curling over the surface of the water, and in a
few minutes we too shall have it.

On it came: the short and lumbering motion of the yacht ceased;
she heeled gently over, and the table swung steadily as with increasing velocity the vessel displaced the water, and flung it in sparkling
sheets from her bows. Next minute the master's voice gave comfortable assurance from the skylight—"The breeze was true, and
before sunset there would be plenty of it."

Those who prefer the security of the king's highway to breasting
" the pathless deep," build upon the certainty with which their jour-
neyings shall terminate, and argue that there is safer dependence
in trusting to post-horses than to the agency of " wanton winds." No
doubt there is; the worst delay will arise from a lost shoe or a broken
trace. The traveller has few contingencies to dread; he will reach
the Bear for breakfast, and the Lion for dinner; and, if he be a bor-
rower from the night, he will be surely at the Swan, his halting-place,

ere the town-clock has ceased striking and the drum has beaten its
reveille. To me that very regularity is not to be endured; the wheels
grate over the same gravel that the thousand which preceded them
have pressed before; the same hedge, the same paling meets the eye;
there hangs the well-remembered sign; that waiter has been there
these ten years,—ay, the same laughing barmaid, and obsequious
boots, and bustling hostler, all with a smile of welcome, cold, mechanical, and insincere; not even the novelty of a new face among
them,—all rooted to their places like the milestones themselves. Pish!
one wearies of the road; it has no danger, no interest, no excitement.
Give me the deep blue water; its very insecurity has charms for me.
Is it calm?—mark yon cloud-bank in the south! There is wind
there, for a thousand! It comes, but right ahead. No matter; my
life for it, it will shift ere morning. Let it but change a point or
two, and we shall lie our course. It comes—and fair at last, and,
rushing forward with augmenting speed, the gallant vessel disparts
the sparkling waters, and the keel cleaves the wave that keel never
cleft before; and objects fade, and objects rise, while, " like a thing
of life," the good ship hurries on. Cold must that spirit be which
owns no elemental influence, nor feels buoyant as the bark that bears
him onward to his destination!

As dinner ended, the altered motion of the yacht announced that
we had rounded Ushet Point, and left the shelter of the island. We
were now in the channel which separates Rathlin from the Scotch
coast, and the cutter felt the rising swell as her sharp bows plunged
in the wave, and flung it aside as if in scorn. The hissing noise with
which the smooth and coppered sides slipped through the yielding
waters marked our increased velocity. Yet we experienced little
inconvenience; on the morocco-cushioned sofa even a Roman might
have reclined in comfort. To every movement of the yacht the table
gave an accommodating swing: fragile porcelain and frail decanter
remained there in full security; and, though the wine-glass was filled
to the brim, the rosewood surface on which it stood was unstained by
a single drop. Human luxury cannot surpass that which a well-
appointed yacht affords.

When we left the cabin for the deck, a new scene and a new sky
were presented. Evening was closing in; the light blue clouds of
morning were succeeded by a dark and lowering atmosphere; the
wind was freshening, and it came in partial squalls, accompanied by
drizzling rain. Rathlin, and the Irish highlands were fading fast
away, while the tower on the Mull of Cantire flung its sparkling light
over the dark waters, as if soliciting our approach. Two or three
colliers we had passed, were steering for the Clyde close astern;
while a Glasgow steamer, bound for Derry, came puffing by, and in a
short time was lost in the increasing haze.

Is there on earth or sea an object of more interest or beauty than
that lone building which relieves the benighted voyager from his uncertainty? In nothing has modern intelligence been more usefully
displayed than in the superior lighting of the British seas. Harbour,
and rock, and shoal, have each their distinguishing beacon; and, when
he once sees the chalk cliffs of his native island, the returning mariner
may count himself at home. Light after light rises from the murky
horizon: there, flaring with the brilliancy of a fixed star; here, meteor-

like, shooting out its stream of fire, and momentarily disappearing. On, nothing doubting, speeds the adventurous sailor, until the anchor falls from the bows, and the vessel " safely rides."

The light upon Cantire burns steadily, and in moderate weather it is visible at the distance of fifteen miles. It stands high, being upwards of two hundred and thirty feet above the level of the sea. We skirted the base of the cliff it occupies, and steered for the little island of Sanna. Momentarily the sea rose, the night grew worse, the dim and hazy twilight faded away, the wind piped louder, and the rain came down in torrents. When the weather looked threatening the cutter had been put under easy canvass, and now a further reduction was required. The mainsail was double-reefed, the third jib shifted for a smaller one, all above and below " made snug," and on we hurried.

The night was dark as a witch's cauldron when, rounding Sanna, we caught the Pladda lights, placed on opposite towers, and bearing from each other N. and S. It was easy to discover that we had got the shelter of the land, as the pitching motion of the yacht changed to a rushing velocity; but, though we found a smoother sea, the wind freshened, the rain fell with unabated violence, and the breeze, striking us in sudden gusts as it roared through the openings of the islands, half-flooded the deck with a boiling sea that broke over the bows, or forced itself through the lee-scuppers. Anxious to end our dreary navigation, " Carry on!" was the word, and light after light rose, and was lost successively. We passed the lights on Cumray; and, presently, that on Toward, in Dumbarton, minutely revolving, burst on the sight after its brief eclipse with dazzling brilliancy; while from the opposite shores of the Frith the beacons of Air and Trune were now and then distinctly visible. Our last meteor guide told that our midnight voyage was nearly ended, and the pier-light of Greenock enabled us to feel our way through a crowd of shipping abreast the town. " Stand by, for'ard!—let go!" The anchor fell, the chain went clattering through the hawse-hole; in a few seconds the cutter swung head to wind, and there we were, safe as in a wet dock!

We descended to the cabin, first discarding our outward coverings at the foot of the companion ladder. We came down like mermen, distilling from every limb, water of earth and sky in pretty equal proportions; but, glory to the Prophet and Macintosh! Flushing petticoats, pea-jackets, sou'westers, and India-rubber boots, proved garments of such excellent endurance, notwithstanding a three hours' pitiless pelting of spray and rain, that we shuffled off our slough, and showed in good and dry condition, as if we had the while been snug in the royal mail, or, drier yet, engaged at a meeting of the Temperance Society. And then came supper,—they *can* cook in yachts!—and we had run ninety miles since dinner; and that lobster salad, and those broiled bones, with the joyous prospect which bottles of varied tint upon yonder locker-head present, all would make—ay—a teetotaller himself forswear his vows for ever.

All is snug for the night. The men have shifted their wet clothes, and, as their supper is preparing, they crowd around the galley fire; and jest and " laugh suppressed " are audible. What a change these few brief minutes have effected! To the dreary darkness of a flooded deck, the luxury of this lighted and luxurious cabin has succeeded. The wind whistles through the shrouds, the rain falls spattering on the skylight,—what matter?—*we* heed them not; they merely recall the discomfort of the past, which gives a heightened zest to the pleasure of the passing hour. On rolled " the sandman" Time! the dial's finger silently pointing at his stealthy course, and warning us to separate.

Presently every sound below was hushed. All felt that repose which comfort succeeding hardship can best produce. In my own cabin I listened for a brief space to the growling of the storm; sleep laid his " leaden mace upon my lids;" I turned indolently in my cot, muttering with the honest Boatswain in the " Tempest,"

" Blow till thou burst thy wind, if room enough!"

and next moment was " fast as a watchman."

THE KEY OF GRANADA.

" Many of the families of Ghar el Milah are descendants of the Spanish Moors; and, though none of them have retained any portion of the language of Spain, yet many still possess the keys of their houses in Granada and other towns."—*Sir Grenville Temple's " Barbary States."*

I.

I KEEP the key,—though banish'd
  From blest Granada long,
Our glorious race has vanish'd,
  Or lives alone in song.
Though strangers in Alhambra
  May, idly musing, gaze
On all the dying splendours
  That round her ruins blaze;
Those towers had once a home for me,
And still I keep the sacred key!

II.

Alas! my eyes may never
  That lovely land behold,
Where many a gentle river
  Flows over sands of gold.
The sparkling waves of Darro
  For me may flow in vain;
No Moorish foot may wander
  In lost, but cherish'd Spain!
Yet once her walls had room for me,
And still I keep the sacred key!

III.

There often comes in slumber
  A vision sad and clear,
When through Elvira's portals
  Abdalla's hosts appear.
The keys of lost Granada
  To other hands are given,
And all the power of ages
  One fatal hour has riven!
No name,—no home remains for me,—
But still I keep the sacred key!

GLORVINA, THE MAID OF MEATH.

(Concluded from Vol. I. page 619.)

THE board was spread. He sat at it abstracted for a time. The dead silence of the place at last recalled him to himself. He was alone! He sprang from his seat, and darted breathlessly to the outward door! No one was in sight. Niall heaved a sigh that seemed to rend his breast, as he wished that the eyes which looked in vain were closed for ever. He returned to the table of repast; he took a small chain of hair from his neck; he laid it on the cover that was before him: he approached the door again. But the keepsake, that had never left its seat for many a year, was too precious to him to be so discarded. He returned: he lifted it, and, thrusting it into his bosom, pressed it again and again to his heart, then again and again to his lips, drinking his own tears, that fell fast and thick upon the loved and about-to-be-relinquished token; he looked at it as well as he could through his blinded eyes, convulsively sobbing forth the name of Glorvina. He made one effort, as it were a thing which called for all the power of resolution, to achieve that he desired to accomplish; and, violently casting the gift of Glorvina down again, he tore himself away!

Oh, the feet which retrace in disappointment the path which they trod in hope, how they move! Through how different a region do they bear us—and yet the same! Niall's limbs bore him from the retreat of Glorvina as if they acted in obedience to a spirit repugnant to his own. He cast his eyes this way and that way to divert his thoughts from the subject that engrossed them, and fix them upon the beauties of the landscape; but there was no landscape there. Mountain, wood, torrent, river, lake, were obliterated! Nothing was present but Glorvina. Rich she stood before him in the bursting bloom of young womanhood! Features, complexion, figure, voice—everything changed; and, oh, with what enhancing! Her eyes, in which, four years before, sprightliness, frankness, kindness, and unconsciousness used to shine,—what looked from them now? New spirits! things of the soul which time brings forth in season. Expression,—that face of the heart,—the thousand things that it told in the moment or two that Niall looked upon the face of Glorvina! A faintness came over the young man; his limbs seemed suddenly to fail him; he felt as if his respiration were about to stop; he stood still, he staggered, utter unconsciousness succeeded.

Niall opened his eyes. Slowly recollection returned. He was aware that he had fainted, but certainly not in the place where he was reclining,—a bank a few paces from the road. The repulse he had met with from Glorvina returned to his recollection in full force. He sighed, and thrust his hand into his bosom to press it to his overcharged heart. His hand felt something there it did not expect to meet! It drew forth the token of Glorvina! Niall could scarce believe his vision. He looked again and again at the precious gift; he pressed it to his lips; he thrust it into his breast; snatched it thence to his lips again, and looked at it again; divided between incredulity and certainty, past agony and present rapture. He looked about him; no one was in sight. "How came it here?" exclaimed he to himself. "Glorvina! Glorvina!" he continued, in tender accents, "was it thy hand that placed it here? Hast thou been near me when I knew it not? Didst thou follow me in pity,—perhaps, O transporting thought! in kindness,—guessing from the untasted repast and the abandoned pledge that Niall had departed in despair? If so, then art thou still my own Glorvina! then shalt thou yet become the wife of Niall!"

"The wife of Niall!" repeated the echo, and echo after echo took it up.

Niall listened till the last reverberation died away.

"The wife of Niall!" he reiterated, in a yet louder voice, in the tone of which exultation and joy were mingled.

"The wife of Niall!" cried the voice of the unseen lips.

"Once more, kind spirit!" exclaimed Niall; "once more!"

"Once more!" returned the echo.

"The wife of Niall!" ejaculated the youth, exerting his voice to its utmost capacity; but he heard not the voice of the echo. The arms of Glorvina were clasped about his neck, and her bright face was laid upon his cheek!

"Companion of my childhood!—friend!—brother!" she exclaimed; and would have gone on, but checked herself, looked in his eyes for a moment, her forehead and her cheeks one blush, and buried her face in his breast.

"Glorvina! Glorvina!" was all that Niall could utter in the intervals of the kisses which he printed thick upon her shining hair. "Glorvina! Glorvina!"

"Come!" said Glorvina, with a voice of music such as harp never yet awakened; "come!" and straight led the way to her retreat.

Slow was their gait as they walked side by side, touching each other. They spake not many words for a time. With the youth all language seemed to be concentred in the name of Glorvina; in the name of Niall with the maid. Suddenly Niall paused.

"How many a time," exclaimed Niall, "when I have been miles and miles away, have I thought of the days when we used to walk thus! only my arm used then to be around your waist, while yours was laid upon my shoulder. Are we not the same Niall and Glorvina we were then?" The maid paused in her turn. She hesitated, but the next second her arm was on the shoulder of Niall; Niall's arm was again the girdle of Glorvina's waist. Language began to flow. Glorvina related minutely, as maiden modesty would permit her, the cause of her secluded retirement and reported death. As she spake, Niall drew her closer to him, and she shrank not; he leaned his cheek to hers, and she drew not away; he drank her breath as it issued in thrilling melody from her lips, and she breathed it yet more freely; she ceased, and those lips were in contact with his own, and not compulsively. Simultaneously Niall and Glorvina paused once more; they gazed—they cast a glance of thankfulness to heaven—gazed again—and, speechless and motionless, stood locked in one another's arms.

"Glorvina!" cried a voice.

The maid started and turned. Malachi stood before his daughter, the bard behind him.

"Niall !" said Malachi. The youth was at the feet of the king. In a moment the maid was there also. Malachi stood with folded arms, looking thoughtfully and somewhat sternly down upon the prostrate pair. No one broke silence for a time.

The bard was the first to speak.

"Malachi," said the bard, "what is so strong as destiny? Whose speed is so swift? Whose foot is so sure? Who can outrace it, or elude it? Thy stratagem is found out. The Dane asks for thy fair child, although thou told'st him she was in the custody of the tomb. If thou showest her not to him, he will search for her. Niall has come in time. The voice of the prophetic Psalter has called him hither; he has come to espouse thy fair child; a bride thou must present her to the Dane. In the feast must begin the fray; by the fray will the peace be begotten that shall give safety and repose to the land. Malachi, reach forth thy hands! Lift thy children from the earth, and take them to thy bosom; and bow thy head in reverence to Fate!"

The aged king obeyed. He raised Glorvina and Niall from the earth; he placed his daughter's hand in that of the youth: he extended his arms; they threw themselves into them.

* * * * *

Bright shone the hall of Malachi at the bridal feast in honour of the nuptials of Niall and Glorvina; rapturously it rang with the harp and with the voice of many a minstrel; but the string of the bard was silent; his thoughts were not at the board; his absent looks rebuked the hour of mirth and gratulation; watchfulness was in them, and anxiety, and alarm. Still the mirth halted not, nor slackened. The king was joyous; on the countenances of Niall and Glorvina sat the smile of supreme content; the spirits of the guests were quickening fast with hilarity; and dancing eyes saluted every new visitor as he entered,—for the gates of the castle were thrown open to all. Suddenly the eyes of the whole assembly were turned upon the bard. He had started from his seat, and stood in the attitude of one who listens.

"Hark!" he cried. He was obeyed. The uproar of the banquet subsided into breathless attention; yet nothing was heard, though the bard stood listening still. The feast was slowly renewed.

"Cormack," said Malachi, in a tone of mingled good-nature and sarcasm, "what did you call upon us to listen to?"

"The sound of steps that come!" replied the bard with solemnity, and slowly resuming his seat.

"It is the steps of thy fingers along the strings then!" rejoined the king. "Come!—strike! A joyful strain!"

"No joyful strain I strike," said the bard, "till the land shall be free from him whose footsteps now are turned towards thy threshold, and shall cross it ere the feast is half gone by."

"No joyful strain thou 'lt strike till then!" said the king. "Come, take thy harp, old man, and show thy skill; and play not the prophet when it befits thee to be the reveller!"

The bard responded not by word, action, or look, to the command or request of Malachi. He sat, all expectation, on the watch for something that his ear was waiting for.

"Nay, then," said the king, "an thou wilt not play the bard, whose office 'tis, thy master will do it for thee!" and Malachi pushed back his seat, and reached to the harp, which stood neglected beside the bard: he drew it towards him; his breast supported it; he extended his arms, and spread his fingers over the strings. "Now!" said Malachi.

"Now!" said the bard, starting up again, as the harsh blast of a trumpet arrested the hand of the king on the point of beginning the strain. Malachi started up too. All were upon their feet; and every eye was fixed upon the portal of the hall, beneath which stood Turgesius with a group of attendants.

"He is come!" said the bard. "The feast is not crowned without the fray! He is come!" he repeated, as Malachi strode from his place, and with extended hand approached the visitor, who smilingly bowed to his welcome, and followed him to the head of the board, round which he cast his eyes till they alighted upon Glorvina. Malachi pointed to the seat beside himself, as Niall half gave place.

"No!—there!" said Turgesius, pointing to the side of Glorvina. He approached the place where she sat with a cheek now as white as her nuptial vest; the person next her mechanically resigned his seat, and the rover took it.

"The cup!" cried Turgesius. It was handed to him. With kindling eyes he lifted it, holding it for a second or two at full length; then, turning his gaze upon the bride, he gave "The health of Glorvina!"

"Glorvina!—Glorvina and Niall!" rang around the board. The Dane started to his feet, snatching the cup from his lips, that were about to touch it; and lifting it commandingly on high, "Glorvina!" he repeated, casting a glance of haughty defiance round him; and, taking a deep draught, with another glance at the company, sat down, riveting his eyes upon the bride.

The cloud of wrath overcast the bright face of Niall as he watched the licentious Dane. Frequently did he start, as upon the point of giving way to some rash impulse, and then immediately check himself. Now and then he looked towards the king, and turned away in disappointment to see that Malachi thought of nothing but the feast, and noted not the daring gaze which the rover kept bending on his child. He looked round the board, and saw with satisfaction that he was not the only one in whom festivity had given place to indignation; and, with the smile of fixed resolve, he interchanged glances with eyes lighted up with spirits like his own.

Turgesius plied the cup; and, as he drained it, waxed more and more audacious. Regardless of the sufferings of the fair maid who sat lost in confusion, he praised aloud the charms of Glorvina, and gave utterance to the unholy passion with which they had inspired him. Nor had he arrived at the limits of his presumption yet. He caught her delicate hand, and held it in spite of her gentle, remonstrating resistance. He dared to raise it to his lips, and hold it there, covering it with kisses, till, the dread of consequences lost in the dismay of outraged modesty, the royal maid by a sudden effort wrested it from him, at the same time springing upon her feet with the design of flying from the board; but the bold stranger, anticipating her, was up as soon as she, and, grasping her by the rich swell of her white arms, constrained her from departing.

"No!" cried Turgesius, bending his insolent gaze upon the now burning face and neck of Glorvina. "No! enchanting one! Thus may not the Dane be served by the woman that inflames his soul with love," and at the same moment attempted to throw his arms around her.

"Desist, robber!" thundered forth the voice of Niall, and, at the same moment, a goblet directed by his unerring aim stretched the Dane upon the floor. Outcry at once took place of revelry. The attendants of Turgesius, baring their weapons, rushed in the direction of Niall, but stopped short at the sight of treble the number of their glaives waving around him. They looked not for such hinderance. Since the Dane had got the upper hand, the Irish youth had been forbidden the practice or wearing of arms. They stopped, and stood irresolute. The voice of the king restored order.

Malachi had hitherto sat strangely passive. He noted not the distress of Glorvina, the audacity of the Dane, or the gathering wrath of Niall; but the act of violence which had just taken place aroused him from his abstraction. He rose; and, extending his hand, commanded in a voice of impressive authority that the sword should be sheathed, and the seats resumed. Then calling to his attendants, he pointed to his prostrate guest, and signed to them to raise him, assisting them himself, and giving directions that he should be conveyed to his own chamber, and laid upon his own couch. This being performed, he motioned to Glorvina to withdraw from the hall, which she precipitately did, followed by her bridemaidens and other female friends, and casting an anxious, commiserating look upon Niall, whose wonder at the meaning of such a farewell was raised to astonishment, when, turning towards the king, he encountered the stern, repelling, and indignant gaze of Malachi.

"Niall!" said the king, in a voice of suppressed rage, "depart our castle! Depart our realms! Withdraw from all alliance with our house! Our honour has been stained by thee to-night in thy unparalleled violation of the rights of hospitality. This roof never witnessed before now, the person of a guest profaned by a blow from its master, or from its master's friend. Consummation awaits not the rites that have been performed to-day. The obligation of those rites shall be dissolved! We mingle blood no further! Thou art henceforward an alien—an outlaw; and at the peril of thy life thou crossest, after this, our threshold, or the confines of our rule!" So saying, Malachi resumed his seat, and sat pointing in the direction of the door. Niall stood for a moment or two without attempting to move. His countenance, his limbs, his tongue seemed frozen by dismay and despair. At length he clasped his hands, and lifting them along with his eyes, to heaven, turned slowly from the king, and strode from the bridal feast.

Niall felt his cloak twitched as he issued from the portal. It was the bard, who had quitted the hall before him, and remained waiting for the young man.

"Niall," said the reverend man, "wilt thou now believe in the song of Destiny? From the knowledge of the past confide for the future. Hear what the Psalter saith:—'*The Dane shall rise from the couch, and shall sit at the feast again; but in the fray that shall follow that feast, he shall fall to rise no more.*' The mountains are lofty in Moran, my son, where Slieve Dannard sits, with his feet in the sea, his head in the cloud, and his back to the lake of the lonely shieling. Turn thy steed thither! Lo, the sound of his feet! He is coming to receive thee."

One on horseback appeared, leading another steed.

"Mount," cried the bard, "and be ready."

Niall was in the saddle. "Glorvina!" was all he could utter as he wrung the old man's hand. Several others on horseback came up. They were the friends of Niall, who had come to the bridal feast.

"Come!" cried one of them.

"Not yet," interposed the bard. "There are more to join you. Hear you not their horses' feet? You cannot be too many in company. Listen!"

Another came up, and another.

"Spurs!" exclaimed the old man; and the band of friends were in motion, and away. Little they spoke,—merely what sufficed to concert a plan for future meetings; and they dropped off one by one as the destination of each called him from the common track, till three of the party were all that now remained together,—Niall and two others.

"We may progress softly now," remarked one of his companions. "We have crossed the boundaries of Meath, and half an hour will bring my lord to the place where he is to rest."

In the voice of the speaker Niall recognised that of one of the oldest of Malachi's household.

"The place where I am to rest?" echoed Niall.

"Yes, my lord," rejoined the other. "It has been prepared for you; nor must you leave it till night sets in again. You will then forward with all speed till you are met by those who expect you, and will conduct you to where you must repose again. It will take you four nights to reach your place of destination, whither I precede you."

"They who foresaw, have provided," said Niall, sighing.

"They have," responded the other.

"Had I been gifted with their reach of sight," exclaimed the young man, "I should have provided too, and Glorvina were now at my side! I would not have waited for the bridal feast! I would have borne her away the moment the holy man had blessed us."

No further word was uttered, till, suddenly striking down a path that belted a small wood, they came all at once upon a hut, at the door of which they halted.

"Alight!" said Niall's guide.

Niall alighted, but the other kept his saddle; though his companion, the third of the riders, had dismounted, unobserved by Niall till now.

"And now, my lord, good night!" said he that remained on horseback. "The door opens, and light streams from it. You see you are expected. I leave one to wait upon you while I go forward to make preparations for your further progress. So, again good night!" added he, putting spurs to his steed.

Niall entered the hut, the hearth of which was blazing. He threw himself into a seat before the fire, and looked around him. The door of an inner apartment was open. He saw that a couch was ready for him, and such a one as he could hardly expect to meet with, in such an abode.

"Come in !" said the owner of the hut,—an aged woman. " Come in !"

" What 's the matter ?" inquired Niall.

" Thy companion stands without," replied the dame, " and will not come in.   Come in !" she repeated, but with no better success.

"Come in, friend," said Niall. " Nay," added he, " there is no need of ceremony here;" and rising, went to the door, and reached his hand to the other, who hesitatingly took it. " Whoever thou art, we are companions for the time !" exclaimed Niall ; " and, if they have no other couch for thee, I will even give thee share of my own !"

Niall felt that his companion trembled as he pulled towards him the hand that he held. A seat, hastily placed, received the figure, which, but for the now supporting arms of Niall, would have fallen. Niall quickly threw open the folds of an ample cloak to give the owner air. What was his amazement to discover the form of a fe- male ! His heart stopped for a second or two at the thought that flashed across him ! Another moment decided a question almost as momentous to him as that of life or death, when, removing a hat that was slouched over the face of the stranger, the bridegroom be- held his bride ! Niall gazed upon his Glorvina half-swooning in his arms !

"Revive!—revive, my loved one !   My own !—my bride !—my wife !—my Glorvina !—revive !" rapidly ejaculated Niall. " Not so bright breaks the sun out of the storm, as thou, sweetest, my vision now ! Where, a moment ago, could I have found, in my soul, hope —comfort—anything that belongs to happiness ?—and, lo ! now it overflows, full beyond measure with content—bliss—transport ! Re- vive, my Glorvina ! Speak to me ! Thy form is in my arms ! They feel that they surround thee, yet with a doubt. Assure me 'tis thy- self! Pour on my entranced ear the music of thy rich voice ! Con- vince me that it is indeed reality !—no dream—no vision—but Glor- vina—my own Glorvina encircled within my arms—enfolded to the breast of Niall !"

Half-suspended animation became suddenly restored ; the blood rushed to the face and neck of the fair bride ; she made an effort as if she would be released from the embrace in which she sat locked, but it resisted her. She desisted. She fixed her full eyes upon her lover. Affection, and modesty, and honour, were blended in the gaze which they bent upon him ! The soul of Niall felt subdued. His arms, gradually relaxing their pressure, fell from the lovely form which they could have held prisoner for ever. He dropped on his knee at her feet ; he caught her hand, and pressed it to his lips with the fervour and deference of duteous, idolizing love.

"Niall," said Glorvina, "I am thy bride ; I have plighted my troth to thee ! Whatever be my worth,—in person, feature, heart, and mind,—I am thine !—all thine !—thine, as the hand that now is locked in thy own is a part of me ! Yet—" She faltered, and her eyes fell ; and she raised them not again till she had concluded what she meant to say. " Yet," she resumed, "I had not left my father's roof this night to follow thee, but from the dread of outrage when thou wast no longer near me. I came with thee—unknown to thee—for protection; for by thy side alone I feel security. I feel I have a right to find it!—nowhere so entitled to it! nowhere so sure to meet it!"

Glorvina ceased. Niall, still kneeling, kept gazing upon her face, watching her lids till she would raise them. Slowly she lifted them, as again and again he breathed her sweet name; till at length her eyes encountered Niall's, beaming with reverence and love. He drew her gently towards him. She did not resist. She bowed her fair head till it rested on his shoulder; her arm half encircled his neck! It was a moment of unutterable bliss,—yet but a moment! The very next was one of alarm. The hoofs of a steed were heard. Niall darted towards the door; his sword flew from its scabbard.

"Who comes?" he exclaimed, in a voice of defiance.

"A friend," replied the horseman; "but a friend who is the fore-runner of foes. You are pursued. I had only a dozen minutes the start of them,—if so much! Listen to the words of one who loves thee—the words of Cormack—of the bard. 'Tell him,' said he, 'thus saith the Psalter:—*The land must obtain her freedom ere the bride-groom his rights. What the altar shall grant must be enjoyed by means of the sword!* Niall must journey on to the lake of the lonely shieling! Thither shall gather to him the choice and true among the sons of the land. Them shall he train in arms. Them shall he bring with him to fetch his bride, long wedded ere a wife. Glorvina must return! Niall stood confounded; but Glorvina was herself. She rose from her seat. She approached the door, and listened.

"They are at hand!" she cried. "I hear their trampling. Niall, I am resolved. 'Tis vain to resist fate. Its hand it is that severs us for the present. Thy life is in peril if they find thee. I go to meet them. I will thereby stop pursuit. Farewell!"

Niall heard not. Glorvina reached her hand to the horseman, who helped her up behind him. Niall saw it not! She extended her white arms towards him; he moved not. Once more she said fare-well, and not a word did he utter in reply. She departed. Niall took no more note of her vanishing form, than the post of the door against which he was leaning.

*   *   *   *

Malachi impatiently awaited the return of those whom he had des-patched in pursuit of his daughter; whose flight, a Dane imposed upon the confidence of Malachi as a spy, had betrayed to the king. Sternly the father fixed his eyes upon his child as she entered; but with amazement encountered looks as firm, as indignant as his own. He forgot the reproaches that stood ready upon his lips. He gazed, but spake not. Glorvina broke silence.

"Why hast thou taken back by force," said the maid, "what thou gavest of free will? To whose custody behoves it thee to give thy child—her husband's, or the ravisher's? Didst thou not sanction the vow? Didst thou not say 'amen' to the blessing? Why are they then of no avail, and through thee? Did not thy command as a father cease when thou resignedst me to a husband? Why is it then resumed, and that husband alive? Did not the holy man pronounce us one? Why stand I here then in thy castle without him by my side ? Love, honour, obedience, did I swear to render him; why have I been constrained to desert him, and by the father too who listened to the oath ?"

The maiden paused. Malachi remained silent. Yet longer she awaited his reply; still he spake not.

"Thou hast welcomed in thy hall," she resumed, "whom thou shouldst have laid dead at thy threshold!" Her eyes now flashed as she spoke. "Thou hast extended the hand where thou shouldst have opposed the sword, though thou, and thine, and all allied to thee, had perished by the sword. Thou, a king, hast made friends with a robber, who, after stripping thy neighbours, advanced to plunder thee; and holdest that friendship on at the risk of dishonour to thy child,—whose modesty was outraged at thy board with impunity from thee to the offender, and with injury to him who dared resent the wrong. The dread of similar insult—if not of worse, stronger than the opposition of maiden reserve, compelled that child—unasked, unexpected, unpermitted—to fly for protection where protection had been promised, accepted, and sanctioned, but never experienced yet; and scarce had she found it when she was wrested from it, and brought back—brought back to the hall which the spoiler, whom she dreads, is as free to enter as she! And now—" She broke off. The eyes of Malachi were fixed on the ground; confusion, and care, and regret, were in his looks; a tear was trickling down his cheek! The maiden essayed to go on, but could not. Resolution wavered—it yielded more and more—it melted utterly away; she rushed towards her father, and fell, kneeling at his feet, and dissolved into tears. Malachi threw his arms around his child, lifted her to his breast, and held her there, mingling his tears with hers; both unconscious that Turgesius had entered the apartment, and stood glaring upon them.

"She is found then?" said Turgesius. The father and child started, and withdrew from one another's embrace. "'Tis well!" continued he; "and now I will speak to thee what I have long borne in my mind to tell thee. I love thy daughter."

Malachi stared at the Dane. His self-possession seemed to have utterly left him. Not so was it with Glorvina. She drew her tall and stately figure up till it towered again, as she stood collected with an expression of calm scorn upon her brow and lip. Her eyes were cast coldly down; her arms were folded upon her breast; she moved no more than a statue.

"I love thy daughter," repeated the Dane impatiently.

"Well ?" faltered forth Malachi.

"Well !" echoed the Dane. "Dost thou not comprehend my speech? Is it not enough to say I love her? Need I tell thee I would *have* what I love? Requirest thou such wasting of words? Well, then, I love thy child, and desire that thou wilt give her to me!"

Malachi mechanically moved his hand in the direction of his belt, but his sword was not there. He rose—he advanced towards Turgesius—he fixed upon him a look of fire—his lips trembling, and his cheek wavering between red and pale, his hands clenched and trembling. Turgesius in spite of himself drew back a pace.

"Dane," said the king, in the voice of rage suppressed, yet ready to break forth, "dost thou ask me for the honour of my child? Dost thou offer to bring shame upon the roof that has given thee welcome, refreshment, and repose,—the roof of a king!—a king of ancient line!—a warrior, and thy host!"

Turgesius stood momentarily abashed.

"Thy honour!" at length he cried, "the honour of thy child can stand in no peril from me—a conqueror who profits wherever he smiles!—whose favour is honour, wealth, life!" he added emphatically,—"life, without which wealth and honour are of little avail! Come!" continued he, suddenly grasping the wrists of the old king as if in cordiality. "Come! Be no wrath between us! Thy armed men are few, and those less thy subjects than my slaves! My bands hover on the borders of thy kingdom; a part of them are here with their master in the very heart of it. True thou hast said. Thou hast been my host; thou hast received me as thy friend! I would not thou shouldst turn me into thy foe; for little, as thou knowest, it would avail thee. Talk not of things that are only imaginary, but pay heed to those that are real; for it is they that concern thee most. I love thy daughter. Give her to me, and 'tis well! Refuse her to me, and it is well still—for I will have her!"

"Not with life in her!" exclaimed the frantic father, suddenly freeing himself from the hold of the Dane, rushing up to his daughter, plucking from her hair the large golden pin that held her tresses up, and pointing it to her heart. Turgesius stood transfixed. Glorvina never started nor flinched; but leaned her cheek forward upon her father's breast, looking up in his face and smiling. The king arrested his hand. The savage stood lost in amaze.

"I thank thee, O my father!" Glorvina at length exclaimed; "thou lovest indeed thy child! It is destiny, and not thou, that has afflicted her. But—listen to thy Glorvina. On one condition I consent to leave thy hall, and present me at the castle of Turgesius to await his pleasure."

"Name it, fair maiden!" cried Turgesius, his eyes sparkling up.

"Twenty fair cousins have I," resumed Glorvina, "whose beauty far surpasses mine. They shall accompany me to the hold of Turgesius; he shall compare them with me, and if he finds one among them whom he prefers, her shall he take as my ransom. I doubt not of their consent. In ten days we shall present ourselves at his gate. Agrees he to wait that time, and retire to his hold till it expires? The conqueror of a king is not unworthy a king's daughter!"

Malachi stared in amaze upon his child. Not so Turgesius. The countenance of the libertine was lighted up with triumph. "Be it so!" he exclaimed. "At the expiration of ten days I shall expect thee, attended as thou promisest; but if thou exceedest the time the half of another day, thou wilt not blame me, fair one, if I come to fetch thee?" He then approached Malachi, and taking the hand of the king without questioning whether it was given or not, shook it. Glorvina's hand next endured his obstrusive courtesy. He clasped it, raised it to his audacious lips, kissed it; and, turning exultingly away, with confident tread strode down the hall, and, summoning his attendants, departed from the castle.

*   *   *   *   *

Ere a week had elapsed, the solitudes of Moran were peopled with the youth of the adjacent country. From miles they gathered; one' spirit animating the breasts of all, one resolve,—to free the land, or perish! · Readily ·they placed themselves under the command of Niall. He had won fame even while yet a boy. Then he had no competitor in the feats of strength or dexterity; while his ever-modest, generous bearing, divested defeat of chagrin on the part of the unsuccessful. Since then, he had sojourned with the Saxon, whose' art of warfare he had thoroughly mastered, trained by the greatest captain of that nation. With avidity his young countrymen availed themselves of his instructions, and learned a mode of attack and defence superior to that they had hitherto known. They practised incessantly the advance, the retreat, the wheel, the close and open order, the line, and the square, the use of the javelin, the sword, and the shield. Hour after hour their numbers swelled. The first quarter of the moon had witnessed the commencement of their gathering; the fourth looked upon them, a host prepared, and almost equal to give battle to the Dane.

"Welcome, son of Cuthell!" exclaimed Niall, to a youth who, on a steed of foam, drew near. "Welcome! You see what a company we have here to greet you," continued he. "You see how we banquet! You like our revelry, and are come to make one among us! You are welcome, son of Cuthell! right welcome!"

The youth gazed with wonder upon the bands that, reclined upon the borders of the lake of the lonely shieling, were enjoying a moment's repose in an interval of practice; then, turning upon Niall a look full of sad import, alighted, took him kindly by the hand, and led him yet further apart from the companions of his exile.

"Niall!" began the young man, "it is a stout heart that defies the point of the spear, or the edge of the glaive; but greater is the fortitude that cowers not before the unseen weapons of misfortune. My soul is heavy with the tidings that I bring. Shall I speak them? Will Niall hear them, and not allow his manly spirit to faint?"

"Speak them!" said Niall. "Stay! Whom concern they? The evil thou wouldst avert hath nearly come to pass. My soul sickens already! To whom do the tidings relate that demand such preparation? To whom *can* they relate but to Glorvina?" The head of Niall dropped upon his breast.

"Injury," rejoined the other, "hath ever its solace with the brave, —revenge!"

"It has!" exclaimed Niall, rearing his head, and directing towards his friend a glance of fire. "Is the maid in danger, or hath she suffered wrong? the wedded maid that plighted her troth to Niall: the bride that has not pressed the bridal couch?"

"The couch that she shall press with another," resumed the young man, "is spread for her in the castle of Turgesius!" He paused, alarmed at the looks of Niall, from whose face the blood had fled.

"Go on!" said Niall, after a time, articulating with difficulty; and, with clenched hands, folding his arms tightly upon his breast. "Go on!" he repeated, observing that the young man hesitated. "Tell me the whole! It is worse, I see, than I feared; but go on! Keep nothing from me!"

"Turgesius has demanded thy bride for his mistress, and Glorvina
——" The son of Cuthell stopped short, as if what was to follow
was more than he had fortitude to give utterance to.

"Has consented?" interrogated Niall, with a look of furious distraction.

"Has consented," rejoined the young man.

Niall stood transfixed for a minute or two; then smote his forehead fiercely with his hand, groaned, and cast himself upon the
earth.

The son of Cuthell left him to himself for a time. He spake
not to him till he saw that his passion had got vent in tears; then
he accosted him.

"Revenge," said he, "stands upon its feet. It braces its arm for
the blow! Not to see thee thus did I spur my steed into foam soon
as I learned the news. Within a month did Glorvina promise to
surrender herself to the arms of the rover. Five days remain un-
expired. Up! Call thy friends around thee! inform them of the
wrong, the dishonour that awaits thee. Ask them to avenge thee.
Not a spear but will be grasped; not a foot but will be ready! You
shall march upon the castle of Malachi. You shall demand your
bride. You shall have her!"

Niall sprang from the ground; he hastened towards his bands;
his looks and pace spoke the errand of wrath and impatience. His
friends were on their feet without the summons of his tongue. They
simultaneously closed around him when he drew near, eagerness
and inquiry in their eyes, whose sparkling vouched for spirits that
were not slow to kindle.

Niall told what he came to say; no voice replied to him. Silently the warriors formed themselves into the order of march; then
turned their eyes upon Niall, waiting his command. He raised his
sword aloft, and his eyes went along with it, followed by the eyes of
all his little host. Slowly he bent the knee. Not a knee besides
but also kissed the earth.

"To Meath!" exclaimed Niall, springing up.

"To Meath!" shouted every warrior, as the whole stood erect.

Niall placed himself in the van; he moved on; they followed
him.

The last morning of the month lighted up the towers of Malachi;
but gloomy was the brow of their lord. He paced his hall with
hurried steps, every now and then casting an uneasy glance towards
the door that communicated with the interior of the castle. The
bard was seated near the exterior portal, his harp reclining on his
breast, his arms extended across his frame; his fingers spread over its
strings. Lively and loud was the chord that he struck, and bold was
the strain that he began.

"What kind of strain is that?" demanded the king, suddenly stopping, and directing towards the aged man a look of reproachful displeasure.

"The strain befits the day and the deed," replied the bard, and
went on.

"Peace!" commanded Malachi.

"Not till the feet are announced," rejoined the bard, "that bring the strife which maketh peace;" and he resumed the strain with new, redoubled fire, nor paused till the portal resounded with the summons of one impatient for admittance.

The portal opened. Pale and breathless was he that passed in.

"Thy news?" demanded Malachi.

He whom he accosted tried to find utterance, but could not. He had come in speed; his strength and breath were exhausted. He stood for a minute or two, tottering; then staggered towards a seat.

"A friend is coming," said the bard; "but he wears the face of a foe. Nor does he come alone; but prepared to demand what was forbidden;—to take what was withheld. Niall, with a host of warriors, is at thy gate. Thy bands that watch thy foe have left thy friend free to approach thee; but he comes in the form of the avenger."

Scarcely had the bard pronounced the last word when the hall was half filled with armed men; Niall at their head. Jaded, yet fierce, were his looks. He strode at once up to the king, and stood silent for a time, confronting him.

"Niall!" said the king, confounded; and paused.

"Yes," said Niall, "it is I! the son-in-law of thy own election, come to demand his rights! Where is my bride, king of Meath? Where is thy daughter? the wedded maid who, denied to the arms of her bridegroom, has consented to surrender herself to unhallowed embraces! O, Malachi! accursed was the day when thou gavest welcome to the stranger, whose summons at thy gate was the knock which he gave with the hilt of his sword,—was the blast of the horn of war! Low lies the glory of thy race! From the king of a people art thou shrunk into the minion of a robber, who, not content with making a mockery of thy crown, brings openly pollution to thy blood! Where is thy child? Does the roof of her father still shelter her head? or does she hang it in shame beneath that of Turgesius? Where is she? Reply, O king, and promptly! for desperation grasps the weapons that we bring, and which we have sworn shall receive no sheaths at our hands but the breasts of those who dishonour us!"

So spake the youth, his glaive in his hand, his frame trembling with high-wrought passion, his eye flashing, and his cheek on fire with the hectic of rage, when Glorvina entered the hall.

She did not hang her head; she bore it proudly erect. A tiara of gems encircled her brow; fair fell a robe of green from her graceful shoulders. A girdle of gold round her waist confined the folds of her under-dress, swelling luxuriantly upwards and downwards, and falling to within an inch of her ancles, each of which a palm of a moderate span might encircle. She advanced three or four paces into the apartment, right in the direction of Niall, and then stood still; still fixing her eyes steadily upon her bridegroom with an expression in which neither defiance nor deprecation, neither reproach nor fear, neither recklessness nor shame, but love—all love— was apparent. Niall scarcely breathed! An awe came over his chafed spirit as he surveyed his bride. The more he looked, the more the clouds of wrath rolled away from his soul, until not a vestige of tempest remained. He uttered tenderly the name of Glorvina. He cast down his eyes in repentant humility; he approached her, half hesitating, without raising them. He sank on his knee at her feet; Glorvina recoiled at the posture of her lover. She extended her shining arms; she caught his hands in hers; she almost raised him herself from the earth, and vanished with him from the hall.

＊　　　＊　　　＊　　　＊　　　＊

The Dane looked from the ramparts of his castle. Twenty of his chiefs—the choicest—were about him. Expectation was painted in the looks of all. Their eyes were directed towards the same quarter.

"They come!" at length exclaimed Turgesius. "The maiden hath kept her word. Yonder they issue from the wood!"

"Those are soldiers!" remarked one.

"Her attendants," rejoined Turgesius; "she comes as a royal maiden should!"

"Then she is well attended. I'll answer for a hundred spears already; and more are coming on."

"Let them!" said Turgesius. "Though they double the number, it were but twenty for each fair virgin, and the princess to go without. Turn out our bands, that we may receive them with all due courtesy!"

Turgesius and his chiefs descended; they issued from the castle-gate; the bands of the Dane were drawn up ready to give salutation to the visiters. The Irish party drew near; they halted within fifty paces of the walls, and, unfolding their ranks, presented to the eyes of the Dane, Glorvina and her kinswomen, faithful to the appointment of the royal maid. All were veiled. Turgesius and his chiefs approached them; and Glorvina, when they drew near, removed the thick gauze from her face.

"Chieftain!" she spake, "I am here to keep my word. Conduct us into thy castle. Compare me there with my kinswomen. If thou findest amongst them, her whom thou deemest more deserving thy love than I, accept her in place of me, and let me return to my father."

"Be it so!" said Turgesius, casting a significant glance around him upon his chiefs; and led the way, Glorvina and her companions following.

They passed into the hall of banquet. Turgesius led Glorvina to the head of the board, but not to place her there. He turned; and, as she looked down the chamber along with him, she saw that his chiefs had likewise entered it, and her respiration became difficult, and a chill passed over her frame.

"Chiefs!" cried Turgesius, "you see what choice of beauty the bounty of Malachi has presented to your lord; but he cares not to avail himself of it. He asks not a damsel even to remove her veil, content with the charms of the fair Glorvina. Her does he lead to the banquet which has been prepared for her within. Welcome ye the daughters of Meath! Leave them no cause to tax the sons of the Dane with want of gallantry." Turgesius took the hand of Glorvina.

"Stay!" interposed the maid: "the Irish maiden sits not at the banquet with the glaive in the girdle of the warrior; for the cup engenders ire as well as mirth, and blood may flow as well as wine. Before my kinswomen withdraw their veils, let thy chieftains deposit their weapons without the hall, and each as he returns accept the first maiden that commits herself to his courtesy, and conduct her to her seat, nor ask her to remove the guard of modesty till all are in their places."

The chiefs waited not for the reply of Turgesius. They passed quickly out of the hall; they returned unarmed. All was performed as Glorvina prescribed. She waited not for the invitation of Turgesius. Of her own accord she entered the apartment prepared for the rover and herself. Closely he followed her. The door was closed after him. He sprang towards her, and caught her to his breast. She shrieked, and disengaged herself. Again he approached her; but stopped short at the sight of a dagger, which gleamed in her hand.

"Listen!" cried Glorvina.

Her injunction was unneeded: sounds, not of revelry but of anguish, proceeded from the hall, with a noise as of heavy weights cast violently upon the floor. Turgesius grew pale. His eyes glared with alarm and inquiry.

"Listen!" again cried the maid. Sounds came from without as though the storm of battle were on. Turgesius waxed paler still. Surprise and terror seemed to have bereft him of the power of motion. He shook from head to foot.

"Behold!" exclaimed Glorvina, as the door of the apartment was burst open, and Niall presented himself, grasping a reeking brand. The robber tottered. Life was almost extinct as the youth, twisting his hand in the grey hairs of Turgesius, dragged him from the apartment to his doom.

Not a Dane survived that day.

A second bridal feast graced the hall of Malachi. Niall and Glorvina were the bridegroom and the bride. The bard sat beside them with his harp; but that harp was not silent now, nor sad. No guest unbidden came to the door of that hall. No fray turned the tide of their revelry. And when the bright Glorvina retired, with downcast eyes and crimsoned cheek, the bridegroom himself arose, and, bowing to the king, lifted the brimming cup, and, having cast his eyes around the board, drank

"To Glorvina, the Heroine of Meath!"

PHELIM O'TOOLE'S
NINE *MUSE*-INGS ON HIS NATIVE COUNTY.

Tune—" *Cruiskeen lawn.*"

Let others spend their time
In roaming foreign clime,
To furnish them with rhyme
 For books:
They 'll never find a scene
Like Wicklow's valleys green,
Wet-nurs'd, the hills between,
 With brooks—
  Brooks—brooks,—
Wet-nurs'd, the hills between,
 With brooks!

Oh! if I had a station
In that part of creation,
I'd study the first CAWS *like rooks—*
 Rooks—rooks,—
I'd study the first CAWS *like rooks!*

II.

Oh! how the Morning loves
To climb the *Sugar-Loaves,**
And purple their dwarf groves
 Of heath!
While cottage smoke below
Reflects the bloomy glow,
As up it winds, and slow,
 Its wreath—
  Wreath—wreath,—
As up it winds, and slow,
 Its wreath!

Oh! how a man does wonder him
When he 'as the big CONE-UNDER-HIM,
And ask'd to guess his home beneath—
 'Neath—'neath,—
And ask'd to guess his home beneath!

III.

And there 's the *Dargle* deep,
Where breezeless waters sleep,
Or down their windings creep
 With fear;
Lest, by their pebbly tread,
They shake some lily's head,
And cause, untimely shed,
 A tear—

Tear—tear,—
And cause, untimely shed,
 A tear!

Oh! my native Dargle,
Long may you rinse and gargle
Your rocky throat with stream so clear,
 Clear—clear—
Your rocky throat with stream so clear!

IV.

And there is *Luggalaw,*
A gem without a flaw,
With lake, and glen, and shaw,
 So still;
The new moon loves to sip
Its dew with her young lip,
Then takes a ling'ring trip
 O'er hill—
  Hill—hill,—
Then takes a ling'ring trip
 O'er hill!

Oh! hungry bards might dally
For ever in this valley,
And always get their fancy's fill—
 Fill—fill,—
And always get their fancy's fill!

V.

And there 's the " *Divil's Glin,*"
That devil ne'er was in,
Nor anything like sin
 To blight:
The Morning hurries there
To scent the myrtle air;
She 'd stop, if she might dare,
 Till night—
  Night—night,—
She 'd stop, if she might dare,
 Till night!

Oh! ye glassy streamlets,
That bore the rocks like gimlets,
There's nothing like your crystal bright,
 Bright—bright,—
There's nothing like your crystal bright!

* Two hills in the county of Wicklow, so called from their conical shape.

VI.

And there 's Ovoca's vale,
And classic Annadale,*
Where Psyche's gentle tale
　　Was told :
Where MOORE's fam'd waters meet,
And mix a draught more sweet
Than flow'd at Pindus' feet
　　Of old—
　　Old—old,—
Than flow'd at Pindus' feet
　　Of old !

Oh ! all it wants is whiskey
To make it taste more frisky ;
Then ev'ry drop would be worth gold—
　　Gold—gold,—
Then ev'ry drop would be worth gold !

VII.

And there 's the *Waterfall,*
That lulls its summer hall
To sleep with voice as small
　　As bee's :
But when the winter rills
Burst from the inward hills,
A rock-rent thunder fills
　　The breeze—
　　Breeze—breeze,—
A rock-rent thunder fills
　　The breeze !

Oh ! if the LAND *was taught her*
To FALL *as well as* WATER,
How much it would poor tenants please,
　　Please—please,—
How much it would poor tenants please !

VIII.

And if you have a mind
For sweet, sad thoughts inclined,
In *Glendalough* you 'll find
　　Them nigh :—
Kathleen and Kevin's tale
So sorrows that deep vale,
That birds all songless sail
　　Its sky—
　　Its sky—sky,—
That birds all songless sail
　　Its sky !

Oh ! cruel Saint was Kevin
To shun her eyes' blue heaven,
Then drown her in the lake hard by—
　　By—by,—
Would I have sarved her so ?—not I !

IX.

And there 's—But what 's the use
Of praising *Scalp* or *Douce ?—*
The wide world can't produce
　　Such sights :
So I will sing adieu
To Wicklow's hills so blue,
And green vales glittering through
　　Dim lights—
　　Lights—lights,—
And green vales glittering through
　　Dim lights !

Oh ! I could from December
Until the next November
MUSE *on this way both days and nights,*
　　Nights—nights,—
MUSE *on this way both days and nights !*

---

* The residence of the late Mrs. Henry Tighe, the charming authoress of
" Psyche."

SONG OF THE MONTH. No. X.

October, 1837.

I.

You may talk of St. Valentine all his month round,
   And discourse about June for some brace of days longer;
But no saint in the Kalendar ever was found,
   Throughout the whole year, either merrier or stronger
Than his reverence to whom you must now fill your glass,—
   Many years to him, whether tipsy or sober!—
And his name when you 've heard, you will let the malt pass,
   Singing " Hip, hip, hurrah! here 's success to October!"

II.

Were I Dan Maclise, his sweet saintship I 'd paint
   With his face like John Reeve's, and in each hand a rummer;
And write underneath, " Oh! good luck to the saint
   Who comes in the days between winter and summer!"
Yes, the jolly gay chap has well chosen his time,
   He is here as the leaves are beginning to yellow,
For he knows it is not when the grapes are in prime
   That their juice is most fit for a hearty gay fellow.

III.

And though, without leave from the council or pope,
   In Bentley's Miscellany I canonize him
Thus late in the day, still I 'm not without hope
   There are some who, perhaps, will not wholly despise him:
Tis for such lads as they are, and each jolly lass,
   Who can smile on them whether they 're tipsy or sober,
That new saints should be made. Come, then, fill up each glass,
   And " Hip, hip, hurrah! one cheer more for October!"

THE POISONERS OF THE SEVENTEENTH CENTURY.

BY GEORGE HOGARTH.

No. II.

OUR Scottish Solomon, King James the First, amongst other instances of wisdom, was especially addicted to favourites. During his whole reign he was governed by a succession of minions. His prime favourite, Buckingham, (the celebrated "Steeny,") was preceded in his affections by a man little less remarkable, the Earl of Somerset. Robert Carr, a young man of a respectable Scotch family, appeared at court very soon after James's accession to the English crown. At a tilting-match, where the king was present, Carr by an accident was thrown from his horse, and had his leg broken. The king, who had been struck with his handsome figure, made him be attended by his own surgeons, visited him daily, and soon became immoderately fond of his society. The young favourite did not neglect the means of advancement; before many months were over he was knighted and made a gentleman of the bedchamber, and from that time became all-powerful at court. There is a letter from Lord Thomas Howard to Sir John Harrington, written about the year 1608, which shows the feelings of the courtiers upon the subject. "Carr," says the writer, "hath all the favours, as I told you before. The king teacheth him Latin every morning, and I think some one should teach him English too; for he is a Scottish lad, and hath much need of better language. The king doth much covet his presence: the ladies, too, are not behind hand in their admiration; for, I tell you, good knight, this fellow is straight-limbed, well-favoured, and smooth-faced, with some sort of cunning and show of modesty, though, God wot, he well knoweth when to show his impudence. Your lady is virtuous, and somewhat of a good housewife; has lived in a court in her time, and I believe you may venture her forth again; but I know those would not so quietly rest, were Carr to leer on their wives, as some do perceive, yea, and like it well too they should be so noticed. If any mischance be to be wished, 'tis breaking a leg in the king's presence; for this fellow owes all his favour to that bout. I think he hath better reason to speak well of his own horse than the king's roan jennet. We are almost worn out in our endeavours to keep pace with this fellow in his duty and labour to gain favour, but in vain; where it endeth I cannot guess, but honours are talked of speedily for him." These honours speedily followed, Carr having been soon afterwards created Viscount Rochester.

Robert, Earl of Essex, the son of the unfortunate favourite of Queen Elizabeth, had married, in the year 1603, the Lady Frances Howard, eldest daughter of the Earl of Suffolk. The earl was only fourteen, and his bride a year younger. Immediately after the marriage the young earl was sent abroad on his travels, the countess remaining at court,—of which she was one of the brightest ornaments. Under a form, however, of singular loveliness, she concealed a mind of not less singular depravity. When Essex returned, after a few years' absence, he found her affections quite estranged from him. She had conceived a passion for the handsome favourite, and received her husband with contemptuous coldness; while she endeavoured, by her arts and allurements, to captivate the object of her guilty flame. To these means she added others more peculiarly characteristic of the age. There was a woman of the name of Turner, a servant or dependant of the countess's family, and with whom she appears to have associated much in her childhood and youth. This woman was of an atrocious character, and soon succeeded in making her patroness as wicked as herself. Mrs. Turner, as well as the countess, had an illicit amour; and they were in the habit of resorting to a Dr. Forman, a celebrated quack and dealer in magic, in order, by means of love-philters and conjurations, to obtain the objects of their wishes.

Whether Dr. Forman's charms prevailed, or the countess's own were sufficient, Rochester was soon caught; and a guilty *liaison* was formed between them.

Sir Thomas Overbury was then Lord Rochester's secretary. He was an able and accomplished man, in the prime of life, of a bold and aspiring disposition; and, being high in the good graces of the reigning favourite, appeared to be on the road to political distinction. To the raw youth, who had had " greatness thrust upon him " so rapidly, the services of a man of parts and experience were invaluable; and Overbury, by acting as the guide and counsellor of the favourite, directed, in a great measure, the movements of majesty itself.

Rochester made Overbury the confidant of his intrigue with Lady Essex; and the secretary, in order to pay his court to his patron, encouraged and assisted him in the prosecution of it. He even composed the *billets-doux* which the illiterate lover sent to his *inamorata*.

The countess, not content with the clandestine indulgence of her adulterous passion, now conceived the idea of getting rid of her husband. The intercourse between her and Rochester had become so shameless and open that it was loudly talked of by the world; and it appeared evident that a divorce from her husband, followed by a marriage with her lover, was the only way to prevent their separation. The countess, therefore, instituted proceedings against her husband for a divorce, on grounds to which only a shameless and abandoned woman could think of resorting. The favourite gained the king's sanction and support to this scandalous suit; and, after a course of procedure which is a disgrace to the judicature of that age, a sentence of divorce was pronounced by judges influenced and intimidated by the king himself, whose interference was grossly arbitrary and indecent. Within six weeks after the divorce, Lady Essex was married to Rochester, whom the king had previously created Earl of Somerset.

While his patron's connexion with Lady Essex was merely an adulterous intrigue, Overbury had no objection to it; but he seems to have been shocked and frightened at the idea of Lord Rochester's marrying a woman of whose atrocious character he was well aware. He, therefore, earnestly dissuaded Rochester from this marriage. One night, when they were walking together in the gallery at Whitehall, Overbury made use of the most earnest remonstrances.

" Well, my lord," he said, " if you do marry that base woman you will utterly ruin your honour and yourself. You shall never do it by my advice, or with my consent; and, if you do, you had best look to stand fast."

"My own legs are strong enough to bear me up," cried Rochester, stung with such language applied to a woman whose fascinations retained all their power over him; "but, in faith, I will be even with you for this." So saying, he flung away in a rage, and left the place. The conference was terminated with such heat that the words of the speakers were overheard by persons in an adjoining room, who soon had cause to remember them.

Rochester allowed his resentment apparently to subside, and treated his secretary as before. He even requested the king, as a mark of favour, to appoint Overbury ambassador to Russia. The king complied; and Overbury accepted the appointment with great alacrity. But this act of kindness, as it seemed to be, on the part of Somerset, was the first step to a deep and deadly revenge for the insult to the woman whom he had resolved to marry, and whose fury he had roused by informing her of what had passed.

Having allowed Overbury to accept the office which he had procured for him, Somerset now advised him to decline it. "If you serve as ambassador," he said, "I shall not be able to do you so much good as if you remain with me. If you are blamed, or even committed for refusing," he added, "never mind: I will take care that you meet with no harm." Overbury, in an evil hour, listened to this perfidious counsel, sent his resignation to the king, and was instantly sent to the Tower.

Sent to the Tower for declining to accept an office! Even so. Such was the "Divine right" of an absolute king, in England, in the seventeenth century. Without even the shadow, or the accusation, of a crime, Sir Thomas Overbury was immured in a dungeon, because he declined the honour of being sent as ambassador to Russia.

This act of tyranny was committed at the instigation of the favourite; and Overbury, in the Tower, was entirely in the hands of his enemies. Somerset, in the first place, obtained from the king the dismissal of the lieutenant of the Tower, and the appointment, in his stead, of Sir Jervis Elwes, one of Somerset's creatures. One Richard Weston, who had been shopman to an apothecary, was made underkeeper, and specially charged with the custody of Overbury. This man had been an agent of Lady Essex in her secret transactions with Dr. Forman and Mrs. Turner, and in affording opportunities for her guilty meetings with Lord Rochester at Mrs. Turner's house, and elsewhere, and was quite ready to perpetrate any deed of darkness which they might desire. Weston, thus become Overbury's keeper, confined him so closely that he was scarcely permitted to see the light of day; and debarred him from all intercourse with his family, relations, and friends.*

The associates in wickedness lost no time in commencing their operations on their victim, whom they had determined to destroy by degrees, so as to prevent suspicion. Weston, on the very day he be-

---

* This close imprisonment, it must be observed, was not the unauthorised act of a subordinate, but the result of an express order from the king: and his majesty was equally rigorous in enforcing as in issuing this order; for Winwood tells us that "Sir Robert Killigrew was committed to the Fleet *from the council-table* for having some little speech with Sir Thomas Overbury, who called to him as he passed by his window, as he came from visiting Sir Walter Raleigh."

came Overbury's keeper, administered to him a slow poison, provided by Mrs. Turner; and, from that time, some poisonous substance was mingled with every article of food or drink which was given him. "He never ate white salt," said one of the witnesses on the trials which afterwards took place, "but there was white arsenic put into it. Once he desired pig, and Mrs. Turner put into it *lapis costitus* (lunar caustic). At another time he had two partridges sent him from the court; and water and onions being the sauce, Mrs. Turner put in cantharides instead of pepper; so that there was scarce any thing that he did eat but there was some poison mixed."

Under such treatment Overbury's constitution (which seems to have been of extraordinary strength) began to give way. Relying on Rochester's promise, that his refusal to accept the embassy should bring him to no harm, he daily expected his release. After remaining in this state for three or four weeks, he wrote to Rochester, urging him to remember his promise, and received for answer that "the time would not suffer; but, as soon as possible might be, he would hasten his delivery;" a promise which he certainly intended to fulfil, though not in the sense in which it was meant to be understood. By way of "hastening his delivery," Rochester sent him a letter, containing a white powder, which he desired him to take. "It will," he said, "make you more sick; but fear not: I will make this a means for your delivery, and the recovery of your health." Unsuspicious of treachery, Overbury took the powder, which acted upon him violently, and (as he indeed expected) increased his sickness. Weston afterwards confessed that it was arsenic.

In this situation Overbury languished for two months, growing worse and worse. His suspicions being now, to some extent, awakened, he wrote to Rochester: "Sir,—I wonder you have not yet found means to effect my delivery; but I remember you said you would be even with me, and so indeed you are: but, assure yourself, my lord, if you do not release me, but suffer me thus to die, my blood will be required at your hands." Overbury appears to have remembered Rochester's threat that he would be even with him for the manner in which he had spoken of Lady Essex; but never seems to have dreamed that more was meant than to punish him by a protracted imprisonment. He therefore was satisfied with the explanations and excuses sent him by Lord Rochester, who affected, at the same time, to show the utmost anxiety for his comfort. He was daily visited by creatures of Lord Rochester and Lady Essex, who delivered him encouraging messages from Rochester, and pretended to furnish him with various comforts in the articles of food and drink, which he could not otherwise have had in the Tower. To gratify a sickly appetite he expressed a wish for tarts and jellies, which were provided by Mrs. Turner, and sent to Elwes, the lieutenant of the Tower, to be given to Overbury, by Lord Rochester and Lady Essex. These sweetmeats were not poisoned at first; but the poisoned ones were accompanied by a letter from Lady Essex to Elwes, in which she said, "I was bid to tell you that in the tarts and jellies there are *letters*, but in the wine none; and of that you may take yourself, and give your wife, but, of the other, not. Give him these tarts and jelly this night, and all shall be well." The meaning of the word, *letters*, is sufficiently evident; but the countess afterwards removed any doubt on the subject, by confessing, on her trial, that "by *letters* she meant poison." Rochester appears to have been then residing at some little distance from town; for Lady Essex was the immediate agent in these transactions, and carried on a correspondence with Rochester on the subject. In one of his letters to her he expressed his wonder "that things were not yet despatched;" on which she sent instructions to Weston to despatch Overbury quickly. Weston's answer was, that he had already given him as much as would poison twenty men. Still, however, the victim survived. He was now reduced to extremity; but the patience of his destroyers was exhausted, and they put an end to his sufferings by a dose of corrosive sublimate. He died in October 1613, having been for nearly six months in their hands. His body, carelessly wrapped in a sheet, was buried in a pit on the very day of his death, without having been seen by any of his friends, or the holding of a coroner's inquest; though, as Elwes admitted on his trial, the duty of the lieutenant of the Tower was, that if any prisoner died there, his body was to be viewed, and an inquisition taken by the coroner. These circumstances excited suspicion, and Overbury's relations were persuaded to take some steps towards the prosecution of an inquiry: but the attempt was defeated by the power and influence of the noble criminals.

The marriage between Rochester, now Earl of Somerset, and Lady Essex, took place in February 1614, four months after the close of this tragedy. It was celebrated with a pomp and splendour more befitting the nuptials of a prince than those of a subject. The king himself gave away the bride. A masque, according to the fashion of the times, was exhibited by the courtiers, and another by the gentlemen of Gray's Inn; their repugnance to this act of sycophancy having been overcome, it is said, by the persuasions of Bacon,—a man whose moral deficiencies formed a strange contrast to his almost superhuman vastness of intellect. A splendid banquet, too, was given by the City, at which the king, queen, and all the court, were present. But the public knew enough of the open profligacy of this brilliant pair to look upon them with indignation,—a feeling accompanied with abhorrence of the dark deeds already strongly suspected.

Somerset was now at the height of his greatness; but he no longer possessed the qualities which had gained him the king's favour. His appearance and manners underwent a total change. His countenance became care-worn and haggard; his dress neglected; his manners morose and gloomy. The alteration was apparent to all; and the king became weary of one who no longer ministered to his amusement. His majesty had now, too, found a new favourite,— George Villiers, afterwards the famous Duke of Buckingham, who gained James's affections by the same means as Somerset himself had done,—a handsome person, graceful manners, quick parts, and courtly obsequiousness. These two men became rivals and enemies. Somerset was universally odious from his arrogance and rapacity; and Villiers was looked upon with favour as the probable instrument of his fall. Somerset, now aware of his danger, and trembling for the discovery of his guilt when he might no longer have the king for a protector, availed himself of his remaining influence with James to obtain from him a pardon for all past offences. This he begged as a safeguard against the consequences of any errors into which he might have fallen in the high offices which he had held, and the secret and important affairs with which it had been his majesty's pleasure to intrust him. Strange to say, the king signed a document, whereby he pardoned "all manner of treasons, misprisions of treasons, murders, felonies, and outrages whatsoever, committed, or to be committed," by Somerset. But, when this deed was carried to the Lord Chancellor, he absolutely refused to affix the great seal to it, declaring it to be absolutely illegal. No importunity could prevail on him to yield; and Somerset remained without the shield with which he had endeavoured to provide himself.

The rivalry between the favourites went on increasing; but the Earl of Somerset's rank and standing still gave him the ascendancy. The king wished them reconciled; and, for this purpose, desired Villiers to wait on Somerset with a tender of his duty and attachment. But the haughty earl, though he had received a hint that the king expected this offer to be graciously received, spurned at it. "I will none of your service," was his answer, "and you shall none of my favour. I will, if I can, break your neck, and of that be confident." It was immediately after this interview that an inquiry was set on foot into the circumstances of Overbury's murder; and the supposition of a contemporary writer is not improbable, that, "had Somerset complied with Villiers, Overbury's death had still been raked up in his own ashes."

The first step that appears to have been taken in this inquiry was a private examination of Sir Jervis Elwes, the lieutenant of the Tower, by the king himself, who piqued himself on his skill in conducting judicial investigations; in which, indeed, he had acquired great experience during his turbulent reign in Scotland. Pressed by the king's questions, Elwes admitted his knowledge of Weston's intention to poison his prisoner, but denied his own participation in the crime. Weston, being apprehended and examined, admitted circumstances which involved Mrs. Turner, and the Earl and Countess of Somerset. The king issued his warrant for the commitment of the earl and countess to private custody, which was executed on the 15th October 1615. The circumstances attending this arrest, as related by a contemporary, Sir Anthony Weldon, in his "*Court and Character of King James*," are curious, and characteristic of that monarch.

"The day," says this writer, "the king went from Whitehall to Theobald's, and so to Royston, the king sent for all the judges, (his lords and servants encircling him,) where, kneeling down in the midst, he used these words:—'My lords the judges, it is lately come to my hearing that you have now in examination a business of poisoning. Lord, in what a miserable condition shall this kingdom be, (the only famous nation for hospitality in the world,) if our tables should become such a snare as none could eat without danger of life, and that Italian custom should be introduced among us! Therefore, my lords, I charge you, as you will answer it at that great and dreadful day of judgment, that you examine it strictly, without favour, affection, or partiality; and, if you shall spare any guilty of this crime, God's curse light on you and your posterity; and, if *I* spare any that are guilty, God's ucrse light on me and my posterity for ever!'"

We shall presently see how his majesty kept this solemn vow, uttered in such awful terms. "The king, with this," continues Weldon, "took his farewell for a time of London, and was accompanied with Somerset to Royston, where, no sooner he brought him, but instantly took leave, little imagining what viper lay among the herbs; nor must I forget to let you know how perfect the king was in the art of dissimulation, or, to give it his own phrase, kingcraft. The Earl of Somerset never parted from him with more seeming affection than at this time, when he knew Somerset would never see him more; and, had you seen that seeming affection,—as the author himself did,—you would rather have believed he was in his rising than setting. The earl, when he kissed his hand, the king hung about his neck, slabbering his cheeks, saying, 'For God's sake, when shall I see thee again? On my soul I shall neither eat nor sleep until you come again.' The earl told him 'On Monday,'—this being the Friday. 'For God's sake, let me!' said the king. 'Shall I? shall I?' then lolled about his neck. 'Then, for God's sake, give thy lady this kiss for me!' In the same manner at the stairs' head, at the middle of the stairs, and at the stairs' foot. The earl was not in his coach when the king used these very words in the hearing of four servants, one of whom was Somerset's great creature, and of the bed-chamber, who reported it instantly to the author of this history; 'I shall never see his face more.'"

It afterwards appeared that, when Somerset returned to London, he found that his wife had received the fatal tidings of Weston's apprehension. There was an apothecary of the name of Franklin who had been employed by the countess and Mrs. Turner to procure the poisons. At a late hour in the night Mrs. Turner was despatched to bring this man to the earl's house. When he arrived, he found the countess in a state of violent agitation. "Weston," she said, "was taken; he should likely be seized immediately, and they should all be hanged." She went into an inner room, where Franklin heard her conversing with her husband. On her return she again urged Franklin to be silent, and made him swear not to reveal any thing. "The lords," she told him, "if they examine you, will put you in the hope of a pardon upon confession: but believe them not; for, when they have got out of you what they want, we shall all be hanged." "Nay, madam," said Mrs. Turner, who was in the room, "I will not be hanged for you both." That same night, or next morning, the earl and countess, with Mrs. Turner, were arrested, and committed to prison.

Weston was first tried. At first, by the direction of Serjeant Yelverton, "an obliged servant of the house of Howard," he stood mute, and refused to plead; but, after a few days, the terror of being pressed to death overcame his resolution, and he pleaded "Not guilty." The circumstances already detailed, in which he was concerned, were fully proved. He himself confessed that he had been the medium of the correspondence carried on between Lord Rochester and Lady Essex, not only in regard to the poisoning of Overbury, but during their adulterous intercourse; and he also confessed that, after Overbury's death he had received, as a reward, one hundred and eighty pounds from the countess, by the hands of Mrs. Turner. He was convicted, and executed at Tyburn. At the time of his execution, Sir John Holles and Sir John Wentworth, friends of the Earl of Somerset, went to Tyburn, and urged Weston to deny what he had before confessed; but he refused to do so: and these gentlemen were afterwards prosecuted in the Star-Chamber for traducing the king's justice in these proceedings.

The next trial was that of Mrs. Turner. It excited intense interest, as it involved, besides the murder of Overbury, the circumstances of Lady Essex's connexion with Rochester. Some letters from the countess to Mrs. Turner, and Forman the conjuror, were read, and are preserved in the record of the proceedings. To Mrs. Turner, (whom she addresses "Sweet Turner,") after complaining of her misery in her husband's society, and giving vent to her passion for Rochester, she says, " As you have taken pains all this while for me, so now do all you can, for I was never so unhappy as now ; for I am not able to endure the miseries that are coming upon me, but I cannot be happy so long as this man liveth : therefore, *pray for me*,(!) for I have need, and I should be better if I had your company to ease my mind. Let *him* know this ill news " (her husband's insisting on cohabiting with her); if I can get this done, you shall have as much money as you can demand : this is fair-play. Your sister, FRANCES ESSEX." In a letter to Forman, she says, " Sweet father,—I must still crave your love, although I hope I have it, and shall deserve it better hereafter. Keep the lord [Rochester] still to me, for that I desire; and be careful you name me not to anybody, for we have so many spies that you must use all your wits,— and all little enough, for the world is against me, and the heavens favour me not. Only happy in your love, I hope you will do me good ; and, if I be ungrateful, let all mischief come unto me. My lord is lusty and merry, and drinketh with his men ; and all the content he gives me is to abuse me, and use me as doggedly as before. I think I shall never be happy in this world, because he hinders my good; and will ever, I think so. Remember, I beg, for God's sake, and get me out from this vile place. Your affectionate loving daughter, FRANCES ESSEX." Some of the magical implements made use of by these wretches, such as images, pictures, &c. were exhibited in court. " At the showing of these," says the account in the *State Trials*, " there was heard a crack from the scaffolds, which caused great fear, tumult, and confusion among the spectators, and throughout the hall ; every one fearing hurt, as if the devil had been present, and grown angry to have his workmanship showed by such as were not his scholars. There was also a note showed in the court made by Dr. Forman, and written on parchment, signifying what ladies loved what lords in court; but the Lord Chief Justice would not suffer it to be read openly in court." The scandal of the day was, that Coke suppressed the note because he found his own wife's name at the beginning of it.

Mrs. Turner's share in the death of Overbury was amply proved ; and Coke pronounced sentence upon her, telling her that she had been guilty of the seven deadly sins, among which he enumerated witchcraft and popery. " Upon the Wednesday following," says the account of the trial, " she was brought from the sheriff's in a coach to Newgate, and was there put into a cart ; and, *casting money often among the people as she went*, she was carried to Tyburn, where she was executed, and whither many men and women of fashion came in coaches to see her die; to whom she made a speech, desiring them not to rejoice at her fall, but to take example by her. She exhorted them to serve God, and abandon pride and all other sins; related her breeding with the Countess of Somerset, having had no other means to maintain her and her children but what came from the countess; and said further, that, when her hand was once in the business, she knew the revealing it would be her overthrow. The which, with other like speeches, and great penitency there showed, moved the spectators to great pity and grief for her."

Immediately after Mrs. Turner's execution, Sir Jervis Elwes, the lieutenant of the Tower, was brought to trial. He was convicted upon the evidence of the correspondence which he had held with the Earl and Countess of Somerset, and also with the Earl of Northampton, the countess's uncle; from which it appeared that that nobleman had been deeply implicated in Overbury's murder. By the letters read on this and some of the other trials it was shown that Northampton was not only aware of Somerset's adulterous intercourse with his niece, but had aided them in carrying it on; that he had been a principal promoter of the scandalous divorce, and the equally scandalous marriage which followed it; and that he was not only privy to the murder, but actively instrumental in the steps taken to conceal the crime. He was, however, freed by his death the preceding year from the earthly retribution which would now have overtaken him. In the course of this trial the name of Sir Thomas Monson, the chief falconer, was also implicated; it having appeared that through his recommendation Weston had been employed as Overbury's keeper, and that he was at least aware of the crime. One of the principal pieces of evidence was the voluntary confession of Franklin the apothecary, who had been employed to provide the poisons. This man, among many other things, said, " Mrs. Turner came to me from the countess, and wished me from her to get the strongest poison I could for Sir Thomas Overbury. Accordingly I bought seven, viz. aquafortis, white arsenic, mercury, powder of diamonds, lapis costitus (lunar caustic), great spiders, and cantharides: all these were given to Sir Thomas Overbury at several times." He declared also, that the lieutenant knew of these poisons: "for that appeared," he said, "by many letters which he writ to the Countess of Essex, which I saw, and thereby knew that he knew of this matter."—" For these poisons," he further said, " the countess sent me rewards. She sent many times gold by Mrs. Turner. She afterwards wrote unto me to buy more poisons. I went unto her, and told her I was weary of it; and I besought her upon my knees that she would use me no more in these matters: but she importuned me, bade me go, and enticed me with fair speeches and rewards; so she overcame me, and did bewitch me." The cause of the poisoning, he said, as the countess told him, was because Sir Thomas Overbury would pry so far into their suit (the divorce) as he would put them down. He added, that, on the marriage-day of the countess with Somerset, (which was after Overbury's death,) she sent him twenty pounds by Mrs. Turner, and he was to have been paid by the countess two hundred pounds per annum during his life. The Lord Chief Justice, when he produced Franklin's confession upon this trial, prefaced his reading of it by informing the court that this poor man, not knowing Sir Jervis should come to his trial, had come to him that morning at five o'clock, and told him that he was much troubled in his conscience, and could not rest until he had made his confession: " and it is such a one," added the Chief Justice, " as the eye of England never saw, nor the ear of Christendom ever heard." Sir Jervis, who had defended himself strenuously against the other articles of evidence, was struck dumb by this unexpected disclosure. He was found guilty, condemned, and executed, after having at the place of execution made a full confession of his guilt.

Franklin was then tried, convicted, and executed, on his own confession alone, to which, as it was entirely voluntary, he seems really to have been prompted by remorse. In passing sentence upon him, the Lord Chief Justice said, that, " knowing as much as he knew, if this had not been found out, neither the court, city, nor any particular family, had escaped the malice of this wicked cruelty."

Sir Thomas Monson was next arraigned, and strongly exhorted by the crown lawyers to confess his crime; one of them (Hyde) declaring him to be " as guilty as the guiltiest." The trial, however, was brought to a strange and abrupt conclusion. In the middle of the preliminary proceedings the culprit was suddenly carried off from the bar by a party of yeomen of his majesty's guard, and taken to the Tower, from whence he was soon afterwards liberated without further trial. This singular interference is ascribed to some mysterious expressions dropped by the Lord Chief Justice. " But the Lord Chief Justice Coke," says Sir Anthony Weldon, " in his rhetorical flourishes at Monson's arraignment, vented some expressions as if he could discover more than the death of a private person; intimating, though not plainly, that Overbury's untimely remove had in it something of retaliation, as if he had been guilty of the same crime towards Prince Henry; blessing himself with admiration at the horror of such actions. In which he flew so high a pitch that he was taken down by a court lure; Sir Thomas Monson's trial laid aside, and he soon after set at liberty; and the Lord Chief Justice's wings were clipt for it ever after." There can be no doubt that the conduct of Coke on these trials was used as a handle against him by his rival and enemy, Bacon, to deprive him of the royal favour; and, that the manner in which his language on the above and other occasions was represented (or misrepresented) to the king, was one cause, at least, of his removal from his office a few months afterwards. But this was not the only mystery connected with this matter.

All these trials took place in close succession between the 19th of October and the 4th of December 1615; but the principal criminals were not tried till May following. During this interval the earl and countess were frequently examined, and many efforts were made to bring them to confession. On the 24th of May the countess was arraigned before a commission of the peers. A graphic account of her demeanour is given in the *State Trials*. The Clerk of the Crown addressed her:

" ' Frances, Countess of Somerset, hold up thy hand !'

" She did so, and held it till Mr. Lieutenant told her she might put it down; and then he read the indictment. The Countess of Somerset, all the while the indictment was reading, stood, looking pale, trembled, and shed some tears; and at the first naming of Weston in the indictment, put her fan before her face, and there held it half covered till the indictment was read.

"*Clerk.*—'Frances, Countess of Somerset, what sayest thou? Art thou guilty of this felony and murder, or not guilty?'

"The Lady Somerset, making an obeisance to the Lord High Steward, answered, '*Guilty*,' with a low voice, but wonderful fearful."

After the proceedings consequent on this confession, she was asked in the usual form what she could say for herself why judgment of death should not be pronounced against her. Her answer was,

"I can much aggravate, but nothing extenuate, my fault. I desire mercy, and that the lords will intercede for me with the king."

"This," says the account, "she spake humbly, fearfully, and so low, that the Lord Steward could not hear it; but Mr. Attorney repeated it."

The Lord High Steward then sentenced her to the punishment of the law.

The earl's trial took place on the following day. He refused to follow his wife's example, and pleaded Not guilty. The most remarkable feature of this trial is the correspondence between Somerset and his victim. The following passages are striking.

In Overbury's first letter to Somerset, after his imprisonment, he said,

"Is this the fruit of my care and love to you? Be these the fruits of common secrets, common dangers? As a man, you cannot suffer me to lie in this misery; yet your behaviour betrays you. All I entreat of you is, that you will free me from this place, and that we may part friends. Drive me not to extremities, lest I should say something that you and I both repent. And I pray God that you may not repent the omission of this my counsel in this place whence I now write this letter."

Overbury afterwards writes,

"This comes under seal, and therefore I shall be bold. You told my brother Ledcate that my unreverend style might make you neglect me. With what face could you do this, who know you owe me for all the fortune, wit, and understanding that you have."

*   *   *   *   *

"Yet this shall not long serve your turn; for you and I, ere it be long, will come to a public trial of another nature,—I upon the rack, and you at your ease, and yet I must say nothing! When I heard (notwithstanding my misery) how you went to your woman, curled your hair, and in the mean time send me nineteen projects how I should cast about for my liberty, and give me a long account of the pains you have taken, and then go out of town! I wonder to see how much you should neglect him to whom such secrets of all kinds have passed."

*   *   *   *   *

"Well, all this vacation I have written the story between you and me; how I have lost my friends for your sake; what hazard I have run; what secrets have passed betwixt us; how, after you had won that woman by my letters, you then concealed all your after proceedings from me; and how upon this there came many breaches between us; of the vow you made to be even with me, and sending for me twice that day that I was caught in the trap, persuading me that it was a plot of mine enemies to send me beyond sea, and urging me not to accept it, assuring me to free me from any long trouble. On Tuesday I made an end of this, and on Friday sent it to a friend of mine under eight seals; and if you persist still to use me thus, assure yourself it shall be published. Whether I live or die, your shame shall never die, but ever remain to the world, to make you the most odious man living."

Overbury is aware that he has been betrayed and entrapped, and is left by his treacherous patron to languish in a dungeon. He addresses him in the bitterest and most indignant language, and threatens him with a desperate and fatal revenge. He remembers, too, the threat which had been applied to himself; knows himself to be in the power of the man who used it; feels himself to be dying by inches, of maladies which the most rigorous confinement could not have produced; and yet it never enters his mind that his unscrupulous enemy may have determined, by his death, to get rid of him and his dangerous secrets!

The evidence of Overbury's father is affecting. "After my son was committed," he said, "I heard that he was very sick. I went to the court and delivered a petition to the king, the effect whereof was, that, in respect of my son's sickness, some physicians might have access unto him. The king answered, that his own physician should go to him; and then instantly sent him word by Sir W. Button that his physician should presently go. Upon this, I only addressed myself to my Lord of Somerset, and none else, who said my son should be presently delivered, but dissuaded me from presenting any more petitions to the king; which notwithstanding, I (seeing his freedom still delayed) did deliver a petition to the king to that purpose, who said I should have present answer. And my Lord of Somerset told me he should be suddenly relieved; but with this, that neither I nor my wife must press to see him, because that might protract his delivery, nor deliver any more petitions to the king, because that might stir his enemies up against him; and then," added the poor old man, "he wrote a letter to my wife, to dissuade her from any longer stay in London."

This letter was, "Mrs. Overbury,—Your stay here in town can nothing avail your son's delivery; therefore I would advise you to retire into the country, and doubt not before your coming home you shall hear he is a free man."

Thus did this monster amuse the unhappy parents with delusive hopes till all was over; and he then wrote to the aged father the following unparalleled letter:

"Sir,—Your son's love to me got him the malice of many, and they cast those knots on his fortune that have cost him his life; so, in a kind, there is none guilty of his death but I; and you can have no more cause to commiserate the death of a son, than I of a friend. But, though he be dead, you shall find me as ready as ever I was to do all the courtesies that I possibly can to you and your wife, or your children. In the mean time I desire pardon from you and your wife for your lost son, though I esteem my loss the greater. And for his brother that is in France, I desire his return, that he may succeed his brother in my love."

Somerset defended himself stoutly. His desperate situation seems

to have sharpened his faculties. He cross-examined the witnesses
with much acuteness and presence of mind, made ingenious objections
to their testimony, and laboured to explain away the facts which
could not be denied. From eight in the morning till seven at night
he exerted himself with an energy worthy of a better cause; but in
vain. He was found guilty by the unanimous voice of his judges.
He then desired a death according to his degree; but this was denied
him, and he received the usual sentence of the law.

Thus were these great criminals brought to justice; and they received, it may be supposed, the punishment of their crimes. No:
they were pardoned by the king,—nay more, received especial marks
of royal favour! They were imprisoned in the Tower till January
1621, when the king, by an order in council, granted them the liberty
of retiring to a country-house. "Whereas his Majesty is graciously
pleased," thus ran the order, "to enlarge and set at liberty the Earl
of Somerset and his lady, now prisoners in the Tower of London, and
that nevertheless it is thought fit that both the said earl and his lady
be confined to some convenient place; it is therefore, according to his
majesty's gracious pleasure and command, ordered that the Earl of
Somerset and his lady do repair either to Greys or Cowsham, the Lord
Wallingford's houses in the county of Oxon, and remain confined to
one or other of the said houses, and within three miles' compass of
either of the same, until further order be given by his majesty." In
1624, they both obtained full pardons; the lady, on the ground that
"the process and judgment against her were not as of a principal,
but as of an accessary before the fact;" and the earl, merely on the
ground of the king's regard for his family. Nor was this all: his
majesty granted the earl an income of four thousand pounds a-year
out of his forfeited estate; and, what was still worse, in order to save
this minion from disgrace, committed a gross outrage on the order of
knighthood to which he belonged. "The king," says Camden, "ordered that the arms of the Earl of Somerset, notwithstanding his
being condemned of felony, should not be removed out of the chapel
at Windsor, and that felony should not be reckoned amongst the disgraces for those who were to be excluded from the order of St.
George; which was without precedent." Without precedent indeed!

Remembering the king's solemn vow when, kneeling in the midst
of the judges whom he had summoned into his presence, he exclaimed,
"If you shall spare any guilty of this crime, God's curse light on
you and your posterity; and, if *I* spare any that are guilty, God's
curse light on me and my posterity for ever!" how are we to account
for so flagrant a violation of it? Even had he not so earnestly called
down the curse of Heaven upon his head, he was bound by the strongest
obligations of public justice not to screen from condign punishment
criminals so atrocious. Nor can we ascribe his failure in so sacred a
duty to personal regard for Somerset. His attachment to him was
long since extinguished; a newer favourite had engrossed his capricious affection. Fear, not love, seems to have been the cause of his
forbearance.

Before Somerset's trial, mysterious circumstances were remarked,
both in his conduct and in that of the king. It is stated by several
historians that the earl, while in the Tower, loudly asserted that the
king durst not bring him to trial; and there is still extant a letter
from him to the king, written immediately after his condemnation,

in which he desires that his estate may be continued to him entire, in a style rather of expostulation and demand than of humble supplication. There is a studied obscurity in the style of this letter, as if it darkly hinted at things meant to be understood only by him to whom it was addressed; but its tone indicates that it was meant to impress the king with the dread of a secret which the writer had it in his power to reveal.

The king, on the other hand, showed the most extreme anxiety about the earl's behaviour and the event of the trial. He himself selected certain persons to examine Somerset in secret, among whom was Bacon. They had the king's instructions to work upon the earl's obstinate temper by every method of persuasion and terror: now to give him hopes of the king's compassion and mercy, and now to impress him with the certainty of conviction and punishment. Moreover, the king ordered Bacon (then Attorney-General) to put in writing every possible case which might arise at the trial out of Somerset's behaviour. Bacon accordingly drew up a paper of this sort, on which the king with his own hand made some marginal notes. Bacon having said, " All these points of mercy and favour to Somerset are to be understood with this limitation,—if he do not, by his contemptuous and insolent carriage at the bar, make himself incapable and unworthy of them," the king's remark in the margin was, " That danger is well to be foreseen, lest he upon one part commit unpardonable errors, and I on the other part seem to punish him in the spirit of revenge." Why this solicitude to prevent the "danger" of Somerset's adopting a " contemptuous and insolent carriage at the bar ?" And what were the "unpardonable errors" it might lead him to commit? No error could be so unpardonable as the crime he had already committed; and we are led, therefore, to the inference that the king wished it to be understood, that though he was ready to pardon the crime of which Somerset should be convicted, provided he conducted himself *discreetly* on his trial, yet an error *on this score* should be held as unpardonable.

Notwithstanding all these precautions and pains taken to bring Somerset to a *safe* frame of mind, he appears to have been very untractable; and the king's dread of his conduct during his trial, and anxiety to know the result, seem to have amounted to agony. His behaviour cannot be so well described as in the words of Sir Anthony Weldon.

" And now for the last act enters Somerset himself upon the stage, who, being told, as the manner is, by the lieutenant, that he must provide to go next day to his trial, did absolutely refuse it, and said they should carry him in his bed; that the king had assured him he should not come to any trial, neither durst the king to bring him to trial. This was in a high strain, and in a language not well understood by George Moore, [Sir George Moore, lieutenant in the room of Elwes,] that made Moore quiver and shake; and, however he was accounted a wise man, yet he was near at his wit's end. Yet away goes Moore to Greenwich, as late as it was, being twelve at night; bounceth at the back-stairs as if mad; to whom came Jo. Loveston, one of the grooms, out of his bed, inquiring the reason of that distemper at so late a season. Moore tells him he must speak with the king. Loverton replies, ' He is quiet,' which in the Scottish dialect is, fast asleep. Moore says, ' You must wake him.' Moore was called in (the chamber left to the king and Moore). He tells the king those passages, and desired to be directed by the king, for he was gone beyond his own reason to hear such bold and undutiful expressions from a faulty subject against a just sovereign. The king falls into a passion of tears : ' On my soul, Moore, I wot not what to do : thou art a wise man ; help me in this great strait, and thou shalt find thou dost it for a thankful master ;' with other sad expressions. Moore leaves the king in that passion, but assures him he will prove the utmost of his wit to serve his majesty. Sir George Moore returns to Somerset about three o'clock next morning of that day he was to come to trial, enters Somerset's chamber, tells him he had been with the king, found him a most affectionate master unto him, and full of grace in his intentions towards him. ' But,' said he, ' to satisfy justice you must appear, although you return instantly again without any further procedure ; only you shall know your enemies and their malice, though they shall have no power over you.' With this trick of wit he allayed his fury, and got him quietly, about eight in the morning, to the Hall ; yet feared his former bold language might revert again, and, being brought by this trick into the toil, might have more enraged him to fly out into some strange discovery, that he had two servants placed on each side of him, with a cloak on their arms, giving them a peremptory order that if Somerset did any way fly out on the king, they should instantly hoodwink him with that cloak, take him violently from the bar, and carry him away ; for which he would secure them from any danger, and they should not want a bountiful reward. But the earl, finding himself overreached, recollected a better temper, and went on calmly in his trial, where he held the company until seven at night. But who had . seen the king's restless motion all that day, sending to every boat he saw landing at the bridge, and cursing all that came without tidings, would have easily judged all was not right, and that there had been some grounds for his fear of Somerset's boldness. But at last one bringing him word he was condemned, and the passages, all was quiet."

The reader will remember that the abrupt termination of the proceedings against Sir Thomas Monson, who was carried off from the bar by a party of yeomen of the guard, was caused by the Lord Chief Justice's having made some indiscreet allusion to suspicions regarding the death of Prince Henry, the king's eldest son, which had taken place in 1612, about four years before the time of these trials.

This young prince at a very early age displayed talents and virtues which endeared him to the nation. The accounts of his short life are pleasing and interesting. He was thus described when he was twelve years old, in a letter from the French ambassador. " None of his pleasures savour in the least of a child. He is a particular lover of horses, and what belongs to them ; but is not fond of hunting ; and, when he does engage in it, it is rather for the pleasure of galloping than for any which the dogs give him. He is fond of playing at tennis, and at another Scotch diversion very like mall ;* but always with persons older than himself, as if he despised those of his own age. He studies two hours in the day, and employs the rest of his time in tossing the pike, or leaping, or shooting with the bow, or throwing the bar, or vaulting, or some other exercise of that kind ; and he is never idle. He is very kind to his dependents, supports their inte-

* The national, and still favourite game of *golf*.

rests against all persons whatsoever, and urges all that he undertakes for them or others with such zeal as ensures it success; for, besides his exerting his whole strength to compass what he desires, he is already feared by those who have the management of affairs, and especially by the Earl of Salisbury, who appears to be greatly apprehensive of the prince's ascendency; as the prince, on the other hand, shows little esteem for his lordship." This high-spirited and magnanimous boy could not fail to be aware of the faults and vices of his father's character. He entertained great admiration for Sir Walter Raleigh; was often heard to exclaim, "No king but my father would keep such a bird in a cage;" and his aversion to the Earl of Salisbury was understood to have arisen from that nobleman's share in Raleigh's ruin.* His strong sense of religion rendered his father's habit of profane swearing repulsive to him. "Once," we are told by Coke, "when the prince was hunting the stag, it chanced the stag, being spent, crossed the road where a butcher and his dog were travelling. The dog killed the stag, which was so great that the butcher could not carry him off. When the huntsman and the company came up, they fell at odds with the butcher, and endeavoured to incense the prince against him; to whom the prince soberly replied, 'What! if the butcher's dog killed the stag, how could the butcher help it?' They replied, if his father had been served so, he would have sworn as no man could have endured it. 'Away!' replied the prince, 'all the pleasure in the world is not worth an oath.'"

A young prince, who, at twelve years old, was "feared by those who had the management of affairs," must, when he grew up, have been a formidable object to a worthless minion like Carr. He disliked this man from the first; and his aversion grew into a rooted hatred. When Carr was made Viscount Rochester, Henry, then about fourteen, as we are told by Osborn, "contemned so far his father's election of Rochester, that he was reported either to have struck him on the back with his racket, or very hardly forborne it." The prince continued to express on all occasions an abhorrence of favourites, and an utter contempt of Carr; and made no secret of his resolution to humble both him and the family into which he was allied if ever he came to the throne.

Carr, then, must necessarily have feared and hated the prince; and it is hardly to be supposed that such feelings would remain passive in a mind like his. Henry did not enjoy his father's favour. The king's "genius was rebuked" in the presence of a son so much his superior in every moral and intellectual quality; and he was jealous of the esteem and admiration in which the youth was held by the nation. "The vivacity, spirit, and activity of the prince," says Dr. Birch, "soon gave umbrage to his father's court, which grew extremely jealous of him."—"The king," says Osborn, "though he would not deny any thing the prince plainly desired, yet it appeared

---

* The king afterwards stripped Raleigh of his estate for the purpose of bestowing it upon his favourite, Carr. "When the Lady Raleigh and her children on their knees implored the king's compassion, they could get no other answer from him but that he ' mun ha the land,' he ' mun ha it for Carr!' But let it be remembered, too, that Prince Henry, who had all the amiable qualities his father wanted, never left soliciting him till he had obtained the manor of Sherborne, with an intention to restore it to Raleigh, its just owner; though by his untimely death this good intention did not take effect."—*Life of Raleigh*.

rather the result of fear and outward compliance than love or natural affection; being harder drawn to confer an honour or pardon, in cases of desert, upon a retainer of the prince, than a stranger." The prince himself, in a letter written within a few weeks of his death, excused himself from applying on behalf of a friend, for some piece of court favour, "because, as matters now go here, I will deal in no businesses of importance for some respects." At this time Carr was in the height of his power; and this position of the prince at his father's court must be ascribed in no small degree to the influence of the favourite.

Prince Henry died on the 6th of November 1612, (at the age of eighteen,) of an illness under which he had laboured for two or three weeks. The symptoms (as detailed by Dr. Birch in his Life of the prince) were of the most violent kind; dreadful affections of the stomach and bowels, excessive thirst, burning heat, blackness of the tongue, convulsions, and delirium. The physicians "could not tell what to make of the distemper," were confounded by "the strangeness of the disease," and differed in their opinions as to its treatment. The day after the prince's death his body was opened by order of the king; and the report of the physicians who examined it does not indicate the operation of poison. They say, in particular, "his stomach was without any manner of fault or imperfection."

The grief of the nation pervaded all ranks, and almost all parties. The king himself, however, manifested the utmost insensibility. Only three days after the prince's death, Carr (then Lord Rochester) wrote, by the king's orders, to the English ambassador at Paris, directing him to resume the marriage treaty, which had been begun for Prince Henry, in the name of his brother Charles. After a very short interval, all persons were prohibited from appearing in mourning before the king; and orders were given that the preparations for the Christmas festivities should proceed without interruption. The Earl of Dorset, in a letter written at this time to the English ambassador in France, uses these expressions: "That our rising sun is set ere scarcely he had shone, and that with him all our glory lies buried, you know and do lament as well as we; *and better than some do, and more truly*, or else you are not a man, and sensible of this kingdom's loss."

Suspicions that the young prince had come foully by his death became prevalent immediately after that event. They were by no means of that vague and unmeaning kind which the untimely end of an illustrious person is apt to occasion among the vulgar. " The queen," says Dr. Welwood, " to her dying day could never be dissuaded from the opinion that her beloved son had foul play done him." Bishop Burnet, in his History of his own time, says, that Charles the First declared that the prince, his brother, had been poisoned by the means of the Viscount Rochester, afterwards Earl of Somerset. And contemporary writers afford innumerable proofs of this opinion having been entertained by persons engaged in public affairs, and conversant with the transactions of the time.

The opinions of modern writers, as may be supposed, are divided on a question so dark and mysterious. "Violent reports were propagated," says Hume, "as if Henry had been carried off by poison; but the physicians, on opening his body, found no symptoms to confirm such an opinion. The bold and criminal malignity of men's tongues and pens spared not even the king on the occasion; but that prince's character seems rather to have failed in the extreme of facility and humanity, than in that of cruelty and violence." Hume's facts, it is notorious, often assume the colouring of his political feelings; of which a pretty strong instance occurs in this very case of Sir Thomas Overbury, whose imprisonment in the Tower, says this historian, "James intended as *a slight punishment for his disobedience*" in refusing to go as ambassador to Russia. James ordered Overbury to be most rigorously confined, and even sent a gentleman to the Tower for having simply exchanged a word with the prisoner. Nay, more: James knew all along that Overbury was languishing in his dungeon; having received, and disregarded, repeated petitions from his afflicted father for his release. And this, according to Hume, was intended by James as a slight punishment for what was, in truth, no offence.

In the preface, by Lord Holland, to Fox's History of the early part of the reign of James the Second, we find the opinion of that illustrious statesman upon the subject. Lord Holland, speaking of Mr. Fox's historical researches, and his correspondence with the Earl of Lauderdale and others of his friends respecting them, says: " Even while his undertaking was yet fresh, in the course of an inquiry into some matters relating to the trial of Somerset, in King James the First's reign, he says to his correspondent, ' But what is all this, you will say, to my history? Certainly nothing; but one historical inquiry leads to another: and I recollect that the impression upon my mind was, that there was more reason than is generally allowed for suspecting that Prince Henry was poisoned by Somerset, and that the king knew of it after the fact. This is not, to be sure, to my present purpose; but I have thought of prefixing to my work, if ever it should be finished, a disquisition upon Hume's history of the Stuarts; and in no part of it would his partiality appear stronger than in James the First.' "

For ourselves, we shall not pretend to penetrate a mystery which is now, perhaps, for ever inscrutable. But the events which we have related form an impressive and instructive page of the great book of human life.

The guilty pair, who were the chief actors in these tragic scenes, though they escaped the death which they had merited, did not escape, even in life, the retribution of their crimes. They suffered " a living death." For many years they resided together, in the house allotted to them as their place of banishment, detested by the world and by each other. The unceasing torments of an evil conscience were embittered by mutual hatred so rancorous and implacable, that they passed year after year in the same dwelling without the interchange of a single word. Their doom may be likened to that so fearfully described in the tale of the Caliph Vathek. It seemed as if their punishment was begun ere yet they had tasted of death. The everlasting fire was already burning in their hearts; hope, the last and most precious of Heaven's blessings, had forsaken them for ever; and they read in each other's eyes nothing but rage, aversion, and despair. So they lived, in seclusion and solitude, till their existence was forgotten; and, of those who have commemorated their crimes, hardly any one has cared to record the periods when, one after the other, they dropped into eternity. 2 c 2

AN EXCELLENT OFFER.

BY MARMADUKE BLAKE.

" It 's an excellent offer—so plain and handsome !"

The above contradictory description was applied by Mrs. Gibbs to the contents of a letter which a few hours previously, had been received by her husband, Mr. John Gibbs, of Adelaide Crescent, Camberwell.

Mr. and Mrs. Gibbs were rather elderly : a stranger would have taken them to be brother and sister ; for, having lived together during the greater part of a long life, not only had their habits and modes of thought become congenial, but even the expression of their respective features had assumed a strong resemblance.

On the evening in which it is our purpose to introduce the reader to their acquaintance, Mr. and Mrs. Gibbs occupied the precise position which they had at the same hour occupied evening after evening for the preceding forty years ; that is, Mrs. Gibbs was by the side of the table with her " work," and Mr. Gibbs sate with his feet upon the fender, an open book by his side, on which his spectacles were deposited, while his body was assuming a backward inclination, which was occasionally checked by a sudden bobbing forward of the head, accompanied by a pulmonary effort of a most profound description.

" A little more, and I should have been asleep," said Mr. Gibbs ; and, as the remark had escaped from the lips of that gentleman once every evening during nearly half a century, it did not seem to Mrs. Gibbs to call for any particular reply.

" I was speaking, my dear," said she, " of Mr. Paine's offer."

" And I," responded Mr. Gibbs, " was thinking upon the very same subject at the moment when you spoke ; I was thinking that we must keep our eyes open to the advantages which are now presented."

Mr. Gibbs took a glass of wine, resumed his horizontal position, and seemed disposed to nod.

" Well, my dear,—now do rouse up,—if we are to accept Mr. Paine as a son-in-law, what will young Langton say to us ?"

" I hope," said Mr. Gibbs, rubbing his eyes and yawning most uncomfortably,—" I hope Mr. Langton doesn't dream——"

" Why, my dear," interrupted the lady, " you must allow, we *have* given him a little encouragement."

" Not at all—not at all," was the reply ; " nothing could be further from my intention : if indeed he had such an idea as you seem to intimate, I 'm sure it has never been encouraged by me ; he may have fancied otherwise, but anything of the sort on my part was mere manner, I assure you."

Mrs. Gibbs seemed satisfied, and the conversation on Mr. Paine's offer was resumed.

" He is so very respectable," said Mr. Gibbs, " and at a very suitable age for Caroline ; two giddy people together would never do any good : I don't think much good ever comes of early marriages."

" We were neither of us of age when *we* married," interposed Mrs. Gibbs : " I hope you consider that case to have been an exception."

Mr. Gibbs was still dozy, and he nodded his head just at the right moment. The lady continued.

"If I were asked to *choose* a husband for my daughter, I shouldn't hesitate to give her Paine."

"Nor I either," replied Gibbs, who misunderstood his wife; "it would be entirely for her own good."

"He is a very pleasant man," ruminated Mrs. Gibbs.

"He has a thorough knowledge of the world, a great deal of philosophy, and——"

"A nice house in the Regent's Park."

We need not further pursue the interesting dialogue; suffice it to say that it terminated in a decision favourable to Mr. Paine, and a comfortable belief that if Mr. Charles Langton should go out of his mind, it would be entirely his own fault, as any encouragement which he might fancy to have been given, was only to be attributed to Mr. Gibbs's "manner."

Mr. and Mrs. Gibbs were "early people;" the clock struck ten, the housemaid and cook were heard ascending to their places of repose. Mrs. Gibbs followed, while her husband commenced, according to nightly custom, a perambulation in the dark, in order to see that everything was right; and having descended into the kitchen, and peeped into the cellar, and put his foot into a dish of water and red wafers set as a black-beetle trap, and knocked his forehead against a half-open door, he felt, as he said, satisfied in his mind, and could go to sleep in the most comfortable manner.

"What a beautiful night!" said the gentleman as he placed the extinguisher on his candle and the bright light of the moon entered his dressing-room. He manifested, however, no romantic desire to sit and watch her silent progress, so in a short time her beams were falling on the unconscious features of Mr. and Mrs. Gibbs.

The night was beautiful indeed,—so beautiful that we can only hope to bring it to the mind's eye of our matter-of-fact friends by stating that it was one of those evenings when the moon attains a brilliancy so extraordinary, that "you may see to pick up a pin;" having arrived at which point, we have been accustomed to believe lunar brightness can no further go.

The number of moonlight nights which shed their influence upon us during a passing year is of very small amount; and yet, when we suffer memory to look through "the waves of time," how much of moonlight is brought upon the mind. Day after day passes away, and although they give birth to new events and unlooked-for changes, yet they leave no more impression behind than we should experience after a survey of the fragmental patterns of a kaleidoscope,—each movement produces a variation, but there is nevertheless a general sameness of character which is altogether destructive of a permanent effect;—but in the lives of all men there have been moonlight "passages" which stand alone in their recollection, and which come upon them in after years, remembered as the periods when the heart, escaping from the stifling struggles of daily life, assumed a freer action,— moments in which they made resolutions which perhaps were broken, but which nevertheless it is some credit to them only to have made.

By daylight we are apt to consider mankind in the mass; by moonlight we invariably individualize,—we feel more deeply how mysteriously we stand, lonely in the midst of countless multitudes, and we draw more closely to our hearts those who have sought to lighten

> "The heavy and the weary weight
> Of all this unintelligible world."

Reader, when you take a retrospect of life, we will answer for it that your fancy turns to some moonlight game with happy schoolfellows beneath a row of ancient elms, which threw their long cold shadows upon the greensward by the side of a village church. Let your fancy wander on, there is moonlight still: you roam, perchance, near the same church, and a gentle maiden is by your side; but you do not choose the elm-walk now, because the "school-boys" divert themselves thereon, and you prefer a semi-solitary stroll. Onward still: you are mixing in the bustle and heat of life; and there are moonlight hours when the thought of your vain career comes upon your mind, and you form in your heart new resolves, and pant with higher aspirations. Onward once more: and the scene is drawing to a close, the mist is on your sight, and memory wanders o'er a field of graves; and now how often do you lift your aching eyes to the silent and trembling stars, and suffer fancies to dwell upon your mind, that perchance from those orbs the spirits of the dead may be permitted to look down!

We only intended to venture a few words upon this subject, but we are afraid that we have written a "discourse."

There is a range of hill running from Westerham to Sevenoaks, the neighbourhood of which abounds with quiet scenery of surpassing beauty; and during the period in which Mr. and Mrs. Gibbs's dialogue took place, the young lady to whom it referred was indulging in a pleasant stroll in the garden of a cottage which stood in one of the little valleys at the foot of this range, and in which dwelt the parents of the young gentleman who was the companion of her walk, and who was the identical person whom Mr. Gibbs so strenuously stated to have received no "encouragement" whatever.

They wandered round a lawn encircled by a shrubbery path, which was glittering in the silver light: they were very silent, but they felt all that youth can feel, although an occasional exclamation of "How beautiful this is!" was all that mutually escaped their lips. A midsummer night and a garden-path are capable of imparting much power to the most delicate young ladies; and instances are by no means rare of some who would have shrunk from the prospect of an excursion extending to a mile from home, who will nevertheless stroll unrepiningly in company with a cousin or a friend two or three hundred times round a gravel-walk!

There was a happy family within doors,—brothers and sisters,— the light from the cottage-windows shining on the shrubs in front, and the merry laugh sounding from within: occasionally they were interrupted in their stroll, and messages were sent to know "whether they were coming in,—and that the grass was wet, and the night-air dangerous, and Miss Gibbs very delicate," &c. &c. &c.; to which messages replies were given that "they were *not* walking on the grass, and that the air was exceedingly mild, and that Miss Gibbs had a headache, and found herself better out of doors;" and then they were told that it was past ten o'clock,—and they promised to come in directly : and Mr. Langton only asked Caroline to take one turn more, and during that time he took Miss Gibbs's arm ; and then he must walk once more round, and " this should positively be the last ;" and so they took another turn, and this time his arm gently encircled her waist ; and as they came in, there was a little hesitation while they were scraping their feet, and Caroline upon entering looked a little confused, and Mr. Langton seemed remarkably buoyant, and he rattled on for an hour or two, till his mother declared that there was " no getting him to bed ;" and after Caroline and his mother and sisters had retired, he entered into an elaborate speech to his father concerning his prospects in life, which was only discontinued upon the discovery that his respectable parent had been asleep for upwards of an hour.

The reader who compares the stern reality of our opening scene with the poetic character of that by which it was succeeded, will have little difficulty in anticipating the result : the first disclosed the decision upon a plan which it had long been the chief object of a worldly man to effect ; the latter was the idle dream of a boy and girl who knew nothing of the world, and still less of themselves.

On the morning subsequent to his moonlight walk, cool reflection had operated on the mind of Mr. Langton so far as to reduce the ardour with which he desired to communicate to his father his design of immediately entering into some active pursuit, with the view of sharing with an amiable partner an income which he was quite sure he could not fail to realize, but which as yet existed only in his own imagination. Nevertheless, although the daylight had thus produced its usual effect, and had given a matter-of-fact turn to his thoughts, he felt that he really did love Caroline, although it might be prudent to wait some few years before he made a formal declaration to that effect. Like most other young persons, he imagined that it was the easiest thing in the world to live on with unshaken affection, however distant might be the realization of his hopes : he was little aware of the numberless and apparently trivial influences which, during a period of prolonged separation or suspense, tend effectually to give a new colour to the views of those who have thus drawn upon futurity.

As he seated himself at the breakfast-table, he received from Caroline, in return for one of those

" Looks and signs
We see and feel, but none defines,"

a very kind glance, which assured him that he was the object of kind thoughts : he fancied that Fate had already twined the wreath that was to bring their happy fortune within one bright round,—that their love would be sanctified by the very difficulties with which he might have to contend before he could make her his wife,—that, with her as the reward of his exertions, he could not fail to succeed, and that to her influence alone he should proudly attribute whatever honours he might ultimately gain :—that look across the breakfast-table, unobserved by others, was the source from whence his imagination found no difficulty in tracing the Nile-like current of his future career !

We want to compress into one paper, events which were brought about by the course of several years ; we must therefore hurry the reader over a few facts which perhaps he will have anticipated already.

Shortly after the consultation between Mr. and Mrs. Gibbs, Caroline received a letter from them, written in a tone of more than ordinary affection, interweaved with some little sermon-like passages touching the implicit obedience which children should at all times bestow upon their parents, and enforcing the same by the observation that those who had lived in the world nearly sixty years must of course in that time have acquired a nice sensibility of the manner in which to deal with the affections of the young. It concluded by requiring her immediate return to town; it gave their best love to Mr. and Mrs. Langton, and their compliments to Mr. Charles.

On Caroline's return the arrangements respecting Mr. Paine were fully detailed. Caroline cried, and Mrs. Gibbs said it was very natural she should dislike to leave her mother,—that she would consult her wishes in every way,—that she lived only in the happiness of her child, but that she must *insist* upon her acceptance of Mr. Paine : and then Caroline's friends were entreated to come and see her as often as possible, and they were particularly requested by Mrs. Gibbs not to put any idle fancies into her head which might prejudice her against the match; and one young lady of four-and-thirty, who had once possessed some charms, and who had flirted away all her chances, was desired to come and "cheer her up" whenever she could find time : the said young lady having for the last five years been in the habit of expressing a contempt for *very* young men, and an extreme desire to become the wife of some "nice old gentleman who kept his carriage."

After the detail of these circumstances, it will not be thought surprising that at a period of seven years from the opening of our story Caroline had long been the wife of Mr. Paine; and, having become the mother of three children, had made every effort, although perhaps she had not succeeded, to forget the moonlight walk in which she had been "*so* happy" with Charles Langton.

Mr. Paine was a merchant. His father, who had been a warehouseman in Friday-street, had, as is the custom of warehousemen, amassed a considerable fortune ; and, although he had not been known to think very highly of himself while he was in indifferent circumstances, his own estimate of his value as a man, gradually grew with the strength of his pocket. His friends considered this a very proper view, and towards the end of his life he became much respected. Some time before his death he had purchased for his son a partnership in a house of "high standing," in which that gentleman had gradually risen from junior partner until he became the head of the firm. He inherited along with his father's wealth a great similarity of disposition ; and his ideas of the importance of the "house," and consequently of his own importance as the head of the firm, had become the all-absorbing feature of his mind. Now this, although it told with admirable effect in Broad-street, was scarcely calculated to astonish his West-end connexions, nor was it likely to give that freedom of manner which forms the peculiar charm of domestic life.

Mr. Paine, on account of his mercantile standing, had been elected to a directorship of a prosperous insurance company; and as he was accustomed to look in daily at the office of the establishment, where he found himself surrounded by bowing clerks, and porters in bright waistcoats, who never heard a whisper from his voice without raising their hands to their hats, he became very deeply impressed with the idea that he really was an extraordinary person. No doubt he was so; but it was the misfortune of Mr. Paine that he never contemplated that "unbending of the bow" which is rather necessary to make home happy, and consequently when he returned from town he was cold and formal, in order to produce an impression on his servants, similar to that which gratified him in the City; and when he took his seat at the dinner-table there was hardly any variation from the manner which characterised him as chairman at the weekly meetings of the company, each remark being delivered in a style which sounded very much like a Resolution of " the Board."

Men choose their acquaintances as they choose their wives, and are very apt to select those whose qualities differ most widely from their own. Acting upon this principle, Mr. Paine had become intimate with a person to whom he condescended in a more than ordinary degree.

This person was Mr. Hartley Fraser, an unmarried man, at about the middle, or, as it is very pleasantly termed, the prime of life. He was of good family and small income; which latter circumstance he always assigned as the cause of his determination to live single, although it was attributed by some to a habit of ease and self-indulgence which he was now not disposed to correct. He knew and liked everybody in the world; and his philanthropy was not thrown away, for he was universally sought after, and in the making up of parties was always spoken of as a very desirable man. He humoured the foibles and flattered the caprices of his friends; the ladies liked him because he was " so useful," and the men spoke well of him because he never became a rival. He had always avowed his intention of remaining unwived, since, to use his own words, he found that he could drag on quietly enough with six or seven hundred a year as a bachelor, and he felt no inclination to go back in the world by becoming the proprietor of an expensive wife and a needy " establishment."

His manner, which, as we have already stated, was quite antithetical to Mr. Paine's, was as easy and kind as possible; and his stiff friend was never able to unravel the means by which, in the absence of a cast-iron stateliness, he invariably seemed to produce a feeling of deference in the minds of those with whom he came in contact. Though professing poverty, he never borrowed. His appearance was extremely good; while in conversation he rarely spoke of himself, and, if ever he did so, it was with an air of so little reserve, that his hearer could not help entertaining an idea that he was the most candid person in the world.

Mr. Paine felt quite proud of his popular acquaintance; and, as pride was the only attribute through which it was possible to gratify or wound that gentleman's feelings, of course he entertained as much regard for him as he could under any circumstances feel for any one. Fraser was therefore a frequent visitor at his house, which, despite of the governor's formality, was pleasant enough, for Caroline was always kind and cheerful, and " the children" were never visible.

Mr. Fraser soon became aware that his visits were rendered more frequent by the attraction of Caroline's society, while she could not sometimes help acknowledging to herself that her husband's selfish coldness was not placed in the most favourable light by a contrast with his agreeable friend. This was a dangerous discovery; but just at the period when it might have led to serious inroads on her happiness, an accident occurred which gave a new turn to her thoughts, and which tended to a catastrophe as unforeseen as it was fatal.

At an early hour in the afternoon a servant who had charge of the children would frequently request permission to take the eldest, a fine boy six years of age, for a short walk. Her consideration for the health and mental improvement of her young charge invariably induced her to wend her way to Oxford-street, where, by a strange coincidence, she invariably met a young gentleman in a flour-sprinkled jacket who emerged from a neighbouring baker's, and with whom, though they only met on these occasions, it afterwards appeared she was "keeping company." During the period of their conversation the child was told to "play about;" and, with that inherent love of liberty which dwells in the human mind, the boy made a point of availing himself of this permission by forthwith getting into all those spots which at other times he had been taught to shun. Occasionally a foot would become fixed between the iron gratings of an area in such a manner that he was unable to extract it; and then he would immediately roar as though he had been placed there by some tyrannical nursery-maid, and a crowd would collect to sympathise with his pangs, and at length to witness his extrication. At other times the gutter would seem to offer irresistible attraction; and in all cases the attentive guardian to whom he was entrusted consented not to tell her "missus" of his delinquencies if he would promise not to say a word about the young man from the baker's. This system was carried on till it had nearly terminated in a serious event. The child, having on one occasion stepped off the footway, was thrown down in attempting to escape from a carriage that was furiously approaching: in another instant the horses would have trampled upon him, had not a young man who observed his frightful situation rushed, heedless of danger, to the horses' heads, and, with the aid of the coachman, arrested their progress. The stranger learned from the boy his name and residence, conveyed him home, and, after giving an account of the accident, left a card with the footman to whom he delivered the child. About an hour afterwards the guardian angel returned in great alarm, when she was immediately favoured with unlimited leave of absence, and thereby enabled, literally as well as metaphorically, to "keep company" with her interesting friend.

On the following morning, a paragraph, which ran as follows, decorated the columns of the Morning Post.

" Yesterday, as Lady Crushmore's carriage was going down Oxford-street, it nearly passed over a child who had fallen before the horses: the boy was, however, rescued by a person who happened to witness his perilous situation. We merely notice the circumstance in order that we may have the satisfaction of recording a noble instance of humanity on the part of Lady Crushmore, who would not suffer the coachman to drive on until he had inquired whether the child was hurt."

It would be impossible to describe Caroline's feelings when she received the account of the accident: she took the card which had been left by the stranger, but in the excitement of the moment she did not heed the name, and, throwing it on one side, she pressed the terrified boy to her breast with hysteric minglings of tears and laughter. That afternoon Mr. Paine returned in company with Fraser; and, as he entered, he received an account of what had happened. He was by no means moved, but went into the matter, and asked questions in a most cool and dignified manner.

"Really," he said, "I think this is a case we ought not to look over; and therefore I must move, that is, I would suggest, that the boy should receive a very severe whipping."

The motion, not being seconded, fell to the ground, and Mr. Paine continued,

"Have you learned the name of the person by whom he was accompanied home?"

Caroline recollected the card, and, without looking at it, handed it to her husband.

"Langton—Charles Langton, Raymond Buildings," ruminated Mr. Paine; "I don't know the name."

"Good heavens!" exclaimed Caroline; "Charles Langton?"

"Yes, my dear; is there anything so extraordinary in the name—is he any connexion of your family?"

"Yes—no—that is, my father had a very old friend of the name of Langton, who lived near Sevenoaks."

"Ah," said the amiable Paine, who prided himself on the sarcastic, "Raymond Buildings are within a stone's throw of Sevenoaks."

Mr. Paine had not observed any great peculiarity in Caroline's manner; but he was excessively fond of giving utterance to an occasional sneer, which was the highest effort of his conversational power. But with Fraser, who had been a silent spectator of the scene, the emotion which Caroline betrayed when the card was read did not pass unnoticed or unremembered.

Mr. Paine having on the subsequent day made strict inquiries as to the respectability of the man who had saved his child, condescended to forward a note of thanks and an invitation to dine. This was immediately accepted, for Langton was not ignorant that the mother of the boy was his early friend; and, although circumstances were so sadly altered, he could not resist an opportunity of renewing the acquaintance.

The dinner to which he thus had the honour of being invited, went off rather flatly. There was a large party, principally composed of that class of persons who get their heads muddled in wool and tallow speculations during the day, and who attempt to become particularly brilliant and exclusive in the evening, when unfortunately it generally happens that, despite their best exertions,

"Let them dress, let them talk, let them act as they will,
The scent of the city will hang round them still."

Fraser, to whom Mr. Paine always looked as the enlivener of his otherwise cold dinners, was on this occasion unusually quiet, Langton and Caroline were mutually embarrassed, and Mr. Paine's platitudes grew more and more tiresome, till at length, when the dessert made its appearance, he took an opportunity of effecting an elaborate speech, the object of which was to impress upon his friends the sensation which would have been created if the eldest child and only son of Mr. Paine, of the firm of Paine, Grubb, and Jones, had been the victim of any serious accident, and the gratitude which in consequence they ought to entertain to the person by whom such an event had been arrested.

"A shock so calamitous," he said, "has been averted by the intrepid conduct of Mr. Langton; and I must therefore beg that he will accept the cordial thanks of this meeting,—that is, of myself and friends,—for the courage and presence of mind which he so seasonably displayed."

This speech exhibited such a style of pompous foolery, that during its delivery Fraser was tempted to glance at Caroline with peculiar significance, which seemed to intimate a considerable degree of contempt for her husband, and an idea that a similar feeling could not be altogether a stranger to her bosom.

Langton observed all this; and although it was with little surprise, for he knew that love is more easily alienated by pride than any other sentiment, yet he could not help feeling the most sincere regret that Caroline had entered upon that dangerous path, the first step of which is the condescending to show to any man a feeling of this nature.

"I have not learned to love her less," he said, when afterwards meditating on this circumstance, "and I love her too well to see her comfort or fame lightly lost while it may be in my power to save her. It was always her nature to be easily led by the influence of others; and although her pliant disposition may have linked her destiny with one whom it is evident she can never love, yet she may still be saved from a more fearful sacrifice. I will see her, and in the recollection of our early friendship, as well as in the recent claim which I have acquired upon her feelings, I will venture to speak boldly and sincerely. In warning her of the precipice on which she stands, she must not, however, be violently aroused to a sense of danger which perhaps she has not yet acknowledged to herself. I must first gently win her back to that spirit of confidence which we formerly knew, and, if I succeed in my ultimate aim, how slight in comparison will seem the peril from which I have saved the child, to that from which I shall have rescued the mother!"

Alas! that the morality of the young, which is so strong in thought, should be so weak in practice as it ever is. Here was another stone added to that pavement which is said to be composed of good intentions.

From this time he became a frequent visitor in the Regent's Park, and the result of this course will be best given in the description of an interview between himself and Caroline which took place about three months afterwards.

"Caroline," said he, as during a morning call, which had been prolonged to a most unfashionable extent, he sate alone by her side, "I find you the same kind being that you always were; it is from that tenderness of feeling, which under happier circumstances would have given additional value to your character, that I now dread an inroad on your peace. You confess that you are wearied with the cold and monotonous routine of your daily life, and that it is your fate to be linked with one who is incapable of understanding or returning any deep emotion of the heart; can you then wonder that I should tremble for your peace, when I see you flattered by the attentions of a man from whom I am afraid you have not been sufficiently discreet to conceal the disquiet which you suffer?"

"Indeed, indeed you have mistaken me," exclaimed Caroline. "I have neither been flattered by his attention, nor have I in any way confided in him: to you only have I spoken thus. I was wrong, very wrong, in doing so; but you entreated me to speak without reserve, and it is hardly kind of you now to tax me with the fault." As she said this, the tears started to her eyes, and as Langton gazed upon her he knew that the very confidence which had appeared so dangerous when he imagined it to be given to another, was now unreservedly bestowed upon himself: did he remember his indignant anticipations of broken happiness and degraded character on the part of Caroline, or did he apply to himself those rules which he had deemed so necessary to be considered by another? Alas! no. He took her hand, and said in a voice which faltered with emotion,

"Caroline, dear Caroline, I cannot bear to see you give way thus. Come, come, we must not have any tears: you may be very happy yet."

"No," she said, making a vain attempt to repress her sobs, "I do not hope to be happy,—I have not deserved to be so; for I knew, when they wished me joy on my wedding-day, that my happiness was gone for ever. But I must not talk thus to you, Charles; I have no right to trouble you with sorrows of my own seeking. Besides," she continued, smiling bitterly through her tears, "you are about to be married to one who cannot fail to love you, and I must claim no share in your thoughts. Believe me, I will conquer every emotion that you desire to be repressed. I will endeavour to be all that you would wish to see me,—indeed I will: only tell me that you are not offended,—that you do not think less kindly of me than you have always done,—and that you will sometimes think of her who, while she lives, can never cease to think and pray for you." She buried her face in her hands and wept bitterly. "Don't, don't speak to me now," she said, as her tears flowed more quickly; and Langton, taking her hand, felt them falling on his own. At that moment he considered himself pre-eminently wretched; he pressed her head upon his shoulder, bidding her be more calm, and, as he imprinted one kiss upon her forehead,—a servant entered the room.

"Did you ring, sir?"

"No!" said Langton furiously, and the intruder disappeared. Servants always think you ring at the very moment when you wish you were in a wilderness!

The party who received Mr. Langton's impetuous negative was a fat housemaid of extreme sensibility; and as the sensibility of housemaids is usually concentrated upon themselves, of course, in the description of the indignity she had received, any very delicate consideration for the character of her mistress could not be, expected to find a place. A committee was immediately formed in the pantry, where she related the "undelicate" conduct of that lady to her sympathising colleagues, and several strong resolutions were immediately carried expressive of their unqualified admiration of virtue in general, and their particular disapprobation of the deviation from its strict rules which had just been detailed; but as the said committee could not perceive any particular benefit to themselves that was

likely to result from a disclosure to Mr. Paine, they determined to
let the matter drop, and merely to suffer it to exist as an occasional
topic to give intensity to those sublime denunciations of the wickedness of their betters in which they were accustomed to indulge round
the kitchen fire, when their thoughts were glowing beneath the sti-
mulus of an occasional bottle of wine which had been abstracted from
the cellars of their "injured master."

Of course, however, it was not to be expected that the knowledge
of the circumstance should be concealed from their immediate circle
of acquaintance; and as the green-grocer wished he might drop if he
ever breathed a syllable about it, and the milkwoman thanked Heaven
that she never was a mischief-maker, of course the insulted housemaid "didn't mind telling them," upon their promise of profound secrecy; which was especially necessary, as, with the exception of the
servants on each side of Mr. Paine's, and the nurserymaid opposite,
not a soul knew a word about the matter.

Now it so happened that the watchful being who had been discharged on account of the affair in Oxford-street, was one of those
amiable characters by whom forgiveness of injuries is accounted a
duty. She had carried out this principle so far, that, although she
had been desired never to enter the house again, she would occasionally call after dark to see her old fellow-servants, with whom she
would sometimes take a glass of ale, in order to show how completely
she had subdued those feelings of animosity which she might be expected to entertain towards the person at whose cost it was provided. She always seemed to take the same interest in the family
as she had formerly done, and, with a spirit of Christian charity
which did honour to her nature, she would sometimes declare " that
although they had injured *her*, yet she hoped it would never come
home to them,"

Any concealment from a person of this disposition was of course
unnecessary; and, when she was made acquainted with the circumstance, her horror was unlimited. " Poor Mr. Paine, who was so
much of a gentleman!—and Mrs. Paine, too, who always seemed to
love the dear children so!—who would take care of them now?—and
then *that* Mr. Langton, she always said from the first she never liked
him! But no," she continued, her goodness of disposition again overmastering every other feeling, " I won't believe it,—I can't do so;
though I know, Mary, that you wouldn't tell a falsehood for the
world, and, if you couldn't speak well of anybody, would rather say
nothin' at all."

The reader will be surprised to learn that, although Mr. Paine's
servants had acted with such praiseworthy reserve, a letter was received by that gentleman at the insurance office of which he was
chairman, (the seal bearing the royal arms, which had been produced
by the application of a sixpence; and the post-mark giving indications
of the existence of a place called "Goswell-street Road,") the purport of which was as follows:

" SIR,—Nothin but my ankziety for your peas of mind could in-
dews me to writ this letter, which i am afeard will set your fealings
in a flame, & cause you grate distres. i am sorry to say your con-
fidens is abused, and that you have little idere of the fallshood which
will be found in what i am goin to relate.

" Your wife is untrew—the young man who pickt up Master Eddard when he *would* run into the rode, is one of her old bows. You may depend upon my assurance, for altho' there is an animus signatur at the bottom of this, the writer is a steddy young woman and knows what wickedness is.

" If you don't take warnin by what I have writ you will peraps be unhappy all the rest of your days, and so I hope you will.

" From your sincere well-wisher,

" J. J."

It is said that, for the deprivation of one sense, compensation is not unfrequently given by an increased action which is acquired to the remainder; and those who have seen men cut off from the enjoyment of some long-cherished feeling at the moment when its gratification seemed most essential to their happiness, must have admired the benevolence with which Providence has thus bestowed upon the mind a capability, when it is deprived of one pursuit, of falling back with redoubled ardour upon another. But Mr. Paine was an exception to this rule; he was rather the incarnation of a single feeling than a sharer in the complicated emotions of mankind. Pride was the only thing that he was conscious of,—the one point from which all his ideas radiated; and, when this was destroyed, his existence might virtually be considered at an end.

From the moment that he had received the wretched scrawl, the alteration which took place in this unhappy man was of the most extraordinary kind. He had never been suspicious, for, loveless though he was, the possibility that *his* wife could sink to frailty had never entered into his mind; but, when the idea was once aroused, he seemed without hesitation to receive it as a truth; and that that truth should be forced upon him by the agency of a person who was evidently of the lowest class was an aggravation of the keenest kind. His spirit was from that day broken. Homage seemed a mockery, for he felt that the most despised among those who showed him reverence possessed a more enviable lot than it could ever be his fate to know again.

For a few days the secret remained fixed in his own heart,—that heart which had sought to citadel itself in its indomitable pride, and which was now crushed and powerless. At length to Fraser, by whom his altered manner had been remarked, he ventured to ask, with an air of forced coldness, " Whether it had ever occurred to him that Mr. Langton had been in the habit of paying more than proper attentions to the mother of the boy whom he had rescued? —he did not mean to hint that those attentions had been encouraged or received—that of course was out of the question; but still——"

He hesitated; and Fraser, deceived by the quietude of his manner, thought it a very good opportunity to say a few words upon a subject that had given him some little annoyance. He readily avowed " that he entertained no very high opinion of the gentleman in question, but" (of course) " his opinion of Mrs. Paine's correct feeling was so strong that he thought the matter need cause very little discomfort. Nevertheless, he imagined it would be as well to intimate to Mr. Langton that his constant attendance in the Regent's Park was no longer expected or desired."

This was the confirmation that was sought—the vulgar letter was accurate enough—all the world were pointing at him. Fraser had noticed it, but in delicacy to his feelings, and in gallantry to his wife, had forborne to speak more explicitly: he had no remedy; wronged as he was, he had no remedy. He might go into a court of justice, and there, in consideration of his shame being recorded upon oath, he might receive a sum equal to about a tithe of his yearly income. He might kill the man; and then also the world, with whom suspicion only might exist at present, would be certified of the fact. No; his course was run,—there was but one way left for him to pursue.

It was dusk on a summer's evening, a few days after this, that Caroline and Langton met for the last time.

"Charles," she said, "it is not a resolution lightly formed; it has cost me a struggle which I knew I should experience, but which I never expected to have conquered, you must not see me more! Nay, do not utter one word of remonstrance; you may by so doing make the separation more bitter, but you cannot shake my resolution. I dare not trust myself to say all that now rushes to my mind; yet, perhaps, parting as we do for ever, I may be forgiven for saying that I always loved you: this I could not help; but, with such a feeling, I ought to have shown more strength of mind than to have sacrificed your happiness and my own even to a parent's wish. I failed to do so, and it is right that the penalty should be borne. Farewell! You can appreciate all that I now suffer, and you will tell me that you love me better for the determination which I have made. Believe me, a time will come when you will praise God that I had sufficient strength to endure the agony of this trial. We have been very foolish,—we ought never to have met; but thank Heaven that, having met, we have escaped from guilt. There, now leave me—pray leave me, and——"

At this moment they were interrupted by a hasty knock at the street-door; they stood still for a moment: it was Mr. Paine. He seemed, upon entering, to make some inquiries of the servant: he ascended the stairs, paused for an instant at the drawing-room door, as if about to open it, and then with a hurried step ascended to his dressing-room above. Caroline and Langton moved not; they seemed to dread some coming event, and yet they had no definite ground for fear. Several minutes elapsed: at length Langton smiled and was about to speak, when they heard a heavy, lumbering fall upon the floor above, followed by a long, low groan, the sound of which was never afterwards forgotten.

We willingly draw a veil over the circumstances of this scene, and have only now to detail the events to which it ultimately led.

The parting between Caroline and Langton on that dreadful night was *final:* he made an attempt to see her once more during the period of her suffering, but this she positively refused. The suicide of her unhappy husband caused some little talk at the time; but as it was proved, to the satisfaction of a coroner's jury, that his death took place on a Wednesday, and that upon that day he had written a short note which he had dated "Thursday," they without hesitation returned a verdict of "Temporary Insanity," and the newspapers saw no reason for departing from their usual plan, by attributing the rash act to any other cause than the unsuccessful result of some speculations on the Stock Exchange.

The world, (that is to say, those immediate connexions who became acquainted with the circumstances of the case,) upon a retrospect of the affair, condemned Mr. Paine for his pride, Mr. Fraser for his politeness, and Caroline and Langton for their indiscretion ;—the only persons mentioned in our story with whom the said "world" found no fault were—Mr. and Mrs. Gibbs !

Mr. Paine had made no alteration in his will, and a large portion of his property was left to his widow during her life. Caroline passed some years in deep seclusion, devoting herself to the education of her children, and seeking consolation in the exercises of religion, wherein alone she could hope that it might be found. She died at the commencement of the present year; and an extract from a letter addressed to Langton, which was discovered among her papers, may serve to conclude her history, and to impart a moral which may not be altogether vain.

"You will perhaps be surprised at this request," (she had entreated that he would undertake the guardianship of her children,) "but, after all that I have suffered, I could not feel one moment's peace if I thought it possible that in the course of events a similar fate might attend upon them. Edward will require little care,—to the girls my anxiety is directed: the destiny of women is too often fixed when they possess little power of judging wisely for themselves; and, even if they should possess this power, strength of character is required to enable them to resist all other influences, and to abide firmly by the judgment they have formed. Remembering that my fate was thus rendered unhappy, you will not hesitate to guard my children against the misery I have endured. Watch over them, I entreat you; and let that love which, when it was bestowed upon me, could lead only to sorrow, descend upon them with the consciousness of purity. I know that you will do this; I know, above all, that in affairs of the heart you will consult their feelings of affection rather than their dreams of pride; and while, on the one hand, you prohibit a union that might degrade them, you will, on the other, be equally cautious never to *enforce* the acceptance of 'an excellent offer.' "

THE AUTOBIOGRAPHY OF A GOOD JOKE.

THE diamond is precious from its scarcity, and, for the same reason, a new thought is beyond all price. Unluckily for us moderns, the ages who came before us have seized upon all the best thoughts, and it is but rarely indeed that we can stumble upon a new one. In the pride of superior knowledge, we sometimes imagine that we have succeeded in coining a new thought in the mint of our own brain; but, ten to one, if we make any researches into the matter, we shall find our bran new thought in some musty volume whose author lived a thousand years ago. This is exceedingly provoking, and has often led me to imagine that the ancients (so miscalled) have been guilty of the most atrocious plagiarisms from us, who are the real ancients of the world. It seems as if by some unhallowed species of second-sight they have been enabled to see down the dim vistas of futurity, and have thus forestalled us in the possession of the choicest thoughts and the most original ideas. This is especially the case with regard to jokes; all the best of them are as old as the hills. On rare occasions some commanding genius astonishes the world by a new joke; but this is an event,—the event of the year in which the grand thing is uttered. Hardly has it seen the light ere it passes with the utmost celerity from mouth to mouth; it makes the tour of all the tables in the kingdom, and is reproduced in newspapers and magazines, until no corner of the land has been unhonoured and ungladdened by its presence. Reader! it was once my fortune to be the creator, the Ποιητής, of a witticism of surpassing excellence,—of a joke which, as soon as it proceeded from my brain, made a dozen professed wits ready to burst with envy at my superior genius! Many a time since, has that bright scintillation of intellectual light brought smiles into the faces, and gladness into the hearts of millions! and many a joyous cachinnation has it caused, to the sensible diminution of apothecaries' bills and undertakers' fees! If I had been a diner-out, I might have provided myself with dinners for two years upon the strength of it; but I was contented with the honour, and left the profit to the smaller wits, who, by a process well known to themselves, contrive to extract venison out of jests, and champagne out of puns. For years I have reposed on my laurels as the inventor of a new thought; and, but for the hope that there were still more worlds to conquer, I would have folded my arms in dignified resignation, and acknowledged to myself that I had not lived in vain. About a month ago, however, my complacent pride in my production received a severe check; and circumstances ensued which have led me to doubt whether in these degenerate days it is possible for a man to imagine any new thought. I was in the society of half a dozen men of real wit, but of no pretension,—men of too joyous a nature to be envious of my achievement,—when one of them actually uttered my joke,—the joke upon which I pride myself,—coolly looking me in the face, and asserting that he was the author of it. I felt at first indignant at so dishonest an act; but, convinced of my own

George Cruikshank fecit

The Autobiography of a ...

right, I smiled contemptuously, and said nothing. My friend noticed the smile, and saw that it was not one of mirth but of scorn, and has ever since treated me with the most marked coolness. When I returned home I retired to my chamber, and throwing myself into my comfortable arm-chair, I indulged in a melancholy reverie upon the vanity of human exertion, and the disposition so common among mankind to rob the great of their dearly-acquired glory. "Even Homer," said I to myself, "did not escape the universal fate. Some deny his very existence, and assert that his sublime epic was the combined work of several ballad-mongers; others, again, generously acknowledge his existence, but still assert that he was no poet, but the mere singer of the verses that abler men composed! And, if Homer has not escaped detraction and injustice, shall I?" These, and similar thoughts, gradually growing more and more confused and indistinct, occupied my attention for a full hour. A bottle of champagne, corked up and untasted, stood upon the table before me. It was just the dim faint dawn of early morning; and in the grey obscurity I could plainly distinguish the black bottle as it stood between me and the window. Notwithstanding the hour, I felt half-inclined to take a draught of the generous juice it contained, and was stretching forth my hand for that purpose, when, to my great surprise, the bottle gave a sudden turn, and commenced dancing round the table. Gradually two arms sprouted forth from its sides; and, giving them a joyous twirl, the bottle skipped about more nimbly than before, and to my eyes seemed endeavouring to 'dance a Highland fling. I thought this very extraordinary behaviour on the part of the bottle. I rubbed my eyes, but I was wide awake. I pinched myself, and came to the same conclusion. As I continued to gaze, the mysterious bottle grew larger and larger, and suddenly sprung up as tall as myself. Immediately afterwards, the cork, which had become supernaturally large and round, changed colour, and turned to a ruddy hue; and I could by degrees distinguish a pair of sparkling eyes, and a whole set of rubicund features smiling upon me with the most benign expression. The forehead of this apparition was high and bald, and marked with wrinkles,—not of decrepitude, but of a hale old age,—while a few thin grey hairs hung straggling over his temples. As soon as my astonishment was able to vent itself in words, I addressed the apparition in a query, which has since become extremely popular, and called out to it, "Who are you?"

Ere it had time to reply to this classical question, my eyes fell upon a roll of parchment which it held in its hand, and on which were inscribed the magic words of my joke.

"Do you not know me?" said this Eidolon of my wit, pointing to the scroll. "I am the joke upon which you pride yourself, and, although I say it myself, one of the best jokes that ever was uttered. Don't you know me?"

"I can't say that I should have recognised you," said I, as I felt my heart yearning with paternal kindness towards him; "but— Come to my arms, my son, my progeny!"

"Aha! ha! ha!" said the Joke, looking at me with very unfilial impertinence, and holding his sides with laughter.

"The contempt with which you treat me is exceedingly unbecoming," said I with much warmth, and with the air of an offended parent; "and, what is more, sir, it is unfeeling and unnatural—'tis past a joke, sir!"

"'Tis no joke!" said the Joke, still laughing with all his might, and peering at me from the corners of his eyes, the only parts of those orbits which mirth permitted to remain open; "really, my good friend, the honour to which you lay claim is nowise yours. Lord bless your foolish vanity! I was a patriarch before the days of your great grandfather!"

"Pooh, pooh!" said I, "it cannot be! You know that you are my production;—you cannot be serious in denying it."

"I am not often serious," said the Joke, putting on a look of comic gravity; "but there is no reason for so much solemnity in telling an unimportant truth. However, we will not argue the point; I will proceed at once to tell you my history, to convince you how little claim you have to the honours of paternity in my case."

"I shall be very happy," said I, with more reverence than I had yet assumed towards my mysterious visitor.

"For fear you should find me dry," said the Joke, "get a bottle of wine."

I did as I was desired, drew the cork, filled two glasses, one of which I handed to the Joke, who, nodding good-humouredly at me, commenced the following narrative.

THE JOKE'S STORY.

"I have not the slightest recollection of my progenitors; like the great Pharaohs who built the pyramids, their names have sunk into oblivion in the lapse of ages. They must, however, have lived more than thirty centuries ago, as my reminiscences extend nearly as far back as that period. I could, if I would, draw many curious pictures of the state of society in those early ages, having mixed all my life with persons of every rank and condition, and traversed many celebrated regions. I say it with pride that I have always delighted to follow in the track of civilization, and claim as a great honour to myself and the other members of my fraternity, that we have in some degree contributed to hasten the mighty march of human intelligence. It is only savage nations who are too solemn and too stupid to appreciate a joke, and upon these people I never condescended to throw myself away. One of my earliest introductions to society took place about two thousand five hundred years ago, among a company of merchants who were traversing the great deserts of Arabia. Methinks I see their faces now, and the very spot where they first made acquaintance with me. It was towards sunset, under a palm-tree, beside a fountain, where the caravan had stopped to drink the refreshing waters. It has been often said that grave people love a joke, and it was a grave old trader who showed me off on this occasion, to the infinite delight of his companions, who laughed at my humour till the tears ran down their cheeks. In this manner I traversed the whole of civilized Asia, and visited at different periods the luxurious tables of Sardanapalus and Ahasuerus, and brought smiles into the faces of the queenly beauties of their courts. From Asia I passed into Greece, and I remember that I used often to sit with the soldiers round their watch-fires at the siege of Troy. At a much later period I was introduced to Homer, and shall always remember with pleasure that I was the means of procuring him a supper when, but for me, he would have gone without one. The poor peasants to whom the still poorer bard applied for a supper and a lodging, had no relish for poetry; but they understood a joke, and the bard brought me forth for their entertainment; and, while my self-love was flattered by their hearty laughter, his wants were supplied by their generous hospitality. But I was not only acquainted with Homer, for Aristophanes very happily introduced me into, one of his lost comedies. Anacreon and I were boon companions; and, while upon this part of my career, you will permit me to give vent to a little honest pride, by informing you in few words that I once brought a smile into the grave face of the divine Plato; that I was introduced into an argument by no less an orator than Demosthenes; that I was familiarly known to Esop; that I supped with Socrates; and was equally well received in the court of Philip of Macedon and the camp of his victorious son. Still a humble follower in the train of civilization, I passed over to Rome. I was not very well received by the stiff, stern men of the republic; but in the age of Augustus I was universally admired. The first time that I excited any attention was at the table of Mecænas, when Horace was present. I may mention by the way that it was Horace himself who, in a *tête-à-tête*, first made known my merits to his illustrious patron, and the latter took the first opportunity of showing me off. I was never in my life more flattered than at the enthusiastic reception I met from the men of genius there assembled, although I have since thought that I was somewhat indebted for my success to the wealth and station of the illustrious joker. However that may be, my success was certain; and so much was I courted, that I was compelled to visit every house in Rome where wit and good-humour stood any chance of being appreciated. After living in this manner for about a hundred years, I took it into my head to go to sleep; and I slept so long, that, when I awoke, I found the victorious Hun in the streets of the city. This was no time for me to show my face; and, seeing so little prospect of happy times for me and my race, I thought I could not do better than go to sleep again. I did so, and when I awoke this second time found myself at the gay court of old king René of Provence. Among the bright ladies and amorous troubadours who held their revels there, I was much esteemed. There was, however, I am bound in candour to admit, some falling-off in my glory about this period. I was admitted to the tables of the great, it is true; but I was looked upon as a humble dependent, and obliged to eat out of the same platter with the hired jester. I could not tolerate this unworthy treatment for ever, and it had such an effect upon me that I soon lost much of my wonted spirit and humour. In fact, I was continually robbed of my point by these professed wits, and often made to look uncommonly stupid; so much so, that my friends sometimes doubted of my identity, and denied that I was the same joke they had been accustomed to laugh at. I contrived, however, to be revenged occasionally upon the unlucky jesters who introduced me *mal-à-propos*. They used to forget that their masters were not always in a humour to be tickled by a joke, and a sound drubbing was very often the only reward of their ill-timed merriment. This was some slight consolation to me; but I could not tolerate long the low society of these hired buffoons, and, as I did not feel sleepy, I was obliged to think of some scheme by which I might escape the continual wear and tear, and loss of polish, that I suffered at their hands. I at last resolved to shut myself up in a monastery, and lead a life of tranquillity and seclusion. You need not smile because so merry a personage as myself chose to be immured within the walls of a monastery, for I assure you that in the intellectual society of the monks,—the only intellectual society that one could meet with in those days,—I was soon restored to my original brightness. I lived so well and so luxuriously among these good people, that I quickly grew sleek and lazy, and somehow or other I fell into a doze, from which I was not awakened until a wit in the reign of Elizabeth stumbled upon me, and again brought me out into the busy world. I ran a splendid career in England."

"Did you?" said I, interrupting the Joke at this part of his narrative, and appealing to him with considerable energy of manner, for I began to be apprehensive that some of my friends, more learned than myself, might have discovered the antiquity of my "joke," and would quiz me on the subject. I restrained my impetuosity, however, and, with some alarm depicted in my countenance, I asked him in a trembling voice, "Did you—did you—ever—meet with—Joe Miller?"

"D— Joe Miller!" said the Joke with much vivacity; "I suffered more from the dread of that fellow than I ever suffered in my life. I had the greatest difficulty in keeping out of his way, and I only managed it by going to sleep again. You awoke me from that slumber, when, like many others who came before you, you passed me off as your own. You remember you got much credit for me, as all ever have done who have good sense enough to introduce me only at a proper time, and wit enough to launch me forth with all my native grace and brilliancy about me."

"Then you are not a Joe?" said I, much relieved.

"A Joe!" said the Joke, reddening with anger. "Have I not told you already that I am not? Do you mean to insult me by the vile insinuation that I ever showed my face in such despicable company? Do you think, sir, that I am a pun?"

"Oh, by no means," said I; "I assure you I meant no offence."

"You did, sir," replied the Joke, striking his fist upon the table with great vehemence. Immediately afterwards I observed that his face became dreadfully distorted, and he shook his head convulsively from side to side. As I continued to gaze without the power of saying a single word to calm the irritation I had so unintentionally raised, I noticed that his neck grew every instant longer and longer, until his chin seemed to be fully two feet from his shoulders. I was unable to endure the sight, and rising up, half frantic with nervous excitement, I put my hand convulsively upon his head, with the benevolent intention of squeezing it down to its proper level. He glared furiously at me with his swollen eyes, and, horrible to relate, just as I came in contact with him, his head flew off with a tremendous explosion, and bounced right through a chimney-glass that ornamented my mantel-piece. The glass flew in shivers round me. In a dreadful state of alarm I rang the bell for assistance, and sank down overpowered upon the chair.

"Beggin' your honour's pardon for being so bould," said my tiger, a good-natured Irish boy named Phelim, who had entered at the summons, " I think your honour had better drink a bottle of soda-water and go to bed."

" Where 's his head, Phelim ?" said I.

" Your own, or the bed's ?" said Phelim.

" The Joke 's," replied I.

"Och, you must mane your own ; it 's light enough, I dare say," said Phelim as he pulled my boots off. " You took a dhrop too much last night, anyhow."

" Phelim," said I solemnly, " did you hear nothing ?"

" To be sure I did," said Phelim. " Haven't you, like a drunken baste as you are, (begging your pardon for my bouldness,) been trying to broach that bottle of champagne at this early hour of the mornin', and haven't you driven the cork through the lookin'-glass ?"

I looked at the bottle ; it was uncorked, and the champagne was even at that moment sparkling over the neck of the bottle, and running over my books and papers.

" A pretty piece of work you have made of it," said Phelim, picking up the cork and pointing to the looking-glass.

" 'Twas a good joke," said I, although my faith was somewhat staggered by Phelim's explanation.

" Troth, an' I 'm glad you take it so asy," said Phelim, ramming the cork into the bottle; " you 'll find it a dear one when the landlady brings in her bill for the lookin'-glass. But never mind it, sir, now. Go to bed and get sober."

I took Phelim's advice, and went to bed. To this day I am unable positively to decide whether his explanation was the true one or not. I incline, however, to the belief that I was *not* drunk, but that the illustrious JOKE actually visited me in *propriá personá*. I am the more inclined to this belief from the remarkable coherency of his narrative, which I now leave, without a word of comment, to the consideration of the curious.

THE SECRET.

TRANSLATED FROM THE FRENCH OF M. PAUL DE KOCK.

NATHALIE DE HAUTEVILLE at the age of twenty-two had been for three years a widow. She was one of the most beautiful women in Paris; a brunette, with large black eyes, and one of those fascinating faces whose charm consists more in expression than in regularity of features, and in which are portrayed at once all the elegance of the Frenchwoman, all the vivacity of the Italian, and all the fire of a daughter of Spain.

When she married, at eighteen, a man of nearly three times her age, Nathalie, a mere child in character, had not bestowed a thought on any thing beyond her wedding dresses, her marriage presents, and the delight of being called Madame. Her husband was as generous to her as he was rich. Twelve months had passed in a continued round of gaiety and amusement, when M. de Hauteville was suddenly attacked by a disease which carried him off in a few days, and left his young widow to mourn for a husband as she would have mourned for the loss of a friend and protector.

But, at eighteen, sorrow soon passes away; the heart is so new to every feeling, to every illusion. Madame de Hauteville found that she was courted by the world; that she was invited everywhere; and that, by her fortune and her position, she was called upon to become an ornament of society. Yet she felt that she was too young to live without a mentor, and to go out alone; so she asked her uncle, M. d'Ablaincourt, to come and live with her.

M. d'Ablaincourt was an old bachelor: one love only, had he ever known, and the object of that was—himself. His love for himself was paramount; and, if ever he went so far as to show any liking for any other individual, he must have received from that individual such attention as to make him a gainer by their intimacy. M. d'Ablaincourt was an egotist; but, at the same time, a well-bred, à well-mannered egotist. He had all the air of devoting himself to the wishes of others, whilst he was exclusively occupied in compassing his own; he would appear to be taking a lively interest in those around him, whilst, in reality, he never felt any interest in anybody but himself. Too thoughtless to do harm, he was as little disposed to do good, unless it were for his own advantage. In short, he liked to be at his ease, and to be surrounded with all the enjoyments which luxury could invent. Such was the character of M. d'Ablaincourt, who readily acceded to his niece's proposal, because Nathalie, though a little giddy, had a good and affectionate heart, and would load him with kindnesses and attentions.

M. d'Ablaincourt went out into the world with his niece, because he had not yet lost his relish for its pleasures; but, if an invitation came for any party which he thought held out no amusement for him, he would turn to her, and say, "I am afraid, my dear, you will not like this party; there will be nothing at all but play. I shall be very happy to take you; you know I always do exactly as you wish, but I think you will find it dull." And Nathalie, who was all con-

George Cruikshank fc.

fidence in her uncle, never failed to answer, " You are quite right, uncle ; it will be much better for us not to go."

So it was with everything else. M. d'Ablaincourt, who, without wishing to be thought so, was an excessive *gourmand,* said one day to his niece, " You know, my dear, I am no *gourmand ;* I care very little myself how things are served up, and am always satisfied with what is laid before me ; but your cook puts too much salt in everything, which is not wholesome for a young woman ; and then, she sends up her dishes in a careless, slovenly way, which is very annoying to me on your account, as you often give dinners. The other day there were six people at table, and the spinage was badly dressed. You must consider what people will say of your management when they see such neglect. They will say that Madame de Hauteville has no idea of having things as they ought to be ; and this may do you harm, as there are persons who notice everything."

" What you say is very true, dear uncle ; will you take the trouble of looking out for a good cook for me ?"

" To be sure, my love ; you know I think nothing of trouble when I can be of service to you."

" How lucky I am in having you always by me to tell me of all these little things, which I should never think of !" said Nathalie, kissing her uncle ; and he, good old man, forthwith discharged the cook who dressed the spinage badly, to make way for one who shone particularly in all *his* favourite dishes.

Another time some improvements were to be made in the garden ; for instance, the trees in front of the old gentleman's windows were to be felled, because they might occasion a dampness which would be dangerous for Nathalie. And then, the elegant calash was to be exchanged for a landau, as being a carriage in which a young lady could be much more at her ease. So minutely attentive was M. d'Ablaincourt to the comforts and enjoyments of his niece !

Nathalie was somewhat of a coquette : accustomed to conquest, she used to listen with a smile to the numerous proposals which were made to her, and sent off all suitors to her uncle, telling them, " Before I can give you any hope, I must know what M. d'Ablaincourt thinks of you."

Had her heart favoured any individual, it is probable that the answer of Nathalie would have been different ; but, as it was, she thought nothing could be more agreeable than to please all, and be the slave of none.

The old gentleman, for his part, being master in his niece's house, was not at all anxious that she should marry again. A nephew might be less inclined to give way, less indulgent to him than Nathalie, so that he never failed to find some serious fault in every fresh aspirant to the hand of the pretty widow, and, as in every other case, he seemed to be thinking of nothing but her happiness.

In addition to his egotism, and his fondness for good living, M. d'Ablaincourt had of late years been seized with a violent passion for *tric-trac.* His favourite pastime, his highest delight, was this game ; but, unfortunately for him, it was one very little played. The ladies do not like it in a room, because it is noisy ; the gentlemen prefer *bouillotte* or *écarté ;* so that the old gentleman very seldom found an opportunity of indulging his propensity. If any of his niece's visitors did happen to play, he seized upon them for the whole evening;—there was no possibility of escape. But, as they did not come to the pretty widow's for the sake of a game at *tric-trac* with the old uncle, many were the nights he sighed in vain for somebody to play with.

To please her uncle, Nathalie attempted to learn; but in vain. She was too giddy to give the necessary attention, and was continually making mistakes: the uncle scolded; and at last, Nathalie, throwing away dice and dice-box, said, " It is no use,—I never can learn this game."

" I am sorry for it," answered M. d'Ablaincourt, "very sorry; it would have given you so much pleasure. I only wished to teach it you for your own amusement."

Such was the state of affairs, when, at a very large party, where Nathalie was allowed to stand unrivalled for personal beauty and elegance of dress, was announced M. d'Apremont, a captain in the navy.

Nathalie expected to see a blunt, gruff old sailor, with a wooden leg, and a black patch on his eye. To her great astonishment there entered a tall, handsome young man, with a graceful figure and commanding air, and without either a wooden leg or a black patch.

Armand d'Apremont had entered the service very early in life; his whole soul was in his profession ; and, though only thirty, he had risen to the rank of captain. His family property was considerable, and he had increased his fortune by his own exertions. Under these circumstances it is not surprising that, after fifteen years spent at sea, he should have yielded to a longing for repose ; yet he never could be persuaded to listen to the solicitations of his friends, who urged him to marry: hitherto he had only laughed at love as a passion unworthy of a sailor.

The sight of Nathalie changed all his ideas, — the whole man underwent a sudden revolution. He watched her dancing, and could look nowhere else. All the other beauties in the room passed before him but as vain shadows, so busy were his eyes in following the graceful movements of the young widow.

"Who is that lovely creature who dances so beautifully ?" at last he exclaimed to a person next him.

" That is Madame de Hauteville, a young widow. You admire her, captain?"

" I think her enchanting."

" She is very beautiful ! And her mental qualifications are at least equal to her personal charms. But you must ask her to dance, and then you will be able to judge for yourself."

" *I* ask her to dance ! I never danced in my life!" and for the first time Armand felt that this was a deficiency in his education. However, he went and stood close to the beauty, watching an opportunity of entering into conversation with her. Once he was on the very point of succeeding, when a young man came up, and led her away to the quadrille. Poor Armand bit his lips, and was obliged again to content himself with admiring her dancing. This whole evening he made no further advances, but he did not lose sight of his enchantress for an instant.

The captain's behaviour did not pass unobserved by Nathalie,—so soon do women see what effect they produce,—and, although she did not appear to notice it, she felt secretly not a little flattered ; for D'Apremont had been described to her as a man who was far from agreeable in the society of ladies, and who had never been known to pay a single compliment. And Nathalie said to herself, " What fun it would be to hear him make love !"

D'Apremont, who, before he had seen Nathalie, went very little into society, particularly to balls, from henceforth never missed going wherever he had a chance of meeting his fair widow. He had succeeded in speaking to her, and had done his utmost to render himself agreeable. His behaviour was entirely changed, and the world was not more slow than usual in discovering the cause, or in commenting upon the marked attention which he paid to Nathalie.

" Mind you are not caught, captain !" a good-natured friend would say. " Madame de Hauteville is a coquette, who will but make a toy of your love, and a joke of your sighs." And to Nathalie some equally kind friend would say, " The captain is an original, a bear, with every fault that a sailor can possess. He is passionate, he is obstinate, he swears, he smokes. You will never make anything of him."

In spite of these charitable warnings,—the result, perhaps, of envy and jealousy,—the sailor and the coquette enjoyed a mutual pleasure in each other's society. Whenever D'Apremont was on the point of forgetting himself, and letting out an expression a little too nautical, Nathalie looked at him with a slight frown. He stopped short, stammered, and dared not finish his sentence, so afraid was he of seeing a harsh look on that pretty face. Nor is it a slight proof of the mighty power of love that it can thus implant fear in the breast of a sailor.

Some rumours of his niece's new conquest had reached the ears of M. d'Ablaincourt ; but he had paid but little attention to them, thinking that this new admirer would share the fate of all the others, and that it would be very easy to get him dismissed. Yet the report had so far increased, that when Nathalie one day told her uncle that she had asked the captain to her house, the old gentleman almost flew into a passion, and said, with a vehemence quite uncommon to him, " You have acted very wrong, Nathalie ; you do not consult me as you ought. I am told that Captain d'Apremont is a blunt, unpolished, quarrelsome —— He is always behind your chair, and he has never even asked *me* how I did. There was no necessity at all for you to ask him. You know, my dear," added he, softening his tone, " all I say is for your good ; but indeed you are too thoughtless."

Nathalie, quite afraid that she had acted very inconsiderately, was going to put off the captain ; but this the uncle did not require :—he thought he should be able to prevent too frequent a repetition of his visits.

It is a trite observation, that the most important events in life are frequently the result of the most trivial incidents,—that on a mere thread, which chance has flung in our way, may hang our whole future destiny. Such was the case in the present instance : to the game of *tric-trac* it was owing that Madame de Hauteville became Madame d'Apremont. The captain was an excellent player ; and happening in the course of conversation to broach the subject, M. d'Ablaincourt caught at him immediately, and proposed a game. D'Apremont consented; and, having understood that it was necessary to play the agreeable to the old uncle, spent the whole evening at *tric-trac*.

When everybody was gone, Nathalie complained of the captain's want of gallantry,—that he had hardly paid her any attention at all.

"You were quite right," said she pettishly to her uncle; "sailors are very disagreeable people. I am very sorry I ever asked M. d'Apremont."

"On the contrary, my dear," replied the old bachelor, "we had formed quite an erroneous opinion of M. d'Apremont. I found him so agreeable and so well-bred, that I have asked him to come very often to play with me,—I mean, to pay his court to you. He is a very clever, gentlemanlike young man."

Nathalie, seeing that the captain had won the heart of her uncle, pardoned his want of attention to her. Thanks to *tric-trac*, and to his being necessary to M. d'Ablaincourt's amusement, he came very often to the house, and at last succeeded in winning the heart of the young widow. One morning she came, her face covered with blushes, to tell her uncle that M. d'Apremont had proposed to her, and to ask his advice.

The old gentleman thought for a few minutes, and he said to himself, "If she refuses him, there will be an end to his visits here; no more *tric-trac*. If she accepts him, he will be one of the family; I shall always be able to nail him for a game;" and the answer was, "You cannot do better than accept him."

The happiness of Nathalie was complete, for she really loved Armand; but, as a woman never should seem to yield too easily, she sent for the captain to dictate her conditions.

"If it is true that you love me," she began.

"*If* it is true! Oh, madame, I swear by all——"

"Allow me to speak first. If you love me, you will not hesitate to give me the proofs I demand."

"Whatever you ask, I——"

"In the first place, you must no longer swear as you do occasionally; it is a shocking habit before a lady: secondly, — and on this point I insist more particularly,—you must give up smoking, for I hate the smell of a pipe of tobacco; in short, I never will have a husband who smokes."

Armand heaved a sigh, and answered, "To please you I will submit to anything,—I will give up smoking."

Her conditions being thus acceded to, the fair widow could no longer withhold her hand, and in a short time Armand and Nathalie reappeared in the world as a newly-married and happy couple. Yet the world was not satisfied. "How could that affected flirt marry a sailor?" said one. "So, the rough captain has let himself be caught by the pretty widow's coquetry," said another. "This is a couple ill-matched enough."

Poor judges of the human heart are they who imagine a resemblance of disposition to be essential to love! On the contrary, the most happy effects are produced by contrast: mark but the union of light and shade; and is not strength wanting to uphold weakness :—the wild bursts of mirth to dispel melancholy? You join together two kindred tempers, two similar organisations, and what is the result? 'Tis as the blind leading the blind.

Our young couple passed the first few months after their marriage in undisturbed happiness. Yet in the midst of the rapture he experienced in the society of his lovely bride, Armand sometimes became pensive, his brow was contracted, and his eyes betrayed a secret uneasiness: but this lasted not; it was but as a fleeting cloud, which passes without leaving a trace. Nathalie had not hitherto perceived it. After some time, however, these moments of restlessness and gloom recurred so frequently as no longer to escape her observation.

" What is the matter, my love?" said she to her husband one day when she saw him stamping his foot with impatience; "what makes you so cross?"

" Nothing, nothing at all!" answered the captain, as if ashamed of having lost his self-possession. " With whom do you think I should be cross?"

" Indeed, my dear, I know not; but I have fancied several times that I perceived a something impatient in your manner. If I have unconsciously done anything to vex you, do tell me, that it may never happen again."

The captain kissed his wife affectionately, and again assured her that she was mistaken. For some days he manifested none of those emotions which had so disturbed Nathalie; but at length the same thing occurred again: Armand forgot himself once more, and she racked her brain to guess what cause her husband could have for this uneasiness. Not being satisfied with her own solution of the problem, she communicated her thoughts to her uncle, who replied immediately, " Yes, my dear, you are quite right; I am sure something must be the matter with D'Apremont; for several times lately, at *tric-trac* he has looked round with an abstracted air, passed his hand across his temples, and finished by making an egregious blunder."

" But, my good uncle, what can the mystery be? My husband must have some secret which preys upon his mind, and he does not choose to trust me with it."

" Very likely; there are many things which a man cannot tell his wife."

" Which a man cannot tell his wife! That is a thing I do not understand. I expect my husband to tell me everything, to have no mysteries with me, as I have none with him. I can never be happy so long as he on whom I have bestowed my heart, keeps any secret from me."

M. d'Ablaincourt, to comfort his niece, or rather, perhaps, to cut short a conversation which began to bore him, promised to do his utmost to discover the cause of his nephew's uneasiness; but he went no further than trying to make him play oftener at *tric-trac*, as being an excellent method of keeping him in good humour.

Early in the summer they left Paris for a beautiful property belonging to the captain in the neighbourhood of Fontainebleau. He appeared still as fond of his wife as ever; to afford her pleasure was his delight, to anticipate her wishes his study; but, as she was not fond of walking, he begged to be allowed to take a stroll into the country every day after dinner. This was too natural a request to be denied; and after dinner, whether they were alone or not, out went Armand, and returned in the best humour imaginable. Still Nathalie was far from being satisfied; her suspicions returned, and she said to herself, "My husband has no longer the serious, gloomy look he used to wear in Paris; but it is only since he has gone out every evening after dinner. Sometimes he is away two hours,—where can he go? —and he always likes to be alone. There is some mystery in his conduct, and I shall never be happy until I have found it out."

Sometimes Nathalie thought of having her husband followed; but this was a step too repugnant to her feelings. To take a servant into her confidence, to place a spy on the path of a man the business of whose life seemed to be to give her pleasure, she felt would be wrong, and she gave up the idea. To her uncle alone she ventured to disclose her anxiety, and he simply answered, "True, your husband plays less at *tric-trac*, but still he does play; and as to my following him in his walks, it is out of the question, for he has very good legs, and I have very bad ones;—I should be fatiguing myself to no purpose."

One day that Madame d'Apremont gave a party, a young man present said, laughing, to the master of the house,

"What were you doing yesterday, Armand, in the disguise of a peasant at the window of a little cottage about half a mile from hence? If my horse had not started, I was coming to ask if you were feeding your sheep."

"My husband in the disguise of a peasant!" exclaimed Nathalie, fixing her eyes upon Armand in amazement.

"Oh! Edward has made a mistake," replied the captain, endeavouring to conceal a visible embarrassment; "he must have taken somebody else for me."

"Very likely," said the young man, hurt at the impression which his words had made upon Nathalie, and perceiving that he had been guilty of an indiscretion; "I must have been deceived."

"How was the man dressed?" asked Nathalie. "Where was the cottage?"

"Really I know the country so little, I should have some difficulty in finding the spot. As for the man, he had on a blue smock-frock, with a sort of cap on his head. I don't know what could have put it into my head that it was the captain, as it is not the carnival."

Madame d'Apremont said no more on the subject, but remained persuaded that it *was* her husband. The assumption of a disguise proved that he was engaged in some extraordinary intrigue, and in a flood of tears poor Nathalie complained of the bitterness of her lot in having married a man of mysteries.

Whether secrets of this nature are the only ones which women can keep, far be it from me to decide; but certain it is that they always connect some infidelity with those of our sex. Madame d'Apremont did not form an exception to this general observation, and in a fit of jealousy she begged to return to town. Her husband consented immediately, and in a few days they were in Paris. Here the captain again betrayed the same symptoms of discontent, until one day he said to his wife, "My dear, a walk after dinner does me a great deal of good. During the latter part of our stay in the country I was quite well in consequence. You can easily conceive that an old sailor wants exercise, and that he cannot remain cooped up in a room or a theatre all the evening."

"Oh! very easily," replied Nathalie, biting her lips with spleen; "go and take your walk, if it does you good."

"But, my love, if it annoys you——"

"Oh! not in the least; take your walk; I have no objection."

So the husband took his evening walk, returned in excellent spirits, and again every sign of impatience had vanished.

"My husband is carrying on some intrigue: he loves another, and cannot live without seeing her," said poor Nathalie to herself. "This is the secret of his strange conduct, of his ill-humour, and of his walks. I am very, very wretched; and the more so that when he is with me he is all kindness, all attention! I know not how I can tell him that he is a monster, a traitor! But tell him I must, or my heart will burst! Yet if I could but get some undeniable proof of his faithlessness. Oh! yes, I will have some proof." And with a swelling heart, and eyes full of tears, she rushed into her uncle's room, crying that "she was the most miserable woman alive!"

"What is the matter?" said the old gentleman, burying himself in his arm-chair. "What has happened?"

"Every day after dinner," answered his niece, sobbing, "my husband goes out to walk, as he did in the country, and stays away two hours. When he returns, he is always cheerful and gay, gives me a thousand little marks of his attention, and swears that he adores me as he did the day of our marriage. Oh! my good uncle, I can bear it no longer!—You must see that this is all treachery and deceit. Armand is playing me false."

"He plays less with me at *tric-trac*," was the answer of the imperturbable uncle; "but still——"

"My dear uncle, if you do not help me to discover this mystery, I shall die of grief—I shall commit some rash act—I shall get separated from my husband. Oh! my good uncle, you who are so kind, so ready to oblige, do render me this service,—do find out where my husband goes every evening."

"There can be no doubt about my readiness to oblige, seeing that it has been the business of my life; but really I do not know how I can serve you."

"Again I repeat, that, if this mystery is not cleared up, you will lose your niece."

M. d'Ablaincourt had no wish to lose his niece, or, for the matter of that, his nephew either. He felt that any rupture between the young couple would disturb the quiet, easy life he was now enjoying, and he therefore decided upon taking some steps to restore peace. He pretended to follow the captain; but, finding this fatiguing, he returned slowly home after a certain time, and said to his niece, "I have followed your husband more than six times, and he walks very quietly alone."

"Where, where, my dear uncle?"

"Sometimes one way, and sometimes another; so that all your suspicions are entirely without foundation."

Nathalie was not duped by this answer, though she pretended to place implicit confidence in her uncle's words. Determined on discovering the truth, she sent for a little errand-boy, who stood always at the corner of their house, and whom she had heard more than once praised for his quickness and intelligence. Having ascertained that he knew her husband by sight, she said to him, "M. d'Apremont goes out every evening. To-morrow you must follow him, watch where he goes, and bring me back word immediately. And take care not to be seen."

The boy promised to execute her orders faithfully, and Nathalie awaited the morrow with that impatience of which the jealous alone can form any idea. At length the moment arrived, the captain went out, and the little messenger was on his track. Trembling, and in a fever of agitation, Nathalie sat counting the minutes and seconds as they passed until the return of the boy. Three quarters of an hour had elapsed when he made his appearance, covered with dust, and in a violent perspiration.

"Well," said Nathalie in an altered tone of voice, "what have you seen? Tell me everything."

"Why, ma'am, I followed the master, taking care he shouldn't see 'me—and a long chase it was—to the Vieille Rue du Temple in the Marais. There he went into a queer-looking sort of a house,—I forget the number, but I should know it again,—in an alley, and there was no porter."

"No porter!—in an alley!—Oh, the wretch!"

"As soon as the master had gone in," continued the boy, "I went in too. He kept on going up stairs till he got to the third floor, and then he took out a key and opened the door."

"The monster!—he opened the door himself,—he has a key,— and my uncle to take his part! You are quite sure he opened the door himself,—that he did not knock?"

"Quite sure, ma'am; and, when I heard him shut the door, I went up softly and peeped in at the keyhole: as there were only two doors, I soon found the right one; and there I saw the master dragging a great wooden chest across the room, and then he began to undress himself."

"To undress himself!—O Heavens!—Go on."

"I couldn't see into the corner of the room where he was; but presently he came out dressed in a grey smock, with a Greek cap on his head. And so, ma'am, I thought you'd like to know all I'd seen, and I ran with all my might to tell you."

"You are a very good boy. You must now go and fetch a coach directly, get up with the coachman, and direct him to the house."

Nathalie, meanwhile, flew to her room, put on a bonnet and shawl, rushed down to her uncle crying out, "My husband has betrayed me, —I am going to catch him;" and before the old gentleman could extract another word from her, she was out of the house, in the coach, and gone. In the Vieille Rue du Temple the coach stopped; Nathalie got out, pale, trembling, and scarcely able to support herself. The boy showed her the entrance, and she declined his further attendance. With the help of the hand-rail she ascended a dark narrow staircase till she reached the third story, when she had just force enough left to throw herself against the door, and cry out,

"Let me in, or I shall die!"

The door opened, the captain received her in his arms, and she saw nothing but her husband alone, in a smock and a Greek cap, smoking a superb Turkish pipe.

"My wife!" exclaimed Armand in utter amazement.

" Yes, sir," replied Nathalie, resuming her self-command,—" your injured wife, who has discovered your perfidy, and has been made acquainted with your disguise, and who has come in person to unravel the mystery of your conduct."

" What, Nathalie!—could you, then, suppose that I loved another? You wish to fathom the mystery,—here it is ;" and he showed her the pipe. " Before our marriage you forbade me to smoke, and I promised to obey. For some months I kept my promise most faithfully. Oh! Nathalie, if you did but know what I suffered in consequence,—the fretfulness, the depression of spirits under which I laboured for hours together!—it was my old friend that I missed, my darling pipe that I sighed for in vain! At last I could hold out no longer; and, when we were in the country, happening to go into a cottage where an old man was smoking, I asked him if he could afford me a place of refuge, and at the same time lend me a smock and a hat; for I was afraid that my clothes might betray me. Our arrangements were soon made; and, thanks to this precaution, you had not the slightest suspicion of the real cause of my daily absence. Shortly afterwards you determined upon returning to Paris; and, being obliged to find a new way of indulging myself with my pipe, I took this little garret, and brought hither my old dress. You are now, my love, in possession of the whole mystery, and I trust you will pardon my disobedience. You see I have done everything in my power to conceal it from you."

Nathalie threw herself into her husband's arms, and cried out in an ecstasy of delight,

" So this is really all!—how happy I am! From henceforth, dearest, you shall smoke as much as you like at home; you shall not have to hide yourself for that!" and away she went to her uncle with a face all beaming with joy, to tell him that Armand loved her, adored her still,—it was only that he smoked. " But now," added she, " I am so happy, that he shall smoke as much as he likes."

" The best plan will be," said M. d'Ablaincourt, " for your husband to smoke as he plays at *tric-trac*; and so," thought the old gentleman, " I shall be sure of my game every evening."

" My dear Nathalie," said the captain, " though I shall take advantage of the permission you so kindly give me, still I shall be equally careful not to annoy you, and shall take the same precautions as before."

" Oh! Armand, you are really too good; but I am so happy at being undeceived in my suspicions, that I think now, I quite like the smell of a pipe."

SHAKSPEARE PAPERS.—No. IV.

MIDSUMMER NIGHT'S DREAM.
BOTTOM, THE WEAVER.

" Some men are born with a silver spoon in their mouths, and others with a wooden ladle."—*Ancient Proverb.*

" Then did the sun on dunghill shine."—*Ancient Pistol.*

It has often been remarked that it is impossible to play the enchanted scenes of Bottom with any effect. In reading the poem we idealize the ass-head; we can conceive that it represents in some grotesque sort the various passions and emotions of its wearer; that it assumes a character of dull jocosity, or duller sapience, in his conversations with Titania and the fairies; and when calling for the assistance of Messrs. Peas-blossom and Mustard-seed to scratch his head, or of the Queen to procure him a peck of provender or a bottle of hay, it expresses some puzzled wonder of the new sensations its wearer must experience in tinglings never felt before, and cravings for food until then unsuited to his appetite. But on the stage this is impossible. As the manager cannot procure for his fairies representatives of such tiny dimensions as to be in danger of being overflown by the bursting of the honey-bag of an humble-bee, so it is impossible that the art of the property-man can furnish Bottom with an ass-head capable of expressing the mixed feelings of humanity and asinity which actuate the metamorphosed weaver. It is but a paste-board head, and that is all. The jest is over the first moment after his appearance; and, having laughed at it once, we cannot laugh at it any more. As in the case of a man who, at a masquerade, has chosen a character depending for its attraction merely on costume,— we may admire a Don Quixote, if properly bedecked in Mambrino's helmet and the other habiliments of the Knight of La Mancha, at a first glance, but we think him scarcely worthy of a second.

So it is with the Bottom of the stage; the Bottom of the poem is a different person. Shakspeare in many parts of his plays drops hints, " vocal to the intelligent," that he feels the difficulty of bringing his ideas adequately before the minds of theatrical spectators. In the opening address of the Chorus of Henry V. he asks pardon for having dared

" On this unworthy scaffold to bring forth
So great an object. Can this cockpit hold
The vasty fields of France ? or, may we cram
Within this wooden O, the very casques
That did affright the air at Agincourt ?"

and requests his audience to piece out the imperfections of the theatre with their thoughts. This is an apology for the ordinary and physical defects of any stage,—especially an ill-furnished one; and it requires no great straining of our imaginary forces to submit to them. Even Ducrow himself, with appliances and means to boot a hundred-fold more magnificent and copious than any that were at the command of Shakspeare, does not deceive us into the belief that his fifty horses, trained and managed with surpassing skill, and mounted by agile and practised riders, dressed in splendid and carefully-considered costumes, are actually fighting the battle of Waterloo, but we willingly lend ourselves to the delusion. In like manner, we may be sure that in the days of Queen Elizabeth the audience of the Globe complied with the advice of Chorus, and,

> " Minding true things by what their mockeries be,"

were contented that

> " Four or five most vile and ragged foils
> Right ill-disposed, in brawl ridiculous,"

should serve to represent to their imagination the name of Agincourt.

We consent to this just as we do to Greeks and Romans speaking English on the stage of London, or French on that of Paris; or to men of any country speaking in verse at all; or to all the other demands made upon our belief in playing. We can dispense with the assistance of such downright matter-of-fact interpreters as those who volunteer their services to assure us that the lion in Pyramus and Thisbe is not a lion in good earnest, but merely Snug the joiner. But there are difficulties of a more subtle and metaphysical kind to be got over, and to these, too, Shakspeare not unfrequently alludes. In the play before us,—Midsummer Night's Dream,—for example, when Hippolita speaks scornfully of the tragedy in which Bottom holds so conspicuous a part, Theseus answers, that the best of this kind (scenic performances) are but shadows, and the worst no worse if imagination amend them. She answers that it must be *your* imagination then, not *theirs.* He retorts with a joke on the vanity of actors, and the conversation is immediately changed. The meaning of the Duke is, that, however we may laugh at the silliness of Bottom and his companions in their ridiculous play, the author labours under no more than the common calamity of dramatists. They are all but dealers in shadowy representations of life; and if the worst among them can set the mind of the spectator at work, he is equal to the best. The answer to Theseus is, that none but the best, or, at all events, those who approach to excellence, can call with success upon imagination to invest their shadows with substance. Such playwrights as Quince the carpenter,—and they abound in every literature and every theatre,—draw our attention so much to the absurdity of the performance actually going on before us, that we have no inclination to trouble ourselves with considering what substance in the background their shadows should have represented. Shakspeare intended the remark as a compliment or a consolation to less successful wooers of the comic or the tragic Muse, and touches briefly on the matter; but it was also intended as an excuse for the want of effect upon the stage of some of the finer touches of such dramatists as himself, and an appeal to all true judges of poetry to bring it before the tribunal of their own imagination; making but a matter of secondary inquiry how it appears in a theatre, as delivered by those who, whatever others may think of them, would, if taken at their own estimation, " pass for excellent men." His own magnificent creation of fairy land in the Athenian wood must have been in his mind, and he asks an indulgent play of fancy not more for Oberon and Titania, the glittering rulers of the elements, who meet

> "—— on hill, in dale, forest, or mead,
>   By paved fountain, or by rushy brook,
>   Or on the beached margent of the sea,
>   To dance their ringlets to the whistling wind,"

than for the shrewd and knavish Robin Goodfellow, the lord of practical jokes, or the dull and conceited Bottom, " the shallowest thick-
skin of the barren sort," rapt so wondrously from his loom and
shuttle, his threads and thrums, to be the favoured lover of the
Queen of Faëry, fresh from the spiced Indian air, and lulled with
dances and delight amid the fragrance of the sweetest flowers, filling
with their luscious perfume a moonlighted forest.

One part of Bottom's character is easily understood, and is often
well acted. Amid his own companions he is the cock of the walk.
His genius is admitted without hesitation. When he is lost in the
wood, Quince gives up the play as marred. There is no man in
Athens able to take the first part in tragedy but himself. Flute declares that he has the best wit of any handicraftman in the city.
This does not satisfy the still warmer admirer,* who insists on the
goodliness of his person, and the fineness of his voice. When it seems
hopeless that he should appear, the cause of the stage is given up as
utterly lost. When he returns, it is hailed as the " courageous day,"
and the " happy hour," which is to restore the legitimate drama. It is
no wonder that this perpetual flattery fills him with a most inordinate
opinion of his own powers. There is not a part in the play which
he cannot perform. As a lover, he promises to make the audience
weep; but his talent is still more shining in the Herculean vein of a
tyrant. The manliness of his countenance, he admits, incapacitates
him from acting the part of a heroine; but, give him a mask, and
he is sure to captivate by the soft melody of his voice. But, lest it
should be thought this melodious softness was alone his characteristic, he claims the part of the lion, which he is to discharge with so
terrific a roar as to call forth the marked approbation of the warlike
Duke; and yet, when the danger is suggested of frightening the

---

* Act iv. sc. 2. Athens.—Quince's House.—Enter Quince, Flute, Snout,
and Starveling.
  " *Qui.* Have you sent to Bottom's house yet, &c. ?
  Flu. He hath simply the best wit of any man in Athens.
  Qui. Yea, and the best person too; and he is a very paramour for a sweet
voice.
  Flu. You must say paragon; a paramour is, God bless us ! a thing of
naught."
I propose that the second admirer's speech be given to Snout, who else has not
anything to say, and is introduced on the stage to no purpose. The few words
he says elsewhere in the play are all ridiculous; and the mistake of " paramour "
for " paragon " is more appropriate to him than to Quince, who corrects the *ca-
cology* of Bottom himself. [Act. iii. sc. 1.
        " *Pyr.* Thisby, the flower of odious savours sweet.
          Qui. Odours—odours."]
And, besides, Quince, the playwright, manager, and ballad-monger,
  [" I 'll get Peter Quince to write a ballad of this dream," says Bottom,]
is of too much importance in the company to be rebuked by so inferior a personage as Flute. In the original draft of their play Snout was to perform Pyramus's father, and Quince, Thisbe's father, but those parts are omitted; Snout is
the representative of Wall, and Quince has no part assigned him. Perhaps this
was intentional, as another proof of bungling.

ladies, who all, Amazons as they were, must be daunted by sounds so fear-inspiring, he professes himself gifted with a power of compass capable of imitating, even in the character of a roaring lion, the gentleness of the sucking dove, or the sweetness of the nightingale. He is equally fit for all parts, and in all parts calculated to outshine the rest. This is allowed; but, as it is impossible that he can perform them all, he is restricted to the principal. It is with the softest compliments that he is induced to abandon the parts of Thisbe and the lion for that of Pyramus. Quince assures him that he can play none other, because " Pyramus is a sweet-faced man; a proper man as one shall see in a summer's day ; a most lovely, gentlemanlike man ; *therefore* YOU must undertake it." What man of woman born could resist flattery so unsparingly administered? the well-puffed performer consents, and though he knows nothing of the play, and is unable to tell whether the part for which he is cast is that of a lover or a tyrant, undertakes to discharge it with a calm and heroic indifference as to the colour of the beard he is to wear, being confident, under any circumstances, of success, whether that most important part of the costume be straw-coloured or orange-tawny, French crown or purple in grain. With equal confidence he gets through his performance. The wit of the courtiers, or the presence of the Duke, have no effect upon his nerves. He alone speaks to the audience in his own character, not for a moment sinking the personal consequence of Bottom in the assumed port of Pyramus. He sets Theseus right on a point of the play with cool importance ; and replies to the jest of Demetrius (which he does not understand) with the self-command of ignorant indifference. We may be sure that he was abundantly contented with his appearance, and retired to drink in, with ear well deserving of the promotion it had attained under the patronage of Robin Goodfellow, the applause of his companions. It is true that Oberon designates him as a " hateful fool;" that Puck stigmatizes him as the greatest blockhead of the set ; that the audience of wits and courtiers before whom he has performed vote him to be an ass : but what matter is that ? He mixes not with them ; he hears not their sarcasms ; he could not understand their criticisms; and, in the congenial company of the crew of patches and base mechanicals who admire him, lives happy in the fame of being *the* Nicholas Bottom, who, by consent, to him universal and world-encompassing, is voted to be *the* Pyramus, —*the* prop of the stage,—*the* sole support of the drama.

Self-conceit, as great and undisguised as that of poor Bottom, is to be found in all classes and in all circles, and is especially pardonable in what it is considered genteel or learned to call " the histrionic profession." The triumphs of the player are evanescent. In no other department of intellect, real or simulated, does the applause bestowed upon the living artist bear so melancholy a disproportion to the repute awaiting him after the generation passes which has witnessed his exertions. According to the poet himself, the poor player

> " Struts and frets his hour upon the stage,
> And then is heard no more."

Shakspeare's own rank as a performer was not high, and his reflections on the business of an actor are in general splenetic and discontented. He might have said,—though indeed it would not have fitted with the mood of mind of the despairing tyrant into whose mouth the reflection is put,—that the well-graced actor, who leaves the scene not merely after strutting and fretting, but after exhibiting power and genius to the utmost degree at which his art can aim, amid the thundering applause,—or, what is a deeper tribute, the breathless silence of excited and agitated thousands,—is destined ere long to an oblivion as undisturbed as that of his humbler fellow-artist, whose prattle is without contradiction voted to be tedious. Kemble is fading fast from our view. The gossip connected with every thing about Johnson keeps Garrick before us, but the interest concerning him daily becomes less and less. Of Betterton, Booth, Quin, we remember little more than the names. The Lowins and Burbages of the days of Shakspeare are known only to the dramatic antiquary, or the poring commentator, anxious to preserve every scrap of information that may bear upon the elucidation of a text, or aid towards the history of the author. With the sense of this transitory fame before them, it is only natural that players should grasp at as much as comes within their reach while they have power of doing so. It would be a curious speculation to inquire which personally has the greater enjoyment,—the author, neglected in life, and working for immortal renown, or the actor living among huzzas, and consigned to forgetfulness the moment that his hour is past. I suppose, on the usual principle of compensation, each finds in himself springs of happiness and self-comfort. The dim distance, in its shadowy and limitless grandeur, fills with solemn musings the soul of the one; the gorgeous gilding of the sunny scenery in the foreground kindles with rapturous joy the heart of the other. Shenstone lays it down as a principle, that, if it were left to our choice whether all persons should speak ill of us to our faces, and with applause behind our backs, or, *vice versâ,* that the applause should be lavished upon ourselves, and the ill-speaking kept for our absence, we should choose the latter; because, if we never heard the evil report, we should know nothing about our bad reputation, while, on the contrary, the good opinion others entertained of us would be of no avail if nothing reached our ears but words of anger or reproach. Since, after all, it is from within, and not from without, the sources of joy or sorrow bubble up, it does not matter so very much as the sensitive Lord of Leasowes imagines what the opinions of others concerning us may be,—at least as compared with those which, right or wrong, we form of ourselves. The question is of no great practical importance; and yet it would be somewhat curious to speculate in the manner of Hamlet, if we could do so, on the feelings of Kean and Wordsworth in the zenith of the popularity of the former, when he was worshipped as a demi-god by the unquestionable, or, at least, the scarce-questioned dispensers of daily renown; while the other by the recognised oracles of critical sagacity was set down as a jackass more obtuse than that belaboured by his own Peter Bell.

Pardon, therefore, the wearers of the sock and buskin for being obnoxious to such criticism as that lavished by Quince upon Bottom. We have no traces left us of what constituted the ordinary puffery of the Elizabethan days; but, as human nature is the same in all ages, we must suppose the trade to have been in its own way as vigorously carried on then as now. And, without hinting at anything personal, do we not week after week find attached to every performer making (whether with justice or not is no part of the consideration) pretensions to the omnifarious abilities of Bottom, some Peter Quince, who sticks to that Bottom with the tenacity of a leech, and is ready to swear that *he*, the Bottom, is the only man in Athens; that his appearance spreads an universal joy; his occultation involves the world in dramatical eclipse; that his performance of the lover can only be surpassed by his performance of the tyrant; and that it must puzzle an impartial public to decide whether nature and art, genius and study, designed him for a heroine couchant, or a rampant lion. To this it is little wonder that the object of applause lets down his ears too often donkey-like, and permits himself to be scratched by a Master Cobweb, spun though he be by a bottle-bellied spider, or a Master Peas-blossom, who can only claim Mistress Squash for his mother and Master Peascod for his father. In Peter Quince, Shakspeare shadowed forth, by anticipation, Sheridan's Puff. Quince is a fool, and Puff a rogue; and yet I think the criticism of the elder reviewer just as valuable. It is in the end as useful to the object of applause to be told, in plain terms, that he alone can act Pyramus because he is a sweet-faced man, a proper man, a most lovely, gentlemanlike man, as to have the same flummery administered under the guise of mock philosophy, with gabbling intonations about breadth, profoundness, depth, length, thickness, and so forth; which, being interpreted, signify, in many cases, " I know nothing about acting or writing, but I do know that you can give me a box or a dinner, and therefore let me play to your Bottom, Quince the carpenter, in an ass's head, intended as a representation of Aristotle the Stagirite."

Alas! I am wandering far away from the forest. I can only plead that my guide has led me into my own congenial land of newspaper from his native soil of poetry. But he never long remains out of his own domain, and the jokes and jests upon the unlucky company who undertook to perform

> " A tedious brief scene of young Pyramus
> And his love Thisbe, very tragical mirth,"

are but intrusive matter amid the romantic loves, all chivalrous and a little classical, of Theseus and Hippolita, and the jealousies unearthly, and yet so earthly, of Fairy Land. The romance of early Greece was sometimes strangely confused by the romance of the middle ages. It would take a long essay on the mixture of legends derived from all ages and countries to account for the production of such a personage as the " Duke ycleped Theseus " and his following; and the fairy mythology of the most authentic superstitions would be ransacked in vain to discover exact authorities for the Shakspearian Oberon and Titania. But, no matter whence derived, the author knew well that in his hands the chivalrous and classical, the airy and the imaginative, were safe. It was necessary for his drama to introduce among his fairy party a creature of earth's mould, and he has so done it as in the midst of his mirth to convey a picturesque satire on the fortune which governs the world, and upon those passions which elsewhere he had with agitating pathos to depict. As Romeo, the gentleman, is *the* unlucky man of Shakspeare, so here does he exhibit Bottom, the blockhead, as *the* lucky man, as him on whom Fortune showers her favours beyond measure.

This is the part of the character which cannot be performed. It is here that the greatest talent of the actor must fail in answering the demand made by the author upon our imagination. The utmost lavish of poetry, not only of high conception, but of the most elaborate working in the musical construction of the verse, and a somewhat recondite searching after all the topics favourable to the display of poetic eloquence in the ornamental style, is employed in the description of the fairy scenes and those who dwell therein. Language more brilliantly bejewelled with whatever tropes and figures rhetoricians catalogue in their books is not to be found than what is scattered forth with copious hand in Midsummer Night's Dream. The compliment to Queen Elizabeth,

> " In maiden meditation fancy-free,"

was of necessity sugared with all the sweets that the *bon-bon* box of the poet could supply; but it is not more ornamented than the passages all around. The pastoral images of Corin

> " Playing on pipes of corn, and versing love
> To amorous Phillida ;"

the homely consequences resulting from the fairy quarrel,

> " The ox hath therefore stretch'd his yoke in vain,
> The ploughman lost his sweat, and the green corn
> Hath rotted ere his youth attain'd a beard ;
> The fold stands empty in the drowned field,
> And crows are fatted with the murrain flock ;"

and so on, are ostentatiously contrasted with misfortunes more metaphorically related :

> " We see
> The seasons alter; hoary-headed frosts
> Fall on the fresh lap of the crimson rose ;
> And on old Hyems' chin and icy crown
> An odorous chaplet of sweet summer buds
> Is, as in mockery, set."

The mermaid chaunting on the back of her dolphin; the fair vestal throned in the west; the bank blowing with wild thyme, and decked with oxlip and nodding violet; the roundelay of the fairies singing their queen to sleep; and a hundred images beside of aërial grace and mythic beauty, are showered upon us; and in the midst of these splendours is tumbled in Bottom the weaver, blockhead by original formation, and rendered doubly ridiculous by his partial change into a literal jackass. He, the most unfitted for the scene of all conceivable personages, makes his appearance, not as one to be expelled with loathing and derision, but to be instantly accepted as the chosen lover of the Queen of the Fairies. The gallant train of Theseus traverse the forest, but they are not the objects of such fortune. The lady, under the oppression of the glamour cast upon her eyes by the juice of love-in-idleness, reserves her raptures for an absurd clown. Such are the tricks of Fortune.

Oberon himself, angry as he is with the caprices of his queen, does not anticipate any such object for her charmed affections. He is determined that she is to be captivated by " some vile thing," but he thinks only of

> " Ounce, or cat, or bear,
> Pard, or boar with bristled hair,"

animals suggesting ideas of spite or terror; but he does not dream that, under the superintendence of Puck, spirit of mischief, she is to be enamoured of the head of an ass surmounting the body of a weaver. It is so nevertheless; and the love of the lady is as desperate as the deformity of her choice. He is an angel that wakes her from her flowery bed; a gentle mortal, whose enchanting note wins her ear, while his beauteous shape enthralls her eye; one who is as wise as he is beautiful; one for whom all the magic treasures of the fairy kingdom are to be with surpassing profusion dispensed. For him she gathers whatever wealth and delicacies the Land of Faëry can boast. Her most airy spirits are ordered to be kind and courteous to this *gentleman*,—for into that impossible character has the blindness of her love transmuted the clumsy and conceited clown. Apricocks and dewberries, purple grapes, green figs, and mulberries, are to feed his coarse palate; the thighs of bees, kindled at the eyes of fiery glow-worms, are to light him to his flower-decked bed; wings plucked from painted butterflies are to fan the moonbeams from him as he sleeps; and in the very desperation of her intoxicating passion she feels that there is nothing which should not be yielded to the strange idol of her soul. She mourns over the restraints which separate her from the object of her burning affection, and thinks that the moon and the flowers participate in her sorrow.

> " The moon, methinks, looks with a watery eye,
> And when she weeps, weeps every little flower,
> *Lamenting some enforced chastity.*"

Abstracting the poetry, we see the same thing every day in the plain prose of the world. Many is the Titania driven by some unintelligible magic so to waste her love. Some juice, potent as that of Puck, —the true Cupid of such errant passions,—often converts in the eyes of woman the grossest defects into resistless charms. The lady of youth and beauty will pass by the attractions best calculated to captivate the opposite sex, to fling herself at the feet of age or ugliness. Another, decked with graces, accomplishments, and the gifts of genius, and full of all the sensibilities of refinement, will squander her affections on some good-for-nothing *roué*, whose degraded habits and pursuits banish him far away from the polished scenes which she adorns. The lady of sixteen quarters will languish for him who has no arms but those which nature has bestowed; from the midst of the gilded *salon* a soft sigh may be directed towards the thin-clad tenant of a garret; and the heiress of millions may wish them sunken in the sea if they form a barrier between her and the penniless lad toiling for his livelihood,

> "Lord of his presence, and no land beside."

Fielding has told us all this in his own way, in a distich, (put, I believe, into the mouth of Lord Grizzle; but, as I have not the illustrious tragedy in which it appears, before me, I am not certain, and must therefore leave it to my readers to verify this important point.) Love

> " Lords into cellars bears,
> And bids the brawny porter walk up stairs."

Tom Thumb and Midsummer Night's Dream preach the one doctrine. It would be amusing to trace the courses of thought by which the heterogeneous minds of Fielding and Shakspeare came to the same conclusion.

Ill-mated loves are generally but of short duration on the side of the nobler party, and she awakes to lament her folly. The fate of those who suffer like Titania is the hardest. The man who is deprived of external graces of appearance may have the power of captivating by those of the mind: wit, polish, fame, may compensate for the want of youth or personal attractions. In poverty or lowly birth may be found all that may worthily inspire devoted affection—

> " The rank is but the guinea's stamp,
>   The man 's the gowd for a' that."

In the very dunghill of dissipation and disgrace will be raked up occasionally a lurking pearl or two of honourable feeling, or kind emotion, or irregular talent, which may be dwelt upon by the fond eye, wilfully averting its gaze from the miserable mass in which they are buried. But woe unto the unhappy lady who, like Titania, is obliged to confess, when the enchantment has passed by, that she was " enamoured of an *ass !*" She must indeed "loathe his visage," and the memory of all connected with him is destined ever to be attended by a strong sensation of disgust.

But the ass himself of whom she was enamoured has not been the less a favourite of Fortune, less happy and self-complacent, because of her late repentance. He proceeds onward as luckily as ever. Bottom, during the time that he attracts the attentions of Titania, never for a moment thinks there is anything extraordinary in the matter. He takes the love of the Queen of the Fairies as a thing of course, orders about her tiny attendants as if they were so many apprentices at his loom, and dwells in Fairy Land unobservant of its wonders, as quietly as if he were still in his workshop. Great is the courage and self-possession of an ass-head. Theseus would have bent in reverent awe before Titania. Bottom treats her as carelessly as if she were the wench of the next-door tapster. Even Christopher Sly,* when he finds himself transmuted into a lord, shows some signs of astonish-

---

* In comparing the characters of Sly and Bottom, we must be struck with the remarkable profusion of picturesque and classical allusions with which both these buffoons are surrounded. I have quoted some of the passages from Midsummer Night's Dream above. The Induction to the Taming of the Shrew is equally rich. There, too, we have the sylvan scenery and the cheerful sport of the huntsman, and there we also have references to Apollo and Semiramis; to Cytherea all in sedges hid; to Io as she was a maid; to Daphne roaming through a thorny wood. The coincidence is not casual. Shakspeare desired to elevate the scenes in which such grovelling characters played the principal part by all the artificial graces of poetry, and to prevent them from degenerating into mere farce. As I am on the subject, I cannot refrain from observing that the remarks of Bishop Hurd on the character of the Lord in the Induction to the Taming of the Shrew are marked by a ridiculous impertinence, and an ignorance of criticism truly astonishing. They are made to swell, however, the strange farrago of notes gathered by the variorum editors. The next editor may safely spare them.

I have not troubled my readers with verbal criticism in this paper, but I shall here venture on one conjectural emendation. Hermia, chiding Demetrius, says, Act iii. sc. 2,

> " If thou hast slain Lysander in his sleep,
>   Being o'er shoes in blood, wade in *the* deep,
>   And kill me too."   Should

ment. He does not accommodate himself to surrounding circumstances. The first order he gives is for a pot of small ale ; and after all the elegant luxuries of his new situation have been placed ostentatiously before him,—after he has smelt sweet savours, and felt soft things,—after he begins to think he is

> "A lord indeed,
> And not a tinker nor Christopher[o] Sly ;"

even then nature—or habit, which stands in the place of nature,— recurs invincible, and once more he calls for a pot of the smallest ale. (I may again cite Fielding in illustration of Shakspeare ; for do we not read, in the Covent Garden tragedy, of the consolation that

> " Cold small beer is to the waking drunkard ;"

and do we not hear the voice of Christopher Sly praying, for God's sake, in the midst of his lordly honours, for a draught of that unlordly but long-accustomed beverage ?) In the Arabian Nights' Entertainments a similar trick is played by the Caliph Haroun Al-raschid upon Abou Hassan, and he submits, with much reluctance, to believe himself the Commander of the Faithful. But having in vain sought how to explain the enigma, he yields to the belief, and then performs all the parts assigned to him, whether of business or pleasure, of counsel or gallantry, with the easy self-possession of a practised gentleman. Bottom has none of the scruples of the tinker of Burton-heath, or the *bon vivant* of Bagdad. He sits down amid the fairies as one of themselves without any astonishment; but so far from assuming, like Abou Hassan, the manners of the court where he has been so strangely intruded, he brings the language and bearing of the booth into the glittering circle of Queen Titania. He would have behaved in the same manner on the throne of the caliph, or in the bedizened chamber of the lord ; and the ass-head would have victoriously carried him through.

Shakspeare has not taken the trouble of working out the conclusion of the adventure of Sly ; and the manner in which it is finished in the old play where he found him, is trifling and common-place. The Arabian novelist repeats the jest upon his hero, and concludes by placing him as a favourite in the court of the amused caliph. This is the natural ending of such an adventure ; but, as Bottom's was supernatural, it was to conclude differently. He is therefore dismissed to his ordinary course of life, unaffected by what has passed. He admits at first that it is wonderful, but soon thinks it is nothing more than a fit subject for a ballad in honour of his own name. He falls at once to his old habit of dictating, boasting, and swaggering, and makes no reference to what has happened to him in the forest. It was no more than an ordinary passage in his daily life. Fortune knew where to bestow her favours.

Adieu then, Bottom the weaver ! and long may you go onward prospering in your course ! But the prayer is needless, for you carry about you the infallible talisman of the ass-head. ~~You will~~ be always

---

Should we not read " *knee* deep ?" As you are already over your shoes, wade on until the bloody tide reaches your knees. In Shakspeare's time *knee* was generally spelt *kne* ; and between *the* and *kne* there is not much difference in writing.

sure of finding a Queen of the Fairies to heap her favours upon you, while to brighter eyes and nobler natures she remains invisible or averse. Be you ever the chosen representative of the romantic and the tender before dukes and princesses; and if the judicious laugh at your efforts, despise them in return, setting down their criticism to envy. This you have a right to do. Have they, with all their wisdom and wit, captivated the heart of a Titania as you have done? Not they—nor will they ever. Prosper therefore, with undoubting heart despising the rabble of the wise. Go on your path rejoicing; assert loudly your claim to fill every character in life; and you may be quite sure that as long as the noble race of the Bottoms continues to exist, the chances of extraordinary good luck will fall to their lot, while in the ordinary course of life they will never be unattended by the plausive criticism of a Peter Quince.

LADY BLUE'S BALL.

BY MRS. C. B. WILSON.

" So warmly we met," and so closely were jumbled,
　　Like pigeons in pies, for the rooms were too small;
I was fearful my new satin dress would be tumbled,
　　As I gasp'd in a corner at Lady Blue's ball.
Some attempted to dance, but ran 'gainst each other;
　　Some flirted, some fainted; but *this* agreed all,
They had ne'er before witness'd a crowd or a smother,
　　Till jamm'd on the staircase at Lady Blue's ball!

A dance! 'tis a heaven, if a girl's not neglected,
　　And has plenty of partners to come at her call;
And many a mirror's bright surface reflected
　　Soft smiles and warm blushes at Lady Blue's ball!
Mammas sat aside, (for eldest sons looking,)
　　Whose daughters had beauty, but no cash at all;
Younger brothers (in thought) were the bright thousands booking
　　Of those girls who *had* fortunes at Lady Blue's ball.

And some they were waltzing, and others quadrilling,
　　" All pair'd, but not match'd," young and old, short and tall:
While some in sly corners were cooing and billing
　　Notes at sight, and of hand, at my Lady Blue's ball.
Thus Fashion's gay crowd goes on flirting and whirling,
　　As they mingle together, the great with the small;
And what's life but a dance, too, where, twisting and twirling,
　　We jostle each other, to get through the ball!

THE MAN WITH THE CLUB FOOT.

TALE (THE SECOND) OF ST. LUKE'S.

" You must know, sir, that our family is of very distinguished origin. My father was descended from the ancient L——s, of L—— Hall, in Leicestershire ; my mother is from the sole remaining branch of the renowned family of *Maxwell ;*—of course you must remember, sir, what great actions have been achieved by the *Maxwells* in olden time ?"

" My memory is not very good in such particulars," said I, to the elegant young man with whom I was speaking ; " pray proceed with your narration, and never mind your ancestors."

" Not mind my ancestors !" returned L——, a little angrily ; " but perhaps you are right, sir, after all ; the *living* ought to claim our attention more than the dead. Well ! we were left in the deepest distress,— my excellent mother, and myself, her only child. I will not trouble you in detailing how my poor father, by a hundred improvident and extravagant ways contrived to dwindle down his property ; too proud to embark in any profession except the army, and afterwards too poor to enter it. He died of—of—a broken heart when I was about twelve years old. I did nothing but devise schemes after this event to retrieve our wretched circumstances when I became old enough. A thousand plans, wild and visionary, passed through my brain ; I could not sleep at night for projects and inventions. I became fevered, restless, taciturn, irritable, and absent. One day, when I had arrived at the age of fifteen, on returning from a solitary walk, weary and exhausted, with a lump of clayey substance, wrapped up carefully, in my hands, which I had extracted from the side of a canal at a great distance from my home, believing it to contain some most precious qualities which might lead to my making a rapid fortune, I was forcibly struck with the extreme dejection of my mother, and the want of all preparation in our little parlour. I could not understand it at first ; but the truth came home slowly, heavily upon my heart. She had no longer the means of procuring her son and herself another meal !" Here L—— paused, and looked for sympathy.

" Did not the distress of your mother rouse you, L——, into immediate action ?" said I.

" No, sir," replied my companion, with an emphasis that made me start ; " would you have had a son of the ancient house of L—— go and work upon the highway ? to degrade himself with trade ? or——"

" Surely this had been better than seeing a mother starve, young gentleman," said I mildly ; " but I interrupt you. Tell me what effect was produced upon your mind by the knowledge of your situation. What did you do ?"

" You shall hear, sir, in due time," continued he gloomily ; " but I suppose the relation will cause you some displeasure. We cannot always be masters of ourselves, or of our own actions."

" But we *ought* to be so, Mr. L—— ; there is no slavery so bad as the slavery of the passions. Then are we slaves indeed," and I looked full upon him.

L—— resumed : " You shall know the exact truth, sir ; I will at any rate be strictly impartial. When I was convinced that we had not a meal left in the world,—convinced by remembering the bareness of the walls, and now missing several articles of furniture that had disappeared without my before perceiving it,—I seized my hat, and, totally disregarding the pathetic appeal of my mother's voice,—the beseeching accents of her who had never yet spoken to me a reproachful word from my earliest recollections,—' to be calm, and hope that better times would come,' I darted out of the house like an arrow from the bow, and, coward as I was, after wandering about for hours to summon resolution for the act, rushed to the river about a mile from the village, and threw myself into its rapid current. There I soon lost all recollection of myself and my misery. The last sound I heard was the gurgling of waters in my ears and throat; the last sensation I experienced was that I should not now die the languishing death of famine. My mother's image was before me; then it grew indistinct, and all was darkness, vagueness, insensibility." L—— again paused.

"Then you have actually committed the crime of suicide, young man!" I exclaimed reproachfully; "I trust you have been repentant for it. Your intention was to destroy yourself; the motive makes the crime."

"My narrative, sir, is of events, not of my own feelings," replied Mr. L—— proudly; "if you are already disgusted with my conduct as a boy, perhaps it might be better that you knew not of it as a man. Perhaps I had better stop here?"

"That is according to your own pleasure, my dear sir," said I, affecting an indifference that I did not feel; but wishing to curb the irritability of my young companion.

"Most strange were my emotions," continued he, after a pause and a smile, "on life returning to my bosom,—that is active life; for I suppose the principle itself was not absolutely extinct. What is your opinion, sir, as a medical man? Can life be rekindled in the human breast when once fairly extinguished? for my part I think it can, and that mine is a renewed life. You smile, sir, but I should wish an answer to my question;" and again that proud, yet beautiful, lip of his, curled with impatience, whilst he took a stride across the apartment.

"Can life ever be extinguished?" I demanded.

"Certainly," replied Mr. L——, looking at me as if he thought I was insane, or jesting with him. "Are we not living in one great hospital, amidst the dying and the dead? Are we sure of our existence a single hour? Must we not all die at last?"

"Let each one speak for himself, Falkner L——," said I impressively; "I am sure of the perpetuity of mine own existence; it can never perish."

"Oh! *that* is your meaning, is it?" sarcastically exclaimed my opponent. "I am no divine, and my question related to that existence I know of. I wished to learn whether I have been absolutely dead? since, if so, I can account better for many of those thoughts and sensations that now puzzle and perplex me exceedingly. But I will not press my inquiry further on you; perhaps you know as little about these things as myself;" and he pressed his hand upon his forehead, whilst a sigh he sought to restrain would be heard.

"Go on with your story, L——," said I ; "we will discuss this subject about existence and a future state another time ; what were your sensations on recovering the use of your senses ? for you must have been brought to life, I conclude, somehow or other."

"I found myself lying on the grass," continued Mr. L——, "quite wet, but with an agreeable warmth within, from some cordial that had been administered to me. I gazed at first, unconsciously, upon the clouds sailing by upon the blue ocean of immensity above my head. I felt myself calm and composed as that depth of sky, fathomless, unsearchable,—for memory was not yet awakened in me, —and *the present* was to me peaceful, holy. Oh, that such moments should be lost ! I thought the moon some new and beautiful appearance just rising from creation. I was roused into recollection thus :

"'Are you able, young man, now to walk ?' said a hoarse unpleasing voice near me ; 'your mother, perchance, is uneasy at your absence ; and she should be spared from the bitter knowledge that her only, her beloved son, intended to have deserted her in her moment of deep affliction. Hide this from her ; it will be a pious secret. Conceal your intention of self-destruction from her.'

"During the whole of this speech my entire being seemed to be undergoing a change, rapid and powerful. I awakened as from a trance. I felt the enormity of my past conduct. My mother's tenderness ! her uncomplaining sufferings ! the sacrifices she had made to procure me the necessaries of life ! her total absence of all selfishness ! her privations ! her patience ! all rose before me. And how had I requited her ?—by base desertion, by cruel ingratitude ! My heart was softened, and, boy-like, I burst into tears.

"'Showers should produce blossoms, — blossoms fruit !' said the same croaking discordant voice close to my ear. '*Tears* are showers for good resolutions; they should not be unproductive. Your mother, young man ! think of your mother !'

"I started upon my feet, and was going hastily home, when it struck me that this man must have plucked me out of the water ; so I turned to thank him. I had not yet set my eyes upon him. A short, squabby figure met my gaze, with a head of extraordinary size, round which hung dark elfish locks ; his eyes were immensely large, and had a most melancholy expression, yet they were strongly tinctured with benevolence, and had a most searching quality,—something that seemed not of this earth. My reason still tottered on its throne: the delusion again darted across my mind that I was not in the same state of existence as formerly, and that this strange-looking being was one of the inhabitants of the new one, in which I found myself. I looked at him again curiously, inquiringly ; and found that, in addition to his uncouth globular form, enormous head, and eyes with bushy brows, he had an excrescence on his shoulder known commonly by the name of '*a hump*,' and had one short, distorted *club-foot !*"

As Mr. L—— told me this, he turned unusually pale, and a cold shudder passed like a blighting wind over him. I knew he had been subject to all sorts of fancies and wild conjectures, the offspring of a heated imagination ; so I only coolly observed,

"Oh ! your preserver, then, it seems, was a poor hunchback ! I wonder how he fished you out of the river ? — how he had the strength to do it ?"

Mr. L—— answered me only with a most mysterious look, and another shudder. I took out my watch, and struck the hour; it had the desired effect, for he was sensitive in the highest degree.

"I will not detain you long," said he, in a deprecating tone, "your time is precious;" and thus he continued: —"I stammered out my thanks for the service he had done me; but my knees knocked against each other, and my teeth chattered in my head. I was on the point of falling."

"'You have caught a severe cold, I suppose,' exclaimed the man with the club-foot; 'but it might have been worse. Here, take another draught of this cordial, which has been the means already of doing you some service. Hesitate not; you will find instant relief; I composed it myself in the island of Ceylon, from the rarest spices, and have often proved its efficacy.' He approached me; he only reached my waist; and, what was most strange, I heard not the slightest sound as he moved his feet! Feet!—shall I call them *feet?*—he had but one; the other resembled the gnarled, disproportioned fragment of the root of an old oak-tree; it had a sort of cradle, on which it rested; it was tipped with brass, and of expensive workmanship. I could draw you the exact pattern of this shoe."

"What matters the shape of a deformed man's shoe?" said I; "a little larger, or a little smaller, makes all the difference, I suppose, between them. They are very expert in manufacturing these *helps* in Germany; we cannot approach them in such things. There is a man now at Hambro', who ——"

"This shoe was never made in Germany!" interrupted Mr. L——, with a deep sepulchral tone of voice; and again he shuddered, whilst a spasm shook his frame.

"Very likely not," said I, with a tone of perfect nonchalance; "perhaps it was one of Sheldrake's shoes; but it is of little consequence:—you and I will never want one of such construction; that is one comfort, however."

"No," he replied musingly, "not for ourselves: but in my family perchance it may be wanted. Tell me, sir, are these deformities hereditary?" and his eyes seemed to penetrate my inmost thoughts.

"Did you mean the *shoe* or the *foot*, L——?" I asked jestingly; "one is as likely as the other; but shall we never get beyond or above this piece of leather, or prunella? I declare we have been standing in this man's shoes half an hour at least; they pinch me to death."

"I would not stand in that man's shoes for a single moment, to gain an entire world!" impressively pronounced poor L——, casting up his eyes to heaven.

"Yet," said I, "one of them might fit you better than the other; for I suppose that brass-bitted piece of machinery must be rather uncomfortable to walk with. It would make, too, such a devil of a noise!" and I again had recourse to my watch.

"It made no noise at all, I tell you!" vehemently cried out poor Falkner L——; "no satin slipper of a lady ever trod so silently. A rose-leaf dropping on the ground might have made a louder sound; but you do not credit me."

"Pooh, pooh!" cried I; "the water was still in your ears; that was the reason you could not hear the clatter of the mailed shoe."

"Has the water been in my ears these ten—nay, more,—eleven summers and winters since, nights and days?" inquired my companion petulantly. "No one can, no one will, understand me,—nay, I scarce can comprehend myself. That accursed cordial that he gave me!"

"I should like to have a glass of it this moment, for I feel much exhausted," said I.

"I beg your pardon, I ought to have thought of it myself;" and he rang the bell for a tray and wine. We partook of some potted meats. I drank a couple of glasses of Madeira, my friend one of water; the tray was removed, and I took up my hat.

"Will you not hear me to the end?" inquired L——, fixing his dejected eyes upon me with an expression so appealing, so touching, that I could not resist them.

"When will that *end* arrive?" said I, playfully. "Did you drink the cordial that this little rotundity offered to you?"

"Yes, I drained it to the bottom. So very delicious was its taste, so grateful to my exhausted frame and spirits, that I left not a drop in the globular vessel that contained it. I returned to him the flask."

"'Thou art not yet cured of *thy selfishness*, young man,' said the man with the club-foot, in a severe tone which made his voice appear more harsh and grating even than before. 'Couldst thou not have spared a single drop out of that vessel for the next intended suicide I may chance to meet with? Fortunately I have been more provident than thou hast been considerate; I have not exhausted my whole mine of wealth upon thee. Thy mother, boy, has spoiled thy nature, I see, by indulgence. Go, and think of others as well as of thyself.' With this, the strange being I had been speaking with, shaking his coarse and wiry locks at me, trundled himself away,—for walking it did not seem; and I again perceived *that not the slightest sound came from his steps!*"

"On entering my mother's small but neat abode, she threw her arms around my neck, and wept for joy at seeing me.

"'My beloved Falkner! I am so glad you are returned! I have such delightful news to tell you;—but you are wet, pale, hungry too I doubt not; but that shall not be for long. I have plenty of every thing good in the house; food of every description, and ready for eating, too,—so we will begin: but change your clothes first, Falkner! Why, my dear, dear boy, you must have tumbled into the river,—perhaps in trying to catch fish for your mother's supper;—but we do not want fish now.'

"After changing my wet apparel for the only other suit I had, and that none of the best, we sat down opposite to each other at the clean-scowered deal table,—the others had been parted with previously. We had no cloth,—they too had disappeared one by one long before; but hunger is not over fastidious. A cold fowl was placed upon the table: a tongue, and a bottle of wine, with plenty of fine wheaten bread, cheese, and butter. The word 'selfishness' rung in my ears during dinner; I was resolved to pluck this abominable vice from my bosom even to the very roots. When we had ate and were filled, I began to question my mother how she had been able to procure these dainties.

"'They were sent from the tavern, Falkner, by a *very old friend*

of mine,—one I have not seen for many, many years. He has taken
our spare apartments at a price twenty times beyond their value, and
has given me a month's rent in advance. He is gone now to order
in furniture from C—— both for himself and us. We shall never
know want again! My darling son will now be provided for, according to his birth;' and my mother shed tears of joy.

"All this appeared to me exceedingly strange; but, then, it was
delightful also. I complained, however, very soon of fatigue, when
my tender mother insisted on having my bed warmed, on account of
my ' *tumble into the water ;*' and, bringing me a glass of mulled spiced
wine, she kissed my forehead, and departed.

"I did not wake till noon. What a change had been effected
ere that time, in our white-washed cottage! New handsome carpets
were spread over the floors; chairs and tables placed in perfect order
against the walls, and of the best quality. Room was left on one side
our parlour for a grand piano, which my mother's friend would
procure for her use from London. He had already ransacked a considerable market-town near us, and had contrived to get together tolerable things, but not of the quality he wished: he had gone now to
London for the purpose of purchasing the piano, and many other luxuries he thought she needed; but would return in the course of a
week, and take up his abode as——

"'And who is this friend of yours, my dear mother?' I inquired.
'You say you have known him long. Why has he not sooner attended to your wants?'

"'For a simple reason, Falkner,' she replied; 'he knew not of
them; he is but just arrived in England.'

"'Is he a *relation*, mother? I trust he is, and a very near one too,
or——' and I hesitated. 'I am but a young adviser, yet I feel that
a female,—a handsome one, too,—a descendant from the proud family of the Maxwells, ought not to be obliged to any one who is
an alien in blood and name. I cannot suffer *my* mother to be degraded. We may perish, but we will not be disgraced.'

"My mother heard me patiently to the end; then, smiling sweetly
on me, told me she admired me for my delicacy of feeling and regard
for her honour, but that I need be under no apprehension on her account, as her dear and valued old friend was her very nearest relative; also, 'We are sisters' children, Falkner, and in childhood were
most intimate. You should hear him on the organ, Falkner; he
would rival St. Cecilia herself on that celestial instrument. He
wishes now to know in what way he can benefit my son? Have
you ever thought of a profession?'

"'Thought of one! Oh, mother! Have I thought of anything
else? Who can look at those bright orbs moving above us without
longing to be acquainted with their relative positions, their bearings
on each other. Let me be an astronomer, I conjure you, but let
me not learn of any common master; let me understand the wonders
of magnetic and electrical influence, the causes of universal gravitation; whether the infinite expanse above and around me be an entire void—a vacuum, or full of invisible ether, from which matter is
formed the subtle essence which, when called together by its Maker's
voice, thickens and hardens into worlds like this I tread on.'

"I was now mounted on the hobby that had for the last three

years—nay, more, from my very infancy,—carried me on its back, enjoying my day-dreams, and bearing me oft into dark labyrinths of abstruse speculations. This was the first time I had ever ventured to mount it, except in privacy; for there is a secret delight in keeping these same ambling nags, you know, from the sight of others. They are ready at all hours during the day, as well as night, saddled and bridled for our use."

"And so is my Bucephalus, Mr. L——," said I, interrupting him. "I dare say the poor beast is wondering what his master is about this length of time."

"I beg your pardon; I am a long time telling my story," said my companion; "but I wished to show you how very soon the favourite occupation of my mind, indulging in vain abstractions, put to flight all my prudence, my high sense of honour, and delicacy to my mother's fame. To have my ardent wishes gratified with regard to my studies made me forget that perhaps it might be improper to purchase them at such expense; but my *selfishness* was not wholly departed from me.

"My mother seemed perfectly astonished at hearing what was my desire for the future; but she wrote off that night to consult 'her friend,' whose answer was most propitious. 'He knew a very learned man in Germany, who could instruct me in all these matters, a Dr. Hettmann, a great philosopher and astronomer,—something, too, of an astrologer to boot,—who was certain to receive as a pupil any relative of Mr. Maxwell's; and, as for the means, he begged my mother not to consider about those, but to prepare my equipment, and he would himself take me over to the doctor, by way of Rotterdam, to Vienna, and settle every arrangement on my account.' And so the preparations were begun immediately.

"With that inconsistency with which very young men generally act and think, it struck me forcibly that I could not, ought not, to leave my mother thus domesticated in the same house even with her near relation, and I absent; so, with a very high air of importance, conceit, as well as temper, I told her, 'I should *not* go to Germany after all, for I should have enough to do to protect her against the evil designs of this accursed relative of hers, who I wished heartily was at the bottom of the Black Sea—the Red one was too good for him.'

"'Do not alarm yourself, my dear Falkner,' said she meekly, and confusedly casting down her eyes; 'there shall be no impropriety on my part. You shall never have cause to blush for your mother. The morning previous to your setting off under the escort of my friend, I intend giving him my hand at C—— church, and trust you will be present at our nuptials.'

"I have no doubt, sir, I jumped from my chair a foot and a half at hearing this proposition," said L——. "I asked her if I had heard aright? and felt that my lips quivered with emotion, and that a cold damp was on my brow.

"'It is a long story, Falkner,' said my mother, 'and I have not the heart to enter into it now; suffice it to say I was engaged to my cousin, Mr. Maxwell, before I saw your father: *after* I had seen him, I could not fulfil my prior engagement. With a generosity I could not copy, I was relieved from it by him, and he went abroad. But now, though late, I shall do my best to make my first affianced *lover*

2 F 2

happy.' 'Lover!' thought I. From my very soul I detested this abominable Mr. Maxwell. Once or twice I contemplated shooting him, as a kind of rival; at any rate to interpose my authority—to interdict the ceremony, to me so loathsome; but then again I thought of our former poverty, our threatened starvation, of my wretched prospects without the aid of this odious father-in-law. In the end, after a fearful tempest in my mind, and then a fit of gloom and ill-humour, I moodily made up my mind *not* to prevent my mother's marriage with her cousin; especially as a box of Dollond's best mathematical instruments, with a quadrant and telescope, were sent down to me as a present from this hated Mr. Maxwell. 'I will endeavour to behave decently when he arrives, and give her to him, if I can, at the altar,' thought I.

"Two days after, a plain travelling-carriage stopped at our garden gate; my heart beat wildly—I looked at my mother; she was calm and pale as usual, but her eyes were anxiously, deprecatingly, cast on me. I understood the appealing glances that came from them. 'Mother,' said I, 'fear not; I will behave magnificently!—you shall see how well I will treat him.' I heard the carriage-door slap to; I expected to hear the footsteps of the ardent, thriving bridegroom coming up the little gravel-walk leading from the gate to the parlour; but all was quiet. 'Shall I go to meet him?' I inquired in the plenitude of my intended patronage. There was no need; *the intended bridegroom stood before me*,—the man to whom I was to give away my tender, my beloved, my beautiful mother. There, in all his native deformity, with his large head, enormous eyes, and dark elf looks, stood *the man with the club-foot!*

"I will tell you the rest of my story another time—not now—not now!" and Falkner L—— rushed from the apartment. I left the house immediately.

As I rode home to my own house, half a dozen miles distant, I pondered upon the narrative I had just heard. "Perchance," thought I, "the root of this malady is left; it may grow again. I fear he is not quite recovered. I will see him at any rate to-morrow."

L—— fully expected me, and smiled as I entered; but he looked paler than usual, and his hand was feverish. I spoke cheerfully to him; told him some little gossip I had picked up by the way; read him a paragraph or two from a London paper—the crack article of the day; descanted on the weather, as all Englishmen do, and prophesied respecting it for the next four-and-twenty hours. It was his turn next. After a moment's silence, and a sort of struggle with his feelings, he took up the thread of his discourse, but not where he had left off.

"You must have perceived, sir," began my young friend, "that I am of a wayward temper, and have been spoiled by overweening indulgence. My father—but he is in the grave; let me not disturb his ashes more than necessary;—I told you he had died of a broken heart. I am ashamed of the prevarication; his heart certainly was broken, but *his own hand* assisted the slower operations of nature. He would not brook delay; so ran a sword into that princely organ, and made it stop."

So fearfully pale now looked poor Falkner, that I handed him a glass of wine standing ready on the table, and made him drink it, saying in as cheerful a tone as I could muster up, "Come, come, my dear L——, you have begun now at quite a different part of your story; we must not retrograde. I want to know what you said or did to this same extraordinary-looking being who wanted to be your father-in-law,—this *man with the club-foot;* what did you say to him ?"

"Astonishment chained up my tongue," answered L——, "and disgust to his person turned me sick. On the other hand, gratitude whispered to me that he had saved my life : and self-interest suggested that without his aid, however revolting his person might be, there was nothing left to us but penury and wretchedness. Suspended as between two attractive powers did I stand, my eyes wildly gazing on him, and my brain actually whirling amidst these conflicting emotions."

" 'Falkner,' said my mother, 'speak to me !—you alarm me greatly ! Why do you look as if you saw a spirit ? Randolph, has my son ever beheld you before this moment, for there is recognition in his gaze ? He was an infant only when you saved his life thirteen years ago.' 'He has seen me only for two minutes,' croaked out that same harsh unmusical voice : 'he fell by some chance into the mill-stream the other day, and I helped him out again. To judge by his looks, he would not have done the same thing by me, if I had given him the same chance ;' and the monster laughed.

"I roused myself at length from the spell that bound me. 'Mother,' cried I vehemently, 'I must speak to you alone ;' the man with the club-foot moved instantly and silently from the apartment.

" 'This cannot be,' I exclaimed passionately, 'that you can call this hideous wretch your husband ! Nature herself must shudder only at the thought. Deformed, stunted, odious, revolting !—Mother, the very touch of his hand would be a profanation to the dead. My mother sighed. 'And yet, Falkner, how much happier should I have been had I not been dazzled from my plighted faith by exterior advantages alone, and passed my life with one whose qualities are like the fairest diamond placed in a rude shagreen casket. My son, you have not yet looked upon the brilliancy *within.* Read that paper, Falkner, and be just.' My mother quitted the room as she spoke.

"For the first time in my life I perceived a counteracting influence in opposition to my own in the breast of my tender mother, and the thought enraged me beyond all bounds. Again I meditated self-destruction; again gloomily conceived the thought that I would immolate this intruding wretch, and thus free us both from his persevering attentions. 'It shall be done,' I exclaimed aloud, clenching my hands together in a delirium of passion; 'I have learned a few secrets from Nature in my wanderings alone with her, and one of them I will prove this very evening on——'

" '*Your benefactor, Falkner !*' interrupted the raven-like croaking of Randolph Maxwell, looking up into my face with those large melancholy eyes of his, and laying his hand on mine. I was taken unawares, and was surprised to find that this same hand of his was delicately white, and soft as that of a woman's. It had on a ring of surpassing brilliancy, which attracted my eyes even in the midst of this exciting scene, so boyish and unfixed at that time was my mind. Was it that the ring itself possessed some powerful spell over my wayward thoughts? or that the hand, looking like a *human one*,—nay, even beautiful in its kind,—made the owner of it appear at that moment like a being of the same nature as my own? By an impulse I could not control, I extended my own towards him, and I fancied I saw a moisture in those large melancholy eyes of his. 'Emma, my betrothed Emma,' called out that voice, made only for the society of crocodiles and croaking birds of prey, 'come hither, Emma, and behold thy Randolph and thy son *friends*.' She entered at the call, and pressed our united hands between her own. Then all the loathing and abhorrence of my nature against that inexplicable being returned, and with as much violence as before. But I covered it over with artifice, cloaked it with politeness, obscured it from observation by taciturnity and sullenness. Like a martyr I submitted to my fate; so, the next morning I accompanied this ill-matched pair to the church of C——, and saw them married, forcing myself to give away my almost idolised parent to a thing resembling an ourangoutang. How did I long to spurn the reptile I looked down upon, with my foot! to crush him to pieces as I would a bloated toad!

"That very evening my new father-in-law and myself set off to Germany, my mother having previously put into my hands once more, that paper she had before wished me to read. I thrust it into my pocket. Her blessing to us both, as we seated ourselves in the carriage of the dwarf, still rings in my ears.

"'Farewell, dear Randolph! Farewell, beloved son! For my sake, Randolph, be kind to this *unfortunate* boy!' Thus did the dwarf answer: 'I swear to you by that faith which has been so powerfully proved, to be careful and indulgent to your son. Write to me, my——' he would have added '*beloved wife*;' but catching, I suppose, some strange and threatening expression in my eyes, he changed it into 'my dear and earliest friend!' I felt choking, but would not give way to the tenderness of nature;—I would not say, 'God bless you, best and kindest of mothers!' I threw myself back into the carriage, and, overpowered with various emotions, I wept like an infant. But be it remembered, sir, I was not then sixteen years old. At length a healing slumber closed up my senses. I know not how long it lasted, for when I awoke I was alone; the carriage was standing without horses in an inn-yard; my companion would not have me disturbed, and was gone himself into the house to give orders for our accommodation there that night.

"My mother had used a word in parting that became to me as a constant goad; nay, it entered into my very soul. '*Her unfortunate boy!*' Why should she use the word *unfortunate*? I had been told from infancy, (and I firmly believed what had been so often asserted,) that I was eminently handsome. Both my parents had been distinguished for their great personal attractions, and I had been assured that I possessed in a still higher degree than they did the exterior gifts and graces of nature. Then, as to mental ones, had I not been born a poet, philosopher, everything that was great and noble?—for so my doting parents always said in my hearing. Why then did she now call me *unfortunate*, especially when she had provided for me so august a patron in her second husband? I have since fully known what she meant by this term *unfortunate*."

Poor L—— at this time rose from his chair, and gazed up vacantly into the clouds. I knew what he was thinking of, but the subject was too delicate for me to touch on.

He continued:

"I forgot the paper I had thrust into my pocket when I left my mother. We travelled on together wrapt up each in our own thoughts, for I could not force myself to converse with him, although sometimes I was astonished at the depth and genius of his observations. They fell like brilliant gems around me, but I would not pick them up, or even admire their lustre. At length wearied, I suppose, with my obstinacy, he took a book out of the pocket of the carriage, and began to read. This I considered an indignity, an insult, and with marks of temper sought immediately for another. In this mood we reached the house of the celebrated *Scheele*, in Vienna, where it was agreed I should for some months reside, that I might learn something of chemistry before I began my astronomical researches.

"Not a word was said to me on money matters; all this was arranged without my knowledge. I found a pocket-book on my toilet, containing most ample means for my private expenses, but it was unaccompanied with a single line. No leave was taken of me; but when I arose one morning I was told by the family of the Professor Scheele that 'my friend' had departed at an early hour, leaving me in charge of them, bespeaking their kindest attentions for me, and paying most liberally for me in advance.

"'Tis *all beyond* my comprehension," said Falkner L——— after a pause, and repeating to himself that line of Milton,

> "And found no end, in wandering mazes lost."

Then abruptly he continued thus:

"I learned all sorts of splendid nonsense from Professor Scheele, for I know not its utility. I went from him to the renowned Berzelius, and laid in a stock of more. I studied astronomy under a relation of the famous Schiller, and alchemy from a nephew of Jang Stilling. But what availed all these acquisitions? One fixed idea was ever like an incubus upon my soul,—the thought of my mother's marriage with this club-footed hunchback. Years passed on; and though invited, implored, to return to England, yet I could not endure the thought of seeing her *the wife* of so distorted a little wretch. She wrote to me ever 'of his nobleness, his generosity:' I felt the latter in the plenitude of his allowance to her son; but I was haunted perpetually by his image, hovering like an imp of darkness over a form moulded by the Graces. I hated my own country because it contained him, and yet I could think of nothing else. I became melancholy, morose, obstinate, taciturn, irritable to excess.

"One day, in clearing out my writing-desk, a paper came into my hand that I had no recollection of; it turned out to be the very one my mother had put into my hands just before my departure. These were the words. It was a letter from 'the Man with the club-foot' to herself.

"'To Emma, the beloved of my heart,—Think you that I am blind to my own imperfections?—that I am fool enough to suppose that this warped and twisted person of mine is a thing to be beloved, to be caressed? I have been conscious of my own deformities from a very child; and then it was that you, many years my junior, and accustomed to the sight of my exterior hideousness from your birth, cared not for it, but gave me the blessing of your companionship, and taught me to hope you could endure my presence through life. So did I delude myself; so did you guilelessly assist me in the delusion. I believed I should call you my own; you sanctioned this belief. But when the fascinating L—— arrived, how soon did I perceive my fatal mistake! I saw it long before my Emma even suspected it, and—why should I pain you now by telling you what I then suffered? enough, you know how I acted;—the hunchback preferred your happiness to his own.

" ' Emma, it is unnecessary now to tell you how I employed myself during seventeen years, and how much I thought of those days when my beautiful cousin would gaze fondly in my eyes, and call me ' her dear Randolph !' Need I say what unexpected delight I experienced when once I was enabled to save her child, then a very cherub, and still beautiful as herself, from destruction? You know all this; and how, after this transaction, blessed with her gratitude, I departed for Ceylon. Was I not loaded also with the knowledge and the misery that she, my beloved one, was not happy? I could not stay to witness her regrets.

" ' I went to Ceylon. It was with a miser's feeling that I hoarded up riches in that island, which contains more riches than any other part of the world. I trafficked in diamonds; I tried experiments with spices; I found hidden treasure; and, as I amassed wealth almost beyond calculation, I constantly said to myself, ' All this is for her,—*she will need it.*'

" ' And is it not thine own, thou idol of my heart?—and is it not thy darling son's? But think not that Randolph Maxwell's love is tainted by vile selfishness. I know, I feel my *person* must be abhorrent to my lovely cousin now—it is not like her L——'s; my mind she has some knowledge of. Let our marriage, then, beloved one! be only of the mind; let me live with you, gaze on you, hope that I disgust you not, and you will make your faithful cousin happy. I ask no more. Your child is mine; I have no other; he is the heir of my possessions, and herewith I make over to him and you, wealth enough to satisfy the most craving of our species;—everything, except a small pittance in case you should wish my absence, is yours. And now, Emma, we understand each other, and I think we ever shall. If your son——'

" But here the paper was skilfully divided; my mother would not suffer me to know the opinion Randolph Maxwell had of her wayward Falkner. Oh! that I had read this letter before!—it would have saved me hundreds of hours of anguish; but, now that I had done so, I formed an instant resolution of returning to England and my mother. Having always the means by me, I put no curb to my inclinations; I never had done so in my life, and, to my mother's astonishment, arrived there without informing her she might expect me. Enchantment seemed to have been used, for a palace had risen up close to our former white-washed cottage. I forgot my mother had apprised me. By an expensive process, full-grown trees of every kind had been transplanted to the new abode; it was imbedded in the midst of costly firs and flowering shrubs. I flew to her and tenderly embraced her. I even inquired respectfully for *the man with the club-foot.* I began myself to honour him. My mother's countenance changed as I mentioned his name, and an unknown kind of dread came over me. 'Let me know the worst at once,' said I, ' for,'—in short, I thought then, as now, that he had more than mortal agency.

" ' *The worst* will 'soon be told you, Falkner,' said my mother sadly. 'My cousin Randolph is dying : he has been in a declining state for the last two years. He eats nothing, never sleeps, and I shall soon lose a being of such exemplary worth, that I fear it will break my heart. It is impossible to describe to you the nobleness, the disinterested attachment of this creature, now at the very point of death. But here comes Dr. E——; he has been with my poor Randolph for the last two hours ; he will tell us what he thinks of his malady;'—and you, sir, came into the room."

" Do you remember this circumstance, doctor ?" said Falkner to me, " do you remember coming in from the bedside of your patient to the room where my mother and myself were sitting,—do you remember how closely I questioned you ?"

" *I do*," answered I dryly, " and also what passed in the sick man's chamber. But proceed with your narration—I think you have not much more to say."

" Is it then still a profound *secret* what that man, or devil,—I know not which he is,—communicated to you at that time ?" inquired poor L——, looking at me with eyes that seemed to search my very soul. " You told us, doctor, he was dying, and I thought so too myself afterwards ; for I was prevailed on to visit him you both called *my benefactor !*—Oh God ! oh God ! what is the reason that he did not die ? —that in a few days he—this hunchback—rose from that couch where we all expected he would close for ever those melancholy eyes ? Instead of our carrying him to the churchyard, and burying him deep, deep there, he broke his plighted faith to my ill-used mother, and rose from his couch to *become the partner of hers*—her veritable husband ! Was it not this accursed knowledge that utterly destroyed me ? Did I not rave then, beat my breast, and become a madman ? Did I not attempt the life of her who gave me birth ? And was I not prevented from fulfilling my design by this same loathsome being, who bound my hands together with a strength as if he had been a giant ; not the pigmy that he is ?—He overcame me—I remember this, now, full well."

" All this is nothing new to me," said I, " for I attended you all the time of your illness, *and you have been very bad indeed.* But what then ? These clouds will pass away, and the sun, the brilliant star of your mind, will be much brighter than it has ever been. Can you bear Falkner L—— to hear what passed in the sick chamber of him you have called by such opprobrious names ?"

" Before I answer you, doctor, you must resolve me one question," and the brow of the young man darkened :—" How long have I been ill ?" This was whispered rather than spoken.

" Exactly ten months," I replied. " Is that your question ?" and I smiled upon him, for I knew what was in his mind.

" No," he answered ; " it is only the scaffolding about it. It shall out," cried poor L—— furiously, " and on its reply depends whether I will ever speak again to man or woman during my short remnant of life. It is a question to me of vital importance indeed !" I am reluctant to give it utterance, so much disgust do I feel with this whole affair; yet I have a burning desire *to know*, and I will be satisfied."

"So had our first parents, L——," said I; "but they found the fruit of the tree of knowledge bitter and indigestive. *Wisdom* is always preferable to *knowledge;* for it yields content, calmness, holiness. But what is your question? I think I know its purport—out with it."

"Has my mother given birth to a child of that abominable man with the club-foot?" cried poor L—— almost inaudibly, with a lip quivering, an eye flaming; "is there *another* little wretch upon this earth inheriting the deformities of that monster?—a creature doomed to walk in shoes that give no sound, and therefore of magic and unlawful make?"

"What nonsense you talk, L——!" cried I. "Why, I took up those very shoes and examined them curiously, when I visited the sick chamber of their owner. I was struck with their strange make, and was much pleased with the invention, which is a German one; and I mean to write over for a pair or two of boots, made on this same construction, as I dislike creaking appendages to my feet of all things; for it sounds so *material,* you know. The soles of these are elastic and hollow, filled, moreover, with gas, which makes the wearer light-footed. We—that is, you and I—do not want such inventions to our *heads,* you know," I said a little archly; "we are light-headed enough without the assistance of German mechanists; but for their shoes we thank them."

"Perhaps they have helped us a little to be light-headed too, notwithstanding," retorted L—— with a spirit I was delighted to see. "German philosophy may produce the same effects on the head as German boots on the feet. But you astonish me by what you say! Elastic hollow soles!—then there was no necromancy in them after all! But still you have not answered my question, doctor."

"All in good time, L——; let me first put one category to you. What should make you have such a dreadful abhorrence to infants? —are they not the most interesting beings in the universe?—does not heaven lie about them then? As for inheriting a club-foot, that is all stuff. The children of Socrates did not inherit his snub nose, nor the mind either of him who chanced to have this *nez retroussé.*"

"What am I to infer from this preamble?" demanded L—— with a face as white as death.

"Why, that you have as lovely a little sister as ever opened a pair of eyes upon this earthly scene—such a pair of eyes, too!—large, dark, magnificent eyes,—much handsomer than yours, L——, and they are not much to be found fault with. In short, my little god-daughter Emma is a perfect beauty, of about three weeks old,—and I am ready to enter the lists with any one who is bold enough to deny the full power of her infantine charms."

There was a long pause after this.

"And her feet?" inquired L——, gasping for breath, "has she— club feet?"

"Pshaw! you never expected more than one; her father ——." But he wildly interrupted me.

"Oh! name him not!—name him not!—Deceiver!—liar!—hypocrite!—I knew it would come to this!—this is what has maddened me—I knew it would be so!"

"Then you have been a seer and a prophet," replied I, "all along. Allow me to bow to your superior wisdom. I never dreamed of such a thing; yet would it not have been as it has turned out, but for my advice, my judgment."

"What on earth could *you* have had to do with this wretched business?" inquired L——. "Pray, pray, do not confuse me more than you can help."

"I am going rather to enlighten you, L——," said I, "and must ·beg you seriously to attend now to me. You know that I was summoned to attend upon Mr. Randolph Maxwell, the first cousin of your mother. Well, I found him in almost a dying state,—weak, exhausted, dejected in the extreme, without a wish to live. I inquired into the symptoms of his malady. I could gain no information from his words; but those melancholy yet beautiful eyes of his gave me a suspicion. Having obtained a clue, and *not* having the same contemptible and erroneous opinion of my patient as yourself, I arrived at length at the truth, and found that this '*demon*,' as you are pleased to call him, was falling a sacrifice to his high sense of honour, and delicacy to his idolised wife's feelings. He had adored her ever, and believed firmly, when he wrote that last epistle to her which you saw, that he was capable of keeping his word; that the society of his Emma as a friend and sister only would fully satisfy every desire of his heart. But in living with her, in receiving her smiles, and hearing himself called 'Randolph,' 'dear Randolph,' by lips so lovely and beloved, he found that he was human, and had human wishes to gratify. Thus, like Tantalus, did he languish and droop, yet without a hope, uttering a complaint, or making a single effort to draw her compassion, or even to let his sufferings be understood by her. By heavens! L——, that man, small as he is in stature, deformed and unpleasant to look upon, is one of the greatest heroes, ay, martyrs, let it be added,—I speak as a medical man,—that history has to boast of!"— I paused as I said this, and waited for some observation from my young friend; but he merely leaned his cheek upon his hand, and cast his eyes upon the ground.—"Shall I proceed?" asked I.

"I can finish the narrative myself," said he: "you communicated the state of her friend, of course, to my mother, and she,—to save his life,——"

"—Told me," cried I, "that she had now been so long accustomed to his presence, so familiarised with his uncouth appearance, that she scarcely noticed his deformities; that his attentions, his delicacy, his devotedness to her for so long a time, had taken from her all repugnance to his person; and that she could truly say, 'she loved him even as he was.'" L—— groaned aloud. "Oh!" continued I, "I wish I could describe to you the feelings of this man with the *club-foot*,—this being so despised, so loathed by you,—when I repeated to him, word for word, what his adored wife had imparted to me,—when the delightful conviction stole into his mind that there was one woman in the world, and that one the most valued and the most lovely, who could look upon him, dwarf, hunchback as he was, with eyes of returning affection,—that he was loved in some measure with a return. —After all, L——, what is there in the outside?"

"Is my mother happy?" at length inquired L—— with a burning cheek, but a softening tone of voice.

. " The only drawback on her felicity is from the waywardness, the morbid temper, and the cruel prejudices of her only son," said I. " What is there in a mere form, the husk, the shell, the covering of the immortal mind? Would you have treated Socrates as you have treated Mr. Maxwell ?—thus have despised Alexander Pope ?"

" *Socrates had not a club-foot*," answered he ; but I fancied that an air of pleasantry accompanied the observation : " Pope had not this deformity."

" But other great men had," I replied, " who were as inferior to the gentleman we have been speaking of in *true heroism*, as they excelled him in other mere personal attractions. Remember the adage, L——, ' Handsome is who handsome does.' "

" Doctor E——," exclaimed Falkner L——, after a pause of an entire minute, for I noted it by my stop-watch,—" Doctor E——, I will see this infant sister of mine ; I will see its—its father also ; I will be one of that happy family.—Oh, what a monster of prejudice have I been until this very hour !"

" You say right, my dear L—— ; prejudice does make monsters of mankind,—*it has made you mad*, — but happily you are restored. Look not in future on the outside of the cup and platter ; for be assured that the pearl beyond all price is to be found within. Prejudice and pride are, according to my experience, the causes of more lunacy even than the use of ardent spirits, or the goad of poverty, that eateth into the very soul."

I had the great satisfaction of seeing that very evening a lovely female infant, dressed in a white cassimere cloak and hood, trimmed with swansdown and rich lace, in the arms of the young man, who caressed the child with every mark of affection, and called her " his dear, dear little sister !" I smiled to myself also at seeing this same young man looking with pleased delight on its small perfect ivory feet, which I took care to display ; and much pleased was I in hearing him for the first time in his life say with sincerity,

" *My dear Mr. Maxwell*, I thank you from my very heart for the kindness you have shown to this beloved lady, your happy wife, and the forbearance you have evinced towards her wayward and insulting son.—Am I forgiven ?"

" From my very soul !" said a voice, now heard without disgust, notwithstanding its croaking and discordant tone. It was that of " The Man with the Club-Foot."

FULL REPORT OF THE
FIRST MEETING OF THE MUDFOG ASSOCIATION
FOR THE ADVANCEMENT OF EVERYTHING.

WE have made the most unparalleled and extraordinary exertions to place before our readers a complete and accurate account of the proceedings at the late grand meeting of the Mudfog association, holden in the town of Mudfog; it affords us great happiness to lay the result before them, in the shape of various communications received from our able, talented, and graphic correspondent, expressly sent down for the purpose, who has immortalised us, himself, Mudfog, and the association, all at one and the same time. We have been, indeed, for some days unable to determine who will transmit the greatest name to posterity; ourselves, who sent our correspondent down; our correspondent, who wrote an account of the matter; or the association, who gave our correspondent something to write about. We rather incline to the opinion that we are the greatest man of the party, inasmuch as the notion of an exclusive and authentic report originated with us; this may be prejudice: it may arise from a prepossession on our part in our own favour. Be it so. We have no doubt that every gentleman concerned in this mighty assemblage is troubled with the same complaint in a greater or less degree; and it is a consolation to us to know that we have at least this feeling in common with the great scientific stars, the brilliant and extraordinary luminaries, whose speculations we record.

We give our correspondent's letters in the order in which they reached us. Any attempt at amalgamating them into one beautiful whole, would only destroy that glowing tone, that dash of wildness, and rich vein of picturesque interest, which pervade them throughout.

" Mudfog, Monday night, seven o'clock.

"WE are in a state of great excitement here. Nothing is spoken of, but the approaching meeting of the association. The inn-doors are thronged with waiters anxiously looking for the expected arrivals; and the numerous bills which are wafered up in the windows of private houses, intimating that there are beds to let within, give the streets a very animated and cheerful appearance, the wafers being of a great variety of colours, and the monotony of printed inscriptions being relieved by every possible size and style of hand-writing. It is confidently rumoured that Professors Snore, Doze, and Wheezy have engaged three beds and a sitting-room at the Pig and Tinder-box. I give you the rumour as it has reached me; but I cannot, as yet, vouch for its accuracy. The moment I have been enabled to obtain any certain information upon this interesting point, you may depend upon receiving it."

" Half-past seven.

"I HAVE just returned from a personal interview with the landlord of the Pig and Tinder-box. He speaks confidently of the probability of Professors Snore, Doze, and Wheezy taking up their residence at his house during the sitting of the association, but denies that the beds have been yet engaged; in which representation he is confirmed by the chambermaid,—a girl of artless manners, and interesting appearance. The boots denies that it is at all likely that Professors Snore, Doze, and Wheezy will put up here; but I have reason to believe that this man has been suborned by the proprietor of the Original Pig, which is the opposition hotel. Amidst such conflicting testimony it is difficult to arrive at the real truth; but you may depend upon receiving authentic information upon this point the moment the fact is ascertained. The excitement still continues. A boy fell through the window of the pastrycook's shop at the corner of the High-street about half an hour ago, which has occasioned much confusion. The general impression is, that it was an accident. Pray Heaven it may prove so!"

" Tuesday, noon.

"At an early hour this morning the bells of all the churches struck seven o'clock; the effect of which, in the present lively state of the town, was extremely singular. While I was at breakfast, a yellow gig, drawn by a dark grey horse, with a patch of white over his right eyelid, proceeded at a rapid pace in the direction of the Original Pig stables; it is currently reported that this gentleman has arrived here for the purpose of attending the association, and, from what I have heard, I consider it extremely probable, although nothing decisive is yet known regarding him. You may conceive the anxiety with which we are all looking forward to the arrival of the four o'clock coach this afternoon.

"Notwithstanding the excited state of the populace, no outrage has yet been committed, owing to the admirable discipline and discretion of the police, who are nowhere to be seen. A barrel-organ is playing opposite my window, and groups of people, offering fish and vegetables for sale, parade the streets. With these exceptions everything is quiet, and I trust will continue so."

" Five o'clock.

"It is now ascertained beyond all doubt that Professors Snore, Doze, and Wheezy will *not* repair to the Pig and Tinder-box, but have actually engaged apartments at the Original Pig. This intelligence is *exclusive;* and I leave you and your readers to draw their own inferences from it. Why Professor Wheezy, of all people in the world, should repair to the Original Pig in preference to the Pig and Tinder-box, it is not easy to conceive. The professor is a man who should be above all such petty feelings. Some people here, openly impute treachery and a distinct breach of faith to Professors Snore and Doze; while others, again, are disposed to acquit them of any culpability in the transaction, and to insinuate that the blame rests solely with Professor Wheezy. I own that I incline to the latter opinion; and, although it gives me great pain to speak in terms of censure or disapprobation of a man of such transcendent genius and acquirements, still I am bound to say, that if my suspicions be well founded, and if all the reports which have reached my ears be true, I really do not well know what to make of the matter.

"Mr. Slug, so celebrated for his statistical researches, arrived this afternoon by the four o'clock stage. His complexion is a dark purple, and he has a habit of sighing constantly. He looked extremely well, and appeared in high health and spirits. Mr. Woodensconse also came down in the same conveyance. The distinguished gentleman was fast asleep on his arrival, and I am informed by the guard that he had been so, the whole way. He was, no doubt, preparing for his approaching fatigues; but what gigantic visions must those be, that flit through the brain of such a man, when his body is in a state of torpidity!

"The influx of visitors increases every moment. I am told (I know not how truly) that two post-chaises have arrived at the Original Pig within the last half-hour; and I myself observed a wheelbarrow, containing three carpet-bags and a bundle, entering the yard of the Pig and Tinder-box no longer ago than five minutes since. The people are still quietly pursuing their ordinary occupations; but there is a wildness in their eyes, and an unwonted rigidity in the muscles of their countenances, which shows to the observant spectator that their expectations are strained to the very utmost pitch. I fear, unless some very extraordinary arrivals take place to-night, that consequences may arise from this popular ferment, which every man of sense and feeling would deplore."

" Twenty minutes past six.

"I HAVE just heard that the boy who fell through the pastrycook's window last night, has died of the fright. He was suddenly called upon to pay three and sixpence for the damage done, and his constitution, it seems, was not strong enough to bear up against the shock. The inquest, it is said, will be held to-morrow."

" Three-quarters past seven.

"PROFESSORS Muff and Nogo have just driven up to the hotel door; they at once ordered dinner with great condescension. We are all very much delighted with the urbanity of their manners, and the ease with which they adapt themselves to the forms and ceremonies of ordinary life. Immediately on their arrival they sent for the head-waiter, and privately requested him to purchase a live dog,—as cheap a one as he could meet with,—and to send him up after dinner, with a pie-board, a knife and fork, and a clean plate. It is conjectured that some experiments will be tried upon the dog to-night; if any particulars should transpire, I will forward them by express."

" Half-past eight.

" THE animal has been procured. He is a pug-dog, of rather intelligent appearance, in good condition, and with very short legs. He has been tied to a curtain-peg in a dark room, and is howling dreadfully."

" Ten minutes to nine.

" THE dog has just been rung for. With an instinct which would appear almost the result of reason, the sagacious animal seized the waiter by the calf of the leg when he approached to take him, and made a desperate, though ineffectual resistance. I have not been able to procure admission to the apartment occupied by the scientific gentlemen; but, judging from the sounds which reached my ears when I stood upon the landing-place outside the door, just now, I should be disposed to say that the dog had retreated growling beneath some article of furniture, and was keeping the professors at bay. This conjecture is confirmed by the testimony of the ostler, who, after peeping through the keyhole, assures me that he distinctly saw Professor Nogo on his knees, holding forth a small bottle of prussic acid, to which the animal, who was crouched beneath an arm-chair, obstinately declined to smell. You cannot imagine the feverish state of irritation we are in, lest the interests of science should be sacrificed to the prejudices of a brute creature, who is not endowed with sufficient sense to foresee the incalculable benefits which the whole human race may derive from so very slight a concession on his part."

" Nine o'clock.

" THE dog's tail and ears have been sent down stairs to be washed; from which circumstance we infer that the animal is no more. His forelegs have been delivered to the boots to be brushed, which strengthens the supposition."

" Half after ten.

" MY feelings are so overpowered by what has taken place in the course of the last hour and a half, that I have scarcely strength to detail the rapid succession of events which have quite bewildered all those who are cognizant of their occurrence. It appears that the pug-dog mentioned in my last was surreptitiously obtained,—stolen, in fact,—by some person attached to the stable department, from an unmarried lady resident in this town. Frantic on discovering the loss of her favourite, the lady rushed distractedly into the street, calling in the most heart-rending and pathetic manner upon the passengers to restore her, her Augustus,—for so the deceased was named, in affectionate remembrance of a former lover of his mistress, to whom he bore a striking personal resemblance, which renders the circumstance additionally affecting. I am not yet in a condition to inform you what circumstances induced the bereaved lady to direct her steps to the hotel which had witnessed the last struggles of her *protege*. I can only state that she arrived there, at the very instant when his detached members were passing through the passage on a small tray. Her shrieks still reverberate in my ears! I grieve to say that the expressive features of Professor Muff were much scratched and lacerated by the injured lady; and that Professor Nogo, besides sustaining several severe bites, has lost some handfuls of hair from the same cause. It must be some consolation to these gentlemen to know that their ardent attachment to scientific pursuits has alone occasioned these unpleasant consequences; for which the sympathy of a grateful country will sufficiently reward them. The unfortunate lady remains at the Pig and Tinder-box, and up to this time is reported in a very precarious state.

" I need scarcely tell you that this unlooked-for catastrophe has cast a damp and gloom upon us in the midst of our exhilaration; natural in any case, but greatly enhanced in this, by the amiable qualities of the deceased animal, who appears to have been much and deservedly respected by the whole of his acquaintance."

" *Twelve o'clock.*

" I TAKE the last opportunity before sealing my parcel to inform you that the boy who fell through the pastrycook's window is not dead, as was universally believed, but alive and well. The report appears to have had its origin in his mysterious disappearance. He was found half an hour since on the premises of a sweet-stuff maker, where a raffle had been announced for a second-hand seal-skin cap and a tambourine; and where—a sufficient number of members not having been obtained at first—he had patiently waited until the list was completed. This fortunate discovery has in some degree restored our gaiety and cheerfulness. It is proposed to get up a subscription for him without delay.

" Everybody is nervously anxious to see what to-morrow will bring forth. If any one should arrive in the course of the night, I have left strict directions to be called immediately. I should have sat up, indeed, but the agitating events of this day have been too much for me.

" No news yet, of either of the Professors Snore, Doze, or Wheezy. It is very strange!"

" *Wednesday afternoon.*

" ALL is now over; and, upon one point at least, I am at length enabled to set the minds of your readers at rest. The three professors arrived at ten minutes after two o'clock, and, instead of taking up their quarters at the Original Pig, as it was uni-

versally understood in the course of yesterday that they would
assuredly have done, drove straight to the Pig and Tinder-box,
where they threw off the mask at once, and openly announced
their intention of remaining. Professor Wheezy *may* reconcile this
very extraordinary conduct with *his* notions of fair and equitable
dealing, but I would recommend Professor Wheezy to be cautious
how he presumes too far upon his well-earned reputation. How
such a man as Professor Snore, or, which is still more extraordinary, such an individual as Professor Doze, can quietly allow
himself to be mixed up with such proceedings as these, you will
naturally inquire. Upon this head, rumour is silent; I have
my speculations, but forbear to give utterance to them just
now."

" Four o'clock.

" THE town is filling fast; eighteenpence has been offered
for a bed, and refused. Several gentlemen were under the necessity last night of sleeping in the brick-fields, and on the steps
of doors, for which they were taken before the magistrates in a
body this morning, and committed to prison as vagrants for
various terms. One of these persons I understand to be a highly-respectable tinker, of great practical skill, who had forwarded
a paper to the president of Section D. Mechanical Science, on
the construction of pipkins with copper bottoms and safety-
valves, of which report speaks highly. The incarceration of this
gentleman is greatly to be regretted, as his absence will preclude
any discussion on the subject.

" The bills are being taken down in all directions, and lodgings are being secured on almost any terms. I have heard of
fifteen shillings a week for two rooms, exclusive of coals and
attendance, but I can scarcely believe it. The excitement is
dreadful. I was informed this morning that the civil authorities, apprehensive of some outbreak of popular feeling, had
commanded a recruiting sergeant and two corporals to be under
arms; and that, with the view of not irritating the people un-
necessarily by their presence, they had been requested to take
up their position before daybreak in a turnpike, distant about a
quarter of a mile from the town. The vigour and promptness
of these measures cannot be too highly extolled.

" Intelligence has just been brought me, that an elderly female, in a state of inebriety, has declared in the open street her
intention to 'do' for Mr. Slug. Some statistical returns compiled by that gentleman, relative to the consumption of raw
spirituous liquors in this place, are supposed to be the cause of
the wretch's animosity. It is added, that this declaration was
loudly cheered by a crowd of persons who had assembled on the
spot; and that one man had the boldness to designate Mr. Slug
aloud by the opprobrious epithet of 'Stick-in-the-mud!' It is
earnestly to be hoped that now, when the moment has arrived
for their interference, the magistrates will not shrink from the

exercise of that power which is vested in them by the constitution of our common country."

"*Half-past ten.*

" THE disturbance, I am happy to inform you, has been completely quelled, and the ringleader taken into custody. She had a pail of cold water thrown over her, previous to being locked up, and expresses great contrition and uneasiness. We are all in a fever of anticipation about to-morrow; but, now that we are within a few hours of the meeting of the association, and at last enjoy the proud consciousness of having its illustrious members amongst us, I trust and hope everything may go off peaceably. I shall send you a full report of to-morrow's proceedings by the night coach."

" *Eleven o'clock.*

" I OPEN my letter to say that nothing whatever has occurred since I folded it up."

" *Thursday.*

" THE sun rose this morning at the usual hour. I did not observe anything particular in the aspect of the glorious planet, except that he appeared to me (it might have been a delusion of my heightened fancy) to shine with more than common brilliancy, and to shed a refulgent lustre upon the town, such as I had never observed before. This is the more extraordinary, as the sky was perfectly cloudless, and the atmosphere peculiarly fine. At half-past nine o'clock the general committee assembled, with the last year's president in the chair. The report of the council was read; and one passage, which stated that the council had corresponded with no less than three thousand five hundred and seventy-one persons, (all of whom paid their own postage,) on no fewer than seven thousand two hundred and forty-three topics, was received with a degree of enthusiasm which no efforts could suppress. The various committees and sections having been appointed, and the mere formal business transacted, the great proceedings of the meeting commenced at eleven o'clock precisely. I had the happiness of occupying a most eligible position at that time, in

" SECTION A.——ZOOLOGY AND BOTANY.

"GREAT ROOM, PIG AND TINDER-BOX.

" PRESIDENT—PROFESSOR SNORE. VICE-PRESIDENTS—PROFESSORS DOZE
AND WHEEZY.

"The scene at this moment was particularly striking. The sun streamed through the windows of the apartments, and tinted the whole scene with its brilliant rays, bringing out in strong relief the noble visages of the professors and scientific gentlemen, who, some with bald heads, some with red heads, some with brown heads, some with grey heads, some with black heads, some with block heads, presented a *coup-d'œil* which no

2 G 2

eye-witness will readily forget. In front of these gentlemen
were papers and inkstands; and round the room, on elevated
benches extending as far as the forms could reach, were assembled a brilliant concourse of those lovely and elegant women for which Mudfog is justly acknowledged to be without a
rival in the whole world. The contrast between their fair faces
and the dark coats and trousers of the scientific gentlemen I
shall never cease to remember while Memory holds her seat.

"Time having been allowed for a slight confusion, occasioned
by the falling down of the greater part of the platforms, to
subside, the president called on one of the secretaries to read
a communication entitled, 'Some remarks on the industrious
fleas, with considerations on the importance of establishing infant schools among that numerous class of society ; of directing
their industry to useful and practical ends ; and of applying
the surplus fruits thereof, towards providing for them a comfortable and respectable maintenance in their old age.'

"The Author stated, that, having long turned his attention to
the moral and social condition of these interesting animals, he
had been induced to visit an exhibition in Regent-street, London, commonly known by the designation of 'The Industrious
Fleas.' He had there seen many fleas, occupied certainly in various pursuits and avocations, but occupied, he was bound to
add, in a manner which no man of well-regulated mind could
fail to regard with sorrow and regret. One flea, reduced to the
level of a beast of burden, was drawing about a miniature gig,
containing a particularly small effigy of his Grace the Duke of
Wellington ; while another was staggering beneath the weight of
a golden model of his great adversary Napoleon Bonaparte.
Some, brought up as mountebanks and ballet-dancers, were performing a figure-dance (he regretted to observe, that, of the
fleas so employed, several were females) ; others were in training,
in a small card-board box, for pedestrians,—mere sporting characters—and two were actually engaged in the cold-blooded and
barbarous occupation of duelling ; a pursuit from which humanity recoiled with horror and disgust. He suggested that
measures should be immediately taken to employ the labour of
these fleas as part and parcel of the productive power of the
country, which might easily be done by the establishment among
them of infant schools and houses of industry, in which a system of virtuous education, based upon sound principles, should
be observed, and moral precepts strictly inculcated. He proposed that every flea who presumed to exhibit, for hire, music or
dancing, or any species of theatrical entertainment, without a
licence, should be considered a vagabond, and treated accordingly ; in which respect he only placed him upon a level with
the rest of mankind. He would further suggest that their labour
should be placed under the control and regulation of the state,
who should set apart from the profits, a fund for the support of

superannuated or disabled fleas, their widows and orphans. With this view, he proposed that liberal premiums should be offered for the three best designs for a general almshouse; from which —as insect architecture was well known to be in a very advanced and perfect state—we might possibly derive many valuable hints for the improvement of our metropolitan universities, national galleries, and other public edifices.

" THE PRESIDENT wished to be informed how the ingenious gentleman proposed to open a communication with fleas generally, in the first instance, so that they might be thoroughly imbued with a sense of the advantages they must necessarily derive from changing their mode of life, and applying themselves to honest labour. This appeared to him, the only difficulty.

" The AUTHOR submitted that this difficulty was easily overcome, or rather that there was no difficulty at all in the case. Obviously the course to be pursued, if her Majesty's government could be prevailed upon to take up the plan, would be, to secure at a remunerative salary the individual to whom he had alluded as presiding over the exhibition in Regent-street at the period of his visit. That gentleman would at once be able to put himself in communication with the mass of the fleas, and to instruct them in pursuance of some general plan of education, to be sanctioned by Parliament, until such time as the more intelligent among them were advanced enough to officiate as teachers to the rest.

" The President and several members of the section highly complimented the author of the paper last read, on his most ingenious and important treatise. It was determined that the subject should be recommended to the immediate consideration of the council.

" MR. WIGSBY produced a cauliflower somewhat larger than a chaise-umbrella, which had been raised by no other artificial means than the simple application of highly carbonated soda-water as manure. He explained that by scooping out the head, which would afford a new and delicious species of nourishment for the poor, a parachute, in principle something similar to that constructed by M. Garnerin, was at once obtained: the stalk of course being kept downwards. He added that he was perfectly willing to make a descent from a height of not less than three miles and a quarter; and had in fact already proposed the same to the proprietors of Vauxhall Gardens, who in the handsomest manner at once consented to his wishes, and appointed an early day next summer for the undertaking; merely stipulating that the rim of the cauliflower should be previously broken in three or four places to ensure the safety of the descent.

" THE PRESIDENT congratulated the public on the *grand gala* in store for them, and warmly eulogised the proprietors of the establishment alluded to, for their love of science, and regard for

the safety of human life, both of which did them the highest
honour.

"A Member wished to know how many thousand additional
lamps the royal property would be illuminated with, on the
night after the descent.

"Mr. WIGSBY replied that the point was not yet finally decided; but he believed it was proposed, over and above the ordinary illuminations, to exhibit in various devices eight millions
and a half of additional lamps.

"The Member expressed himself much gratified with this
announcement.

"Mr. BLUNDERUM delighted the section with a most interesting and valuable paper 'on the last moments of the learned
pig,' which produced a very strong impression upon the assembly, the account being compiled from the personal recollections of his favourite attendant.   The account stated in the
most emphatic terms that the animal's name was not Toby, but
Solomon; and distinctly proved that he could have no near relatives in the profession, as many designing persons had falsely
stated, inasmuch as his father, mother, brothers and sisters,
had all fallen victims to the butcher at different times.   An
uncle of his, indeed, had with very great labour been traced to
a sty in Somers Town; but as he was in a very infirm state at
the time, being afflicted with measles, and shortly afterwards
disappeared, there appeared too much reason to conjecture that
he had been converted into sausages.   The disorder of the
learned pig was originally a severe cold, which, being aggravated by excessive trough indulgence, finally settled upon the
lungs, and terminated in a general decay of the constitution.
A melancholy instance of a presentiment entertained by the
animal of his approaching dissolution, was recorded.   After
gratifying a numerous and fashionable company with his performances, in which no falling-off whatever, was visible, he fixed
his eyes on the biographer, and, turning to the watch which
lay on the floor, and on which he was accustomed to point out
the hour, deliberately passed his snout twice round the dial.
In precisely four-and-twenty hours from that time he had
ceased to exist!

"PROFESSOR WHEEZY inquired whether, previous to his demise, the animal had expressed, by signs or otherwise, any
wishes regarding the disposal of his little property.

"Mr. BLUNDERUM replied, that, when the biographer took up
the pack of cards at the conclusion of the performance, the
animal grunted several times in a significant manner, and nodded his head as he was accustomed to do, when gratified.   From
these gestures it was understood that he wished the attendant
to keep the cards, which he had ever since done.   He had not
expressed any wish relative to his watch, which had accordingly
been pawned by the same individual.

" The PRESIDENT wished to know whether any member of the section had ever seen or conversed with the pig-faced lady, who was reported to have worn a black velvet mask, and to have taken her meals from a golden trough.

" After some hesitation a Member replied that the pig-faced lady was his mother-in-law, and that he trusted the president would not violate the sanctity of private life.

" The PRESIDENT begged pardon. He had considered the pig-faced lady a public character. Would the honourable member object to state, with a view to the advancement of science, whether she was in any way connected with the learned pig ?

" The Member replied in the same low tone, that, as the question appeared to involve a suspicion that the learned pig might be his half-brother, he must decline answering it.

" SECTION B.——ANATOMY AND MEDICINE.

"COACH-HOUSE, PIG AND TINDER-BOX.

"PRESIDENT—DR. TOORELL. VICE-PRESIDENTS—PROFESSORS MUFF AND NOGO.

" DR. KUTANKUMAGEN (of Moscow) read to the section a report of a case which had occurred within his own practice, strikingly illustrative of the power of medicine, as exemplified in his successful treatment of a virulent disorder. He had been called in to visit the patient on the 1st of April 1837. He was then labouring under symptoms peculiarly alarming to any medical man. His frame was stout and muscular, his step firm and elastic, his cheeks plump and red, his voice loud, his appetite good, his pulse full and round. He was in the constant habit of eating three meals *per diem*, and of drinking at least one bottle of wine, and one glass of spirituous liquors diluted with water, in the course of the four-and-twenty hours. He laughed constantly, and in so hearty a manner that it was terrible to hear him. By dint of powerful medicine, low diet, and bleeding, the symptoms in the course of three days perceptibly decreased. A rigid perseverance in the same course of treatment for only one week, accompanied with small doses of water-gruel, weak broth, and barley-water, led to their entire disappearance. In the course of a month he was sufficiently recovered to be carried down stairs by two nurses, and to enjoy an airing in a close carriage, supported by soft pillows. At the present moment he was restored so far as to walk about, with the slight assistance of a crutch and a boy. It would perhaps be gratifying to the section to learn that he ate little, drank little, slept little, and was never heard to laugh by any accident whatever.

" DR. W. R. FEE, in complimenting the honourable member upon the triumphant cure he had effected, begged to ask whether the patient still bled freely ?

" DR. KUTANKUMAGEN replied in the affirmative.

"Dr. W. R. Fee.—And you found that he bled freely during the whole course of the disorder?

"Dr. Kutankumagen.—Oh dear, yes; most freely.

"Dr. Neeshawts supposed, that if the patient had not submitted to be bled with great readiness and perseverance, so extraordinary a cure could never, in fact, have been accomplished. Dr. Kutankumagen rejoined, certainly not.

"Mr. Knight Bell (M.R.C.S.) exhibited a wax preparation of the interior of a gentleman who in early life had inadvertently swallowed a door-key. It was a curious fact that a medical student of dissipated habits, being present at the *post mortem* examination, found means to escape unobserved from the room, with that portion of the coats of the stomach upon which an exact model of the instrument was distinctly impressed, with which he hastened to a locksmith of doubtful character, who made a new key from the pattern so shown to him. With this key the medical student entered the house of the deceased gentleman, and committed a burglary to a large amount, for which he was subsequently tried and executed.

". The President wished to know what became of the original key after the lapse of years. Mr. Knight Bell replied that the gentleman was always much accustomed to punch, and it was supposed the acid had gradually devoured it.

"Dr. Neeshawts and several of the members were of opinion that the key must have lain very cold and heavy upon the gentleman's stomach.

"Mr. Knight Bell believed it did at first. It was worthy of remark, perhaps, that for some years the gentleman was troubled with a night-mare, under the influence of which, he always imagined himself a wine-cellar door.

". "Professor Muff related a very extraordinary and convincing proof of the wonderful efficacy of the system of infinitesimal doses, which the section were doubtless aware was based upon the theory that the very minutest amount of any given drug, properly dispersed through the human frame, would be productive of precisely the same result as a very large dose administered in the usual manner. Thus, the fortieth part of a grain of calomel was supposed to be equal to a five-grain calomel pill, and so on in proportion throughout the whole range of medicine. He had tried the experiment in a curious manner upon a publican who had been brought into the hospital with a broken head, and was cured upon the infinitesimal system in the incredibly short space of three months. This man was a hard drinker. He (Professor Muff) had dispersed three drops of rum through a bucket of water, and requested the man to drink the whole. What was the result? Before he had drunk a quart, he was in a state of beastly intoxication; and five other men were made dead-drunk with the remainder.

"The President wished to know whether an infinitesimal

dose of soda-water would have recovered them? Professor Muff replied that the twenty-fifth part of a tea-spoonful, properly administered to each patient would have sobered him immediately. The President remarked that this was a most important discovery, and he hoped the Lord Mayor and Court of Aldermen would patronise it immediately.

" A Member begged to be informed whether it would be possible to administer—say, the twentieth part of a grain of bread and cheese to all grown-up paupers, and the fortieth part to children, with the same satisfying effect as their present allowance.

" Professor Muff was willing to stake his professional reputation on the perfect adequacy of such a quantity of food to the support of human life—in workhouses; the addition of the fifteenth part of a grain of pudding twice a week, would render it a high diet.

" Professor Nogo called the attention of the section to a very extraordinary case of animal magnetism. A private watchman, being merely looked at by the operator from the opposite side of a wide street, was at once observed to be in a very drowsy and languid state. He was followed to his box, and being once slightly rubbed on the palms of the hands, fell into a sound sleep, in which he continued without intermission for ten hours.

" SECTION C.—STATISTICS.

" HAY-LOFT, ORIGINAL PIG.

" PRESIDENT—MR. WOODENSCONSE. VICE-PRESIDENTS—MR. LEDBRAIN AND MR. TIMBERED.

" Mr. Slug stated to the section the result of some calculations he had made with great difficulty and labour, regarding the state of infant education among the middle classes of London. He found that, within a circle of three miles from the Elephant and Castle, the following were the names and numbers of children's books principally in circulation :—

" Jack the Giant-killer	.	.	.	7,943
Ditto and Bean-stalk		.	.	8,621
Ditto and Eleven Brothers		.	.	2,845
Ditto and Jill	.	.	.	1,998
		Total	. .	21,407

" He found that the proportion of Robinson Crusoes to Philip Quarlls was as four and a half to one; and that the preponderance of Valentine and Orsons over Goody Two Shoeses was as three and an eighth of the former to half a one of the latter : a comparison of Seven Champions with Simple Simons gave the same result. The ignorance that prevailed, was lamentable. One child, on being asked whether he would rather be Saint George of England or a respectable tallow-chandler, instantly replied, 'Taint George of Ingling.' Another, a little boy of

eight years old, was found to be firmly impressed with a belief
in the existence of dragons, and openly stated that it was his intention when he grew up, to rush forth sword in hand for the
deliverance of captive princesses, and the promiscuous slaughter
of giants.   Not one child among the number interrogated had
ever heard of Mungo Park,—some inquiring whether he was at
all connected with the black man that swept the crossing ; and
others whether he was in any way related to the Regent's Park.
They had not the slightest conception of the commonest principles of mathematics, and considered Sinbad the Sailor the most
enterprising voyager that the world had ever produced.

"A Member strongly deprecating the use of all the other
books mentioned, suggested that Jack and Jill might perhaps
be exempted from the general censure, inasmuch as the hero
and heroine, in the very outset of the tale, were depicted as going *up* a hill to fetch a pail of water, which was a laborious and
useful occupation,—supposing the family linen was being washed, for instance.

" Mr. Slug feared that the moral effect of this passage was
more than counterbalanced by another in a subsequent part of
the poem, in which very gross allusion was made to the mode in
which the heroine was personally chastised by her mother

"' For laughing at Jack's disaster ;'

besides, the whole work had this one great fault, *it was not
true.*

" The President complimented the honourable member on
the excellent distinction he had drawn.   Several other members,
too, dwelt upon the immense and urgent necessity of storing the
minds of children with nothing but facts and figures ; which process the President very forcibly remarked, had made them (the
section) the men they were.

" Mr. Slug then stated some curious calculations respecting
the dogs'-meat barrows of London.   He found that the total
number of small carts and barrows engaged in dispensing provision to the cats and dogs of the metropolis, was one thousand
seven hundred and forty-three.   The average number of skewers
delivered daily with the provender, by each dogs'-meat cart or
barrow was thirty-six.   Now; multiplying the number of skewers
so delivered, by the number of barrows, a total of sixty-two
thousand seven hundred and forty-eight skewers daily would
be obtained.   Allowing that, of these sixty-two thousand seven
hundred and forty-eight skewers, the odd two thousand seven
hundred and forty-eight were accidentally devoured with the
meat, by the most voracious of the animals supplied, it followed
that sixty thousand skewers per day, or the enormous number
of twenty-one millions nine hundred thousand skewers annually,
were wasted in the kennels and dust-holes of London ; which,
if collected and warehoused, would in ten years' time afford a
mass of timber more than sufficient for the construction of a

first-rate vessel of war for the use of her Majesty's navy, to be called ' The Royal Skewer,' and to become under that name the terror of all the enemies of this island.

"MR. X. LEDBRAIN read a very ingenious communication, from which it appeared that the total number of legs belonging to the manufacturing population of one great town in Yorkshire was, in round numbers, forty thousand, while the total number of chair and stool legs in their houses was only thirty thousand, which, upon the very favourable average of three legs to a seat, yielded only ten thousand seats in all. From this calculation it would appear,—not taking wooden or cork legs into the account, but allowing two legs to every person,—that ten thousand individuals (one-half of the whole population) were either destitute of any rest for their legs at all, or passed the whole of their leisure time in sitting upon boxes.

"SECTION D.—MECHANICAL SCIENCE.

"COACH HOUSE, ORIGINAL PIG.

"PRESIDENT—MR. CARTER. VICE-PRESIDENTS—MR. TRUCK AND MR. WAGHORN.

" PROFESSOR QUEERSPECK exhibited an elegant model of a portable railway, neatly mounted in a green case, for the waistcoat pocket. By attaching this beautiful instrument to his boots, any Bank or public-office clerk could transport himself from his place of residence to his place of business, at the easy rate of sixty-five miles an hour, which, to gentlemen of sedentary pursuits, would be an incalculable advantage.

" THE PRESIDENT was desirous of knowing whether it was necessary to have a level surface on which the gentleman was to run.

" PROFESSOR QEERSPECK explained that City gentlemen would run in trains, being handcuffed together to prevent confusion or unpleasantness. For instance, trains would start every morning at eight, nine, and ten o'clock, from Camden Town, Islington, Camberwell, Hackney, and various other places in which City gentlemen are accustomed to reside. It would be necessary to have a level, but he had provided for this difficulty by proposing that the best line that the circumstances would admit of, should be taken through the sewers which undermine the streets of the metropolis, and which, well lighted by jets from the gas-pipes which run immediately above them, would form a pleasant and commodious arcade, especially in winter-time, when the inconvenient custom of carrying umbrellas, now so general, could be wholly dispensed with. In reply to another question, Professor Queerspeck stated that no substitute for the purposes to which these arcades were at present devoted had yet occurred to him, but that he hoped no fanciful objection on this head would be allowed to interfere with so great an undertaking.

" MR. JOBBA produced a forcing-machine on a novel plan, for

bringing joint-stock railway shares prematurely to a premium. The instrument was in the form of an elegant gilt weather-glass of most dazzling appearance, and was worked behind, by strings, after the manner of a pantomime trick, the strings being always pulled by the directors of the company to which the machine belonged. The quicksilver was so ingeniously placed, that when the acting directors held shares in their pockets, figures denoting very small expenses and very large returns appeared upon the glass; but the moment the directors parted with these pieces of paper, the estimate of needful expenditure suddenly increased itself to an immense extent, while the statements of certain profits became reduced in the same proportion. Mr. Jobba stated that the machine had been in constant requisition for some months past, and he had never once known it to fail.

" A Member expressed his opinion that it was extremely neat and pretty. He wished to know whether it was not liable to accidental derangement? Mr. Jobba said that the whole machine was undoubtedly liable to be blown up, but that was the only objection to it.

" PROFESSOR NOGO arrived from the anatomical section to exhibit a model of a safety fire-escape, which could be fixed at any time, in less than half an hour. and by means of which, the youngest or most infirm persons (successfully resisting the progress of the flames until it was quite ready) could be preserved if they merely balanced themselves for a few minutes on the sill of their bed-room window, and got into the escape without falling into the street. The Professor stated that the number of boys who had been rescued in the day-time by this machine from houses which were not on fire, was almost incredible. Not a conflagration had occurred in the whole of London for many months past to which the escape had not been carried on the very next day, and put in action before a concourse of persons.

" THE PRESIDENT inquired whether there was not some difficulty in ascertaining which was the top of the machine, and which the bottom, in cases of pressing emergency?

" PROFESSOR NOGO explained that of course it could not be expected to act quite as well when there was a fire, as when there was not a fire; but in the former case he thought it would be of equal service whether the top were up or down."

———

With the last section, our correspondent concludes his most able and faithful Report, which will never cease to reflect credit upon him for his scientific attainments, and upon us for our enterprising spirit. It is needless to take a review of the subjects which have been discussed; of the mode in which they have been examined; of the great truths which they have elicited. They are now before the world, and we leave them to read, to consider, and to profit.

The place of meeting for next year has undergone discussion, and has at length been decided; regard being had to, and evidence being taken upon, the goodness of its wines, the supply of its markets, the hospitality of its inhabitants, and the quality of its hotels. We hope at this next meeting our correspondent may again be present, and that we may be once more the means of placing his communications before the world. Until that period we have been prevailed upon to allow this number of our Miscellany to be retailed to the public, or wholesaled to the trade, without any advance upon our usual price.

We have only to add, that the committees are now broken up, and that Mudfog is once again restored to its accustomed tranquillity,—that Professors and Members have had balls, and *soirées*, and suppers, and great mutual complimentations, and have at length dispersed to their several homes,—whither all good wishes and joys attend them, until next year !

Signed   Boz.

A REMONSTRATORY ODE TO MR. CROSS.

BY JOYCE JOCUND.

Good Mr. Cross ! we hate the fuss
And flames of your Vesuvius,
Whose roaring quite convinces us,
  As each successive shock
    Grows louder,
That you deem a dose of powder,
With its deafening noise,
As good as medicine given to girls and boys
  Suffering with measles or small-pock ;—
In short we do believe, beyond a doubt,
You physic us to bring th' ERUPTION—*out !*

In vain soft balmy sleep one courts,
On exhibition nights ; all sorts
Of terrible and strange reports
  Drive rest away, and mock it.
Think you our wives can quiet keep,
Or that a child *can* go to sleep
  The while you " squib and *rocket ?*"
I tell you, sir, I cannot count
The dangers to our daughters' fame ;
But this I 'll publish to their shame,
They find their *sparks*, and feel love's flame
  Increasing in *a*-MOUNT !
And tho' I 'm no amusement hater,
Yet, by my study of LAV-A-ter,
Vesuvius is a dangerous—*crater !*

Bethink you, on some gala night,
Whether you 'd much enjoy the sight
Of beasts and birds all taking flight,
  And from the gardens, making out,
Should your ERUPTION, with its jars,
Just chance to break their cages' bars.
  That were indeed a " breaking out"
    And din
I rather think you 'd be for " driving in !"

Come, Mr. CROSS, for once do try
To be good-natured, and your name belie ;
Indulge no more these furious fiery fits ;
  Let such freaks cease,
Blow up your Mount Vesuvius—all to *bits*,
  And prithee let us have—" a LITTLE PEACE !"

MEMOIR OF BEAU NASH.

RICHARD NASH—or Beau Nash, as he is commonly called—was born at Swansea, in the autumn of the year 1674. His father possessed a moderate income, which he derived from a partnership in a glass manufactory; and his mother was niece to Colonel Poyer, a chivalrous old Cavalier, who was executed by order of Cromwell for defending Pembroke Castle against the assaults of the Roundheads. At the usual age young Nash was sent to a private school at Carmarthen, whence in due time he was transferred to Jesus College, Oxford, where he distinguished himself by an extraordinary and precocious genius for intrigue and gallantry. Before he was seventeen, he had got himself into at least a dozen delicate dilemmas; and, but for the seasonable interference of his college tutor, would have married a female of abandoned character, whose wit and beauty had completely turned his brain.

Disheartened by such licentious conduct, his father abruptly recalled him from the university, and purchased him a commission in the army; a profession of which he soon grew weary, the more especially as he had little besides the slender pay of an ensign to support him. Finding, however, that it was necessary to make some sort of exertion in order to obtain a decent livelihood, our Beau entered himself as a law-student in the Temple, and for some months applied himself assiduously to study. But his natural volatility soon regained its usual ascendency over him, and, dismissing all thoughts of acquiring fortune and reputation as a lawyer, he set up for a man of wit and fashion about town, dressing, as one of his biographers observes, " to the very edge of his finances," exhibiting himself conspicuously in the side-boxes of the theatres, cultivating the acquaintance of young men of rank and wealth, and practising those arts of address and persuasion for which he was afterwards so celebrated.

It was while he was a student in the Temple that a circumstance occurred which gave a wondrous lift to his sense of self-importance, and brought him before the gay world in the very way he most preferred. It seems that it had been long the custom of the different inns of court to entertain our sovereigns on their accession to the crown with a dramatic pageant; and, on the accession of William the Third, Nash was appointed to conduct this entertainment, a task which he fulfilled so much to his Majesty's satisfaction, that he made him an offer of knighthood. But he refused this honour, at the same time hinting that he should have no objection to be made one of the Poor Knights of Windsor, for then he should have a fortune sufficient to maintain his new dignity. The King smiled, but took no further notice of this broad hint, for he was not one to give pensions without value received; and jokes, even of the first water, always ranked low in his estimation.

This affair of the pageant procured Nash many associates among the rich and the titled, who were delighted by his good-humoured vivacity, his easy assurance, his clever after-dinner stories, and his familiar acquaintance with the habits of town life. Many characteristic anecdotes are told of him at this gay period of his life. On one oc-

London Richard Bentley, Sept. 1837

casion, when called on by the masters of the Temple for certain accounts, among other items he made this odd charge, "For making one man happy, ten pounds." "What is the meaning of this, sir?" said one of the dignitaries in his gravest and most authoritative manner. "Why, to tell you the truth," replied Nash, "I happened a few days ago to overhear a poor man, who had a large family, say that ten pounds would make him happy for life, and I could not resist the opportunity of trying the experiment." The masters were so much struck with the singularity of this explanation, that they not only allowed the charge, but even insisted on doubling it, in testimony of their approbation of Nash's benevolence. On another occasion, having gone down on a sporting excursion to York, our thoughtless Beau lost all his money at the gaming-table; and on applying for assistance to a college friend whom he met with in the city, was promised the loan of fifty pounds, provided he would stand at the great door of the Minster in a blanket, just as the people were coming out of church. Nash unhesitatingly agreed to do so, but had not stood there long before he was discovered by the dean, who had some slight acquaintance with him. "What!" exclaimed the divine, "Mr. Nash in masquerade?" "Not so, reverend sir; I am merely doing penance for keeping bad company;" saying which, he pointed to his companion, who was not a little annoyed at finding the laugh thus unexpectedly turned against him. A few days afterwards, Nash won another wager by riding naked through a country village on a cow, a freak which in those times was considered a clever practical joke!

But the strangest of all his adventures is the following. He was once invited by some convivial officers of the navy on board a frigate that had just received sailing orders for the Mediterranean; and, after spending some hours in revelry, found that during his debauch the vessel had set sail, and that to return to land was wholly out of the question. He accordingly, nothing loth, made the whole voyage with his boon companions, and in the course of it was engaged in action, and severely wounded in the leg, while one of his friends was shot dead by his side. In after years Nash was singularly fond of repeating this story; but as he was apt, like Foote's liar, to be occasionally "poetical in his prose," his hearers always received it with a wholesome distrust. "I don't believe one word about your having been kidnapped on board ship," said a lady of distinction to him one day in the Bath pump-room. "Fact, upon my honour," replied the unabashed Beau; "and, if you will step with me into another room, I shall be happy to show you my leg, which will convince you whether I speak truth or not."

On his return from this naval trip, Nash, who had now reached the age of thirty, and had neither fortune nor profession to rely on for support, turned his whole attention to gambling. He encountered the usual vicissitudes attendant on this course of life, sometimes winning, but more frequently losing, but always bearing his reverses with equanimity. *Vive la bagatelle!* was his motto. He was not one to sit down and despond because luck had gone against him. If it rained one day, he felt sure it would clear up the next; so, shrugged his shoulders, and waited patiently the approach of more sunny weather.

We now come to the great epoch in Nash's life,—his accession to the throne of fashion! About the year 1705, a short visit paid by

Queen Anne to Bath had the effect of directing the eyes of the gay world to that city. Our Beau, among others, was attracted to it; and, having amassed a large sum by gambling, soon made himself conspicuous by the splendour of his equipage, his trim attire, courteous manners, and invincible good-humour. In those primitive days Bath was little better than an ordinary country town; but Nash, with the prophetic eye of taste, discerned its capabilities as a fashionable watering-place, and by adroitly flattering the local authorities, and worming himself into the good graces of all the most influential inhabitants, succeeded in obtaining the appointment of Master of the Ceremonies, with sole and uncontrolled power to raise subscriptions for building pump-rooms, laying out public walks, and making whatever improvements he might think expedient. From this period down nearly to the day of his death, Nash was, to all intents and purposes, sovereign of the city. King George might rule at St. James's, but King Richard ruled at Bath.

> " The eagle he was lord above,
> But Rob was lord below."

One of the first reforms projected by the new monarch was in the dress of his subjects. Previous to his accession to the throne it had invariably been the custom for gentlemen to dance in boots. Nash resolved to put a stop to this barbarism, and accordingly issued a ukase ordering his people never henceforth to make their appearance at the Assembly Rooms, save in pumps, silk stockings, and all the finery of full dress. For some time this arbitrary mandate was resisted by more than one Bath Hampden; but perseverance at length gained the day, and the patriots surrendered at discretion. But not only was Nash omnipotent at the city of Bladud, but he subdued also Tunbridge Wells to his authority. In fact, he was as successful a despot as Napoleon, with this difference in his favour,—that he ruled by the force of address, while the other ruled solely by force of arms. Napoleon tamed refractory subjects by threats of exile or imprisonment; Nash, by threats of epigrams in the county newspapers.

Having crushed rebellion by the strong arm of power, and brought to a successful issue the important question of boots, or no boots, our Beau next proceeded to draw up a social code, which in the strictness with which it was enforced, and the benefits it conferred on the community for whose use it was intended, may vie with the famous *Code Napoléon*. " I shall go down to posterity," said the French emperor, " with my code in my hand." Nash has come down to posterity with his code also in his hand. We have diligently perused this celebrated document, which, although it contains as many violations of grammar as a king's speech, is remarkable for the good sense and simplicity of its directions. On the conduct, in particular, to be observed by both sexes at public assemblies, it is shrewd and explicit to a degree. Here Nash showed himself the very incarnation of punctilious etiquette. Even royalty itself endeavoured in vain to mitigate the severity of his decrees. The Princess Amelia having one night humbly requested him to permit her to join in one more country-dance after the hour of breaking up had arrived, Nash assured her that the "established rules of Bath resembled the laws of Lycurgus, which would admit of no alteration without an utter overthrow of all legitimate authority." Of course, as a member of the

constitutional House of Brunswick, her Royal Highness succumbed
to the force of this logic.

One of Nash's special objects of dislike, and against which he
pointed the whole artillery of his sarcasm, was a white apron, then
much worn by ladies at public assemblies. To such an extent did
he carry his abhorrence of this article of female apparel, that he actually stripped the Duchess of Queensberry one evening at a ball,
"and threw her apron," says his biographer, "upon the hinder benches
among the ladies' women;" a significant hint which had all the good
effect he could have desired. If Peter the Great has been universally
praised for his address in prevailing on his countrywomen to adopt
European costumes, surely Richard the Great deserves equal credit
for having been able to persuade his female subjects to lay aside
their darling prejudices in favour of aprons!

Nash had now been upwards of three years Master of the Ceremonies at Bath; and such was the attention which he paid to its
amusements, and so numerous the improvements he made in the architecture and public walks of the city, that it soon became the most
fashionable watering-place in the empire. But even this did not
satisfy his thirst for notoriety, and accordingly he founded another
kingdom at Tunbridge Wells, whither he was in the habit of travelling
once a year, in a post-chariot drawn by six greys, with out-riders,
French horns, and all the paraphernalia of royalty. His arrival at
this picturesque spot was always followed by that of the nobility and
gentry, who regarded him as their "Sir Oracle." Even the announcement, "Nash is coming," was quite sufficient to raise the price of
lodgings, and set every adventurer on the *qui vive*.

And here it may be asked, how was it that Nash, who started on
his career without a sixpence in his pocket, and was generally unsuccessful at play, contrived for so many years to maintain such a
splendid establishment? The answer is soon given. He was a sleeping partner in one of the most thriving of the Bath gambling-houses.
Connected with his transactions in this line we give the following
curious anecdotes, which will show that whatever were the defects of
his head, his heart was always in the right place. The Earl of T——,
when a young man, was inordinately addicted to gambling, and in
particular loved to have the King of Bath for his opponent. He was,
however, no match for his majesty, who, after winning several trifling
sums from him, resolved to attempt his cure, foreseeing that otherwise he would fall a prey to adventurers who might not be so for-
bearing as himself. Accordingly he engaged his lordship one evening
in play to a very serious amount, and won from him, first, all his
ready money, then the title-deeds of his estates, and, finally, the very
watch in his pocket and the rings on his fingers. When he had thus
sufficiently punished the young nobleman for his infatuation, Nash
read him a lecture on the flagrant impropriety of attempting to make
money by gambling, when poverty cannot be pleaded in justification
of such conduct; after which he returned him all his winnings, merely
exacting from him a promise that he would never play again! Not
less generously did he behave to an Oxford student who had come
to spend the long vacation at Bath. This greenhorn, who also affected to be a gamester, was lucky enough to win a large sum of
money from our Beau, and after the game was ended, was invited by

him to supper. " Perhaps," said Nash, " you think I have asked you
for the purpose of securing my revenge ; but I can assure you that
my sole motive in requesting your company is, to set you on your
guard, and to entreat you to be warned by my experience, and shun
play as you would the devil.   This is strange advice for one like me
to give ; but I feel for your youth and inexperience, and am convinced that if you do not stop where you now are, you will infallibly
be ruined."   Nash was right.   A few nights afterwards, having lost
his entire fortune at the gaming-table, the young man blew his brains
out !

Though it was one of Nash's foibles to be thought " a lady-killer,"
yet this did not prevent him fróm befriending the fair sex whenever
opportunity offered.   He was the means of exposing many a scheming
libertine, and more than one heiress owed to him her escape from the
snares of penniless adventurers.   About the time of the treaty of
Utrecht, a certain Colonel M——, a gallant, handsome officer of dragoons, was in great favour with all the Bath ladies.   As, however, he
had nothing to depend on but his pay, it was an object with him to
marry for money ; and accordingly he singled out a Miss L——, a
wealthy heiress, whose father was desirous that she should espouse
a nobleman of distinction.   But the colonel had gained her affections ;
whereupon Nash, who was well acquainted with his circumstances,
wrote to the young lady's parents, advising them strongly to put an
end to the connexion, which they did, by abruptly removing her from
Bath.   The disappointed suitor, enraged at the Beau's interference,
instantly sent him a challenge, which was declined ; for, among other
of his prejudices, Nash held the *monomachia* or *duello* in the most unequivocal abhorrence.   Finding his only chance of retrieving his
finances thus cut off, the colonel quitted Bath, where his creditors
were become quite clamorous, and in a fit of desperation hurried over
to the Continent, and joined the Dutch army in Flanders.   Here he
enlisted himself as a volunteer ; while his friends, not hearing of or
from him for a considerable period, gave out that he had been killed
in battle.   Meantime the nobleman, taking advantage of his rival's
absence, pushed his suit with ardour ; but, before he could bring it to
a satisfactory conclusion, the young lady's father died, leaving her
property to the amount of fifteen hundred pounds *per annum !*   It
was at this crisis of her fate that Nash happened to hear that the
colonel had returned to England, but, fearful of being discovered by
his creditors, had changed his name, joined a company of strolling
actors, and was then playing at Peterborough.   On learning these
particulars, our Beau thought that the time was come for him to make
reparation to the colonel, especially as the lady was now of age, and
fully competent to make her own choice of a husband.   He invites
her accordingly to join him and some mutual friends in a short trip
to Peterborough, where they arrive early in the forenoon, and, by
way of passing the evening agreeably, pay a visit to the theatre.
Just as they are entering the box, the colonel appears on the stage.
The young lady recognises him in an instant, and is so much affected
by his altered circumstances, that she faints away.   On regaining
consciousness, she finds him standing beside her.   Nash has brought
him there.   " You thought me your enemy," said the kind-hearted
monarch, "but I was no such thing ; I merely thought one of you

too extravagant, and the other too inexperienced, to be likely to make a happy match of it. But the case is altered now ; if, therefore, you feel inclined to marry, do so in God's name, and d—n him, say I, that would part you !" They were married within the month, and Nash spent many a pleasant day at their villa in the neighbourhood of Bristol.

Mr. Wood, the architect, of Bath, has left on record another anecdote of Nash, which redounds equally to his credit. About the period of his greatest popularity, there came to the city a young lady well known by the name of Sylvia, who, as she was handsome, accomplished, of "gentle blood," and possessed of a large fortune, soon became one of the ruling belles of the day. Among the number of this lady's admirers was a gentleman, nicknamed by his friends the " Goodnatured Man," from his easy and indolent temper. He was of sadly improvident habits ; and having contracted heavy debts, which he was wholly unable to discharge, he was arrested and thrown into prison, which coming to the ears of Sylvia, she went to consult Mr. Nash upon the best means of freeing him from his embarrassments. His majesty strongly endeavoured to persuade her from interfering in the matter ; observing that her interference would be sure to be misconstrued, and that to evince such extreme interest in a young man who had no claim on her consideration further than having occasionally flirted with her in society, would expose her to the cruellest calumnies ; and, moreover, that she could do him no good, for that her entire fortune, ample as it was, would be scarcely sufficient to satisfy the demands of his creditors. The thoughtless and enamoured girl listened to, but was not convinced by, Nash's arguments. She expended a large portion of her property in defraying the " Good-natured Man's" debts ; but before she could accomplish his liberation he died, and she had the mortification to discover that she had not only lost the greatest part of her fortune, but, which was of more value, her reputation also. In this forlorn condition, her spirits broken, and her society avoided by those who had formerly been proud to rank themselves among her flatterers, she accepted the offer of a plausible old demirep, who kept one of the most splendid gaming establishments at Bath, to pay an occasional visit to her rooms, for the hag was shrewd enough to foresee that Sylvia's beauty would prove a powerful magnet of attraction to the libertines who frequented such places. Here Nash used often to meet her, and, believing that she was still innocent, however thoughtless her conduct might be, remonstrated with her in the kindest terms, and at length succeeded in persuading her to take up her residence with Mr. Wood's family in Queen Square. While here, Mr. Wood describes her as having been most exemplary in her habits, seldom going out, but confining herself to the solitude of her chamber, where she spent the greatest portion of her time in reading. About a month after she had been domesticated in his house, business of importance took her host to London ;· and it was during his absence that Sylvia first meditated the idea of suicide. One evening, after having been more than usually cheerful, and amused herself by dandling one of Mr. Wood's children in her arms, she ordered supper to be got ready in the library, and, having spent some hours alone there, went up into her bed-room. On her way, she had to pass through the chamber where her host's children lay asleep, and struck with their happy, innocent countenances, and the consciousness of her own meditated guilt, she burst into tears; but, recovering herself with an effort, hurried into her own apartment, carefully locking the door behind her. She then proceeded to dress herself in white like a bride's-maid, neatly arranged her hair, and, having procured a pink silk girdle, which she lengthened by means of another made of gold thread, placed it on the table, and, throwing herself on the bed, spent some time in reading. About midnight she rose, and, after kneeling for a few minutes in prayer, mounted upon a chair, drove a large nail into the closet-door, and, attaching one end of the girdle to it, fastened the other tightly about her neck, and so hung suspended. Her weight, however, proving too much for it, the girdle broke, and she fell to the floor with violence; but, still resolute to destroy herself, she made a second attempt, in which she unfortunately succeeded. Her death created an extraordinary sensation throughout Bath; the coroner's jury brought in a verdict of lunacy; and Nash, who, with Mr. Wood, was the only friend the poor girl had left, attended her funeral, and did his best to protect her memory from insult.

In the year 1734 Bath was honoured by a visit from the Prince of Orange, and in 1738 by another from the Prince of Wales, both of whom took particular notice of Nash; for which, in return, the grateful Beau erected obelisks in their honour. He had now attained the climax of his popularity. His word was law; his bow an honour; his acquaintance a sure passport into the best circles. The Prince of Wales having made him a present of a magnificent gold snuff-box, the rest of the nobility thought it incumbent on them to follow the example; and, accordingly, it soon became the fashion—a fashion which he most disinterestedly encouraged—to give Nash snuff-boxes. As if this were not sufficient distinction, the corporation, in a paroxysm of gratitude for the benefits which he had conferred on their city, determined on erecting a full-length statue of him in the Pump-room, between the busts of Newton and Pope, which gave rise to one of Lord Chesterfield's wittiest and most caustic epigrams. We subjoin the closing stanza of this brilliant gem:—

> ' The statue, placed the busts between,
>   Adds to the satire strength;
> Wisdom and Wit are little seen,
>   But Folly's at full length."

Poor Nash's brains were half-turned by such brilliant prosperity. He had his levees, where he affected all the airs of a legitimate monarch; his buffoons, his parasites, and even his poet-laureate. But, so far was he from being satisfied with the flatteries constantly lavished on him, that his appetite "grew by what it fed upon." If a beggar in the street called him " Your honour," he always bowed low to the compliment; but if he called him " Your lordship," he would give him every farthing he had about him. He has even been known, when in London, to stand a whole day at the window of the Smyrna Coffee-house, merely in the hope of receiving a passing bow from the Prince of Wales or the Duchess of Marlborough!

The numerous dedications to Nash are not the least curious proofs of his universal celebrity. Some of these are such exquisite samples of the servile, that we cannot resist the temptation of extracting a sentence or two from them. One is from a noted highwayman, who was taken up for attempting to rob and murder a Dr. Handcock. This scamp, whose name was Baxter, published a book, dated from Taunton jail, exposing the tricks of thieves and gamblers, which he dedicated to Nash, as follows: " As your honour's wisdom, humanity, and interest, are the friend of the virtuous, I make bold to lay at your honour's feet the following work," &c. Another dedication is from a professor of cookery, who says, " As much as the oak exceeds the bramble, so do you, honoured sir, exceed the rest of mankind in benevolence, charity, and every other virtue that adorns, ennobles, and refines the human species. I have, therefore, made bold to prefix your name, though without your permission, to the following volume, which stands in need of such a patron." We next find a musical composer essaying the complimentary. " To whom," asks this sycophantic dedicator, " could I presume to offer these, my first attempts at musical composition, but to the great encourager of all polite arts; for your generosity knows no bounds, nor are you more famed for that dignity of mind which ennobles and gives a grace to every part of your conduct, than for that humanity and beneficence, which make you the friend and benefactor of all mankind !" These dedications, and a hundred others of the same calibre, which might have turned the stomach of an ostrich, Nash digested with uncommon facility. But it was with the flatteries of the poets that he used to be most tickled; and many a hungry browser on Parnassus has been rescued by his thirst for praise from the fangs of an unimaginative bailiff.

But the hour was at hand when this Wolsey of the fashionable world was doomed to experience the caprice and neglect of those circles whom he had so long ruled with despotic authority. His sun had attained its meridian, and was already journeying westward. Intoxicated with self-conceit, and firmly persuaded that he was the first man of the age, he began to lay aside those magic arts of address to which he owed all his success; became morose and fidgety; and took a pleasure in speaking unpleasant truths, which he mistook for wit. He was, besides, getting fast on in years; and age, which brings wisdom to some, to men like Nash is apt to bring nothing but petulance and imbecility. But he was not splenetic without reason; for his fortune, which he had never husbanded, diminished rapidly, and he had no earthly means left of recruiting it. His greatest grievance, however, was the gradual dropping off of his old friends the nobility, who, it is said, exerted all their influence with the corporation of Bath to get him superannuated, and Quin, the actor, appointed Master of the Ceremonies in his stead. This unparalleled ingratitude, as he called it, stung Nash to the quick, and he threatened to take his revenge of a degenerate aristocracy by writing his memoirs ! His intention, however, was never carried into effect; which is a pity, for, judging by the few scraps of composition he left behind, his book would have been a literary phænomenon of the first water.

Nash was now become a confirmed old dotard; nevertheless, he still aped the character of a young beau,—still continued to haunt like a spectre the scenes of his departed glory. Though the snows of eighty-six winters were whitening on his head, it was still his proud-

est ambition to "settle the fashion of a lady's cap," and assign her
her proper station in a country-dance.   This, which, to say the worst
of it, was but harmless drivelling, roused against him the pious wrath
of the more straight-laced among the Somersetshire clergy, who
pelted him with the most minaceous pamphlets; exhorted him to quit
the assembly-room for the church, and to repent of those colossal
enormities of which they charitably took for granted he had been
guilty.   One of these clerical pamphleteers addressed him in the following indulgent terms : " Repent ! repent ! or wretched will you be,
silly, vain old man, to eternity !   The blood of souls will be laid to
your charge; God's jealousy, like a consuming flame, will smoke
against you, as you yourself will see in that day when the mountains
shall quake, and the hills melt, and the earth be burned up at his
presence."   Another says, " God will bring you to judgment.   He
sees me now I write; he will observe you while you read.   He
notes down my words; he will also note down your consequent procedure.   Not then upon me, not upon me, but upon your own soul
will the neglecting or despising my sayings turn."   How different
these fanatical fulminations from the honied flatteries, in the shape of
poems and dedications, on which Nash's vanity had been so long
fed !

The poor old man was now hourly decaying; but this quite as
much from grief as age.   The season of snuff-boxes was over; the
great had altogether forgotten him; and he was preserved from
utter penury solely by the munificence of the Bath corporation, who
granted him ten guineas the first Monday of every month.   For some
weeks previous to his decease it was evident that his last hour was at
hand; but he himself would never admit it.   He clung to life with all
the tenacity of a Johnson; and roundly asserted that he was in robust
health at the very moment when he was treading, with palsied head
and tottering limbs, on the threshold of the grave.   At length his exhausted powers wholly gave way, and he expired in the eighty-
seventh year of his age, at his house in St. John's Court, Bath, in the
spring of 1761.

No sooner was his death known than the press teemed with tributes to his memory.   The Muses were called on to lament the
eclipse of the brightest luminary of the age; and epitaphs were written on him,—one in Latin, and another in English,—by two of the
most accomplished scholars in the kingdom.   That in Latin, by Dr.
King, is a fine sample of mock-solemnity, comparing Nash, as a legis-
lator, with Solon and Lycurgus, and giving him the preference to
both.   But, in his own capital, the sensation occasioned by our Beau's
decease was unexampled.   The very day after, the corporation, with
the mayor at their head, met in full and solemn conclave, and voted
nem. con. fifty pounds towards defraying their monarch's funeral expenses.   The corpse lay four days in state; after which it was conveyed to the Abbey Church, in the midst of one of the greatest
crowds that had ever assembled in Bath.   The following week, the
principal local journal commented on the mournful event as follows :
" Sorrow sate on every face, and even children lisped that their sovereign was no more.   The peasant discontinued his toil; the ox
rested from the plough; all nature seemed to sympathise with our
loss ; and—the muffled bells rung a peal of bob-major !"   It must be

confessed, to our shame, that we have no such newspaper writing as this now-a-days. We have become as unimaginative as steam-engines, and no longer indulge in those astounding bursts of eloquence and sensibility which used to electrify our grandfathers and grandmothers.

In person Nash was large and awkward, with harsh, strong, and irregular features. Nevertheless, he was popular with women, and not unsuccessful as a gallant; for he dressed showily, had some wit, abundance of small talk, and was by no means encumbered with modesty. He used frequently to say of himself, that he was, "like Nestor, a man of three generations." The Beau of his youth, he would observe, was stiff, solemn, and formal to a degree; visiting his mistress, as Jupiter visited Semele, in state; toasting her on bended knees; and languishing, a timid suppliant, at her feet, by the hour together. The Beau of his manhood was just the reverse; being a pert, grinning, lively chatterbox,—such as we meet with in Congreve's comedies; ready for any absurd, *outré* display of sentiment; and deeming it an exalted proof of gallantry to eat "a pair of his idol's shoes tossed up in a fricassee." The Beau of his old age was a still more extraordinary character, for his whole secret in intrigue consisted in perfect indifference. If his mistress honoured him with her approbation, well; if not, she might let it alone. He had no notion of breaking his heart for love. Women were as plentiful as mushrooms, and always to be had for the asking. Nash was a great theorist on all matters of sentiment. It was a favourite maxim with him that good-humour and fine clothes were enough to ruin a nunnery; but that "flummery," or the art of saying nothings, was worth them both put together. Women, he used to say, dote upon lively nonsense; always talk to them, therefore, in the language they best understand. The instant you begin to converse rationally with them the game is up, which is the reason why learned men make such indifferent lovers.

Next to his powers of gallantry, Nash piqued himself on his wit. But he was by no means remarkable for this quality, though never did mortal man labour harder to say good things. His best jokes were always cracked unawares. The majority of them are well known to the world, for Smollett, with the coolest effrontery, has transferred them, unacknowledged, into his own novels. We will, however, give one or two of them. Meeting one morning, in the Pump-room, a lady who was deformed, Nash asked her where she came from. Her reply was, "Straight from London." "Then, madam," replied the Beau, "you must have been confoundedly warped by the way." Doctor Cheney, on some occasion having recommended to him a vegetable diet, he tartly observed, "I suppose you would have me go grazing and eating thistles like Nebuchadnezzar!" "No, no," said the doctor, who was also a wag, "there needs no such metamorphosis; your ears are quite long enough already." Being once confined to his house by sickness, the same physician drew up a prescription for him, and, calling on his patient next day, found him up and well. "I 'm glad you had the good sense to follow my prescription, Mr. Nash," quoth the leech. "Follow it!" exclaimed the other. "Egad, if I had, I should have broke my neck, for I flung it out of my bedroom window." We are not without our suspicions that this last witticism is a regular Joe Miller, for we have detected it in at least a dozen different publications. But this is not to be wondered at, for your good joke is the greatest of travellers. The "facetiæ" of the old Greek wag, Hierocles, have been naturalised in every language of Europe.

Though convivial in his youth, yet, for the greatest portion of his life, Nash was rigidly abstemious in his habits. He loved plain dishes, seldom remained long at table, and usually contented himself with two glasses of wine. But he liked to see his friends enjoy themselves, and would encourage them in these elegant and emphatic terms: "Eat, gentlemen, — eat and drink, in God's name; spare, and the devil choke you!" His favourite meal was supper; and so fond was he of potatoes, which he called the English pine-apple, that he used to eat them, like fruit, after dinner. He was also remarkable for his love of early rising, being seldom in bed after four in summer, and five in winter. His generosity and benevolence were unbounded. He gave away enormous sums in charity, and founded a hospital at Bath, the expenses of which for a time almost beggared him. Though he had a great respect for rank, yet he discouraged anything like aristocratic assumption; and, whenever he heard a young lord boasting of his family, never failed to put him down with a sneer. In this respect he resembles the late John Kemble, of whom it is recorded, that, when dining with the Dukes of Hamilton and Gordon, who were boasting somewhat ostentatiously of the antiquity of their blood, he lost all patience, and put an abrupt stop to their egotism by exclaiming, "D—n both your bloods; pass the bottle!" Owing to his frequent intercourse with small poets, Nash fancied that he was a judge of the art. A volume of Pope, who was his favourite writer, generally lay on his table, though we question much whether he ever got beyond the "Rape of the Lock." This, however, was a production every way calculated to please him; and, accordingly,—a rich trait of character,—he was never weary of repeating the lines,

"Sir Plume, of amber *snuff-box* justly vain,
And the nice conduct of a clouded cane."

Though he had mixed so much with the world, yet Nash was a man of great simplicity of character. He imagined that others were as frank and sincere as himself; and, in his connexion with the gambling establishments at Bath and Tunbridge Wells, never kept an account, but trusted entirely to the honour of his partners. He was never married, though he once made proposals to a young lady, whose parents favoured his suit, for he was then at the summit of his celebrity. She, however, declined his addresses; but, apprehensive of her father's indignation, went to Nash, and candidly told him that her affections were fixed upon another. He immediately sent for his rival; gave him the lady with his own hand; and reconciled her parents to the match by settling on her a fortune equal to that which they proposed to give her. Unfortunately, however, his generosity was thrown away; for soon after her marriage she ran away with her footman, and her husband died of grief.

Late in life Nash set up for a teller of good stories, which he would repeat half-a-dozen times in the same day. As he seldom allowed truth to stand in the way of a point, his anecdotes were sometimes amusing, despite the "says he's" and "says I's" with which he stuffed them *usque ad nauseam*. The surest way to gain his favour,—next to dedicating a work to him,—was to laugh, in the right place, at his conceits, and call him an "odd fellow;" for, like the majority of mankind, he looked upon eccentricity as a sure test of genius. But, indeed, vanity was his ruling foible. He had numerous other weaknesses; but this, "like Aaron's serpent, swallowed all the rest." He considered his office to be the most important in the world, and himself the greatest man in it. Yet he was not naturally devoid of good sense; but, having been long accustomed to pursue trifles, his mind insensibly shrunk to the size of the petty objects on which it was employed. Even the most frivolous duties of his office he discharged with the gravest punctiliousness; and, though overflowing with the milk of human kindness, never forgave a breach of his regulations. The man might relent; but the Master of the Ceremonies was inexorable!

The influence that Nash had on the social character of his age was greater than has been generally supposed. Men of far more exalted pretensions than he have not effected one half the good. He was the first who promoted a taste for elegant amusements, and an ease of address, among a people notorious for their anti-gregarious habits, and reserved and awkward bearing. The disposition for familiar intercourse, which—encouraged by his example—strangers acquired at Bath and Tunbridge Wells, they carried with them to the metropolis, and whatever other place they might visit; and thus the whole kingdom became gradually more refined and social in its character. When it is borne in mind that Nash laid the foundation of this wholesome change without any help from birth, fortune, connexions, or superior intellect; that, with nothing but his good-humour and his address to support his claims, he reigned the undisputed monarch of the empire of fashion for upwards of half a century; though we cannot affirm that he was a great man, it is impossible to deny that he was an extraordinary one.

GRUB-STREET NEWS.

ACRES is made by Sheridan to say, "The best terms will grow obsolete." This, every day's experience proves to be true. "What a shocking bad hat!" "There he goes with his eye out!" and "Flare up!" were doomed to make way for "Who are you?"—as "All round my hat," with the public street vocalists, has been superseded by "Jump, Jim Crow."

But it may be remarked that popular phrases founded on a well-known fact have had a longer duration than those which cannot be proved to have any such origin.

The cry of "*Nosey!*" at the theatres, when it was wished that the music should play up, which arose about a century ago in honour of Mr. Cervetto, whose nasal promontory used to adorn the Drury-lane orchestra, survived till a very late period, and indeed has hardly yet fallen into desuetude; and "*Grub-street news*" is still spoken of by our elder *quidnuncs*, though probably they would be puzzled to tell, not the meaning of the sentence, but how those words came to convey the meaning they embody.

It has been said that they took their rise from the circumstance of a set of needy scribblers having established themselves in Grub-street, a mean narrow passage leading from Chiswell-street to Fore-street, now dignified with the name of Milton-street, and thence sending forth fabricated intelligence. This may be true; but still there was a founder of this hopeful colony, whose name has not been preserved. It is intended in this paper to fill up the *hiatus* in history which has so long been deplored. George Iland appears to have been the man.

In the early part of the reign of Charles the Second, some very bold inventions were hazarded, and given to the world duly attested, with as good a set of signatures appended as Morison's pills can command now. They somehow attracted the notice of those in authority, and one of the marvellous narratives launched in the year 1661 was thought worthy to be made the subject of an official investigation. Some curiosity will be felt to know what sort of a narrative it could be that received this singular honour. A verbatim copy is therefore subjoined. The original filled six pages, and was adorned with a grotesque engraving, which it is hardly worth while to transcribe. The title-page ran thus:

"A STRANGE AND TRUE

RELATION

OF A WONDERFUL AND TERRIBLE

EARTH-QUAKE,

That happened at HEREFORD on *Tuesday* last, being the first of this present *October* 1661,

Whereby

A Church-Steeple and many gallant Houses were thrown down to the ground, and several of the Inhabitants slain; with the terrible Thunder-claps and violent Storm of great Hail-stones that then fell, which were about the bigness of an Egge, many Cattle being thereby utterly destroyed as they were feeding in the Field.

Also,

The prodigious and wonderful Apparitions that was seen in the Air, to the great amazement of all Spectators, who beheld two perfect Armes and Hands: In the Right-Hand being graspt a great broad Sword, and in the Left, a Bowl full of Blood, from whence they heard a most strange and loud Voice, to the wonderful astonishing of all present, the fright whereof causing divers Women to fall in Travel, amongst whom the Clerk's Wife, named *Margaret Pelmore*, fell in labour and brought forth three Male-Children, who had all Teeth, and spake as soon as they were born, and presently after gave up the Ghost and died together; the like having never been known before in any Age!

"The Truth hereof is witnessed by

Francis Smalman,	*Nicholas Finch,* Gent.
and *Henry Cross,*	*James Tulley,* Gent.
Churchwardens.	*George Cox,*
Peter Philpot,	*Robert Morris,*
Constable.	*Thomas Welford,* &c.

"London, Printed for J. J. 1661."

"A

"TRUE AND PERFECT RELATION OF THE TERRIBLE EARTH-QUAKE, GREAT CLAPS OF THUNDER, AND MIGHTY HAIL-STONES, WHICH HAPNED AT HEREFORD, ON TUESDAY LAST, THE FIRST OF THIS PRESENT OCTOBER, &c.

"Before I mention any further concerning this strange and sudden Accident, which hath so lately befaln at Hereford, and that this Real and Authentique Truth may not seem doubtful, I shall put the Reader hereof in minde to take notice and remember the several Disasters that hath befaln, not long since, in and about London, which I need not here to declare, yet none so wonderful or worthy of observation as this; but let it not seem strange, for we know, and often read, that the Lord doth sometimes manifest his will unto the World in Wonders and Signes, thereby in some part to shew his Omnipotency, and let them know that he is still the Almighty God, and that he sees and knows all our ways, how slight soever we make thereof. Then how can we praise him sufficiently, when we hear of this strange Disaster that did so lately befal at Hereford, in that he was pleased to keep the like from us here in London, we being as sinful as any? But he that is all Mighty and all Powerful, is also all Goodness and all Merciful, whereon depends the best hopes of all good Christians.

"And now to descend to the subject I was before speaking of, which was of the violent Tempest, and terrible Earth-quake, &c. that hapned at Hereford, be pleased to observe the true Relation thereof, which is thus:

"On Tuesday last, being the first of this present October 1661, about 2 of the clock after Noon, there hapned a great and violent storm to arise, to the amazing and astonishing of all the inhabitants. The first beginning was with a most terrible Winde, which continued for the space of 2 hours, with such vehemency, that it forced the Tiles off the Houses, insomuch that none durst come out at their doors; in the midst of which storm was blown down the Steeple of a Church, and many brave Houses, the falling whereof hath killed some persons, but what they are, or whom, we yet know not.

"Then the Air began to be darkned, but, suddenly clearing again, the people began to look abroad; and so continuing for a while, all assuredly thought the storm to be over: but contrary to their hopes, about 6 or 7 of the clock in the evening, their ears were solicited with unwonted Claps of Thunder; and, more to augment their fear, presently fell such Hail-stones, that the like was never seen in any Age before, each Hail-stone being about the bigness of an Egge, which several gentlemen of quality affirm, here present in London, who certifie that they destroyed the Cattle in the Field, and did much other harm.

" Then followed a terrible and fearful Earth-quake, which continued almost for the space of half an hour, which so amazed the inhabitants, that they thought the last Day had been come; and immediately appeared a great brightness, as if it had been Noon-day, but
was presently overcast with a Black Cloud, out of which appeared a
perfect Armes and Hands; in the right-hand was grasped a great
broad Sword, and in the left a Cup, or Boul, as they conceived, full
of Blood.

" Having glutted their eyes with amazement, and filled their hearts
with great fear, with beholding these prodigious Apparitions, more to
astonish both them and us, appeared to their eyes a piece of Corn,
ground, ready to mow, and a Sythe lying by, from whence they heard
a most strange and loud voice, which said, ' Woe, woe to thee, and to
the inhabitants thereof, for he cometh that is to come, and ye shall
all see him !'

" At the conclusion of these words, the people made a grievous
cry, as indeed they might, and many Women that were with Child,
through extream fear, fel in travel; but none so wonderful to be
taken notice of, as Mrs. Margaret Pelmore, the Clerk's Wife of the
Town, who, for the space of twenty Weeks, wanting her bodily health,
had sought for cure of the Doctors: This Margaret Pelmore at that
very instant fell in travel, being exceedingly affrighted, and brought
forth 3 Male Children, who had all teeth, and spake as soon as they
were born. The first said, ' The Day is appointed which no Man
can shun.' The second demanded, ' Where would be found sufficient
alive to bury the Dead ?' And the third said, ' Where will there
be Corn enough to satisfie the hungry and needy ?'

" As soon as they had spoken these words, they all immediately
gave up the Ghost and died, to the great astonishing and amazement
of all present; and the Mother of the said Children doth at this moment lie Distracted, and raging in such extream manner, that none
can tell, as yet, whether she will live or die !

" The truth whereof is witnessed by

Francis Smalman,	*James Tulley,*
Henry Cross,	*George Cox,*
Churchwardens.	*John Groom,*
Peter Philpot,	*Robert Maurice,*
Constable.	*Thomas Welford,*
Nicholas Finch.	And divers others.

" FINIS."

Such was the experiment then made on public credulity. The
inquiry which has been mentioned is proved to have taken place by
a paper found some years ago in the State Paper Office, attached to
the pamphlet itself, which was marked, " Examinaçon of Jo. Jones,"
and dated " 20th 8ber, 1661." The examination is reported as
follows :

" This Examinate saith that he had a share in the printing of the
booke of an Earth quake at Hereford, but did not Print it; and that
it was printed in Mr. Alsop's house in grub streete where one Geo.
Iland, who brought the coppy, liveth.

" JOHN JONES."

SONG OF THE MONTH. No. XI.

November, 1837.

Of all the months that compose the year,
From January chill, to December drear,
  Commend us to November;
For, sure as its period comes around,
Good fellows are over the wine-cup found,—
  'Twas so since we remember.

Let April boast of its sunny showers,
Let May exult in its gay young flowers,
  And June in its heat and its light;
This, this is the month to surpass them all,
While wine-cups circle in wood-lit hall,
  And wit flashes on through the night.

What flowers can vie with the charms we view
Around us then? Love's rosiest hue
  To woman's cheek is given.
No shower is like the tear of the grape,
In its rainbow Joy has his happiest shape,
  And each tint is direct from heaven.

If mists veil the earth, and if storms arise,
And darkness broods gloomily over the skies,
  And the gusty wind sullenly moans;
Let them e'en do their worst:—we care not a pin,
Though it 's dreary without, we are merry within
  As we listen to music's gay tones.

Then of all the months that compose the year,
From January chill, to December drear,
  Commend us to November;
For, sure as its period comes around,
Good fellows are over the wine-cup found,—
  And 'twas so since we remember.

OLIVER TWIST;

OR, THE PARISH BOY'S PROGRESS.

BY BOZ.

ILLUSTRATED BY GEORGE CRUIKSHANK.

CHAPTER THE SIXTEENTH

RELATES WHAT BECAME OF OLIVER TWIST, AFTER HE HAD BEEN CLAIMED
BY NANCY.

THE narrow streets and courts at length terminated in a large
open space, scattered about which, were pens for beasts, and
other indications of a cattle-market. Sikes slackened his pace
when they reached this spot, the girl being quite unable to support any longer the rapid rate at which they had hitherto
walked; and, turning to Oliver, commanded him roughly to
take hold of Nancy's hand.

"Do you hear?" growled Sikes, as Oliver hesitated, and
looked round.

They were in a dark corner, quite out of the track of passengers, and Oliver saw but too plainly that resistance would
be of no avail. He held out his hand, which Nancy clasped
tight in hers.

"Give me the other," said Sikes, seizing Oliver's unoccupied
hand. "Here, Bull's-eye!"

The dog looked up, and growled.

"See here, boy!" said Sikes, putting his other hand to Oliver's
throat, and uttering a savage oath; "if he speaks ever so soft
a word, hold him! D'ye mind?"

The dog growled again, and, licking his lips, eyed Oliver as
if he were anxious to attach himself to his windpipe without
any unnecessary delay.

"He's as willing as a Christian, strike me blind if he isn't!"
said Sikes, regarding the animal with a kind of grim and ferocious approval. "Now you know what you've got to expect,
master, so call away as quick as you like; the dog will soon
stop that game. Get on, young 'un!"

Bull's-eye wagged his tail in acknowledgment of this unusually endearing form of speech, and, giving vent to another
admonitory growl for the benefit of Oliver, led the way onward.

It was Smithfield that they were crossing, although it might
have been Grosvenor Square, for anything Oliver knew to the
contrary. The night was dark and foggy, and it was just beginning to rain. The lights in the shops could scarcely struggle
through the heavy mist, which thickened every moment, and
shrouded the streets and houses in gloom, rendering the strange
place still stranger in Oliver's eyes, and making his uncertainty
the more dismal and depressing.

George Cruikshank

They had hurried on a few paces, when a deep church-bell struck the hour. With its first stroke his two conductors stopped, and turned their heads in the direction whence the sound proceeded.

"Eight o'clock, Bill," said Nancy, when the bell ceased.

"What's the good of telling me that; I can hear, can't I?" replied Sikes.

"I wonder whether *they* can hear it," said Nancy.

"Of course they can," replied Sikes. "It was Bartlemy time when I was shopped, and there warn't a penny trumpet in the fair as I couldn't hear the squeaking on. Arter I was locked up for the night, the row and din outside made the thundering old jail so silent, that I could almost have beat my brains out against the iron plates of the door."

"Poor fellows!" said Nancy, who still had her face turned towards the quarter in which the bell had sounded. "Oh, Bill, such fine young chaps as them!"

"Yes; that's all you women think of," answered Sikes. "Fine young chaps! Well, they're as good as dead; so it don't much matter."

With this consolation Mr. Sikes appeared to repress a rising tendency to jealousy, and, clasping Oliver's wrist more firmly, told him to step out again.

"Wait a minute," said the girl: "I wouldn't hurry by, if it was you that was coming out to be hung the next time eight o'clock struck, Bill. I'd walk round and round the place till I dropped, if the snow was on the ground, and I hadn't a shawl to cover me."

"And what good would that do?" inquired the unsentimental Mr. Sikes. "Unless you could pitch over a file and twenty yards of good stout rope, you might as well be walking fifty mile off, or not walking at all, for all the good it would do me. Come on, will you, and don't stand preaching there."

The girl burst into a laugh, drew her shawl more closely round her, and they walked away. But Oliver felt her hand tremble; and, looking up in her face as they passed a gas-lamp, saw that it had turned a deadly white.

They walked on, by little-frequented and dirty ways, for a full half-hour, meeting very few people, for it now rained heavily, and those they did meet appearing from their looks to hold much the same position in society as Mr. Sikes himself. At length they turned into a very filthy narrow street, nearly full of old-clothes shops; and the dog, running forward as if conscious that there was now no further occasion for his keeping on guard, stopped before the door of a shop which was closed and apparently untenanted, for the house was in a ruinous condition, and upon the door was nailed a board intimating that it was to let, which looked as if it had hung there for many years.

"All right," said Sikes, looking cautiously about.

Nancy stooped below the shutters, and Oliver heard the sound of a bell. They crossed to the opposite side of the street, and stood for a few moments under a lamp. A noise, as if a sash-window were gently raised, was heard, and soon afterwards the door softly opened; upon which Mr. Sikes seized the terrified boy by the collar with very little ceremony, and all three were quickly inside the house.

The passage was perfectly dark, and they waited while the person who had let them in, chained and barred the door.

" Anybody here ?" inquired Sikes.

" No," replied a voice, which Oliver thought he had heard before.

" Is the old 'un here ?" asked the robber.

" Yes," replied the voice; " and precious down in the mouth he has been. Won't he be glad to see you ? Oh, no."

The style of this reply, as well as the voice which delivered it, seemed familiar to Oliver's ears; but it was impossible to distinguish even the form of the speaker in the darkness.

" Let 's have a glim," said Sikes, " or we shall go breaking our necks, or treading on the dog. Look after your legs if you do, that 's all."

" Stand still a moment, and I 'll get you one," replied the voice. The receding footsteps of the speaker were heard, and in another minute the form of Mr. John Dawkins, otherwise the artful Dodger, appeared, bearing in his right hand a tallow candle stuck in the end of a cleft stick.

The young gentleman did not stop to bestow any other mark of recognition upon Oliver than a humorous grin; but, turning away, beckoned the visitors to follow him down a flight of stairs. They crossed an empty kitchen, and, opening the door of a low earthy-smelling room, which seemed to have been built in a small back-yard, were received with a shout of laughter.

" Oh, my wig, my wig !" cried Master Charles Bates, from whose lungs the laughter had proceeded; " here he is ! oh, cry, here he is ! Oh, Fagin, look at him; Fagin, do look at him ! I can't bear it; it is such a jolly game, I can't bear it. Hold me, somebody, while I laugh it out."

With this irrepressible ebullition of mirth, Master Bates laid himself flat on the floor, and kicked convulsively for five minutes in an ecstasy of facetious joy. Then, jumping to his feet, he snatched the cleft stick from the Dodger, and, advancing to Oliver, viewed him round and round, while the Jew, taking off his night-cap, made a great number of low bows to the bewildered boy; the Artful meantime, who was of a rather saturnine disposition, and seldom gave way to merriment when it interfered with business, rifling his pockets with steady assiduity.

" Look at his togs, Fagin !" said Charley, putting the light so close to Oliver's new jacket as nearly to set him on fire. " Look

at his togs !—superfine cloth, and the heavy-swell cut ! Oh,
my eye, what a game ! And his books, too ;—nothing but a
gentleman, Fagin !"

"Delighted to see you looking so well, my dear," said the
Jew, bowing with mock humility. "The Artful shall give you
another suit, my dear, for fear you should spoil that Sunday
one. Why didn't you write, my dear, and say you were coming ?—we 'd have got something warm for supper."

At this, Master Bates roared again, so loud that Fagin himself relaxed, and even the Dodger smiled ; but as the Artful
drew forth the five-pound note at that instant, it is doubtful
whether the sally or the discovery awakened his merriment.

"Hallo ! what's that ?" inquired Sikes, stepping forward as
the Jew seized the note. "That's mine, Fagin."

"No, no, my dear," said the Jew. "Mine, Bill, mine ;
you shall have the books."

"If that ain't mine !" said Sikes, putting on his hat with a
determined air,—"mine and Nancy's, that is,—I 'll take the
boy back again."

The Jew started, and Oliver started too, though from a very
different cause, for he hoped that the dispute might really end
in his being taken back.

"Come, hand it over, will you ?" said Sikes.

"This is hardly fair, Bill ; hardly fair, is it, Nancy ?" inquired the Jew.

"Fair, or not fair," retorted Sikes, "hand it over, I tell you !
Do you think Nancy and me has got nothing else to do with
our precious time but to spend it in scouting arter and kidnap-
ping every young boy as gets grabbed through you ? Give it
here, you avaricious old skeleton ; give it here !"

With this gentle remonstrance, Mr. Sikes plucked the note
from between the Jew's finger and thumb ; and, looking the old
man coolly in the face, folded it up small, and tied it in his
neckerchief.

"That's for our share of the trouble," said Sikes ; "and not
half enough, neither. You may keep the books, if you 're fond
of reading ; and if not, you can sell 'em."

"They 're very pretty," said Charley Bates, who with sundry
grimaces had been affecting to read one of the volumes in question ; "beautiful writing, isn't it, Oliver ?" and at sight of the
dismayed look with which Oliver regarded his tormentors, Master Bates, who was blessed with a lively sense of the ludicrous,
fell into another ecstasy more boisterous than the first.

"They belong to the old gentleman," said Oliver, wringing
his hands,—"to the good, kind old gentleman who took me into
his house, and had me nursed when I was near dying of the
fever. Oh, pray send them back ; send him back the books
and money ! Keep me here all my life long ; but pray, pray

send them back! He 'll think I stole them ;—the old lady, all of them that were so kind to me, will think I stole them. Oh, do have mercy upon me, and send them back!"

With these words, which were uttered with all the energy of passionate grief, Oliver fell upon his knees at the Jew's feet, and beat his hands together in perfect desperation.

"The boy 's right," remarked Fagin, looking covertly round, and knitting his shaggy eyebrows into a hard knot. "You 're right, Oliver, you 're right; they *will* think you have stolen 'em. Ha! ha!" chuckled the Jew, rubbing his hands; "it couldn't have happened better if we had chosen our time!"

"Of course it couldn't," replied Sikes; "I know'd that, directly I see him coming through Clerkenwell with the books under his arm. It 's all right enough. They 're soft-hearted psalm-singers, or they wouldn't have took him in at all, and they 'll ask no questions arter him, fear they should be obliged to prosecute, and so get him lagged. He 's safe enough."

Oliver had looked from one to the other while these words were being spoken, as if he were bewildered and could scarcely understand what passed; but when Bill Sikes concluded, he jumped suddenly to his feet, and tore wildly from the room, uttering shrieks for help that made the bare old house echo to the roof.

"Keep back the dog, Bill!" cried Nancy, springing before the door, and closing it as the Jew and his two pupils darted out in pursuit; "keep back the dog; he 'll tear the boy to pieces."

"Serve him right!" cried Sikes, struggling to disengage himself from the girl's grasp. "Stand off from me, or I 'll split your skull against the wall!"

"I don't care for that, Bill; I don't care for that," screamed the girl, struggling violently with the man: "the child shan't be torn down by the dog, unless you kill me first."

"Shan't he!" said Sikes, setting his teeth fiercely. "I 'll soon do that, if you don't keep off."

The housebreaker flung the girl from him to the further end of the room, just as the Jew and the two boys returned, dragging Oliver among them.

"What 's the matter here?" said the Jew, looking round.

"The girl 's gone mad, I think," replied Sikes savagely.

"No, she hasn't," said Nancy, pale and breathless from the scuffle; "no, she hasn't, Fagin: don't think it."

"Then keep quiet, will you?" said the Jew with a threatening look.

"No, I won't do that either," replied Nancy, speaking very loud. "Come, what do you think of that?"

Mr. Fagin was sufficiently well acquainted with the manners and customs of that particular species of humanity to which Miss Nancy belonged, to feel tolerably certain that it would be ráther unsafe to prolong any conversation with her at present. With the view of diverting the attention of the company, he turned to Oliver.

"So you wanted to get away, my dear, did you ?" said the Jew, taking up a jagged and knotted club which lay in a corner of the fire-place ; " eh ?"

Oliver made no reply, but he watched the Jew's motions and breathed quickly.

"Wanted to get assistance,—called for the police, did you ?" sneered the Jew, catching the boy by the arm. " We'll cure you of that, my dear."

The Jew inflicted a smart blow on Oliver's shoulders with the club, and was raising it for a second, when the girl, rushing forward, wrested it from his hand, 'and flung it into the fire with a force that brought some of the glowing coals whirling out into the room.

"I won't stand by and see it done, Fagin," cried the girl. "You've got the boy, and what more would you have ? Let him be—let him be, or I shall put that mark on some of you that will bring me to the gallows before my time !"

The girl stamped her foot violently on the floor as she vented this threat; and with her lips compressed, and her hands clench-ed, looked alternately at the Jew and the other robber, her face quite colourless from the passion of rage into which she had gradually worked herself.

"Why, Nancy !" said the Jew in a soothing tone, after a pause, during which he and Mr. Sikes had stared at one another in a disconcerted manner, " you—you 're more clever than ever to-night. Ha! ha! my dear, you are acting beautifully."

"Am I !" said the girl. " Take care I don't overdo it : you will be the worse for it, Fagin, if I do ; and so I tell you in good time to keep clear of me."

There is something about a roused woman, especially if she add to all her other strong passions the fierce impulses of reck-lessness and despair, which few men like to provoke. The Jew saw that it would be hopeless to affect any further mistake re-garding the reality of Miss Nancy's rage ; and, shrinking invo-luntarily back, a few paces, cast a glance, half-imploring and half-cowardly, at Sikes, as if to hint that he was the fittest per-son to pursue the dialogue.

Mr. Sikes thus mutely appealed to, and possibly feeling his personal pride and influence interested in the immediate reduc-tion of Miss Nancy to reason, gave utterance to about a couple of score of curses and threats, the rapid delivery of which re-flected great credit on the fertility of his invention. As they produced no visible effect on the object against whom they were discharged, however, he resorted to more tangible arguments.

"What do you mean by this ?" said Sikes, backing the in-quiry with a very common imprecation concerning the most beautiful of human features, which, if it were heard above, only once out of every fifty thousand times it is uttered below, would render blindness as common a disorder as measles ; " what do you mean by it ?   Burn my body ! do you know who you are, and what you are ?"

" Oh, yes, I know all about it," replied the girl, laughing hysterically, and shaking her head from side to side with a poor assumption of indifference.

" Well, then, keep quiet," rejoined Sikes with a growl like that he was accustomed to use when addressing his dog, " or I 'll quiet you for a good long time to come."

The girl laughed again, even less composedly than before, and, darting a hasty look at Sikes, turned her face aside, and bit her lip till the blood came.

" You 're a nice one," added Sikes, as he surveyed her with a contemptuous air, " to take up the humane and genteel side ! A pretty subject for the child, as you call him, to make a friend of !"

" God Almighty help me, I am !" cried the girl passionately ; " and I wish I had been struck dead in the street, or changed places with them we passed so near to-night, before I had lent a hand in bringing him here. He 's a thief, a liar, a devil, all that 's bad, from this night forth ; isn't that enough for the old wretch without blows ?"

" Come, come, Sikes," said the Jew, appealing to him in a remonstratory tone, and motioning towards the boys, who were eagerly attentive to all that passed ; " we must have civil words, —civil words, Bill !"

" Civil words !" cried the girl, whose passion was frightful to see. " Civil words, you villain ! Yes ; you deserve 'em from me. I thieved for you when I was a child not half as old as this (pointing to Oliver). I have been in the same trade, and in the same service, for twelve years since ; don't you know it ? Speak out ! don't you know it ?"

" Well, well !" replied the Jew, with an attempt at pacification ; " and, if you have, it 's your living !"

" Ah, it is !" returned the girl, not speaking, but pouring out the words in one continuous and vehement scream. " It is my living, and the cold, wet, dirty streets are my home ; and you 're the wretch that drove me to them long ago, and that 'll keep me there day and night, day and night, till I die !"

" I shall do you a mischief !" interposed the Jew, goaded by these reproaches ; " a mischief worse than that, if you say much more !"

The girl said nothing more ; but, tearing her hair and dress in a transport of phrensy, made such a rush at the Jew as would probably have left signal marks of her revenge upon him, had not her wrists been seized by Sikes at the right moment ; upon which she made a few ineffectual struggles, and fainted.

"She's all right now," said Sikes, laying her down in a corner. "She's uncommon strong in the arms when she's up in
this way."

The Jew wiped his forehead, and smiled, as if it were a relief
to have the disturbance over; but neither he, nor Sikes, nor
the dog, nor the boys, seemed to consider it in any other light
than a common occurrence incidental to business.

"It's the worst of having to do with women," said the Jew,
replacing the club; "but they're clever, and we can't get on in
our line without 'em.—Charley, show Oliver to bed."

"I suppose he'd better not wear his best clothes to-morrow,
Fagin, had he?" inquired Charley Bates.

"Certainly not," replied the Jew, reciprocating the grin with
which Charley put the question.

Master Bates, apparently much delighted with his commission, took the cleft stick, and led Oliver into an adjacent
kitchen, where there were two or three of the beds on which he
had slept before; and here, with many uncontrollable bursts of
laughter, he produced the identical old suit of clothes which
Oliver had so much congratulated himself upon leaving off at
Mr. Brownlow's, and the accidental display of which to Fagin
by the Jew who purchased them, had been the very first clue received of his whereabout.

"Pull off the smart ones," said Charley, "and I'll give 'em
to Fagin to take care of. What fun it is!"

Poor Oliver unwillingly complied; and Master Bates, rolling
up the new clothes under his arm, departed from the room,
leaving Oliver in the dark, and locking the door behind him.

The noise of Charley's laughter, and the voice of Miss Betsy,
who opportunely arrived to throw water over her friend, and
perform other feminine offices for the promotion of her recovery,
might have kept many people awake under more happy circumstances than those in which Oliver was placed; but he was sick
and weary, and soon fell sound asleep.

CHAPTER THE SEVENTEENTH.

OLIVER'S DESTINY CONTINUING UNPROPITIOUS, BRINGS A GREAT MAN TO LONDON TO INJURE HIS REPUTATION.

IT is the custom on the stage in all good, murderous melo-
dramas, to present the tragic and the comic scenes in as regular
alternation as the layers of red and white in a side of streaky,
well-cured bacon. The hero sinks upon his straw bed, weighed
down by fetters and misfortunes; and, in the next scene, his
faithful but unconscious squire regales the audience with a
comic song. We behold with throbbing bosoms the heroine
in the grasp of a proud and ruthless baron, her virtue and her
life alike in danger, drawing forth her dagger to preserve the
one at the cost of the other; and, just as our expectations are
wrought up to the highest pitch, a whistle is heard, and we are

straightway transported to the great hall of the castle, where a grey-headed seneschal sings a funny chorus with a funnier body of vassals, who are free of all sorts of places from church vaults to palaces, and roam about in company, carolling perpetually.

Such changes appear absurd ; but they are by no means unnatural. The transitions in real life from well-spread boards to death-beds, and from mourning weeds to holiday garments, are not a whit less startling, only there we are busy actors instead of passive lookers-on, which makes a vast difference ; the actors in the mimic life of the theatre are blind to violent transitions and abrupt impulses of passion or feeling, which, presented before the eyes of mere spectators, are at once condemned as outrageous and preposterous.

As sudden shiftings of the scene, and rapid changes of time and place, are not only sanctioned in books by long usage, but are by many considered as the great art of authorship,—an author's skill in his craft being by such critics chiefly estimated with relation to the dilemmas in which he leaves his characters at the end of almost every chapter,—this brief introduction to the present one may perhaps be deemed unnecessary. But I have set it in this place because I am anxious to disclaim at once the slightest desire to tantalise my readers by leaving young Oliver Twist in situations of doubt and difficulty, and then flying off at a tangent to impertinent matters, which have nothing to do with him. My sole desire is to proceed straight through this history with all convenient despatch, carrying my reader along with me if I can, and, if not, leaving him to take some more pleasant route for a chapter or two, and join me again afterwards if he will. Indeed, there is so much to do, that I have no room for digressions, even if I possessed the inclination ; and I merely make this one in order to set myself quite right with the reader, between whom and the historian it is essentially necessary that perfect faith should be kept, and a good understanding preserved. The advantage of this amicable explanation is, that when I say, as I do now, that I am going back directly to the town in which Oliver Twist was born, the reader will at once take it for granted that I have good and substantial reasons for making the journey, or I would not ask him to accompany me on any account.

Mr. Bumble emerged at early morning from the workhouse gate, and walked, with portly carriage and commanding steps, up the High-street. He was in the full bloom and pride of beadleism ; his cocked hat and coat were dazzling in the morning sun, and he clutched his cane with all the vigorous tenacity of health and power. Mr. Bumble always carried his head high, but this morning it was higher than usual ; there was an abstraction in his eye, and an elevation in his air, which might have warned an observant stranger that thoughts were passing in the beadle's mind, too great for utterance.

Mr. Bumble stopped not to converse with the small shop-keepers and others who spoke to him deferentially as he passed along. He merely returned their salutations with a wave of his hand, and relaxed not in his dignified pace until he reached the farm where Mrs. Mann tended the infant paupers with a parish care.

"Drat that beadle!" said Mrs. Mann, hearing the well-known impatient shaking at the garden gate. "If it isn't him at this time in the morning!—Lauk, Mr. Bumble, only think of its being you! Well, dear me, it *is* a pleasure this is! Come into the parlour, sir, please."

The first sentence was addressed to Susan, and the exclamations of delight were spoken to Mr. Bumble as the good lady unlocked the garden gate, and showed him with great attention and respect into the house.

"Mrs. Mann," said Mr. Bumble,—not sitting upon, or dropping himself into a seat, as any common jackanapes would, but letting himself gradually and slowly down into a chair,—"Mrs. Mann, ma'am, good morning!"

"Well, and good morning to you, sir," replied Mrs. Mann, with many smiles; "and hoping you find yourself well, sir?"

"So-so, Mrs. Mann," replied the beadle. "A porochial life is not a bed of roses, Mrs. Mann."

"Ah, that it isn't indeed, Mr. Bumble," rejoined the lady. And all the infant paupers might have chorused the rejoinder with great propriety if they had heard it.

"A porochial life, ma'am," continued Mr. Bumble, striking the table with his cane, "is a life of worry, and vexation, and hardihood; but all public characters, as I may say, must suffer prosecution."

Mrs. Mann, not very well knowing what the beadle meant, raised her hands with a look of sympathy, and sighed.

"Ah! You may well sigh, Mrs. Mann!" said the beadle.

Finding she had done right, Mrs. Mann sighed again, evidently to the satisfaction of the public character, who, repressing a complacent smile by looking sternly at his cocked hat, said,

"Mrs. Mann, I am a going to London."

"Lauk, Mr. Bumble!" said Mrs. Mann, starting back.

"To London, ma'am," resumed the inflexible beadle, "by coach; I, and two paupers, Mrs. Mann. A legal action is coming on about a settlement, and the board has appointed me —me, Mrs. Mann—to depose to the matter before the quarter-sessions at Clerkinwell; and I very much question," added Mr. Bumble, drawing himself up, "whether the Clerkinwell Sessions will not find themselves in the wrong box before they have done with me."

"Oh! you mustn't be too hard upon them, sir," said Mrs. Mann coaxingly.

"The Clerkinwell Sessions have brought it upon themselves,

ma'am," replied Mr. Bumble; "and if the Clerkinwell Sessions find that they come off rather worse than they expected, the Clerkinwell Sessions have only themselves to thank."

There was so much determination and depth of purpose about the menacing manner in which Mr. Bumble delivered himself of these words, that Mrs. Mann appeared quite awed by them. At length she said,

"You 're going by coach, sir? I thought it was always usual to send them paupers in carts."

"That 's when they 're ill, Mrs. Mann," said the beadle. "We put the sick paupers into open carts in the rainy weather, to prevent their taking cold."

"Oh!" said Mrs. Mann.

"The opposition coach contracts for these two, and takes them cheap," said Mr. Bumble. "They are both in a very low state, and we find it would come two pound cheaper to move 'em than to bury 'em,—that is, if we can throw 'em upon another parish, which I think we shall be able to do, if they don't die upon the road to spite us. Ha! ha! ha!"

When Mr. Bumble had laughed a little while, his eyes again encountered the cocked hat, and he became grave.

"We are forgetting business, ma'am," said the beadle;— "here is your porochial stipend for the month."

Wherewith Mr. Bumble produced some silver money, rolled up in paper, from his pocket-book, and requested a receipt, which Mrs. Mann wrote.

"It 's very much blotted, sir," said the farmer of infants; "but it 's formal enough, I dare say. Thank you, Mr. Bumble, sir; I am very much obliged to you, I 'm sure."

Mr. Bumble nodded blandly in acknowledgment of Mrs. Mann's curtsey, and inquired how the children were.

"Bless their dear little hearts!" said Mrs. Mann with emotion, "they 're as well as can be, the dears! Of course, except the two that died last week, and little Dick."

"Isn't that boy no better?" inquired Mr. Bumble. Mrs. Mann shook her head.

"He 's a ill-conditioned, vicious, bad-disposed porochial child that," said Mr. Bumble angrily. "Where is he?"

"I 'll bring him to you in one minute, sir," replied Mrs. Mann. "Here, you Dick!"

After some calling, Dick was discovered; and having had his face put under the pump, and dried upon Mrs. Mann's gown, he was led into the awful presence of Mr. Bumble, the beadle.

The child was pale and thin; his cheeks were sunken, and his eyes large and bright. The scanty parish dress, the livery of his misery, hung loosely upon his feeble body; and his young limbs had wasted away like those of an old man.

Such was the little being that stood trembling beneath Mr. Bumble's glance, not daring to lift his eyes from the floor, and dreading even to hear the beadle's voice.

"Can't you look at the gentleman, you obstinate boy?" said Mrs. Mann.

The child meekly raised his eyes, and encountered those of Mr. Bumble.

"What 's the matter with you, porochial Dick?" inquired Mr. Bumble with well-timed jocularity.

"Nothing, sir," replied the child faintly.

"I should think not," said Mrs. Mann, who had of course laughed very much at Mr. Bumble's exquisite humour. "You want for nothing, I 'm sure."

"I should like——" faltered the child.

"Hey-day!" interposed Mrs. Mann, "I suppose you 're going to say that you *do* want for something, now? Why, you little wretch——"

"Stop, Mrs. Mann, stop!" said the beadle, raising his hand with a show of authority. "Like what, sir; eh?"

"I should like," faltered the child, "if somebody that can write, would put a few words down for me on a piece of paper, and fold it up, and seal it, and keep it for me after I am laid in the ground."

"Why, what does the boy mean?" exclaimed Mr. Bumble, on whom the earnest manner and wan aspect of the child had made some impression, accustomed as he was to such things. "What do you mean, sir?"

"I should like," said the child, "to leave my dear love to poor Oliver Twist, and to let him know how often I have sat by myself and cried to think of his wandering about in the dark nights with nobody to help him; and I should like to tell him," said the child, pressing his small hands together, and speaking with great fervour, "that I was glad to die when I was very young; for, perhaps, if I lived to be a man, and grew old, my little sister, who is in heaven, might forget me, or be unlike me; and it would be so much happier if we were both children there together."

Mr. Bumble surveyed the little speaker from head to foot with indescribable astonishment, and, turning to his companion, said, "They 're all in one story, Mrs. Mann. That out-dacious Oliver has demoralised them all!"

"I couldn't have believed it, sir!" said Mrs. Mann, holding up her hands, and looking malignantly at Dick. "I never see such a hardened little wretch!"

"Take him away, ma'am!" said Mr. Bumble imperiously. "This must be stated to the board, Mrs. Mann."

"I hope the gentlemen will understand that it isn't my fault, sir?" said Mrs. Mann, whimpering pathetically.

"They shall understand that, ma'am; they shall be acquainted with the true state of the case," said Mr. Bumble pompously. "There; take him away. I can't bear the sight of him."

Dick was immediately taken away, and locked up in the coal-cellar; and Mr. Bumble shortly afterwards took himself away to prepare for his journey.

At six o'clock next morning, Mr. Bumble having exchanged his cocked hat for a round one, and encased his person in a blue great-coat with a cape to it, took his place on the outside of the coach, accompanied by the criminals whose settlement was disputed, with whom, in due course of time, he arrived in London, having experienced no other crosses by the way than those which originated in the perverse behaviour of the two paupers, who persisted in shivering, and complaining of the cold in a manner which, Mr. Bumble declared, caused his teeth to chatter in his head, and made him feel quite uncomfortable, although he had a great-coat on.

Having disposed of these evil-minded persons for the night, Mr. Bumble sat himself down in the house at which the coach stopped, and took a temperate dinner of steaks, oyster-sauce, and porter: putting a glass of hot gin-and-water on the mantel-piece, he drew his chair to the fire, and, with sundry moral reflections on the too-prevalent sin of discontent and complaining, he then composed himself comfortably to read the paper.

The very first paragraph upon which Mr. Bumble's eyes rested, was the following advertisement.

"FIVE GUINEAS REWARD.

"WHEREAS a young boy, named Oliver Twist, absconded, or was enticed, on Thursday evening last, from his home at Pentonville, and has not since been heard of; the above reward will be paid to any person who will give such information as may lead to the discovery of the said Oliver Twist, or tend to throw any light upon his previous history, in which the advertiser is for many reasons warmly interested."

And then followed a full description of Oliver's dress, person, appearance, and disappearance, with the name and address of Mr. Brownlow at full length.

Mr. Bumble opened his eyes, read the advertisement slowly and carefully three several times, and in something more than five minutes was on his way to Pentonville, having actually in his excitement left the glass of hot gin-and-water untasted on the mantel-piece.

"Is Mr. Brownlow at home?" inquired Mr. Bumble of the girl who opened the door.

To this inquiry the girl returned the not uncommon, but rather evasive reply of, "I don't know—where do you come from?"

Mr. Bumble no sooner uttered Oliver's name in explanation of his errand, than Mrs. Bedwin, who had been listening at the parlour-door, hastened into the passage in a breathless state.

"Come in—come in," said the old lady: "I knew we should hear of him. Poor dear! I knew we should,—I was certain of it. Bless his heart! I said so all along."

Having said this, the worthy old lady hurried back into the

parlour again, and, seating herself on a sofa, burst into tears. The girl, who was not quite so susceptible, had run up-stairs meanwhile, and now returned with a request that Mr. Bumble would follow her immediately, which he did.

He was shown into the little back study, where sat Mr. Brownlow and his friend Mr. Grimwig, with decanters and glasses before them : the latter gentleman eyed him closely, and at once burst into the exclamation,

" A beadle—a parish beadle, or I 'll eat my head !"

" Pray don't interrupt just now," said Mr. Brownlow. " Take a seat, will you ?"

Mr. Bumble sat himself down, quite confounded by the oddity of Mr. Grimwig's manner. Mr. Brownlow moved the lamp so as to obtain an uninterrupted view of the beadle's countenance, and said with a little impatience,

" Now, sir, you come in consequence of having seen the advertisement ?"—" Yes, sir," said Mr. Bumble.

" And you *are* a beadle, are you not ?" inquired Mr. Grimwig.

" I am a porochial beadle, gentlemen," rejoined Mr. Bumble proudly.

" Of course," observed Mr. Grimwig aside to his friend. " I knew he was. His great-coat is a parochial cut, and he looks a beadle all over."

Mr. Brownlow gently shook his head to impose silence on his friend, and resumed :

" Do you know where this poor boy is now ?"

" No more than nobody," replied Mr. Bumble.

" Well, what *do* you know of him ?" inquired the old gentleman. " Speak out, my friend, if you have anything to say. What do you know of him ?"

" You don't happen to know any good of him, do you ?" said Mr. Grimwig caustically, after an attentive perusal of Mr. Bumble's features.

Mr. Bumble caught at the inquiry very quickly, and shook his head with portentous solemnity.

" You see this ?" said Mr. Grimwig, looking triumphantly at Mr. Brownlow.

Mr. Brownlow looked apprehensively at Bumble's pursed-up countenance, and requested him to communicate what he knew regarding Oliver, in as few words as possible.

Mr. Bumble put down his hat, unbuttoned his coat, folded his arms, inclined his head in a retrospective manner, and, after a few moments' reflection, commenced his story.

It would be tedious if given in the beadle's words, occupying as it did some twenty minutes in the telling; but the sum and substance of it was, that Oliver was a foundling, born of low and vicious parents, who had from his birth displayed no better qualities than treachery, ingratitude, and malice, and who had terminated his brief career in the place of his birth, by making a sanguinary and cowardly attack on an unoffending lad, and then running away in the night-time from his master's house. In proof of his really being the person he represented himself, Mr. Bumble laid upon the table the papers he had brought to town, and, folding his arms again, awaited Mr. Brownlow's observations.

"I fear it is all too true," said the old gentleman sorrowfully, after looking over the papers. "This is not much for your intelligence; but I would gladly have given you treble the money, sir, if it had been favourable to the boy."

It is not at all improbable that if Mr. Bumble had been possessed with this information at an earlier period of the interview, he might have imparted a very different colouring to his little history. It was too late to do it now, however; so he shook his head gravely, and, pocketing the five guineas, withdrew.

Mr. Brownlow paced the room to and fro for some minutes, evidently so much disturbed by the beadle's tale, that even Mr. Grimwig forbore to vex him further. At length he stopped, and rang the bell violently.

"Mrs. Bedwin," said Mr. Brownlow when the housekeeper appeared, "that boy, Oliver, is an impostor."

"It can't be, sir; it cannot be," said the old lady energetically.

"I tell you he is," retorted the old gentleman sharply. "What do you mean by 'can't be'? We have just heard a full account of him from his birth; and he has been a thorough-paced little villain all his life."

"I never will believe it, sir," replied the old lady, firmly.

"You old women never believe anything but quack-doctors and lying story-books," growled Mr. Grimwig. "I knew it all along. Why didn't you take my advice in the beginning; you would, if he hadn't had a fever, I suppose,—eh? He was interesting, wasn't he? Interesting! Bah!" and Mr. Grimwig poked the fire with a flourish.

"He was a dear, grateful, gentle child, sir," retorted Mrs. Bedwin indignantly. "I know what children are, sir, and have done these forty years; and people who can't say the same shouldn't say anything about them—that's my opinion."

This was a hard hit at Mr. Grimwig, who was a bachelor; but as it extorted nothing from that gentleman but a smile, the old lady tossed her head and smoothed down her apron, preparatory to another speech, when she was stopped by Mr. Brownlow.

"Silence!" said the old gentleman, feigning an anger he was far from feeling. "Never let me hear the boy's name again: I rang to tell you that. Never—never, on any pretence, mind. You may leave the room, Mrs. Bedwin. Remember; I am in earnest."

There were sad hearts at Mr. Brownlow's that night. Oliver's sank within him when he thought of his good, kind friends; but it was well for him that he could not know what they had heard, or it would have broken outright.

THE CONFESSIONS OF AN ELDERLY GENTLEMAN;

CONTAINING HIS LAST LOVE.

WITH AN ILLUSTRATION BY GEORGE CRUIKSHANK.

THE Countess of Blessington need not be afraid that I shall interfere with her work in the unhappy tale which I am about to begin; my scene will be laid in a very different walk of life, and the lady whose charms have wounded my heart bear no resemblance whatever to the aristocratic beauties which grace the book of the Countess. My arrangement ever goes upon an opposite principle to hers; her elderly gentleman proceeds from first to last, getting through his fates and fortunes in regular rotation, as if they were so many letters of the alphabet, from A to Z: I read mine backward, in the manner of Turks, Jews, and other infidels; for worse than Turk or Jew have I been treated by the fair sex !

When I confess to being an elderly gentleman, I leave my readers to their own conjectures as to the precise figure of my age. It is sufficient to say that I have arrived at the shady side of fifty,—how much further, it is unnecessary to add. I have been always what is called a man in easy circumstances. My father worked hard in industrious pursuits, and left me, his only son, a tolerably snug thing. I started in life with some five or six thousand pounds, a good business as a tobacconist, a large stock-in-trade, excellent credit and connexion, not a farthing of debt, and no encumbrance in the world. In fact, I had, one way or another, about a thousand a year, with no great quantity of trouble. I liked business, and stuck to it; became respected in my trade and my ward; and have frequently filled the important office of common-councilman with considerable vigour and popularity. As I never went into rash speculations, and put by something every year, my means are now about double what they were some thirty-five years ago, when Mr. Gayless, sen. departing this life, left the firm of Gayless, Son, and Company, to my management.

It is not to be wondered at, that a man in such circumstances should occasionally allow himself relaxation from his labours. I entered heartily into all the civic festivities; and, at my snug bachelor's country-house on Fortress Terrace, Kentish Town, did the thing genteelly enough every now and then. Many an excursion have I made up and down the river, to Greenwich, Richmond, Blackwall, &c.; have spent my summer at Margate, and once went to the Lakes of Westmoreland. Some of that party proposed to me to go over to see the Lakes of Killarney; but I had by that time come to years of discretion, and was not such a fool as to trust myself among the Irish. I however did go once to Paris, but, not understanding the language, I did not take much interest in the conversation of the Frenchmen; and as for talking to English people, why I can do that at home, without distressing my purse or person.

The younger portion of my fair readers may be anxious to know what is the personal appearance of him who takes the liberty of addressing them. I have always noticed that young ladies are very curious on this point; and it is difficult, if not impossible, to persuade them how irrational is their anxiety. It is in vain to quote to them the venerable maxims of antiquity, such as, "It is not handsome is, but handsome does," or, "When Poverty enters the door, Love flies out at the window," or, "All is not gold that glitters," or many more adages of equal wisdom. It is generally of no avail to dilate upon the merits of mind and intellect to persons whose thoughts run after glossy locks and sparkling eyes, and to whose imagination a well-filled ledger is of secondary importance to a well-tripped quadrille. In my own knowledge, a young lady of our ward refused to accept the hand of a thriving bill-broker in Spital-square,—a highly respectable middle-aged man, who had made a mint of money by sharp application to his business,—and chose a young barrister of the Inner Temple, whose bill, to my certain knowledge, was refused discount by the Spital-square broker at twenty-five per cent. I have been assured by officers in the army that the case has sometimes occurred of girls in garrison towns preferring an ensign to a major of many years' service; and I have heard, on authority which I have reason to credit, of a West-end lady rejecting an actual governor of a colony, on the ground that he was a withered fellow as old and prosy as her grandfather,—as if there was anything disgraceful in that,—and shortly afterwards cocking her cap at a penniless dog, because he had romantic eyes, and wrote rubbish in albums and pocket-books. I really have no patience with such stuff. Middle-aged ladies are far less fastidious.

If I must delineate myself, however, here goes. So far from deteriorating by age, I think I have improved, like Madeira. A miniature of me, taken in my twenty-first year by an eminent artist who lived in Gutter-lane, and drew undeniable likenesses at an hour's sitting for half-a-guinea, forms a great contrast to one by Chalon, painted much more than twenty years afterward. You really would never think them to represent the same man, and yet both are extremely alike. I was in my youth a sallow-faced lad, with hollow cheeks, immense staring eyes, and long thin sandy hair, plastered to the side of my head. By the course of living which I have led in the city, the sallow complexion has been replaced by a durable red, the lean cheek is now comfortably plumped out, the eyes pursed round and contracted by substantial layers of fat, and the long hair having in general taken its departure has left the remainder considerably improved by the substitution of a floating silver for the soapy red. Then, my stature, which, like that of many celebrated men of ancient and modern times, cannot be said to be lofty, gave me somewhat an air of insignificance when I was thin-gutted and slim; but, when it is taken in conjunction with the rotundity I have attained in the progress of time, no one can say that I do not fill a respectable space in the public eye. I have also conformed to modern fashions; and when depicted by Chalon in a flowing mantle, with " *Jour à gauche* " (whatever that may mean) written under it, I am as grand as an officer of hussars with his martial cloak about him, and quite as distinct a thing from the effigy of Mr. M'Dawbs, of Gutter-lane, as the eau de Portugal which now perfumes my person, is, from the smell of the tobacco which filled my garments with the odour of the shop when first I commenced my amorous adventures.

Such was I, and such am I; and I have now said, I think, enough to introduce me to the public. My story is briefly this:—On the 23rd of last December, just before the snow, I had occasion to go on some mercantile business to Edinburgh, and booked myself at a certain hotel, which must be nameless, for the journey—then rendered perilous by the weather. I bade adieu to my friends at a genial dinner given, on the 22nd, in the coffee-room, where I cheered their drooping spirits by perpetual bumpers of port, and all the consolation that my oratory could supply. I urged that travelling inside, even in Christmas week, in a stage-coach, was nothing nearly so dangerous as flying in a balloon; that we were not to think of Napoleon's army perishing in the snows of Russia, but rather of the bark that carried the fortunes of Cæsar; that great occasions required more than ordinary exertions; and that the last advices concerning the house of Screw, Longcut, and Co. in the High-street, rendered it highly probable that their acceptances would not be met unless I was personally in Edinburgh within a week. These and other arguments I urged with an eloquence which, to those who were swallowing my wine, seemed resistless. Some of my own bagmen, who had for years travelled in black rappee or Irish blackguard, shag, canaster, or such commodities, treated the adventure as a matter of smoke; others, not of such veteran experience, regarded my departure as an act of rashness not far short of insanity. " To do such a thing," said my old neighbour, Joe Grabble, candlestick-maker and deputy, " at your time of life !"

I had swallowed perhaps too much port, and, feeling warmer than usual, I did not much relish this observation. " At my time of life, Joe," said I; " what of that? It is not years that make a man younger or older; it is the spirits, Joe,—the life, the sprightliness, the air. There is no such thing now, Joe, as an old man, an elderly man, to be found anywhere but on the stage. Certainly, if people poke themselves eternally upon a high stool behind a desk in a murky counting-house in the city, and wear such an odd quiz of a dress as you do, they must be accounted old."

" And yet," said Joe, " I am four years younger than you. Don't you remember how we were together at school at old Muddlehead's, at the back of Honey-lane-market, in the year seventeen hundred and eighty-fou—?"

" There is no need," said I, interrupting him, " of quoting dates. It is not considered genteel in good society. I do not admit your statement to be correct."

" I'll prove it from the parish register," said Joe Grabble.

" Don't interrupt, Joe," said I; " interrupting is not considered genteel in good society. I neither admit nor deny your assertion; but how does that affect my argument? I maintain that in every particular I am as young as I was thirty years ago."

" And quite as ready to go philandering," said Joe, with a sneer.

" Quite," replied I, " or more so. Nay, I venture to say that I could at this moment make myself as acceptable to that pretty young woman at the bar, as nine-tenths of the perfumed dandies of the West-end."

" By your purse, no doubt," said Joe, " if even that would obtain you common civility."

I was piqued at this; and, under the impulse of the moment and the wine, I performed the rash act of betting a rump and dozen for the present company, against five shillings, that she would acknowledge that I was a man of gaiety and gallantry calculated to win a lady's heart before I left London, short as was the remaining space. Joe caught at the bet, and it was booked in a moment. The party broke up about nine o'clock, and I could not help observing something like a suppressed horselaugh on their countenances. I confess that, when I was left alone, I began to repent of my precipitancy.

But faint heart never won fair lady; so, by a series of manœuvring with which long practice had rendered me perfect, I fairly, in the course of an hour, entrenched myself in the bar, and, at about ten o'clock, was to be found diligently discussing a fragrant remnant of broiled chicken and mushroom, and hobnobbing with the queen of the pay department in sundry small glasses of brandy and water, extracted from the grand reservoir of the tumbler placed before me. So far all was propitious; but, as Old Nick would have it, in less than ten minutes the party was joined by a mustachoed fellow, who had come fresh from fighting—or pretending to fight—for Donna Isabella, or Don Carlos,—Heaven knows which, (I dare say he didn't,)—and was full of Bilboa, and San Sebastian, and Espartero, and Alaix pursuing Gomez, and Zumalacarregui, and General Evans, and all that style of talk, for which women have open ears. I am sure that I could have bought the fellow body and soul—at least all his property real and personal — for fifty pounds; but there he sate, crowing me down whenever I ventured to edge in a word, by some story of a siege, or a battle, or a march, ninety-nine hundred parts of his stories being nothing more nor less than lies. I know I should have been sorry to have bulled or beared in Spanish on the strength of them; but the girl (her name is Sarah) swallowed them all with open mouth, scarcely deigning to cast a look upon me. With mouth equally open, he swallowed the supper and the brandy for which I was paying ; shutting mine every time I attempted to say a word by asking me had I ever served abroad. I never was so provoked in my life ; and, when I saw him press her hand, I could have knocked him down, only that I have no practice in that line, which is sometimes considered to be doubly hazardous.

I saw little chance of winning my wager, and was in no slight degree out of temper; but all things, smooth or rough, must have an end, and at last it was time that we should retire. My Spanish hero desired to be called at four,—I don't know why,—and Sarah said, with a most fascinating smile,

"You may depend upon 't, sir; for, if there was no one else as would call you, I'd call you myself."

"Never," said he, kissing her hand, "did Boots appear so beautiful !"

"Devil take you !" muttered I, as I moved up stairs with a rolling motion; for the perils of the journey, the annoyance of the supper-table, the anticipation of the lost dinner and unwon lady, aided, perhaps, by what I had swallowed, tended somewhat to make my footsteps unsteady.

My mustachoed companion and I were shown into adjacent rooms, and I fell sulkily asleep. About four o'clock I was aroused by a knocking, as I at first thought, at my own room, but which I soon found to be at that of my neighbour. I immediately caught the silver sound of the voice of Sarah summoning its tenant.

"It's just a-gone the three ke-waters, sir, and you ought to be up."

"I am up already, dear girl," responded a voice from inside, in tones as soft as the potations at my expense of the preceding night would permit; "I shall be ready to start in a jiffy."

The words were hardly spoken when I heard him emerging, luggage in hand, which he seemed to carry with little difficulty.

"Good-b'ye, dear," said he; "forgive this trouble."

"It's none in the least in life, sir," said she.

And then—god of jealousy!—he kissed her.

"For shame, sir!" said Sarah. "You mustn't. I never permit it; never!"

And he kissed her again; on which she, having, I suppose, exhausted her stock of indignation in the speech already made, offered no observation. He skipped down stairs, and I heard her say, with a sigh, "What a nice man!"

The amorous thought rose softly over my mind. "Avaunt!" said I, "thou green-eyed monster; make way for Cupid, little god of love. Is my rump and my dozen yet lost? No. As the song says,

> "When should lovers breathe their vows?
> When should ladies hear them?
> When the dew is on the boughs,
> When none else is near them."

Whether the dew was on the boughs, or not, I could not tell; but it was certain that none else was near us. With the rapidity of thought I jumped out of bed, upsetting a jug full of half-frozen water, which splashed all over, every wretch of an icicle penetrating to my very marrow, but not cooling the ardour of my love. After knocking my head in the dark against every object in the room, and cutting my shins in various places, I at last succeeded in finding my dressing-gown knee smalls, and slippers, and, so clad, presented myself at the top of the staircase before the barmaid. She was leaning over the balustrade, looking down through the deep well after the departing stranger, whose final exit was announced by the slamming of the gate after him by the porter. I could not help thinking of Fanny Kemble in the balcony scene of Romeo and Juliet.

She sighed, and I stood forward.

"Oh!" she screamed. "Lor' have mercy upon us! what's this?"

"Be not afraid," said I, "Sarah; I am no ghost."

"Oh, no," said she, recovering, "I didn't suppose you were; but I thought you were a Guy Fawkes."

"No, angelic girl, I am not a Guy Fawkes; another flame is mine!" and I caught her hand, endeavouring to apply it to my lips.

"Get along, you old ——" I am not quite certain what the angelic Sarah called me; but I think it was a masculine sheep, or a goat.

"Sarah!" said I, "let me press this fair hand to my lips."

Sarah saved me the trouble. She gave me—not a lady's "slap," which we all know is rather an encouragement than otherwise,—but a very vigorous, well-planted, scientific blow, which loosened my two fore-teeth; and then skipped up stairs, shut herself in her room, and locked the door.

I followed, stumbled up stairs, and approached in the dark towards

the keyhole, whence shone the beams of her candle. I was about
to explain that innocence had nothing to fear from me, when a somewhat unintelligible scuffling up the stairs was followed by a very
intelligible barking. The house-dog, roused by the commotion,
was abroad,—an animal more horrid even than the schoolmaster,—
and, before I could convey a word as to the purity of my intentions,
he had caught me by the calf of the leg so as to make his cursed fangs
meet in my flesh, and bring the blood down into my slippers. I
do not pretend to be Alexander or Julius Cæsar, and I confess that
my first emotion, when the brute let me loose for a moment, and
prepared, with another fierce howl, for a fresh invasion of my personal
comforts, was to fly,—I had not time to reflect in what direction ;
but, as my enemy came from below, it was natural that my flight
should be upwards. Accordingly, up stairs I stumbled as I could,
and the dog after me, barking and snapping every moment, fortunately without inflicting any further wound. I soon reached the top of
the staircase, and, as further flight was hopeless, I was obliged to
throw myself astride across the balustrade, which was high enough to
prevent him from getting at me without giving himself more inconvenience than it seems he thought the occasion called for.

Here was a situation for a respectable citizen, tobacconist, and
gallant! The darkness was intense ; but I knew by an occasional
snappish bark whenever I ventured to stir, or to make the slightest
noise, that the dog was couching underneath me, ready for a spring.
The thermometer must have been several yards beneath the freezing
point, and I had nothing to guard me from the cold but a night-gown
and shirt. I was barelegged and barefooted, having lost my slippers
in the run. The uneasy seat on which I was perched was as hard
as iron, and colder than ice. I had received various bruises in the
adventures of the last few minutes, but I forgot them in the smarting
pain of my leg, rendered acute to the last degree by exposure to the
frost. And then I knew perfectly well, that, if I did not keep my seat
with the dexterity of a Ducrow, I was exposed by falling on one side
to be mangled by a beast of a dog watching my descent with a malignant pleasure, and, on the other, to be dashed to pieces by tumbling down from the top to the bottom of the house. The sufferings
of Mazeppa were nothing compared to mine. He was, at least, safe
from all danger of falling off his unruly steed. They had the humanity to tie him on.

Here I remained, with my bedroom candle in my hand,—I don't
know how long, but it seemed an eternity,—until at length the dog
began to retire by degrees, backwards, like the champion's horse at
the coronation of George the Fourth, keeping his eyes fixed upon me
all the time. I watched him with intense interest as he slowly receded down the stairs. He stopped a long time peeping over one
stair so that nothing of him was visible but his two great glaring
eyes, and then they disappeared. I listened. He had gone.

I gently descended ; cold and wretched as I was, I actually smiled
as I gathered my dressing-gown about me, preparatory to returning
to bed. Hark! He was coming back again, tearing up the stairs
like a wild bull. I caught sight of his eyes. With a violent spring I
caught at and climbed to the top of an old press that stood on the
landing, just as the villanous animal reared himself against it, scratch-

ing and tearing to get at me, and gnashing his teeth in disappointment. Such teeth too!

" Why, what is the matter ?" cried the beauteous Sarah, opening her chamber door, and putting forth a candle and a nightcap.

" Sarah, my dear !" I exclaimed, " call off the dog, lovely vision !"

" Get along with you !" said Sarah ; " and don't call me a lovely vision, or I 'll scream out of my window into the street. It serves you right !"

" Serves me right, Sarah !" I exclaimed, in a voice which I am quite certain was very touching. " You 'll not leave me here, Sarah ; look, look at this dreadful animal !"

" You 're a great deal safer there than anywhere else," said Sarah ; and she drew in her head again, and locked the door, leaving me and the dog gazing at each other with looks of mutual hatred.

How long I continued in this position I feel it impossible to guess ; It appeared to me rather more than the duration of a whole life. I was not even soothed by the deep snoring which penetrated from the sleeping apartment of the fair cause of all my woes, and indicated that she was in the oblivious land of dreams.

I suppose I should have been compelled to await the coming of daylight, and the wakening of the household, before my release from my melancholy situation, if fortune had not so far favoured me as to excite, by way of diversion, a disturbance below stairs, which called off my guardian fiend. I never heard a more cheerful sound than that of his feet trotting down stairs ; and, as soon as I ascertained that the coast was clear, I descended, and tumbled at once into bed, much annoyed both in mind and body. The genial heat of the blankets, however, soon produced its natural effect, and I forgot my sorrows in slumber. When I woke it was broad daylight,—as broad, I mean, as daylight condescends to be in December, — an uneasy sensation surprised me. Had I missed the coach? Devoting the waiters to the infernal gods, I put my·hand under my pillow for my watch ; but no watch was there. Sleep was completely banished from my eyes, and I jumped out of bed to make the necessary inquiries ; when, to my additional horror and astonishment, I found my clothes also had vanished. I rang the bell violently, and summoned the whole *posse comitatûs* of the house, whom I accused, in the loftiest tones, of misdemeanors of all descriptions. In return, I was asked who and what I was, and what brought me there ; and one of the waiters suggested an instant search of the room, as he had shrewd suspicions that I was the man with the carpet-bag, who went about robbing hotels. After a scene of much tumult, the appearance of Boots at last cut the knot. I was, it seems, " No. 12, wot was to ha' gone by the Edenbry coach at six o'clock that morning, but wot had changed somehow into No. 11, wot went at four."

" And why," said I, " didn't you knock at No. 12 ?"

" So I did," said Boots ; " I knocked fit to wake the dead, and, as there warn't no answer, I didn't like to wake the living ; I didn't knock no more, 'specially as Sarah ——"

" What of Sarah ?" I asked in haste.

" ——'Specially as Sarah was going by at the time, and told me not to disturb you, for she knowd you had been uneasy in the night, and wanted a rest in the morning."

"I waited for no further explanation, but rushed to my room, and dressed myself as fast as I could, casting many a rueful glance on my dilapidated countenance, and many a reflection equally rueful on the adventures of the night.

My place was lost, and the money I paid for it; that was certain: but going to Edinburgh was indispensable. I proceeded, therefore, to book myself again; and, on doing so, found Joe Grabble in the coffee-room talking to Sarah. He had returned, like Paul Pry, in quest of his umbrella, or something else he had forgotten the night before, and I arrived just in time to hear him ask if I was off. The reply was by no means flattering to my vanity.

"I do not know nothink about him," said the indignant damsel, "except that, whether he's off or on, he's a nasty old willin."

"Hey-day, Peter!" exclaimed Joe. "So you are not gone? What is this Sarah says about you?"

"May I explain," said I, approaching her with a bow, "fair Sarah?"

"I don't want your conversation at no price," was the reply. "You're an old wretch as I wouldn't touch with a pair of tongs!"

"Hey-day!" cried Joe. "This is not precisely the character you expected. The rump and dozen ——"

But the subject is too painful to be pursued. My misfortunes were, however, not yet at an end. I started that evening by the mail. We had not got twenty miles from town when the snow-storm began. I was one of its victims. The mail stuck somewhere in Yorkshire, where we were snowed up and half starved for four days, and succeeded only after a thousand perils, the details of which may be read most pathetically related in the newspapers of the period, in reaching our destination. When there, I lost little time in repairing to our agent, —a W.S. of the name of M'Cracken,—who has a handsome flat in Nicholson-street, not far from the College. He welcomed me cordially; but there was something dolorous in his tone, nevertheless.

"Sit ye down, Master Gayless; sit ye down, and tak' a glass o' wine; it wull do ye guid after yer lang and cauld journey. I hae been looking for ye for some days."

"What about the house of Screw and Longcut?" I inquired, with much anxiety.

"I am vera sorry to say, naething guid."

"Failed?"

"Why, jest that; they cam' down three days ago. They struggled an' struggled, but it wad no do."

"What is the state of their affairs?"

"Oh! bad—bad—saxpence in the pund forby. But, why were you no here by the cotch o' whilk ye advised me. That cotch cam' in safe eneuch; and it puzzled me quite to see yer name bookit in the waybill, an' ye no come. I did no ken what to do. I suppose some accident detained you?"

"It was indeed an accident," replied I faintly, laying down my untasted glass.

"I hope it's of nae consequence elsewhere," said M'Cracken, "because it is unco unlucky _here;_ for if ye had been in E'nbro' on the Saturday, I think—indeed I am sure—that we wad hae squeezed ten or twelve shillings in the pund out o' them,—for they were in hopes o' remittances to keep up; but, when the Monday cam', they saw the game was gane, and they are now clane dished. So you see, Mr. Gayless, ye're after the fair."

" After the *fair,* indeed," said I; for men can pun even in misery.

What my man of business told me, proved to be true. The dividend will not be sixpence in the pound, and it is more than six hundred and fifty pounds odd out of my pocket. I had the expense (including that of a lost place) of a journey to Edinburgh and back for nothing. I was snowed up on the road, and frozen up on the top of a staircase. I lost a pair of teeth, and paid the dentist for another. I was bumped and bruised, bullied by a barmaid, and hunted by a dog. I paid my rump and dozen amid the never-ending jokes of those who were eating and drinking them; and I cannot look forward to the next dog-days without having before my eyes the horrors of hydrophobia.

Such was my last love!

MY FATHER'S OLD HALL.

BY MRS. CORNWELL BARON WILSON.

I.

Though the dreams of ambition are faded and o'er,
And the world with its glitter can charm us no more;
Tho' the sunbeams of fancy less vividly play,
And in reason's calm twilight are melting away;
Still thought loves to wander, entranced in the maze
Of the joys and the hopes of those earlier days.
Fond mem'ry delights life's best moments to call
In the scene of my childhood, my Father's Old Hall!

II.

Oh! light were the hearts which have met 'neath the dome
Of that once gaily throng'd, but now desolate home;
And light were the spirits that crowded the hearth
Of social enjoyment and innocent mirth;
When the laugh echo'd round at the wit-sparkling jest,
And the roses of innocence bloom'd in each breast;
Whose fragrance, once shed, Time can never recall,
Like the garlands we wreath'd round my Father's Old Hall!

III.

Now scatter'd, dispers'd, 'mid the heartless and proud,
Where wander the steps of that once happy crowd?
Some have toil'd the steep rock towards the temple of Fame,
To snatch from her altars a wreath and a name;
Some have sought honour's death on the field or the wave;
Some have found in the land of the stranger *a grave!*
The chain is now broken, the links sever'd all,
That united the hearts in my Father's Old Hall!

· PORTRAIT GALLERY.—No. IV.

CANNON FAMILY.—JOURNEY TO BOULOGNE.

When Alexander the Great was gazetted commander-in-chief of the Macedonian forces, and was concocting the eighteen manœuvres at the Horse-guards of that celebrated country; when he was about fighting Darius, Xerxes, and Porus; when Cæsar was invading Gaul and Britain; when the Benedictine monks were compiling "*L'Art de verifier les dates ;*" when Sterne was writing Tristram Shandy; when Burton was anatomizing melancholy; when the companions of Columbus were puzzling their brains to find out how an egg could stand on end; when Mrs. Glass was concocting her cookery-book, and Bayle his dictionary; their minds were as smooth and as calm as a fish-pond, a milk-bowl, a butter-boat, an oil-cruet, compared with the speculative and prospective anxieties of all the Cannons as they were rattled on towards Dover, on their way to the land of promise, where milk and honey were to be found flowing,—longevity in apothecaries' shops, — modesty purchased at milliners' counters,—and decorum taught by opera-dancers. In these Utopian dreams, England was considered an uninhabitable region of fogs, mists, tyranny, corruption, consumption, and chilblains; the fate of Nineveh was denounced on London,—the modern Babylon; and, had it been burning from Chelsea bun-house to Aldgate pump, and from the Elephant and Castle to the Wheatsheaf at Paddington, the Cannons would not have dared to cast " a lingering look behind them" without dreading the lot of the Lots.

After their due share of impositions, thanks and curses, maledictions or valedictions, as they had been " genteel " or " shabby " with waiters, chambermaids, boots, porters, postilions, and hostlers on the road, the party arrived at Dover, and of course " put up," or rather, were " put down," at the Ship. But here fresh reasons for abhorring England were in store. When the waiters saw the arms of the Cannons on their panels, and the dragon, and the motto " *Crepo.*" they all crowded round the travellers; but, like many apparently good things in this world, the inside of the fruit did not appear as attractive as its external bloom; and as the Cannons tumbled out, or jumped out, or rolled out, or staggered out of their vehicles, with all sorts of parcels and bundles, in brown and whity-brown paper, and pocket-handkerchiefs of silk and of cotton, without any of those neat and elegant cases containing all sorts of necessary articles for travellers in health or in sickness, and which form an invariable part of fashionable travellers' luggage, the waiters and the lookers-on seemed to consider the Cannons with looks that, without much knowledge of physiognomy, might have been interpreted " These people have no business here." They were reluctantly shown into a parlour, and to bed-rooms at the top of the house, with the usual formal apology, " Sorry, ma'am, we can't afford better accommodation; our house is quite full: the Duke of Scratchenburg and his *suet* is just come over from Germany, and the Prince of Hesse Humbuginstein is hourly looked for. Coming—going—coming—oh, Lord, what a life! going—going directly !"

The Cannons were hungry; dinner was ordered *immediately*. Now it was the height of presumption—nay, of impudence—on the part of a hungry citizen, without courier or *valet de chambre*, or supporters, to his arms, to make use of such an aristocratic adverb. *Immediately* implies servitude, slavery, servility, at the nod of a master,—ay, and of an accidental master, an interloper in command. Is a free-born Englishman to run helter-skelter up and down stairs at the risk of breaking his neck, to hurry the cook, to expose himself to a forfeit of one shilling (not being a gentleman) by swearing and cursing in the teeth of the 19 Geo. 2. c. 21, when the cook tells the officious waiter not to bother him, or, if the weather is hot and the fire is fierce, bids him, by a natural association of ideas, to go to h—; and all this because an ex-tallow-chandler is hungry, and wants an *immediate* dinner! Forbid it, glorious constitution! forbid it, bill of rights!

Old Commodus Cannon pulled the bell until the rope remained in his hand unconnected with its usual companion; for be it known for the information of impatient voyagers, that in modest apartments the said ropes are only attached by slender ties, which give way when vigorously jerked, that servants may not be disturbed. At last a waiter, bearing in his knitted brows the apprehension of a miserable shilling " tip " on departure, came in to inform the party that dinner would be served as soon as possible, but that the Duke of Scratchenburg and Prince Hesse Humbuginstein's dinners busied every hand in the house; but, if the gentlemen *chose*, there was a hot joint serving up in the coffee-room.

Cannon was outrageous, and swore that he would go to another hotel.

" You are perfectly welcome to do so, sir, if you like."

" I 'll represent your behaviour to all our friends!" exclaimed Mrs. Cannon.

" None of our acquaintance shall ever put up in this house," added Miss Cannon.

" Then, ladies," replied the waiter, with a ludicrous heavy sigh, " we shall be obliged to shut up shop!"

At last an apology for a dinner was served; beefsteaks, potatoes, and a gooseberry tart. No oyster sauce!—the last oyster had been served to his Grace! No fish!—the last turbot had been served to his Serene Highness!

" Your port wine and your sherry are execrable!"

" His Grace thought them excellent."

Cannon was bubbling over, but he philosophized over a glass of punch; and his family comforted themselves, over a cup of tea, with the thoughts of their speedy departure from " horrible England."

Peter Cannon complained in the coffee-room of the treatment they had experienced, and he felt not a little annoyed when his interlocutor, a perfect stranger, observed that " they would have been much more comfortable had they put up at a second or third-rate hotel." They seemed created for wanton insult. Cornelius Cannon strolled out to inquire if there was anything to be seen in Dover; an insolent groom told him that, if he would go up to the Castle, he might see " a *rum cannon* " that carried a ball to Calais. Had he been a gentleman, Cornelius must have called him out, for he fancied that the term " *rum cannon* " had been a personality.

The next morning the packet was to sail. Here again fresh out-rages were heaped upon them. They were asked for the keys of their trunks, to be examined at the custom-house!

"Why, what the deuce do they fancy I can have to export?" ex-claimed Commodus Cannon.

"Why, sir, perhaps it might be some machinery."

There was something wantonly offensive in the insinuation that a man like Mr. Commodus Cannon should smuggle out a steam-engine, an improved loom, or a paper-mill, in his luggage! What could have been the cause of all these indignities? Simply this, as it was subsequently discovered: Sam Surly, being hungry, and not over nice, despite a brown and gold-laced red-collared livery, and military cockade, had gone to the *tap* to enjoy a pull of half-and-half; and, unaccustomed to travel, had gone into the kitchen for some " vic-tuals," instead of joining the board of the other under-gentlemen in the house. On the other hand, Sukey Simper, both for the sake of comfort and economy, had brought with her a bottle of rum, and some loaf-sugar wrapped up in brown paper, and, having been shown to her attic quarters, forthwith prepared a potation to refresh herself after her journey: neither being aware that it is part and parcel of a ser-vant's duty in a respectable family to run up a heavy score at their master's expense. Now, Sam Surly had also picked up an old Yorkshire acquaintance, with whom he repaired to another eating-house, where, over a bowl of generous *humpty-dumpty*, Sam was prevailed upon to take charge of a *small parcel* of little articles for a present at Boulogne, and, to avoid paying *freight*, he was recommend-ed to conceal the said trifles in his capacious corduroy unmention-ables.

As Messrs. Cannons were perambulating the streets of Dover, they observed sundry gentlemen, some of them lords, wearing sailors' jackets and hats, and they therefore determined to turn out in a ma-rine costume; for which purpose they hied to a Jew slop-seller for their outfit. Mr. Cannon, senior, donned a pea-coatie, with a pair of ample blue trousers, and a glazed hat with a jaunty riband; while his sons soon strutted about the town in yacht-club uniforms, with their hands knowingly thrust in the pockets of their jackets, resplendent with anchored buttons. They felt satisfied that they had produced " the desired effect," for every one stared at them as they stalked along in "rank entire," Commodus Cannon leading the van, and the ladies—enraptured at the appearance of the male part of the family —bringing up the rear. They were certainly annoyed by the im-pertinent observations of the vulgar people, boys and girls, who, with the usual English bad taste, did not know better,—who would titter, and exclaim, " I say, there goes the horse-marines !"

"No, no," cried another; " it 's the famous Sea Cook and his sons wot uncovered the Sandwich Islands !"

"I say, commodore, how are they all in the *Fleet ?*" roared out a costermonger.

" Poor old gentleman! his eyebrows are worn out, looking out for squalls through a *grating ?*" said a fourth.

While a boatswain sang out, and whistled in Cannon's ear,

" Yer, yer ! man the sides ! there 's the flying Dutchman coming on board !"

" Sing out for Captain Yokell, cockswain !" bellowed an impertinent sailor.

Now, strange to say, these observations, which might have offended some sensitive persons, highly gratified our travellers. They had already obtained what they so ardently desired—*notoriety*, and had a chance of seeing their names in *print*; for, even when a man is abused and ridiculed, if it is in *print*, the sting carries with it its own antidote. He becomes public property ; he is something ; " There goes that confounded ass, Mr. Such-a-one ! there goes that rum cove, Mr. What 's-his-name !" Then, if he can but get himself caricatured, he is a made man. Were it not for the gratification derived from such publicity, would so many people walk, and talk, and dress, or undress, in the absurd manner we daily witness in our lounges ? A certain lord was honoured with an hebdomadary flare-up by a certain weekly paper as regularly as church-bells are rung on the sabbath. It was expected that his lordship would have purchased the editor's silence,—absurd expectation ! One might as well expect that a jolly prebend would decline sitting in half-a-dozen stalls at the same time. No, no ; the editor abused on until he was tired of abusing *gratis* ; when his lordship was so much annoyed that he paid to have scurrilous article inserted, forwarded by himself.

Two packets were about starting, a French one and an English one. The Cannons were resolved to punish their ungrateful countrymen, and embarked under the colours of France. A numerous French family were repairing on board ; and, as the gentlemen wore a red riband in their button-holes, our party concluded they were noblemen. The two families were grouped near each other ; and the French, with their usual condescension, honoured the Cannons with their countenance, conversing as well as persons scarcely acquainted with each other's language can conveniently converse.

The morning was fine ; but lowering clouds and a white sun would have induced experienced mariners to expect a fresh breeze. With great volubility of execrations the Gaul got under weigh, and paddled on slowly, while the English packet shot by like a dart. The French captain smiled at this swiftness, and, shrugging up his shoulders, exclaimed,

" *Ces Anglais ! ça n'a pas d'expérience !—nous verrons tout à l'heure !*" he added, rubbing his hands with delight.

The influence of dress is wonderful. A certain costume seems to impart to the wearer, ideas pertaining to the class of society which he then personates. A lawyer's wig and gown make a man fancy that he could plead, and he regrets that he was not brought up to the bar. A civilian, who attends a fancy ball in a splendid uniform, is inspired with courageous ideas, which a free potation of *refreshment* fans into a martial ardour. Now the Cannons did truly consider themselves sailors. The young men walked up and down the deck boldly, endeavouring to show how they could tread a plank or a seam on " sea legs" without staggering, although there was no more motion than under Kew-bridge ; and then they would cast a knowing eye at the compass as they passed the binnacle, to ascertain if the helmsman steered judiciously, although the compass was as little known to them as the Koran. Then they would suddenly stop, and look at the sky ; then suck their fingers, and hold them up, to *see* which way the wind blew; and, when their cigars were out they would whistle or hum "*Rule Britannia!*" or, "*You gentlemen of England, who live at home at ease,*" while they were lighting other havannahs.

Old Cannon was equally busy; but he was seated amongst the ladies, *encouraging* them against sea-sickness, which he said was all nonsense, and, if they were *very* sick, recommended them most particularly to turn their faces to the wind, and to keep their veils before them not to *see* the *sea*. Then to the French gentlemen he endeavoured to describe the battles of the Nile and of Trafalgar; and the Frenchmen of course concluded from his age, language, and appearance, that he was at least an admiral.

A "*cat's-paw,*" as the sailors call it, had now ruffled the surface of the water, and the vessel commenced heaving; ere long, most of the passengers assisted the packet in conjugating the verb "heave;" when, strange to say, the powers of the pea-jacket and the anchor-buttons were exhausted, and all the Cannons were drawn out, — a broadside of unutterable misery. Old Cannon roared out "*he was a-dying,*" and begged they would send for a doctor; and while he was rolling, and twisting, and twining upon the deck in agony, the cabin-boy was cleansing him with a wet swab. As to the Miss Cannons, they were assisted below,—not by their brothers, who, with dismay in their countenances, were "*holding on*" at every thing and every one they could catch, until a sudden regurgitation made them rush in desperation to the bulwark, with closed eyes and extended arms. Strange to say, the French gentlemen were not sick! possibly their red riband was more effectual than blue jackets; but they indulged their mirth at the expense of old Cannon, exclaiming,

"*Mais, voyez donc, ce pauvre Monsieur de Trafalgar!*"

It now was blowing fresh, and, to add to their misery, the paddles, by some mismanagement of the engineer, got obstructed, and the vessel was completely water-logged.

The French passengers got frightened, and began shaking old Cannon, roaring out,

"*Monsieur de Trafalgar, à la manœuvre! à la manœuvre!*"

"Oh Lord! oh Lord!" exclaimed the old man in a piteous tone, "are we arrived?"

"*No, sare! we sall all arriver down to de bottom. Mon Dieu! mon Dieu!*"

"*Monsieur de Trafalgar, you do see! vat is de matter!*" exclaimed a poor Frenchwoman, who had rolled over him,

The captain swore that it all arose from their having an English steam-engine, which his owner had insisted upon. Fortunately for the party, there happened to be an English sailor on board, who had all the while been sleeping on the bows, and who started at the uproar and the loud curses of the French crew: every one giving an advice which no one followed and all contradicted. He jumped down below, and in a few moments all was right again. When he returned upon deck, the captain, with a smile of importance, observed,

"*I do suppose, sare, dat you have been vere long time in France; dat is de metod of which we do make use in circonstances similar.*"

"*Circumstances similar!*" exclaimed Jack, as he thrust a quid in his cheek, " then, why the h— didn't you do it yourself, you beggar?" and off he went to roost, as the Frenchman, pale with rage, muttered a " *sacré Godam !*"

Soon, however, the harbour of Boulogne was made, and the crowd of its idle inhabitants were congregated as usual on the pier, to variegate the sameness of their amusements by the arrival of fresh food for curiosity and gossip regularly supplied by the packets. Unfortunately it was low water, and the steamer could not get in ; it therefore became necessary that the passengers should be landed on the backs of fisherwomen, who are always ready saddled on these occasions for the carriage of voyagers. Great were the cries and the shrieks of the Miss Cannons and their mamma when thus mounted ; but old Cannon, recovered from his sickness, seemed quite delighted. He jumped upon the shoulders of a fat old woman, who staggered under the weight, with a " *'Cré chien, qu'il est lourd !*" But Mr. Cannon was not satisfied with his natural weight, and, wishing to show the natives that he could ride *à l'Anglaise,* he stuck his knees in the sides of his biped steed, and began rising in his saddle, despite the tottering *Boulonnaire,* who was roaring out, " *'Cré Dieu, Monsieur l'Anglais ! est-ce que vous êtes enragé ! Nom d'un Dieu ! vous m'ereintes ! Ah Jesus, je n'en puis plus !*" and, suiting the action to the word, down she rolled in the mud, pitching her rider head over heels, amidst convulsive roars of international laughter.

This accident did not halt the cavalcade, and Cannon's affectionate spouse and children endeavoured in vain to rein in their chargers. On they trotted until they landed them at the pier, leaving Cannon in the hands of the fisherwoman, who not only insisted upon her fare in the most vehement language, but on compensation for the damage occasioned by her fall, which she justly attributed to his bad riding.

The old gentleman, soused to the skin, was most anxious to reach some hotel where he could put on dry clothes; but he was in France, — and plans of comfort are not of easy execution in that land of freedom. He was stopped with his whole generation at the custom-house, where fresh annoyances awaited them. It had never occurred to him that in pacific times a passport was required, and he had neglected this necessary measure. In vain he roared out that his name was Cannon. " Were you the pope's park of artillery," replied the insolent scrivener of the police, " you must be *en règle.*" While this warm discussion was going on, Commodus heard loud shrieks in a room into which his wife and daughters had been politely pushed. He asked for admittance in vain, bawling out that they were the Miss Cannons. It was indeed his astonished young ladies, whom a custom-house female official insisted upon searching. Another more terrific alarm shook his nerves ; a terrible *fracas* took place at the door, and he thought he heard the voice of Sam Surly cursing the entire French nation in the most eloquent Yorkshire dialect. Alas! it was he ; but in what a degraded situation,—what a disgraceful condition for a free-born British yeoman ! and yet we are at peace with the Gaul ! Sam was stretched upon the ground, surrounded by what appeared to Cannon to be soldiers, with drawn swords, threatening his life, while he was emphatically denouncing their limbs. But, oh, horror ! another soldier was pulling off his corduroys in presence of the multitude ; while another, and another, and another were drawing out of them about two hundred yards of bobbinet! This operation over, the *douanier* proceeded to draw out a specification, or *procès verbal*, not only regarding the seizure, but a black eye and a bloody nose that Sam had inflicted on "*des soldats Français*," for which his life alone could atone; but an English gentleman standing by, assured Cannon that a napoleon would manage these *braves*, if they had been half kicked to death. Money settled the business, and all the party proceeded toward the town, surrounded by a crowd of curious people in roars of laughter; the male part of the family were swearing most copiously, the ladies crying most piteously, and Sam Surly offering to box any one for a pot of porter.

The name of Cannon had passed from mouth to mouth, and had reached Stubb's corner before the party. This celebrated laboratory of reputation and crucible of character is simply the front of a circulating library,—a very emporium of works of fiction. A group of idlers were, as usual, assembled at this saluting battery, who loaded so soon as the approach of what a wag called the *battering train* was announced.

This spot proved to the Cannon family a second baptismal fount, for, as they passed by, they all received cognominations according to their external appearance, which ever after have stuck to them. Commodus Cannon, a short, plump, dapper man, was called the Mortar; Mrs. Cannon, also of respectable *embonpoint,* and of a *tournure* between an apple dumpling and a raspberry bolster-pudding, was named the Howitzer; Miss Molly, a tall slight figure, was favoured with the appellation of the Culverin; Biddy, a squat cherub-looking girl, was basely named the Pateraro; Lucy, who had rather a cast in each eye, which had induced the wits of Muckford to christen her Miss Wednesday (as they pretended that she looked both ways to Sunday,)—Miss Lucy, those pernicious sponsors called the Swivel; Kitty, a stout, short, beautiful creature, in whose form graceful undulations made up for length, they nicknamed the Carronade. The senior of the junior Cannons was a Short Nine; George, a Four Pounder; Cornelius, a Cohorn; Peter, a Long Six; and Oliver, a Pétard, the most horrible and degrading patronymic that could be bestowed upon any poor traveller in France.

At last, after passing under this volley from Fort Stubb, they all arrived, more dead than alive, at a hotel. Here, to their additional comfort, they were informed that half of the ladies' things that had not been made up were seized, or, in other words, made over to the *douaniers.* Exhausted and despairing, they asked for some soup, expecting a bowl of mock-turtle or of gravy. A *potage de vermicelle* was served up, the sight of which was not very encouraging for digestive organs just recovering from an inverted peristaltic motion. Cannon tasted it, and swore it was nothing but "hot water and worms." Miss Molly told him he ought to be ashamed of himself, before strangers, not to know wermichelly. Cannon swore lustily that they might swallow the wormy-jelly themselves, and asked for some other *potage*. A *soupe maigre*, made of sorrel and chervil, followed. Cannon had scarcely tasted the sour mixture, when he swore he was poisoned with oxalic acid, and roared out for a doctor, when he was informed to his utter dismay that all the doctors in the town had struck.

Doctors strike!—never heard of such a thing. To be sure, they may strike a death-blow now and then; but doctors striking was a new sort of a conspiracy. The French waiters only shrugged up their shoulders with a " *Que voulez vous, monsieur !*" a most tantalizing reply to a man who cannot get anything that he wants.

An English resident in the room explained matters. " We have, sir," he said, " several British practitioners in this place : many of them are men of considerable merit ; but the learned body have just been thrown into a revolution by a Scotch physician, a Dr. M'Crusoe. The usual fee here, is a five-franc piece, or four shillings and twopence English ; a sum so very small that many English are ashamed to tender it. M'Crusoe therefore proposed to his brethren that they should claim a higher remuneration."

" Jantlemen," he said, " it's dero-gatory tul the deegnety of a pheeseecian like huz, who hae received a leeberal eeducation, mare aspeecially mysel', wha grauduated at Mo-dern Authens, tul accep' sic a pautry fee as four an' tippence. No maun intertains mare contemp' for siller than aw do ; but the varry least we aught tul expec' is ten fraunks for day veesits, an' eleven fraunks for nighet calls ; fare from the varry heegh price of oil and caundles, at the varry lowest caulculation, it costs me mare than ten *baubees per noctem* to keep my noghcturnal lamp in pro-per trim. An' aw therefore houp in this deceesion we wull support each eather ho-nestly and leeberally. Aw need na remind jantlemen of yere erudeetion of the wee bit deformed body Æsop's fable, o' the bundle o' stucks, or o' the faucees of the Ro-man leectors, union cone-stitutes straingth. Therefore aw repeat it, aw trust ye wull enforce this raigulation like men o' indepaindence, an' conscious of the deegnity o' science."

All the doctors acquiesced in the expediency of his project, and to that effect signed a resolution, with which M'Crusoe walked off, and read the document with a loud and audible voice, as sternly as a magistrate could read the riot act, at Stubb's corner. The indignation of the community knew no bounds ; their wrath foamed and bubbled like the falls of Niagara ; they swore by the heads of Galen and Esculapius that they would rather die of the pip, expire in all the agonies of hepatitis, gastritis, enteritis, and all the *itises* that were ever known, than give one *centime* more than five francs ; nay, in their fury, they swore they would throw themselves into the hands of French doctors, and swallow a gallon of *tisane* a day for a fifteen-pence fee ; and hundreds of letters were sent off to Scotland for cheap doctors.

This was what Dr. M'Crusoe wanted : he immediately circulated himself in every hole and corner to inform the public that,

" In consequence of illeeberality o' ma breethren, under exusting cercumstaunces, aw feel mysel' called upon by pheelauntropy and humaunity to tak' whatever ma patients can afford to gie me."

Such was the state of the faculty of Boulogne when Cannon swore he was poisoned. A French doctor came and ordered him four grains of tartar emetic in a gallon of hot water ; and as French doctors are very kind and attentive to their patients, acting both as physicians and nurses, Cannon's attendant had the extreme benevolence to remain with him until he had not only swallowed, but restored, every *minim* of this bounteous potation, which really amounted to the full capacity that Cannon possessed of containing fluids.

Whether there was anything deleterious or not in the *soupe à l'oreille*, it is difficult to say; but the ladies were afflicted all night with what physicians call *tormina*, and *tenesmus*, and *intus-susceptio*, and *iliac passion*, and *borborygma* in their *epigastric* and their *hypochondriac* regions; for all and several of which, the French doctor duly irrigated them with hot water and syrup of gum, threatening them with a *cuirasse de sangsues* if they were not better in the morning, as he said that they all laboured under an *entero-epiplo-hydromphalo-gastrite*: while poor Cannon, writhing under the effect of *l'eau émétisée* was denounced as being threatened with *entero-epiplomphale, entero-merocèle, entero-sarcocèle*, and *entero-ischiocèle*. Sick as they all were, they looked upon the native practitioner as a very learned man, and gladly gave thirty sous *a head* for so much information, when an impudent English quack would have asked them ten francs for merely telling them that they had what is vulgarly called the mulligrubs.

After an intolerable night, Morpheus was shedding his poppies over the exhausted travellers, when they were all roused by the most alarming cries; and Miss Lucy Cannon and Molly Cannon were dragged out of their beds by two French gentlemen, who had just jumped out of theirs, and, clasped in their arms, were forthwith carried out into the court-yard.

THE RELICS OF ST. PIUS.

SAINT PIUS was a holy man,
  And held in detestation
The wicked course that others ran,
  So lived upon starvation.

He thought the world so bad a place
  That decent folks should fly it;
And, dreaming of a life of grace,
  Determin'd straight to try it.

A cavern was his only house,
  Of limited expansion,
And not a solitary mouse
  Durst venture near his mansion.

He told his beads from morn to night,
  Nor gave a thought to dinner;
And, while his faith absorb'd him quite,
  He ev'ry day grew thinner.

Vain ev'ry hint by Nature given,
  His saintship would not mind her;
At length his soul flew back to heaven,
  And left her bones behind her.

Some centuries were gone and past,
  And all forgot his story,
Until a sisterhood at last
  Reviv'd his fame and glory.

To Rome was sent a handsome fee,
  And pious letter fitted,
Requesting that his bones might be
  Without delay transmitted.

The holy see with sacred zeal
  Their relic hoards turn'd over,
The skeleton, from head to heel,
  Of Pius to discover;

And having sought with caution deep,
   To pious tears affected,
They recognised the blessed heap
   So anxiously expected.

And now the town, that would be made
   Illustrious beyond measure,
Was all alive with gay parade
   To welcome such a treasure.

The bishop, in his robes of state,
   Each monk and priest attending,
Stood rev'rently within the gate
   To view the train descending;

The holy train that far had gone
   To meet the sacred relic,
And now with joyous hymns came on,
   Most like a band angelic.

The nuns the splendid robes prepare,
   Each chain, and flower, and feather;
And now they claim the surgeon's care
   To join the bones together.

The head, the arms, the trunk, he found,
   And placed in due rotation;
But, when the legs he reached, around
   He stared in consternation!

In vain he twirl'd them both about,
   Took one, and then took t' other,
For one turn'd in, and one turn'd out,
   Still following his brother.

Two odd left legs alone he saw,
   Two left legs! 'tis amazing!
"Two left legs!" cried the nuns, with awe
   And anxious wonder gazing.

The wonder reach'd the list'ning crowd,
   And all the cry repeated;
While some press'd on with laughter loud,
   And some in fear retreated.

The bishop scarce a smile repress'd,
   The pilgrims stood astounded;
The mob, with many a gibe and jest,
   The holy bones surrounded.

The abbess and her vestal train,
   The blest Annunciation,
With horror saw the threaten'd stain
   On Pius' reputation.

" Cease, cease! ungrateful race!" cried she,
   " This tumult and derision,
And know the truth has been to me
   Revealed in a vision!

" The saint who now, enthron'd in heav'n,
   Bestows on us such glory,
Had *two* left legs by Nature given,
   And, lo! they are before ye!

" Then let us hope he will no more
   His blessed prayers deny us,
While we, with zeal elate, adore
   The left legs of St. Pius."

C. S. L.

DARBY THE SWIFT;

OR,

THE LONGEST WAY ROUND IS THE SHORTEST WAY HOME.

CHAPTER III.

"*Tipsy dance and jollity.*"—*L'Allegro.*

A FULL hour after Darby's departure I ventured to open the little dog-eared volume which he had thrown upon my table. The title-page was a curious specimen of that lingual learning which is so often to be met with in the remotest districts of Ireland. Gentle reader, a description of it would only spoil it; I therefore lay it before you as it appeared to me then, with this slight difference,—that the printer informs me he has no *letter* that can adequately express or imitate the rustic simplicity, the careless elegance both of the character and setting up. It was as follows:

THE DARBIAD!

A BACCHI-SALTANT EPIC. IN ONE BOOK.

AUCTORE CLAUDICANTE KELLIO.

Containing an Account of a Great Festival given at "The Three Blacks," by one Mr. Darby Ryan, on the occasion of his coming into his Fortune, and all the Songs an' Dances as perform'd there in honor to him.

Dulce est desipere in loco.

Printed by Mary Brady, ×, her mark, at the sign of the Cross Quills in Monk's Lane, opposit the Friary. Price sixpence; and to be had of all Flyin' Stationers, and Dancin' Masthers.

I could not but admire the classical taste and ingenuity with which Mr. Kelly, the author, had Latinized his name. He had read, no doubt, that Ovid was called Naso from the excessive size of his nose; and, with a delicacy peculiar to himself, had elegantly concealed the vulgar cognomen of *Lame* Kelly,—by which he was known,—in the more pompous-sounding Roman appellation of *Claudicante!* *Kellio*, too, was another "*curiosa felicitas;*" for, while it was in perfect accordance with grammatical accuracy, it sounded like an ingenious anagram of O'Kelly, an ancient Irish name. But, to the poem itself.

INVOCATION.

INSPIRE me, Phœbus! in the song I sing,
And to my aid the nine twin-sisters bring;
No common deeds I celebrate or praise—
DARBY THE SWIFT is hero of my lays!

AFTER a hurling-match by Darby won,
Although his nose had suffered in the fun,
He, with his rivals, now no longer foes,
To the Three Blacks in peaceful triumph goes !
Two blacks already had he in the fray,
But whereabouts I won't presume to say :
'T would spoil the beauty of a hero's mien,
Though by the candles' glare they scarce were seen.

Many were met ; of sisters, brothers, cousins,
Aunts, uncles, nieces, sweethearts, wives, some dozens.

First, Widow Higgins, with her daughters three,
Bedizen'd out as fine as fine could be,
Came on her low-back'd car, with feather-bed,
And ornamental quilt upon it spread.
She look'd a queen from the luxurious East
Reclining on an ottoman :—the beast
That drew her, chicks and all, drew seventy stone at least !
And he to horse was what to man is monkey,
In epics 't would be *bathos*, or I 'd call him donkey.

But (who can read the secret book of Fate ?)
Just as the party pass'd the inn-yard gate,
A startled pig—a young and timorous thing
That in a puddle had been weltering—
Woke from some rapturous dream, and in its fright
Rush'd 'tween the nag's forelegs, who, woful sight !
Employ'd his hinder ones so wondrous well,
That Widow Higgins, bed, and daughters, fell
(Alas, my muse !) into the porker's bath !
Oh, day turn'd night ! oh, pleasure sour'd to wrath !

But soon they did recover mirth, and jok'd,
For 'twas the feather-bed alone that soak'd
The stagnant pool :—no stain's impurity
Defil'd their rainbow-riband'd dimity,
Save one ; and that was on the widow's *crupper*,
Who said, " I wish they 'd *scald* that pig for supper !"

Next came Miss Duff, in a light pea-green plush,
That beautifully show'd her blue-red blush.
Miss Reeves soon follow'd, spite of summer weather,
In pelerine of goose-down, and a feather.
The two Miss Gallaghers, the four Miss Bradys,
With I know not how many other ladies.
Amongst them Nelly Jones, with her first child,
That squeak'd and squall'd ; then, cock-a-doodle, smiled.
Reader ! I tell this for your private list'ning,
To have the clargy at his feast, a christ'ning
Our Darby thought would be a trick with art in
To *nail* the presence of big Father Martin,
Who was the *bochel-bhui* of jolly sinners,
At wakes or christ'nings, weddings, deaths, or dinners !
Suppose Jack Falstaff had ta'en holy orders,
And then I 'll say your fancy somewhat borders
Upon the plumpy truth of this round priest,
Who ne'er refus'd his blessing to a feast.

One slender damsel, that seem'd not fifteen,
With younger brother, in the throng was seen ;
Shy and confused, as when a violet,
Suddenly snatch'd from its dark-green retreat,

First meets the gaudy glaring of the day,
And seems to close its beauty from the ray
Of unaccustom'd light that rudely prys
Into its gentle, modest, azure eyes.
What led her thither I could never learn.
But, hark! who comes? it is Miss Pebby Byrne,
All spick and span, to grace our hero's feast ;—
And last, Miss Reilly, who, tho' last, not least,
Contributes by her dress and portly mien
To swell the splendour of the joyous scene.
Juno herself ne'er walk'd with such an air!
A bright-blue band encircled her red hair,
Clasp'd on her forehead by a neat shoe-buckle!
Her dress was gaudy,—though as coarse as huckle-*
Back, or the web call'd linsey-woolsey,—flowing
In graceful negligence; tho' sometimes showing
It had been out for a more sylphid shape,
As sundry pins, o'ertir'd, releas'd the cape!

But now the christ'ning's o'er: of wine and cakes
First Father Martin, then each fair, partakes;
The youths incline to porter and potcheen.
Miss Reilly condescends to be the queen,
Presiding o'er the rites of dear bohea,
Whose incense in one corner you might see
Rising in volumes from four sacred stills,
Which, as Miss Reilly empties, Darby fills
With boiling fluid from a cauldron spoutless,
That had been ages at the Three Blacks, doubtless.

But now the pipes are smoking both and playing:
"Come, boys!" says Father Martin, "no delaying!
Let's have a song. Come, you first, Tommy Byrne,
And then we'll get a stave all round in turn."
Tommy, obedient, put his *dudheen*† in
His waistcoat pocket, and thus did begin:—

Tune—"Alley Croker."

I.

Your furreners, that come abroad
    Into our Irish nation,
Expectin' nothin' else but fraud
    And cut-throat dissertation;
What is't they find on landin' first
    But hundred *millia-fulthas*,
And kindness that we still have nurs'd?
    Tho' slav'ry near has spoilth us!
        Wirra! wirra! wirrasthrue!
        Wouldn't Erin's glory,
            With the pen
            Of clever men,
        Make a weepin' story?

II.

Says one,—"You lazy pisant! why
    Parmit that pig so durty
To sleep beside you, when a sty
    He'd find more clane and purty?"—
They little know that gratitude
    To us was early sint, sir!
And so we think no place too good
    For him that pays the rint, sir!
        Wirra! wirra! wirrasthrue!
        Wouldn't Erin's glory,
            With the pen
            Of clever men,
        Make a dacent story?

Here a loud squeak of grunting praise was heard
From the new pig-house in the stable-yard:
Th' applause awhile the minstrel's music drown'd;
But soon he did resume, and all around
Remark'd how much his voice of late improv'd in sound.

* The usual spelling of this word is "huckaback;" but I suppose Mr. Kelly's excuse would be " *licet facere verba.*"
† *Dudheen,* short pipe.

III.

Another says,—"You idle dog,
  Why do ye lock your door up,
And every sason quit your bog
  To thravel into Europe?"
Sure we would gladly stop at home
  The whole year round, and labour,
But for the harvest-pence we roam

To pick up in the neighbour-
  Hood of England, wirrasthrue!
  Wouldn't Erin's glory,
    With the pen
    Of clever men,
  Make a pleasant story?

[I could not help laying the book down at this passage to reflect whether the imputation of idleness can be justly thrown upon the Irish. Men who year after year toil through the perils and privations of a journey into another land for the sake of a few shillings, can scarcely be termed lazy; and it is to be regretted that some mode of employment at home is not devised by those in whose power it is to meli-orate and tranquillise their condition.]

IV.

St. Patrick (many days to him!)
  Thought *he* kilt all the varmin
That through the land did crawl or swim,
  But he left their cousins-giarmin!
He never dreamt of two-legg'd snakes,
  Or toads that were toad-eathers,
Or those *dartlukers** the law makes

To hunt our fellow-crathurs!
    (*Chorus, boys!*)
Wirra! wirra! wirrasthrue!
  Isn't Erin's glory,
    By sword and pen
    Of wicked men,
  Made a dismal story?

"Success, avourneen!" cried the jolly friar,
"An' may yir whistle, *'lanna!* never tire!
Now for a toast, my boys, or sentiment,
An' here is one from me with your consent:
' A saddle prickly as a porcupine,
A pair of breeches like a cobweb fine,
High-trottin' horse, and many a mile to go,
For him that to ould Ireland proves a foe!'"

  Miss Biddy Reilly was the siren next
Knock'd down for melody: she seem'd perplext,
And said: "Upon my conscience—ralely—now—
I—Tommy, sing for me—well, anyhow,
I 've nothin' new to trate ye with—"

                      "No matther!"
(From all parts of the room,) "sing *Stoney Batther!*"

  With that she hem'd to clear her pipe, and through
Her bright-red curls her radish fingers drew;
Then looking round, and smiling as she look'd,
(While many a heart upon her bait she hook'd,)
Her ditty once, twice, she commenced too high,—
At last she found the key;—then, with a sigh
Long-drawn and deep, her quivering voice she woke,
Which rose and curl'd—ay, gracefully as smoke
Seen at a distance—misty-wreathing—dimly
  Issuing from some wood-bound cottage *chimley.*

I.

In Stoney Batther
  There liv'd a man,
By trade a hatther,
  And *a* good wan:
The best of baver
  He used to buy;

Till a deceiver,
  Passing by,
Said,—"For a crown
  I 'll sell ye this."
"Come in," says he,
  "Let 's see what 'tis."

* *Dartluker*, the Irish name for a peculiar kind of leech that preys upon a small fish called *pinkeen.*

II.

"The finest skin, sir,
  You ever saw;
Without or in, sir,
  There's not a flaw!
No hat or bonnet
  You ever made,
With gloss upon it
  Of such a shade!"
"Then put it down,"
  The hatther cried;
"And here's yir crown,
  And thanks beside."

III.

But, oh! what wondher
  When he did find
The wicked plundher
  The rogue design'd!
"My cat is missin',"
  (Says he,) "black Min,
They've cut yir wizzin,—
  I've bought yir skin!
Of neighbours' cats,"
  Then wild he swore,
"I'll make my hats
  For evermore!"

Miss Biddy Reilly ceased her pensive ditty,
  And, with a look that made his rivals jealous,
She call'd upon our hero, who, quite witty,
  Express'd a hope they would excuse his bellows,
As he had lately caught *cold* in the water,
'Stead of an *eel* that he was lookin' a'ter!
A loud horse-laugh first trumpets Darby's praise,
Then thus his low bass voice he high did raise.

Tune—"Young Charly Reilly."

I.

Beside a mountin,
Where many a fountin,
Beyant all countin',
  Ran swift and clear,
A valley flourish'd
That Nature nourish'd,
For she *dhuc-a-dhurrish'd**
  Her last drop there!
And said, at partin',
To Father Martin,
"There's more of *art* in
  Some spots of earth;
But, by this whiskey,
That makes me frisky,
In Ballanisky
  Myself had birth?"

II.

In this inclosure,
With great composure,
And hedge of osier,
  A cabin grew;
And, sweeter in it
Than any linnet
Could sing, or spinnet,
  A maiden, too!
Her time went gaily
Both night and daily,
Till Rodhrick Haly
  Pierc'd thro' her heart:
Oh! if he'd spoken,
Or giv'n one token,
Sure 'twouldn't have broken
  With love's keen dart!

III.

She thought his fancy
Was bent on Nancy
Or Judy Clancy,
  Two sisthers fair:
Though in his bosom,
You can't accuse him,
But *she* did strew some
  Love-nettles there!
For all that, never
Could he endeavour
His lips to sever,
  And say, "Dear Kate!"
The lad was bashful,
'Caze not being cashful;
But she was rashful,
  As I'll relate.

IV.

One Sunday mornin',
All danger scornin',
Without a warnin'
  She left her home;
And to a valley
She forth did sally
That lay in Bally-
  Hinch-a-dhrome!
A while she wandher'd—
And then she pondher'd—
At last she squandher'd
  Her *rason* quite;
And in a pool there,
Like any fool there,
She soon did cool there
  Her burnin' spite!

Our hero ceas'd; and from the multitude
The suck-tongue sounds of pity that ensued
Would warm a stoic in his coldest mood: }

* *Dhuc-a-Dhurrish*, the drink at the door.

Ducks on a pond, when gobblin' up duck-meat,
Ne'er smack'd a music half so sadly sweet!
Miss Biddy Reilly's long-lash'd eyes of jet
Were red (as rivalling her hair) and wet!
Some inward feeling caus'd this outward woe;
But what it was but love for Darby, I don't know!

But now *tay-tay* and coffee-*tay* are done,
And of the night begins the raal fun:
The dance is nam'd, and straightway on the floor
Two dozen couple start,—I might say more.
But Darby interposes, and cries, " Stop!
Afore we have a reel let 's have a hop:
First—boy an' girl; then girl relieve the girl,
Next boy the boy, till all round have a whirl!
Miss Reilly an' myself will lead the first;—
Come, piper! squeeze yir bags until they burst!
' *Tatther Jack Welsh*,' or ' *Smash the Windows*,' play,
' *The wind that shakes the barley*,' ' *Flow'rs in May*,'
Or any rantin' roarin' lilt ye know:
What! ' *Ligrum Cuss?*' hurroo! then here we go!"

" He spake: and, to confirm his words," they all
Sate down obedient in the festive hall!
None but himself and Biddy upward stood,
All eyes were on them of the multitude!
But how shall I describe the wondrous pair,
Terpsichore! that worshipp'd thee then there?
Such grace, such action, on a malt-house floor,
Was never seen or heard of, e'en, before!
O'Ryan's arms at stiff right angles to
His body were, which to the gazer's view
Betray'd no motion; while his legs below
Seem'd all *St. Vitus'* nimblest shakes to know!
With knees bent inward, heels turn'd out, and toes
That seem'd contending like two deadly foes
For one small spot of earth, he digg'd the ground,
And sent the mortar pulveriz'd around!
" Look at his feet!" was the admiring cry;
" Hold down the light that we may closely spy:
There 's double-shuffle for ye! hoo! success!
He 'd dance upon a penny-piece, or less!"

Meanwhile, Miss Reilly, with her hands aside,
A varied change of steps and movements plied;
Now bold advancing in her partner's face,
Now shooting by a side-slip to a place
The farthest on the floor:—at every turn,
As round and graceful as a spinning churn!

But, ah! not long was she the dance's queen;
For young *Kate Duff*, who owed her long a spleen,
Swift as the lightning from a cloud of gloom,
Shot from a dim-lit corner of the room,
And sent the frowning Biddy to her seat,
Who mutter'd something that I can't repeat!

Long Curly next our hero's post relieves,
And *Kitty Duff* gives place to *Nelly Reeves*:
Curly, the piper's son, *Ned Joyce*, supplants;
The blind old father knows his step, and chants
The lilt with double force: *Miss Higgins* next
Sets down *Miss Reeves*; *Ned Joyce* retires, half vext,

For *Knock-knee'd Phelim*, who, despite his *pins*,
Applause from all for *heel-and-toeing* wins!

Thus did they trip it for a goodly hour;
When, oh! what charm there is in music's pow'r!
Old Joyce the piper seizes a short stay
To change his pipes:—and, what's the merry lay
They now lilt up?—' *The Priest in his Boots*,' and. lo!
(Whether 'twas all concerted I don't know,)
Fat *Widow Higgins*, 'midst the general shout,
By *Father Martin* is led waddling out!

Oh! how they tramp'd and stamp'd, and flounc'd and bounc'd!
A mercy 'twas they trod on the ground-floor,
For through a loft they surely would have pounc'd—
As 'twas, the earth was trembling to its' core:
Sure such *flochoolah* dancers ne'er were seen before!

A FEW ENQUIRIES.

MORTAL, in thy brief career,
Ranger of this nether sphere,
Tell me truly, have thine eyes
View'd earth's hidden mysteries?
Hast thou seen the dark blue sea,
Its bosom heaving tranquilly
To the wooing breath of night?
Hast thou watch'd the quiv'ring light,
Where the silver moonbeams dance,
Scatter'd o'er its broad expanse?
Likening the giant deep
To a sobbing child asleep,
O'er whose cheeks and visage fair
Smiles that wait on infant care
Chase the tear-drops trickling there?
Hast thou ever watch'd that sea
Rising in its majesty,
When its mighty depths are rent
By the rushing element,
And its waves exultingly
Revel in their liberty?
Hast thou ever, pale with doubt,
View'd the fatal waterspout,
Or the whirlpool's treach'rous wave
Luring seamen to their grave?
Hast thou climb'd o'er Alpine snows,
When the day is at its close,
When the storm its fury spends,
And the avalanche descends,
Hurling a terrific death
On the mountaineer beneath?
Hast thou on Arabia's soil,
Faint with heat, and worn with toil,
Bow'd beneath the simoom's blast,
Till its deadly breath was past?

Hast thou e'er pursued thy way
'Neath the red sun's burning ray?
And, when hope was almost gone,
Has the mirage lured thee on
With its waves that ever flee,
And but mock thy misery?
Hast thou watch'd the torrent's force
Dashing onward in its course,
Till, in one tremendous leap,
Its waters sink into the deep?
Hast thou seen the lava glide
Down the steep volcano's side?
Hast thou seen the misty light
Of the comet's erring flight?
Or the rainbow's azure span,
Or the huge leviathan,
Or the meteor in the air,
Or the lion in his lair,
Or the thousand things that be
In the blue depths of the sea?

Mortal, in thy brief career,
Ranger of this nether sphere,
Thou that hast a wand'rer been,
Tell me truly, hast thou seen
Of fire, ocean, earth, and air,
Such things—beautiful and rare?
If 't has been thine to behold
Nature's hidden charms unroll'd,
All her features to peruse
Deck'd in all their varied hues;
If so blest thy lot has been,—
Why, what a deal you must have seen!

NIGHTS AT SEA;

Or, Sketches of Naval Life during the War.

BY THE OLD SAILOR.

No. V.

THE FRENCH CAPTAIN'S STORY.

> " But, in these cases,
> We shall have judgment here ; that we but teach
> Bloody instructions, which, being taught, return
> To plague the inventor : this even-handed justice
> Commends the ingredients of our poisoned chalice
> To our own lips."   *Macbeth.*

WE left Lord Eustace Dash in his gallant frigate, with the prize in company, running down into the gulf of Genoa, and a strange sail in sight. His lordship swept the horizon with his glass till his keen eye caught the desired object in the field, and in an instant he was as fixed and stationary as a statue. The moon was rising, and her glorious light shone upon the distant sails, which looked like a silver speck on the dark zone of the horizon. Intense and eager was the gaze of the noble captain, and breathless attention pervaded every individual on the forecastle ; even old Savage, the boatswain, suffered his rattan to be motionless, and the tongue of Jack Sheavehole was still. At length Lord Eustace raised himself from his recumbent position ; every ear was awaiting the announcement of the stranger's character ; the boatswain approached his commander rather nearer than etiquette allowed, so eager was he to obtain the information. " Mr. Sinnitt!" said his lordship, and old Savage opened his mouth as well as his ears to catch all that would be uttered. " Mr. Sinnitt!" repeated his lordship ; and, that officer's response being heard, the important communication would next be made. " Mr. Sinnitt, trim sails in chase," said the captain, and walked aft to resume his station near the taffrail.

" Now that 's what I calls onprincipled," uttered the boatswain, in a low tone, to his mate : "here we are, rambadgering right down somewhere away to the back of November, in chase of the Flying Dutchman, I supposes : but whether yon 's she or not may I be bamfoozled into a kettle-drummer if I know, and the skipper arn't never got the politeness to inform us. Well, the sarvice is going to——"

" Trim sails !" shouted Mr. Sinnitt, from the quarter-deck ; and then was heard the twittering of Jack Sheavehole's pipe, and a rattling of ropes as the braces were hauled in, the tacks and sheets arranged, till every square inch of canvass performed its own especial and proper duty. Lord Eustace hailed the Hippolito to continue her course, though the Spankaway should do otherwise ; and then rejoined Citizen Captain Begaud, who still retained his position, apparently abstracted from all that was passing around him.

" I have another hour to spare, Monsieur," said his lordship ; " your star, as you call it, is certainly none of the brightest to-night, and I own I am desirous of hearing the finish of your narrative. Will you favour me by proceeding ?"

"I will, my lord," returned the Frenchman; "and I am the more inclined to do so, from a presentiment that hangs over me that my days—ay, even my hours—are numbered. How, when, or where the fatal blow may be given, or whether by friend or foe, I cannot even conjecture; but still I am convinced of the fact, and wish to disburthen my mind before my departure."

"Such presentiments are unworthy a brave man," said Lord Eustace. "You shall dine with me in Plymouth, Captain Begaud. I fancy you take the loss of your frigate too much to heart, though you may be well excused doing so. You fought her nobly, and that rascally first-lieutenant of yours, merits a hangman's noose, though I have cause to thank him; but, there, d— it! a coward is my utter abhorrence. Come, come, Monsieur! your nation is not proverbial for despondency. You will marry the countess yet,—that is, if she be not already your wife."

A thrilling shudder passed over the Frenchman's frame. "Never, never!" exclaimed he, with startling vehemence, as he covered his eyes with his hands, as if to shut out some terrific vision. "No, no, my lord!—no,—it is past,—it is gone! Ha! ha! ha!—hell itself lends me its laugh whenever I think of it!"

There was something so demoniac and unearthly in the agonised chuckle of the Frenchman, that Lord Eustace turned a penetrating look upon him, as if he actually expected to see the Prince of Evil by his side.

"I had no intention of wounding your feelings, Monsieur, and regret that I have done so," said the generous Englishman.

"I know it; I am well aware of it," responded Begaud. "You will presently judge for yourself. But, to proceed. After my audience with Louis the Sixteenth, the grandson of that wretch whose misdeeds laid the foundation of the revolution; who, if he did not sanction, at least did nothing to prevent the murder of his own son, together with his princess; who broke the heart of his queen, and revelled in abomination—— What was the Parc aux Cerfs?—I have seen it, Monsieur; I know it all!—the receptacle for his victims,—mere children, whom he taught to read, and write, and pray;—yet, horrible depravity! he made them the companions of his disgusting orgies! Yes; he would nightly kneel with them, and afterwards carry round the crucifix that they might kiss it; and then selecting —— Bah! my soul sickens at the thought of such a monster! my heart swells almost to bursting! The daughter of Madame T—— had been there! but I have had my full revenge! Revenge! revenge on whom? Ay, that's the question; it is a hidden mystery! the understanding cannot solve it! the innocent suffer for the guilty!

"After leaving the royal presence, fresh apparel was furnished to me, a chamber and ante-room were set apart for my use, and, on the morrow, I — the sworn enemy to the Bourbons! the outcast, whose parents perished in the fête of 1770! the adorer of the young Countess de M——, who but a few hours before cherished his affection in despair!—I became an *attaché* to the household of the queen,—though in reality engaged in the confidential service of Monsieur Calonne. Thus both were exposed to my secret scrutiny; my star was in the ascendant! I felt the importance of the part I was called upon to enact; and Fate seemed to be weaving for me a web to catch the royal victims in its trammels!" He drew a convulsive respiration. "I little thought then, that my own soul would be meshed in the snares which were laid for others!

"There was something strange in the unusual reliance which M. Calonne placed upon my fidelity. I was to watch the court party, who flattered whilst they hated the queen; I was especially instructed to notice those who had audience of the king: in fact, I engaged to watch over the interests of my employer by every possible means, fully convinced that by so doing I should be the better able to promote my own. You will say this was a dishonourable occupation, my lord. I grant it; but then, you must remember the bias of my mind,—my oath to Madame T——, (which I considered religiously binding upon my conscience, though she was in all probability numbered with the dead,)—and there was, also, the bewitching felicity of being near to the young countess, whom my very soul ardently adored.

"The courtiers had raised Calonne from comparative obscurity to the high and important office which he held; but this they did to suit their own purposes, not to forward his. But the wily minister soon ascertained that his position would be scarcely tenable, unless by some bold stroke the chances should turn in his favour; or else, by rendering the profligacy of the aristocracy so odious to the people,—especially the middle classes,—that he might fall back upon the latter, and become their leader. Economy had been the object of his predecessors, Neckar and Turgot; but Calonne started a new theory, which he followed up with avidity,—namely, that profusion best contributed to, and formed, the wealth of a state. Paradoxical as this most certainly was, the courtiers could not, or would not, see through it. They hailed the absurdity with the utmost applause, and henceforth extravagant profusion became the order of the day, and soon degenerated into the very extremes of profligacy. The aristocracy delighted in this, for they bore none of the burthens; and history will perhaps record that Calonne acted with self-conceit and ignorance. He did no such thing, my lord; he saw that Neckar, by creating provincial assemblies, had laid the first stone of a republican form of government; that the middle classes, though by far the least in numerical strength, had thereby acquired an influence it was impossible to control; and therefore, as I said before, he endeavoured to take advantage of events as they stood, so as to cajole one party whilst he negociated with the other. Loans were raised to meet the expenditure, and thus the burthens of the people were increased, the revenue of four hundred millions of francs was exceeded by at least one hundred and fifty millions. Complaints, though not loud, were deep. La Fayette was the leader of the popular cause. He advocated the rights of human nature, and he was looked up to, with reverence and esteem. He demanded the convocation of a representative assembly, and M. Calonne secretly encouraged this demand, that he might be the better enabled to enforce his schemes upon the nobility for the payment of the deficit.

"In this emergency, and the more securely to carry out his plans, the minister proposed to assemble the chiefs of the privileged orders, —the Notables: they met at Versailles; Calonne explained the financial state of the nation, declared the amount of his deficit, and suggested the necessity of equalising the taxes, and levying them alike on the *noblesse* and the clergy, as well as on the commonalty. Need I say how distasteful this was to the individuals he addressed? Need I describe their violent opposition to the proposal, and their determination to crush the man who had the hardihood to bring it before them? His enemies were numerous. The pretended friends, who had elevated him to power to suit their own nefarious arrangements, now united with his avowed foes; whilst the defalcation brought him into disrepute with the middle classes, and every engine was set at work to effect his overthrow. The press, the clergy, and the *noblesse* took the lead; and the fate of Calonne seemed to be fully decided upon. But, under a show of ostentatious vanity and inflated ambition, the minister concealed consummate penetration and skilful tactics. If the Notables had acceded to his wishes, his end would be answered, and himself continued in power; if they refused, they involved themselves in an odium which would have due weight with the adherents of La Fayette, and to them he hoped to be enabled to look for support when the court should fail him.

"I have been minute, my lord, in these particulars, that you may the better understand what has yet to come, for it was about this time that I made my engagement to serve Calonne; and I was not long in ascertaining that, though apparently the superficial prodigal, and the frivolous man of fashion, there was yet an energetic boldness about him that would, if thwarted in his views, urge him to some deed of desperation. In most instances he behaved to me with the utmost familiarity; but I strongly suspected that, through some secret agency of which I was held in ignorance, he kept up a communication with the disaffected amongst the middle orders; nor was it long before the fact was fully revealed to me, for the individual who had been the accustomed means of correspondence was seized with sudden illness, and negociations were for a time suspended. It was an anxious and trying period for the minister; he stood upon a pinnacle from which a powerful party were concentrating all their force to hurl him, whilst the illness of the agent had separated him from those who, proud in their republicanism, would not of themselves seek him, and yet it was from them alone that he now anticipated succour.

"In his extremity Calonne fixed his attention upon me, and openly and frankly did he communicate his wishes: his pleasing address and fascinating manners were at first, however, vainly brought into play; I suffered them to make but little impression on my mind. To quit the court,—where I was in great favour with her majesty,—and to leave the presence of her whom my soul so ardently worshipped, seemed to be a sacrifice of such magnitude, that I felt I had not the resolution to make it, and therefore I respectfully declined. 'Such, then, is your resolve?' said the minister. I bowed acquiescence. 'I shall not ask your reasons,' continued he, with a smile of mingling scorn and pride, 'they are well known to me; but it is right that you should correctly know the situation in which you are placed. Who has been the architect of your present prosperity? Mark, young man! the hand that raised the structure can also prostrate it to the dust. I have entrusted too much to your keeping, not to make the depository safe. It is true, I have found you faithful; but, if it had been

otherwise——' He paused for a moment, and then rapidly added,
' Young man, there is such a place as the Bastille ! there is such an
instrument of execution as the guillotine !' I smiled in defiance, for
threats never produced any other feeling in me. He observed it,
and added, ' It is well your personal courage prompts you to surmount
all apprehensions of either, and induces you to brave the worst; but
reflect !' and his keen eye was fixed upon me : ' the former would
prove a delightful bower for a love-sick youth ; there you may in heavy
fetters deplore the harshness of fortune, and curse the hour that saw
you recklessly rend asunder the rosy bonds of Cupid for the iron safeguards of a stern gailor.' He saw he had touched me, though I strove
to conceal all emotion ; and he went on. ' But what will become of
the lovely being whom you worship ? Amidst the gaiety and licentiousness of a court she will soon forget the child of fortune—Jacques
Begaud ! and, though I believe she is not altogether insensible to
your merits, yet the memory of ladies is as evanescent as a flower, it
soon fades away ; and other arms will enfold that loveliness in their
embrace ! some other head will be pillowed on that fair bosom !
another——' ' Hold !' exclaimed I, affecting an indifference, from a
hope that the secret of my affection was still secure within my own
keeping ; ' hold, Monsieur ! you are coming to conclusions before you
are aware that you have the slightest ground for them. I am yet
free from——' ' It is now my turn to cry 'hold !' ' said he, interrupting me, and that, too, in a voice and manner that betokened his
full sense of the advantage he had obtained ; ' do you imagine, Jacques,
that one so well versed in the workings of human nature as myself
can be easily deceived ? Your love for the young Countess de
M——! Ay, that flush of the cheek becomes you ! I have seen it
before, young man ! Those flashing eyes are traitors to your confidence ! they revealed it to me from the first moment of your entering the royal closet ! Your wandering in the forest,—the eagerness
with which you complied with my request to attend me to the château,—the delight you manifested when first within the walls of the
palace,—all these I knew must have some actuating motive ; nor was
I long in discovering it. Subsequent occurrences have confirmed my
penetration, and——' ' You have not been over-generously employed, Monsieur,' said I, somewhat humbled.—' Young man,' returned
he, ' bear witness by your own feelings that self-interest is the go-
verning principle of our actions. Circumstanced as I was, I deemed
it necessary to ensure your services through a more powerful sentiment than mere gratitude to Monsieur Calonne, and the sequel shows
that I am right. I might command,' continued he proudly, ' and
fear no denial ; but I solicit,' he added mildly, and with a smile ;
' will you refuse me, Jacques ?'—' You do me too much honour, Monsieur,' responded I, fully aware that further subterfuge would be
useless ; ' I own I love the countess.' — ' And what hope have
you of making her your own, Jacques Begaud ?' inquired he eagerly,
but in a tone of mournful commiseration. ' What hope can you
have ? Etiquette imposes an impassable barrier between you ; what,
then, can break it down ?' He paused, and a vague sense of his meaning crossed my mind. ' What,' continued he,—' what I ask you is
to annihilate all obstacles, and unite two hearts that fervently affect
each other ?' I remained silent. ' To show that I trust you, Jacques,

I will answer my own question. Popular feeling,—the popular voice, —La Fayette,—and the representative assembly,—liberty and equality! do you understand me now?'—'I do,' returned I; and, oh! how often have those very words 'liberty and equality' rung in my ears since then! they seemed a prophetic intimation of events that afterwards occurred. I own that I was not really inimical to his proposal, for my pledge to my injured relative, and my inherent detestation of monarchy, still retained a powerful influence over my mind; but I wished, by withholding my acquiescence for a time, to enhance the value of compliance. How hazardous it is for inexperience to endeavour to cope with long-practised subtlety! Monsieur Calonne had read my inmost heart, whilst I foolishly imagined it was a sealed book! he played a skilful game, and at length, without quitting the court, (which soon returned to Versailles,) I became the creature of his will.

"My first attempt at negotiation was to be at the residence of a celebrated fortune-teller at Paris, — one who would have been crushed by the persecution of the clergy, many of her predictions had been so singularly fulfilled that both the ecclesiastical and the civil power were afraid to meddle with her; superstitious awe held them in abeyance, and she triumphed in despite of both. My embassy was to deliver a packet into her hands, and to receive a secret communication in reply. I readily found the dwelling, for my directions were too clear to be mistaken: it was enclosed within a capacious court-yard, the walls of which were old, and in some parts dilapidated, but, nevertheless, there was a frowning strength about them that typified a stern resistance. The house itself was of ancient structure, with small narrow windows, which seemed more like loop-holes to a fortification than apertures to admit light and air, but they were very numerous; and the exterior masonry had been cut away at an angle of full fifty degrees on each side, so as to command a tolerably wide range over every part of the court-yard, except that which lay immediately beneath. There was not, altogether, an appearance of actual poverty in the exterior; but it rather resembled the habitation of an ancient family in decay, proud of splendour, yet without the means of adequately sustaining it. An aged porter admitted me on my giving a required signal; but, though his years appeared to be many, there was a piercing keenness in his eyes, at variance with the silvery whiteness of his hair. His scrutiny was peculiarly searching, though scarcely more than momentary; and, having satisfied himself, he preceded me through a long narrow passage, and then up a flight of stairs, to an apartment rather meanly furnished, where he demanded my business. I requested an interview with *la sorcière*, as it was only with herself I could communicate. He hesitated; but at length left me for about a quarter of an hour, and at his return bade me follow him. I obeyed; and we passed through several rooms, of no great pretensions as it regarded furniture,—there was, however, sufficient in each for use, and every one seemed adapted to receive different inmates.

"At length we reached the end of a long gallery, and stopped in a small closet-like place, but well filled with light, and containing numerous emblems of the divining art of the being who ruled as mistress of the whole. There were globes of considerable magnitude, diagrams of the heavenly bodies, curious geometrical figures, two enormous skulls on pedestals, a human skeleton in a glass-case, stuffed snakes, mirrors that unnaturally enlarged the human features,—in short, the place was literally crowded with strange things to attract, or rather to distract, the attention. Here we lingered a few minutes, and then a small door was thrown open, into an extremely dark passage hung with black cloth, and lighted only by a diminutive lamp, that scarcely sent its feeble rays from one extremity to the other; the sombre appearance was well calculated to strike terror, and bewilder the weak minds that traversed its gloom. 'Pass on,' said my conductor; 'open the farther door! I quit you here.' I obeyed without hesitation, though I must own that, when I heard the portal close heavily behind me, and the key harshly grating in the lock, a sickening sensation crept over my spirit, and I was almost fainting with the closeness of the place. I pushed on with what haste I could, and, throwing open the door at the extremity, burst at once from darkness and gloom into a scene of resplendent brightness that dazzled the eyes; and, before I could recover my senses, I felt myself enclosed in the arms of some one who, by her dress, I concluded was the sibyl herself. Such a greeting appalled me, from its being so totally unexpected; but a well-remembered voice soon dispelled alarm. I was in the embrace of my venerable relative,—she who had influenced every action of my early life;—it was Madame T—— !

"Need I tell you that I was at once thrown into the very centre of the vortex of sedition? That this powerful woman, who had gained an ascendency that was as extensive as it was astonishing, quickly introduced me to the disaffected of the times, whom she actually ruled with a despotism they could not counteract? Need I tell you that my position at court, and the confidential favour of Calonne, were immediately turned to her advantage, so as to render her more absolute? She had unbounded wealth at her command, supplied from the treasury of the Duke d'Orleans; for, whilst she held council with La Fayette, Mirabeau, and others, the representatives of the middle classes,—who, in humbling the *noblesse*, had no idea of abolishing monarchy, — she also secretly encouraged the leaders of the mob, several of whom were sheltered in her house. I will not, however, weary you with details of politics; suffice it to say that Calonne was thrown down by those who had elevated him, whilst I retained my station about the royal person, was gradually raised to honour and trust, and became the companion, the favoured lover of the young countess. But the utmost caution was requisite: in public a restrained distance was preserved, for the purpose of concealment; in the hours of stolen privacy our very souls were firmly knit together.

"Oh! my lord, it is not possible to tell the commotions which constantly agitated my mind. I saw the relative whom I had revered from infancy almost, incessantly engaged in overturning the throne, and annihilating royalty. She held an unaccountable control over my actions, and urged me on in the same career with herself; whilst the innocence of the queen, and my affection for the countess, stirred up the better feelings of my nature, and prompted me to fly from Paris. But the noble young lady's attachment to her royal mistress prevailed over every other sentiment, and she would not leave the queen. Day by day the crisis gradually approached. I ventured to reason with Madame T——, and was silenced by reproach; had she used threats we might have been saved. From thenceforth I was narrowly watched; my position with the countess became known; and the sibyl of Paris, to my surprise, rather encouraged than opposed it,—nay, she bade me look forward, as Calonne had done, to popular supremacy as most conducive to the happiness I sought.

"The king, weak and fickle, one moment yielding, and the next annulling his consent, destitute of bold and energetic persons to guide or to defend him, and practised on by treacherous counsellors, became little more than a cipher in authority, though a rallying-point for conspiracy. Monsieur, the revolution had commenced! It called into action, men of ardent passions and extensive talent. The court, the Count d'Artois, the Polignacs, could not cope with them. Liberality gained the ascendency. The *noblesse* and the clergy, after making a show of resistance to popular demands, hurled themselves into the revolutionary torrent, and were swept away. My detestation of monarchy had been to my heart like the life-streams that supplied the channels of existence; yet, when I saw the fated king in his retirement, amidst his family, with his children on his knees, and the beautiful white arms of the queen around his neck, compunctious visitings would swell my breast; for I knew the national assembly which had been convened was to be the destruction of Louis, and I, on whom benefits had been showered, was sworn an accessory to his downfall!"

"Really, Citizen Captain," said his lordship, rather warmly, "you worked the devil's traverse with a vengeance! Upon my word, you have been a—ha, hem!—excuse my English blood. There's something yet to come; pray proceed. One may gather a useful lesson even from—I beg pardon—proceed."

"An impulse I cannot counteract impels me to continue," returned Begaud proudly, "or, otherwise, my tongue should be silent. If you are an unwilling listener, my lord, have the politeness to say so; all that I desire is a hearer, not a judge."

"True, true!" responded Lord Eustace. "I have to apologise for my warmth. Believe me I am all attention."

"Step by step," continued the French captain, "the revolution proceeded. The chambers became united,—not for the purpose of resisting popular demands, but that by their embrace they might hug each other, to the death of both. The royal sitting took place; the assembly insisted on concessions, well knowing that the sceptre was passing away from the royal grasp; and Louis menaced in return, being, however, wholly destitute of influence or power to carry his menaces into operation;—he was the braggart of the morning, the shrinking imbecile of sun-set. It was shortly after this that the Count d'Artois undertook to stop the revolutionary torrent. He might as well have attempted to control the lightning's forked flash, or tried to have silenced the rolling of the thunder. Arms were seized; bloodshed followed. The Bastille—ha! ha!—the Bastille came down! the populace triumphed! the physical strength of the lower orders had developed itself as superior to every other appliance, and threatened to overwhelm the middle classes, who had stirred up the ponderous and mighty engine to perpetrate devastation. The joy of Madame T—— became unbounded; but her schemes had not yet arrived at the full maturity she wished. Her idol, La Fayette, it is true, was rising to the zenith; but she deceived even him. The Duke d'Orleans was her prompter; his gold was scattered by her amongst the mob with a profuse hand; and neither Bailly, (who had been created mayor of Paris,) La Fayette, nor the leaders of true liberty, were aware of the extent to which corruption was carried to further revolutionary designs, and bribe the mob to renewed sedition.

"Constant in my attendance upon the royal family, I was also assiduous in my attention to the young countess. Monsieur, if ever hearts truly loved, those hearts were ours! Yet, apart from each other, how different were our actions! Hers was all-confiding, fond attachment and devotion; whilst, at the same time, she persisted in following and in sharing the fortunes of her royal mistress. I almost idolized Amelie, and would cheerfully have sacrificed my life to have preserved hers; but I still retained my deadly hatred to monarchy, and had registered an oath to work its overthrow. Oh, Monsieur! had Louis been born in a private station, his amiability would have gained him the love, the estimation of all; but he was a king, and it was against the crown the battery was levelled. Had the *noblesse,* had the clergy acquiesced in the reasonable plans at first proposed, and then stood firm by the throne, the middle classes must have partially yielded; but they first abandoned their own position, and then deserted their monarch.

"Mirabeau arose: La Fayette began to doubt his powers to allay the revolutionary phrensy; he wished to preserve the monarchical form of government, and opposed the insurrectionary movements with an armed force; but Mirabeau died, and, according to his own prediction, the faction soon tore the last shreds of monarchy asunder. The king attempted to escape; I aided that attempt, Monsieur; and glad should I have been, had the royal family attained a place of safety! But the scheme was frustrated, and frustrated by whom? by Madame T——, whose intelligence, independent of myself, had placed the fugitives within the power of the Orleanists. Amelie, at the earnest request of the queen, remained behind, so that the numbers might not attract notice; but she was at the earliest opportunity to follow Marie Antoinette. That opportunity never offered itself. The royal family were brought back to Paris. Petion and Robespierre clamoured for a republic. In vain Bailly and La Fayette dyed the Champ de Mars with the blood of democrats. The new legislative assembly mocked and insulted the monarch. They began their sitting in puerility; they terminated their decrees in blood!

"The Tuileries was soon afterwards invaded by the mob, and Louis's head assumed the symbol of revolution; the crown was already crushed, the red cap had taken its position even upon the monarch's brow; royalty was no more, and my heart exulted in its annihilation. Still I pitied the fate of the Bourbons. The people feared them; there seemed something in the very name of king which stirred up feelings no earthly power could subdue. The secrecy I had observed with Madame T—— relative to the flight of the royal family had exposed me to suspicion; and my condemnation would have been sealed but for the timely rescue of my aged relative, who saved me from assassination; but I no longer held influence with either party. I exhorted the countess to fly with me; but the noble and heroic woman remained firm to her

2 N 2

duty, and I determined rather to perish with her than leave her to the remorseless cruelty of the rabble.

"The northern armies were rapidly marching to the frontiers unresisted. The prisons of Paris were crowded with royalists, and such as were suspected of favouring their views; and, as circumstances had excited a strong feeling against me, I was at length consigned to the Abbaye; but an emissary of Madame T—— assured me that it was more for security than punishment. Horrible were the spectacles that daily succeeded each other. The stones of the court-yard of the Abbaye reddened with the blood of victims till the day of immolation crowned the demons of revolution with a wreath that hell itself might envy. I had been called before Maillard, and questioned; my replies appeared to be satisfactory; I was commanded to act as secretary to this wholesale murderer. A table was placed in the court-yard, at which Maillard took his seat, with a knife yet reeking with blood before him. On either side were arranged about a dozen of the lowest order of *sans culottes*, to form the mockery of a tribunal, whilst near the entrance stood a ruthless band of sanguinary assassins armed with knives and mallets. The portal was thrown open, a carriage drove in, and from it alighted an ecclesiastic, his robes torn and soiled, his face the semblance of despair, his step, as he descended, feeble,—for he was aged and weak. His feet touched the ground, Maillard raised his bloody token, a blow from a mallet felled him to the earth, the wretches closed upon their victim, and beat and wounded him till his last convulsive shudder proclaimed that life was extinct! Another presented himself; but he was young and active, and he sprang at once into the midst of the assassins, and stood proudly erect. For the moment the hired tools of vengeance were appalled; but again the knife was raised, and rage returned with redoubled energy for having suffered a recoil! Another and another succeeded as the carriages drove in. Age and infirmity had their brief career shortened! Youth and strength were cut off in their prime! The sacred character of priest was no protection; and, Monsieur, I registered the names of twenty-three ecclesiastics whose mangled bodies were piled against the wall. There was yet another; but he was saved almost by miracle, and his preservation is yet to me unaccountable.

"I will not go over the events of that day. Every being within the prison was massacred except the women, and one or two who were saved by their intercession. Goblets of blood—the blood of aristocrats— were handed to daughters and wives, as the test of safety to a parent or a husband; and the disgusting draughts were swallowed with a horrid eagerness lest it should be supposed they shrunk from the task. Monsieur, my very soul sickened. I had hated monarchy; but I had never contemplated the possibility of such enormities as I was then compelled to witness. The infuriated beasts of the wildest forest could not be compared to these hyenas in human form; for, whereas instinct would lead the first to rend their prey for food without the ingenuity of torture, the latter called in the aid of human invention to prolong the sufferings of their victims, for the purpose of glutting their worst and most baneful passions.

"I was released, and sought the residence of Madame T——; but I found that even her protection would not avail me. The torrent

.had reached even to her, and she feared being carried away by its eddies. There was but one alternative,—a commission in the army of the North. This was accepted; but, previous to my departure, (though only a few hours were allowed,) I endeavoured to obtain intelligence of Amelie. She was in the Temple with her fated mistress, and I was hurried off to join the Duke de Chartres* on the frontiers. La Fayette was induced to give himself up to the enemy, who erected the finger of menace before they had power to execute. A manifesto was published, summoning the Parisians to return to their allegiance, and, in case of refusal, threatening to deliver them up to military execution. Bah! Monsieur, it was gasconade! and by whom was this precious document drawn up? By the very man who had first set the revolutionary machine in motion, and who now imagined that the Parisians, having plucked forth the sword and thrown away the scabbard, were to be terrified by mere threats; it was my old master, Monsieur Calonne. This act of his, brought the unfortunate Louis more hurriedly to the scaffold.

" I was present under Dumouriez at Valmy, where the allies, as if panic-stricken, showed the futility of their threats, for we were victorious. Conquest succeeded to conquest. The battle of Jemmapes was fought, and Belgium became ours. It was whilst prosecuting a hazardous march that intelligence reached me that Louis was no more. Madame T——'s revenge was satiated; but she herself perished near the guillotine, an awful instance of fearful retribution. She had hurried in disguise to the place of slaughter, and obtained a near approach to the fatal instrument. Her joy at seeing the axe fall was unbounded; she shrieked with delight, and, being recognised, was raised upon the shoulders of the women, and in the madness of the moment was worshipped with enthusiastic fervour: they bore her along through the swelling crowds, and, amidst their awe and homage, she cried for fresh victims,—'The queen! the queen!' Her shout was reiterated by the mob, in whom the sight of royal blood had quickened the tiger-like ferocity of their sanguinary thirst for gore; and they were hurrying towards the prison of the bereaved wife and wretched mother, when a *garde du corps*, in female attire, fought his way to the head of the procession. He, too, had witnessed the murder of his royal master; and, terror for his own fate inspiring him with a desire to fall at once, he formed the determination to have a companion in his exit. He stood before the shouting mob, who were compelling every one to do obeisance to their idol; he stooped down, as if in obedience to their mandate; but, making a sudden spring, like the panther from his lair, or the snake from his coil, he gripped the sibyl by the throat, dragged her to the earth, and stabbed her to the heart! 'Twas the work of an instant; the sound of her voice had scarcely died away in the distance as she stirred up the vindictiveness of the populace, when she lay extended on the frost-bound ground a lifeless corpse. The *garde du corps* was instantly seized, and in a short time his dissevered limbs were scattered through the Place Louis Quinze. Thus terminated the life of Madame T——, and the queen was spared a little longer.

" Anxious for the security of Amelie, I requested leave of absence, but it was refused me,—'my services were required with the

* The present King of the French.

army.' Again, and again, at intervals, I renewed my application,
with no better success; till, goaded by agony, I threw up my commission, and returned to Paris, where I found Robespierre the leader
of the day. The queen had shared the fate of her royal consort, and
the countess was under condemnation in a dungeon of the Conciergerie. Maddened and desperate, I sought out Danton, and endeavoured to enlist him on my side for the preservation of her I loved;
but he had argued himself into cold-blooded policy, and recommended my abandoning Amelie to her fate. With difficulty I was allowed
an interview with the devoted lady; and, oh! Monsieur, language
cannot describe the bitterness of those moments! Her affection was
unchanged and unsubdued. She was calm and collected, though
there was the prospect of only a few hours' division between her and
eternity. Young and beautiful, though somewhat wasted by distress
and hunger, I could not look upon her resigned and heroic conduct
but as something too valuable for my possession, and only worthy of
that heaven to which she was hastening. We parted; and I left her
with the assurance that no means should be left untried to preserve
her life. I hurried to Robespierre, and met Danton coming out; a
cold sick shuddering rushed through my heart; nevertheless, I entered the bureau of the tyrant, who commenced a rapid series of questions relative to the defection of Dumouriez, (who had passed over to
the enemy,) and the state of the army of the North. Repeatedly did
I attempt to introduce the object of my visit, and as often did he
foil me. The insatiate monster! the consummate villain! At length
I obtained a hearing, described my services, promised the most implicit compliance with every order he might give, provided the life of
the countess was granted me as a boon. 'Her attachment to the queen,'
said he, 'has rendered her conspicuous, and these are not times in
which to suffer the milk of human kindness to overflow the current of
a just retribution.'—'Her devotion to her mistress ought to excite admiration, Monsieur Citizen,' returned I; 'but I will answer with my
own existence that henceforth she will cause no trouble, but bend to
the will of the nation.'—'You promise well,' said he, 'and, did it rest
with me, the pardon might be easily accomplished; but we want re-
cruits to meet the enemy, and they refuse to join our standard, lest,
during their absence, the aristocrats should again usurp the power,
and revenge themselves on the families and friends of those who are
in the field. Young man, I fear the case is hopeless.'—'You want
trusty servants, Citizen,' rejoined I,—'men on whom you can rely
with confidence that they will neither desert nor betray the interests of the nation. Save the life of this innocent, and you bind me
yours for ever.' He held me for some time in conversation. I entreated, I implored,—nay more, I wept! and the drops that were
wrung from my eyes were like boiling and scalding blood rushing
from my heart. He seemed moved to compassion; tears stole down
his cheeks! Bah! the wretch was mocking me! no soft distilment
of generous sympathy was ever wormed from out his breast! 'I
have an important duty for you to execute;' said he, 'perform it with
fidelity, and the pardon shall be granted.'—'But the time is short,'
remonstrated I; 'Citizen Danton——!' 'You are right,' he answered,
and, hastily snatching a piece of paper, he hurriedly wrote a few
lines, which he presented to me. 'This will stay the execution,'

he added; 'Danton is not to be trusted.'—'The pardon, Monsieur Citizen!' exhorted I; 'let me but see her released, and I am yours, soul and body!'—'The populace, my friend,' returned he; 'the populace and Danton! Has she not seduced a brave officer from the defence of his country? Believe me, she is more safe within the walls of the Conciergerie than if exposed to popular violence.'—'As my wife, Monsieur,' responded I, 'she will immediately return with me to the army. Grant me her pardon and her liberty, let the rest fall upon my head.'—'You are wilful,' said he, somewhat sternly; 'but take your wish.' Again he wrote, and once more I received a document, that seemed like renewed light, and hope, and life to me. 'You will return here,' continued he, 'when your mission is accomplished; I have business for you. Use despatch now, but do not fail hereafter.'

"With a bold step and a bounding heart I hurried from his presence, and ran toward the prison. In one of the streets I met a *fiacre* accompanied by the officers of justice, and I knew it was some poor wretch whose hours were numbered; and, oh! how did my spirit exult in the thought that Amelie—my own Amelie—would be rescued from a similar fate! I stopped not to ascertain who the condemned prisoner was; but with my quickest speed presented myself at the prison gate. I showed my paper, the porter admitted me; and, oh! Monsieur, what tongue can tell the joyous and eager delight that held a sainted fête within my breast! In a few minutes I should hold her within my arms, should clasp her in my embrace, and lead her forth to freedom. And yet I trembled: the perspiration stood in big drops upon my face. I felt a sickness steal over me; though not a fear, not a doubt arose in my mind of Amelie's liberty. The head gaoler was engaged; but in a time,—though short, it was an age to me,—he came; I delivered the document into his hands; he read it, shook his head, and, whilst a suffocating sensation almost stifled every faculty, I heard him say, 'I fear you are too late. Amelie de M—— has already departed for the place of execution!'"

Here vivid recollection appeared to overcome the Frenchman's strength of mind; he paced the deck athwart-ships with impetuous strides; the picture of desolation was probably present to his imagination in all its horrors; and Lord Eustace could not behold his apparent agony unmoved, but he did not speak, rather preferring to leave nature to its own operations. In a few minutes the captive grew more composed; he again placed himself by his lordship's side, folded his arms, and proceeded.

"Yes, my lord, she had indeed departed, and was the inmate of that *fiacre* I had passed on my hurried way to the prison. The truth instantly flashed upon me; in my disregard for the sufferings of another, I had consigned her to an ignominious end. I had the pardon in my hand. I might be her murderer!—Might be? there was a hope in that surmise; and, resuming the document, I flew rather than ran towards the fatal spot. People stared at my headlong speed, and gave way before me. I saw the guillotine, with the prostituted figure of Liberty presiding over it. My breath began to fail; but yet I shouted. There was a commotion in the crowd as I held up the paper high above my head. I rushed forward. The few persons who had collected opened a passage, and I reached the scaffold at the very moment the axe fell, and the decapitated trunk of the young and beautiful, sent forth its gush of blood to waste the fountain of life! At first I stood speechless with horror and amazement; but when the head was raised, and I saw those tresses I had loved to weave amongst my fingers, stained with gore, —when I beheld the cheek that had been pressed to mine still quivering in the last death-pang,—phrensy drove reason from her seat. I raved till the air rang with my maledictions. I cursed the Convention, and denounced the monsters Robespierre and Danton. The guard were about to seize my person, when a young man caught me by the arm, claimed me as his brother, and declared I was a lunatic, escaped from the control of my keepers. He dragged me away with him to his lodgings, and, when my fit of passion was passed, I recognised the youth I had saved from drowning during the earthquake of Messina.

"That night we quitted Paris together, for he would not suffer me to remain alone, and despair had fixed a melancholy upon my mind that rendered all places alike to my despondency. For a time we sojourned in the country; but my friend received orders to join the army employed against Toulon, and I accompanied him. He had been a pupil in the artillery school of Brienne; he was soon raised to eminence by his skill and judgment, and the whole artillery department of the army before Toulon was placed at his disposal. Through his talent and intrepidity Toulon fell; and I obtained by his recommendation a lucrative office, and ultimately rose through the several grades to that in which you found me,—*capitaine de frégate*. Monsieur, the youth of Messina, the artillery officer who snatched me from the myrmidons of Robespierre, is now the First Consul of the French nation,—Napoleon Buonaparte!"

Here Citizen Begaud ceased. The chase was closing nearly within hail, and, without exchanging another word, Lord Eustace walked to the gangway.

LINES

Occasioned by the death of the Count Borowlaski, a Polish dwarf, whose height was under thirty-six inches, and who died at Durham, on the 5th of September last, aged ninety-eight.

A SPIRIT brave, yet gentle, has dwelt, as it appears,
Within three feet of flesh for near one hundred years;
Which causes wonder, like his constitution, strong,
That one so *short alive* should be *alive so long!*

J. S.

A CHAPTER ON WIDOWS.

WIDOWS! A very ticklish subject to handle, no doubt; but one on which a great deal may be said. An interesting subject, too,—what more so? What class of persons in the universe *so* interesting as weed-wearing women? We are not sure that on paper they have ever been treated as they deserve. We don't think they have been considered as they ought to be: their past, their present, and their future, have not been speculated upon; their position in the world has not been decided. They have simply been spoken of *as* widows, in the gross: the various circumstances of widowhood have never been distinguished; as if those circumstances did not subdivide and classify, giving peculiar immunities to some, and fixing peculiar obligations on others; as if every good woman who has the fortune, or misfortune, to call in an undertaker, is placed in precisely the same situation as far as society is concerned, or ought to be judged or guided by the same rules. We shall begin with a definition; not because any one can doubt what a widow is, but because we have a reason.

A widow is—"a woman who has lost her husband." We must here premise that it is no part of our present plan to say a syllable about those whose husbands have taken themselves off—the dear departed,—and not been heard of, Heaven knows how long: nor of those who have lost the affection, and attention, and care of their husbands; for, however much they may be widows as to the comforts and endearments of married life, they are not widows for our purpose.

We shall define a widow in other words. A widow is—" a woman whose husband is dead." This would not be sufficiently intelligible unless we were to add "dead by due course of nature, accident, or physic," because there is such a thing as a man being dead in law; and as we have ever carefully eschewed all things pertaining, directly or indirectly, to that dangerous " essence," as far as volition could assist us, so we intend to eschew them. We mean, then, dead in fact, and comfortably buried, or otherwise safely disposed of.

And now, having settled a definition, let us proceed to the division of our subject.

We propose to treat of young widows, middle-aged widows, and old widows; to speak of them the truth, and nothing but the truth, and, if not the whole of it, sufficient we trust to show that they have merited our attention.

A young widow must be on the tender side of twenty-eight; the tough side begins, and ten additional years limit, middle-aged widow-hood; while all from thirty-eight to a hundred must take rank, in this army at least, as granny-dears.

A young widow!—to what emotions of tenderness and pity do these words give rise! With what a vivid scene of wretchedness is the mind oppressed! Do they not tell us a tale—and how briefly too!—of joy and sorrow, rejoicing and wailing?—happy anticipations and blighted hopes crowded into one little space? In our mind's eye, we see a fair and blushing bride, an animated ardent bridegroom, a group of happy friends, favours, and festivals; in the background of the picture, a grave. One is missing from the party, never to return; gone from the light and warmth of love, to the cold but constant embrace of the tomb,—from the *few living* to the *many dead!* The atmosphere was sweet, and life-instilling; an arc of promise was above us: that arc has vanished, that atmosphere has changed,—it is thick, oppressive, dank! Hope's lamp flickers, as if it would go out for ever.

This is undoubtedly the cambric-pocket-handkerchief view of the matter, making, as some would say, the "devils" very blue indeed; but it is one that strikes many, perhaps all, who are not of a fishy or froggy temperament: at the same time, we will admit the brush is dipped in the darkest colours, and that we might have been a little less sombre by imagining the defunct a fat and apoplectic old fool, who had only decided upon going to church when he ought to have been looking to the church-yard; in which case, "a young widow," instead of drawing on the deep wells of the heart, draws upon our cheerful congratulations, and stands forth "redeemed, regenerated, and disenthralled by the irresistible genius of universal emancipation."

Whether under the melancholy or the happy circumstances to which we have alluded, a young widow is a very different being to what she has ever been before; in identity of person she is the same, but there is no identity of position; as regards society, there is no identity of rights, privileges, licences, or liabilities. The great difference as regards herself is, that, for the first time in her life, she is her own protector: many things that she could not do as a girl, and dare not do as a wife, are now open to her. She has been "made a woman of," and is a very independent person. After languishing a fitting time in calm retirement and seclusion, having "that within which passeth outward show," she reappears to the world decked in "the trappings and the suits of woe." We purposely use the word "decked," because in its most familiar sense it implies "adorned," at least as applied to the "craft" we are now convoying. We should very much like to be told, and very much like to see, a more interesting sight than a young widow, when, after having been laid up in ordinary the ordinary time, she leaves her moorings, in proper "rig and trim," to prosecute the remainder of the voyage of life. The black flag is up, and no doubt she means mischief; but all is fair and above board. No mystery is made of the metal she carries, the port she is bound for. She may take a prize, or make one; but it must be by great gallantry if she is captured.

To drop metaphor: a young widow is, we repeat, an extremely delightful and highly privileged creature. Mark her in society,—we do not care how limited or how extensive,—and she bears the palm in the interest that is excited. We will give a showy animated girl of eighteen the benefit of a first appearance; we will allow her to have excited the attention of the room, to be the observed of all observers; every one shall be asking, "Who is the young lady in pink crape?" —she shall have danced and sung herself into full-blown importance, —she shall have turned as many heads as she has times in her waltzing;—and then, a little late in the evening, we will introduce, very quietly,—no loud double-knocking at the door, no voices of servants echoing her name, no rustling of silks or satins, — a young widow! just " one year off;" she shall slide gently into the room, seeming to shun observation, as they all do, (lest perchance some ill-natured person should wonder what business they have there,)—and, contented with a simple recognition from her host or hostess, she shall occupy some " silent nook," and rest satisfied in its shade. Presently, some one shall chance to *speak* of her as " a young widow,"—the lady of the house, for instance, who usually occupies every leisure moment in informing groups of her old visitors the names and et-ceteras of her young ones, — she shall happen to say, " Excuse me one moment, I *must* go and speak to poor Mrs. Willow."

" *Poor* Mrs. Willow!—what can that mean?" wonder all who hear it.

And then the lady comes back, and explains that Mrs. W. is a widow.

" Poor thing !" says one.

" Only think !" says another.

" How very young !" says a third.

" Any children ?" asks a fourth.

" I thought she looked melancholy !" observes a fifth; and then, after staring at the object of their commiseration and curiosity sufficiently long to be sure they will know her again, they separate with the view of advertising the interesting intelligence. It being known to four old women, and one middle-aged man who doesn't dance, it speedily spreads over the whole room ; and, provided no one intimates off-hand a superior case of affliction in the person of any one present, the young widow has to bear the brunt of a very wholesale inspection. There is also a great deal of wonder ; people wonder in classes :—the elderly, What her husband died of,—the young ladies, Whether she has any family,—the gentlemen, Whether she has any money. During all this wonderment, " the young lady in pink crape" is entirely forgotten.

Now, if the young widow should happen to feel at all " at home," and chooses to " come out" a little, mark what follows : " the young lady in pink crape" has to dance the remainder of the evening with red-haired, freckled, pock-marked, snub-nosed, flat-footed fellows, with whom she would not have touched gloves an hour ago, while all the stylish staff that then surrounded her, are doing homage at another shrine.

And no wonder !—A girl may be very agreeable and " all that," as people say when they want to cut description short ; but it's impossible she can hold a candle to a young widow. She is obliged to be circumspect in all she says,—to weigh every word,—to cripple her conversation, lest she should be thought forward ; but, worse than this, she is so deuced simple and credulous, that a man with a fine flowing tongue is apt to mislead her, and place himself in a false position before he gets through a set of quadrilles ; whereas with the other partner it is *tout au contraire.* " Old birds are not to be caught with chaff;" and old the youngest widow is, in " the ways of men," compared with the bread-and-butter portion of the unmarried world. You may rattle on as much as you please, so may she ; you neither of you mean anything, and both of you know it : besides, no one has a right to forbid it ; you are your own master, she her own mistress. Dance ten times in an evening with her, and call in the morning. What then!—she has her own house, her own servants. What more?—she is—able to take care of herself.

So much for a young widow in society, or those scenes of life in which the actors and actresses play more immediately against one another; scenes in which tragedy, comedy, melo-drama, and farce—the last predominating—are brought before us. Now, if we step behind the scenes, and look a little into the privacy of the domestic circle, and observe her as one of the " select few," we fancy we shall still find her maintaining her pre-eminence as an intelligent companion and delightful friend. When we use the term " intelligent," we do not presume to say that she is necessarily more acute than she was as a coy maiden, or than the virgin of our acquaintance, as touching any branch of historical, artistical, or scientific information; but we mean intelligent in an unobtrusive but every-day-available knowledge of " men and things,"—in other words, a knowledge of the world. She has pushed off from shore, and has learnt a little of the current of life, its eddies, shoals, and quicksands. She has lost the dangerous confidence of inexperience, without having acquired an uncharitable distrust; and smiles at the greenness of girlhood, without assuming the infallibility of age. She is not too old to have sympathy for youth, nor so young as to slight the experience of years. In her past, joy and sorrow have commingled; in her future, hope is chastened by reason.

Some imaginative people of bygone centuries decided that fire produced all things, and that this fire was inclosed in the earth. Of fire, Vesta was the goddess; or, as the Romans sometimes thought, Vesta herself was fire. Ovid is our authority for this:

" Nec tu aliud Vestam quàm vivam intellige flammam."

The same gentleman, also, synonymizes her with another element:

" ——Tellus Vestaque numen idem est."

Now, whether Vesta was fire, or fire Vesta, or whether the earth and Vesta were one and the same fire, we are not in a condition to determine; and as there are no muniments of any Insurance Office to throw light on the matter,—even the " Sun" had not then begun business in this line,—the curiosity of the curious must remain unquenched. This, however we know, that Vesta's waiting-women;—we beg their pardon, the goddess's lady's-maids,—the Vestales of her Temple, had, beyond the usual routine of their business, such as dressing and undressing her; waiting her whims, and getting up her linen, the onerous charge of watching and guarding the holy fire, and lighting it once a year, whether it required lighting or not. The first of March was the appointed day for this ceremony: though the first of April might have been, under all the circumstances, a more appropriate anniversary. We have no distinct records as to whether these young women were familiar with the application of flint and steel to tinder, or whether the royal-born Lucifer had, in those days, taken out a patent for his matches; there is little reason for regret, however, in this uncertainty, inasmuch as neither the one nor the other could have been made use of. The holy fire might be supplied from no common flame, and they had therefore to ask " the favour of a light" from the pure and unpolluted rays of the Sun.

Now we humbly conceive that our motive for introducing this interesting little classical episode must be obvious from its conclusion.

We were talking of one—though certainly not in any probability a Vestal virgin—whose "sacred flame" had gone out, and we felt we should be expected to say something of its re-lighting. Thinking, preparatory to writing, we recollected all that we *have* written, and we were interested and amused with the identity of means employed for a common end two thousand years ago and in the present day; as it then was, so it now is, managed by *attraction.*

It has just occurred to our reflective mind, that the imaginative people before-mentioned must have been figurative also; and meant by earth, human clay,—and by the fire therein, love. We should like to know what love will *not* do; and, until we are told, we shall deem it capable, as the ancients did fire, of producing everything.

And now a few words upon the marriage of a young widow. We might be expected to discuss the question of second marriages generally, and weigh the arguments pro and con,—the romance against the reality of life; but we decline doing so at present, on the ground that, right or wrong, young widows at any rate have ever had, if possible, and even will have, a second string to their bow, should grim Death rudely snap the first,—a second arrow to their quiver, should the first be lost " beyond recovery."

She marries again,—may we say, loves? If she has loved before, we may not. *He* is in the grave, and her "heart is in the coffin there." But she marries; and, though she may exclaim,

> " No more—no more,—oh! never more on me
> The freshness of the heart can fall like dew,"

in the spirit of the words,—she takes nothing from their truth by substituting one reading for another:

> " No more—no more,—oh! never more on me
> The *greenness* of the heart," &c.

And this, there is no doubt, she does, as she embarks in matrimony with comfortable confidence a second time.

It is believed that many very sensible men have married young widows. Without saying whether we believe it, we may observe that *we* have never done anything of the kind, and never intend: This declaration is not inconsistent with perfect sincerity in all we have said. We have been treating of young widows *as* widows, not as wives. Our objections to any transformation on our own account are many; we shall give only one,—our extreme diffidence and modesty, which would never allow us to be judged by comparison as to the essentials of a good husband. So strong, indeed, is our feeling on this point, that, notwithstanding our extreme prepossession in their favour, we verily believe that the most fascinating relict that ever lived, with the best fortune that was ever funded, might say to us by her manner, as plainly as a brass-plate on a street-door, " Please to ring the bell-e," only to suffer defeat and disappointment.

And now we approach the second division, and proceed to pay our respects to middle-aged widows; generally, stout, healthy-looking women with seven children. We have omitted, by-the-bye, to observe, that young widows cannot have more than two, or at the most three, without losing caste. Seven children form a very interesting family, and confer considerable importance on their proprietor, of whose melancholy bereavement they are perpetual advertisements. In proportion to the number of pledges presented to a husband, is a wife's love for him; or, if this be not invariable, at any rate in proportion to her little ones is her sorrow for his loss; particularly when he dies leaving nothing behind him but the "regret of a large circle of friends." For some time, the afflicted woman places great reliance on an extensive sympathy, and has very little doubt that some one will some day do something: godfathers and godmothers rise into importance, and directors of the Blue-coat School are at a premium. If she be fortunate, her motherly pride is gratified before long by gazing on her first-born with a trimmed head and yellow cotton stockings; and by this time she generally finds out she has nothing more to expect from any one but—herself.

We have begun with the poor and heavily-burthened middle-aged widows, because they are by far the most numerous of the class. It is a singular thing, that we seldom meet with a middle-aged widow with a small family, or a large provision. The young and the old are frequently wealthy; not so the other unfortunates. We suppose the reason of this is, that the harassing cares of an increasing family kill off a prodigious number of men; and, inasmuch as these cares would not have existed had Fortune been propitious, they make their exit in poverty.

Occasionally, however, we meet with a middle-aged widow without children, and with fortune, or a comfortable independence. Of such a one we shall say a word or two. Generally speaking, she looks with extreme resignation on the affliction that has overtaken her; and, when she speaks of it, does so in the most Christian spirit. Of all widows, she is the most sure that "everything is for the best;" and, as she has no living duplicates of the lost original, her bosom is less frequently rent by recollections of the past. Anxious, however, to prove her appreciation of the holy state, and offer the best testimony of her sense of one good husband, she rarely omits taking a second; and, purely to diminish the chance of having twice in her life to mourn the loss of her heart's idol, she generally selects one some ten or fifteen years younger than herself. We say "selects," because it is very well known, that, though maids are wooed, widows are not. The first time a woman marries is very frequently to please another; the second time, invariably herself: she therefore takes the whole management of the matter into her own hands. We think that this is quite as it should be: it stands to reason that a woman of seven or eight and thirty, who has been married, should know a great deal more about married life than a young gentleman of twenty-five, who has not. And then he gets a nice motherly woman to take care of him, and keep him out of mischief, and has the interest of her money to forward him in his profession or business,—the principal has been too carefully settled on the lady to be in any risk.

We do occasionally encounter some "*rara avis in terris*"—a middle-aged widow who thinks nothing of further matrimony; and so convinced are we of the "dangerous tendency" of such characters, that we would at once consign them to perpetual imprisonment. If they declared their resolution in time, we would undoubtedly try it, by burying them with their first lover, or burning them Hindoo fashion ; for, supposing them to have no children, to what possible good end can they propose to live ? It is our firm belief that they know too much to be at perfect liberty, with safety to society ; and they must of necessity be so thoroughly idle, beyond knitting purses and reading novels, as to make mischief the end and aim of their existence. We ask fearlessly of our readers this question—"Did you ever in your lives know an unmarrying, middle-aged, childless widow, who was not a disagreeable, slanderous, and strife-inducing creature ?" If you ever did, you ought to have tickled her to death,—so as to have avoided disfigurement,—and sent her in a glass-case to the British Museum.

Perhaps it will be said by some, that they have known such a woman as we have just enquired about, and that they don't think she merited any such fate ; perhaps they will say that she was a very harmless, pleasant person, and only remained single because she held her heart sacred to her departed lord. Cross-grained and ugly middle-aged widows may occasionally foster this romance ; as also may those whose husbands have exemplified by their wills that jealousy may outlive life, by decreeing that their flower should lose its sweetness upon another presuming to wear it,—in other words, that, upon a second marriage, the worldly advantages of the first should determine.

There is a class of men in the world, who go through two-thirds of their life single, and who, if you were to believe them, never entertain the remotest notion of being "bothered with a wife." In some instances this arises from an early indulgence in dissipation ; and, from keeping very equivocal company. In their own opinion they are extremely knowing, and are continually wondering "how men can make such asses of themselves" as to put their necks into the matrimonial noose ; if you attempt to argue with them on the stupidity, if not baseness of their creed, they assure you confidently that "women are all alike." We once made a fellow of this sort ashamed of himself, when, having ended a long tirade, which was a coarse amplification of Pope's line,

"But every woman is at heart a rake,"

we asked him, with sufficient emphasis, "Who his mother and sisters were *living* with ?"

Another portion of the ring-renouncers are men who are so abominably selfish, that they would not share an atom of their worldly substance with the most perfect specimen of "the precious porcelain of human clay" that the world could produce them ;—men who look with horror on the expenses of an establishment, and live in miserable hugger-muggery on some first-floor, sponging on their friends to the extremity of meanness ;—men who look upon children with as much horror as that with which they would view a fall in the funds or the stoppage of their banker, and see nothing in them but a draft upon their pockets.

There is yet another body of solitaries, much smaller in number though, than either of the other two;—men who underrate themselves, and who are so extremely diffident and bashful as never to have "popped the question," though their tongues have often had the itch to do it;—men who people their room, as they sit over the fire, with an amiable woman and half-a-dozen little ones, and, when they rub their eyes into the reality of their nothingness, sigh for the happiness of some envied friend. It was necessary that we should make this digression.

We left the middle-aged widow with a large family and small means, convinced that, having got one child provided for,—enabling every one to speak of a kind act as though they had something to do with it,—she had then only to rely upon herself. She *does* rely upon herself; and, in nine hundred and ninety-nine cases out of a thousand, her own resources are sufficient to change her state. Men may make fools of girls, but women make fools of men. In this work of retribution, middle-aged widows with families pre-eminently take the lead. They work particularly on those gentlemen whom we have here introduced; and more particularly and successfully on the first and third class, though the second are not unfrequently made examples of. It will be said that the first class are fools to hand: so they are; and, when caught, they find it out themselves. They are flies, buzzing about and blowing every fair fame they are not scared from. The widow spreads her web of flattery and flirtation; and when the poor insect ventures boldly in, confident that he can at any moment "take wing and away," she rolls him round and round in her meshes, as a spider does a blue-bottle,—or, to use a very expressive idiom, she "twists him round her finger," ring-shape. The consequential, slanderous, and boasting booby sinks into the insignificance of a caged monkey, and lives and dies a miserable Jerry Sneak! Look into society, and you will find many of them.

We admit it is a hard fate for a man, whose only failing, perhaps, has been his modesty, to be secured for the purpose of feeding the hungry and clothing the naked; but then it must be remembered that, had not a widow proposed to him, he would never have had courage to propose to anybody, and that he gets a companion for life and a ready-made family, instead of lingering on in envy and despair.

Seeing that we have called all widows old, who are on the grave side of forty, we feel that we have the most difficult portion of our subject to discuss,—difficult, and, we may add, delicate, because so very few of those who are obnoxious to what we may say, will be inclined to admit it; indeed, if we had any hope of getting over this difficulty by throwing in ten or fifteen years more, we would do so, and date only from fifty or fifty-five. We know, however, that this would not extricate us, and so prefer adhering to our original scale. Widows of forty and upwards command very little of the sympathy that waits on those bereaved in earlier life. The reason of this, perhaps, is, that they are not themselves so interesting. It is astonishing how much we feel through our eyes. We are told that "Pity is akin to love," and we might enter into some curious speculations as to the various deductions to be drawn from these words. Supposing we see a young creature of one-and-twenty, in all the freshness of life and first grief, who has buried a lover in a husband after two or three years of unalloyed happiness; she has an infant, perhaps, in each arm. Do we pity her? Deeply,—acutely; we could almost weep for her. Well; we meet a woman in the autumn of life, whose summer has been passed with the first and only object of her affections; hearts that yearned towards each other in youth, time has made one; in every inclination, wish, hope, fear, they have heightened the pleasures of life by a mutual enjoyment of them, and alleviated its sorrows by sharing them together. Death has divorced them, and we see her—alone! We are very sorry for her, and her four or five children; it is "a sad loss:"—we say so, and of course we mean it; but are we as sensitive to this picture as to that?

If we make second marriages a principal feature in this dissertation on widows, we do so because it is their "being's end and aim," as is incontrovertibly proved by their all but universality. Old widows, even if poor, sometimes lend an able hand in the retaliation of which we have before spoken; but, unfortunately, they also very frequently, when they happen to have wealth, become themselves objects of scorn and derision. Perhaps the most offensive creature in existence, and, save one, the most contemptible, is the worn-out, toothless, hairless, wrinkled jade, who attempts,

> " —— Unholy mimickry of Nature's work!
> To recreate, with frail and mortal things,
> Her withered face;"

and then, upon the strength of a long purse, puts herself up, a decayed vessel, to Dutch auction, herself proclaiming what she is worth, to be knocked down—we are almost unmanly enough to wish it were not figuratively— to some needy young spendthrift, of whose grandmother she must have been a juvenile contemporary. Widows of this stamp are almost always women raised from low stations, from whom, perhaps, little delicacy or refinement is to be expected. There is hardly a season in which some carcase-butcher's or grocer's wealthy relict is not the talk, and wonder, and emetic of the town.

We must not conclude with exceptions, however, where they create so unfavourable an impression; we will rather turn to those portly and obliging widows who, after looking a little about them as single women, fall in with some comfortable old gentleman who very much wants a housekeeper, and somebody to mix his grog o' nights, and at once agree to take the situation. The old boy puts all his affairs into her hands, and they rub on together cosily enough the remainder of their days. Every one admits it to be "a very suitable match;" if an objection be made by anybody, it merely comes from some expectant nephews or nieces.

There *are* widows we think, we must admit it, who, widows once, remain so for ever, and from inclination, or rather from disinclination to encourage any impression, or even thought, that might weaken or interfere with the memory of the past; but we must repeat that they are never young, and rarely middle-aged widows: they are women past the meridian of their days, whose griefs, not violent or obtrusive, have yet been solemn and absorbing; women who have lost the vanity of believing they can accommodate themselves to any man; and, dwelling on the happiness they *have* enjoyed, cherish its recollection as an act of devotion to one "not dead, but gone before."

They wear their "weeds" as long as they are of this world; and there is always a quietness, if not gravity of demeanour, that perfectly assorts with them. In society they are always respected; by those who know them, loved; they do not hesitate to talk of their married life, and live over many of its scenes, to those who are interested in listening: herein they differ from married widows, if we may use the expression, who very rarely talk of their first union to any one but their husbands; they, perhaps, hear of it something too much, and too often!

And now, having passed our compliments and paid our respects, we must take our leave. We have been guilty of one rudeness,—we have had all the talk to ourselves: in return, we promise to be patient listeners, should any fair controversialist think fit to propound her views on this "highly-interesting and important subject."

PETRARCH IN LONDON.

I.

Near Battersea a lonely flower grew,
  It was in truth a sweet and lovely thing:
  The skies smiled on its blossoming,
And poured into its breast their balmy dew;
Its breath was fragrant as the month of May;
  Its face was fairer than the mist that veils
Aurora's self, ere she has bid the day
  Laugh on the hills, and smile upon the dales.
Fairest of all!—companions she had none;
  For Fate had torn them from her tender side.
She seemed a virgin suing to be won,
  And yet all-shrinking in her modest pride.
This cauliflower,—which I now call a flower,—
I took into my arms, and boiled that very hour.

II.

The Irish hodman, on his ladder high,
  Surveys each chimney-pot that smokes around,
  Then turns his anxious eyes upon the ground
To where his pipe doth in his jacket lie:
Sweet thoughts of "'bacco," and the opium feel
  That lays a handcuff on Care's iron wrist,
Come o'er his mind; and pots of porter steal,
  Illusive settling on his outstretched fist!
Entranced he stands: the tenants of his hod
  Fall down before the spirits of his heart;
Till Reason interferes her magic rod,
  "Puts out his pipe," and shows his bricks apart,
So 'twas with me: Ambition once did fix
An airy structure, which fell down "like bricks!"

ADVENTURES IN PARIS.

BY TOBY ALLSPY.

THE FIVE FLOORS.

THE Boulevards may be said to perform for Paris the functions fulfilled by the cestus of Venus towards that amphibious goddess, by surrounding it with a magic girdle of fascinations. Every sort and variety of entertainment is to be found comprised in their cincture of the city,—from the stately Académie de Musique and Italian Opera (full of dandies and dowagers), to the trestles of rope-dancers, amphitheatres of dancing-dogs, and galleries of wax-work, (full of ploughboys and pickpockets,)—and every species of domicile, from the gorgeous hôtel to the humble stalls of the venders of liquorice-water and *galette*. At one extremity we have the costly *menu* of the Café de Paris, with its *ortolans* and *poudings à la Nessebrode ;* at the other, the greasy *fricots* of La Courtille. The Café Turc brays forth with Tolbecque, and an orchestra of trumpets and bassoons; the *guinguettes* of the Faubourg St. Antoine scrape away with their solitary fiddle. Every species of shop and merchandize, from the sumptuous *magazin* of Le Revenant to the *boutique à vingt-cinq sous ;* every species of temple, from the Parthenonic Madeleine, to that aërial shrine of liberty, the site of the Bastille. Every gradation of display between splendour and misery is epitomized in the circuit of the Boulevards.

Play, opera, farce, feats of equestrianism, funambulism, somnambulism, and humbugism of every colour, industrious fleas, and idle vendors of magic eye-salve, successively arrest the attention ; while in the vicinity of the Café Tortoni, famous for the coldness of its ices and heat of its quarrels, the *courtier marron* plies his trade of trickery ; stock-jobbing has full possession of the *pavé ;* and almost within hearing of the knowing ears of the Jockey-Club, and the ears polite of the *Club Anglais,* bulls and bears outbellow the fashionable jabber of the Boulevards.

On emerging from the head-quarters of English Paris,—the Rue de la Paix,—to the Boulevards des Capucines and des Italiens, the eye is dazzled by gilding, gas-light, plate-glass, scagliola, or moulu, varnished counters, and panelling in grotesque and arabesque, interspersed with glittering mirrors, as appliances and means of getting off the lowest goods at the highest rate. A little further, and by an imperceptible gradation, vice succeeds to frivolity. Instead of milliners and jewellers, we find billiard-tables and gambling-houses, deepening at length, into the more tremendous hazards of the Stock Exchange. After passing the vicinity of the Bourse, we come, naturally enough, to the quarter of the Jews ; passing through the speculative neighbourhood of Le Passage des Panoramas, which is but a splendid game of chance materialised into stone and marble.

Next to this gaudy section of the modern Babylon dwells solid trade,—the streets of St. Denis and St. Martin,—accompanied by such theatres and such coffee-houses as might be expected to minister to the sensual and intellectual delights of the *marchand en gros ;* melodrama, and the Porte St. Martin,—the *Cadran Bleu,* and its unctuous *cuisine.* The vicinage of Rag Fair (the *marché aux vieux linges*) succeeds; then the Boulevard still bearing the name of Beau-marchais (the mansion formerly inhabited by the creator of Figaro being appropriately occupied by a refinery of salt); and lastly, in the wake of rags and wits, the site of the Bastille,—the rallying-point of the most seditious parish of Paris, the republican quarter of the ma-nufacturers, the tremendous Faubourg St. Antoine.

It was precisely at the boundary limit between the pleasure and business sections of the Boulevards, at the corner of the Rue du Fau-bourg Montmartre, on an airy second-floor with a projecting balcony, commanding a view of the sporting world to the right, and the trading world to the left,—the idle west, and active east,—that there lived a certain Monsieur Georges,—a little wizened man, of doubtful age, doubtful fortune, doubtful reputation. Everything about him was equivocal. In Paris people occupy themselves far less than in London with the affairs of their neighbours: the great have something bet-ter to do, the little something worse; the rich being too busy with play, the poor too busy with work, to have leisure for the dirty scan-dals which spring up like *fungi* in that region of lords and lackeys, Grosvenor Square. Nevertheless, the porter's lodge of every Pa-risian house is a chartered temple of echo, having a gossipry and a jargon of its own. The porter's lodge knits stockings, reads novels, and composes romances; peeps into letters, interrogates chamber-maids, and confederates with duns. A man loose in his habits had need be very close in his domestics, in order to escape the detection of his porter's lodge.

Yet, in spite of fifteen years' domiciliation in that polished corner of the Boulevards, Monsieur Georges, though far from a beauty, was still a mystery. *Madame la portière* had never been able to dis-cover whether "Georges" was a surname given by father to son, or a Christian name given by godfather to godson. She sometimes thought him a single man, sometimes a double, nay, sometimes a treble. Curious varieties of the fair sex occasionally visited the bal-conied saloon,—young, old, and middle-aged,—shabby-genteels who passed for poor relations, and glaring tawdry who passed for worse. There was no roost in his abode, however, either for the birds with fine feathers, or the birds without. Monsieur Georges's foible was not that of hospitality. His interests were too intimately cared for by a ferocious *femme de confiance*, who set himself and his house in order, and caused his establishment to be designated in the neigh-bourhood as that of Georges and the Dragon.

If not generous, however, the little man was strictly just; he gave nothing, but he kept nothing back. He paid his way with the praise-worthy punctuality remarkable in those who never pay an inch of the way for other people.

It is a hard thing, by-the-bye, that while male designations leave the facts of the man's bachelorhood uncertain, a spinster is specially pointed out by the malice of conventional phraseology. Mr. or Mon-sieur may be married or single, as he pleases; but Mrs. and Madame assume, even on the direction of a letter, their airs of matronly su-periority over Miss or Mademoiselle. While her master rejoiced in his ambiguity as *Monsieur* Georges, *Mademoiselle* Berthe was de-signated to mankind and womankind in all the odium of spinster-hood; and exclamations of "old maid" and "*chissie*" followed her daily passage past the porter's lodge, the moment the " grim white woman " reached the first floor.

Among those who indulged in the acrimonious apostrophe, the most persevering, if not the loudest, was an urchin of some fourteen years old, whom Monsieur Georges had added to his establishment two years before, by way of Jack Nasty, foot-page, or errand-boy, under an engagement to clean Monsieur Georges and the housekeeper's shoes, without dirtying the ante-room with his own; to work much, eat little, sleep less; to keep his ears open, and his mouth shut; his hands full, and his stomach empty; his legs were to be evermore running, his tongue never. Now, little Auguste, (Auguste in the parlour, and Guguste in the porter's lodge,) though reared in a provincial foundling hospital, where infants are fed, like sheep, on a common, by the score, and washed, like pocket-handkerchiefs, by the dozen, had unluckily both a will and an appetite of his own. Cleaning Mademoiselle Berthe's shoes inspired him with a fancy for standing in them; and, on more than one occasion, he was found to have encroached upon the housekeeper's breakfast of coffee and cream, instead of contenting himself with wholesome filtred water. He was forthwith accused of being a greedy pig, as well as of making a litter in the apartments; till, after six months of faultiness and fault-finding, Monsieur Georges pronounced him to be an incorrigible *gamin*, sentenced him to " bring firing at requiring," and blacken shoes as usual, but to have his bed in an attic under the roof, (Parisianly called, after the famous Parisian architect, a *mansarde*,) and his board in the porter's lodge, where the board was exceedingly hard; Madame Grégoire,—the knitter of stockings, reader of novels, and coiner of romances for the corner-house of the Rue Montmartre,—having consented to feed and cherish him at the rate of twenty-five francs per month, *id est,* five weekly shillings lawful coin of her Majesty's realm. Monsieur Georges perhaps intended to starve the saucy *gamin* into submission; he *did* almost succeed in starving him into an atrophy.

Guguste, however, was a lad of spirit, and could hunger cheerfully under the housekeeping of the kind-hearted Madame Grégoire, who made up for the scantiness of her cheer by the abundance of her cheerfulness, buttered her parsnips with fine words, and gave the poor half-clothed *gamin* the place nearest the *chauffrette*, (fire she had none,) while Mademoiselle Berthe made the apartment on the second floor too hot to hold him. Madame Grégoire,—whose only daughter was the wife of a puppet-showman, and whose only grandson, a seller of sparrows *rouged et noired* into bullfinches, or whitewashed into canaries, on the Pont Neuf,—transferred a considerable portion of her unclaimed dividends of maternal tenderness to the little orphan. Her son was a soldier, serving (as she said) at Algiers in the Indies, and by no means likely to enter into rivalship with the slave of Monsieur Georges and Mademoiselle Berthe's household.

" 'Tis a strange thing, my dear child," mumbled the old woman to Guguste, as they sat down together one day to their six o'clock soup, (a composition of hot water, cabbage-stalks, half an ounce of bacon, and a peck of salt,) " that so long as I have held the string*

---

* The business of a porter in Paris is to open the gates of the house to comers and goers after dusk, by means of a cord, which is fixed in the lodge.

in this house, not a drop of wine, either in piece or bottle, has ever gone through the gateway to the address of Monsieur Georges! Every month comes the supply of chocolate from Marquise's for Monsieur, and from the Golden Bee a cargo of Bourbon coffee and beetroot sugar for the housekeeper; but of wine not a pint."

"Neither Georges nor the Dragon are honest souls enough to trust themselves with their cups," said the knowing *gamin*. "Wine tells truth, they say. None but an ass talks now-a-days of truth lying at the bottom of a well;—'tis in the bottom of a hogshead of claret. Ma'mselle Berthe, who can do nothing but lie, is the liar in the well. *She* can't keep her head above water."

"But Monsieur Georges, who need entertain no fear of making too free with his own secrets after a glass or two, inasmuch as no living mortal ever dips with him in the dish;—surely Monsieur might indulge on Sundays, and fête days, and the like?"

"And so he does indulge, Maman Grégoire,—so he does! Some folks like their champagne, some their burgundy. Master loves to take an internal hot-bath after the English fashion."

"A tea-drinker? *sacristie!* what effeminacy!" exclaimed the old woman, bravely swallowing, out of a spoon of *métal d'Alger*, a large mouthful of tepid cabbage water. "I recollect seeing tea made upon the stage, in the farce of 'Madame Pochet et Madame Gibou.' *Jésu!* what nastiness! I really wonder at Monsieur Georges! So spruce and so cleanly a gentleman as he looks, when, every evening just as St. Philip's church chimes the half-hour after seven, '*Le cordon, s'il vous plait*,' gives me notice of his exit! His superfine blue coat and garnet-coloured velvet waistcoat without a speck of dust upon them!"

"Thanks to *me!*" interposed Guguste.

"His *toupet* shining with *huile antique*."

"Thanks to *me!*" continued Guguste.

"His boots varnished like looking-glasses."

"Thanks to *me!*" pursued Guguste.

"His hat smoothed as with an iron."

"Thanks to *me*,—thanks to *me!*"

"His *jabot* plaited as if by machinery, and white as snow; while his great diamond studs look out like eyes of fire from the frilling,—"

"Thank to—no, not thanks to *me!*" cried Guguste. "I must own that Ma'mselle Berthe, who is so much in the starch line, still presides in the washing and ironing department; and, as to the brilliants, which you say shine in the dark like cats' eyes, master keeps them like the apple of his own."

"I wonder what makes him so wonderful particular about his dress after nightfall?" said Madame Grégoire, peering through her spectacles into the face which she was preparing to cross-examine. "Humph?"

"Can't say," replied Guguste, tilting the soup-tureen to transfer the last drop of warm salt-water to his own plate.

"You mean *won't;* you *could* fast enough if you would, child!" said Madame Grégoire pettishly.

"Bah!" cried the *gamin*, (who was perhaps of opinion that the kicks, which, more than half-pence, constituted his salary in Monsieur Georges's service, formed a tie upon his discretions,)—"how can *you*, Ma'me Grégoire, who are such a very sensible woman, imagine it possible, that while I am clearing away the dinner things down stairs in the porter's lodge, or up stairs in Ma'mselle Berthe's chamber, I can have an eye to master's proceedings after he has crossed his threshold! Maybe he goes to the opera."

"Three nights in the week. But the other four?"

"There are fifteen theatres open, as I 've heard tell, in the city and the suburbs," quoth Guguste drily.

"But, gentlemen as *is* gentlemen (which is what Monsieur Georges calls himself, however he may be called by others,) don't put on diamond studs and embroidered waistcoats, to go to the playhouses!"

"Don't they? How should I know?" demanded Guguste, polishing the pewter spoon on his sleeve as he was accustomed to do those of his master's double-threaded silver. "What do I see of playhouses?"

"Why, you ungrateful child! didn't I give you a ticket for the pit of the Porte St. Martin, for that moving piece, 'The Spectre Abbot,' on the night of Ma'mselle Isoline's benefit, the deputy-double of the general-utility *jeune première*, who lodges up stairs in the back attic, next but one to your own?"

"Yes; I saw 'The Spectre Abbot,' and Ma'mselle Isoline into the bargain, with three-quarters of a yard of red calico hanging to her waist, to represent the 'Bleeding Nun;' but I didn't take any notice whether the gentleman whose elbows were jammed into my sides wore diamond studs or velvet waistcoats."

"At all events you must perceive that the highly-respectable gentleman who occupies our splendid first-floor apartment, (Monsieur Boncoeur, the deputy,) goes out every evening in his carriage in a very different costume?"

"Monsieur Boncoeur, in his carriage, need not hoist a flag of gentility. Monsieur Georges, on foot, might be hustled off the pavement but for his brilliants."

"More likely *for* them," said the porteress.

"Besides, Monsieur Boncoeur is, as you say, such a very respectable-looking gentleman! His dark, square-cut coat, and pepper-and-salts; his broad-brimmed hat, and sad-coloured gloves; his whole outward man seems to have been taken measure of as the picture of respectability! And see what that very respectability has brought him to! Partner in one of the first houses in the Rue Bergère; deputy in the chamber; *marguillier* of the parish; a ribbon in his button-hole; and the picture of himself and his ribbon face to face with the portrait of Louis Philippe, at the gallery of the Exposition, for all the world as if they 'd a little word to say to each other in public. Lord bless you! Monsieur Boncoeur's respectable grey whiskers, respectable speckled stockings, respectable great-coat and umbrella, are worth a couple of hundred thousand francs a year to the banking-house in the Rue Bergère, as vouchers for the square-toeishness of the firm!"

"Lord love thee, child! at thy years how shouldst thou know so much of the world!" cried Madame Grégoire, removing her spectacles after this tirade, as if all further perspicacity were superfluous.

"By being thrown upon it from the moment I had years to count," cried the urchin. "A foundling hospital, Ma'me Grég. is a famous whetstone, against which no one can rub without sharpening his wits !"

"But, since thine are so sharp, boy, how comes it thou hast never discovered whither Monsieur Georges directs his steps every evening, winter and summer, at half-past seven."

"Because 'tis my business to know, and I prefer my pleasure. I've some sort of *right*, you see, to interest myself in master's proceedings; but in those of Monsieur Boncoeur of the first floor, Ma'mselle Isoline of the attic, Madame la Baronne de Gimbecque, the pretty lady with the handsome *cachemires*, *coupé*, and black eyes, who lodges in the *entrésol*, and Madame Courson, the widow lady, on the *troisième*, I've nothing but wrong; and, accordingly, not a step do they take with which I am not conversant. I could tell you, if you wanted to know, where Madame Courson's poor, little, pale, patient daughter, Demoiselle Claire——"

"Thank ye,—thank ye! I fancy I know more of my lodgers than *you* do! All I ask you, is, concerning your master. Monsieur Georges is the only inmate of this house for whom it has ever been my fortune to pull the string without discovering, before the end of the first term, the source of his income, where he came from, whither he was going, and——

"Good evening, grandmamma!" squeaked a voice at the moveable pane of the glass-door,—the arrow-slit, or *meurtrière*, through which every porteress is privileged to parley with visitors at meal-times or in windy weather.

"'Tis Dodo!" exclaimed Guguste, rising to open the latch for the lean and impish-looking grandson of Madame Grégoire, whose wistful glances in eyeing the empty tureen plainly indicated that his visit had been miscalculated by a quarter of an hour.

"Mother desired me to call and inquire after the rheumatic pain in your right shoulder," continued Dodo, (the short for Dodore,— which is short for Theodore, in cockney Parisian.)

"'Twas in my left, and it has left me," said the old woman peevishly; "and don't sit on that chair, child. The knitting-needles in the stocking may do you a mischief. How 's your mother?"

"Mamma 's got a cold, sitting out in the showers yesterday afternoon, to finish shaving a poodle which a customer was werry particular to get done in time to go out to dinner."

"Humph! I fancied, Dodo, *you* had taken that part of the business off her hands. I thought she made over the scissors to you at Michaelmas last?"

"And so she did for anything of plain work," replied the brat; "but this was a choice customer, and a bit of fancy work; a great big grey *barbet*, which stands as high as a rocking-horse, whose master is curious in his shaving. The gentleman 's a poet, what does the off-rights *romantique* for Victor Hugo's plaything playhouse at the Porte St. Antoine; and, as the vulgars is apt to have their poodles lion-fashion, Monsieur Eugène gives hisn a mane and forelock; which, with cropped ears, looks for all the world like a unicorn!"

"What an ass!" cried Madame Grégoire contemptuously, tapping her snuff-box. "These poet and player folk makes themselves notorious, and fancies themselves famous!"

"And how goes on your own business, Dodo?" demanded Guguste, assuming in the presence of the starveling of nine years old the airs of a man of the world.

"Pretty smart, thank ye. I've just set up two new sparrow-traps in a ditch under the barrack-wall at Montrouge; and last week I sold a pair of as fine canaries as a coating of plaster of Paris and gamboge could make 'em, to a fine English lady in a carriage, as was crossing the bridge to the flower-market. Gave the brace of birds for nine francs, one of which I slipped into the hand of her *laquais de place*. But then I was out of business, you see, for three days a'twards, for fear of the police."

"Dodo, you'll be disgracing your family one of these days by being took up!" said Madame Grégoire impressively. "I remember my respectable first-floor, Monsieur Boncoeur, bringing home a piping bullfinch last year he'd bought on the Boulevards, whose red breast washed off the first showery day, all as one as Ma'mselle Isoline's rouge after a flood of tears in a melodrame! The poor dear gentleman had half a mind to have up the seller of the impositious bird before the commissary of the district; only, as he'd paid for it with an old coat unbeknownst to his valet, and an old coat not being lawful coin of the realm, there was a doubt in his mind about his power of bringing the vagabond to justice."

"Which? Himself, or the impositious bird, or the industrious fowler as was arning a living for his family?" inquired Guguste.

"Hush!" cried Madame Grégoire, laying her hand on the cord as Monsieur Georges' thin voice was heard giving utterance to his usual evening cry of "*Le cordon !*" Guguste slunk behind her high-backed chair as his tyrant passed the window,—his withered, sallow face enlivened by his gold-mounted spectacles, and his mean person coquetted into consequence, perforce of velvet and trinkets. Burnished from top to toe, he was the very moral of one of Giroux's toys, the very *immoral* of a *chevalier d'industrie*.

Certain that his master's exit would be the signal for his being fetched out of that, by the shrill summons of Ma'mselle Berthe to set the place in order, and make up the fire, (against the arrival of her cousin, Madame Dosne, an ex-box-opener of the Ambigu Comique, who occupied a chamber in the story above, and was admitted to the honour of seeing her prim relative play patience, and of sipping a glass of sugar and water with her on a long winter's evening,) Guguste flitted upward to the discharge of his duties, leaving the skinny imp of the Pont Neuf and his grandam to commune of domestic matters. While waiting the summons of Monsieur Boncoeur's demure-looking footman to open the gate for the demure-looking chariot of that highly demure and respectable individual, Madame Grégoire accordingly interrogated the boy concerning his father's absence from the sweets of his domestic hearth.

"Papa is making a tour in the south," replied the imp. "He passed the summer in the Pyrenees. The Pyrenees are quite in fashion in papa's line of business!"

"Ay, 'tis well for him that Gothon likes him to lead such a rambling life!" said Madame Grégoire in a moralizing tone. "When my poor daughter thought proper to marry a showman, I told her how it would be! To think, now, of a child of mine, a respectable *portière* in the same house, of the same parish, for forty years' standing."

" The house?"

" The *house*, ignoramus !—The house is a century old, built by the Regent Duke of Orleans, father of his unfortunate majesty, Louis XIV, as you might read in history, —if you knew how to read.—To think of a child of mine, I say, squatting on a wooden stool, like a wild Indian, winter and summer, with nothing but a cold river under her feet, and cold oil-cloth over her head, on the look-out for a poodle in want of clipping, or some mouse-eaten-out-of-house-and-home baker in want of a tabby kitten ! I protest I never think of my poor Gothon and her stock-in-trade,—her cage of cats on one side, and her string of puppies on the other,—without bitter anguish of soul. Why can't your father stay at home, Dodore, and set up in the Champs Elysées, or at the *barrières*, like other respectable men of his profession, to be nearer home ?"

" Bless your heart !" remonstrated Dodo, " papa took up his station three years ago, on the way along the Allée d'Antin, to the Suspension Bridge. But it all but made a bankrupt of him ! There was too much competition. Pierre the Savoyard, who had his show-box within fifty yards, has such a winning way with him that not a nurse-maid, or English lord coming out of Lepage's shooting-gallery, but used to throw silver to Pierre, where papa took only the brownest of copper. At last, a nasty, good-for-nothing, designing Jesuit of a fellow set up in opposition to both on 'em ; Scripture pieces, with Jepfa's daughters, and Dalily and Goliar, a hand-organ, and Dutch pug as held an old hat, and what not. Papa bore it as long as he was able ; but what was the good of opposition atween friends ? He 'd nothing in his box but worn-out things, as old as Methusalem or Jerusalem, or whatever it is, such as the battle of Marengo, and the Pyramids, and the landing of Xerxes in the Hellyspunt and a pack of low-lived fancies. So mamma persuaded him to try the provinces (where, as all the world knows, the stalest bread goes down) ; and so, from fair to fair, he 's been touring it this twelve-month."

" Poor Gothon !"

" Mamma doesn't fret. She says I shall soon be old enough to take papa's business off his shoulders, and then he 'll be able to retire comfortable ; and she 'll give up her stall on the Pont Neuf, and the kitten and canary line, to sister Mary."

Madame Grégoire was about to remonstrate against this perpetuation of open-air commerce in her posterity, when Monsieur Boncoeur's signal was given ; and, lo, the well-varnished, well-stuffed, but plain chariot of the thriving banker, rolled after his fat and bean-fed horses out of the court-yard.

Some minutes afterwards, his portly *femme de ménage*, Madame Alexandre, stepped into the lodge for a few minutes' gossip with the porteress previous to proceeding to her evening's *Boston* with the grocer's lady at the opposite corner. The comely housekeeper, in her silk-cloak and bonnet, was naturally an object of dislike and envy to the withered *portière*, in her ragged merino gown and dingy calico cap. But Christmas was approaching. Her *étrennes* for New Year's Day (to the sum total of which, the first-floor contributed three-fourths) were seldom absent from Madame Grégoire's calculations. Besides, Monsieur Boncoeur's housekeeper was to be conciliated as a connecting link in her chain of domestic investigation; for Madame Alexandre not only afforded her quota of information concerning her own and her master's affairs, but, in pure pryingness of spirit, contrived to see through stone-walls, and hear down chimneys, while striving to put this and that together concerning those of her fellow-lodgers.

"Well, Madame Grégoire, what is the best news with us this evening?" demanded the jolly dame, as soon as the porteress had despatched her hungry grandson home to his mamma, the kittens and canaries. "I'm just stepping out, you see, for my little game with the Pruins. Poor people, they can't do without me! If I warn't with them before the clock struck eight, I should be having them here after me; and, to be filling the house with visitors during master's absence, is a thing I'm not in the habit of doing, as nobody knows, better than yourself. Indeed, it's a matter of conscience that takes me out the moment his back is turned. As a *femme de confiance*, I'm bound to see there's no waste; and where there's visitors there *must* be tippling and stuffing; so, out of regard to Monsieur Boncoeur's property, I'm seldom in the house ten minutes after him. I hope I know my duty by so respectable a master better than to make away with his goods like Ma'mselle Berthe up yonder, who keeps open house like a lady, with as many rings at her bells of an evening as e'er a duchess in the land! But, as I was saying, Madame Grégoire,— (Dearie me, I thought I wasn't by no means comfortable! I've been sitting on the knitting-needles! lucky my cloak was wadded!)—as I was saying, have you made out anything further about them Coursons?"

"Scarce a syllable more than the first day they took possession! One knowed they was respectable, 'cause our proprietor is exceeding particular about references, — (there isn't a partic'larer landlord from one end of the Boulevards to t'other!)—and one knowed they was *poor*, 'cause their moveables came on a porter's truck, instead of occupying a cart and horse, as becomes a creditable lodger, or instead of occupying three vans of the *administration des déménagemens*, as was the case, I remember, when our respectable first-floor moved in."

Madame Alexandre smiled a neat and appropriate smile of acknowledgment for her master; while the porteress took breath, a pinch of snuff, and proceeded.

"But as to their origin, and sitch, I know no more than Adam! Not an acquaintance in the parish! I even put the water-carrier upon asking about the neighbourhood; but no such name as Courson was ever heard of! How do we know, pray, who we've got among us? Courson may be a sham name, such as we reads of in Monsieur Jules Janin's novels!"

"Such rubbish, indeed!" said Madame Alexandre, with a sneer, intended, like the epithet, to apply to the lodgers on the third-floor, ignored by the water-carrier and public-houses in the neighbourhood, *not* to Monsieur Janin's novels, which were probably familiar to them all.

"Would you believe it, ma'am? there's the saucy minx of a

daughter (Ma'mselle Claire, I think, you told me was her name,) has the owdacity to bid me good morning or good evening if I haps to meet her on the stairs, affable-like, as if she felt me her inferiorer! Me! Now I don't know, Ma'me Grégoire, what your opinion may be, but *I* holds (and so does my friends, the Pruins,) that the upper domestics of the first-floor is on a 'quality with the lodgers of the third, that keeps no domestics at all."

"Certainly, ma'am, certainly," replied the porteress, still harping on the amount of her New Year's gift. "But have you made out nothing of these people's occupations? You're two floors nigher to 'em than me. If I was in *your* place——"

"If you was in that of the housekeeper of Monsieur Georges, you mean! Ma'mselle Berthe's store-closet looks clean into Ma'mselle Claire's room."

"Looks dirty in," emended the prying porteress.

"And, if Ma'mselle Berthe wasn't as dry as a handful of deal shavings, maybe I might have demeaned myself to ask her in a friendly way how the young lady passed her mornings. But Ma'mselle Berthe (the *chissie!*) condescends to hold just about as much communication with me as one of the chayney mandarins on the top of master's cabinet,—shakes her head by way of salutation, and not a word!"

"But, Guguste (Monsieur Georges's little lad of all work and no play) assured me he saw Ma'mselle Courson ring at Monsieur Boncoeur's bell the other day, and deliver a letter to the footman."

"Oho! that dirty little *gamin* plays the spy upon those who rings at Monsieur Boncoeur's bell, do he?" cried the housekeeper, reddening. "Very dirty behaviour, I must confess!"

"But, my dear madam, my dear friend," whined the porteress in a tone of deprecation, "did not you yourself inform me that Monsieur Boncoeur's footman carried up on Sunday se'nnight, by Monsieur Boncoeur's desire, to Ma'mselle Claire, a box of apricot marmalade, and the last number of the '*Follet*'?"

"I said no such thing, ma'am, as I remember. The marmalade and the journal was both lawfully directed to Madame Courson. I never so much as insinnivated a word of an intention of attention to Mademoiselle!"

"Then I miscomprehended, ma'am; in which I'm the more to blame, because, from the highly-respectable character of the mansion for which I have the honour to pull the string, (there isn't, as I said before, a more partic'larer landlord than the proprietor from one end of the Boulevarts to t'other,) I might have known that even the letters of a gentleman so distinguished as my first-floor would never have been received by Ma'mselle, the daughter of Madame Courson."

"*That's* all you know about it,—is it?" cried the lusty housekeeper, crimsoning with pique. "Then be so good as to tell me what makes such a young lady as Ma'mselle, Madame Courson's daughter, write written letters to so distinguished a gentleman as your first-floor? Answer me that!"

"She couldn't be guilty of anything so heinous!" cried the porteress, aghast.

"I tell you she *was!*"

"You *must* be mistaken!"

" Seeing is believing, Madame Grégoire !"

" Ay ! you may have seen her *deliver* a written letter, poor dear, from her mamma, in all probability ?"

" No such thing !—from herself."

" Now, how can you possibly know ! Did you see her write it ? Do you even know her handwriting ?"

" I know her signature,—' Claire de Courson ;' and you told me your werry self, that the agreement for the lodgings was signed by her mother as ' Emilie de Courson.' "

" But the signature was inside the written letter. How could you see *that ?*"

" No matter ; I did see it with my two eyes as plain as I see you."

" And that's plain enough," muttered Guguste, who, having crept back unobserved into the room, was skulking in a corner.

" Why, sure you didn't go to peep ?" said the porteress, with a knowing look of inquiry and accusation.

" What a one you are !" cried Madame Alexandre, trying to turn off jocularly her self-betrayal. " But, not to haggle with partic'lars of how the letter came into my hands, into my hands it came ; and what should it be, but a private confidential *tête-à-tête* epistle from the young lady, saying how Monsieur Boncoeur's reputation for benevolence was up in the neighbourhood, and how he seemed inclined to befriend her poor mother, (the apricot marmalade, you know !) and how it would be a great charity (no, not charity,—act of humanity the shabby-genteels calls it,) if he would exert his interest to procure for her mamma a privilege to sell stamps, a *bureau de papier timbré ;* for which, of course, his petitioner was ever bound to pray, and so forth."

" I hope they don't think of setting up anything in the shop or office line in a house like ourn ?" cried Madame Grégoire, with dignity. " They 'll find theirself plaguily out of their reckoning !— for I must say it, who shouldn't say it, that there isn't a more partic'larer landlord."

" I 'll just tell you what," ruthlessly interrupted Madame Alexandre, twitching her silk cloak, as if meditating departure. " To-night's Monday, you know."

" Yes, I *do* know."

" And that 's the reception-night, you know, of the Minister of the Home Department."

" No, I didn't know."

" And, as sure as life,——"

" Lord lovee, Ma'me Alexandre, don't use that profane expression ! There 's nothing less sure than life !" cried Madame G. while Auguste groaned in the background.

" As sure as a gun, then——"

Again Auguste groaned.

" —Master 's gone this evening to the hotel of the *Ministre de l'Interieur*, to present Ma'mselle Claire's petition for a stamp-office."

" Do you raally think things of that sort are done in that sort of straight-for'ard way ?" demanded the porteress. " *I* fancied that, when you wanted anything of government, you got a word said for you to the cousin of some clerk-of-a-deputy-to-an-under-commissioner, with, maybe, a genteel little offering, to make it go down,—such as a Savoy cake, or a China rose-tree in a flower-pot."

"Nonsense! You're thinking of folks of your own species," said the housekeeper disdainfully.

"You forget that my master, Monsieur Boncoeur,'s a representative of the nation, a governor of the Bank of France, and a *marguillier* of the parish. Master's a right to go straight an end to the king, and tell his majesty any little wish he may have ungratified. And, if he *should* think proper to mention to Louis Philippe Ma'mselle Claire's desire that her mamma should set up a bureau for stamps, her business is done!"

They were interrupted by the starting up of Guguste, who was crouching behind them, and placed an admonitory finger on his lip to impose silence upon Madame Grégoire's meditated rejoinder, just as a very white hand, holding a very black key, was intruded into the room through the porter's window; and the silvery accents of Mademoiselle Courson were heard, announcing to the porteress that she was going out for half an hour; and that, though her mother remained at home, she was indisposed, and could receive no visitors."

"*Visitors*, indeed! Who ever comes to visit *them*, I should like to know!" muttered Madame Grégoire, after pulling the *cordon* to admit of the young lady's egress.

"She certainly *had* a bundle under her arm!" cried Madame Alexandre, who had been watching the young lady through the window. "Now, how I *should* like to know where she's going."

"To the pharmacy, for medicine for her mother, or to the herborist for lime-blossoms, to make *tisanne*," said Guguste, who shrewdly anticipated a request on the part of the elderly ladies that he would arise and play the spy upon the movements of Mademoiselle Claire.

"Pho! pho! The old lady's only trouble-sick, which would be a deal worse than body-sick, only that it don't require no physic," observed the porteress.

"Then she's gone to the laundress."

"Laundress, indeed!" cried the fat housekeeper; "as if low-lived people like the third-floor wasn't their own laundress!"

"Pardon me, my dear Ma'me Alexandre," cried the porteress. "You know we don't allow no hanging out in *this* house. There's not a more partic'larer landlord in ——"

"'Tis my true and honest belief," interrupted the lady in the silk-cloak, "that the girl is gone to the Mont de Piété! I said to Robert, our footman, when he was taking up master's apricot marmalade, that 'twould be a deal more to the purpose if he took up a good dish of cutlets, or a *fricandeau;* for, as you and I was agreeing t' other day, my dear Ma'me Grégoire, not an ounce of anything eatable beyond daily bread ever goes up these blessed stairs to the third-floor. And, what's more, I've noticed strange changes in Miss and Madam since they took up in the house; I don't mean in point of growing thin and meagre, 'cause care alone, without starving, will bring the poor body of a poor soul down to nothing. But, the day as their goods came in, Ma'mselle Courson had as good a cloak over her shoulders as the one on mine (which cost me a good hundred and thirty livres in the Passage de l'Orme,) and Ma'mselle Claire's having a velvet collar doubtless might be counted at twenty more. What 's become of it, I should like to know ?"

" Ay, what 's become of it, eh ?" added the porteress, tapping her box.

" *Certes !* people that *has* a comfortable cloak is apt to put it on such nights as this !" rejoined the housekeeper; "but I say nothing."

" The young lady may have lent it to her mamma, who is indisposed," pleaded Guguste. " Fuel is ris' within the week. I don't suppose they 've too much fire."

" Lent it to her mamma, indeed !" cried Madame Alexandre. " Why, Madame Courson has as handsome a Thibet shawl as ever came out of Ternaux's factory."

" *Had,*" emended the porteress. " I haven't seen the red shawl on her shoulders these three weeks. On that point I has my suspicions."

A single rap, Parisian-wise, at the *porte cochère,* produced the usual professional tug at the *cordon.* The gate flew open ; and, peeping in at the window-pane, was seen the rubicund face of Monsieur Paul Emile Pruin, the grocer, come in search of his loitering guest.

" So, so, so !" cried he, on detecting her in the thick of gossip with the grandmamma of Dodore. " *This* is the way you keep your appointments, *ma belle voisine ?* Haven't we had the hearth made up these three quarters of an hour, candles snuffed, (*bougies de l'étoile,* always a-snuffing !) a fresh bottle of *groseille frambroisée* ready to be uncorked, and a batch of *biscuits de Rheims* ready to be opened ?— Saw *Monsieur le Député's* carriage bowl out, and been hoping ever since to see you bowl in. Poor Madame Paul in the fidgets, as if she 'd swallowed a flight of swallows,—up and down,—in and out. Sent me over with the umbrella to look after you."

" Thank you,—thank you !" cried Madame Alexandre. " 'Tis the first of the month, you see," she continued, winking at the blind old porteress (to whom a nod and wink were much alike) to back her apologies. " I 'd my little postage account to settle with my good friend here. But now I 'm at your service. *Allons !*"

" Guguste, my dear, show the lantern to Madame Alexandre over the *ruisseau,*" said the porteress, turning round to look for her boarder. But Guguste had disappeared. He had perhaps sneaked away to track the mysterious footsteps of Mademoiselle de Courson.

MARTIAL IN TOWN.

THE SERVANT OUT OF LIVERY.

DANDLE ! when thou art asked abroad,
It is not for thy wit reward :
We know that thou canst draw a cork ;
In carving, use thy knife and fork ;
Canst hand the tea-cups round at tea,
And hold an urchin on each knee ;
Canst sort the cards, set tables right,
And see old ladies home at night :
With talents of such vast display,
Thou 'rt but a servant for the day !

ASTRONOMICAL AGITATION.

REFORM OF THE SOLAR SYSTEM.

FROM OUR OWN REPORTER.

YESTERDAY, a numerous and highly respectable meeting of gentlemen and ladies interested in the stability of the solar system was held, pursuant to advertisement in the Vox Stellarum, True Sun, &c. at the sign of the Great Bear in the North Hemisphere, at One P. M. (sidereal time).

Long before the hour named, the neighbouring constellations were crowded with a brilliant assemblage of all the beauty and fashion of the upper regions. Amongst the glittering throng we noticed nearly all the stars of any magnitude occupying their accustomed places, together with deputations from various influential bodies interested in the support of the system; the principal Nebulæ, several Signs of the Zodiac, a deputation from the Electro-magnetic Grand Junction Company, and from the Galvanic Branch Association, his Highness the Meridian with several degrees of Longitude, the Equator with the Latitudinarian party, the Torrid Zone and his Tropics, their High Mightinesses the Hurricanes, Mr. Monsoon and the Trades' Union of the South Hemisphere, the Æthereal and Atmospheric Alliance Company, and, though last not least, their Royal Highnesses the Planets, who came in state, attended by a guard of honour of their Satellites in rings and belts, under a royal salute of Thunder and Lightning.

The great Area of the Constellation was brilliantly lit with Zodiacal light. Notwithstanding the exertions of a strong party of the Centrifugal Police Force, assisted by the Comets from the out-stations under Inspector Halley, and a detachment of the South African Asteroids, (sent by Sir W. Herschel from head-quarters at the Cape,) the atmospheric pressure was nearly insupportable, and several of the ladies were nearly absorbed by the crowd. Ceres, Pallas, and Vesta appeared to suffer intensely; and we deeply regret to state that one of the Pleiads is still missing, to the great regret of her lovely sisters and their brilliant circle. The disorderly conduct of a White Squall (introduced by Mr. Monsoon) was as conspicuous as the undeviating and steady regularity of the members of the Trades' Union. Discordant cries of "Adjourn!" "Adjourn to the Milky Way!" quite drowned the music of the Spheres.

On the arrival of the Planets, the meeting accordingly adjourned to the Via Lactea. Cassiopea's Chair (kindly lent for the occasion) was impartially, if not brilliantly, filled by our old and steady friend the Pole Star; his fair neighbour and *protegée*, Aurora Borealis, acted as secretary, and excited universal admiration by her brilliant rapidity.

The Man in the Moon then rose, and said he had been deputed by the Sidereal and Solar System Self-supporting Societies, to lay before the meeting a statement of their reasons for assembling. His indifference to all sublunary considerations was well known, and he was utterly incapable of casting reflections upon any body; but he must solemnly declare that the constant annoyances and insults which he received from his neighbours the Terrestrials were enough to inflame the temper of a Fixed Star. (Cheers from the Sidereal benches.) He had heard much of Tellurian attractions; but he was fortunately not of a warm temperament, and he would never so far deviate from the orbit of moral rectitude as to yield to them. The very idea of forming a Tellurian connexion was repulsive to him: and with his Eccentric tendency, unless he were warmly supported by the Influential Members of the System, and by that admirable institution the Centrifugal Force, he trembled for the consequences of the continuance of such conduct on the part of the Earth; he should hazard his very Equilibrium, and expose himself to an attack of Parabola. ("Shame!" and groans.) Ever since that scoundrel Daniel O'Rourke had obtruded himself upon him, he had had no peace: the sanctity of Sidereal society had been invaded, and the mysteries of the Lunarian Œconomy unveiled. (Loud cries of "Shame!" from Mars and Venus.) He had been, in common with many of those whom he was addressing, travestied at the Terrestrial theatres. (A voice, "The Olympic!") He had been exposed to the naked eye by astronomical lecturers, without even the decent intervention of a spy-glass. Whichever way he turned his phase, they followed him. But he would proceed at once to that which had principally induced him to address them; he meant the Monster Balloon (Confusion) and its crew. (Cries of "Down with 'em!" "Nebulize 'em!" "Tip 'em the Meteorics!" &c.) Yes, they had defied the elements, violated the whole of the Gravitation laws, and endangered the stability of the system itself. (Cheers.) He (the Honourable Lunarian) did not know where they would stop. Other aeronauts had respected Lunatic and Sidereal dignity, and had had the decency to perform their antics by daylight; but these Balloon Monsters, these vile Misouranists had done it burglariously, and by starlight. He had indeed been spared the indignity of beholding them; but all celestial security was at an end, and he did not know when he rose any evening, whether he should be allowed to set again in peace."

(The worthy Luminary, overpowered by his feelings, sank beneath the Horizon in a Halo of tears, amidst thunders of applause.)

The Winds rose all at once, and attempted to make themselves heard; and many of the Siderealists being anxious to neutralize all opposition, much irregularity and many disturbances ensued, but, the Fixed Stars surrounding the Chair, and the Centrifugal Force interfering, order was restored, and

Mr. Zephyr, of the Trades' Union, in a scarcely audible whisper, commenced by expressing his regret at the surface of the meeting having been ruffled by anything which had *fallen from the Moon.* (Corruscations of laughter.) The Moon rose to order. "It was a vile slander of the grovelling Terrestrials,—he never let anything fall: the meteoric stones—" ("Order, order!") "Mr. Zephyr proceeded. He had expected a breeze, but was quite unprepared for such a blowing up. (Cheers.) His own course had been uniformly steady, and the principles by which he was actuated were now ascertained and appreciated by high and low. He was neither a Lunatic nor a Terrestrial, but of the Atmospheric Juste Milieu,—in short, an Aerialist. Whilst he opposed all undue Planetary influence, and disliked a Sidereal ascendency, he abhorred a Vacuum, and was deeply interested in the stability of the Solar System. He could with confidence appeal to his worthy neighbours the Tropics, and to the whole constituency of the Torrid Zone for the confirmation of his assertions. ("Hear, hear!" from Cancer and Capricorn.) He had been accused of blowing hot and cold, (Ironical cheers from Messrs. Boreas and Auster,) but that was merely because he was not violent,—not a regular Destructive, like some of his neighbours, who were always kicking up a dust, and never knew when to stop. (Cheers from the Trades.) But he would no longer deviate from his course. It must, he thought, be clear to the least reflecting surfaces, that these large meetings had a tendency to cause disturbances, and to lead to serious irregularities. Many of the Stars would be out all night, and he feared that some of their Royal Highnesses the Planets would find it impossible to perform their necessary revolutions in proper time. How could they expect to find Honourable Luminaries ready to undertake the onerous duties of acting as Morning Stars if all this night-work were to be allowed? How was it possible, for instance, for Jupiter to go his circuit, or for Georgium Sidus to keep his distance? ("Order!") He looked upon the Balloon and its crew as mere trifles, light as air. There was no danger of their rising above their own petty sphere. It was quite clear that they were within the Gravitation laws: if they transgressed them, they would be very soon placed *in vacuo*, and the full penalty levied under the Newton act. That penalty amounted to a prohibition, for it not only inflicted sixteen feet perpendicular for the first second, but went on in a rapidly-increasing proportion. He must be excused for disbelieving the alleged Eccentricity of the worthy Luminary who rose last. He thought his anticipations of premature Parabola mere moonshine; he appeared to him to have viewed the light in which he was regarded by the Terrestrials through a most distorted medium. He could assure him that he had lately become the observed of all observers. The Fixed Stars were much better appreciated, and were considered as peculiarly well calculated for their places: even the Nebulæ were beginning to be properly estimated; and a very graphic account of the Double Stars had made them better known, and had displayed their peculiar sympathies, and numerous and unprecedented attractions. Even the necessity of Periodical Revolutions was now admitted below as well as above, and there appeared a strong tendency to a system of Universal Centralization. His worthy friends the Atmospherics would bear him out in saying that the doctrine of ' Pressure from without' was understood and acted on to its fullest extent, and that an important Displacement was generally anticipated. He begged to be allowed to subside by moving an adjournment *sine die*." (At this period our reporter was obliged to leave; but we are happy to say there was every prospect of Mr. Zephyr's motion being carried.)

THE ADVENTURES OF A TALE.

BY THE HON. MRS. ERSKINE NORTON.

"I could [and will] a tale unfold!"—*Hamlet.*

It is with indignation such only as a literary composition, conscious of its own high value, and smarting under injustice and neglect, can be supposed to feel, that I lift up my voice from behind the serried ranks of my companions, long tales and short, the light effusion of three pages, or the decided weight of three volumes; serious tales or gay; moral or profane; fine French or low Irish; tales without an end, and tales that ought never to have had a beginning; tales in ponderous verse or in gossamer prose; the delicate and brittle ware called travellers' tales; or those more substantial and important-looking matters, political economy tales. I say, that from behind this prodigious phalanx I rise up like Erskine from behind the big-wigs of the first law-court he addressed, elevating myself as the young counsellor on his bench, and making myself heard,—not, it is true, in the general cause of justice, liberty, humanity, and so forth, but in that cause in which all, if not eloquent, are at least earnest and sincere,—in the cause of self.

It is said that Minerva (a goddess) sprang from the brain of Jupiter without a mamma; I, Seraphina (a tale), issued forth from the lovely head (I am not quite so sure of the brain) of a fair romantic young lady, without a papa;—at least so I presume, for my composition is purely feminine; my slight and delicate texture could only have been woven by an unassisted female imagination.

While yet in embryo, I was christened Seraphina, and was to be composed in three or four reasonably long letters (ladies' letters, crossed and re-crossed with different coloured inks,) to Clementina. My respected parent decided that there was nothing equal to the epistolary form for describing the sentiments and adventures of a heroine; for, who like herself can lay open all those finer and minuter feelings of the inmost heart, pouring into the ear of sympathising friendship every wish, every hope, every thought? Soul meets soul, even through the vulgar medium of pens, ink, and paper; "thoughts that glow and words that burn," are traced by the delicate fingers that "resume the pen," with a celerity altogether surprising; no agitation can delay, no fatigue can excuse; the half-dozen sheets of foolscap that are to be run over before she can lay her throbbing temples on her pillow, her white drapery (i. e. her night-gown) floating round her, her long hair unbound (very much out of curl), her snowy feet on the cold marble (she has lost her slippers), her door carefully locked, but her trellised casement left open, that the pale moonbeams may peep through it; her lamp is decaying, her hands are trembling, her eyes swimming in tears;—*n'importe*, the six sheets of foolscap are finished! O, there is nothing like the epistolary form! Seraphina shall be in letters to Clementina;

> "Sure, letters were invented for some wretch's aid,
> Some absent lover, or some captive maid."—Pope.

I can just recollect, as I began to assume form and consistency, how much and how dearly I was fondled by my young and doting mother; indeed, at times, I ran some danger of being killed by kindness. While transcribing some of the deeply affecting scenes and sentiments with which I abound, I was nearly obliterated by her tears, my material parts being composed with a very fine pen and very pale ink ; at other times, when the stronger passions took possession of the scene, and revenge, hatred, and fury predominated, she would crush me in her hand, " her eyes in a fine frenzy rolling," and throw me to the other end of the room. Of course she had some difficulty in smoothing me out again. Nevertheless I grew in stature, and in favour with mamma, myself, and four young ladies, her neighbours, (all under fifteen,) who were at home for the holidays. On the assembling of this little coterie, I was mysteriously brought forth from my perfumed drawer, where I lay covered with dried rose-leaves, and read by the author of my being, in a way in which an author only can read. My young auditory listened in profound attention and admiration, secretly resolving that they too would try their unfledged wings in authorship, when they had left off school and finished their education. Except to these four interesting girls, my existence was a profound secret.

My composition is certainly enough to excite emulation, however hopeless. I am (though I say it myself) an exquisite tale. My heroine is a model of beauty, virtue, tenderness, and thrilling sensibility ; " a perfect wonder that the world ne'er saw ;" therefore the world ought the more to appreciate so rare a conception. Her mother was a suffering angel on earth ; but, happily for herself, she removed to a more congenial abode, while her cherub child was yet in infancy. The surviving parent is, of course, a horrid tyrant, who cannot comprehend the highly-wrought sensibilities of his daughter, and therefore will not give way to them. There is the suitor favoured by the father, and the lover favoured by the daughter. There are a locking up, an elopement, delicate and dubious situations full of excitement, misapprehensions of all kinds, a false female friend, libertine lords, fine unfeeling ladies, dark stormy nights, and a catastrophe of the most extraordinary, pathetic, and soul-subduing interest. And then my descriptions of nature ! my silver moon and diamond stars ! my rustling trees ! my woodbine, jessamine, and violets !

A little conceit I acknowledge to, when copied on pale pink, gilt-edged paper, curiously ornamented with embossed loves and doves, written in a neat small running-hand, the tails of my letters prettily curled, plenty of dashes, and very few stops, I was thus headed :

SERAPHINA ; OR, SUFFERING SENSIBILITY.

A TALE.

BY A FAIR UNKNOWN.

" Love rules the camp, the court, the grove,
    And man below, and saints above,
    For love is heaven, and heaven is love."
                                        Lay of the Last Minstrel.

I was highly scented, and sealed in green wax, with a device of Cupid tormenting a heart.

The dignified Half-yearly was selected for my debut. It rarely admitted literature of my class, and such only of acknowledged merit ; consequently it was considered my proper and natural medium. From it, I was to be commented on and extracted in the monthlies, as well in Edinburgh and Dublin as in London; I was to be pirated by the Americans and translated by the French; and at the end of the year I was, by express permission, to appear in one of the most fashionable annuals, my tenderest scene forming the subject of a gorgeous frontispiece, on which the most celebrated artists were to lavish their talents. The identification of the "Fair Unknown" was to become the puzzle of the season; and already many scenes of admiring wonder on the part of others, and of dignified modesty on her own, had been played off in the active imagination of my dear parent: the acknowledgement of Evelina by its young authoress to her father, and the final recognition of the *Great* Unknown, were her models.

At length, with this dazzling perspective before me, I was dismissed from the maternal embrace. Betty the housemaid slipped with me out of the street-door, holding me with a piece of white paper between her finger and thumb, to prevent her soiling my envelope; while my mother watched us from the window with tears in her eyes. On reaching the twopenny post-office, Betty without any ceremony pushed me through a slit beneath a window, and, to my great discomposure, I fell head over heels into a dirty box full of all sorts of queer-looking epistles. As might be expected, I painfully felt this my first tumble (for I cannot call it *step*) into real from imaginary life. I had scarcely time to recover from the shock before the box was withdrawn, and we were all turned out by a fat woman on a horrid thing called a counter, where we were *sorted*, as she termed it, and distributed, with a rapidity that was quite confounding, to three or four shabby-looking men having bags under their arms. I, being the first turned out, was the last the post-mistress clawed up. She retained me a full minute, twirled me round, examined my seal, thrust her great finger between my delicate side folds, and brought me up to her eye to peer if possible into my inside, when the monster who held his bag open to receive me, called out,

"Come, mistress,—can't wait no longer!"

"Well," she replied, "bless me, if this don't look for all the world like a walentine!" and into the bag she reluctantly dropped me, writhing as I was with pain and indignation.

When I had somewhat smoothed my ruffled plumes, I ventured to look round on my fellow-travellers, in search of some congenial spirit with whom I might beguile the tediousness of time, as we jolted along on the shoulders of the postman; but I looked round in vain. My nearest neighbour, to my great annoyance, was a butcher's bill, with whom every jolt brought me in contact; the dirty thing had a wet wafer prest down by a greasy thumb. I shrank from it with horror, and fell back on an epistle from a young gentleman at school, which was at least clean, and in fair round characters; so I attended to what it had to say. The date took up a large portion of the paper, and then: "My dear mamma,—I have the pleasure to inform you that our Christmas vacation begins on the 20th. I am very well. I hope you are very well. I hope my papa is very well; and my brothers and sisters, my uncles, aunts, and cousins. I beg my duty to my papa, my love to my brothers and sisters, my respects to my uncles and aunts, and my remembrances to my cousins; and believe me your dutiful son." I sighed, and turned to a business-like looking letter, directed in a precise hand to Messrs. ——, in some dark

lane in the city. The names of the persons addressed, and a very
exact date, took up, as in the schoolboy's letter, a vast deal of room,
and then it began : "Gentlemen,—We beg to acknowledge your
favour of the 1st instant—" I could not get any further, for I was
suddenly attracted by a smart-looking and very highly scented affair, sealed, and directed to a lord; but was disappointed on finding
it was only a Bond-street perfumer's little yearly account of one
hundred and fifty pounds for perfumes, fine soaps, cold-cream, and
tooth-brushes. There was no other very close to me, so I ventured gently to push my way to a curiously folded epistle directed
to Miss Matilda Dandeville, Oxford-street : "Dear Tilly,—Pray send
me, as soon as you can, my close bonnet, for my nose is nearly off
from wearing my pink silk and blonde this freezing weather. Full
of life and fun here ! Shall tell you all when we meet. It will be
your turn next; meantime, business, business ! money, money ! Love
to all inquiring friends." I felt disgusted. Do not gentlemen and
ladies write by the twopenny-post? Nothing but duns, bills, business, and money ! Is there no sense, sentiment, or sensibility, to
be found in a twopenny-postbag? I certainly did observe some
fashionable-looking letters, and one decidedly with a coronet; but
they were too far down, quite unattainable; so I drew myself up as
much apart as possible from the things by which I was so unhappily
surrounded, and remained the rest of the way in dignified stillness.
My wounded feelings were somewhat soothed by observing the awe,
mingled with curiosity, with which I was regarded; and somewhat
amused by the perfumer's genteel account turning its back on the
butcher's bill, and the lady of the pink and blonde squeezing herself
into a corner to avoid contact with a housemaid. The schoolboy
alone was at perfect liberty,—and a great annoyance he was,—evidently delighting to jumble us all together by a single jump, and
constantly peering at my seal, trying to read my address, and touching my embossed and gilded edges.

At length we reached our district, and that nervous sound, the
postman's rap, was heard in rapid succession down the street; heads
were popped out at windows, and doors were opened, and pence
ready, before we reached. Out hopped the housemaid, out jumped
the school-boy; and, as my fellow-travellers departed, I sank gradually lower, until I arrived among the genteel-looking letters I had
spied at a distance; a slight shuffle was perceptible among them:
their black and red seals were erected with great gravity, and my
pink dye became almost crimson when I found that, from the gaiety
of my attire, they evidently thought me "no better than I should
be;" however I had scarcely time to feel uneasy, so swift were our
evolutions, and so completely were we all turned topsy-turvy every
time the postman's hand was introduced among us, and that was every
minute; the big-wigs lost their dignity, and as to me, I felt my seal
crack like a lady's stay-lace; I thought my envelope was torn away,
and that I myself would have been displayed. Shocked at the
very idea of such a catastrophe, I sank senseless to the bottom of the
bag, and only recovered on being violently shaken from it, and hearing my brutal conductor exclaim: "Why, here it is, to be sure;
and if it isn't the walentine itself, I declare !" He seized his pence,
and, folding up his empty bag, strode off.

I found myself in the hands of a respectable man-servant out of livery, who, after having examined me with a look of surprise, introduced me up stairs into rather a dark and heavy drawing-room, with, however, a cheerful fire, bookcases, and portraits of distinguished authors. I lay for some time on a circular table, which was covered with newspapers and periodicals: there was a dead silence; if I had had a heart, it would have beaten audibly. At length a side-door opened, and a young gentleman stept in from an adjoining room; he glanced his eyes over the table, evidently in search of letters from the post; and, when he saw me, he smiled, and, picking me up, carried me into the room he had just left. I am sure he must have felt me tremble in his grasp. In this apartment, the only furniture was chairs and three writing-tables, the two smaller of which were occupied by my bearer and another young gentleman; but at that in the centre was seated a grave elderly personage, rather large in person, with bushy eyebrows, and keen penetrating eyes. I, who was extremely ignorant at that time, and had heard much of the knowledge, power, and dignity of the Half-yearly, without exactly knowing what it was, took this gentlemen for it himself. My introducer held me up to his young companion, and a stifled laugh passed between them; but, recovering his gravity, he laid me on the Half-yearly's desk, as near under his spectacles as he could bring me without interrupting his pen. The old gentleman started, frowned, and, lowering his head, looked at me from above his spectacles, (an awful way of looking, as is well known,) inquiring gruffly, "What's this?" "A letter by the twopenny, sir; a lady's verses I should think, by its appearance." "D—— ladies' verses! Take it away." "Shall we open it, sir?" "Don't pester me!" and in an instant afterwards he was lost in his important meditations.

The two young gentlemen cut round my seal, and perused the note of the Fair Unknown, with tears—but not of sympathy. I was then taken up, and passages here and there recited in an under-tone with mock gravity, eliciting, in spite of their dread of their superior, bursts of irrepressible laughter: these, at last, attracted his attention, and, looking over his shoulder, he angrily inquired what they were about. "Pray, sir, do look at this! it is quite a curiosity;" and my note was handed to him.

"A fair unknown, with that modesty which ever accompanies genius; with faltering accent, timid step, and eyes that seek the ground, presumes to lay at the feet of the great Half-yearly the first-born of her imagination! She prays him not to spurn the babe; but to take it, cherish it, and usher it into the world!—It is his own!"

"Mine!" exclaimed the Half-yearly, settling his wig; "I hope she does not mean to swear it to me; such scrapes are marvellously difficult to get out of. Wafer up the babe, if you please, gentlemen, in a sheet of foolscap, (its proper swaddling band,) and add a sentence to our Notices to Correspondents."

In a few weeks after this memorable scene, my young and tender parent was at breakfast with her family, when her father entered, carrying a new Half-yearly, with leaves uncut, and hot from the press, under his arm. My mother's heart leaped in her bosom, her face became scarlet, and her mouthful of bread and butter nearly choked her. Her father dawdled a little over the advertisements and answers to correspondents: at the latter he smiled. "What amuses you, sir?" inquired his anxious daughter in a tone of forced calmness: he read, " A Fair Unknown is earnestly requested to send for her babe immediately; the Half-yearly having no intention of cherishing, fostering, furthering, or fathering it in any way whatever." It was well for his thunderstricken auditor that the reader became immediately too much absorbed in a political paper to notice the effect of this appalling blow. She made her escape unobserved: I was instantly sent for, torn from my coarse envelope, and pressed to her agonised bosom.

Her four friends had returned to school, she could not therefore have the benefit of their advice and condolence; and, to tell truth, she did not appear much to regret this circumstance,—the mortification of their presence would have been too great.

Betty was not even let into the secret: I was placed in a plain white envelope, accompanied by a note much less romantic than the first, addressed to a Monthly; and, being sealed with a more respectable and well-behaved seal, she hid me in her muff, and dropped me herself into the same dirty box as before.

The Monthly was not nearly so terrible a person as the Half-yearly. He was not at home on my arrival in the evening, and I was laid with several other very literary-looking letters on a table in his dressing-room, near a good fire, with a lamp ready to light, a pair of slippers on the hearth-rug, and a large easy chair with a dressing-gown thrown over it. All this looked sociable and comfortable; and, feeling quite in spirits, I curtsied respectfully to a moral paper, shook hands with a political argument, chatted with a *jeu d'esprit*, and flirted with a sonnet.

The Monthly returned home about midnight in exceeding good humour, humming an opera tune; he lit his lamp, donned his dressing-gown, thrust his feet into his slippers, and, having mused a little while over the fire, ventured a glance at the table. "The deuce take it, what a lot there are of them!" he exclaimed; "politics, morality, and poetry I am not fit for to-night, that's very clear; something entertaining—what's this?" (taking up me)—"a woman's hand—prose—a tale—just the very thing!" and forthwith I was begun.

Reader, can you imagine—no, you cannot, so there is no use in appealing to your sympathy—the state of agitation I was in? He read amazingly fast, and hummed and ha'ed as he proceeded; and, to my utter astonishment, at one of my most pathetic appeals he burst into a fit of laughter: in short—I grieve to say it—but I fear the Monthly, as indeed he himself had hinted, had indulged a little too freely,—had taken a little drop too much; for, soon after this unaccountable explosion of merriment, he yawned, settled himself more decidedly in his chair, read very much slower, and at last, on observing that he turned over two of my pages at once without finding it out, I ventured to look up, and, behold! his eyes were closing,—sleep was creeping over him! I lay aghast, every moment inclining more and more backwards, till I reposed upon his knee. The pangs of wounded pride, acute as they were, began to give way to apprehensions of the most serious nature; his hold momentarily relaxed, and at length I fell—fell over the fender, reader! and there I lay, roasting like a Spanish priest cooked by a French soldier, (the French, they say, are excellent cooks,) until he should discover the hidden treasures of his monastery.

Alas! I thought *my* treasures were lost for ever to the literary world! There they lay, scorching and melting, until at last fortunately a cinder, inspired no doubt by the Muses, leapt out to my protection, and, by destroying a small portion, saved the remainder; for the smell of fire became so strong, that a servant, who had just let himself into the house from a high-life-below-stairs party, came rushing in with a nose extended to its utmost width, rousing and alarming his sleeping master. "Deuce take it!" exclaimed the Monthly on perceiving me, "in ten minutes more we should have been all set on fire by this d—d *soporific* (I think that is what he called me). Who would have thought it had spirit enough to burn!" The next morning I was despatched home, without a single line, not even an apology, for my miserable condition.

The curse of Cain was upon me: my own mother (who had become engaged in the creation of another offspring) received me with mortifying coolness, and beheld my burnt and disfigured tale with horror and contempt. She gave up all thoughts of the London annuals, (her new pet was intended for one of them,) and, having coarsely repaired me, I was put into the general post, addressed to a country annual, the "Rosebud" of Diddle-town.

The glowing aspirations of youth were chilled, misfortune had set her seal upon me; but, although hope was diminished, pride remained unquelled, for, as I glided over high-ways, and jolted over by-ways, in the Diddle-town coach, I recalled to my recollection all that I had heard (especially while I lay smothered up for six weeks on the learned Half-yearly's table) of the many great luminaries of literature who had struggled into light and life through the dark and chilling mists of neglect, ignorance, and envy. I had no doubt but that I should yet burst forth from my cloud, astonishing and dazzling the weak eyes which had hitherto refused to encounter, or were incapable of dwelling upon, my beauty and brilliancy.

On being presented to the Diddle-town editor, he immediately seized upon me with great glee, and carried me off, without reading me, to the printer's devil; and, to my utter astonishment, I found myself in the process of printing an hour after my arrival. Although this consummation had long been devoutly wished, I cannot say I was much flattered at its mode.

I appeared in the "Rosebud" of Diddle-town. The editor gave out that I was the production of a celebrated lady-author, anonymous on the occasion to all but him. I was demurely listened to by a coterie of old maids, who, on my conclusion, curtsied to the reader and curtsied to each other, sighed, and inquired if there were a picture; I was hummed over by two or three lazy half-pay officers; I was spelt over by a cottage-full of young lace-makers; and I was wept over by the Diddle-town milliners' apprentice girls.

But my desire for a larger and nobler sphere of action can no longer be suppressed: I am determined to make known that I exist, and to inform the reading world, and all who, like many great philosophers of old, are eager to seek what they are never likely to find, that the Tale of Seraphina reposes in all its neglected sweetness, and unappreciated, because unappreciable beauty, on the leaves of the "Rosebud" of Diddle-town.

WHEN AND WHY THE DEVIL INVENTED BRANDY.

A POPULAR TRADITION FROM THE DUCHY OF SAXE-MEININGEN;
TRANSLATED FOR
THE BENEFIT OF THE TEMPERANCE SOCIETIES.*

MANY years ago, our village (Steinbach) and Winterstein (in the Duchy of Saxe-Gotha) disputed about the common boundaries. Witnesses were called from both sides; but the dispute could not be brought to an end, because each of them spoke in favour of his own village. Amongst these witnesses were two men,—the one a native of Steinbach, and the other of Winterstein,—who had been instructed in magic by the devil, to whom they had sold their souls.

These two men in one and the same night conceived a resolution to erect false boundary-stones, to which they intended to give an appearance of antiquity by the help of magic, so that people might suppose they had stood there for many years. Both of them, in the figures of fiery men, went up the hill where was the boundary in dispute. Neither of them knew of the intentions of the other. When they met on the hill, he who arrived the last, asked the other,

"What he was doing there?"

"That is no concern of yours!" answered this; "tell me first what *you* are doing here?"

"I will place boundary-stones, and settle the limits as they ought to be,"

"That I have done already, and there you see the stones; and, as the stones go, so goes the boundary."

"You are wrong, for the boundary goes this way; and my master told me that I was in the right."

"Pray, who is your master? A fine gentleman must he be!"

"My master is the devil. Are you satisfied now? and do you feel respect for me?"

"That is a lie! for the devil is *my* master; and he told me that I was right; and, therefore, get off as quick as you can, or you shall see!"

So saying, they threw themselves upon each other; but the man of our village proved too strong for the other, to whom he gave such a blow on the mouth that his head flew off and rolled down the hill. The fiery man without a head quickly ran after it to catch it, and fix it on again; but he did not succeed in doing so before he arrived at the spot where the little brook, which flows down the hill, enters the Emse.

---

* Germany is very rich in popular traditions. The nursery-tales collected by the brothers Grimm are known in this country by two translations. The present tale is written in the very words of an inhabitant of Steinbach, situate in Saxe-Meiningen, at one mile's distance from the watering-place of Liebenstein, and containing two hundred and seventy houses, with one thousand three hundred and thirty inhabitants, amongst whom are a hundred and sixty cutlers, and eighty locksmiths. The inhabitants participate in the principal fancies of those regions,—singing-birds, flowers, song, and music. The music bands of Steinbach are some of the best of Germany, and are the delight of its principal fairs. In our translation we have kept as close as possible to the words of the man who related it.

Meanwhile, our man, who gave the blow, looked from the hill how the other chased his own head, when on a sudden a third fiery man stood before him, who asked,

" What he had done there ?"

" That is no concern of yours !" answered our man; "and, if you do not go your ways immediately, I 'll treat you just as I have the other."

" Have you no more respect for me ? and don't you know that I am your master, the devil ?"

" And, if you are the devil himself, I care not a straw for you ! Go to h— !"

" And that I 'll do," said the devil; " but not without you."

Thus saying, the devil stooped to carry him away on his shoulders; but our man, watching his opportunity, caught his neck between his two legs, and then, laying his hands on him, and holding him down to the ground, he said,

" Now you are in my power; and now you shall feel what my hands are able to do. You have during your life broken the neck of many a poor man; you shall now learn yourself how it feels!"

Thus saying, he set about to screw the devil's neck round with all his might; but, when the devil saw that our man was in earnest, he gave him good words, and prayed him not to do so, and not to smother him, promising to do anything he might require.

" As I hear you speaking so piteously," said our man, " I 'll let you loose; but not before you have returned to me the bond by which I sold you my soul. And, moreover, you must swear to me by your own grandmother, not to claim any part in me; and, during all your life hereafter, never to take any man's bond for his soul."

The devil, though not pleased with these conditions, yet, for the safety of his own neck, could not but return the bond, and even swear by his grandmother what our man had ordered him to do.

But, as soon as the devil found himself free, he jumped on his legs, and, retiring a few paces lest the other might take him unawares a second time, he said,

" Now I am free; and now I must tell you that, though I have returned your bond, and sworn not to claim any part in you, I have not promised you not to break your own neck; and that I shall do now, and upon this very spot you shall die for having throttled me, and for having been about to smother me."

The devil then rushed upon him in order to kill him; but our man ran away straight into the wood, the devil after him. But, coming to an old beech which was hollow, and had likewise an opening beneath, he quickly crept into it and hid himself, and the devil would have certainly missed him had not his toe peeped out from the hole; but, his toe being all fiery, and glistening through the darkness, the devil found out where he had hid himself, and stept near to catch him by the toe. But he in the tree, hearing him come, dragged back his toe, and climbed higher up. The devil then crept likewise into the tree. The other climbed still higher up, and the devil pursued him, until at last our man reached another hole high up, through which he crept out. As soon as he was out, he quickly shut the hole, and jumped as quickly down to fasten the opening below. And this he did with magic, and did it so well that the devil himself, nor his grandmother, could have opened it.   Having performed this, he went his ways.

Thus the devil sat in the old beech-tree, and could not come out, though he bethought himself for a long time how to do so.   Thus he was kept in the beech ; and during that time many of our own people, when going to Winterstein or coming from it, heard him bleating and grunting.   At last, amongst a large lot of trees, the old beech was cut down, and the devil regained his freedom.   The first thing he did was to hasten down below, and see how matters stood there.   It was as empty as a church during the week, and not a single soul was to be heard or seen there ; for the devil not having returned for so long a while, and no one knowing where he was, not a single soul had arrived. And that broke the heart of the devil's grandmother, who died with grief ; and, when she was dead, all the souls who were then there ran away, and went straight to heaven.   Thus the devil stood quite alone, without knowing how to get new souls, for he had forsworn to take the bond of any man more, and this was then the only mode in which he would get souls.   And thus he stood there ruminating, and was near to pull out his horns from his head with grief and despair, when he hit upon an idea.   While he had been in his beech, which stood on the old Hart-place, he had, to while away his time, bethought himself of many things, and amongst others he invented brandy.   That he remembered in the midst of his grief, and he conceived at once it would be the best means of getting hold of new souls.

He immediately went to Nordhausen, and made himself a distiller ; and burnt brandy as much as he could, which he sent into all the world.   And he showed to all the men of Nordhausen how brandy was made, promising them great riches if they learnt it, and made brandy like him.   And the men of Nordhausen did not oblige him to say it twice, for they all became distillers, and made brandy like him.   And thus it happened that to the present day there is no other place in the world where there is so much of brandy burned as at Nordhausen.*

And so it turned out as the devil expected.   Whenever people got a little brandy into their stomachs they began to swear, and d—d their souls to the devil ; so that the devil got them when they were dead without taking any bond from them, and without serving them, as he was obliged to do before, when he sought a man's soul. When the brandy rose into their heads, they collared each other, and fought, and broke their necks ; so that the devil was saved all the trouble he had had before in wringing them.   And, if the devil had had before the greatest pains to be imagined in order to get a poor soul a week for his hell, they came now by their own accord by dozens and scores every day ; and scarcely a year passed before hell was too small to hold them.   The devil was then obliged to build a new hell at the side of the old one, for the sake of giving them accommodation.

In one word, since the devil got loose from the beech on the Hart-place, since that time brandy was introduced into the world ; and, since we have brandy, it may be said "that the devil is loosened," as our proverb goes.

* Literally true.

THE WIT IN SPITE OF HIMSELF.

BY RICHARD JOHNS.

READER, are you a wit? If so, are you a whit the better for so being?

The mere imputation of being a facetious fellow has cost me so dearly, that I can well imagine what fearful consequences the actual possession of a real patent from the court of Momus involves. For mine own part, I may truly say *my* offences against the gravity of society ought to have been denominated accidents. Unwittingly have I offended: I have no pretension to the art of " making a good hit," cutting up a private acquaintance or a public character, " back-biting," or giving " a slap in the face." I am no alchymist at retorts, to be able to transmute the missile aimed at me, into a crown of triumph. If I say a sharp thing, it is because I did not perceive its point; or I would not have meddled with it. I never had the knack of running other men's jokes to death by clapping riders to them; and as to mine own, such as they are, any one is welcome to the credit of them who will take their responsibilities.

But, ere the speculative reader closes the bargain, let him " listen to my tale of woe." My father was a wit and a man of letters: he proved his good sense by marrying a fool,—I beg my mother's pardon; she died soon after I was born, and I only judge by the character she left behind her, to say nothing of her MS. poems and common-place book, which I inherited. When ten years of age, I lost my remaining parent, he being killed in a duel arising out of a christening-dinner; on which occasion he originated the *now* standing joke of wishing the heir " long life to be a better man than his father." The worthy host, who was here hinted at, in his relational position, conceiving the expression implied not only an impossibility, but an impertinence, my progenitor was called out, and incontinently sent home again with a hole pinked in his body, which let the existence out of the wittiest man of his day. With such an example before my mental eyes of the consequences of being a bright ornament of society, is it to be wondered that I determined to be the dullest dolt in my school? Alas! it was declared by all, that a " Winkings" must be a wit and a clever fellow, in spite of my endeavours to prove the contrary.

If I committed the most egregious blunders in my class, there was always somebody to say, " Winkings knows better; he is a wag,—a dry dog; very like a whale, that he can't answer such a simple question;" and the cheek of the " dry dog" was often wetted by tears; and the " wag" found the jest no joke; and, if my ignorance was " very like a whale," it was one on mine own shoulders, since, if I really knew better, I certainly got the worst of it. I have been flogged one moment for pretending to be obtuse, when there was no pretence in the matter; and the next, for saying impudent things to the dominie, which I had never intended. I unconsciously quizzed the ushers, to mine own disgrace; while the writing-master declared, if ever I *did* write, it must be without tuition and by intuition, for I was too busy making the other boys laugh, or worrying them till they cried, to attend to my copy. Such was my character at a school which I quitted early in my nonage, having persuaded my guardians that my education was complete, out of sheer compassion to my master. Had I not left his school, there was a probability of my being his only scholar, so numerous were the complaints from my schoolfellows' parents of " that mischief-making, sly, quarrelsome, impudent little scapegrace, Master Sam Winkings, who, from all they had heard, seemed quite enough to corrupt a whole school." Thus early did my unhappy destiny develope itself; people would have it that I was always saying or imagining evil of them, setting others by the ears for the fun of the fight, and jesting and sneering at all the world holds sacred and respectable.

But in those days unjust accusations were of little consequence to me; if strangers belied me, my immediate relatives were then proud of my " facetious ways," and my " dry humour,—so like his poor father !" Thus lauded and encouraged, matters were at one time going on so pleasantly that I had some intention of favouring the deceit my friends seemed determined to put on themselves, and, professing myself a wit, take all the honours for my fortuitous smart sayings, rather than be accused of affectation in eternally denying them. The tables, however, were soon turned; and it was well I still stuck to the truth, or disasters might have more speedily befallen me. As it was, I in due course of time offended matter-of-fact uncles by jests that I was unconscious of; shocked the ears of fair cousins by *double entendre* most unmeaningly; and robbed maiden aunts of their good names, when I really meant to compliment their virtues.

But I will at once individualize my misfortunes, and I feel assured of the reader's sympathy. " Sam," said my uncle John, as he was breakfasting with me at my chambers in the Temple, where I did *nothing*, with an air of business: having been called to the bar, "I want to ask your advice; but you really are such a facetious fellow, that you even laugh at a man's misfortunes."

" Indeed, sir, you wrong me," I replied, anxious to justify myself, for I was his reputed heir. " Only state your case, and I will give you as good advice as if I were your fee'd counsel."

" Well, Sam, you must in the first place know," said the old gentleman, " that I shall be obliged to stand an action for assault."

" Sorry for it, uncle : I hope it is not a bad action on your part, or we had better——" I was going to add " compromise, rather than go into court;" but my worthy relative, who was about one of the most irritable men in existence, interrupted me.

" Confound you, sir ! when *will* you leave off your puns ? What bad action did I ever commit in the whole course of my life ?"

" Beg pardon, uncle, you quite misunderstand me," apologised I, wishing to explain.

" No, I don't, Sam," retorted he, shaking his head; " your unhappy propensity is too well known. But I will forgive you this once; only *do* be serious. I tell you, boy, it may cost me a cool hundred, besides expenses."

I again assured him that I was all attention; and as he threw himself back in his chair, in preparation for a lengthy detail, I quietly continued my breakfast, only occasionally putting in a " Yes," " Truly," " Really," and so on, as Uncle John paused for breath.

" I was down at Brighton last week, as you know, Sam : had a dreadful headache, and thought a shower-bath would do me good; so went to the new baths. An attendant almost ran against me in the hall. 'Shower-bath,' said I. 'Yes, sir, in a moment, sir; hot or cold?' 'A hot shower-bath!' exclaimed I in the very extremity of surprise. 'I am not used to be jested with, young man.' The fellow stared as if he did not half understand me; but brushed off, and I walked into the waiting-room. My head throbbed with pain, and not a little with perplexity at what the fellow could mean by a hot shower-bath; I had never heard of such a thing, and thought the rogue was quizzing me. Well, Sam, to go on with my story, I was soon ushered into a little bathing-room, with its tall sentry-box, by the same man I had at first spoken to. 'Get more towels,' said I; there were only three. 'Yes, sir,' and away went my gentleman; while I stripped, and shut myself up in the bath. For the life of me, I could not muster resolution enough, just at first, to pull the string. It is no joke, Sam, to stand the shock of a deluge of cold water. I can assure you it always seems to make my red face hiss again."

"No doubt, sir," said I inadvertently.

"Young gentleman," slowly enunciated my uncle, drawing himself up to his full height in his seat, as if to give greater gravity to his words by causing them to fall from an increased altitude, "it is not becoming in *you* to make such a remark, though *I* may choose to be a little facetious on myself. You need not excuse yourself," he added, seeing I was about to reply; "it is your infirmity; but your wit will one day be your only portion."

What could I do?—I sighed, let Uncle John go on with his narrative, and helped myself to an egg.

"Well, nephew, if you can keep from your jokes for a moment, I will come at once to the assault. I had at last made up my mind to endure the cold shock, so I pulled the cord. Never shall I forget it: down came at least six gallons of boiling water! Yes! I am sure it was boiling: the fellow had done it to spite me. The rascal was entering the room with the towels at that very moment, and I *had* my revenge. I dashed open the door and seized him by the neck. I kicked him, I cuffed him; he cried out 'Murder!' 'You ordered hot water, sir!' I called him a liar, and knocked his head against the wall."

Here my uncle became so animated, that he seemed inclined to enact his story. Reader, I have mentioned that I had helped myself to an egg. Now, there has long been a question as to the proper mode of boiling eggs. I like them put into cold water: thus, by the heat being gradually introduced, the shell is prevented from cracking. My man, on the contrary, is for plunging the egg into water at boiling-point. Obstinate fellow! his perverseness on this occasion cost me a thousand a-year and a house in Lancashire. Uncle John was dashing out his hand towards my wig, which, in all the majesty of curls, decorated a block on the side-table, no doubt fancying that he was again going to throttle the knight of the bath, and I had just discovered my egg-shell full of vile slimy fluid, instead of the luxurious yolk and white it would have contained had my rascal obeyed directions. Behold the consequences! My uncle sprang half out of his seat in the frenzy of scalding recollections; while I on the opposite side of the table rose in an agony of vexation, exclaiming, "Cracked! cracked! D—the fellow, always in hot water!"

Reader, did you ever happen to say an ill-natured thing of a person whom you supposed to have just left the room, but who, in point of fact, not having progressed many yards from the back of your chair, suddenly confronts you to thank you for the attention; if so, you may imagine my uncle's sarcastic acknowledgments. "Thank you, sir; I am very much obliged to you," said the old man, in a moment recovering himself from his menacing attitude; "I humbly thank you. Your wit, sir, will make your fortune. I am cracked, am I? I am always in hot water?" Then, changing his tone as he stalked from his chair to possess himself of his hat, he thundered out, "Mr. Samuel Winkings, no longer nephew of mine,—if a scurvy jest is all your sympathy for your invalid uncle, jeered at and parboiled by a rascally bath waiter, I wish you a very good morning!"

In vain I interposed between the old gentleman and the door; I essayed to explain; I offered to put myself, my servant, upon oath; he would not listen to me. He declared all wits were liars,—that I had provoked him past bearing; and away he went, and away went my hopes in that quarter. Never did he forgive me. He died last week, and the only mention he favours me with, in his will, runs thus: "To Samuel Winkings I leave nothing; he can doubtless live by his wit, and I would not insult him by making him any other provision."

Though Uncle John had discarded me, still Aunt Jemima, a legacy-huntress all her life, could not carry her quarry to earth with her. She must in her turn make a bequest; and it was at one time thought this would be in my favour, till, in an unluckly hour, I irretrievably lost my place in her good graces. Aunt Jem, as she was familiarly called by her nephews and nieces, had "great expectations" from Miss Julia and Miss Maria Beech, very rich ancient maidens, sufficiently her seniors to make it worth while to calculate what they would leave behind them. Of course my aunt laid herself out in every possible way to conciliate these ladies; indeed, among all their acquaintance, her anxiety to please them was only rivalled by a Mr. Smith, an elderly gentleman living at Barking, in Essex. He, like Aunt Jem, took great pleasure in toadyism, though wealthy enough to have afforded himself much more respectable amusements. There was a cross-fire of invitations, and a grand struggle every Christmas between the lady and gentleman legacy-hunters for the possession of the Misses Beech; and, during a stay I was making last year at my aunt's abode in Hampshire, I found that, yielding to her superior powers of persuasion, the worthy spinsters were her own from the approaching Christmas-eve even until Twelfth-day. "Then they positively *must* go to Mr. Smith; he was so pressing, and made *such* a point of it." This delightful announcement was conveyed in a letter to mine aunt, received at breakfast-time, and triumphantly read to me.

"They each of them bring their own maid," said the hospitable lady as she conned over their epistle; "but I do not mind the expense nor the trouble; the Beeches are such pleasant companions. I dare say they won't die worth less than twenty thousand pounds a-piece. Now I hope you intend to make yourself agreeable, Sam. Let us have none of your jests and your dry sayings. They are—they are staid, serious persons, and don't like such things, but are partial to sensible conversation. If I recollect right, the last time Miss Julia was here, she told me she had three thousand pounds in the Long Annuities. Both she and her sister treat me with the greatest confidence. I only wish they would not go to Barking so soon. If we were to make things very agreeable to them, who knows, Sam, but they might break their engagement with that mercenary Mr. Smith?"

Thus ran on my aunt, while I silently acquiesced in all she said.

"Why, Sam, you do not seem pleased at the prospect of company!"

"Indeed, aunt," replied I, "I was only thinking you would like my *room*."

"Will you have *done* with your jests?" said Aunt Jem, suspecting a joke in my literal offer, I knowing that ladies' maids are often more fastidious as to their bedchambers than their mistresses.

"It is very provoking," exclaimed I in a pet, "that you always think I am making some foolish pun. I only wish to do *my* part towards rendering your guests and their attendants comfortable. You know what a fuss they make about their servants; turning the house into a hospital for the slightest cold, and talking of 'dear Mr. Smith's cough medicine!' I was only thinking what I could do, to keep the Beeches from Barking."

I suppose, in my haste to exculpate myself from the charge of punning, I could not have taken due care to elongate the *proper* name of the fair spinsters, and, doubtless, it must have sounded a most *improper* one in the ears of my aunt; for her little eyes seemed actually to emit sparks, as a black cat's back is said to do when ruffled in the dark.

"They are gentlewomen, Mr. Winkings!" cried Aunt Jem, almost choked with indignation, "and their attendants are respectable young persons, while *you* are a disgrace to your family. For shame! for shame!" emphatically continued the angry lady, interrupting the excuses I attempted to make; "I will not listen to you. I beg you will leave my house immediately. Your room is indeed most desirable, as you just now so wittily remarked. I would not subject my friends to the insolent licence of your tongue for worlds!"

Away marched Aunt Jem with the strut of an incensed turkey-cock, and an hour afterwards, I was on my way back to London; nor have I ever been able to convince my mistaken relative of my innocence, and still do I remain under the ban of her displeasure.

It would be wearying the reader to state all I have lost, and all I have suffered from the imputation of being a droll; and so I will content myself with one more instance of my unhappy fatality.

Not long ago I dined with Lord C——, who, though he certainly does not bear the character of being over bright, was still to me a star of great promise, seeing that he had given me assurance of provision under the operation of the "poor laws' bastard legislation," or some such affair, I forget exactly what, since unfortunately it is now no affair of mine.

The dinner in question was the only one I ever got out of his lordship, who on this occasion merely asked me, I believe, on account of my reputation for drollery. In fact, I was intended to be the jack-pudding of the company; but I determined to eat much and say little, for fear of giving offence. This did not suit his lordship, who considered my silence during the early part of the dinner as so much time lost, many of the party having been asked to meet the facetious Sam Winkings.

"We have just had a discussion here," smiled Lord C——, in his attempt to draw me out, "as to the impossibility of real wit making a rankling wound, it being like the clean cut of a razor. For myself, I am but a fool in such matters. What do *you* say, Mr. Winkings?"

"That I am quite of your lordship's opinion," replied I, most deferentially.

Here, a fit of coughing went round the table, which might or might not have covered a laugh; but looks were exchanged, plainly showing me that something was wrong. Little did I think at the time that, in delivering myself of my first actual sentence, in my hurry to agree with our host, I had called him a noodle. The peer was the only one who indulged in a decided cachinnation. Even he did not laugh comfortably; and I began to imagine that I had made one of my unlucky hits.

"I beg pardon, my lord; I only meant perfectly to agree with your lordship," said I, crossing my knife and fork over a delicious slice from a haunch of Southdown, for which my embarrassment had taken away all relish.

"Don't mention it, Mr. Winkings," rejoined Lord C——, getting up a fresh laugh; "I am sorry I disturbed you till after dinner. You don't like ' to eat mutton cold.' How goes the quotation?"

"'And cut blocks with a razor,' my lord," replied I, with the most imperturbable gravity.

The sensation was immense. Several of the guests palpably scowled at me, as if I had been guilty of an impertinence towards our host. Some stifled their risibility, and others laughed outright. Alas! what had I done? Just helped him to the remembrance of a quotation which there can be no doubt his lordship had forgotten, except as it referred to mutton. But I had the reputation for sarcasm, and of course I had made a personal attack on Lord C——, who, acting under this impression, certainly passed the matter off with a great deal of urbanity.

"Glad you hit him so hard," said a caustic old gentleman on my right. "Can't bear to see men of wit asked to be funny. My lord had much better have let well alone."

"In the name of Heaven, sir," cried I, almost at my wits' end, "what *have* I done?"

"Ah, you're a wag," said the caustic old gentleman.

"Indeed, sir, I am not a wag, but the most unfortunate individual in the world."

My neighbour was convulsed with laughter; and it was not until we left my lord's house after that luckless dinner that I elicited from him the particulars of my offence. His lordship has, like my uncle and aunt, of course, left me to live by my wits; fortunately, my caustic little friend thinks they will stand me in excellent stead. He has taken the place of my offended patron, and has actually introduced me to a publisher, for whom I am just now engaged in editing a new edition of facetiæ, in two volumes quarto, comprising the complete reminiscences of the celebrated Joseph Miller.

LEGENDS.

THE LEGEND OF BALLAR.

THE most ancient of the kings of Torry was Ballar the Dane. If tradition does him no injustice, a worse specimen of royalty could not be found among the Holy Alliance. His manners were anything but amiable; his temper violent; his disposition sanguinary and revengeful; while, in his notions regarding the doctrines of "meum and tuum," there was not a looser gentleman of his day.

In personal appearance Ballar was dark, stern, and gigantic; and, in an excess of her bounty, Nature had been graciously pleased to gift him with a third eye. This extra optic was placed in the back of his head; and such was the malignity of its influence that one glance extinguished animal life, a forest was withered by a look, and all those bare and herbless hills upon the mainland which lie in scattered groups beneath the scathed pinnacles of Arygle, may—if tradition can be trusted—date their barrenness to an optical visitation they underwent from their dangerous neighbour the king of Torry. As, even in the darkest character some lighter shading may be found, Ballar,—to give the devil his due,—perfectly aware of the destructive properties of his third eye, kept it carefully concealed by a curtain.

Ballar had "one fair daughter, and no more," and an oracle had foretold that, unless killed by his grandson, he should exist for ever. Determined to outlive Methuselah, Ballar resolved on leaving his native country, and seeking out some abiding place where the celibacy of the young lady might be secured. Accordingly he set out upon his travels, and, after an extensive tour, visited Donegal, and chose Torry for his residence; and, faith! a *nater* spot for a gentleman who wished retirement could not have been selected. There he built a castle for himself, and a prison for his daughter. To "make all right," the young lady was placed under the *surveillance* of twelve virgins; whence the latter were obtained, history doth not say.

Ballar's nearest neighbours on the main were called Gabshegonal, and Kien Mac Caunthca. The latter was possessed of two brave boys, while the former was owner of a white heifer: Glassdhablecana, or "the grey-flanked cow," was the envy of the country. Nothing from Dingle to Donegal could match her; she was a dairy in herself; and Ballar, regardless of justice, and not having the fear of the going judge of assize before him, determined to abstract her if he could. Like other autocrats, he found no difficulty in trumping up a title, for he asserted that those resident on the mainland were his vassals, and claimed and exacted certain seignorial rights, which, much to the satisfaction of persons entering into matrimony, have been allowed to sink into desuetude.

Like those of all bad monarchs, his ministers were no better than himself; and the chiefs of his household, Mool and Mullock, were worthy agents of their three-eyed master. As his demand upon Gab's cow had been peremptorily rejected, the tyrant of Torry determined to obtain by fraud, what force could not effect; and Mool and Mullock received instructions accordingly.

Ballar's intentions having transpired, Gabshegonal assumed the defensive, and called to his assistance the sons of Kien Mac Caunthca. Gab, it appears, was the most celebrated sword-cutler of his day, and he promised to forge a weapon for each of the young men; they undertaking, in return, to watch the grey-flanked cow for a given time.

The elder of the Mao Caunthcas performed his part of the contract with the smith, and obtained the promised sword; and the younger commenced watch and ward in turn. For some time his vigilance secured the white cow; but, unhappily, it occurred to the youth that it would be desirable to have his name engraved on the sword-blade which Gab was then polishing. He ran to the forge to make his wishes known; and, short as his absence was, alas! upon his return the cow was gone! The spoilers were discovered from the top of Arygle; the younger Mac Caunthca observed Mool and Mullock driving Glassdhablecana along the beach; and, without his being able to overtake them, they embarked for Torry with their prey. Enraged at the occurrence, the smith retained the elder brother as a hostage, and swore that, if the cow were not recovered, he would behead him, to avenge her loss.

The unhappy watchman, overwhelmed with grief and shame, fled from his home, and wandered recklessly along the rock-bound coast. To reach Torry was impossible, and he abandoned himself to sorrow and despair.

Suddenly, a little red-haired man appeared unexpectedly at his elbow, and with sympathetic civility inquired the cause of his lamentations. Mac Caunthca informed him of the misfortune, and the red dwarf offered his condolence, and volunteered to assist him to reach the island. Mac embraced the little gentleman and his offer; and, having ascended the summit of Cruicknaneabth, he placed his foot upon the dwarf's hand, who rose with him into the air, and, passing over the small islands between Torry and the main, fast as the wind itself, landed in safety beneath the castle walls of Ballar. Both the youth and his conductor were " the nonce" rendered invisible. With little difficulty the cow was found; and the dwarf engaged that, ere morning, she should be safely returned to her lawful owner, the honest sword-cutler, Gabshegonal.

Whether the little gentleman with the red beard preferred daylight for his aërial trips, does not appear; but, certain it is, that his *protegé* remained that night upon the island, and was introduced by the obliging dwarfs to the prison of the princess, where he remained until dawn broke. Safely was he then conducted to the place he had left on the preceding evening. The red man took an affectionate leave. The grey-flanked cow was before him at the owner's. His brother was released; the promised sword honestly delivered by the maker; and the whole adventure ended prosperously.

Time rolled on. Nine months had elapsed since his visit to the island, when the young Mac Caunthca was honoured by a call from the little red gentleman, who requested his company to make a morning call upon the imprisoned princess. They crossed the arm of the sea with the same rapidity that marked their former flight;

and, on entering the well-remembered tower, what was Mac Caunthca's delight and surprise on finding that he was the father of a large and healthy family ! The princess had just given birth to a son; and the twelve young ladies, following, as in duty bound, the example of their mistress, had each produced "a chopping boy."

But, alas! the pleasures of paternity were speedily ended. Ballar detested children. Twins would drive a Malthusian distracted; and what apology could be offered for thirteen? Nothing remained but to remove the young Mac Caunthcas in double-quick; and the dwarf, with his usual good nature, proposed the means. A curragh* was procured; the tender pledges of the maids of honour were placed in a blanket, and fastened by skewers upon the back of their papa, while the heir to the throne was accommodated in a separate cloth; and with this precious freight the curragh was launched upon the ocean.

Presently the wind freshened, the sea rose, and the frail bark was tossed upon the surface of an angry sea. In the fury of the gale the skewers that secured the blanket gave way; overboard went the progeny of the virgin body-guard; and the young Mac Caunthca reached the mainland with a single son, the heir-presumptive to the throne of Torry.

It may be imagined that the care of an infant would have become a very troublesome charge upon the lover of the island princess; but here, too, the red man stood his friend. The dwarf volunteered to educate the child seven years, then hand him over to his father for seven more, when he, Red-beard, would again receive him for other seven; and thus the grandson of the three-eyed monarch would be disposed of, during nonage. It was done. The boy grew apace; and, indoctrinated at the feet of a gifted Gamaliel like little Red-beard, it is not surprising that the heir of Torry became a finished gentleman.

His first appearance in public is stated to have been at a country wedding; and there Ballar, attended by Mool and Mullock, and his customary suite, was punctual to claim his prerogative. Shocked at the immorality of his grandfather, the dwarf's *protegé* remonstrated with the old gentleman in vain; and, to strengthen his arguments, imprudently confessed the degree of relationship in which they stood. Furious at the discovery, the ancient sinner determined on the youth's destruction; he raised his hand to uncurtain the third eye, but his grandson burst from the house, and ran for shelter to the forge of his relative, Gabshegonal. A hot pursuit took place. Ballar and his "tail" pressed the fugitive closely; and the youth had only time to arm himself with a heated bar, when his truculent relation, with his train, rushed in. Before the eye could be uncovered, by one lucky thrust the heir of Torry annihilated its evil influence, and thus proved satisfactorily that the worst of eyes is no match for red-hot iron.

But, even in death, Ballar evinced no feelings of Christian forgiveness. Calling his grandson to his side, he requested that he would abridge his sufferings by cutting off his head; and then, by placing it upon his own, he assured him that all the knowledge he, Ballar, possessed, should directly be transferred to his grandson, and de-

* A wicker boat covered with a horse-skin, much used by these islanders.

scend like an heir-loom in the family. With the first part of the
request the young gentleman freely complied; but, being awake to
the trickery of his grandsire, he prudently resolved to see what
effect the head would have upon stone before he tried the experiment. The result proved that his suspicions were well-founded. A
drop of poisonous matter fell from the head upon the rock; and a
broken cliff is pointed out upon the island, said to have been dis-
rupted by the head of Ballar resting on it.

The remainder of the legend is happy, as it should be. The
princess in due time became a wife; her son danced at the wedding;
and the maids of honour were provided with husbands, and, though
rather tardily, were " made honest women of" at last. No longer
necessitated to commit their offspring to the ocean by the dozen,
their progeny increased and multiplied; and from the Danish princess, and the virgin train who "bore her company," the present inhabitants of Torry believe themselves to be immediately descended.

LEGEND OF THE CHURCH OF THE SEVEN.

AFTER a dreadful tempest, seven dead bodies, six of which were
male and one female, were found upon the western shore of the
island, with a stone curragh and paddle beside them: both the latter
had been broken against the rocks. The inhabitants speedily collected, and a consultation took place as to the manner in which the
bodies of the unknown strangers should be disposed of. The opinions
of the islanders were divided: some proposed that they should be
interred, others contended that they should be committed to the
waves again; but it was unanimously resolved, that on no account
should they be buried in the churchyard, as they might not have
been true Catholics. To bury was the final determination. A grave
was accordingly prepared, the seven corpses were indiscriminately
thrown in, and the trench closed up.

Next morning, to the great surprise of the islanders, the body of
the female was found separated from those of her unfortunate companions, and lying on the surface of the ground. It was believed
that the lady had been disinterred by that party who had opposed
the bodies being buried on the island, and the corpse was once more
returned to its kindred clay, and the grave securely filled up.

The second morning came, and great was the astonishment of the
inhabitants when it was ascertained that the same occurrence had
taken place, and the grave had surrendered its dead. The body was
inhumed once more, and, to guard against trickery, and secure the
corpse from being disturbed, a watch was placed around the grave.

But when the daylight broke on the third morning, lo! the body
of the unknown had again burst its cerements, and lay once more
upon the surface of the ground. The vigilance of the guard had
proved unavailing, and the consternation of the islanders was unbounded. A grand conclave assembled, and, after much consideration
and debate, it was decided that the departed female had been a *religi-
euse;* and, that as she had eschewed all communion with the coarser sex
while living, so, true to her vows, even after death she had evaded the
society of man. Believing her to be a gentlewoman of extra holiness,

who had departed " in the pride of her purity," it was shrewdly conjectured that there was nothing to prevent her from working miracles. The sick were accordingly brought forward, and a touch from the blessed finger of the defunct nun—for such she proved—removed every malady the flesh is heir to, and left the island without an invalid. To atone for the irreverential mode in which the lady had been treated on former occasions, a magnificent funeral was decreed her ; a stone monument was erected over the sainted remains ; and, that posterity should not be excluded from the virtues of her clay, an opening was left in the south side of the tomb, whence the faithful could obtain a portion of her ashes, and the sick be cured of their ailments. It being considered that one so particular after death would not, when alive, have ventured upon sea with any but the servants of religion, the other six bodies were honourably interred, and a tomb raised to their memory, while " the Church of the Seven" was built to their joint honour, and dedicated to the whole.

To this day the sanctity of the lady's grave remains unimpaired. The ashes retain their virtue ; the pious resort thither to pray, the sick to procure relief from their sufferings. When it is necessary to obtain the holy dust for devout or medicinal purposes, application is made to the oldest member of a particular family, who have enjoyed from time immemorial the blessed privilege of dispensing the saint's clay. The name of the family is Doogan ; and the reason why this high prerogative rests with this favoured lineage is, because their ancestors were the first converts of St. Colomb Kill, and the first of the islanders who received baptism at his hands.

SOME ACCOUNT OF THE LEGENDS OF THE TORRY ISLANDERS.

Torry Island, situated on the north-west coast of Ireland, is probably the least known of any of her Majesty's European possessions. Although so near the main, the communication is difficult and infrequent. The island has but one landing-place, and that can only be entered with leading winds, while, during the prevalence of the others, it is totally unapproachable.

Within the memory of people still alive, the natives of Torry were idolaters. They were ushered into life, and quitted it for the grave, without either rite or ceremony. Marriage was, *à la Martineau*, nothing but " a civil contract," and their notions of the Deity, rude and untutored as Kamschatdales or New Zealanders. Latterly, priests from the main have occasionally landed on the island, and there introduced the formulæ of religion ; but visits dependent on winds and waves are " few and far between," and the state of Torry may still be termed more than demi-savage. When some adventurous beadsman ventures on a clerical descent, during his brief sojourn he finds that his office is no sinecure : children are to be christened by the score ; and couples, who took each other's words, to be married by the dozen. During the long interregnum, a large arrear of omitted ceremonies has accrued, and the daring clerk returns from this "ultima Thule" a weary, if not a wiser man.

Nothing can be more wretched than the appearance of the island and its inhabitants : the one, cold, barren, and uncultivated ; the other, ugly, dwarfish, and ill-shapen. The hovels are filthy to a degree; and all within and about Torry is so sterile and inhospitable, that a dread of being wind-bound deters even the hardiest mariner from approaching its rock-bound shores.

That "holy men" should venture among the Heathen, is, as it ought to be; and that *savans* will go desperate lengths to obtain bones, oyster-shells, and other valuable commodities, is equally true. For spiritual and scientific Quixotes, Torry opens an untried field; and any philosopher who can digest dog-fish, and possesses a skin impervious to entomological assaults, may here discover unknown treasures: none having yet been found—for none have sought them.

It was, probably, expectations such as these that induced the late Sir Charles Geisecke to visit this unfrequented island. Whether his geological discoveries compensated his bodily sufferings, the gentleman who perpetrated his biography leaves a scientific mystery. Certain it is, that in after-life the worthy knight never touched upon this portion of his wanderings without shuddering at the recollection.

Three days he sojourned among the aborigines, and three nights he sheltered in the chief man's hovel. He left Ards House* in good spirits, and fat as a philosopher should be; and when he returned, his own dog, had he possessed one, would not have recognised his luckless owner. He came out a walking skeleton, and the ablutions he underwent would have tried the patience of a Mussulman. He had lost sleep; well, that could be made up for. He lost condition; that too might be restored. But to lose hair, to be clipped like a recruit, and have his garments burned at the point of a pitch-fork,— these indeed would daunt the courage of the most daring entomologist.

Pat Hegarty, the knight's guide, used to recount the sufferings they underwent. Their afflictions by day were bad enough; but these were nothing, compared to their nocturnal visitations. "My! what a place for fleas!" said an English *femme de chambre* who happened to be an accidental listener. "How numerous they must have been!"

"Numerous!" exclaimed the guide, "*mona mon diaoul*, if they had only pulled together, they would have dragged me out of bed!"

Since the knight's excursion, Torry has been more frequently visited. In executing the Ordnance survey, a party of Sappers and Miners were encamped upon the island, and the engineer officer in command amused many of his solitary hours by collecting traditionary tales from the narration of an old man, who was far more intelligent than the rest of the inhabitants. The two foregoing legends were taken from the patriarch's lips, and they afford an additional proof of that fondness which man, in his savage state, ever evinces for traditions that are wonderful and wild.

---

* *Ards* is situated on the main, near the wild promontory of Horn Head, and is the seat of the Stewart family.

George Cruikshank

Master Bates explains a professional technicality.

SONG OF THE MONTH. No. XII.

December, 1837.

ALL hail to thee, thou good old boy, DECEMBER!
Sick of that sullen, sulky Dan November,
 The very sight of thy bald, reverend, jolly,
 Irreverend head, bright crown'd with holly,
 Makes one forswear, as fudge, all melancholy,—
Thou gladdening, glowing, glorious old DECEMBER!

Grey Nestor of the Months! brethren eleven,
Joint heirs with thee of *Eighteen Thirty-seven*,
 Knock'd up by Time, enjoy oblivious slumbers,—
 Old Monthlies out of print—the scarce back numbers,
 Sold out—not one a shop or shelf encumbers,
While thou art but just publish'd—" No. XII.—DECEMBER !"

" Hail, Thane of" Time !—thou genial, warm old sire
Of *Eighteen Thirty-eight !*—Yule log and sea-coal fire
 Be thine, as glad burnt-offerings in thy praise ;
 Long nights—(thou dost not look for length of days)—
 Be thine, old Joy, wassail'd in various ways
Of warm, bright welcome, to hail thy stay, DECEMBER!

Welcome once more, old Master of the Revels,—
PICKWICK of all the Pleasures !—The blue devils,
 Blue looks, blue noses, hide their uncomely faces ;
 Old Gout throws by his crutch—tries cinquepaces ;
 And Youth and Age, Love, Joy, and all the Graces
Are getting parties up, to honour thee, DECEMBER !

Sir-Loins grow fatter ; plums, like good St. Stephen,
Are suff'ring martyrdom ; the spongy leaven
 Is working puddingwards ; old wines, choice cellars,
 Old coats, new gowns, shawls, cloaks, clogs, logs, umbrellas,
 Young girls, old girls, old boys, and old young *fellars*,
Are brushing up to welcome thee, DECEMBER !

Game, poultry, turkeys, pigs, and country cousins
The Town's great maw will swallow down by dozens ;
 Aunts, uncles, brothers, sisters, nieces, *nevies*,
 Will all be book'd and brought up by " the heavies,"
 With other birds of passage, in large levies,
On Christmas-day, to honour thee, DECEMBER !

Bright hearths, bright hearts, bright faces, and bright holly
Will welcome thee, and make thy sojourn jolly !
 The merry misletoe, in hall and kitchen,
 Will make the ugliest of mugs bewitchin' ;
 And who won't kiss them, may he die a ditch in,
For he's no friend of thine, warm-hearted old DECEMBER !

Once more, all hail! with all thy sports and pastimes,
Though few old sports are left us in these last times !—
 May one fair Virgin Girl—the loved at sight one—
 Twelve days from Christmas-tide, her heart a light one,
 As Queen, choose her a King, and choose the right one,
To our great joy, and hers, agreeable old DECEMBER !

            C. W.

OLIVER TWIST;

OR, THE PARISH BOY'S PROGRESS.

BY BOZ.

ILLUSTRATED BY GEORGE CRUIKSHANK.

CHAPTER THE EIGHTEENTH.

HOW OLIVER PASSED HIS TIME IN THE IMPROVING SOCIETY OF HIS REPUTABLE FRIENDS.

About noon next day, when the Dodger and Master Bates had gone out to pursue their customary avocations, Mr. Fagin took the opportunity of reading Oliver a long lecture on the crying sin of ingratitude, of which he clearly demonstrated he had been guilty to no ordinary extent in wilfully absenting himself from the society of his anxious friends, and still more in endeavouring to escape from them after so much trouble and expense had been incurred in his recovery. Mr. Fagin laid great stress on the fact of his having taken Oliver in and cherished him, when without his timely aid he might have perished with hunger; and related the dismal and affecting history of a young lad whom in his philanthropy he had succoured under parallel circumstances, but who, proving unworthy of his confidence, and evincing a desire to communicate with the police, had unfortunately come to be hung at the Old Bailey one morning. Mr. Fagin did not seek to conceal his share in the catastrophe, but lamented with tears in his eyes that the wrong-headed and treacherous behaviour of the young person in question had rendered it necessary that he should become the victim of certain evidence for the crown, which, if it were not precisely true, was indispensably necessary for the safety of him (Mr. Fagin), and a few select friends. Mr. Fagin concluded by drawing a rather disagreeable picture of the discomforts of hanging, and, with great friendliness and politeness of manner, expressed his anxious hope that he might never be obliged to submit Oliver Twist to that unpleasant operation.

Little Oliver's blood ran cold as he listened to the Jew's words, and imperfectly comprehended the dark threats conveyed in them: that it was possible even for justice itself to confound the innocent with the guilty when they were in accidental companionship, he knew already; and that deeply-laid plans for the destruction of inconveniently-knowing, or over-communicative persons, had been really devised and carried out by the old Jew on more occasions than one, he thought by no means unlikely when he recollected the general nature of the altercations between that gentleman and Mr. Sikes, which seemed to bear reference to some foregone conspiracy of the kind. As he glanced timidly up, and met the Jew's searching look, he felt that his pale face and trembling limbs were neither unnoticed nor unrelished by the wary villain.

The Jew smiled hideously, and, patting Oliver on the head, said that if he kept himself quiet, and applied himself to business, he saw they would be very good friends yet. Then taking his hat, and covering himself up in an old patched great-coat, he went out and locked the room-door behind him.

And so Oliver remained all that day, and for the greater part of many subsequent days, seeing nobody between early morning and midnight, and left during the long hours to commune with his own thoughts; which, never failing to revert to his kind friends, and the opinion they must long ago have formed of him, were sad indeed. After the lapse of a week or so, the Jew left the room-door unlocked, and he was at liberty to wander about the house.

It was a very dirty place; but the rooms up stairs had great high wooden mantel-pieces and large doors, with paneled walls and cornices to the ceilings, which, although they were black with neglect and dust, were ornamented in various ways; from all of which tokens Oliver concluded that a long time ago, before the old Jew was born, it had belonged to better people, and had perhaps been quite gay and handsome, dismal and dreary as it looked now.

Spiders had built their webs in the angles of the walls and ceilings; and sometimes, when Oliver walked softly into a room, the mice would scamper across the floor, and run back terrified to their holes: with these exceptions, there was neither sight nor sound of any living thing; and often, when it grew dark, and he was tired of wandering from room to room, he would crouch in the corner of the passage by the street-door, to be as near living people as he could, and to remain there listening and trembling until the Jew or the boys returned.

In all the rooms the mouldering shutters were fast closed, and the bars which held them were screwed tight into the wood; the only light which was admitted making its way through round holes at the top, which made the rooms more gloomy, and filled them with strange shadows. There was a back-garret window, with rusty bars outside, which had no shutter, and out of which Oliver often gazed with a melancholy face for hours together; but nothing was to be descried from it but a confused and crowded mass of house-tops, blackened chimneys, and gable-ends. Sometimes, indeed, a ragged grizzly head might be seen peering over the parapet-wall of a distant house, but it was quickly withdrawn again; and as the window of Oliver's observatory was nailed down, and dimmed with the rain and smoke of years, it was as much as he could do to make out the forms of the different objects beyond, without making any attempt to be seen or heard,—which he had as much chance of being as if he had been inside the ball of St. Paul's Cathedral.

One afternoon, the Dodger and Master Bates being engaged
out that evening, the first-named young gentleman took it into
his head to evince some anxiety regarding the decoration of his
person (which, to do him justice, was by no means an habitual
weakness with him ;) and, with this end and aim, he condescend-
ingly commanded Oliver to assist him in his toilet straightway.

Oliver was but too glad to make himself useful, too happy to
have some faces, however bad, to look upon, and too desirous to
conciliate those about him when he could honestly do so, to
throw any objection in the way of this proposal ; so he at once
expressed his readiness, and, kneeling on the floor, while the
Dodger sat upon the table so that he could take his foot in his
lap, he applied himself to a process which Mr. Dawkins designated as " japanning his trotter-cases," and which phrase, rendered into plain English, signifieth cleaning his boots.

Whether it was the sense of freedom and independence which
a rational animal may be supposed to feel when he sits on a table in an easy attitude, smoking a pipe, swinging one leg carelessly to and fro, and having his boots cleaned all the time without even the past trouble of having taken them off, or the prospective misery of putting them on, to disturb his reflections ;
or whether it was the goodness of the tobacco that soothed the
feelings of the Dodger, or the mildness of the beer that mollified
his thoughts, he was evidently tinctured for the nonce with a
spice of romance and enthusiasm foreign to his general nature.
He looked down on Oliver with a thoughtful countenance for a
brief space, and then, raising his head, and heaving a gentle
sigh, said, half in abstraction, and half to Master Bates,

" What a pity it is he isn't a prig !"

" Ah !" said Master Charles Bates. " He don't know what 's
good for him."

The Dodger sighed again, and resumed his pipe, as did
Charley Bates, and they both smoked for some seconds in
silence.

" I suppose you don't even know what a prig is ?" said the
Dodger mournfully.

" I think I know that," replied Oliver, hastily looking up.
" It 's a th—; you 're one, are you not ?" inquired Oliver,
checking himself.

" I am," replied the Dodger. " I 'd scorn to be anythink
else." Mr. Dawkins gave his hat a ferocious cock after delivering this sentiment, and looked at Master Bates as if to denote
that he would feel obliged by his saying anything to the contrary. " I am," repeated the Dodger ; " so 's Charley ; so 's
Fagin ; so 's Sikes ; so 's Nancy ; so 's Bet ; so we all are, down
to the dog, and he 's the downiest one of the lot."

" And the least given to peaching," added Charley Bates.

" He wouldn't so much as bark in a witness-box, for fear of

committing himself; no, not if you tied him up in one, and left him there without wittles for a fortnight," said the Dodger.

"That he wouldn't; not a bit of it," observed Charley.

"He's a rum dog. Don't he look fierce at any strange cove that laughs or sings when he's in company!" pursued the Dodger. "Won't he growl at all, when he hears a fiddle playing, and don't he hate other dogs as ain't of his breed! Wink-in! Oh, no!"

"He's an out-and-out Christian," said Charley.

This was merely intended as a tribute to the animal's abilities, but it was an appropriate remark in another sense, if Master Bates had only known it; for there are a great many ladies and gentlemen claiming to be out-and-out Christians, between whom and Mr. Sikes's dog there exist very strong and singular points of resemblance.

"Well, well!" said the Dodger, recurring to the point from which they had strayed, with that mindfulness of his profession which influenced all his proceedings. "This hasn't got anything to do with young Green here."

"No more it has," said Charley. "Why don't you put yourself under Fagin, Oliver?"

"And make your fortun' out of hand?" added the Dodger, with a grin.

"And so be able to retire on your property, and do the genteel, as I mean to in the very next leap-year but four that ever comes, and the forty-second Tuesday in Trinity-week," said Charley Bates.

"I don't like it," rejoined Oliver timidly; "I wish they would let me go. I—I—would rather go."

"And Fagin would *rather* not!" rejoined Charley.

Oliver knew this too well; but, thinking it might be dangerous to express his feelings more openly, he only sighed, and went on with his boot-cleaning.

"Go!" exclaimed the Dodger. "Why, where's your spirit? Don't you take any pride out of yourself? Would you go and be dependent on your friends, eh?"

"Oh, blow that!" said Master Bates, drawing two or three silk handkerchiefs from his pocket, and tossing them into a cupboard, "that's too mean, that is!"

"*I* couldn't do it," said the Dodger, with an air of haughty disgust.

"You can leave your friends, though," said Oliver, with a half-smile, "and let them be punished for what you did."

"That," rejoined the Dodger, with a wave of his pipe,— "that was all out of consideration for Fagin, 'cause the traps know that we work together, and he might have got into trouble if we hadn't made our lucky; that was the move, wasn't it, Charley?"

Master Bates nodded assent, and would have spoken, but

that the recollection of Oliver's flight came so suddenly upon
him, that the smoke he was inhaling got entangled with a laugh,
and went up into his head, and down into his throat, and
brought on a fit of coughing and stamping about five minutes
long.

"Look here!" said the Dodger, drawing forth a handful of
shillings and halfpence. "Here's a jolly life! what's the odds
where it comes from? Here, catch hold; there's plenty more
where they were took from. You won't, won't you? oh, you
precious flat!"

"It's naughty, ain't it, Oliver?" inquired Charley Bates.
"He'll come to be scragged, won't he?"

"I don't know what that means," replied Oliver, looking
round.

"Something in this way, old feller," said Charley. As he
said it, Master Bates caught up an end of his neckerchief, and,
holding it erect in the air, dropped his head on his shoulder, and jerked a curious sound through his teeth, thereby indicating, by a lively pantomimic representation that scragging
and hanging were one and the same thing.

"That's what it means," said Charley. "Look how he
stares, Jack; I never did see such prime company as that 'ere
boy; he'll be the death of me, I know he will." And Master
Charles Bates having laughed heartily again, resumed his pipe
with tears in his eyes.

"You've been brought up bad," said the Dodger, surveying
his boots with much satisfaction when Oliver had polished
them. "Fagin will make something of you, though; or you'll
be the first he ever had that turned out unprofitable. You'd
better begin at once, for you'll come to the trade long before
you think of it, and you're only losing time, Oliver."

Master Bates backed this advice with sundry moral admoni-
tions of his own, which being exhausted, he and his friend Mr.
Dawkins launched into a glowing description of the numerous
pleasures incidental to the life they led, interspersed with a variety of hints to Oliver that the best thing he could do, would
be to secure Fagin's favour without more delay by the same
means which they had employed to gain it.

"And always put this in your pipe, Nolly," said the Dodger,
as the Jew was heard unlocking the door above, "if you don't
take fogles and tickers——"

"What's the good of talking in that way?" interposed Master Bates; "he don't know what you mean."

"If you don't take pocket-hankechers and watches," said the
Dodger, reducing his conversation to the level of Oliver's capacity, "some other cove will; so that the coves that lose 'em will
be all the worse, and you'll be all the worse too, and nobody
half a ha'p'orth the better, except the chaps wot gets them—and
you've just as good a right to them as they have."

" To be sure,—to be sure !" said the Jew, who had entered unseen by Oliver. " It all lies in a nutshell, my dear—in a nutshell, take the Dodger's word for it.   Ha ! ha ! he understands the catechism of his trade."

The old man rubbed his hands gleefully together as he corroborated the Dodger's reasoning in these terms, and chuckled with delight at his pupil's proficiency.

The conversation proceeded no farther at this time, for the Jew had returned home accompanied by Miss Betsy, and a gentleman whom Oliver had never seen before, but who was accosted by the Dodger as Tom Chitling, and who, having lingered on the stairs to exchange a few gallantries with the lady, now made his appearance.

Mr. Chitling was older in years than the Dodger, having perhaps numbered eighteen winters ; but there was a degree of deference in his deportment towards that young gentleman which seemed to indicate that he felt himself conscious of a slight inferiority in point of genius and professional acquirements.   He had small twinkling eyes, and a pock-marked face ; wore a fur cap, a dark corduroy jacket, greasy fustian trousers, and an apron.   His wardrobe was, in truth, rather out of repair ; but he excused himself to the company by stating that his " time " was only out an hour before, and that, in consequence of having worn the regimentals for six weeks past, he had not been able to bestow any attention on his private clothes.   Mr. Chitling added, with strong marks of irritation, that the new way of fumigating clothes up yonder was infernal unconstitutional, for it burnt holes in them, and there was no remedy against the county ; the same remark he considered to apply to the regulation mode of cutting the hair, which he held to be decidedly unlawful.   Mr. Chitling wound up his observations by stating that he had not touched a drop of anything for forty-two mortal long hard-working days, and that he " wished he might be busted if he wasn't as dry as a lime-basket !"

" Where do you think the gentleman has come from, Oliver ?" inquired the Jew with a grin, as the other boys put a bottle of spirits on the table.

" I—I—don't know, sir," replied Oliver.

" Who 's that ?" inquired Tom Chitling, casting a contemptuous look at Oliver.

" A young friend of mine, my dear," replied the Jew.

" He 's in luck then," said the young man, with a meaning look at Fagin.   " Never mind where I came from, young 'un ; you 'll find your way there soon enough, I 'll bet a crown !"

At this sally the boys laughed, and, after some more jokes on the same subject, exchanged a few short whispers with Fagin, and withdrew.

After some words apart between the last comer and Fagin, they drew their chairs towards the fire ; and the Jew, telling

Oliver to come and sit by him, led the conversation to the topics most calculated to interest his hearers. These were, the
great advantages of the trade, the proficiency of the Dodger,
the amiability of Charley Bates, and the liberality of the Jew
himself. At length these subjects displayed signs of being thoroughly exhausted, and Mr. Chitling did the same (for the
house of correction becomes fatiguing after a week or two); accordingly Miss Betsy withdrew, and left the party to their repose.

From this day Oliver was seldom left alone, but was placed
in almost constant communication with the two boys, who played the old game with the Jew every day,—whether for their
own improvement, or Oliver's, Mr. Fagin best knew. At other
times the old man would tell them stories of robberies he had
committed in his younger days, mixed up with so much that
was droll and curious, that Oliver could not help laughing
heartily, and showing that he was amused in spite of all his
better feelings.

In short, the wily old Jew had the boy in his toils; and, having prepared his mind by solitude and gloom to prefer any society to the companionship of his own sad thoughts in such a
dreary place, was now slowly instilling into his soul the poison
which he hoped would blacken it and change its hue for ever.

CHAPTER THE NINETEENTH.

IN WHICH A NOTABLE PLAN IS DISCUSSED AND DETERMINED ON.

IT was a chill, damp, windy night, when the Jew, buttoning
his great-coat tight round his shrivelled body, and pulling the
collar up over his ears so as completely to obscure the lower
part of his face, emerged from his den. He paused on the step
as the door was locked and chained behind him; and having
listened while the boys made all secure, and until their retreating footsteps were no longer audible, slunk down the street as
quickly as he could.

The house to which Oliver had been conveyed was in the
neighbourhood of Whitechapel; the Jew stopped for an instant
at the corner of the street, and, glancing suspiciously round,
crossed the road, and struck off in the direction of Spitalfields.

The mud lay thick upon the stones, and a black mist hung
over the streets; the rain fell sluggishly down, and everything
felt cold and clammy to the touch. It seemed just the night
when it befitted such a being as the Jew to be abroad. As he
glided stealthily along, creeping beneath the shelter of the walls
and doorways, the hideous old man seemed like some loathsome
reptile, engendered in the slime and darkness through which he
moved, crawling forth by night in search of some rich offal for
a meal.

He kept on his course through many winding and narrow

ways until he reached Bethnal Green; then, turning suddenly off to the left, he soon became involved in a maze of the mean dirty streets which abound in that close and densely-populated quarter.

The Jew was evidently too familiar with the ground he traversed, however, to be at all bewildered either by the darkness of the night or the intricacies of the way. He hurried through several alleys and streets, and at length turned into one lighted only by a single lamp at the farther end. At the door of a house in this street he knocked, and, having exchanged a few muttered words with the person who opened the door, walked up stairs.

A dog growled as he touched the handle of a door, and a man's voice demanded who was there.

"Only me, Bill; only me, my dear," said the Jew, looking in.

"Bring in your body," said Sikes. "Lie down, you stupid brute! Don't you know the devil when he's got a great-coat on?"

Apparently the dog had been somewhat deceived by Mr. Fagin's outer garment; for as the Jew unbuttoned it, and threw it over the back of a chair, he retired to the corner from which he had risen, wagging his tail as he went, to show that he was as well satisfied as it was in his nature to be.

"Well!" said Sikes.

"Well, my dear," replied the Jew. "Ah! Nancy."

The latter recognition was uttered with just enough of embarrassment to imply a doubt of its reception; for Mr. Fagin and his young friend had not met since she had interfered in behalf of Oliver. All doubts upon the subject, if he had any, were, however, speedily removed by the young lady's behaviour. She took her feet off the fender, pushed back her chair, and bade Fagin draw up his without saying any more about it, for it was a cold night, and no mistake. Miss Nancy prefixed to the word "cold" another adjective, derived from the name of an unpleasant instrument of death, which, as the word is seldom mentioned to ears polite in any other form than as a substantive, I have omitted in this chronicle.

"It *is* cold, Nancy dear," said the Jew, as he warmed his skinny hands over the fire. "It seems to go right through one," added the old man, touching his left side.

"It must be a piercer if it finds its way through your heart," said Mr. Sikes. "Give him something to drink, Nancy. Burn my body, make haste! It's enough to turn a man ill to see his lean old carcase shivering in that way, like a ugly ghost just rose from the grave."

Nancy quickly brought a bottle from a cupboard in which there were many, which, to judge from the diversity of their appearance, were filled with several kinds of liquids ; and Sikes, pouring out a glass of brandy, bade the Jew drink it off.

" Quite enough, quite, thankye Bill," replied the Jew, putting down the glass after just setting his lips to it.

" What ! you 're afraid of our getting the better of you, are you ?" inquired Sikes, fixing his eyes on the Jew ; " ugh !"

With a hoarse grunt of contempt Mr. Sikes seized the glass and emptied it, as a preparatory ceremony to filling it again for himself, which he did at once.

The Jew glanced round the room as his companion tossed down the second glassful ; not in curiosity, for he had seen it often before, but in a restless and suspicious manner which was habitual to him. It was a meanly furnished apartment, with nothing but the contents of the closet to induce the belief that its occupier was anything but a working man ; and with no more suspicious articles displayed to view than two or three heavy bludgeons which stood in a corner, and a " life-preserver " that hung over the mantelpiece.

" There," said Sikes, smacking his lips. " Now I 'm ready."

" For business—eh ?" inquired the Jew.

" For business," replied Sikes ; " so say what you 've got to say."

" About the crib at Chertsey, Bill ?" said the Jew, drawing his chair forward, and speaking in a very low voice.

" Yes. What about it ?" inquired Sikes.

" Ah ! you know what I mean, my dear," said the Jew. " He knows what I mean, Nancy ; don't he ?"

" No, he don't," sneered Mr. Sikes, " or he won't, and that 's the same thing. Speak out, and call things by their right names ; don't sit there winking and blinking, and talking to me in hints, as if you warn't the very first that thought about the robbery. D— your eyes ! wot d'ye mean ?"

" Hush, Bill, hush !" said the Jew, who had in vain attempted to stop this burst of indignation ; " somebody will hear us, my dear ; somebody will hear us."

" Let 'em hear !" said Sikes ; " I don't care." But as Mr. Sikes *did* care, upon reflection, he dropped his voice as he said the words, and grew calmer.

" There, there," said the Jew coaxingly. " It was only my caution—nothing more. Now, my dear, about that crib at Chertsey ; when is it to be done, Bill, eh ?—when is it to be done ? Such plate, my dears, such plate !" said the Jew, rubbing his hands, and elevating his eyebrows in a rapture of anticipation.

" Not at all," replied Sikes coldly.

" Not to be done at all !" echoed the Jew, leaning back in his chair.

" No, not at all," rejoined Sikes ; " at least it can't be a put-up job, as we expected."

"Then it hasn't been properly gone about," said the Jew, turning pale with anger. "Don't tell me!"

"But I will tell you," retorted Sikes. "Who are you that's not to be told? I tell you that Toby Crackit has been hanging about the place for a fortnight, and he can't get one of the servants into a line."

"Do you mean to tell me, Bill," said the Jew, softening as the other grew heated, "that neither of the two men in the house can be got over?"

"Yes, I do mean to tell you so," replied Sikes. "The old lady has had 'em these twenty year; and, if you were to give 'em five hundred pound, they wouldn't be in it."

"But do you mean to say, my dear," remonstrated the Jew, "that the women can't be got over?"

"Not a bit of it," replied Sikes.

"Not by flash Toby Crackit?" said the Jew incredulously. "Think what women are, Bill."

"No; not even by flash Toby Crackit," replied Sikes. "He says he's worn sham whiskers and a canary waistcoat the whole blessed time he's been loitering down there, and it's all of no use."

"He should have tried mustachios and a pair of military trousers, my dear," said the Jew after a few moments' reflection.

"So he did," rejoined Sikes, "and they warn't of no more use than the other plant."

The Jew looked very blank at this information, and, after ruminating for some minutes with his chin sunk on his breast, raised his head, and said with a deep sigh that, if flash Toby Crackit reported aright, he feared the game was up.

"And yet," said the old man, dropping his hands on his knees, "it's a sad thing, my dear, to lose so much when we had set our hearts upon it."

"So it is," said Mr. Sikes; "worse luck!"

A long silence ensued, during which the Jew was plunged in deep thought, with his face wrinkled into an expression of villany perfectly demoniacal. Sikes eyed him furtively from time to time; and Nancy, apparently fearful of irritating the housebreaker, sat with her eyes fixed upon the fire, as if she had been deaf to all that passed.

"Fagin," said Sikes, abruptly breaking the stillness that prevailed, "is it worth fifty shiners extra if it's safely done from the outside?"

"Yes," said the Jew, suddenly rousing himself as if from a trance.

"Is it a bargain?" inquired Sikes.

"Yes, my dear, yes," rejoined the Jew, grasping the other's hand, his eyes glistening and every muscle in his face working with the excitement that the inquiry had awakened.

"Then," said Sikes, thrusting aside the Jew's hand with some disdain, "let it come off as soon as you like. Toby and I were over the garden-wall the night afore last, sounding the panels of the doors and shutters : the crib's barred up at night like a jail, but there's one part we can crack, safe and softly."

" Which is that, Bill ?" asked the Jew eagerly.

" Why," whispered Sikes, " as you cross the lawn——"

" Yes, yes," said the Jew, bending his head forward, with his eyes almost starting out of it.

" Umph !" cried Sikes, stopping short as the girl, scarcely moving her head, looked suddenly round and pointed for an instant to the Jew's face. " Never mind which part it is. You can't do it without me, I know ; but it's best to be on the safe side when one deals with you."

" As you like, my dear, as you like," replied the Jew, biting his lip. " Is there no help wanted but yours and Toby's ?"

" None," said Sikes, " 'cept a centre-bit and a boy ; the first we 've both got ; the second you must find us."

" A boy !" exclaimed the Jew. " Oh ! then it is a panel, eh ?"

" Never mind wot it is !" replied Sikes ; " I want a boy, and he mustn't be a big un. Lord !" said Mr. Sikes reflectively, " if I 'd only got that young boy of Ned, the chimbley-sweeper's ! —he kept him small on purpose, and let him out by the job. But the father gets lagged, and then the Juvenile Delinquent Society comes, and takes the boy away from a trade where he was arning money, teaches him to read and write, and in time makes a 'prentice of him. And so they go on," said Mr. Sikes, his wrath rising with the recollection of his wrongs,—" so they go on ; and, if they 'd got money enough, (which it's a Providence they have not,) we shouldn't have half-a-dozen boys left in the whole trade in a year or two."

" No more we should," acquiesced the Jew, who had been considering during this speech, and had only caught the last sentence. " Bill !"

" What now ?" inquired Sikes.

The Jew nodded his head towards Nancy, who was still gazing at the fire ; and intimated by a sign that he would have her told to leave the room. Sikes shrugged his shoulders impatiently, as if he thought the precaution unnecessary, but complied, nevertheless, by requesting Miss Nancy to fetch him a jug of beer.

" You don't want any beer," said Nancy, folding her arms, and retaining her seat very composedly.

" I tell you I do !" replied Sikes.

" Nonsense !" rejoined the girl, coolly. " Go on, Fagin. I know what he 's going to say, Bill ; he needn't mind me."

The Jew still hesitated, and Sikes looked from one to the other in some surprise.

" Why, you don't mind the old girl, do you, Fagin ?" he asked at length. " You 've known her long enough to trust

her, or the devil 's in it: she ain't one to blab, are you
Nancy ?"

" *I* should think not !" replied the young lady, drawing her
chair up to the table, and putting her elbows upon it.

" No, no, my dear,—I know you 're not," said the Jew ;
" but——" and again the old man paused.

" But wot ?" inquired Sikes.

" I didn't know whether she mightn't p'raps be out of sorts,
you know, my dear, as she was the other night," replied the
Jew.

At this confession Miss Nancy burst into a loud laugh, and,
swallowing a glass of brandy, shook her head with an air of
defiance, and burst into sundry exclamations of " Keep the game
a-going !" " Never say die !" and the like, which seemed at once
to have the effect of re-assuring both gentlemen, for the Jew
nodded his head with a satisfied air, and resumed his seat, as
did Mr. Sikes likewise.

" Now, Fagin," said Miss Nancy with a laugh, " tell Bill
at once about Oliver !"

" Ah ! you 're a clever one, my dear ; the sharpest girl I ever
saw !" said the Jew, patting her on the neck. " It *was* about
Oliver I was going to speak, sure enough. Ha ! ha ! ha !"

" What about him ?" demanded Sikes.

" He 's the boy for you, my dear," replied the Jew in a hoarse
whisper, laying his finger on the side of his nose, and grinning
frightfully.

" He !" exclaimed Sikes.

" Have him, Bill !" said Nancy. " I would if I was in
your place. He mayn't be so much up as any of the others ;
but that 's not what you want if he 's only to open a door for
you. Depend upon it he 's a safe one, Bill."

" I know he is," rejoined Fagin ; " he 's been in good training
these last few weeks, and it 's time he began to work for his
bread ; besides, the others are all too big."

" Well, he is just the size I want," said Mr. Sikes, ruminating.

" And will do everything you want, Bill my dear," interposed the Jew ; " he can't help himself,—that is, if you only
frighten him enough."

" Frighten him !" echoed Sikes. " It 'll be no sham frightening, mind you. If there 's anything queer about him when we
once get into the work,—in for a penny, in for a pound,—you
won't see him alive again, Fagin. Think of that before you
send him. Mark my words !" said the robber, shaking a heavy
crowbar which he had drawn from under the bedstead.

" I 've thought of it all," said the Jew with energy. " I 've—
I 've had my eye upon him, my dears, close: close. Once let
him feel that he is one of us ; once fill his mind with the idea
that he has been a thief, and he 's ours,—ours for his life ! Oho !

It couldn't have come about better!"   The old man crossed his arms upon his breast, and, drawing his head and shoulders into a heap, literally hugged himself for joy.

"Ours!" said Sikes.   "Yours, you mean."

"Perhaps I do, my dear," said the Jew with a shrill chuckle. "Mine, if you like, Bill."

"And wot," said Sikes, scowling fiercely on his agreeable friend,—"wot makes you take so much pains about one chalk-faced kid, when you know there are fifty boys snoozing about Common Garden every night, as you might pick and choose from?"

"Because they're of no use to me, my dear," replied the Jew with some confusion, "not worth the taking; for their looks convict 'em when they get into trouble, and I lose 'em all. With this boy properly managed, my dears, I could do what I couldn't with twenty of them.   Besides," said the Jew, re-covering his self-possession, "he has us now if he could only give us leg-bail again; and he *must* be in the same boat with us; never mind how he came there, it's quite enough for my power over him that he was in a robbery, that's all I want. Now how much better this is, than being obliged to put the poor leetle boy out of the way, which would be dangerous,— and we should lose by it, besides."

"When is it to be done?" asked Nancy, stopping some tur-bulent exclamation on the part of Mr. Sikes, expressive of the disgust with which he received Fagin's affectation of humanity.

"Ah, to be sure," said the Jew, "when is it to be done, Bill?"

"I planned with Toby the night arter to-morrow," rejoined Sikes in a surly voice, "if he heard nothing from me to the contrairy."

"Good," said the Jew; "there's no moon."

"No," rejoined Sikes.

"It's all arranged about bringing off the swag,* is it?" asked the Jew.

Sikes nodded.

"And about——"

"Oh ah, it's all planned," rejoined Sikes, interrupting him; "never mind particulars.   You'd better bring the boy here to-morrow night; I shall get off the stones an hour arter day-break.   Then you hold your tongue, and keep the melting-pot ready, and that's all you'll have to do."

After some discussion in which all three took an active part, it was decided that Nancy should repair to the Jew's next evening, when the night had set in, and bring Oliver away with her: Fagin craftily observing, that, if he evinced any disincli-nation to the task, he would be more willing to accompany the girl, who had so recently interfered in his behalf, than anybody else.   It was also solemnly arranged that poor Oliver should,

* Booty.

for the purposes of the contemplated expedition, be unreservedly consigned to the care and custody of Mr. William Sikes;
and further, that the said Sikes should deal with him as he
thought fit, and should not be held responsible by the Jew for
any mischance or evil that might befal the boy, or any punishment with which it might be necessary to visit him, it being
understood that, to render the compact in this respect binding,
any representations made by Mr. Sikes on his return should
be required to be confirmed and corroborated, in all important
particulars, by the testimony of flash Toby Crackit.

These preliminaries adjusted, Mr. Sikes proceeded to drink
brandy at a furious rate, and to flourish the crowbar in an
alarming manner, yelling forth at the same time most unmusical
snatches of song mingled with wild execrations. At length, in
a fit of professional enthusiasm, he insisted upon producing his
box of housebreaking tools, which he had no sooner stumbled in with, and opened for the purpose of explaining the
nature and properties of the various implements it contained,
and the peculiar beauties of their construction, than he fell over
it upon the floor, and went to sleep where he fell.

"Good night, Nancy!" said the Jew, muffling himself up as
before.

"Good night!"

Their eyes met, and the Jew scrutinised her narrowly. There
was no flinching about the girl. She was as true and earnest in
the matter as Toby Crackit himself could be.

The Jew again bade her good night, and, bestowing a sly
kick upon the prostrate form of Mr. Sikes while her back was
turned, groped down stairs.

"Always the way," muttered the Jew to himself as he turned
homewards. "The worst of these women is, that a very little
thing serves to call up some long-forgotten feeling; and the
best of them is, that it never lasts. Ha! ha! The man against
the child, for a bag of gold!"

Beguiling the time with these pleasant reflections, Mr. Fagin
wended his way through mud and mire to his gloomy abode,
where the Dodger was sitting up, impatiently awaiting his return.

"Is Oliver a-bed? I want to speak to him," was his first remark as they descended the stairs.

"Hours ago," replied the Dodger, throwing open a door.
"Here he is!"

The boy was lying fast asleep on a rude bed upon the floor,
so pale with anxiety, and sadness, and the closeness of his
prison, that he looked like death; not death as it shows in
shroud and coffin, but in the guise it wears when life has just
departed: when a young and gentle spirit has but an instant
fled to heaven, and the gross air of the world has not had time
to breathe upon the changing dust it hallowed.

"Not now," said the Jew turning softly away. "To-
morrow. To-morrow."

THE LONELY GIRL.

SHE walk'd alone in the mingled throng,
    But there were none to greet her ;
The merry dance and the evening song
    To her were one day sweeter.

She was dress'd in the pride of fashion's glare,
    And diamonds round her glitter'd ;
But beneath them lay a soul of care,
    By distant thoughts embitter'd.

I saw her smile as her gallant pass'd,—
    'Twas the smile of the broken-hearted ;
I watch'd her eye as she turn'd away,—
    The tear to that eye had started.

For she thought of the times when she led the dance,
    A stranger to sin and sorrow :
She thought of the times when the joys of to-day
    But sweeten'd the joys of the morrow.

She thought of the cot and the rustic gown,
    And the hearts that once adored her ;
She thought of the parents that bless'd their child,
    Ere vice and falsehood sold her.

For Mary was once the pride of the plain,
    The happiest fair of the fair :
The flute and the cymbal welcomed her then,—
    They were silent unless she was there.

But now there are none to hear her woes,
    Or join in her tale of sorrow,—
To wipe from her eye the penitent tear,
    Or chase away thoughts of the morrow.

Yes, Mary, there 's one whose heart beats for thee yet,
    Who thinks of her child far away,—
Who blesses thee still, in the stranger land,
    Tho' mouldering fast to decay.

She weeps for thee e'en in the midnight hour,
    When Care may have lull'd thee to sleep ;
She prays for her once adored, still beloved child,—
    She prays, but she turns to weep.

She prays to the Power that rules the winds
    That He will ne'er forsake her ;
She prays the prayer of a parent's grief,
    That the God who gave may take her.

Child of sin ! to thy parent speed,
    For she will yet receive thee ;
Her bosom yet will feel thy pangs,
    Her cares will yet relieve thee.

For know that Love can only rest
    Where Virtue guards the way ;
The hand of Vice may prune the plant,—
    Its blossoms soon decay.

THE APPORTIONMENT OF THE WORLD.

FROM SCHILLER.

"TAKE the world!" from his throne on high, God cried;
  " 'Tis my free gift,—a heritage to man!
His attribute for ever. Go! divide;
  Apportion it like brothers, if you can!"

Straight at his bidding, forth on either hand
  Both old and young to take their portion came:
The farmer seized the produce of the land;
  The hunter rush d upon the forest game;

The merchant from all climes his wares did bring;
  The abbot chose the choicest vintages;
On taxes and on customs pounced the king;
  And the priest claim'd the tithe of all as his.

Last of the throng, from wandering far and wide,
  The poet sought the Lord with haggard air;
For, ah! he wildly gazed on every side,
  And saw that nought remain'd for him to share.

"Ah, wo is me! and must I be forgot,
  The trustiest of your subjects, I, alone?"
As thus he bitterly deplored his lot
  He cast himself before the Almighty's throne.

"If in a world of reverie and rhyme
  You ever live," God answer'd, "blame not me.
Where hast thou been? how hast thou pass'd thy time?"
  "I was," replied the poet, "nigh to thee;

"My eyes have gloated on thy glory's blaze;
  My ears have drunk the music of the spheres:
Forgive! that, dazzled, blinded, by the rays
  Of heaven, I have for earth nor eyes nor ears."

"What then remains?" God answered. "All is given;
  The world apportion'd, nought is left to give;
But, if thou wilt abide with me in heaven,
  Come when thou wilt,—best life for thee to live!"

SHAKSPEARE PAPERS.—No. V.

HIS LADIES.—I. LADY MACBETH.

"Then gently scan your brother man,
More gently sister woman."   BURNS.

" Je donne mon avis, non comme bon, mais comme mien."
MONTAIGNE.

THE ladies of Shakspeare have of course riveted the attention, and drawn to them the sympathies, of all who have read or seen his plays. The book-trained critic, weighing words and sentences in his closet; the romantic poet, weaving his verses by grove or stream; the polished occupant of the private box; the unwashed brawler of the gallery; the sedate visitant of the pit, are touched each in his several way by the conjugal devotion and melancholy fate of Desdemona, the high-souled principle of Isabella, the enthusiastic love and tragic end of Juliet, the maternal agonies of Constance, the stern energies of Margaret of Anjou, the lofty resignation of Katharine, the wit and romance of Rosalind, frolic of tongue, but deeply feeling at heart; the accomplished coquetries of Cleopatra, redeemed and almost sanctified by her obedient rushing to welcome death at the call ringing in her ears from the grave of her self-slain husband; the untiring affection of Imogen, Ophelia's stricken heart and maddened brain, or the filial constancy of Cordelia. Less deeply marked, but all in their kind beautiful, are the innocence of Miranda, the sweetness of Anne Page, the meek bearing—beneath the obtrusion of undesired honours—of Anne Boleyn, the playful fondness of Jessica;—but I should run through all the catalogue of Shakspeare's plays were I to continue the enumeration. The task is unnecessary, for they dwell in the hearts of all, of every age, and sex, and condition. They nestle in the bosoms of the wise and the simple, the sedentary and the active, the moody and the merry, the learned and the illiterate, the wit of the club, the rustic of the farm, the soldier in camp, the scholar in college; and it affords a remarkable criterion of their general effect, that, even in those foreign countries which, either from imperfect knowledge, defective taste, or national prejudice, set little value on the plays of Shakspeare,—while Hamlet, Richard, Macbeth, King John, Lear, and Falstaff, are unknown or rejected, the names of Desdemona and Juliet are familiar as household words.

No writer ever created so many female characters, or placed them in situations of such extreme diversity; and in none do we find so lofty an appreciation of female excellence. The stories from which the great dramatists of Athens drew their plots were, in most of their striking incidents, derogatory to woman. The tale of Troy divine, the war of Thebes, the heroic legends, were their favourite, almost their exclusive sources; and the crimes, passions, and misfortunes of Clytemnestra and Medea, Phædra and Jocasta, could only darken the scene. An adulterous spouse aiding in the murder of her long-absent lord, the King of men, returning crowned with conquest; a daughter participating in the ruthless avenging by death inflicted on a mother by a son; an unpitying sorceress killing her children to satiate rage against her husband; a faithless wife endeavouring to force her shameless love on her step-son, and by false accusation consigning him for his refusal to destruction beneath his father's curse; a melancholy queen linked in incestuous nuptials to her own offspring;—these ladies are the heroines of the most renowned of the Greek tragedies! and the consequences of their guilt or misfortune compose the fable of many more.   In some of the Greek plays, as the Eumenides, we have no female characters except the unearthly habitants of heaven or hell; in the most wondrous of them all, Prometheus Fettered, appears only the mythic Io; in the Persians, only the ghost of Atossa, who scarcely appertains to womankind: in some, as Philoctetes, women form no part of the *dramatis personæ*; in others, as the Seven against Thebes, they are of no importance to the action of the piece; or, as in the Suppliants, serve but as the Chorus; and, in many more, are of less than secondary importance.   Euripides often makes them the objects of those ungallant reflections which consign the misogynic dramatist to such summary punishment from the irritated sex in the comedies of Aristophanes; and in the whole number, in the thirty-three plays extant, there are but two women who can affect our nobler or softer emotions.   The tender and unremitting care of Antigone for her blind, forlorn, and aged father, her unbending determination to sacrifice her lover and her life sooner than fail in paying funeral honours to her fallen brother; and, in Alcestis, her resolute urging that her own life should be taken to preserve that of a beloved husband,—invest them with a pathetic and heroic beauty. But, in the one, we are haunted by the horrid recollections of incest and fratricide; and, in the other, we are somewhat indignant that we should be forced to sympathize with an affection squandered upon so heartless a fellow as Admetus, who suffers his wife to perish in his stead with the most undisturbed conviction of the superior value of his own existence, pouring forth all the while the most melodious lamentations over her death, but never for a moment thinking of coming forward to prevent it.   They are beautiful creations, nevertheless.

The Greek dramatists were in a great measure bound to a particular class of subjects; but, in general, the manner in which an author treats the female character, affords one of the main criteria by which the various gradations of genius may be estimated.   By the highest genius woman is always spoken of with a deep feeling of the most reverential delicacy.   Helen is the cause of the war immortalized by the Iliad; but no allusion to her lapse is made throughout the poem save by herself, deploring in bitter accents what she has done.   She wishes that she had died an evil death before she followed Paris; she acknowledges herself to be unworthy of the kindred of those whom she describes as deserving of honour; her conscience suggests that her far-famed brothers, "whom one mother bore," are in the field when the warring chieftains meet in truce, but dare not show themselves among their peers through shame of the disgrace she has entailed upon them; and, at the last, she lays bare her internal feeling that insult is the lot she deserves by the warm gratitude with which she acknowledges, in her bitter lament over the corse of Hector, that he had the generosity never to address her with upbraiding.   The wrath of Achilles is roused for the injury inflicted upon him by carrying off Briseis, dear to his heart, " spear-captured as she was." She is restored by the penitent Agamemnon, with solemn vows that she returns pure and uninsulted. Of Andromache I think it unnecessary to speak. In the Odyssey, it is true, we have Circe and Calypso ; but they are goddesses couching with a mortal, and excite no human passion. We meet them in the region of " *speciosa miracula*," where Cyclops, and Sirius, and Lotus-eaters dwell; where the King of the winds holds his court, and whence is the passage to Erebus. In that glorious mixture of adventure and allegory,—the Voyage of Ulysses,— we may take those island beauties to be the wives and sweethearts whom sailors meet in every port ; or, following the stream of moralists and commentators, look upon the fable to be no more than

" Truth severe in fairy fiction dressed."

In other parts of the poem we might wish for more warm-heartedness in Penelope ; but under her circumstances caution is excusable, and she must be admitted to be a pattern of constancy and devotion. The Helen of the Odyssey is a fine continuation of the Helen of the Iliad. Still full of kindly feminine impulses, still sorrowing when she thinks of the misfortunes she has occasioned, her griefs have lost the intense poignancy with which they afflicted her while leading a life degrading her in her own eyes, and exposing her to affronts of which she could not complain. Restored to the husband of her early affections, consoled by his pardon, and dwelling once more amid the scenes of her youth,—absence from which, and absence so occasioned, she had never ceased to regret in wasting floods of tears,—the Helen of the Odyssey comes before us no longer uttering the accents of cease-less self-reproach, but soothed, if not pacified, in soul. We have the *lull* after the tempest,—the calm following the whirlwind.

Virgil is a great poet indeed, though few will now agree with Scali-ger that he is equal, far less superior, to Homer. Dido is the blot upon the Æneid. The loves of the Carthaginian queen might have made, and in the hands of Virgil would have made, a charming poem, treated separately,—a poem far superior in execution to the Hero and Leander of Musæus, but a work of the same order. As it stands, the episode, if it can be so called, utterly ruins the epic character of the hero. St. Evremond has said that Æneas had all the qualities of a monk ; it is plain that he had not the feelings of a gentleman ; and we cannot wonder that his first wife wandered from his side, and that he met with so violent an opposition when he sought another. Virgil, after his conduct to Dido, had not the courage to introduce him to Lavinia in person, and leaves him undefended to the angry tongue of her mother. The poet was justly punished for his fourth book ; for, in all those which follow, he has not ventured to introduce any female characters but incendiaries, sibyls, shrews, and furies.

When Dante took Virgil as his guide in the infernal regions, he did not follow his master in dwelling on the pleasures or the gentler sorrows of illicit love. His ghostly women appear stern, or subdued of port. The lady who is best known to the English reader, Fran-cesca di Rimini, forms no exception. Nothing can be more grave and solemn than the tale of her hapless passion, as told in the Inferno. It is pervaded throughout by such sorrow and remorse as we might expect to find in a region whence hope is excluded. Accordingly, how far different is its impression from that left on the mind by the same story when told merely as a love-tale by Mr. Leigh Hunt. I do not say this in disparagement of that picturesque and graphic poem, the Story of Rimini, which has been exposed to the most unjustifiable criticism; but to mark the manner in which men of talent and men of genius handle the same subject. The ladies of Tasso, though not vigorously sketched, and in general imitated from the Latin poets,—I speak of his Jerusalem,—are conceived in a spirit of romantic chivalry; and, even when the witching Armida leads Rinaldo astray, the poet diverts our attention from the blandishments of the enchantress to dazzle us by the wonders of magic groves and gardens. Poor Tasso, besides, wishes to persuade us—perhaps in some moody hours he had persuaded himself—that he intended the whole poem for an allegory, in which Armida was to play some edifying part,—I forget what. In the poets of romance we do not look for the severer style of the epic; but the forest-ranging heroines of Ariosto and Spenser, "roaming the woodland, frank and free," have an air of self-confiding independence and maiden freshness, worthy of the leafy scenes through which they move, that renders it impossible to approach them with other thoughts than those of chivalrous deference. If Spenser, in his canto of Jealousy, makes the lady of the victim of that weak passion treat her husband as he had anticipated, why, she errs with no man of mortal mould, but chooses as her mates the jolly satyrs wonning in the wood; and Spenser has his allegory too. Ariosto took no trouble to make explanations, being satisfied, I suppose, with the character given of his poetry by Cardinal Hippolyto; and even he has the grace to beg the ladies, to whose service he had from the beginning dedicated his lays, to avert their eyes when he is about to sing the strange adventures of Giocondo.*

* Orlando Furioso, canto xxii. st. 1, 2, 3.

I.

"Donne, e voi che le donne avete in pregio,
 Per Dio, non date a questa istoria orecchia,
A questa che 'l ostier dire in dispregio,
 È in vostra infamia e biasmo s'apparecchia;
Benche ne macchia vi puo dar ne fregio
 Lingua si vile; e sia l'usanza vecchia,
Che 'l volgare ignorante ognun riprenda,
E parle piu de quel meno intenda.

II.

Lasciate questo canto, che senz' esso
 Puo star l'istoria, e non sara men chiara;
Mettendolo Turpino, anch' io l' ò messo,
 Non per malevolenzia, ne per gara;
Ch' io v' ami oltre mia lingua che l' a·expresso,
 Che mai non fu di celebrarvi avara,
N' ò falto mille prove, e v' o dimostro
Ch' io son ne potrei esser se non vostro.

III.

Passi chi vuol tre carte, o quattro, senza
 Leggerne verso, e chi pur legge vuole
Gli dia quella medesima credenza,
 Che si vuol dare a finzion, e a fole," &c.

which thus may be rollingly Englished,

Ladies, and you to whom ladies are dear,
For God's sake don't lend to this story an ear. [Care

The theme of Milton in Paradise Lost, hardly admits of the developement of ordinary human feelings; but his sole Eve has grace in all her steps, and all her actions too. In Paradise Regained his subject was badly chosen; and he feared, from religious motives, to introduce the Virgin. In Comus his Lady is a model of icy chastity, worthy of the classic verse in which she is embalmed; but Dalilah in Samson Agonistes is the more dramatic conception. Ornate and gay, she makes urgent court to her angry husband, with no better fate than to be by him inexorably repelled. She presses upon him all the topics that could lead to reconciliation, but the sense of his wrongs is too acute to allow of pardon; and at last she bursts away with the consoling reflection that, though spurned by him, and made the object of reproach in Israelitish songs, she shall be hymned and honoured in those of her own country as a deliverer. Milton was unhappy in his wives and daughters; and his domestic manners appear to have been harsh and unamiable. In his prose works, his Tetrachordon for example, he does not display any kindly feeling for the sex; but when he clothed himself in his singing robes, and soared above the cares of every-day life, to expatiate in the purer regions of poetry, the soul of the poet softened and sublimed; like his own Adam, his sterner nature relented; and, though he could not make Samson pardon Dalilah, he will not let her depart unhonoured. In Paradise Lost he had spoken of her, disparagingly,—

> "So rose the Danite strong,
> Herculean Samson, from the harlot lap
> Of Philistæan Dalilah;"

but when she comes before him, as it were, in bodily presence, he

> Care not for fables of slander or blame
> Which this scandalous chronicler flings on your name.
> Spots that can stain you with slight or with wrong
> Cannot be cast by so worthless a tongue.
> Well is it known, as an usage of old,
> That the ignorant vulgar will ever be bold,
> Satire and censure still scattering, and
> Talking the most where they least understand.
> Passed over unread let this canto remain,
> Without it the story will be just as plain.
> As Turpin has put it, so *I* put it too;
> But not from ill-feeling, dear ladies, to you.
> My love to your sex has been shown in my lays;
> To you I have never been niggard of praise;
> And many a proof I have given which secures
> That I am, and can never be other than yours.
> Skip three or four pages, and read not a word;
> Or, if you *will* read it, pray deem it absurd,
> As a story in credit not better or worse
> Than the foolish old tales you were told by the nurse.

I do not mean to defend my doggrel; but I think Ariosto has not yet had an adequate translator in English, or indeed in any language; nor, in my opinion, will he easily find one. The poem is too long, and requires the aid of the music of the original language to carry the reader through. I do not know what metre in English could contend against the prolixity; but I *do* know that Ariosto sadly wants—as what classic in the vernacular languages does not?—a better critic of his text than he has yet found, in Italian.

In the above passage it is somewhat amusing to find Ariosto assuring his readers that they might pass this particular canto, because without it " *puo star l'istoria ;*" as if there were a canto in the whole poem of which the same might not be said.

leaves all the words of reproach to her irritated lord, and suggests to her, topics of self-justification, dismissing her from the stage, not as a faithless wife, but as a heroic woman, who had sacrificed her affections to her country, and who retires after humiliating herself in vain to reap the reward of her patriotic conduct among her people and her kindred.

If we turn from the epic and tragic to the other departments of literature in which genius can be exercised, we shall find the feeling much the same. Those who write from observation of what is going on in the world,—the novelist, the comic writer, the satirist,—must take the world as it is, and lay it before us in its mixture of good and evil. There is no need, however, that the latter should be forcibly thrust upon us. The task of the satirists appears to me the lowest in which talent can be employed. The most famous among them, Juvenal, tells us truly that the *rigidi censura cachinni*—the part chosen by Democritus—is easy to any one. We must rise above it, as he has done in some of his satires,—as in that sublime poem in which the passage occurs, the tenth, or the thirteenth and fourteenth,—and forget the wit or the censor to assume the loftier bearing of the moralist. I should have wondered that the same mind which produced these noble effusions could have perpetrated the enormities of the sixth satire and some others, if I did not reflect that Rome, originally an asylum for robbers, was nothing more than a standing camp, with the virtues and vices, the manners and the feelings of a camp, to the day of its downfall. Rape and violence procured its first women, and it would seem as if the original act had influenced their feelings to the sex throughout. It is certain that theirs is the only literature in the world in which no female character is delineated worthy of the slightest recollection,—a striking circumstance, and well deserving critical investigation; but it would now lead us too far from our subject, from which indeed I have delayed too long already. We must get back to Shakspeare, staying only to remark that if Boccacio and his imitator, Chaucer, have intermingled licentious tales in their miscellaneous collection, they have done so, only in compliance with the supposed necessity of delineating every species of life, and that they hasten to show that they could be of finer spirit when emancipated from the thraldom of custom; that Cervantes chequers the comic of Don Quixote with visions of graceful and romantic beauty; and that such will be found to be the case more or less in every composition that takes firm hold of the human mind. I except, of course, works of morals, science, and philosophy; and under those heads must come the unromantic and unpoetic books of wit, and even buffoonery, if they be doomed to last. Rabelais will live for ever to speak vocally to the intelligent; but mere licentiousness must perish. Indulgence in woman-scorning ribaldry inflicts due punishment upon talent itself, if it be prostituted to such miserable work. The melancholy ability which has been so successful in La Pucelle affords a sufficient reason why its author failed when he attempted a Henriade.

Supereminent over all the great geniuses of the world,—and with no others have I compared him,—is Shakspeare in his women. Homer was not called upon to introduce them in such number or variety, nor could they enter so intimately into the action of his poems.

Still less was there opportunity for their delineation in Milton. But Shakspeare's is the unique merit that, being a dramatist wielding equally the highest tragic and the lowest comic, and therefore compelled to bring females prominently forward in every variety of circumstance, he has carefully avoided themes and situations which might either inspire horror or disgust, or excite licentious feeling. We have in him no Phædra, Clytemnestra, or Medea; no story like those of Jocasta, or Monimia, or the Mysterious Mother. He would have recoiled from what is hinted at in Manfred. Even the Myrrha of Sardanapalus could not have found a place among his heroines. In none of his plots, comic or tragic, does female frailty form an ingredient. The only play in which ladies have been betrayed is Measure for Measure; and there he takes care that their misfortune shall be amended, by marrying Mariana to Angelo, and ordering Claudio to restore honour to Julietta, whom he had wronged. Nowhere else does a similar example occur, and there it is set in strong contrast with the high-toned purity of Isabella. In the instances of slandered women, it seems to delight him to place them triumphant over their slanderers; as Hero in Much Ado about Nothing, Hermione in the Winter's Tale, Imogen in Cymbeline. All his heroes woo with the most honourable views; there is no intrigue in any of his plays, no falsehood to the married bed. Those who offer illicit proposals are exposed to ruin and disgrace. Angelo falls from his lofty station. Prince John is driven from his brother's court. Falstaff, the wit and courtier, becomes a butt, when his evil star leads him to make lawless courtship to the Wives of Windsor. The innocent and natural love of Miranda in the Tempest affords a striking contrast to the coarse and disgusting passion of Dorinda: a character thrust into the play as an improvement by no less a man than Dryden. Here again we may remark how great is the distance which separates genius of the first order even from that which comes nearest to it. The two most detestable women ever drawn by Shakspeare — Regan and Goneril — are both in love with Edmund; but we have no notice of their passion until the moment of their death, and then we find that, wicked as were the thoughts which rankled in their bosoms, no infringement of the laws of chastity was contemplated; marriage was their intention : " I was contracted to them both," says Edmund; " all three now marry in an instant." With his dying breath he bears testimony that in the midst of their crimes they were actuated by the dominant feeling of woman :—

> " Yet Edmund was beloved ;
> The one the other poisoned for his sake,
> And after slew herself."

Emilia is accused by Iago in soliloquy as being suspected of faithlessness to his bed, but he obviously does not believe the charge :—

> " I hate the Moor ;
> And it is thought abroad that 'twixt my sheets
> He has done my office ; *I know not if 't be true,*
> But I, for mere suspicion in that kind,
> Will do as if for surety."

He uses it merely as an additional excuse for hating the Moor; a palliation to his conscience in the career which he is about to pursue. Queen Gertrude's marriage with her brother-in-law is made the subject of severe animadversion; but it does not appear that she had dishonoured herself in the life of her first husband, or was in any manner participant in the crime of Claudius. Hamlet, in the vehemence of his anger, never insinuates such a charge; and the Ghost, rising to moderate his violence, acquits her by his very appearance at such a time, of any heinous degree of guilt. As for the gross theory of Tieck respecting Ophelia, it is almost a national insult. He maintains that she had yielded to Hamlet's passion, and that its natural consequences had driven her to suicide. Such a theory is in direct opposition to the retiring and obedient purity of her character, the tenour of her conversations and soliloquies, the general management of the play, and what I have endeavoured to show is the undeviating current of Shakspeare's ideas. If the German critic propounded this heresy to insult English readers through one of their greatest favourites in revenge for the ungallant reason which the Archbishop of Canterbury,* in Henry V, assigns as the origin of the Salique law, he might be pardoned; but, as it is plainly dictated by a spirit of critical wickedness and blasphemy, I should consign him, in spite of his learning, acuteness, and, Shakspearian knowledge, without compassion, to the avenging hands of Lysistrata.†

Such, in the plays where he had to create the characters, was the course of Shakspeare. In the historical plays, where he had to write by the book, it is not at all different. Scandal is carefully avoided. Many spots lie on the fame of Queen Elinor, but no reference is made to them by the hostile tongue which describes the mother-queen as a second Áté, stirring her son, King John, to blood and strife. Jane Shore, of whom Rowe, a commentator on Shakspeare too, made a heroine, is not introduced on the stage in Richard III. Poor Joan of Arc is used brutally, it must be owned; but it is not till she is driven to the stake that she confesses to an infirmity which not even her barbarous judges can seriously believe. We must observe, besides, that the first part of Henry VI. can scarcely be considered a play of Shakspeare, for he did little more than revise the old play of that name. To the charge of the older dramatist, too, must be set the strange exhibition of Margaret of Anjou mourning over the head of the Duke of Suffolk in the second part. When Shakspeare has that vigorous woman to himself, as in Richard III, she shows no traces of such weakness; she is the heroic asserter of her husband's rights, the unsubdued but not-to-be-comforted mourner over her foully slaughtered son. He makes the scenes of the civil wars sad enough; the father kills the son, the son the father, under the eyes of the pitying king; but there is no hint of outrage on women. He

---

* Henry V. act i. sc. 2. Archbishop Chicheley's argument is

> " The land Salique lies in Germany,
> Between the floods of Sala and of Elbe,
> Where Charles the Great, having subdued the Saxons,
> There left behind and settled certain French,
> *Who, holding in disdain the German women*
> *For some dishonest manners of their life,*
> Established there this law, to wit, no female
> Should be inheritrix in Salique land."

† Aristoph. Lysistr.

contrives to interest us equally in Katharine of Aragon and Anne Boleyn. Everything that poetry can do, is done, to make us forget the faults of Cleopatra, and to incline us to think that a world was well lost for that *petit nez retroussé*. We should in vain search the writings of the Romans themselves for such Roman ladies as those of Coriolanus and Julius Cæsar. In his camps and armies we have much military tumult and railing, but nowhere the introduction of licentious scenes. If Alcibiades be attended by his Phrynia and Timandra, and Falstaff have his poll clawed like a parrot by Doll Tearsheet, the Athenian ladies are introduced as a vehicle for the fierce misanthropy of Timon, and the fair one of Eastcheap acts as a satire upon the impotent desires of the withered elder, the dead elm, whom she clasps in her venal embraces. They are drawn in their true colours: no attempt is made to bedeck them with sentimental graces —to hold them up to sympathetic admiration with the maudlin novelist, or to exhibit them as "interesting young females" with the police reporter. They lift not their brazen fronts in courts and palaces; in obscure corners they ply their obscene trade. We know that it is their vocation, and dismiss them from our minds. There is no corruption to be feared from the example of the inmates of Mr. Overdone's establishment or Mrs. Quickly's tavern. Shakspeare exhibits only one fallen lady in all his plays,—and she is Cressida. But Troilus and Cressida deserves a separate paper, if for no other reason, yet because it is a play in which Shakspeare has handled the same characters as Homer. It is worth while to consider in what points these greatest of poets agree, and in what they differ.

Such, then, is the female character as drawn in Shakspeare. It is pure, honourable, spotless,—ever ready to perform a kind action,— never shrinking from a heroic one. Gentle and submissive where duty or affection bids, — firm and undaunted in resisting the approaches of sin, or shame, or disgrace. Constant in love through every trial,—faithful and fond in all the great relations of life, as wife, as daughter, as sister, as mother, as friend,—witty or refined, tender or romantic, lofty or gay,—her failings shrouded, her good and lovely qualities brought into the brightest light, she appears in the pages of the mighty dramatist as if she were the cherished daughter of a fond father, the idolized mistress of an adoring lover, the very goddess of a kneeling worshipper. I have catalogued most of the female names which adorn the plays. One is absent from the list. She is absent; the dark lady of that stupendous work which, since the Eumenides, bursting upon the stage with appalling howl in quest of the fugitive Orestes, electrified with terror the Athenian audience, has met no equal. I intend to maintain that Lady Macbeth, too, is human in heart and impulse,—that she is not meant to be an embodiment of the Furies.

Macbeth is the gloomiest of the plays. Well may its hero say that he has supped full of horrors. It opens with the incantations of spiteful witches, and concludes with a series of savage combats, stimulated by quenchless hate on one side, and by the desperation inspired by the consciousness of unpardonable crime on the other. In every act we have blood in torrents. The first man who appears on the stage is the *bleeding* captain. The first word uttered by earthly lips is, "What *bloody* man is that?" The tale which the captain relates is full of fearful gashes, reeking wounds, and *bloody* execution. The murder of Duncan in the second act stains the hands of Macbeth so deeply as to render them fit to incarnadine the multitudinous seas, and make the green—one red. His lady imbrues herself in the crimson stream, and gilds the faces of the sleeping grooms with gore. She thus affords a pretence to the thane for slaughtering them in an access of simulated fury.

> " Their hands and faces were all badged with *blood,*
> So were their daggers, which unwiped we found
> Upon their pillows."

Macbeth carefully impresses the sanguinary scene upon his hearers:

> " Here lay Duncan,
> His silver skin laced with his golden *blood,*
> And his gashed stabs looked like a breach in nature
> For ruin's wasteful entrance; there the murderers,
> Steeped in the colours of their trade, their daggers
> Unmannerly breeched in *gore.*"

Direful thoughts immediately follow, and the sky itself participates in the horror. The old man who can well remember threescore and ten, during which time he had witnessed dreadful hours and strange things, considers all as mere trifles, compared with the sore night of Duncan's murder.

> " The heavens,
> Thou seest, as troubled with man's act,
> Threaten his *bloody* stage; by the clock 'tis day,
> And yet dark night strangles the travelling lamp."

The horses of Duncan forget their careful training, and their natural instincts, to break their stalls and eat each other. Gloom, ruin, murder, horrible doubts, unnatural suspicions, portents of dread in earth and heaven, surround us on all sides. In the third act, desperate assassins, incensed by the blows and buffets of the world, weary with disasters, tugged with fortune, willing to wreak their hatred on all mankind, and persuaded that Banquo has been their enemy, set upon and slay him, without remorse and without a word. The prayer of their master to Night, that she would, with

> " *Bloody* and invisible hand,
> Cancel and tear to pieces that great bond "

which kept him in perpetual terror, is in part accomplished; and he who was his enemy in, as he says,

> " Such *bloody* distance,
> That every minute of his being thrusts
> Against my life,"

lies breathless in the dust. The murderers bring the witness of their deed to the very banquet-chamber of the expecting king. They come with *blood* upon the face. The hardened stabber does not communicate the tidings of his exploit in set phrase. He minces not the matter,—his language is not culled from any trim and weeded vocabulary; and the king compliments him in return, in language equally vernacular and unrefined.

> " *Mur.* My lord, his throat is cut; that I did for him.
> *Mac.* Thou art the best o' the cut-throats."

Cheered by this flattering tribute to his merits, the accomplished artist goes on, in all the pride of his profession, to show that he had left no rubs or botches in his work.   Macbeth, after a burst of indignation at the escape of Fleance, recurs to the comfortable assurance of Banquo's death, and asks, in the full certainty of an answer in the affirmative,

> "But Banquo 's safe ?
> *Mur.* Ay, my good lord : safe in a ditch he bides,
>   With twenty trenched gashes on his head!;
>   The least a death to nature.
> *Mac.* Thanks for that."

Presently the gory locks of Banquo's spectre attest the truth of what the murderer has told, and the banquet breaks up by the flight, rather than the retirement, of the astonished guests; leaving Macbeth dismally, but fiercely, pondering over thoughts steeped in slaughter. The very language of the scene is redolent of blood.   The word itself occurs in almost every speech.   At the conclusion of the act, come the outspeaking of suspicions hitherto only muttered, and the determination of the Scottish nobles to make an effort which may give to their tables meat, sleep to their eyes, and free their feasts and banquets from those bloody knives, the fatal hue of which haunted them in their very hours of retirement, relaxation, or festival.

The sanguine stain dyes the fourth act as deeply.   A head severed from the body, and a bloody child, are the first apparitions that rise before the king at the bidding of the weird sisters.   The blood-boltered Banquo is the last to linger upon the stage, and sear the eyes of the amazed tyrant.   The sword of the assassin is soon at work in the castle of Macduff; and his wife and children fly from the deadly blow, shrieking "murder"—in vain. And the fifth act,—from its appalling commencement, when the sleeping lady plies her hopeless task of nightly washing the blood-stained hand, through the continual clangour of trumpets calling, as clamorous harbingers, to blood and death, to its conclusion, when Macduff, with dripping sword, brings in the freshly hewn-off head of the "dead butcher," to lay it at the feet of the victorious Malcolm,—exhibits a sequence of scenes in which deeds and thoughts of horror and violence are perpetually, and almost physically, forced upon the attention of the spectator.   In short, the play is one clot of blood from beginning to end.   It was objected to Alfieri, (by Grimm, I believe,) that he wrote his tragedies not in tears, but blood.   Shakspeare could write in tears when he pleased.   In Macbeth he chose to dip his pen in a darker current.

Nowhere in the course of the play does he seek to beguile us of our tears.   We feel no more interest in the gracious Duncan, in Banquo, in Lady Macduff, than we do in the slaughtered grooms. We feel that they have been brutally murdered ; and, if similar occurrences were to take place in Wapping or Rotherhithe, London would be in commotion.   All the police from A to Z would be set on the alert, the newspapers crammed with paragraphs, and a hot search instigated after the murderer. If taken, he would be duly tried, wondered at, gazed after. convicted, hanged, and forgotten.   We should think no more of his victim than we now think of Hannah Browne.   The other characters of the play, with the exception of the two principal, are nonentities.   We care nothing for Malcolm or Donalbain, or Lenox or Rosse, or the rest of the Scottish nobles.   Pathetic, in-

deed, are the words which burst from Macduff when he hears the
astounding tidings that all his pretty chickens and their dam have
been carried off at one fell swoop; but he soon shakes the woman out
of his eyes, and dreams only of revenge. His companions are slightly
affected by the bloody deed, and grief is in a moment converted into
rage. It is but a short passage of sorrow, and the only one of the
kind. What is equally remarkable is, that we have but one slight
piece of comic in the play,—the few sentences given to the porter;*
and their humour turns upon a gloomy subject for jest,—the occupation of the keeper of the gates of hell. With these two exceptions,
—the brief pathos of Macduff, and the equally brief comedy of the
porter,—all the rest is blood. Tears and laughter have no place in
this cavern of death.

Of such a gory poem, Macbeth is the centre, the moving spirit.
From the beginning, before treason has entered his mind, he appears
as a man delighting in blood. The captain, announcing his deeds
against Macdonwald, introduces him bedabbled in slaughter.

> " For brave Macbeth,—well he deserves that name,—
> Disdaining fortune, with his brandished steel,
> Which smoked with bloody execution,
> Like valour's minion carved out his passage
> Until he faced the slave ;
> And ne'er shook hands, nor bade farewell to him,
> 'Till he unseamed him from the nave to the chops,†
> And fixed his head upon our battlements."

After this desperate backstroke, as Warburton justly calls it,† Macbeth engages in another combat equally sanguinary. He and Banquo

---

* The speech of this porter is in blank verse.
> Here is a knocking indeed ! If a man
> Were porter of hell-gate, he should have old
> Turning the key. Knock—knock—knock ! Who is there,
> In the name of Beelzebub ? Here is a farmer
> That hanged himself [up]on the expectation
> Of plenty : come in time. Have napkins enough
> About you. Here you 'll sweat for it. Knock—knock !
> Who 's there, in the other devil's name ? [I'] faith
> Here 's an equivocator, that could swear
> In both the scales 'gainst either scale ; [one] who
> Committed treason enough for God's sake, yet
> Cannot equivocate to heaven. Oh ! come in,
> Equivocator. Knock—knock—knock ! Who 's there ?
> 'Faith, here 's an English tailor come hither
> For stealing out of a French hose. Come in, tailor.
> Here you may roast your goose.
>   Knock—knock—
>   Never in quiet.
> Who are you ? but this place is too cold for hell.
> I 'll devil-porter it no longer. I had thought
> T' have let in some of all professions,
> That go the primrose-path to th' everlasting darkness.

The alterations I propose are very slight. *Upon* for *on, i'faith* for *'faith,* and the
introduction of the word *one* in a place where it is required. The succeeding dialogue is also in blank verse. So is the sleeping scene of Lady Macbeth ; and that so
palpably, that I wonder it could ever pass for prose.

† Warburton proposes that we should read " from the *nape* to the chops," as a more
probable wound. But this could hardly be called *unseaming* ; and the wound is intentionally horrid to suit the character of the play. So, for the same reason, when
Duncan is murdered, we are made to remark that the old man had much blood in
him.

> " Doubly redoubled strokes upon the foe ;
> Except they meant to bathe in reeking wounds,
> Or memorize another Golgotha,
> I cannot tell."

Hot from such scenes, he is met by the witches. They promise him the kingdom of Scotland. The glittering prize instantly affects his imagination ; he is so wrapt in thought at the very moment of its announcement that he cannot speak. He soon informs us what is the hue of the visions passing through his mind. The witches had told him he was to be king : they had not said a word about the means. He instantly supplies them :

> " Why do I yield to that suggestion
> Whose horrid image doth unfix my hair,
> And make my seated heart knock at my ribs
> Against the use of nature."

The dreaded word itself soon comes :

> " My thought, whose MURDER yet is but fantastical,
> Shakes so my single state of man, that function
> Is smothered in surmise."

To a mind so disposed, temptation is unnecessary. The thing was done. Duncan was marked out for murder before the letter was written to Lady Macbeth, and she only followed the thought of her husband.

Love for him is in fact her guiding passion. She sees that he covets the throne,—that his happiness is wrapt up in the hope of being a king,—and her part is accordingly taken without hesitation. With the blindness of affection, she persuades herself that he is full of the milk of human kindness, and that he would reject false and unholy ways of attaining the object of his desire. She deems it, therefore, her duty to spirit him to the task. Fate and metaphysical aid, she argues, have destined him for the golden round of Scotland. Shall she not lend her assistance ? She does not ask the question twice. She will. Her sex, her woman's breasts, her very nature, oppose the task she has prescribed to herself; but she prays to the ministers of murder, to the spirits that tend on mortal thoughts, to make thick her blood, and stop up the access and passage of remorse; and she succeeds in mustering the desperate courage which bears her through. Her instigation was not in reality wanted. Not merely the murder of Duncan, but of Malcolm, was already resolved on by Macbeth.

> " The Prince of Cumberland ! That is a step
> On which I must fall down, or else o'erleap,
> For in my way it lies. Stars ! hide your fires,
> Let not light see my black and dark desires !"

As the time for the performance of the deed approaches, he is harassed by doubts ; but he scarcely shows any traces of compunction or remorse. He pauses before the crime,—not from any hesitation at its enormity, but for fear of its results,—for fear of the poisoned chalice being returned to his own lips,—for fear of the trumpet-tongued indignation which must attend the discovery of the murder of so popular a prince as Duncan,—one who has borne his faculties so meekly, and loaded Macbeth himself with honours. He is not haunted by any feeling for the sin, any compassion for his victim ;—

the dread of losing the golden opinions he has so lately won, the consequences of failure, alone torment him. His wife has not to suggest murder, for that has been already resolved upon; but to represent the weakness of drawing back, after a resolution has once been formed. She well knows that the momentary qualm will pass off,—that Duncan is to be slain, perhaps when time and place will not so well adhere. Now, she argues,—now it can be done with safety. Macbeth is determined to wade through slaughter to a throne. If he passes this moment, he loses the eagerly desired prize, and lives for ever after, a coward in his own esteem; or he may make the attempt at a moment when detection is so near at hand, that the stroke which sends Duncan to his fate will be but the prelude of the destruction of my husband. She therefore rouses him to do at once that from which she knows nothing but fear of detection deters him; and, feeling that there are no conscientious scruples to overcome, applies herself to show that the present is the most favourable instant. It is for him she thinks—for him she is unsexed—for his ambition she works—for his safety she provides.

Up to the very murder, Macbeth displays no pity—no feeling for anybody but himself. Fear of detection still haunts him, and no other fear.

> "Thou sure and steadfast earth,
> Hear not my steps which way they walk, for fear
> The very stones prate of my whereabout."

As Lady Macbeth says, it is the frustrated attempt, not the crime, that can confound him. When it has been accomplished, he is for a while visited by brain-sick fancies; and to her, who sees the necessity of prompt action, is left the care of providing the measures best calculated to avert the dreaded detection. She makes light of facing the dead, and assures her husband that

> " A little water clears us of this deed.
> How easy it is then !"

Does she indeed feel this? Are these the real emotions of her mind? Does she think that a little water will wash out what has been done, and that it is as easy to make all trace of it vanish from the heart as from the hand? She shall answer us from her sleep, in the loneliness of midnight, in the secrecy of her chamber. Bold was her bearing, reckless and defying her tongue, when her husband was to be served or saved; but the sigh bursting from her heavily-charged breast, and her deep agony when she feels that, so far from its being easy to get rid of the witness of murder, no washing can obliterate the damned spot, no perfume sweeten the hand once redolent of blood, prove that the recklessness and defiance were only assumed. We find at last what she had sacrificed, how dreadful was the struggle she had to subdue. Her nerve, her courage, mental and physical, was unbroken during the night of murder; but horror was already seated in her heart. Even then a touch of what was going on in her bosom breaks forth. When urging Macbeth to act, she speaks as if she held the strongest ties of human nature in contempt.

> " I have given suck, and know
> How tender 'tis to love the babe that milks me :
> I would, when it was smiling in my face,

Have plucked my nipple from his boneless gums,
And dashed the brains out, had I but so sworn
As you have done to this."

Is she indeed so unnatural,—so destitute of maternal, of womanly feeling? No. In the next scene we find her deterred from actual participation in killing Duncan, because he resembled her father in his sleep. This is not the lady to pluck the nipple from the boneless gums of her infant, and dash out its brains. Her language is exaggerated in mere bravado, to taunt Macbeth's infirmity of purpose by a comparison with her own boasted firmness; but if the case had arisen, she who had recoiled from injuring one whose life stood in the way of her husband's hopes from a fancied resemblance to her father, would have seen in the smile of her child a talisman of resistless protection.

The murder done, and her husband on the throne, she is no longer implicated in guilt. She is unhappy in her elevation, and writhes under a troubled spirit in the midst of assumed gaiety. She reflects with a settled melancholy that

" Nought's had, all's spent,
When our desire is got without content.
'Tis safer to be that which we destroy,
Than by destruction dwell in doubtful joy."

This to herself. To cheer her lord, she speaks a different language in the very next line.

" How now, my lord! why do you keep alone,
Of sorriest fancies your companions making;
Using those thoughts which should indeed have died
With those they think on?"

Her own thoughts, we have just seen, were full as sorry as those of her husband; but she can wear a mask. Twice only does she appear after her accession to the throne; once masked, once unmasked. Once seated at high festival, entertaining the nobles of her realm, full of grace and courtesy, performing her stately hospitalities with cheerful countenance, and devising with rare presence of mind excuses for the distracted conduct of her husband. Once again, when all guard is removed, groaning in despair.

The few words she says to Macbeth after the guests have departed, almost driven out by herself, mark that her mind is completely subdued. She remonstrates with him at first for having broken up the feast; but she cannot continue the tone of reproof, when she finds that his thoughts are bent on gloomier objects. Blood is for ever on his tongue. She had ventured to tell him that the visions which startle him, were but the painting of his brain, and that he was unmanned in folly. He takes no heed of what she says, and continues to speculate, at first in distraction, then in dread, and lastly in savage cruelty, upon blood. The apparition of Banquo almost deprives him of his senses. He marvels that such things could be, and complains that a cruel exception to the ordinary laws of nature is permitted in his case. Blood, he says,

" ——has been shed ere now in the olden time,
Ere human statute purged the gentle weal,"—

and in more civilized times also; but, when death came, no further consequences followed. Now not even twenty mortal murders [he remembered the number of deadly gashes reported by the assassin] will keep the victim in his grave. As long as Banquo's ghost remains before him, he speaks in the same distracted strain. When the object of his special wonder, by its vanishing, gives him time to reflect, fear of detection, as usual, is his first feeling.

> " It will have blood, they say ; blood will have blood !'

The most improbable witnesses have detected murder. Stones, trees, magotpies, choughs, have disclosed the secretest man of blood. Then come cruel resolves, to rid himself of his fears. Mercy or remorse is to be henceforward unknown; the firstlings of his heart are to be the firstlings of his hand,—the bloody thought is to be followed instantly by the bloody deed. The tiger is now fully aroused in his soul.

> " I am in blood
> Stept in so far, that, should I wade no more,
> Returning were as tedious as go o'er."

He sees an enemy in every castle ; everywhere he plants his spies ; from every hand he dreads an attempt upon his life. Nearly two centuries after the play was written, the world beheld one of its fairest portions delivered to a rule as bloody as that of the Scottish tyrant; and so true to nature are the conceptions of Shakspeare, that the speeches of mixed terror and cruelty, which he has given to Macbeth, might have been uttered by Robespierre. The atrocities of the Jacobin, after he had stept so far in blood, were dictated by fear. " Robespierre," says a quondam satellite,* " devenait plus sombre ; son air renfrogné repoussait tout le monde ; il ne parlait que d'assassinat, encore d'assassinat, toujours d'assassinat. Il avait peur que son ombre ne l'assassinât." ·

Lady Macbeth sees this grisly resolution, and ceases to remonstrate or interfere. Her soul is bowed down before his, and he communicates with her no longer. He tells her to be ignorant of what he plans, until she can applaud him for what he has done. When he abruptly asks her,

> " How say'st thou,—that Macduff denies his person
> At our great bidding ?"

she, well knowing that she has not said anything about it, and that the question is suggested by his own fear and suspicion, timidly inquires,

> " Have you sent to him, *sir* ?"

The last word is an emphatic proof that she is wholly subjugated. Too well is she aware of the cause, and the consequence, of Macbeth's *sending* after Macduff; but she ventures not to hint. She is no longer the stern-tongued lady urging on the work of death, and taunting her husband for his hesitation. She now addresses him in the humbled tone of an inferior; we now see fright and astonishment seated on her face. He tells her that she marvels at his words, and she would fain persuade herself that they are but the feverish effusions of an overwrought mind. Sadly she says,

> " You lack the season of all nature,—sleep."

* Causes secretes de la Révolution de 9 au 10 Thermidor ; by Vilate, ex-juré révolutionnaire de Paris.

Those are the last words we hear from her waking lips; and with a hope that repose may banish those murky thoughts from her husband's mind, she takes, hand in hand with him, her tearful departure from the stage; and seeks her remorse-haunted chamber, there to indulge in useless reveries of deep-rooted sorrow, and to perish by her own hand amid the crashing ruin of her fortunes, and the fall of that throne which she had so fatally contributed to win.

He now consigns himself wholly to the guidance of the weird sisters; and she takes no part in the horrors which desolate Scotland, and rouse against him the insurrection of the enraged thanes. But she clings to him faithfully in his downfall. All others except the agents of his crimes, and his personal dependents, have abandoned him; but she, with mind diseased, and a heart weighed down by the perilous stuff of recollections that defy the operation of oblivious antidote, follows him to the doomed castle of Dunsinane. It is evident that he returns her affection, by his anxious solicitude about her health, and his melancholy recital of her mental sufferings. He shows it still more clearly by his despairing words when the tidings of her death are announced. Seyton delays to communicate it; but at last the truth must come,—that the queen is dead. It is the overflowing drop in his cup of misfortune.

> "She should have died hereafter;—
> There would have been a time for such a word."

I might have borne it at some other time; but now—now—now that I am deserted by all—penned in my last fortress—feeling that the safeguards in which I trusted are fallacious,—now it is indeed the climax of my calamity, that she, who helped me to rise to what she thought was prosperity and honour,—who clung to me through a career that inspired all else with horror and hate,—and who, in sickness of body, and agony of mind, follows me in the very desperation of my fate, should at such an hour be taken from me,—I am now undone indeed. He then, for the first time, reflects on the brief and uncertain tenure of life. He has long dabbled in death, but it never before touched himself so closely. He is now aweary of the sun —now finds the deep curses which follow him, sufficiently loud to pierce his ear—now discovers that he has already lived long enough —and plunges into the combat, determined, if he has lived the life of a tyrant, to die the death of a soldier, with harness on his back. Surrender or suicide does not enter his mind; with his habitual love of bloodshed, he feels a savage pleasure in dealing gashes all around; and at last, when he finds the charms on which he depended, of no avail, flings himself, after a slight hesitation, into headlong conflict with the man by whose sword he knows he is destined to fall, with all the reckless fury of despair. What had he now to care for? The last tie that bound him to human kind was broken by the death of his wife, and it was time that his tale of sound and fury should come to its appropriate close.

Thus fell he whom Malcolm in the last speech of the play calls "the dead butcher." By the same tongue Lady Macbeth is stigmatised as the fiend-like queen. Except her share in the murder of Duncan,—which is, however, quite sufficient to justify the epithet in the mouth of his son,—she does nothing in the play to deserve the title; and for her crime she has been sufficiently punished by a life of disaster and remorse. She is not the tempter of Macbeth. It does not require much philosophy to pronounce that there were no such beings as the weird sisters; or that the voice that told the Thane of Glamis that he was to be King of Scotland, was that of his own ambition. In his own bosom was brewed the hell-broth, potent to call up visions counselling tyranny and blood; and its ingredients were his own evil passions and criminal hopes. Macbeth himself only believes as much of the predictions of the witches as he desires. The same prophets, who foretold his elevation to the throne, foretold also that the progeny of Banquo would reign; and yet, after the completion of the prophecy so far as he is himself concerned, he endeavours to mar the other part by the murder of Fleance. The weird sisters are, to him, no more than the Evil Spirit which, in Faust, tortures Margaret at her prayers. They are but the personified suggestions of his mind. She, the wife of his bosom, knows the direction of his thoughts; and, bound to him in love, exerts every energy, and sacrifices every feeling, to minister to his hopes and aspirations. This is her sin, and no more. He retains, in all his guilt and crime, a fond feeling for his wife. Even when meditating slaughter, and dreaming of blood, he addresses soft words of conjugal endearment; he calls her " dearest chuck," while devising assassinations, with the fore-knowledge of which he is unwilling to sully her mind. Selfish in ambition, selfish in fear, his character presents no point of attraction but this one merit. Shakspeare gives us no hint as to her personal charms, except when he makes her describe her hand as " little." We may be sure that there were few " more thorough-bred or fairer fingers," in the land of Scotland than those of its queen, whose bearing in public towards Duncan, Banquo, and the nobles, is marked by elegance and majesty; and, in private, by affectionate anxiety for her sanguinary lord. He duly appreciated her feelings, but it is pity that such a woman should have been united to such a man. If she had been less strong of purpose, less worthy of confidence, he would not have disclosed to her his ambitious designs ; less resolute and prompt of thought and action, she would not have been called on to share his guilt; less sensitive or more hardened, she would not have suffered it to prey for ever like a vulture upon her heart. She affords, as I consider it, only another instance of what women will be brought to, by a love which listens to no considerations, which disregards all else beside, when the interests, the wishes, the happiness, the honour, or even the passions, caprices, and failings of the beloved object are concerned; and if the world, in a compassionate mood, will gently scan the softer errors of sister-woman, may we not claim a kindly construing for the motives which plunged into the Aceldama of this blood-washed tragedy the sorely urged and broken-hearted Lady Macbeth ?

ODE TO THE QUEEN.

THOU of the sunny hair,
And brow more sunny and more fair ;
The upraised heaven-blue eye,
That borrows from the sky
Its tint, its brightness, and its majesty ;
A lip half pouting and half curl'd,—
Mercy and Justice met
To speak thy dictates to the world !
    A form, nor tall,
    Nor small,
But bearing up the casket of thy mind,
Like to a classic pillar 'neath an altar set,
For elegance, and not for gorgeousness design'd.

    How can I hope,
Whilst adulations throng
From mouths of wisdom and the great,
To lift my humble song,
    Or cope
With those of higher state,
But that the smile which smiles on all so free
    Must smile on me ?

Oh, that a brow that has not learn'd to frown
Should bear the impress of a royal crown !
That youth, which has not yet seen womanhood,
Should counsel for the aged and the rude !
And that a form, which joyous as a bird has flown,
Should rigid grow, and statue-like upon a throne !

Can thy tiara's light
    Brighten thy fate ?
Or thy great empire's might
    Relieve its weight ?
    Can aught atone
For natural youthful pleasures fled and gone ?
Not gilded pageantry,
Nor boundless sovereignty:
The ocean that thou rulest is more free than thee !
Thy youthful life is coffin'd down
Beneath the chaining trammels of a crown.

But there 's a recompense that 's given,
    That must sustain
    Thy trying hour,—
The all-seeing eye of Heaven
    Blesses thy reign
    And power;
A Nation's love, in acclamations deep,
Mingles even in thy unbroken sleep,
Giving thee back, in many a vision wild,
Thy days of youthful and unfetter'd charm;
And a fond Mother's arm
Pillows her regal child.
Ah, when thou wakest, still that joyful face is seen,
Beaming upon her daughter and her youthful queen !

On the scroll of Fame
  Thy name
  Stands free,—
'Tis but another name for Victory !
Long may it stand
A law,—a beacon,—and a will,—
Till the Omnipotent command
Bids Fame be mute, and the great globe be still !

W. R. V.

SUICIDE.

" Die, and increase the demand for coffins !"
Motto of Undertakers' Mystery.   Free translation.

A CERTAIN philosopher once said, with a degree of truth that proved the strength of his own head and the weakness of the human nature he was anatomizing, that " many men could easily bring themselves to *practise* those things they would in nowise permit to be *preached* to them."   He saw the line of distinction between virtue in *thought* and virtue in action,—the ease with which we could have the former, the difficulty of possessing in practice the latter; he knew how easy it is to be good when and where there is no temptation to the contrary; he knew the proneness of people thus luckily located on the top of Fortune's wheel, to inquire with seeming wonder wherefore they who were being pulverized beneath the bottom of the same,— the pulverization being no jot the pleasanter from the obvious fact of the inquirer's weight being on the top,—why the discontented fellows presumed to be so uncomfortable, when their superiors made so many inquiries after their well-being; he knew that the top wheelmen were but too apt to argue about the fellows below as if they were of themselves, and to conclude that it was as wicked a thing for a man to steal a penny loaf when starving, as for an alderman to do the same thing, whose well-turtled stomach would bring the robbery into an act of wanton appropriation, only to be explained by his superabundant organ of acquisitiveness.   In short, respectable reader, he knew what we all know, after he has made it clear, that the *degree* in which we practise what we will not permit to be preached to us, is proof of human weakness, and measure of the want of health in our personal morals.   It is a confession of our inability to act up to our conception of virtue; and the cherishing the theory of good without making the practice follow after, is a postponement of active virtue *sine die*.   Or if we beat away that pertinacious dun, conscience, by saying, " Ah ! never mind, I 'll start with bran-new morals next year," it is only like moving that a bill be read this day six months,—a humane method of knocking the measure on the head without the unfeeling necessity of saying in so many words that knocking is to be its entertainment.

Now, if I were to say,—which I feel very much disposed to do,— that cutting one's own throat (where there are no kindred feelings to be cut)—" that cutting one's own throat in this case was a very proper

thing,—where a man likes it," I should at once have a cloud of the
schoolmen upon me, each with the weapons his master of the ordnance, Paley, has supplied to him, proving, until breath, temper, and
text were exhausted, that I am a presumptuous puppy in imagining
for one moment that I have any property at all in my own throat,
which is given to me for the good of society, and not to be cut by
and for me, and my proper satisfaction.   This would be the language
of these " top wheelmen,"—fellows who are far too comfortable not to
wish to be as immortal as a corporation, and who therefore doubt my
sanity in not being as jolly as themselves,—like the young princess
to her miserable little subject, " What is the matter with you ?—how
can you cry ? *I* am very happy ?"   " Live," says the archdeacon, as
he wipes his mulligatawnied mouth with his napkin ;—" live," cries he
to the lank-cheeked fellow who has been fished out of the river
against his will, whither he had gone to stop the disagreeable function of breathing on a scanty supply of bread ;—" *live*," cries the archdeacon,—" life you cannot give, life you. cannot take.   You are
placed in this world to run your course ; you must run it accordingly.
How soon it may require your aid, you do not know ; at any rate,
when it is fit you should retire hence, you will be *called* hence ;·rush
not uncalled-for, into the other world.   I am sorry for you; here is
half-a-crown'; and, John," turning to the footman, who has been picking the crumbs of morality falling from the rich man's mouth, " *John,
show this poor man out.*"   The poor man, with a sad aspect and a
slow pace, crawls toward the door ; and looks as if, did not deferential modesty restrain him, he would reply to the good archdeacon in
these words.   As the old man has seen them, and owned, with wonder
at our penetration, that they correctly exhibit the thoughts at that time
passing through his brain, we at once put the reader in possession.
" Live, my dear sir !   I am quite willing to do so ; it is what I have
been in vain struggling to do.   Live ! Have not the slightest objection ;
but then I *must* live : *you*, your honour, have said you could not afford
to keep a conscience, although you doubtless think it a very good
thing among people who *can* afford to do so ; indeed I know well your
writings venerate many things your *acts* do not, for want of this article you cannot afford to keep.   So my abstract admission must be
given to all arguments against suicide in the main, reserving a particular conclusion for myself, *viz.* that to attempt to live without money
is quite as bad as cutting off my legs, in order to pit myself in a
walking-match against Mr. Coates.   I shudder, Mr. Paley, as deeply
as yourself at the general idea of suicide ; but, in reference to particular cases, it 's all a matter of cash.   *You* cannot afford to keep a
conscience, another man cannot afford to keep a mistress, a third
finds the keeping *himself* beyond the capacity of his exchequer : the
first denies himself the luxury of a conscience for the present, the
second puts his lady quietly away, the third puts himself in a pond
quietly and comfortably."   The would-be suicide was quite right : as
the profound estimator of political tactics some time back remarked,
in reference to the gladiatorial exercises of the factions of the day,
" it 's all a matter of 'wittals :'" necessity compels us to do what principle will not hear preached by others ; so that I almost despair of
miseries great as mine making out a claim for mortality, and apprehend that only a few very sensible people will say at the end of my

paper, " There, *go, my good fellow, and hang yourself,* as soon as you can beg, borrow, or steal a sufficient bit of cord for that laudable purpose."

Yet if there be one moral truth clearer, stronger, and less assailable than another, it is that, in some circumstances, " self-murder" is the most virtuous act a man can perform. A burthen to himself, an annoyance to the world, no relatives or connexions to regret his loss, may not an intentional stopping of the breathing function be the best act he can commit for all sides? The utilitarian will say " *Yes,*" among whom we rank the Paleyites, all of whom were and are utilitarians; the old-fashioned addlepates will shake their heads, take snuff, and finally declare that a good deal may be said on both sides.

The above useful reflections, as well as those that immediately follow, had their origin on the third step above high-water mark of Waterloo Bridge.

I was thinking about providing for myself in the flood beneath, and after mature reflection concluded I had better not. They are your " thinkers" about it who never do the thing,—a man who is always thinking about marrying is sure to die an old bachelor. Hamlet thought about killing his uncle so long, that that very immoral elderly gentleman had very nearly slipped through his reflective nephew's fingers; and so a man who thinks about throwing himself in the water is sure to conclude the argument as I did, by turning round and walking up the steps. Indeed death's a nasty thing; we go to it as to a last resource, sharp though sure, as the young woman said on handling the hatchet that was to dissociate her head and shoulders. The watery form of it has its advantages and disadvantages; there is little pain, but it is cold, plashy, sneaking, and kittenkilling in its general style: the warmest imagination cannot save the body from a certain shiver as the thing is contemplated; at least that was my experience on the third step aforementioned. I tried to fancy that it was but a sort of hydrostatic bed without the expense of the India-rubber casing. It was of no use; active memory recurred to the attitudinizings of a fine growing family of young mousers whom in early life I had introduced to the cold comfort of a pail of water; and at the reminiscence my blood ran colder than the water at my feet. With a quiet rippling plash it washed along the step. It sounded to the ear as if old Charon called from the bottom, ready to start over that other stream to which this merely branch canal must conduct us. Bright and tempting it ran at my feet, ready to conceal both me and my sorrows. But the foolish instinct for life prevailed within me; I returned to walk the streets at night,—an employment from which I had thought, ten minutes before, *death* would be a happy relief; a delusion which the being confronted with it soon dissipated. In walking up the steps I felt as one who had been reprieved, to whom life in its worst aspects would be infinitely preferable to that ' hereafter' which the fancy studs with such dimly awful horrors.

" Stuff!" I hear some one say who is reading this perhaps on a full stomach; "nonsense! a happy relief from walking about the streets, indeed! the fellow does not know what to write about." So would not poor old Dr. Johnson have said after one of *his* street vagabondizings, when he sate down to write the essay whose signature " Impransus," indicated the dinnerless state of the writer's stomach;

so would not *he* have said; no, nor his wandering chum, Savage: warm tears would have coursed down their rough cheeks, for they knew what it was in *their* time; and living in the streets, notwithstanding the improvement of the paving, is not much more desirable now than it was in their time, or in the old time before them.

It is only at night,—and that cold, drizzly, and muddy,—you can feel in its full force the misery that is foodless and houseless. In the day the busy streets are thronged with the crowds drifting along, intent on their respective objects. Then, houseless though you be, you feel no consciousness of it from contrast: purposeless as you are, the fact is known to none but yourself, and you enjoy the poor privilege of promenading the pavement free from staring remark or official interruption. But at night, about twelve or half-past, the theatre-frequenters hurrying home, happy shopmen returning from their sweethearts, and attorneys' clerks and small joyous shopboys, cigar in mouth, hastening to their quiet beds, the very poorest Cyprian, perhaps, staggering away in silence and ginny stupor to her squalid room,—then you feel that you are not one of the mass; it is the school-boy sensation of strangeness in a new school, carried up and increased into one's manhood; you are a misfit in society,—of no use; a shoe-black, a hackney-coachman, a costermonger are respectable in your eyes, for each of these holds a department in the great game of life. If you walk fast, the tears come into your eyes at the thought of the sad mockery of people with homes,—for *where* should *you* walk *to?* You slink from street to street, shivering and broken-spirited; afraid to pause, lest the searching eye of the policeman shall for one moment mistake the unfortunate for a thief; and tremblingly shunning to stretch your weary limbs in a doorway, tempting as it looks, that your miseries shall not the next morning be presented to a police office, and published to the world. In fine, you almost feel that the "*world would move on much the same even if you were dead and buried,*"—a root-and-branch cutting-up of one's self-esteem that may be called the last conviction of the dejected.

Many are the poor wretches who for months pass through such an existence as this. If men, enlistment is a last resource: if women, prostitution, paint, gin, and jollity that would look wonderfully *like* happiness were it not so *loud,* low spirits, laudanum, or Waterloo steps; paragraph in newspapers—old story—seduction and suicide— fine young woman—parents in the country; penny-a-liner pockets his fee, and keeps the "*form*" of his female biography open for the next name the same set of circumstances may bring to him.

There is something awfully desolate in walking the streets through a night, passing across that dark gulf of the four-and-twenty which is a sort of temporary banishment from humanity,—that on-and-on purposeless tramp from the coming down of the darkness to the dawning of light, passing perhaps not two persons within the space of a mile; the solitary pad of our feet on the pavement; the sombre and dim hue of the streets relieved by the gas; the seemingly unnatural quiet in a place old custom tells us should be so noisy; the strange feeling that we are watching and thinking, whilst the vast Leviathan of toil, and luxury, and woe, and pleasure, has run its daily course, and is now snatching from the Lethe of sleep the instalment of energy for the next day's career. What passions and aspirations, what purposes of pomp and glory, of wickedness and virtue, what golden glories of the poet's brain quenched, or flickering in the twilight of dream, the strategy of the politician, all plunged into the "death of each day's life!" What a time, what a scene for reflection, with the deep, and awful, and warning gong of old Paul's clock striking two, in a tone which, plain as words, tells us how time with flying foot runs from us,—and all the humbler fry of iron pots in the metropolis plagiarising the sad fact tolled forth by their grave old leader! The streets are completely empty; the very policeman has slunk into some early house, and we feel like the last man.

And who will wonder, after this course repeated with little variation for a respectable period of three or four months, that a man looks upon a dissolution of partnership with this lower life as the best fate open to him? Why should one in this state stay longer among men, when no occupation can be secured which will rescue him from indifference, or shield him from contempt? Why should moralists, like Paley, try to stay his purpose by flinging the salt of their sapiency on his tail, when his only ambition, like Goldsmith's George Primrose, is to *live*, and that humble aim thwarted at every avenue by the grim visage of starvation staring him in the face? It is time he is gone. Let him unlock his soul from its painful prison, and send it cleaving its way in the joy of emancipation to those regions where the wicked cease from troubling, and the weary are at rest. Without wife or children, brothers, sisters, or cousins, grandfathers or grandmothers, dogs, cats, or birds, which can call with the voice either of nature or custom for my personal presence here below, why should *I* be tied by the leg with a moral "ne exeat mundo?" I *am my own*,— not a chop or a cutlet of me belonging to my creditors, for I am out of debt; and surely, I repeat, I may do what I like with my own. "You are *not your own*," again cries my moralist, attempting to throw a net of words over my mind about relative and social duties, society and its incidents, law of civilization, &c.—the whole leading to a sort of conclusion that if the world may not want me *now*, there is no saying the time will not come when it may find out what an indispensable person I am; and upon the dependence of this "may want" I am to hang about in the outer hall of this sublunary state, until those very comfortable fellows within, happen to think of us shivering without, and promote us to the pleasures of their well-plenished table. Truly we must wait long for this,—perhaps until an earthquake comes, and they call for our assistance in fishing them up through the bricks and beams of their fallen chambers.

No, no; Mr. Creech was quite right, if he thought himself so, in writing on the margin of his Lucretius, "When I have finished my translation, I must kill myself." That gentleman took the extended and philosophical view of the subject; life was to him something to be and to do; to be a translator, to do Lucretius, and then to do for the personal estate of Mr. Creech in this world, in order to translate the accidents and chances of personalty into the settled and comfortable remainder of eternity. Cool, philosophical man! what refinement of reflection, to come to regard the act of letting out life with as little perturbation as ordinary men contemplate eating their dinners! To translate Lucretius was his task; performed, he was to kill himself: a silk-weaver has to weave so many yards of his fabric;

done, he promises himself with his wife and little ones a walk in the fields. In both cases there is a duty to fulfil, in both cases the emancipation follows; both must we subject to the same test in endeavouring to settle their respective characters,—the necessity or obligation of the translator on the one hand, or the weaver on the other, loitering in the world, or the workshop, after their work is executed. The only difference is an affair of time and distance; the one being bound, as he thinks, for the *Elysian*, the other and humbler for the *Marylebone* fields.

"Well, my dear sir," cries the reader, "I see you are intent on your *point*. I shall perhaps only waste my lungs and logic in trying to beat you away from your delusion; but reflect, sir, the tendency— how catching—the imitative faculty in man,—lateral organ largely developed." Fiddlestick!—away with your organs and developements! An old gentleman, who has read all qualities of human dealing in a learned spirit, writes as follows:—"All I will venture to assert with confidence is, that there is no reason to apprehend that suicide will become an epidemic malady. Nature has provided too well for that. *Hope and fear are too powerful as inducements* not to frequently *stop the hands of a wretch about to terminate his own life*."

Meanwhile, it is useless blinking the moral fact, that suicide is as natural a result of compared good and evil as any other act in life. In every case (not excepting those of insanity) we shall find it takes that shape. Whether it be Mr. Creech, who sits down and stares death out of countenance with a familiarity that must have disconcerted the conceit of the omnipotent old commissioner,—or one with blasted hopes, like myself,—or blighted ambition, like old Anthony,— or repulsed patriotism, like Brutus,—the process is the same in all,— comparison of the inestimable evils of life with the presumed quiet and rest of the grave, and action in accordance with the conclusion. Men are not cowards for not living to face evils, for the mere sake of facing them without any other result; they are men of policy and magnanimity to quit, when the grappling with them can alone be productive of a self-destruction of a more painful and protracted character, or at best exhibitory of an idle and vain bravery of bearing, of no avail either one way or the other. They are not cowards, and no imputation of cowardice will prevent them following out the clear conceptions that are shaped from their exigencies, any more than it would deter one in a burning ship at sea from casting himself overboard, rather than become an insulated and floating roast; or than it shall prevent me, when I have made an end of this confession, plaiting my garters for the office of strangulation, if after the plait is finished I entertain the same fixed principles on the subject as I do at present.   **M.**

ADVENTURES IN PARIS.

CHAPTER II.

BY TOBY ALLSPY.

THE FIVE FLOORS.

To the best of our belief, Paris is the only city in Europe where a prize is annually distributed for the encouragement of VIRTUE. In England—that Joseph Surface of the civilized globe—we give premiums for the growth of fat sheep and piccotees, we boast of prize-oxen and prize-heartsease; but at present we have no prize-virtue. The celebrated benefaction founded by Monsieur de Monthyon (confided to the administration of the French Academy) consists in annual premiums for the production of the finest trait of moral excellence, and the literary work best calculated to promote its recurrence.

Now, Monsieur Boncœur, of the first-floor of the corner of the Rue Montmartre, might have monopolised the whole Monthyon endowment for the last fifteen years. The whole man was an incarnate virtue; his works, literary or literal, were based upon the strictest morality. From his top-knot to his shoe-tie, propriety predominated. Methodical in his hours and diet, regular as a chronometer in despatch of business, he insured his own ease of mind and body by scrupulous exactitude in the discharge of their duties and pleasures. His apartment was a model of commodiousness,—doors and windows shutting to a hair; not a draught of air, not a creaking hinge, not an unsteady table, not a hard-shutting drawer, not an easy-opening lock in the whole suite. The floors in summer were as polished as their master's demeanour, the carpets in winter as soft as his address. No grand displays of fragile luxury, of Japan porcelain or Bohemian glass, alarmed the anxieties of Monsieur Boncœur's constituency. It was the " comfortable " in perfection,—but nothing more.

What wonder that a man thus basking in the sunshine of prudent prosperity should bask in the favour of the world?—that such an ornament to society should be incorporated in all the learned and charitable societies of the city?—that so worthy a fellow should be a fellow of every academy and literary association? A string of conventional distinctions was attached to Boncœur's name, vying in length with the catalogue of chivalric honours appended in German almanacks to that of Prince Metternich; but, what was more to the purpose, the patronymic thus honoured was inscribed in every public stock or fund, domestic or foreign. His house was a house of universal bondage. Not a railroad could be started by government till Boncœur had been closeted in the stuffy, fussy, great-talking-little-doing cabinet of the Home Department; nor a minister accredited, till he had hinted his hints and inferred his inferences in the sphinxical blue-chamber of the Foreign. The worsted epaulettes of that all-conciliating monarch, the citizen king, were observed to bow lower to their excellent and much-esteemed friend Monsieur Boncœur than to any other of the golden calves invited to feed and ruminate at the royal rack and manger of the Tuileries.

Of all the inhabitants of the house whose *cordon* was pulled by Madame Grégoire, Boncœur may be considered as at once the least and the most domestic. His business lay elsewhere,—his pleasures lay elsewhere; it was only his respectability that lodged in ostentatious comfort in the first-floor of that memorable dwelling. He knew and cared nothing concerning the neighbours. On his progress from his apartment to his carriage, from his carriage back to his apartment, the banker's countenance expressed only a mild, imperturbable magnanimity, looking neither to the right nor left, but enwrapt in reminiscences of the panacean speech he had been delivering to the Chamber, in proof to the kingdom that it paid no taxes, but lay stretched upon a bed of roses. One day, however, when his ascent happened to be more mercurial than usual, he came suddenly in contact with Claire de Courson, whose slight figure was bending under the weight of a piece of furniture which she was carrying up to her mother's room; and her pure complexion became suffused with the deepest blushes as she acknowledged and declined his polite offers of assistance in her task. Next day, Robert the footman, who had been deputed to relieve her from the burthen of the elbow-chair, was commissioned to convey the " Follet " and apricot marmalade in the same direction. Till that memorable epoch, the virtuous Monsieur Boncœur had remained ignorant that the house contained so powerful an incentive to the fulfilment of the Christian commandment to love his neighbour as himself. But it was not too late. The banker was fond of apricot marmalade, and partial to the prettinesses of a fashionable magazine,—his fair neighbour of an age to share his predilections; and, in presenting these saccharine offerings, he did as he would be done by. The virtuous Monsieur Boncœur was too painfully aware, however, of the scandal-mongering propensities of a sinful world to entrust to the remarks of a common staircase and porter's lodge the visits of a bachelor first-floor to a single third-floor, with large grey eyes, long black eyelashes, and the shape of a nymph. His respectable Robert, a corpulent middle-aged footman, might in the first instance represent his high-principled principal, without provoking the espionage of Ma'mselle Berthe, or the commentations of Madame Grégoire. In the intimacy he hoped to establish, all the advances must come down stairs. The man after the king's own heart was too prudent to stir a single step upward.

Beyond the door of the antechamber, however, which was opened by Mademoiselle de Courson in person, the corpulent footman did not penetrate. The young lady returned, in her mother's name, a civil answer of acknowledgment to their wealthy neighbour, stating that the infirmities of her mother's health rendered it impossible for them to receive visitors. The corpulent footman (despising these wretched people,—as wretched people who keep no establishment of servants ought to be despised by a corpulent footman,) immediately settled it in his own mind that the apartment was too shabby and littered to admit of receiving a gentleman of such far-famed respectability as the eminent banker of the Rue Bergère; that the Coursons' furniture was probably mean,—their fare meagre. The utmost stretch of his pampered imagination did not conjecture that their fare consisted of their furniture,—that ever since Madame's arrival with the truck, she had been dining on chairs and breakfasting on feather-beds. Not a soul in the house (except Guguste) had at present noticed that the *meubles* carried down and conveyed away "to be mended" never found their way back again.

Small as were the appetites of the third-floor, it is extremely difficult to feed and lodge two full-grown human beings upon a pension of forty pounds a-year; and, by the recent failure of the notary in whose hands the small funds of Madame de Courson were deposited, this was all that remained to support her and her daughter. On the discovery of their misfortune, indeed, Claire had undertaken to increase her own and her mother's daily bread by assiduous needle-work; but the constant attendance required by the poor and sorrowful invalid rendered it difficult for her daughter to fulfil her good intentions. Till the loss of their property, they had resided, in tolerable comfort, in cheerful rooms on the Quai Voltaire, assisted by an effective servant; but all this had been perforce resigned,—the best part of their goods was sold off, their wardrobe stript of its luxuries, and Claire was fully justified in undertaking, as she did, the service of the kitchen and pantry; for it was clear that their diet must henceforward consist of bread and water. Like most poor people, they were proud; and pride served to increase their privations. Madame de Courson, the widow of an officer, one of the victims of the Russian campaign, had never yet solicited a pecuniary favour from living mortal. She preferred working for her livelihood, or starving; that is, she preferred that her daughter should work for their livelihood, and consequently that they should starve together. It must be owned (*par parenthèse*) that the only favours tendered to her acceptance since she took up her domicile in the corner house, were Monsieur Boncœur's gift of apricot marmalade and loan of a journal, and poor Guguste's earnest entreaty to Mademoiselle, into whose acquaintance he had intruded by carrying up Madame de Courson's first and last batch of wood, to be permitted to black her shoes, and perform other little neighbourly offices of similar delicacy. When, however, the shoes grew thinner and thinner, without being replaced, his aid was more rarely accepted, and at length positively declined; and little Guguste, who was more a man of the world than the corpulent footman, justly concluded that Mademoiselle Claire did not like to expose her attempts at repairing the inevitable fissures to the comments of Monsieur Georges's lad of all work. Still, though tacitly dismissed from her service, the grey-eyed beauty never passed him on the stairs without a word or smile of recognition, even when her heart was sorest and countenance saddest; for Guguste had installed himself her friend. It remained to be seen whether the donor of the apricot marmalade would prove as true a one as the young shoeblack.

Be it not inferred, however, that the amiable attentions of the ragamuffin page were paid solely as a tribute to beauty; they were a tribute to beauty in distress. There were two other particles of the fair sex resident under the same roof, whom most lads of his age would have preferred to the grey-eyed nymph of the third-floor, viz. Madame la Baronne de Gimbecque, a pretty widow, somewhere between twenty-five and fifty years of age, (for in a well-dressed widow it is extremely difficult to determine a woman's age within ten years or so,—none but a lady's husband being admitted to investigate the case before she

"adores,
With head uncover'd, the cosmetic powers;")

and Madame la Baronne de Gimbecque's coquettish waiting-maid, Mademoiselle Aglaé. But for neither of these divinities of the *entresol* had Guguste ever felt inspired with an inclination to wield the blacking-brush! Not that either the widow or the maid was at any moment guilty of a *chaussure* susceptible of such plebeian *enchainement :*—Madame la Baronne walked not only in silk attire, but silken shoes ; while Ma'mselle Aglaé, like Lear's soldiers, was shod with felt, shuffling in slippers all the morning, and reserving prunella or satin for her visits, play-goings, and *bals masqués.*

Madame la Baronne, with a fortune of thirty thousand francs, or twelve hundred pounds, per annum, would have passed in London for a widow of moderate means, and might perhaps have speculated on improving them by marriage. In Paris she passed for a rich one, and occupied herself with her own amusement. It is amazing how much pleasure may be purchased in that circumscript capital at the rate of one hundred pounds per month, particularly in the state of blessedness which is called single. Conscious of her advantage, Madame de Gimbecque was far from anxious to inscribe herself in the register of lodgers in the Rue Montmartre by double entry. France is peculiar in its views of wedded happiness. In England, what is called a well-assorted marriage implies parity of condition, and compatibility of temper ; in Paris, it implies equality of fortune. Five thousand a-year proposes to five thousand a-year,—three hundred per annum to three hundred ; not Lord Thomas to Miss Sophia, or plain Tom to pretty Sophy. Beauty, harp-playing, quadrilling, have nothing to do with it,—all is matter of arithmetic! If the match turn out ill, it is no fault of the matchmakers ; all has been done according to Cocker.

Now Madame la Baronne, like most Frenchwomen, was a capital calculatress. She knew that, though Sophy and Tom are richer with six hundred a-year between them than Sophy with three and Tom with the same pittance, a pretty Madame de Gimbecque, between twenty-five and fifty years of age, is richer as a widow with thirty thousand francs per annum, than as the wife of a man of fashion with sixty. To espouse any man, *un*fashionable, was out of the question,— that is, any man unfashionable with an income only equal to her own. A Crœsus of any age or calling would have brought his own apology ; and she would have added herself and her establishment to that of the respectable banker of the Rue Bergère at a moment's notice. But that consummation was past praying for. A Crœsus would require a Crœsa as his partner for life, as surely as the primitive lion trotted side by side with a lioness into Noah's ark ; and Monsieur Boncœur, if matrimonially inclined, would demand hundreds of thousands per annum to amalgamate with his hundreds of thousands. The charming Adolphes and exquisite Amédées, meanwhile, frequenting Madame de Gimbecque's opera-box, or ambling by her side in the Bois de Boulogne, had either not an unmortgaged estate wherewith to pretend to her hand, or, if successful pretendants, would appropriate after marriage to their own gratification, not only their own thirty thousand, but three-fourths of hers. Very early in her widowhood Madame de Gimbecque came to this conclusion ; and, on giving utterance at her toilet, as she threw off her widow's weeds, to her anti-matrimonial intention, they were confirmed by Mademoiselle Aglaé with so loud an " amen," that a by-stander might have supposed them two lay-nuns pronouncing vows of eternal celibacy.

Madame de Gimbecque, though thus egoistical in her calculations, was nevertheless a light-hearted, good-humoured little woman, who, if she did not go out of her way to do good, did all the good that lay in it. She had been born, bred, married, and widowed according to that matter-of-fact social system of the French which leaves no space for the expansion of the feelings. Nothing like affection had graced her parents' household,—nothing like affection had warmed her own. Her fifteen thousand francs per annum had been married to those of an ex-colonel of cuirassiers, thirty years her senior, who had pretty nearly scolded, sworn, smoked, and expectorated his pretty wife out of patience, when the sour little cherub who sits up aloft keeping watch over matrimonial destinies, took pity on the lady, and took the colonel to itself.

Marianne de Gimbecque, (then *not* between fifty and five-and-twenty, but between five-and-twenty and fifteen,) though an orphan as well as a widow, consoled herself as thoroughly as propriety would admit for this sudden bereavement. She had neither a tie nor a relative in the world; but what pretty Parisian with *trente mille francs de rente* can feel lonely, while there is an opera, a carnival, and a milliner's shop in existence!

The baroness speedily set about improving her solitary hours. She devoted herself to the cultivation of her charms, as an Englishwoman might have done to the cultivation of her mind. Her accomplishments as a cosmetician were really surprising; she studied the art as a branch of natural history; not a perfumer in Paris could have deceived her as to the ingredients of a wash, or chemical compounds of a pommade. She knew what acids would injure the enamel of her teeth, what astringents wither the smooth surface of her cheek, what spirituous infusions turn her sable locks to iron-grey or silver, as well as Berthollet or " Sromfridevé." She could tell what atmospheric changes enabled her to exchange blue ribbons for pink, without compromise of the becoming; and regulated by the phases of the moon her ebbs and flows between cap, hat, and turban.

Nothing could be more artistically managed than the apartment of the little coquette. Nothing, by the way, is so *easy* to render coquettish as an *entresol*, which is, in fact, a series of boudoirs: saloons like those of Devonshire House, or a hall like that of Stafford, *must* be stately and ostentatious; the trickery of prettiness would be as much out of place in such places as rouge and pearl powder on the marble cheek of Michael Angelo's Moses. But a light airy *entresol*, or *mezzonino* story, whose windows, fronting the south, are shaded by Genoese awnings, overhanging balconies, filled with geraniums, heliotropes, and mignonette, — whose anteroom is painted blue stripewise, to represent a tent, and whose dining-room is varnished scagliola fashion,—whose drawing-room is of white and gold, the *fauteuils* and divans of yellow satin, the *cabarets* of pale Saxon blue porcelain, adorned with shepherds, shepherdesses, and garlands of carnations,—the *consoles* of varnished maple, white as snow, or as the single marble table, *taillé en bloc*, which sustains a scentless exotic in a vase of pale-green Sèvres,—whose boudoir is a tent of white muslin, drawn over dove-coloured *gros de Naples*,—whose bed-room is hung with cachemere spotted with palm-leaves, leading to a bath-room altogether spotless, and lined with mirrors;—such an *entresol* is a paradise for a Peri, (whose age is between twenty-five and fifty!) and such was the one inhabited in the Rue du Faubourg Montmartre by Madame la Baronne de Gimbecque !

The household was concomitant.   A page in a neat livery, a powdered-headed middle-aged sobriety of a *maître d'hôtel*, a *chef* of sufficient merit for a lady neither a dinner-giver nor dinner-devotee ; and, to complete the measure, the *soubrette*, the waiting-maid, the spruce, cunning, *pimpante, fringante*, Mademoiselle Aglaé, with her embroidered cambric aprons and pink ribbons ;—one pennyworth of waiting-maid to all this monstrous quantity of male-faction !   The *maître d'hôtel* dusted the china, the page rubbed the floors,—everything but the lady's toilet being performed in France by slaves of the masculine gender.   Monsieur Simon, the sober *maître d'hôtel*, and Lindor, the pert page, sometimes suggested to their mistress's mistress that an additional petticoat would be far more advantageous to the establishment than entertaining a workwoman fifteen days in the month for the care of the household linen ; but the *femme de chambre* would not hear of it.   She chose to be the sole Helen in Troy ; and, though devoid of personal views on either page or butler,—the cook in his white paper *casquette*, or the coachman in his flaxen wig,—resolved to admit no rival near the throne of her soubrettish autocracy.   It was quite plague enough to have the house frequented by Eugène de Marsan, (the handsome cousin-german of the ugly defunct ex-colonel of cuirassiers, Monsieur le Baron Nicodême de Gimbecque,) and Claude de Bercy, (the popular author of seventy-five successful vaudevilles,) without encumbering the little *entresol* (or its double entrance, double staircase, and corridor, appropriately named in Paris "of escape,") with such lumber as a chambermaid.

"Has Madame Oudot sent home my *foulard peignoir ?*" demanded Madame la Baronne of her waiting-maid, as she lay reclining in her marble-bath, whose tepid warmth served to diffuse through the little room the aroma of the eau de Ninon which Mademoiselle Aglaé was sprinkling on the surface.

"*Non, madame !*   Yet I was particular in making her promise it for yesterday, knowing that Madame expected a visit from Monsieur Eugène before she dressed to take her ride."

"Tiresome woman !" cried the lady in the bath,—an apostrophe which Aglaé of course applied to the unpunctual *couturière.*   "Give me the new number of ' Le Bon Ton,' and in five minutes ring for my chocolate, and bring in my warm linen,—not sooner, or it will be cold before I am ready."

The waiting-maid obeyed ; but finding on the marble slab in the corridor the *Constitutionnel*, damp from the press, she held it for a moment over the drying-basket of the bath-linen, and returned to her lady, taking the liberty, as she slowly paced the room, to cast an eye upon the news of the morning.

"*Sacristie ! ce cher Monsieur Boncœur !* another audience of the king !" exclaimed Mademoiselle Aglaé, presenting the paper to her lady, who extended to receive it, a languid hand, humid with the perfumed exhalations of the bath.

"Doubtless about his title," she replied.

"*Title !*" inquired the waiting-maid, fearing she might be about to forfeit the envied distinction of belonging to the only household of quality in the hotel.

" Didn't I tell you that our neighbour overhead had purchased the estate of D'Offémont, and was trying to obtain the royal sanction to assume the name ? Ay, exactly: the King, I perceive, has created him a baron; not D'Offémont, however,—he is to be Baron de Boncœur. What people this government *does* ennoble !"

" Monsieur Boncœur has one of the greatest names in the monied world," remonstrated the waiting-woman: " he is mayor of his *arrondissement*, and *marguiller* of the parish."

" He may be beadle or drum-major, for anything I know or care," said Madame de Gimbecque with sublime contempt; " but I am convinced that in the time of the elder branch he would never have shaken the dust from his feet in the palace of the Tuileries. Ha !—a critique on Claude's new play. Pray remind me, by and by, to send to Monsieur de Bercy the note-case wadded with *vitiver* I have been embroidering for him. *Voyons !* '*Sophie de Melcour,* a drama in three acts. We regret—a-hem !—feeble—diffuse—flat—a-hem !—dialogue full of platitudes—characters full of exaggeration—style stilted—catastrophe contemptible—false taste—corrupt morality.' (This must have been written by some particular friend !) ' We cannot take our leave of Monsieur de Bercy without counselling him to turn his mind to some other branch of literary occupation than the stage, for which the bent of his genius evidently disqualifies this pains-taking but ill-judging young man.' Bah !—Eugène de Marsan's doing, I am convinced ! He knows I dote upon theatrical entertainments; he knows that I bespoke half-a-dozen boxes to give *éclat* to Monsieur de Bercy's piece, and thinks to disgust me by this disparagement. Eugène does not know me; he does not appreciate the generosity of woman's nature ! His abuse of poor Claude's play has put me more in conceit with it than ever. Certainly the style of ' Sophie de Melcour' *is* rather stilted, and nobody can deny the exaggeration of the characters. *I* expected that the catastrophe would cause the damnation of the piece; and as to the dialogue, I could scarcely sit it out without a yawn. Aglaé ! on second thoughts, Monsieur de Marsan is going out of town, and has been plaguing me for the last six months for some little trifle of my own work. I will give *him* the *vitiver* pocket-book: there will be plenty of time hereafter to get up another for Monsieur de Bercy. People so devoted to letters have no time to think of embroidered pocket-books. I dare say Bercy would like one bought at the Petit Dunquerque twice as well. There is no more sentiment in him than in one of his own farces."

Mademoiselle Aglaé was of the same opinion. The *Constitutionnel* having decided that Claude's seventy-sixth vaudeville was not to *run*, she decided that the author of the vaudeville was also at a stand-still. The loss of his *droits d'auteur*, which would probably deprive her of the gold chain and cross promised by her lady's love, determined *his* forfeiture of the embroidered note-case !

While the sacred mysteries of the toilet are proceeding in the bathroom, let us take a peep at the equivocal gentleman of the third-floor; no longer arrayed in velvet or sparkling with solitaires, but engirt in a scanty, washed-out printed calico dressing-gown, torn in the button-holes, and short enough to display at the open wristbands the sleeves of a dirty checked shirt, covering a yellow shrivelled skin, apparently washed out, like the calico. A pair of flannel drawers, yellow as arnotto, covered his shrunk shanks; a pair of old shoes, cut down into agonizing slippers, his stockingless feet; while, enfranchised from the spruce, lustrous *toupet* adorning his brows when exposed to day's or gas-light's garish eye, his mean, narrow, Emperor-of-Austrian forehead recedes into a bare crown, whose denuded ugliness adds thirty years to the age of the full-dressed sallier-forth of the night before. Even his mouth—that critical verifier of age—is strangely oldened; for his set of *Desirabodes* is still freshening in a glass of water on the chimney-piece, while the mumbling, toothless gums, fallen on each other, allow the lanky sallow cheeks to collapse, like the sides of a half-empty balloon.

Such was the unsophisticated man of the individual whose "getting-up" (as Claude de Bercy would have called it) for public representation was one of the miracles of the Palais Royal; a bazaar which, like the pedlar from the fair Lavinian shore, hath "complexions in its pack," and youth and beauty per yard, per ell, or per ounce, exposed in all its plate-glass windows. It was, as we have already stated, usually half-past seven of an evening when the full-dressed effort of art started forth along the Boulevards; it was as invariably three o'clock in the morning, minus a quarter, when it returned again to lay aside its adornments, and subside into the lean and slippered pantaloon. Ma'm-selle Berthe had been three hours snoring when, with a patent key, he nightly let himself in, to deposit his *Desirabodes*, false fronts, whiskers, and calves on his dressing-table; and in the secretaire beside it realities of a more solid nature: bags of silver pieces, rouleaux of golden ones, and now and then a flimsy I O U from some English flat, or an I O U addressed by the Bank of England to millions of English flats, which he rarely ensnugged within the secret-paper-drawer of his *bonheur du jour* without pronouncing a benediction over its senseless form, varying in intensity of expression, indeed, according as the document happened to be accompanied by bags of silver or rouleaux of gold. When wholly *un*accompanied,—sole trophy of his midnight gains,—the fiendish expression of the little mummy's puckered visage deepened into downright demonism.

Meanwhile it was the morning duty of the sour *femme de confiance* to summon the shattered remains of humanity, which she called master, to breakfast. But let it not be inferred from the squalid nature of his personal costume that the board of Monsieur Georges was spread penuriously: his outward man regarded the gratification of others; his inward regarded his own. The colour of his dressing-gown tended not a jot to his selfish enjoyment; but the amber coffee and smoking cream, the spongy bread and *présalé* butter, the slices of hard *saucisson d'Arles* and tender *côtelettes à la minute* in their silver *réchaud*, regarded exclusively his own five senses. It was to ensure to his daily use these sweeteners of human existence that the *chevalier d'industrie* toiled in his loathsome calling from eight o'clock to two per night; it was to ensure them hot and hot, and upon the most moderate terms, that he bore with the angular and acid female who presided over his domestic arrangements the remaining eighteen hours of the twenty-four. A younger and fairer *femme de ménage* would have exacted a nicer toilet, and the daintiest half of the dainties wherewith it was her duty to provide his table. But the *chissie* not only calculated the weight of provisions to be consumed to the thirty-second fraction of an ounce, but was content to eat the drumsticks of the chickens, the wings of the woodcocks, as well as to support the unsightly spectacle of his bald head and nauseous costume.

" Of what were you disputing last night with the old witch, Madame Grégoire, when I passed the porter's lodge?" demanded Monsieur Georges of the perpendicular shrew seated opposite to him, as he swallowed to his own share the twentieth of the two dozen oysters of Murènes provided for their breakfast.

" I only stepped in to pay her the twenty francs for Guguste's monthly board."

" But what was there in *that* to beget a squabble?" demanded the toothless man, in the mumbling chuckle which nothing but long custom enabled his housekeeper to understand. " Had she a complaint to make against the lad?"

" No one has complaints to make of him but *you*," said Ma'mselle Berthe, (forgetting her own venomous impeachment concerning the coffee and cream.) " We disputed because Madame Grégoire, like an ill-conditioned woman as she is, presumed to insult me."

" And what then?—you can make her *étrennes* pay for it."

" *You* can: but what compensation will it be to *me* that you diminish her New-year's gift from twenty francs to ten? She had the impudence to ask me to have an eye to the people on the third-floor! As if I was paid to do the spy-work of the *propriétaire !*"

" And who *are* the people on the third-floor?" demanded Monsieur Georges, who knew and cared very little for the proceedings of any house save the one under government licence in the Rue de Richelieu, amid the blaze of whose Corcel lamps, and glare of whose gilded cornices, he had the honour nightly to assist in fleecing the disloyal subjects of Louis Philippe and the greenhorn foreign visitors to his realms.

" How should I know?"

" Because Madame Grégoire, doubtless, informed you."

" She told me it was a lady and her daughter, about whom she had her doubts."

" *What* doubts?—that they were disreputable people?"

" Bah!—that they were *beggars !*"

" Then why don't the landlord get rid of them?"

" How can he?—they pay their rent."

" Then what did she want you to find out?"

" How the young lady employs herself of a morning, and why the mamma did not choose to receive the visits of that excellent man Monsieur le Baron de Boncœur."

" Is the first-floor made a baron?"

" To be sure he is!—everybody is made something now-a-days. If you had the spirit of a mouse, you would call yourself the Chevalier de Georges."

" I *have* the spirit of a mouse, which is to 'ware trap!" chuckled the dilapidated croupier. " I had a little adventure one season at Bagnères de Bigorre, under the name of the Chevalier St. Georges, which the police may not happen to have forgotten. But to return to the banker: what can he have in view by visiting a couple of beggarly women on a third-floor above the *entresol ?"*

" You are as bad as Ma'me Grégoire! That is just what she inquired of *me*."

" But though you mightn't choose to acquaint *her* with what had come to your knowledge— Hark! a ring at the bell," cried Monsieur Georges, interrupting himself as he shuffled out of his seat, and prepared to retreat into his adjoining chamber. " If 'tis any one for me, say I'm gone out, and shan't be at home till evening."

" Don't flurry yourself," replied the housekeeper, moving towards the ante-room; " 'tis only Guguste, come up to varnish your boots and bring your *toupet* from the barber's. Don't you hear him scratching the panel? That is the signal by which I know his ring from any other person's."

And no sooner had she charily opened the door, and prepared to lock it again after admitting him, than the quick-witted *gamin*, in his fustian blouse, and barret-cap, though thread-bare, set jauntily on one side, insinuated himself into the hated apartment.

" What makes you so late, sirrah?" demanded the mummy in the washed-out calico dressing-gown, grudging the foundling even the savoury steam of the viands that still circled in the eating-room.

" 'Tis only half-after eleven, sir," replied the drudge. " You desired there might be no noise in the apartment till half-after eleven."

" 'Tis three minutes after the half-hour."

" Mademoiselle does not choose me to come in, till breakfast is cleared away, and the things ready to be washed up," said Guguste, not caring to hear.

" In that case you have no right to be here now. But you know my orders, that you are to enter this room with my dressing things every day at half-past eleven. Where have you been idling for the last three minutes?"

" I have not been idling."

" Where have you been working, then?"

" Helping to put up a truckle-bed in Madame Grégoire's back-room. Her son Jules returned at five o'clock this morning from India."

" From India, child?" demanded the gouvernante, peeling the only slice of saucisson left in the dish, and insinuating it between lips as thin as itself.

" From Algiers in the Indies. Monsieur Jules serves in the twenty-third regiment of the line; and, having suffered considerably from the climate, has obtained his furlough."

" Another lazy useless hanger-on in the house! God help us!" ejaculated the housekeeper. " There, go and arrange your master's things in his dressing-room, while I put away breakfast. I will leave the china for you to wash up, outside the kitchen-door. Go!"

And he went,—neither whistling, however, nor with any want of thought. Between his discoveries concerning the Courson family, and the wonderful events he had just heard recited in the metaphorical military prose of Monsieur Jules, (*alias* the slang of the twenty-third regiment of the line,) Guguste had a forty-horse power of cogitation at that moment labouring in his brain!

(To be continued.)

THE LAST OF THE BANDITS.

I much admired, and have often thought of, two pictures of Horace Verney's, which I saw in the *Exposition des Tableaux,* of I forget what year, at Paris; in truth to nature, in conception and character, they leave nothing to desire. They were painted at Rome; and represent, one, the attack of brigands, — and the other, the death and confession of the captain of the gang after their falling into the hands of the dragoons.

Much has been written, too, on the subject of these outcasts of society; but no description of their manner of life and habits can compare with Washington Irving's "Painter's Story," or rather Charles de Chatillon's own adventures, when carried off from Lucien Bonaparte's villa at Frescati, in mistake for that prince.

The times are grown degenerate; brigandage is no longer a profession; bandits, like the Mohicans, are become extinct, and from Terracina to Forli, travellers have now-a-days no chance of meeting with a Paolo Ucelli, a Fiesole Ogagna, a De Cesaris, or a Barbone. I remember traversing that tract at a period when I expected every moment to see some of these freebooters in their picturesque costume peep from behind every projecting rock. Civilization and morality have stifled all sentiment; — the Neapolitan frontier is become a Salvator Rosa without its figures.

When I landed at Civitā Vecchia from the steamer, I inquired of the landlord of the inn whether the redoubtable Barbone was still an inmate of the fortress; and, on his answering in the affirmative, obtained an order to visit the place. Under the escort of one of the Pope's carabiniers, behold me then in the shadow of that colossal edifice!

It was built by Michael Angelo, and, like all his works, whether in architecture, statuary, or painting, is stamped with the grandeur of his genius. Its stupendous bastions, its ponderous gateway, seem built for eternity. Every stone is a rock such as Briareus and his earth-born brothers might have hurled against Jupiter, in that Titanic war described with such sublime obscurity by Hesiod.

The gendarme was, as is common to all the tribe of cicerones, talkative—not respecting the building, for he had never heard of the great architect, but concerning its then inhabitants. He would, if I had listened to him, have recounted the particulars of Signor Barbone's exploits during the seventeen years that he ravaged like a pestilence the Pontifical states. But I expected to obtain information from the fountain-head, and checked his loquacity.

Our hero had, twice before his present captivity, made terms with the Papal government. Once he was placed with Marocco and Garbarone, two worthy confreres, in the seminary of Terracina; and, just as the priests began to consider him an example of contrition and penitence, bore off the youths into the mountains, where this wolf of the fold barbarously murdered all those whose fathers would not, or could not, pay the exorbitant ransom demanded.

One only of the prisoners escaped the proscription, and the circumstance is a curious one. They were bound two and two, and after great privations and fatigues,—for they were dragged into fast-nesses almost inaccessible,—an order was given for their execution. One had already fallen by the stiletto, when his companion invoked Sant' Antonio, the patron saint of brigands, and that name saved him. It is a hint worth knowing. Should any future Barbone arise, re-member to call upon Saint Anthony!

Barbone afterwards became keeper of the château of St. Angelo, the great prison at Rome; but quickly relapsed into his old practices, the last of which exceeded in ferocity the rest.

Not far from Forli, an Englishman of distinction, whose name I will not mention, was stopped on his way to Rome. They plundered the father, and carried off the daughter. On reaching his destination he put a price on Barbone's head; but one morning a box arrived, which, instead of his, contained that of the daughter!

The revolting recollection of this ruffian's cruelty made me pause as I stood in the portal and thought of that of the Inferno, for which it would have been no bad model; and thought, too, of the giants who guarded it, whose arms, as they wildly brandished them, looked in the distance like the vans of windmills (the original, by the by, of Cervantes'). They would have been in excellent keeping with the place. For a moment, I say, I hesitated about entering; but curi-osity got the better of terror, and I resolved to visit the Bagno, a name which in the month of August it well merited.

In the court-yard were walking several of the brigands who be-longed to their monarch's train,—his satellites; but I did not stop to address them. I desired my conductor to show me to the head-quarters of the general, in the interior of the prison.

I found there a great many cells or holes, not unresembling dog-kennels, arched and formed in the massive walls; and, among the rest, the den of the Cacus. He was lying at full length on the floor, which might be eight or ten feet in length; and behind him, almost hid in shade, was crouching another brigand, leaning on his elbows, and stooping low. He was taking his siesta. This bandit was, I afterwards found, Barbone's prime-minister. They were insepara-ble—the tiger and his jackal, or rather, perhaps, wolf.

Barbone raised himself on one arm at my approach, and eyed me with all the hauteur of a prince. He was dressed like the rest, in the usual uniform,—cap, jacket, and coarse trowsers. He by no means corresponded in appearance with one of Horace Verney's brigands. He was a man of a middle height, corpulent in his person, with a countenance that showed no trace of crime: his features were handsome and regular; and his hair, long, black, and curly, hung over his shoulders. He certainly set all Lavater's theories at defiance. As to his head, I leave that to the phrenologists.

He seemed little inclined to enter into conversation; and, fettered as he was, I should have felt as little disposed to trust myself in his den as in that of a bloodhound. However, perceiving that I did not go away, and stood at the entrance, he at last had the courtesy to come forth. I, too, was inclined to address him civilly, with the hope of knowing something of his history and character; so I said to him,

"You are the famous Barbone, of whom I have heard so much, and long wished to see?"

"*Gasparoni, a servirlo,*" said he.

The reply made me smile, for I doubted not he would have served me, if set at liberty, in his own peculiar way.

"You smile," said he; "perhaps you are come to mock me?" He folded his arms, and looked at me sternly.

"I had no such intention," I replied. "You call yourself Gasparoni. I thought your name had been Barbone?"

"So they styled me," he answered, "from the long beard which I formerly wore."

"Pray may I ask you how you happened to be taken?" I observed inquiringly.

"*Preso!*" said he contemptuously; "I was never taken. Not all the troops in the Pontifical states could have taken me. None but eagles could have reached our resorts. There we wanted for nothing, besiege us as they might. The peasants were our friends, and brought us plenty of provisions. We annihilated party after party that they sent against us, till the soldiers would fight no longer. Many of them entered our band, which at one time consisted of nearly one hundred. But I got tired of that savage life. In the summer months it was well enough; but to brave the winter among the mountains,—to sleep on the snows with nothing but our mantles to shelter us,—to be deprived of our wives and children,—not to be able to dispose of our booty without great risk, so that even money was often of no use to us! I could point out where many a napoleon and doppia d'oro is buried. And yet," said he after a pause, "that life, with all its privations and miseries, is preferable to confinement in a prison. Oh! you cannot fancy what the want of liberty is to us mountaineers!—to rot in a dungeon,—not to have the free use of our limbs!" Here he clanked his chains.

After this harangue, which he delivered with great volubility, he folded his arms again, *à la Napoleon,* and a gloom came over him. He seemed to be lost in thought.

"You have said," I observed, "that you were never taken. How then came you here?"

"Here!" he said with emphasis; "I was trepanned—betrayed! The Pope broke his faith; my confessor, his sacred word. I was promised pardon,—full pardon for myself and my brave brothers. We were betrayed—sold; and yet we live in hopes that the holy father will redeem his promise."

"Yes," thought I; "if he *had* done you justice, you would not be here."

"Your name," I said flatteringly, "is well known in Europe. You are the Napoleon of bandits, and worthy of being classed with De Cesaris."

"De Cesaris," said he contemptuously, "*era un miserabile!* He took a poor painter for a prince. Ha! ha! Gasparoni would not have made such a blunder." Here he laughed again with a consciousness of superiority. "The fool, too," said he, "to allow the artist to paint his portrait!—it was like a man's putting his name on a stiletto, and leaving it as evidence against himself."

"Perhaps," said I, "like him, you have no objection to the world's knowing something of your story. Charles de Chatillon has immortalized him; he is become an historical character."

"I have no such ambition," said he. "It matters little what the world thinks of me; but you shall have my history, if you have any curiosity to know it."

"The greatest," I replied.

"It is a short one," observed the bandit.

"I am the son of Rinalda, better known in the Roman annals than I am. She was cruelly injured. Deprived of her lover, Peronti, whom they made a priest, she took a hatred to all mankind—a just one, and taught me to revenge her wrongs on the whole human species; brought me up to brigandage as a profession,—and as good a one as any other, and as honourable! I went very early into the mountains, and joined a band of brave fellows, which, on the death of their captain, I was unanimously chosen to command. Chosen from my merit, I governed them by opinion. They knew that I was brave and prudent. I had many times an opportunity of showing that I had all the qualities that constitute a good general: had I commanded an army, like Napoleon, I should have been as invincible. Once we were besieged in the upper ranges of the Abruzzi by a company of Austrians, at the time those *maledetti tyranni d'Italia* had possession of Naples. We were enclosed on three sides by the troops, and on the other was a precipice of many hundred feet, that plunged, without a shelf or ledge of rock, into the plain. I was at that time detached with nine of my companions; but such was the nature of the crag on which we bivouacked,—so narrow the access to it, that only one person could mount the pass at a time. This our enemies knew, for they lost several men in making a reconnaissance. But our provisions failed us, and we were on the point of giving ourselves up, for fear of starvation, when I discovered an eagle's eyrie, and, to the wonder of our foes, contrived, by plundering it of hares and kids, to support nature for many days. At last the eaglets flew; and then our distress returned, and with it the thought of surrender.

"I recollected, however, that opposite to where a single sentinel had been posted there was a chasm—a fissure—a deep ravine, the top of which was covered with wood; and one dark night, leading my little band, I crawled on hands and knees without being perceived, and poniarded the vidette:—he fell without a groan! We then, after overcoming incredible dangers, reached the brink of the abyss. My troop eyed the gulph with terror. It was narrow; but at the bottom roared a mountain torrent, that from its immeasurable depth looked like a silver thread. I came provided with a rope, to which, when we dare not go down into the plain, we are in the habit of attaching a basket, which we lower to the peasants for provisions; to this rope I adjusted a heavy dagger, and hurled it across the chasm. By good fortune, it got entangled at the first throw among the brushwood, and stuck fast between two of the branches. Having drawn it tight, I fastened it to a tree on our side of the ravine. My companions watched me with anxiety, wondering what next I was about to do. I spoke not a word, but suspended myself over the abyss; and, hand over hand, reached the opposite bank in safety. All followed me, and with like success, save one, whose strength or courage failed him: he unhappily sunk into the boiling gulph, but he was dead long before he reached it; so that his sufferings were less than had he been taken by the Tedeschi. What a supper we made that night! and how soundly we slept! That night—that sleep repaid all our toils!

" Great was the astonishment of our foes when they found we had escaped their snares; and you may by that escape form some notion of the pleasures of a brigand's life.

" But this was not the only time we were near falling into the power of the soldiery. In all my seventeen years of service we were never betrayed but once. You know that one of the great trades in our mountains is that of Carbonari. The wood is of no value but to make charcoal, which principally goes into the markets of Rome and Naples. We always kept on good terms with these gentry. One night we were incautiously—contrary to our usual practice—drinking with them, without having placed a single sentinel, when we found ourselves attacked by an armed party, — not, however, before I heard their arms rattling in the branches; so that we had time to seize our muskets. They were much more numerous than ourselves, but they paid dear for their attack: I killed four with my own hand. I was wounded; but that is nothing—I am full of wounds: look here, and here, and here! The Carbonari fled; but we surprised them afterwards. Who can escape from those intent on revenge!—a time always comes, or soon or late. So with them. We retaliated—terribly retaliated; not a man escaped! Not that I lifted a hand against them,—none ever fell by Gasparoni but in action."

As he said this, his stature seemed to grow; and it was clear that he thought himself a hero. He waited, expecting, no doubt, that I should express my admiration of his exploits; but I remembered the last, and said to him,

" You forget the daughter of the Englishman—her head——"

" *Questo Inglese era un impertinente*," replied he. " Why did he not send the ransom? He knew, or ought to have known, the laws of brigands; we could not have spared her life had we wished it. No; it would have been an act of injustice—of gross partiality."

Here some of the brigands, who had heard his words, came up, and by their gestures gave confirmation of their general's words.

" And who among the band," I inquired, " was the executioner; for, like Louis XI, I suppose you had your Tristan?"

He pointed to the back of the cave, and called Geronymo, the figure whom I had first observed. He came forward.

" *Son qui!*" said the man with a hoarse guttural voice, that might have been mistaken for the howl of a wolf.

I looked at him attentively, and not without a sense of horror and disgust. His long and bony, yet athletic form, might have served as a model for a gladiator, for the muscles protruded like one of Michael Angelo's anatomical figures: his cadaverous sallow countenance pale with crime,—his eyes deep sunk, and overhung by thick bushy eyebrows, and emitting a gloomy light as within caverns,— his thin and straight upper lip, with the lower underhung like that of a dog-fish, fitted him well for the bourreau of Signor Gasparoni.

" So you were the executioner of the Englishman's daughter, Geronymo, eh?" I inquired.

" *Si, signor*," said he, with a grin of satisfaction, that betrayed a pride of office, and a superiority over his fellows.

" *Era molto bella!*" observed one of the bandits behind me.

I looked over my shoulder. The wretch who spoke was a little corpulent man, and reminded me of one of Rubens' satyrs. There was a most revolting leer on his countenance, which suggested to my mind not her death,—which was a mercy,—but the miserable fate that preceded it. I remembered the story of the peasant girl in the Tales of a Traveller, and shuddered.

Turning round again to that iron-visaged wretch, Geronymo, I said to him,

"Have you no remorse, Geronymo, for all the murders you have committed?"

"Remorse!" he replied, as though he did not understand the meaning of the word: "ought not a good soldier to obey the word of command? Whenever the captain said '*Amazza!' amazzava.*"

"*Avete amazzato molte?*" I asked.

"*Si, signor, moltissime,*" he replied, with the greatest nonchalance. His eye lighted up, as he spoke, with a gloomy joy.

I turned from him as from a basilisk, and almost thought I heard the death-rattle of one of his victims.

As I was about to leave the Bagno, I met a capuchin, their confessor. It was the same who had persuaded Gasparoni to deliver himself up to the Roman authorities. I took him aside, and entered into conversation with him. He was a man advanced in age, and of a physiognomy such as I have observed to be common to almost all ecclesiastics in Italy,—heavy, dull, and unmeaning. He told me that Gasparoni and most of his band were very religious, and went regularly to mass and confession. He added, that he had petitioned the holy father for their liberation, and that he had no doubt, if released, that they would now make good subjects.

"The Pope," I observed, "knows them too well by past experience to trust such wretches at large again."

What tales might not this man reveal! but I found he was disinclined to be communicative, and in a hurry to commence his duties. I wished him therefore a *buon giorno*.

When we have voluntarily shut ourselves up in a Bagno with its unhappy inmates, it seems as though the return to liberty was interdicted to us,—that we are the victims to some snare, and that the iron gates of the prison are actually closed on us for ever. But a moment's reflection dissipates the fearful illusion, and we abandon ourselves, as Lucretius describes those who behold a storm at a distance, to the pleasure derived from our own security; or as we do when leaning over the parapet of a precipice. But, at the same time, I rushed through the open doors like a captive on being delivered from his chains, and, having emerged from the gloomy gateway, breathed more freely, inhaled with a new delight the sea-breeze, and stood watching the sun sink slowly through the vaporous atmosphere till it had totally disappeared below the waters. Then I returned to my inn, reflecting that I had perhaps just seen the last of the bandits. And yet the scene I had witnessed left no impression behind it such as I had expected; it furnished no stores to feed the imagination or to awaken the enthusiasm of art. The poetry of banditism has perished in the citadel of Città Vecchia.

THE GLORIES OF GOOD HUMOUR.

BY GODFREY GOODFELLOW.

"Est Ulubris, animus si te non deficit æquus."—Hor.

WHAT a charming thing good humour is! How superexcellent and inestimable a quality, or character, or attribute of the mind! Yes, I unhesitatingly declare there is nothing like it. It is the only true key to the casket of happiness, the real source of all this world's enjoyments, the potent mithridate of misery, the balm of life, the care-dispelling Nepenthe, the rich restoring heavenly elixir drawn by wisdom from the alembic of content.

The good-humoured man is the only true philosopher. He alone knows how to enjoy life. He is wiser far than all the grave *Saturnine* star-gazers and moralists in the world. Is he not? Why, of what use is all our philosophy if it does not enable a man to be merry and live happy? Psha! to give way to grief, to allow the mind to succumb to despondency, is certainly to exhibit our poor humanity in one of the most ridiculous positions in which it could be placed. Diogenes, domiciled in a tub, cuts rather a curious figure amidst the sages of antiquity; and so do a host of others: but, certainly, Heraclitus in tears exhibits the weakness of human nature more glaringly than any of them. Grieving, forsooth! Why, 'tis just as if a man, plunging into the sea, should tie a stone about his neck in order to enable him to swim the better. Grieving is indeed a bad sort of a safety-jacket in a "sea of troubles." No: give me the good-humoured man; the fine, gay, jovial fellow, whom no disasters can depress; the true minion of merriment and fun, whom no sorrows can sadden; the genuine votary of "heart-easing mirth," whose mind, like the lark at sunrise, is ever cheerful and gay;

> "Whose wit can brighten up a winter's day,
> And chase the splenetic dull hours away."

Give me such a man; his philosophy is worth all the dogmas, and rules, and precepts, that ever were expounded in the Academe, the Porch, or the Lycæum.

What should I be now—or, rather, *where* should I be—but for my good humour? Alas! perhaps sailing the Styx in company with Charon; or, not having the ferry money, wandering disconsolate upon the banks, (for it is only the good-humoured, such as Menippus, that can manage to get over passage-free.) But here I am now, a fine, fat, rubicund fellow,—and all, I say it unhesitatingly, owing to my good humour. Good humour, thou hast indeed been to me a true, and kind, and trusty benefactress! Oh! thou fair, and sweet, and lovely thing, in whatever form thou holdest communion with mortals: whether thou art an immaterial essence that blends at will with our mortal bodies or whether thou art something more loving and palpable, —that light, blithe, blue-eyed maid,

> "Whom lovely Venus at a birth,
> With two sister graces more,
> To ivy-crowned Bacchus bore;"

or whether a wild spirit, a lovely Ariel of the air, thou transfusest thyself into all the beautiful things of this world,—the green fields, and the silvery streams, and the sunny skies,—and then, rich with the sheen of their loveliness, comest into the presence-chamber of the mind, fixest thyself in the great senate of the senses, cheering and gladdening all their emotions!—whatever thou art, good humour,—be thou a bodiless essence, a lovely maid, a lively spirit, or any other modification of the mysterious and the beautiful, I love thee; love thee as dearly as ever Orpheus loved his Eurydice, Petrarch his Laura, or Waller his Sacharissa. Thou art the harbinger of comfort, the inductress of joy, the dove that bringest to mortals the olive of happiness and peace. Without thee what were life?—a dull, dreary, uninteresting scene,—a bare, bleak, barren, joyless, empyreanless——

Stop—stop—stop—stop!—halloo, Pegasus! where the devil are you going to? Soho! softly; not quite so high if you please; much as you admire good humour, do, pray! stay a little nearer to the confines of this "visible diurnal sphere."

"Who are you? where do you come from? You have no right to be dealing out such fulsome panegyrics about good humour."

Yes, but I have, though; I am universally acknowledged to be the most good-humoured man on town. The pure blood of the All-wits, the Easymirths, and the Goodfellows, flows in my veins. I am heir to a large property in Merryland, and my residence is at Jollity Hall, a picturesque, romantic spot in the county of Greatlaughter-shire. I intend to start at the next general election for the borough of Gaybright; when I shall bring in such a measure of reform as shall astonish all our modern menders of constitutions.

I have every right, then, to descant upon the merits of good humour; and I do so the rather because men do not sufficiently appreciate them.

Now I fully agree with Dr. Johnson in thinking that "good humour is the quality to which everything in this life owes its power of pleasing." It is the one great source from which spring all those innumerable streams of enjoyment that intersect, and refresh, and beautify the social and moral world. It is, like Fame, "the spur that the clear spirit doth raise" above the fogs, and the damps, and the vapours that so often hang over and darken this sublunary scene. It is the grand moral alkali that completely neutralizes the corrosive acerbity of all this world's cares and sorrows. It is a pure heavenly sunshine illumining the chambers of the soul; a coal from heaven's own golden hearth, that warms into a congenial and ever-during glow all the best and kindliest emotions of our nature.

How different, indeed, would be the condition of the world if a system of good humour were universally established! For what is it but the absence of good humour that is the cause of almost all the troubles of life? All the wars that have desolated the world spring from no other origin. Kings and rulers wanting good humour have fallen out, and whole nations have been set at loggerheads:

"Quicquid delirant reges plectuntur Achivi."

Now, if good humour universally influenced the actions of men, there would be none of these things; war would be at an end. General Evans might then attend to his parliamentary duties. The "mailed Mars"

might " on his altar sit," but it would not be " up to the ears in blood."
He might lay by his lance, and commence smoking the calumet of
peace. Again, we should have no need of that noisy, brawling, troublesome class of men yclept lawyers,—for it is plainly from the absence
of good humour that all the litigation in the world takes its rise. The
gentlemen of the long robe might then leave *silk gowns* to their ladies,
and transfer their pleading to some other court than a court of law.
At all events, the world would be freed from their forensic displays,
for men would be on such *good terms* with each other that there
would be no need of *law terms* to set them right. And also, under a
general system of good humour, we should be freed from all the tur-
moil and contention of politics. Tithes, and church-rates, and corporation bills, would no longer afford such scope for violent and angry
declamation. Would not this be glorious? As for our physicians,
they might shut up shop, for there is no such admirable conservative
of the constitution as good humour,—it being generally admitted that
all diseases take their rise from the prevalence of *bad* humour in the
blood. These disciples of Galen, then,—these knights of the lancet,—
might become philosophers, and study physics instead of physic; or
they might devote themselves to analyse the faculties of the mind,
and thus, instead of physicians, become metaphysicians.

But, indeed, the ramifications are so numerous, that it would not be
easy to follow out and describe all the innumerable advantages that
would result from the establishment of an universal system of good
humour.

And thus we are enabled at once to explain what the poets have
meant by the Golden Age. It was plainly nothing else than the
reign of universal good humour. The proof is quite obvious. Gold
is the most excellent of metals,—good humour is the most excellent
of the qualities of the mind; and therefore, the analogy being so
striking, the poets at once styled this happy period the Golden Age.
And hence it is evident that good humour is the only true philosopher's stone.

> " This is the charm by sages often told,
> Converting all it touches into gold.
> Content can soothe, where'er by Fortune placed :
> Can rear a garden in the desert waste."

In this passage "content" is only another name for good humour.
Cease, then, ye followers of the Hermetic art, cease toiling over your
crucibles; good humour is the true moral alchemy that will really
enrich and ameliorate mankind.

This, then, is the reform bill which I intend to introduce as soon
as I have the honour of a seat in the house; a bill for striking
out, arranging, devising, and establishing some plan by which good
humour may be reduced to a system; so that henceforward it will
be the cardinal principle of life,—the rule by which all the actions of
men shall be guided, regulated, and directed. Let me but pass this;
and then, my country! thy happiness is secured. Let us hear no
more about the ballot, and universal suffrage, and all those Utopian
schemes of our modern speculators. Let us have no more hunting
after a visionary political optimism; good humour is the only one
thing necessary to bring all our civil institutions to a state of
complete perfection. " Give me," said Archimedes, " a point in extra-

mundane space, and I will remove the solid earth from its foundations." "Give me," say I, "good humour, and I will uproot all miseries, and contentions, and quarrellings from the world." Away with all the nostrums of our moralists and philosophers!—good humour is the one sole, infallible panacea for all the ills of life. Misfortunes may lower, and disappointments may assail; but still the mind of the good-humoured man, like a Delos emerging from the deep, rises buoyant above them all. Hurrah, then, for an eternal, cloudless, bright, jovial, unsubduable good humour! Let us have nothing but good humour! Let a cheerful smile be for ever playing upon the happy faces of our lovely wives; let our children be born in good humour, and in good humour let them grow up; let the girls be taught to smile with their mother's smile, and the boys after the manner of their father; and thus we shall be taking the best way to establish and consolidate one vast, wide, universal empire of love, happiness, and joy!

SONG OF THE MODERN TIME.

Oh how the world has alter'd since some fifty years ago,
When coats and shoes would *really* serve to keep out rain and snow;
But double soles and broadcloth,—oh, dear me! how very low
To talk of such old-fashion'd things, when every one must know
That we are well-bred gentlefolks all of the modern time!

We all meet now at midnight's hour, and form a glitt'ring throng,
Where lovely angels walk quadrilles, and ne'er do l'Été wrong,
Where Eastern scents all fresh and sweet, from Rowland's, float along,
And the name of a good old country-dance would sound like a Chinese gong
In the ears of well-bred gentlefolks all of the modern time!

Young ladies now of sage sixteen must give their friends a rout,
And teach the cook and housemaid how to " hand the things about;"
And they must pull Ma's bedstead down, and hurry, scout, and flout,
To have a fine refreshment-room, and lay a supper out
Like well-bred, dashing gentlefolks all of the modern time!

And beardless boys, all brag and noise, must do "the thing that's right,"—
That is,—they'll drink champagne and punch, and keep it up all night;
They'll shout and swear, till, sallying forth at peep of morning's light,
They knock down some old woman just to show how well they fight,
Like brave young English gentlemen all of the modern time!

At the good old hours of twelve and one our grandsires used to dine,
And quaff their horns of nut-brown ale, and eat roast-beef and chine;
But we must have our silver forks, ragouts, and foreign wine,
And not sit down till five or six if we mean to cut a shine,
Like dashing, well-bred gentlefolks all of the modern time!

Our daughters now at ten years old must learn to squall and strum,
And study shakes and quavers under Signor Fee-fo-fum;
They'll play concertos, sing bravuras, rattle, scream, and thrum,
Till you almost wish that you were deaf, and they, poor things! were dumb;
But they must be like young gentlefolks all of the modern time!

Our sons must jabber Latin verbs, and talk of a Greek root,
Before they've left off pinafores, cakes, lollipops, and fruit;
They all have splendid talents that the desk and bar will suit,
Each darling boy would scorn to be "a low mechanic brute;"
They must be well-bred college youths all of the modern time!

But bills will come at Christmas-tide, alas, alack-a-day!
The creditors may call again, " Papa's not in the way;
" He's out of town; but, certainly, next week he'll call and pay;"
And then his name's in the Gazette! and this I mean to say
Oft winds up many gentlefolks all of the modern time!

CAPITAL PUNISHMENTS IN LONDON
EIGHTY YEARS AGO.

EARL FERRERS.

THE sensation created in London by that which has now become no ordinary spectacle,—two public executions in the course of the last few months,—naturally leads the observant mind to contemplate the march of intellect in this great metropolis with respect to the shedding of human blood by judicial authority. It may be interesting to the general reader to lay before him the reflections thus suggested, together with some curious and minute descriptions of scenes witnessed within the last century.

The practice of *Sus per Col*, as described in legal abbreviations, or hanging, is the only mode of putting to death ("pressing to death" excepted) known to the law of England for all felonies short of high or petty treason. In cases of conspiracy against the state, traitors of rank were indulged with the privilege of being beheaded; but meaner offenders, besides other inflictions, were to suffer on the gallows. This distinction necessarily caused the punishment to be regarded as very ungenteel, if an expression of levity may be allowed; and, in consequence, no respectable person, or, at any rate, only here and there one, would choose to be hanged. Earl Ferrers, who was convicted of the murder of his steward in the reign of George the Second, petitioned that he might die by the axe. This was refused. "He has done," said the old king, "de act of de bad man, and he shall die de death of de bad man." The feeling of the monarch was good, but it was rather odd that a king should seem to think the punishment of treason, called by judges "the highest crime known to the law," an ennobling indulgence which ought not to be extended to a simple murderer.

One luxury, however, Lord Ferrers is reported to have secured for the last hour of his life,—a silken rope; but a more important deviation from the common mode, so far as abridgement of bodily pain is concerned, was made on that occasion, for then it was that what is now familiarly called the "drop" was first used. Till that period, to draw a cart from beneath the culprit, or to throw him from a ladder, by turning it round, after he had ascended to a certain height for the halter to be adjusted, had been the practice; but for the wretched peer a scaffold was prepared, part of the floor of which was raised eighteen inches above the rest, which, on the signal of death being given, became flat. The contrivance, however, did not very well succeed, according to the narrative left us by Lord Orford; which, from the remarkable circumstances it details of that memorable exit, and of the usages which then prevailed, is worth transcribing.

The crime for which the nobleman suffered was a most cruel murder. He had been through life a very depraved character. It was doubted if this were the only homicide he had committed; he had separated from his wife, and ill-used his mistress. He, however, met his fate with great firmness. "On the last morning," says Lord Orford in a letter, "he dressed himself in his wedding clothes, and said he thought this, at least, as good an occasion for putting them on, as that for which they were first made." The account proceeds: " Even an awful procession of above two hours, with that mixture of pageantry, shame, and ignominy, nay, and of delay, could not dismount his resolution. He set out from the Tower at nine, amidst thousands of spectators. First went a string of constables; then one of the sheriffs, in his chariot and six, the horses dressed with ribands; next, Lord Ferrers, in his own landau and six, his coachman crying all the way,—guards at each side; the other sheriff's chariot followed empty, with a mourning coach and six, a hearse, and the Horse-guards. Observe, that the empty chariot was that of the other sheriff, who was in the coach with the prisoner, and who was Vaillant the French bookseller in the Strand. How (exclaims Lord Orford to his correspondent) will you decypher all these strange circumstances? A bookseller, in robes and in mourning, sitting as a magistrate by the side of the earl; and, in the evening, everybody going to Vaillant's shop to hear the particulars. I wrote to him, as he serves me, for the account; but he intends to print it. Lord Ferrers, at first, talked on indifferent matters; and, observing the prodigious confluence of people, (the blind was drawn up on his side,) he remarked, ' they never saw a lord hanged, and perhaps will never see another.' One of the dragoons was thrown, by his horse's leg entangling in the hind wheel: Lord Ferrers expressed much concern, and said, ' I hope there will be no death to-day but mine;' and was pleased when Vaillant told him the man was not hurt. Vaillant made excuses to him for performing the duties of his office in person. ' For that,' said the earl, ' I am much obliged to you: I feared the disagreeableness of the duty might make you depute your under-sheriff. As you are so good as to execute it yourself, I am persuaded the dreadful business will be conducted with more expedition.' The Chaplain of the Tower, who sat backwards, then thought it his turn to speak, and began to talk on religion; but Lord Ferrers received it impatiently. However, the chaplain persevered; and said, he wished to bring his lordship to some confession, or acknowledgment of contrition, for a crime so repugnant to the laws of God and man, and wished him to endeavour to do whatever could be done in so short a time. The earl replied, ' he had done everything he proposed to do, with regard to God and man; and, as to discourses on religion, you and I, sir,' said he to the clergyman, ' shall probably not agree on that subject. The passage is very short; you will not have time to convince me, nor I to refute you; it cannot be ended before we arrive.' The clergyman still insisted, and urged that, at least, the world would expect some satisfaction. Lord Ferrers replied, with some impatience, ' Sir, what have I to do with the world? I am going to pay a forfeit life, which my country has thought proper to take from me; what do I care now what the world thinks of me? But, sir, since you do desire some confession, I will confess one thing to you; I do believe there is a God. As to modes of worship, we had better not talk on them. I always thought Lord Bolingbroke in the wrong to publish his notions on religion: I will not fall into the same error.' The chaplain, seeing that it was in vain to make any more attempts, contented himself with representing to him, that it would be expected from one of his calling, and that even decency required, that some prayer should be used on the scaffold, and asked his leave, at least, to repeat the Lord's Prayer there. Lord Ferrers replied, ' I always thought it a good prayer; you may use it if you please.'

"While these speeches were passing, the procession was stopped by the crowd. The earl said he was dry, and wished for some wine-and-water. The sheriff said, he was sorry to be obliged to refuse him. By late regulations they were enjoined not to let prisoners drink on their way from the place of imprisonment to that of execution, as great indecencies had been formerly committed by the lower species of criminals getting drunk; ' and though,' said he, ' my lord, I might think myself excusable in overlooking this order, out of regard to a person of your lordship's rank, yet there is another reason, which I am sure will weigh with you,—your lordship is sensible of the greatness of the crowd: we must draw up to some tavern; the confluence would be so great, that it would delay the expedition which your lordship seems so much to desire.' He replied he was satisfied, adding, ' Then I must be content with this;' and he took some pigtail tobacco out of his pocket. As they went on, a letter was thrown into his coach; it was from his mistress, to tell him that it was impossible, from the crowd, for her to get round to the spot where he had appointed her to meet and take leave of him, but that she was in a hackney-coach of such a number. He begged Vaillant to order his officers to try to get the hackney-coach up to his. ' My lord,' said Vaillant, ' you have behaved so well hitherto, that I think it is pity to venture unmanning yourself.' He was struck, and was satisfied without seeing her. As they drew nigh, he said, ' I perceive we are almost arrived: it is time to do what little more I have to do;' and then, taking out his watch, gave it to Vaillant, desiring him to accept it as a mark of his gratitude for his kind behaviour; adding, ' It is scarce worth your acceptance, but I have nothing else; it is a stop-watch, and a pretty accurate one.' He gave five guineas to the chaplain, and took out as much for the executioner. Then giving Vaillant a pocket-book, he begged him to deliver it to Mrs. Clifford, his mistress, with what it contained, and with his most tender regards; saying, ' The key of it is to the watch, but I am persuaded you are too much a gentleman to open it.' He destined the remainder of the money in his purse to the same person, and with the same tender regards.

"When they came to Tyburn, his coach was detained some minutes by the conflux of people; but, as soon as the door was opened, he stepped out readily, and mounted the scaffold. It was hung with black by the undertaker, and at the expense of his family. Under the gallows was a new-invented stage, to be struck from under him. He showed no kind of fear or discomposure, only just looking at the gallows with a slight motion of dissatisfaction. He said little, kneeled for a moment to the prayer, said ' Lord have mercy upon me, and forgive me my errors!' and immediately mounted the upper stage. He had come pinioned with a black sash, and was unwilling to have his hands tied, or his face covered, but was persuaded to both. When the rope was put round his neck, he turned pale, but recovered his countenance instantly; and was but seven minutes from leaving the coach, before the signal was given for striking the stage As the machine was new, they were not ready at it: his toes touched it, and he suffered a little, having had time, by their bungling, to raise his cap; but the executioner pulled it down again, and they pulled his legs, so that he was soon out of pain, and quite dead in four minutes. He desired not to be stripped and exposed; and Vaillant promised him, though his outer clothes must be taken off, that his shirt should not. This decency ended with him: the sheriffs fell to eating and drinking on the scaffold, and helped up one of their friends to drink with them, while he was still hanging, which he did for above an hour, and then was conveyed back with the same pomp to Surgeons' Hall, to be dissected. The executioners fought for the rope; and the one who lost it, cried. The mob tore off the black cloth as relics; but the universal crowd behaved with great decency and admiration, as they well might, for sure no exit was ever made with more sensible resolution and with less ostentation."

The contrivance above described has caused the cart to fall into general disuse on such occasions. The change, however, was not suddenly effected. For many years after the death of Lord Ferrers, the triangular gallows at Tyburn maintained its ground, and, on execution-days, the cart passed from Newgate up Giltspur-street, and through Smithfield to Cow-lane; Skinner-street had not then been built, and the crooked lane which turned down by St. Sepulchre's church, as well as Ozier-lane, did not offer sufficient width to admit of the cavalcade passing by either of them with convenience to Holborn-hill.

For centuries the prevailing opinion had been, that executions ought to take place at a distance from the crowded part of the city. Anciently malefactors were put to death at *The Elms* in Smithfield, or rather, between Smithfield and Turnmill-street. But when the houses had increased, so as to encroach on the space which had long been kept open there, it was thought expedient to carry those appointed to die, farther off; and a spot was fixed upon, which received the name of Tyburn, near the beginning of Tottenham-court-road.* When Holborn had been built up to St. Giles's, a farther removal was deemed necessary, and these tragic scenes were carried from one end of Oxford-street to the other,—from the beginning of Tottenham-court-road to the Tyburn of the present day.

But at length, in the reign of George the Third, it was judged better to abandon the parade so long kept up, and to execute the sentence of death in the immediate vicinity of Newgate. This alteration, though many reasons may be urged in its favour, was not universally approved. There were those who apprehended that, in a constitutional point of view, it was dangerous to abate the publicity which had so long attached to the consummation of the last severity of the law. Mr. Horne Tooke was of the number. To hang a felon at the door of his prison, he considered, " the next thing to putting

---

* This fact is not generally known; but a singular proof of the correctness of the above statement has recently been furnished. Within the last three months, the ground having been opened for the common sewer opposite Meux's brewhouse, by the end of Oxford-street, eight or ten, or more, skeletons were discovered. They were supposed to be the remains of suicides, who had been buried there, in the cross roads, under the old law against *felo de se*. One or two of them had perhaps committed self-destruction; but so many could hardly have been collected by the same act in one spot. It is much more probable that the bones there found were those of malefactors, who after execution had been interred under the gallows on which they suffered.

him to death within the walls," and directly approximating towards secret executions.

By degrees, however, the public mind got perfectly reconciled to the change. Much expense and confusion were spared; and the idle were no longer indulged in a disgusting holiday, to witness a spectacle in but too many instances known to produce anything but the impression which might have been desired. The rabble went to the mournful scene as to a public entertainment. The procession to Tyburn, with the prayers and other ceremonies there, occupied a large portion of the day, which many of the spectators closed in dissipation, outrage, and robbery.

Instead of carrying the condemned three miles, and executing the culprits from a cart, an apparatus was now erected close to Newgate; and the awful ceremony, no longer made the business of many hours, was regularly performed at eight o'clock in the morning, and every vestige of the deplorable scene put away between nine and ten. Some of the first executions witnessed at Newgate were most unlike those which have been seen of late years, even before the late king ascended the throne. Not fewer than eighteen or twenty persons were conducted to the scaffold on the same day; and the gallows originally set up in the Old Bailey was so contrived that three cross-beams could be used, and the sufferers were, by this contrivance, disposed in as many rows.

By degrees these spectacles grew less frequent, and the numbers hurried into eternity on each occasion were fewer. The execution of five or six persons on one day became an uncommon sight, and seldom more than two or three suffered together.

This comparatively small sacrifice of life did not make the Old Bailey less attractive on a hanging-day than Tyburn had formerly been, though the rabble were constantly dismissed shortly after the clock struck nine.

About the beginning of the present century, a notorious highwayman of the name of Clark, with five other malefactors, submitted to the last severity of man together. I went before the day had dawned, and very shortly after the preparations had commenced, to the Old Bailey. The spectacle then presented was most picturesque; and to me, whatever it might be to others, most extraordinary. Wooden posts made in a triangular form with rails, and a rod of iron issuing from the tops to pass through holes prepared in strong bars of timber, which they were to sustain, were lying about in every direction. Lighted torches were carried by the workmen and their assistants, the bars being first laid along the ground, nearly on or over the spot where they were to be set up to keep off the crowd, while the preparations went forward for the work of death. The body of the drop had previously been brought out. This did not take to pieces, but was kept, as at present, standing in the yard attached to the prison; and, being placed on wheels, was—I might say *is*, as executions have not wholly ceased,—drawn out at a very early hour. It was curious to notice the interest, the levity, the indifference, which prevailed in the different groups drawn together as the awful hour approached, according to the various humours of the individuals who composed them. When the cross-beam of the gallows was raised to its place, it was gazed on with great eagerness.

2 x 2

As each rail was fixed, to mark the boundary of the space to be kept clear, a mass of men and boys, with here and there a female, ranged themselves close to it. The constables were occasionally seen struggling through the human wall thus formed, and showing their authority—the staff of office, to prove their right to be there; a form by no means unnecessary, as many of them were only to be known by that sign, as in truth they were almost impostors, having only assumed the character in which they appeared, for the day, being engaged by the respectable tradesmen really serving the office, to save them the time that would be consumed, or to spare feelings that must be wounded, if they appeared *in propriâ personâ*.

The scaffold was established at the Debtors'-door, in the widest part of the Old Bailey; and the bar which was placed as above described extended from the further side of the scaffold, to a few feet south of the governor's house. The steps leading to the Felons'-door were soon crowded; and several recesses and niches on that side of the prison were peopled from an early hour with living statues.

Well do I remember the awe with which I heard the chimes of St. Sepulchre's church announce the lapse of another and another quarter of an hour, the calculations which were made of the exact number of minutes which the victims had yet to breathe, and the speculations as to the manner in which they were then engaged, and the deportment which they would assume in the closing scene.

The appearance of the city marshals between seven and eight arranging the constables, announced that the time had nearly arrived. A humourist would have jested at the overacted dignity of the functionaries just named of that day. A Wellington disposing his ranks to meet the fiercest shock of the best warriors of France, could not have given a finer idea of the importance of command, than these civic heroes suggested while placing in Newgate order their crowd of clubmen.

It had been usual to hang black cloth on the chains which ran along three sides of the scaffold. On the occasion now recalled this part of the ceremonial was not omitted. The black was duly paraded; but so beggarly a display in connexion with any public proceeding my *not* "young memory" cannot parallel. It had been so worn and torn, that such a collection of tatters, it might fairly be concluded, could hardly have been found in any part of his Majesty's dominions,—Rosemary-lane, perhaps, excepted. The idlers, who by this time had assembled in great force, and who—the majority of them at all events—evidently considered they had but to enjoy themselves, laughed immoderately, and indulged in all sorts of jokes on this Rag-fair set-out; which, to confess the truth, as their streamers, shaped into all imaginable forms, fluttered in the wind,—bearing in mind the solemnity of the occasion, and the supposed object of the exposure of the sable shreds, namely, mourning,—was the perfection of burlesque.

The hand of St. Sepulchre's clock was pointed at the quarter to eight. Fifteen minutes more, and the unhappy ones appointed to die were expected to ascend that platform from which they were to sink into eternity. The immense multitude extended far up Giltspur-street one way, and almost reached to Ludgate-hill in the opposite direction. In all the houses commanding a view of the gallows the windows were crowded; the ledges without the parapets and roofs were in like manner surmounted by numerous spectators.

It would not be easy to describe the sensation created by the appearance of the very important actors who next came on the stage,—the executioners.

"Here are Jack Ketch and his man!" was the exclamation of almost every individual in the crowd to his neighbour.

There was something in the look of the men which really challenged attention. The principal, or "Jack Ketch himself," as he was called, was a tall, elderly personage. His costume presented a long blue frock-coat, a scarlet waistcoat, and his hose bound with red garters below the knee-buttons of his inexpressibles. He wore a flower in his coat, or carried one in his mouth. He surveyed the eagerly-staring populace, and sustained their gaze with an air of calm indifference, which, however, had nothing of startling effrontery about it. His assistant was a very different figure; he was a coarse-featured, pock-marked, short, thick-set man. All his motions indicated great vivacity; and, if a judgment might be formed from his exterior, he was proud and rejoiced to fill an office of such high distinction, and felt more satisfaction in reflecting on the conspicuous situation in which he was placed, than pity for the poor creatures who almost instantly were to be committed to his professional care. He generally wore dark clothes; but sometimes had a bit of his master's distinguishing finery,—a red waistcoat. He nimbly paced the scaffold on this occasion, and looked on the mob, as I fancied, with an air of mirth or exultation, and presently applied himself, with no bad taste, to tear down the miserable black rags which have been mentioned; and, I believe, since that day they have never reappeared, or anything of the kind in their place. This operation completed, he seemed to confer with the other hangman on the business before them. The tall steps necessary to enable them to attach the halters to the gallows they moved towards the end of the platform near the spot on which the first who came forth was to stand; and, everything now being ready, they composedly waited the coming of the sheriffs with their prisoners.

The clock of St. Sepulchre's church struck eight; a murmur burst from the vast assemblage near it: and the solemn bell of St. Paul's cathedral a moment afterwards confirmed, so to speak, the announcement of the fatal hour. All was expectation. The executioners frequently looked towards the door from which those expected, were to advance, as if to ascertain if they were coming. There was something of excitement in their manner, and a silent indescribable movement among those within the enclosure, that told more distinctly than could speech, that the last scene was about to open.

It was nearly ten minutes after eight when the heavy tone of the prison-bell was heard. Such a sound!—a knell of death sounded for the living, who were then in perfect health, but who were next minute to be consigned to the grave, is well calculated to thrill the most unfeeling. This usage always appeared to me to heighten the solemnity of the scene, and the misery of the convicts for whom it tolled. Yet the authorities deemed it a compliment, or honour, to the sufferer, too great to be conceded in every case. The murderer, for instance, was denied the privilege of hearing it. None but those condemned for the less heinous crimes of forgery, or other capital felony unattended with the spilling of human blood, were *favoured* with the melancholy distinction.

The signal for the bell, I believe, was given at the instant when the brief procession, from the room in which the prisoners were pinioned to the door from which they pass to the final scene of expiation, commenced. The sullen sound was but three or four times repeated when those immediately in front of the prison-entrance saw the white wand of the sheriff approach from within. An officer appeared ascending the ladder, and by his side a man whose solemn aspect indicated with sufficient clearness that he was one of the doomed. The next moment he had passed to the platform, and stood in presence of the gazing populace. When the wand, the insignia of office, was seen, the word was given "Hats off!" and the multitude on every side obeyed the mandate, and stood uncovered.

The unfortunate man who appeared first of the six who were to surrender their lives on this day, was perfectly resigned to his deplorable fate. His eye was bright, his step was firm, and it was impossible for a human being in such circumstances to be more collected, or to deport himself with more propriety. If sorrow at leaving this world oppressed him, hope solaced him with the cheering prospect that it would be his, immediately, to enter on a better. He wore his hat,—such being the usage at that time,—which was removed by the executioners, and placed at one end of the scaffold; and then the clergyman made his appearance. With him the culprit conversed devoutly, but with cheerfulness. His cravat having been taken off, the old executioner elevated himself by the steps, put the fatal noose over the sufferer's head, on which the cap was immediately placed, and the end of the halter being then passed round the beam, was carefully tied. The chain and hook now introduced had not yet been adopted. The companions in woe and death of the unfortunate I have described, quickly followed. Clark was the third or fourth that appeared, and he had the weakness to distinguish himself by the idle bravado of throwing away his hat. To each of them the ordinary addressed a few words. The caps, which had been left up for some moments, were next drawn down over the whole face. A prayer was commenced; but, before it concluded, the minister passed a white handkerchief over his mouth. That was the fatal signal; the drop fell with a dismal noise, and the death-struggle ensued. It was then twenty minutes after eight, and in three or four minutes all appearance of life had ceased. In the same instant that they were suspended the crowd began to withdraw, while those who had been at a distance pressed forward to gain a more distinct view of the appalling spectacle. A cry of horror burst from a portion of the multitude when the floor gave way; but the impression it made was singularly transient. In less than a quarter of an hour cool indifference was everywhere to be marked, and foolish levity and boisterous mirth succeeded to the awe and commiseration lately manifested.

A year or two after this scene, the public mind was violently excited by the case of Governor Wall. This culprit, twenty years before, being then the king's representative at Goree, had caused a man to be flogged so severely that he died. He was present when the punishment was inflicted, and excited the floggers by calling to them, "Cut his liver out!" among other horrible expressions. The crime of whipping a man to death was well calculated to awaken public indignation; but it was not his guilt alone which caused the ferment then witnessed in the metropolis. The belief that, because he had been a governor, mercy was likely to be shown to him, which would be denied to another, probably sealed his doom, and proved a cruel aggravation of his wretched destiny. He was tried on a Wednesday, and ordered for execution on the Friday next following, but was respited till Monday. This was considered an indication that the sentence would not be carried into effect at all, although on the last-mentioned day a vast crowd assembled in the Old Bailey. A second respite had been granted; but this was not generally known, at least to the multitude congregated on the occasion. Great was the disappointment when the hour of seven struck, and no preparations for the execution were visible. Many clung to the expectation that it would yet take place; and several affirmed, untruly I believe, that the apparatus had often been brought out and erected after that hour. I mingled with some of the numerous groups, and listened to the discussions, which were carried on with great vivacity, on the subject of the crime, and probable fate of the criminal. Not till after eight was the idea totally abandoned that the raging thirst of the infuriated populace for his blood would not then be gratified. It was between eight and nine that I had an opportunity of speaking with Mr. Newman, the governor of Newgate, and learned from him that further time had been granted, and that Wall was to suffer on the coming Thursday.

The mob separated with bitter execrations; and the belief that a murderer, whose guilt was of the blackest dye, would escape punishment because he had powerful friends, gained ground throughout the nation. If horror had previously been inspired by his crime, to that personal and political rancour were now added, and the public mind was in a state of violent exasperation. The Thursday arrived, and another crowd assembled in front of Newgate, but doubting much whether the spectacle so ardently desired would at last be offered to their longing eyes. Though the officers were at their posts, and the scaffold in its place, it was still insisted that the governor would escape the fate he merited. The most ridiculous stories were circulated of the influence exercised in his favour, and of the culpable resolution of those who were in power to prevent the administration of justice. These, however, were all confuted when the appointed hour arrived, and the miserable object of public indignation was brought out to suffer like a common offender.

When Governor Wall heard his sentence pronounced on the Wednesday, with whatever dismay it filled him, he prepared to submit to it with resignation. He threw himself, when he had returned to the prison, on his wretched bed, and said he should not rise from it till the officers of justice came to lead him to his fate. The respites granted awakened in him a hope not before entertained, only to render the rigour of the law more dreadful, from the unsettled state of his mind up to the last moment.

He was a remarkably fine man in appearance, standing more than six feet high. When he came on the scaffold, his figure served but to swell the exultation of the crowd. As he advanced, he was greeted with three loud huzzas. When these subsided, a thousand ferocious voices addressed to the executioners the language which the cruel governor was charged with having used while the victim of his severity was writhing under the lash. The furious exclamations were not lost on the criminal; he requested the executioners to perform their part as expeditiously as possible. The drop almost instantly fell, and the shouts of the mob were in that dreadful moment renewed. He struggled long, and it was supposed that his sufferings were greater than those of any other victim on whom the same sentence had been executed. When about to be turned off, Wall entreated that his legs might not be pulled. The wish was respected till his long-protracted agonies compelled the sheriff, in the humane performance of his duty, to order that it should be done in order to terminate his misery. After hanging an hour, he was cut down; and the remains were conveyed in a cart, attended by a joyful rabble, to a house in Castle-street, Saffron-hill, there to be anatomized.

Subsequent to the period of which I have been speaking, an idea was entertained of recurring to the old mode of execution; at least it was revived on one occasion. A triangular gallows was made, and sockets were inserted in the road, opposite Green-arbour-court, to receive the supporting posts. On this, Anne Hurle, convicted of forgery, and a male culprit, were put to death, about thirty years ago. The criminals were brought out at the Felons'-door in a cart, and carried to the upper end of the Old Bailey. There, after the necessary preparations, the ordinary took his leave. The executioner urged the horse forward, and the vehicle was drawn from under the feet of the criminals. The motion caused them to swing backwards and forwards; but this was speedily stopped by the hangman, who leaped from the cart for the purpose. It appeared to the spectators that the victims suffered more than they would have done if executed from the drop. This was probably represented to the city authorities, for the latter method of carrying the law into effect was promptly restored.

It was formerly the usage, when a crime of remarkable atrocity had been committed, to execute the offender near the scene of his guilt. The minds then exercised on these painful subjects judged that a salutary horror would be inspired by the example so afforded, and that localities once dangerous would thus be rendered comparatively secure. Those who were punished capitally for the riots of 1780 suffered in various parts of the town; and, in the year 1790, two incendiaries were hanged in Aldersgate-street, at the eastern end of Long-lane. Since that period there have been few executions in London except in front of Newgate. The last deviation from the regular course was in the case of a sailor named Cashman, who suffered death about the year 1817, in Skinner-street, opposite the house of a gunsmith whose shop he had been concerned in plundering. The gunsmith was anxious that this should not be; but his voice was overruled, and the criminal was carried in a cart to the scaffold. It was then, it should seem, supposed that an awful warning would be given to the dissolute in Skinner-street, which would be in a great measure lost if the executioner performed his work at a distance of some forty yards from the scene of depredation.

Time, which alters everything, effected a remarkable change in this respect; and, however appalling the guilt of the condemned, it was at length presumed to be adequately visited by death in the Old

Bailey. When the fiend-like Burkers were brought to justice, they were sent to their account at the usual place of execution. To mark horror for their crime, or to arrest its progress in the neighbourhood of Shoreditch, it was not thought necessary to erect the gallows in Nova Scotia Gardens.

In the course of the rambling thoughts and recollections here brought together, it has been shown that various alterations have from time to time been made; and one, not the least remarkable, has recently been brought under public notice. Formerly it was usual for the recorder to report the cases of those sentenced at one Old Bailey sessions, to the king in council after the next ensuing sessions. It however not unfrequently happened that, through negligence, or perhaps from a feeling of commiseration for those to whom it must bring death, the report was postponed, till the cases of several sessions remained in arrear. In those days loud were the complaints on the subject of the evil consequences of the delay. The grand argument against it was, that the long interval which separated punishment from crime caused the latter to be forgotten by the public, and the violater of the law was in consequence regarded with sympathy to which he had no just claim: the wrong, the violence which he had perpetrated, were almost wholly lost sight of; and thus the lesson, that an ignominious death would promptly requite a fearful crime, was feebly impressed on the minds of the pitying spectators. Such was the notion when executions followed at some considerable distance from conviction, and the superior efficacy of the course taken with regard to murders was often referred to as being directly in point. Now, this is changed; death for robbery or forgery is hardly known, and he who is sentenced to die for hurrying a fellow-creature out of existence has five or six weeks allowed him to prepare for eternity. In noticing the change, I do not mean to censure it. Time will show whether the course now taken is followed by an increase of homicide: as yet it is too early to pronounce an opinion; but no suspicion of the sort up to the present moment has been entertained.

One strange practice was common to all executions at Newgate: a number of persons were " rubbed for wens," as it was called. Men, women, and children afflicted with them were introduced within the body of the vehicle of death, and elevated so as to be seen by the populace, within a few minutes after the convicts had been turned off. The patients were then indulged with a choice of the individual culprit, from those who had suffered, whose touch was to be applied to the part affected. The hands of the corpse selected were untied by the executioner, and gently moved backwards and forwards for about two minutes, which was supposed sufficient to effect a cure. This custom has now ceased; it was abolished as a piece of contemptible superstition, the continuance of which it would be disgraceful to permit. The executioner was deprived of this lucrative part of his business, without receiving for it any public compensation.

H. T.

A PETER-PINDARIC TO AND OF THE FOG.

IMPARTIAL Fog!
Imperial Smellfungus!
Great Cacafogo! High (and low) Mundungus!
Wherever born,—
Whether in Allan's or in Holland's bog,
Or where the wakeful Morn
Dresses herself by starlight—at the Pole,
Nature's impassable goal;
Or whether born and bred on agueish Essex' shore,
With stagnant waters greenly mantled o'er;—
Thou least-illustrious visitor!
Poking thy foreign way along,
Link-led and stumbling,
Blind-led and fumbling,
And always in the wrong;
Thou great unsung of song!
Inimical to light as an inquisitor,
But not so blood-ferocious,
Dark-hooded, and atrocious;
For, give thee undisturb'd thy gloomy way,—
Uninterrupted, let thee clap
A dark extinguisher on lightsome Day,
On early Morning a night-cap,
And 'tis remarkable how easy,
Though somewhat queasy,
Thou slumberest—how Session-long thy stay!
And very marvellous how
Innocuously quiet!
Passive as Daniel in the lions' den—
The living Daniel—flung to rav'nous men,—
(Delicious picking,
Although no chicken!)
Who lick their longing chaps, and get a precious licking!—
Daniel, who dreads that any row
Should spring up anywhere, and he not breed the riot!

All hail, great Fog! not but a *leetle* rain—
A small, slight drizzling of natural, moist sorrow—
Would make our dark perplexities more plain,
And give us hopes of seeing a to-morrow!
Dear Fog, abate the vigour
Of your full-volumed breath!
Day was a dingy white
Till you " put out the light,"
Like black Othello
When stifling his dear wife to death;
And, here, you've gone and made the comely fellow
A pretty figure,—
A horrid Nigger!

Hear me, if you're a hearkener!—
An English day at best is but a darkener
At any time o' year;
(It costs housekeepers many
A pretty pound and penny
To see *that* clear.)
Look through the lustrous city,
And you will think 'tis pity

That Phœbus—
So shrewd a god, good at a rhyme
        And rebus—
Should waste his precious time
In trying to look down
Upon this independent town;
    And pertinaciously keep poking—
    (While all the city wags are joking
        At his egregious folly
        And failure melancholy)—
Poking his ineffectual beams between the clouds,
Hovering sootily over it in crowds
        To intercept his rays,   .
        And turn them other ways.
    He ought by this time to have known—
        (His chaste, night-wandering sister,
        Who does contrive to glister,
She should have told him)—that London, day and night,
Is better lit by gas than by his sultry light.

Come, brighten up, great Fog, and don't look gloomy
While I can see you—for these eyes grow rheumy!
Clear up, for Heaven's and dear London's sakes:
For, while you 're groping here, there 's sad mistakes
        Making in every possible direction,
        And some without detection!

There 's some one, as I 've struggled through the Strand,
        Has had his hand
In my coat-pocket more than half a minute,
Though there is nothing but one sonnet in it!
La! bless me! well, how odd! why, I declare
It is my own hand I 've detected there!—
I think that wasn't me that trod upon my toes?
There—dear me! why I 've hit some other person's nose!
        Lord! how the Simpson swears,
        And hits about, and tears,
    While I keep snug, and leave the angry ass
    Just room enough to let his passion pass,
And laugh to hear him give himself such ultra-Donkey airs!

Madam, I really beg a person of your charms
        A thousand pardons
For running so unbidden to your arms!
        "Och! for five fardens
Your honour 's wilcum as the flowers in May
    To call agin there any day!
And p'r'aps it 's you don't want a basket-woman?"—
Kitty Malone, by all that 's Irish-human!—
" Och! long life to your honour!   May your eyes
Be iver jist as bright as the Green Island's skies,
        And niver foggy!"
        I add—" Nor groggy;
        Ay, Katty?"
        "'Od dra't ye!"
For if to Kate some female errors fall,
Pay her gin-score, and you whitewash them all.
Now, which way should I turn to escape the Strand?
" Fait', then, it 's handy—turn to your right hand!"
'Gad! I 'm so posed, I know not left from right;
But, here goes—anywhere!   Oh, guide me, Sight!

Heaven bless me ! what
Is this I 've run against, and fix'd it to the spot ?
Bless the dear child ! you really shouldn't stand
                In people's way
                In such a day.
Dear me ! I 've stunn'd her so, she cannot speak,
                Not even shriek !
How pale she turns—white as a Greenland ghost !
                Oh, horror ! what a hue !
                What shall I—can I do ?
Her face is frozen-cold—her eyes all whites !
Here, help ! watch ! murder ! lights ! oh, lights !————
Zounds ! what a fool I am !   Why, here have I
Been wasting all this morbid sympathy—
This tenderness and pity—on *a post !*
Come, that is strange and laughable enough !
Talk of the drolleries of " Blind-man's buff,"
                And " Catch who can,"
                This is as laughable,
                And chaffable,
                To a good-humour'd man !—
(Between parentheses, and just by way
Of taking breath—*sub rosá,* I will say
That I like Blind-man's buff, and I confess it,
                Bless it !
For, in that playful sport, if you 're inclined,
And your hand *sees,* though both your eyes are blind,
        You may, perhaps, catch the petticoat of Miss
                Some one or other,
                Or her still-handsome mother,
                And snatch a kiss,
Which taken impromptu in that lively way,
        In pure Platonic play,
                Is pleasant—very !
                And makes one merry,
And very easily finds ready pardon.)
Well, by this time, I must be near the Garden ?
                Yes, there 's the smell eternal
                Of cabbages infernal,
                Those flatulencies vernal !
And there 's the Hummums—(which my dear friend Stubbs,
Who speaketh through his nose, calls the *Hubbubs !*)—
                Yes, and although the fog 's
Perplexing in th' extreme, this must be Mogg's ?
And this the Arcade which the dear Cockneys call
" *Pie-hay-sir,*"—sounds not like the sounds at all !
Corruption villanous ! I here denounce it,
                And pronounce it
                " *Pi-atz-za,*"
        And rhyme it to " *Buy hat, sir !*"
And there 's the Theatre where solemn SIDDONS,
        And that great " last of all the Romans," KEMBLE,
        Made you for pity weep, or with touch'd passion tremble !
And this is Robins's—Robins, whose Darwin powers
                In making his poetic *flowers*
        (See his advertisements and auctions) tell—
        (While those for sale upon the florists' leads,
                Hard by,
        " Hide their diminish'd heads,"
                And, envious, die)—
                Are known so well !
So far, so good.   Hah ! here is Gliddon's !

And now I am no longer at a loss
　　Which way to go ;
So, here I 'll shoot across
Quick as a fool's bolt from his bow.
　　'Sblood ! what a bump—
　　Not named in Spurzheim—
This cursed, confounded, and confounding pump,
With its large handle stretch'd out to the nor'ward,
Has suddenly developed on my forehead,
　　Which nothing hurts *him !*
How I should like to give some one a thumping !
　　You little scoundrel ! night or day,
　　Whene'er I pass this way,
You d—d young rascal, you are always pumping !
　　Take that—and that—and that !—
　　Och, murder ! if I haven't kick'd
　　(For which I shall get lick'd)
A stout, broad-shoulder'd, five-foot-seven Pat,
　　Just the unlikeliest chap
　　To take a given rap !
" Fly, Fleance, fly !"　Don't stop to " take
Your change," for Heaven's and England's sake !

Well run, for forty-seven !—a tolerable foot-race !
And now I calmly recollect the place,
　　Its ins and outs,
　　And roundabouts,
A batter'd nose and broken shin
Are not too much to pay to win.

　　Pit-pat !
　　What 's that ?
Something that moves soft and slow,
Like graceful dancer in a furbelow !—
　　What are you ?　Ho !
A walking Vestris, with a leg to show ?
　　So be it !
Come, come, you all-engrossing Fog,
You 're " going the whole hog,"
　　And hoggishly won't let me see it !
　　Pit-pat again ! *encore* pit-pat !
Oh, disappointment dire ! a vagabond tom-cat !
Here, Paddy that I kick'd, if you can see,
Kick this great mousing brute in lieu of me !

Well, if again I go out in a fog,
　　May I be call'd a blind man's stupid dog,
　　A bat, a beetle, " *a good-nater'd fellar !*"
Headlong I dive—out of it—into the Cider-cellar !

November, 1837.　　　　　　　　　　　　　PUNCH.

NIGHTS AT SEA;

Or, Sketches of Naval Life during the War.

BY THE OLD SAILOR.

WITH AN ILLUSTRATION BY GEORGE CRUIKSHANK.

No. VI.

JACK AMONG THE MUMMIES.

> " The times have been
> That when the brains were out the man would die,
> And there an end : but now they rise again
> With twenty mortal murders on their crowns,
> To push us from our stools."
>
> SHAKSPEARE.

A STRANGE sail is always a matter of interest in a ship of war ; and no sooner was the canvass set in chase of the brig mentioned in my last, than the forecastle of the Spankaway received its usual group of yarn-spinners, anxious to ascertain the character of the stranger, and what amount of prize-money was likely to be shared in case of her carrying an enemy's flag. There was our old friend Jack Sheavehole, together with Joe Nighthead, Bob Martingal, Bill Buntline, and several others ; and occasionally the warrant-officers, and even the mate of the watch, stopped to chime in with a few words, so as to give life to their conversation.

"It bothers my univarsal knowledge," said old Savage, the boatswain, " to make out what lay the skipper's on ; and as for the chase, mayhap she mayn't turn out to be moonshine arter all."

"How moonshine ?" returned Mr. Bracebit, the carpenter ; " she's plain enough to be seen, and they've made her out to be a brig : there can be no moonshine in that, anyhow."

"But I tell you there is moonshine in it," persevered the boatswain, "a complete bag o' moonshine, unless you can diskiver the right bearings and distance o' the thing. I tell you what it is, Mr. Bracebit, I arn't been these many years man and boy in the sarvice——"

"You should say boy and man, old Pipes," exclaimed the mate of the watch as he stopped short in his walk by the veteran's side.

" And why should I say boy and man, instead of man and boy, Mr. Winterbottom ?" demanded old Savage in anger.

"Because, according to your own maxim, everything should be done ship-shape," replied the other ; " and you was a boy before you was a man."

"He has him there," whispered Jack Sheavehole to his messmate Bob. " I'm bless'd if that arn't plain-sailing, anyhow !"

"Ship-shape do you call it ?" answered the boatswain wrathfully.

" Ay, ay, Muster Winterbottom, mayhap it may be according to your calculations of the jometry of the thing. It's nothing new now-a-days to see the boy put forud afore the man ;" and he laid strong emphasis on the latter words.

"There he hit him again, Jack," observed Bob Martingal in a whisper ; " and I'm blowed if there arn't Gospel truth in that, anyhow !"

"Well, well, don't be angry, old friend," said Mr. Winterbottom, himself somewhat offended; "there's no occasion for being hot upon it; but, if you are, you may go to —— and cool yourself!"

"And a precious queer place that 'ud be for a cold-bath," said the carpenter: ".but let's have no contentions, gentlemen. What do you take the brig to be, Mr. Winterbottom?"

"A ship with her mizen-mast out, bound to Bombay, with a cargo of warming-pans," replied the young officer.

"That arn't being over civil, anyhow," whispered Bob to his messmate; "though mayhap they may want warming-pans in Bumbay as much as they do in the West Ingees. To my thinking, she's a treasure-craft laden with mummies."

"Did you ever fall athwart any o' them there hanimals, Bob?" inquired Joe Nighthead.

"What hanimals do you mean, Joe?" returned Martingal. "For my part, I've seen a little somut of everything."

"I means the mummies," replied Joe, as he squatted down in amidships just before the foremast, in preparation for a yarn, and was soon surrounded by the rest;—"I means the mummies, my boyo."

"No; can't say as I have," answered Bob; "though I've heard somut about 'em, too:—what rig are they?"

"Why, for the matter o' that," said Joe, laughing, "they're broomstick-rig as soon as they makes a brush of it; but I'm blow'd if I hadn't onest as pretty a spree with a whole fleet of mummies as ever any man could fall aboard of in this world, or t'other either."

"What was it, Joe?" asked the boatswain's mate eagerly. "Pay it out handsomely, messmate; but don't pitch us any of Bob's devil's consarns;—let's have it all truth and honesty."

"I'd scorn to deceive *you*, Jack, or anybody else o' my shipmates wot's seamen,", responded Joe reproachfully. "It's all as true as the skipper's a lord, and looks, alongside o' Johnny Cropoh there, like a man alongside of a— But, there,—it arn't honourable to make delusions; and so, shipmates, here goes for a yarn. I was coxswain in the pinnace of the ould Ajax, the Honourable Captain Cochrane, at that 'ere time when Sir Richard Bickerton took command of the fleet, and a flotilla was employed in co-operating with the troops again' Alexandria. Well, shipmates, I was always fond of a bit of gab; and so, the night we lay at a grapplin', waiting for daylight to begin the attack, my officer gets to talking about the place, and what a grand consarn it was in former days for gould and jewels, and sich like; and thinks I to myself, mayhap the Lords of the Admirality will take all that 'ere into account in regard o' the prize-money: and then he overhauls a good deal about the hobbylisks and Clipsypaddyree's Needle, and what not, that I'm blow'd if it didn't quite bamfoozle my larning. Well, we'd four or five days' hard work in the fighting way, and then there was a truce, and my officer run the pinnace aboard of a French prize laden with wine and brandy; so we starts the water out of one of the breakers and fills it with the real stuff, and I man-handled a pair of sodgers' canteens chock-full; and the prize-master, Muster Handsail, an old shipmate of mine, gives me a two-gallon keg to my own cheek, and I stows 'em all snug and safe abaft in the box, and kivers 'em up with my jacket to keep 'em warm. Well, it was just getting dusk in the evening when the skipper claps us alongside, and orders the leftenant to land me well up the lake, so as I might carry a letter from him across to a shore party as manned one of the heavy batteries away inland, at the back of the town.

"Now, in course, shipmates, I warn't by no manner o' means piping my eye to get a cruise on *terror firmer*, seeing as mayhap I might chance to pick up some 'o' the wee things aboot the decks' as likely wud get me a bottle o' rum in England,—for my thoughts kept running on the gould and jewels the leftenant spun the yarn about, and I'd taken a pretty good whack of brandy aboard the prize, though I warn't not in the least tosticated, but ounly a little helevated, just enough to make me walk steady and comfortable. So we run the boat's nose on to the beach, and I catches up my jacket and my canteens, leaving the keg to the marcy of Providence, and strongly dubersome in my mind that I had bid it an etarnal farewell. Howsomever, I shins away with my two canteens filled chock ablock; and 'Bear a hand, Joe!' says the leftenant, 'though I'm blessed if I know what course you're to take, seeing as it's getting as dark as a black fellow's phisog.'—'Never fear, yer honour,' says I; 'ounly let me catch sight o' Clipsypaddyree's Needle for a landmark, and I'm darned if I won't find myself somewhere, anyhow;' and away I starts, shipmates, hand over hand, happy go lucky—all's one to Joe! But it got darker and darker, and the wind came down in sudden gusts, like a marmaid a-sighing; so, to clear my eyes, and keep all square, I was in course compelled to take a nip every now and then out of the canteen, till at last it got so dark, and the breeze freshened into a stiff gale, that the more I took to lighten my way and enable me to steer a straight course, I'm blessed, shipmates, if I didn't grow more dizzy; and as for my headway, why, I believes I headed to every point in the compass:—it was the dark night and the cowld breeze as did it, messmates."

"No doubt in the world on it, Joe," assented Jack Sheavehole; "for if anything could have kept you in good sailing trim, it was the brandy, and the more especially in token o' your drinking it neat;—them dark nights do play the very devil with a fellow's reckoning ashore, in regard of the course and distance, and makes him as apt to steer wild, like a hog in a squall."

"You're right, Jack," continued Nighthead; "and anybody as hears you, may know you speaks from experience o' the thing. Howsomever, there I was,—not a sparkler abroad in the heavens, not a beacon to log my bearings by; and, as I said afore, there I was in a sort of no-man's-land, backing and filling to drop clear of shoals, sometimes just at touch-and-go, and then brought-up all standing, like a haystack a-privateering. At last the weather got into a downright passion, with thunder, lightning, and hail; and 'I'm blessed, Joe,' says I to myself, 'if snug moorings under some klver or other, if it's ounly a strip o' buntin', wouldn't be wastly superior to this here!' But there was no roadstead nor place of shelter, and the way got more rougherer and rougherer, in regard o' the wrecks of ould walls and ould buildings, till I'm blessed if I didn't think I was getting into the latitude and longitude of the dominions of the 'long-shore Davy Jones."

"My eyes, Joe!" exclaimed Martingal, replenishing his quid from an ample "'bacca" box, "but you was hard up, my boy!"

"Indeed and I was, Bob," responded the other; "and I'm blowed if every thing as I seed about me didn't begin to dance jigs and horn-pipes to the whistling of the wind, that I thought all manner of be-devilment had come over me, and so I tries to dance too, to keep 'em company. But it wouldn't do, shipmates, and I capsizes in a sudden squall, and down I went, headforemost."

"It's precious bad work that, Joe," said the old boatswain's mate, shaking his head. "A fellow in an open sea may do somut to claw to wind'ard; but when you're dead upon a lee-shore, it's time to look for your bag. But what did you do, Joe?"

"Why, what could I do, shipmate, but to take another nip at the canteen," responded Joe; "it was all I had in life to hould on by, with a heavy gale strong enough to blow the devil's horns off, and the breakers all round me: my eyes! but it was a reg'lar sneezer. 'Howsomever,' thinks I, 'it won't do, Joe, to be hove down here for a full due—you must at it again, ould chap;' and so I tries to make sail again, and heaves ahead a few fathoms, when down I comes again into a deep hole, and, before you could say Jack Robison, I'm blow'd if I warn't right slap in the middle of a large underground wault, where there was a company o' genelmen stuck up in niches, and peeping over mummy-cases, with great candles in their hands; and in other respects looking for all the world like the forty thieves as I once seed at the play, peeping out of their oil-jars; and there was a scuffling and scrimmaging at t'other eend o' the wault: and, 'Yo hoy!' says I, 'what cheer—what cheer, my hearties!' but not nobody never spoke, and the genelmen in the niches seemed to my thinking to be all groggy, and I'm blessed if ever I seed sich a set o' baboon-visaged fellows in all my days. 'Better luck to us, genelmen,' says I, filling my tot and taking a dram; but not a man on 'em answered. 'Pretty grave messmates I've got,' says I; 'but mayhap you don't hail as messmates, seeing as you arn't yet had a taste o' the stuff. Come, my hearties, I'll pipe to grog, and then I'll sarve it out all ship-shape to any on you as likes.' So I gives a chirp, and 'Grog ahoy!' sings I. Well, shipmates, I'm blessed if one on 'em didn't come down from the far eend o' the wault, and claps me alongside as I was sitting on the ground, and he takes hould o' the tot, knocks his head at me, as much as to say, 'All in good fellowship,' and down went the stuff through a pair o' leather lips in the twinkling of a hand-spik. 'All right, my hearty,' says I, filling the tot again: 'is there any more on you to chime in?'—'Sailor,' says he, in a voice that seemed to come from a fathom and a half down underneath him, for I'm blowed, messmates, if his lips ever moved;—'sailor, you must get out o' this,' says he.—'Lord love your heart,' says I, 'the thing's onpossible; you wouldn't have the conscience to make an honest tar cut and run in sich a rough night as this here.'—'We arn't never got no consciences,' says he; 'we're all dead.'—'Dead!' says I laughing, though, messmates, I own I was a bit flusticated; 'dead!' says I; 'that's gammon you're pitching, and I thinks it's hardly civil on you to try and bamboxter me arter that fashion. Why, didn't I see you myself just now when you spliced the main brace?—dead men don't drink brandy.'—'We're privileged,' sings out a little cock-eyed fellow up in one o' the niches; 'we're the ould ancient kings of Egypt, and I'm Fairer.'—'If there warn't many more fairer nor you,' says I, 'you'd be a cursed ugly set, saving your majesty's presence,' for I thought it best to be civil, Jack, seeing as I had got jammed in with such outlandish company, and not knowing what other privileges they might have had sarved out to 'em besides swallowing brandy. 'Will your majesty like just to take a lime-burner's twist, by way of warming your stumack a bit, and fumigating your hould?' says I, as I poured out the stuff.—'Give it to King Herod, as is moored alongside of you,' says he, 'and keep your thumb out of the measure;' for, shipmates, I'd shoved in my thumb pretty deep, by way of lengthening out the grog, and getting a better allowance of plush. How the ould chap came to observe it, I don't know, unless it was another of their privileges to be up to everything. 'Keep your thumb out!' says he.—'All right, your honour,' says I, handing the little ould fellow the tot; and he nipped it up, and knocked off the stuff in a moment. And 'Pray,' says I, 'may I make bould to ax your honour how long you've been dead?'—'About two thousand years,' says he: and, 'My eyes!' thinks I, 'but you're d—d small for your age.'— 'But, sailor,' says he, 'what brought you here?'—'My legs, your honour,' says I, 'brought me as far as the hatchway; but I'm blowed if I didn't come down by the run into this here consarn.'—'You mustn't stop here, sailor,' says he,—'that's King Herod,—you can have no business with us, seeing as we're all mummies.'—'All what?' says I, 'all dummies?' for I didn't catch very clearly what he said; 'all dummies?' says I. 'Well, I'm bless'd if I didn't think so!'— 'No, no! mummies,' says he again, rather cantankerously; 'not dummies, for we can all talk.'—'Mayhap so, your majesty,' says I, arter taking another bite of the cherry, and handing him a third full tot, taking precious good care to keep my thumb out this time: 'but what am I to rouse out for? It ud take more tackles than one to stir Joe Nighthead from this. I'm in the ground-tier,' says I, 'and amongst all your privileges, though you clap luff upon luff, one live British tar, at a purchase, is worth a thousand dead kings, any day.'— 'Haugh!' says he, as he smacked his leather lips, and the noise was just like a breeze making a short board through a hole in a pair of bellows; 'Haugh!' says he, as soon as he'd bolted the licker, 'it doesn't rest with us, my man: as mummies, we're privileged against all kinds of spirits.'—'Except brandy,' says I.—'I means evil spirits,' says he: 'but if the devil should come his rounds, and find you here upon his own cruising-ground, he'd pick you up and make a prize of you to a sartinty.'—'D— the devil!' says I, as bould as a lion, for I warn't a-going to let the ould fellow think I was afeard of Davy Jones, though I was hard and fast ashore; and 'D— the devil,' says I, 'axing your majesty's pardon; the wagabone has got no call to me, seeing as I'm an honest man, and an honest man's son as defies him.' Well, shipmates, I had my head turned round a little, and something fetches me a crack in the ear, that made all sneer again, and 'Yo hoy! your majesty,' says I; 'just keep your fingers to yourself, if you pleases.'—'I never touched you,' says he; 'but there's one close to you as I can see, though you can't.'—'Gammon!' says I; 'as if your dead-eyes were better than my top-lights.'—But, shipmates, at that moment somut whispers to me,—for may I be rammed and jammed into a penny cannon if I seed anything; but somut whispers to me, Joe Nighthead, I'm here over your shoulder.'—'That's

my name all reg'lar enough, whatever ship's books you got it from,'
says I : ' But who the blazes are you that 's not nothing more than a
woice and no-body ?'—' You knows well enough who I am,' says the
whisper again ; 'and I tell you what it is, Joe, I 've got a job for you to
do.'—' Show me your phisog first,' says I, ' or I 'm blow'd if I 've anything whatsomever to say to you. If you are the underground Davy
Jones, it 's all according to natur, mayhap ; but I never signs articles
unless I knows the owners.'—' But you *do* know *me*, Joe,' says the
woice, that warn't more nor half a woice neither, in regard of its being
more like the sigh of a periwinkle, or the groan of an oyster.—' Not a
bit of it,' says I ; for though I suckspected, shipmates, who the
beggar was, yet I warn't going to let him log it down again me without having hoclar proof, so ' Not a bit of it,' says I ; ' but if you wants
me to do anything in all honour and wartue,'—you see, Jack, I didn't
forget wartue, well knowing that when the devil baits his hook he
claps a ' skylark' on to the eend of it ; so, ' all in honour and wartue,'
says I, ' and Joe 's your man.'—' Do you know who 's alongside of
you ?' says the woice.—' Why, not disactly,' says I : ' he calls himself
King Herod ; but it 's as likely he may be Billy Pitt, for anything I
knows to the contrary.'—' It *is* King Herod,' says the whisper again ;
' the fellow who killed all the Innocents.'—' What innocents ?' axes I,
seeing as I didn't foregather upon his meaning.—' The innocent babbies,' says the woice ; ' he killed them all, and now he 's got a cruising
commission to keep me out o' my just rights, and I daren't attack him
down below here.'—' The ould cannibal !' says I : ' what ! murder
babbies ?—then I 'm blowed if he gets a drop more out of my canteen.'—' Who 's that you 're meaning on ?' says King Herod ; ' who
isn't to get another taste ?'—' Not nobody as consarns you, your honour,' answers I, for I didn't like to open my broadside upon him, in
regard of not knowing but he might have a privilege to man-handle
me again.—' I think you meant me,' says he ; ' but if you didn't, prove
the truth on it by handing me over a full gill.' Well, shipmates, that
was bringing the thing to the pint, and it put me into a sort of quan-
dary ; but ' All in course, your honour,' says I ; ' but I 'm saying,
your majesty, you arn't never got sich a thing as a bite o' pigtail
about you—have you ? seeing as I lost my chaw and my 'bacca-box
in the gale—hove overboard to lighten ship.'—' Yes, I can, my man
—some real Wirginny,' says the king."

"Ha! ha! ha!" laughed the sergeant of marines ; "go it, Joe ;—
you 'll rival Tom Pepper presently. Why, Virginia is only a late
discovery ; such a place wasn't known in the days of Herod, nor tobacco either." ·

"To my thinking it 's wery hodd, Muster Jolly, that you should
shove your oar in where it arn't wanted," muttered Joe. "Why ?—
couldn't they have a Wirginny in Egypt ? and as for the 'bacca, I 'm
blowed if I don't wouch for the truth on it, for out his majesty lugs
a box as big round in dameter as the top of a scuttle-butt, and,
knocking off the lid, ' There 's some of the best as ever was many-
facter'd,' says he. ' I loves a chaw myself, and there 's nothing whatsomever as 'ull beat the best pound pig-tail.'—' Sartinly not, in course,
your honour,' says I ; ' but I 'm blessed if it doesn't double upon my
calculations o' things to think how your majesty, who ought to be in
quod in t'other world, should take your *quid* in this.'—' We 're pri-

vileged, my man,' says he; 'we 're privileged and allowed to take anything, in reason,' and he fixed his glazed eyes with a 'ticing look at the canteen. 'You know,' says he, 'that it 's an ould saying aboard, "the purser makes dead men chaw tobacco."' Well, shipmates, that was a clencher in the way of hargyfication that brought me up all standing; so I hands King Herod the tot again, and I rouses out a long scope of pig-tail out o' the box, and takes another nip at the brandy.—'You won't do it, then, Joe,' says the whisper t'other side of me.—'What is it?' axes I.—'The best pound pigtail,' says King Herod, as if he thought I was speaking to him.—'It's ounly to borrow one of these here mummies for me for about half an hour,' says the woice.—'Which on 'em?' says I.—'This here in the box,' says King Herod. 'Why, I'm thinking your brains are getting all becalmed.' And so they was, shipmates; for, what with the woice at one ear that I couldn't see, and his majesty at the other, who often doubled himself into two or three, I'm blowed if I warn't reg'larly bamboozled in my upper works."

"You was drunk, Joe," said the sergeant of marines; "it's very evident you was *non compos mentis.*"

"And, what if I hadn't a nun compass to steer by?" replied Joe angrily, "is that any reason I should be tosticated? I tell you I warn't drunk, in regard o' the full allowance o' brandy I stowed in my hould to keep me steady and sober. Ax Jack there if it's any way likely I should be drunk."

"It stands to reason, not," argued Jack Sheavehole, "or, what's the use of a fellow having the stuff sarved out at all? Short allowance only brings a mist afore the eyes and circumpollygates the head till everything looms, like Beachy in a fog. But when you've your full whack, it clears the daylights, cherishes the cockles o' your heart, and makes you more handy, 'cause you often sees two first leftenants where there 's ounly one."

"Dat berry true, massa Jack," said Mungo Pearl; "me al'ays sweep de deck more clean when me tink me hab two broom in me hand."

"In course," continued Joe, more soothed: "none but a Jolly would go to say anything again it, or doubt the woracity o' the thing. Well, shipmates, to heave ahead, I'm saying I was reg'larly bambluster-cated when one of the genelmen up in the niches squeaks out, 'King Herod, I'll just thank you for a thimble-full of the stuff.'"

"Did he say 'a thimble-full?'" inquired Sam Slick, the tailor. 'It couldn't be a professional thimble, then, for they never has no tops to 'em. It shows, however, the antickity of thimbles; though I thought they never had any use for them in those days."

"And why not, you lubber?" asked Bob Martingale.

"Simply because their garments were not sewed together as they are in the present day," answered the tailor.

"Tell that to the marines, Sam," said the boatswain's mate; "why what was Clipsypaddyree's needle for, eh? But, get on, Joe; there's no conwincing such ignoramasses."

"Ay, ay, messmate!" uttered Joe. "'Well,' says the genelman in the niche, 'I'll thank you for a thimbleful of that 'ere stuff.'—'With all the pleasure in life, your honour,' says I as I filled up the tot, and was going to carry it to him, but——'Give it to me, I'll take it,' says King Herod;' and up he gets,—my eyes! I never seed such a queer little ould chap in all my life!—and off he bolts to t'other mummy, steering precious wild, by the way; and he tips him the *likser witey*, and then back again he comes, and brings up in his ould anchorage. 'May I make bould to ax your majesty,' says I, 'what the name o' that genelman is as you've just sarved out the stuff to?'—'He's not a genelman, not by no manner o' means,' says he, 'in regard of his being a king.'—'And King who?' axes I.— 'You're werry quizative, Muster Sailor,' says he; 'but it's in the natur o' things to want to know your company. That's King Hanga-bull.'—'And a devilish queer name, too,' says I, 'for a fellow to turn into his hammock with. Is he of Irish distraction?'—'His mother was an Irishman,' says the king, 'and his father came out of a Cart-ridge.'—'And a pretty breed they'd make of it,' says I, 'somut atwixt a salt cod and a marmaid.'—'Will you steal me a mummy?' comes the whisper again; 'you'd better, Joe.'—'No threats, if you please,' says I.—'I never threatened you,' says the king, who thought I was directing my discourse to him; 'but, sailor, I must call over all their names now to see there's none absent without leave,'—and I'm blow'd if he didn't begin with King Fairer; but there was a whole fleet of King Fairers and King Rabshakers, and King Dollyme, and ever so many more, every one answering muster, as if it had been a rope-yarn Sunday for a clean shirt and a shave, till at last I got fairly foozlified, and hove down on my beam-ends as fast asleep as a parish-clerk in sarmon time."

"A pretty yarn you're spinning there, Mister Joe," said old Sa-vage, who it was evident had been listening,—as he had often done both before and since he mounted his uniform coat:—"A pretty yarn you're spinning. I wonder you arn't afeard to pay out the slack o' your lies in that fashion."

"It's all true as Gospel, Muster Savage," responded Joe: "I seed it, and suffered it myself, and afore I dropped asleep—'Mayhap,' thinks I, 'if I could steal a mummy for myself to give to my ould mo-ther, it 'ud be a reg'lar fortin to her,—dead two thousand years, and yet drink brandy and chaw tobacco!' So I sleeps pretty sound, though for how many bells I'm blessed if I can tell; but I was waked up by a raking fire abaft, that warmed my starn, and I sits upright to clear my eyes of the spray, and there laid King Herod alongside of me, with one of the canteens as a pillow, and all the ould chaps had come down out o' their niches, and formed a complete circle round us, that made me fancy all sorts of conjuration and bedevilment; so I jumps up on to my feet, and lets fly my broadsides to starboard and port, now and then throwing out a long shot a-head, and occasionally discharging my starn chasers abaft till I'd floored all the mummies, and the whole place wrung with shouts of laughter, though not a living soul could I see, nor dead uns either,—seeing as they'd nothing but bodies. Well, shipmates, if the thought didn't come over me again about bolting with one on 'em, and so I catches up King Herod, and away I starts up some steps,—for the moon had got the watch on deck by that time, and showed her commodore's light to make every thing plain:—Away I starts with King Herod, who began to hollow out like fun, 'Stop—stop, sailor! stop!—where are you going to take me? I'm Corporal Stunt.'—'Corporal H—!' says I, 'you arn't go-

ing to do me in that way,—you said yourself you was King Herod.'
—'It was all a trick,' says he, again, kicking and sputtering like
blazes; 'I'm not King Herod, I'm ounly Corporal Stunt,' says he.—
'That be d—;' says I, 'you're conwicted by your own mouth. And
didn't the voice tell me you was the barbarous blaggard as murdered
the babbies?'—'Yes,—yes; but I did it myself,' says he.—'I know
you did,' says I, fetching him a poke in the ribs,—for, shipmates, I
made sure he warn't privileged above ground,—'I know you did,' says
I, 'and I'm blessed if the first leftenant shan't bring you to the gangway for it!' And then he shouts out, and I hears the sound of feet
astarn coming up in chase, and I carries on a taut press, till I catches
sight of Clipsypaddyree's needle, that sarved me for a beacon, and I
hears the whole fleet of mummies come 'pad-pad' in my wake, and
hailing from their leather-lungs, 'Stop, sailor—stop!' but I know'd a
trick worth two of that, shipmates; so I made more sail, and the little
ould chap tries to shift ballast so as to bring me down by the head;
but it wouldn't do, and he kept crying out, 'Let me down! pray let
me go, I'm ounly Corporal Stunt!'—'Corporal Stunt or Corporal
Devil,' says I, giving him another punch to keep him quiet; 'I knows
who are you, and I'm blessed if the ould woman shan't have you
packed up in a glass cage for a show! you shall have plenty o' pigtail
and brandy:' and on I carries, every stitch set, and rattling along at a
ten-knot pace, afeard o' nothing but their sending a handful o' mony-
ments arter me from their bow-chasers, that might damage some of
my spars. At last I makes out the battery, and bore up for the entrance, when one of the sodgers, as was sentry, hails, 'Who goes
there?'—'No—no!' says I, seeing as I warn't even a petty officer.—
'That won't do,' says the sodger; 'you must give the countersign.'
—'What the blazes should I know about them there things?' axes I,
'you may see I'm a blue-jacket.'—'You can't pass without the countersign,' says he.—'That be d—d!' says I, 'arn't I got King Herod
here? and arn't there King Fairer, and King Dollyme, and King
Hangabull, and a whole fleet more on 'em in chase!' says I.—'Oh,
Tom Morris, is that you?' says King Herod.—'Yes,' says the sentry;
'why, I say, sailor, you've got hould o' the corporal!'—'Tell that to
the marines,' says I, 'for I knows well enough who he is, and so shall
my ould mother when I gets him home! But, I'm blessed, but here
they come!' and, shipmates, I heard 'em quite plain close aboard o'
me, so that it was all my eye to be backing and filling palavering
there afore the sentry, and get captured, and with that I knocks him
down with King Herod, and in I bolts with my prize right into the
officer's quarters. 'Halloo! who the devil have we got here?' shouts
the lieutenant, starting up from his cot.—'It's not the devil, your
honour,' says I, 'not by no manner o' means; it's Joe Nighthead, and
King Herod,' and I pitches the wagabone upright on to his lower
stancheons afore the officer.—'There, your majesty,' says I, 'now
speak for yourself.'—'Majesty!' says the leftenant, onshipping the
ould fellow's turban and overhauling his face,—'majesty!' why, it's
the corporal — Corporal Stunt; and pray, Muster Corporal, what
cruise have you been on to-night?'—and then there was the clattering
of feet in the battery, and, 'Here they all are, your honour!' says I,
'all the ould ancient kings of Egypt as are rigged out for mummies.
My eyes, take care o' the grog bottles, for them fellows are the

very devil's own at a dram ! Stand by, your honour ! there's King
Dollyme and all on 'em close aboard of us ! but, I'm blowed if I
don't floor some on 'em again as I did in the wault!' Well, messmates, in they came ; but, instead of mummies in their oil jars, I 'm
bless'd if they warn't rigged out like sodger officers, and they stood
laughing at me ready to split their sides when they saw me squaring
away my yards all clear for action."

"But, what was they, Joe?" inquired the boatswain's mate, "they
must have shifted their rigging pretty quick."

"I think I can explain it all," said the sergeant, laughing heartily,
"for I happened to be there at the time, though I had no idea that
our friend Joe here was the man we played the trick on."

"Just mind how you shapes your course, Muster Sergeant !" exclaimed Joe, angrily. "I 'd ounly give you one piece of good ad-
wice,—don't be falling athwart my hawse, or mayhap you may wish
yourself out o' this."

"Don't be testy, Joe," said the sergeant, "on my honour I'll tell
you the truth. Shipmates, the facts are these :—I belonged to the
party in the battery, and went with some of the officers to explore
a burial-ground, not without hopes of picking up a prize or two, as
the report was that the mummies had plates of gold on their breasts.
Corporal Stunt went with us ; and, when we got to the place we
lighted torches and commenced examination, but, if they ever had
any gold about them the French had been there before us, for we
found none. Whilst we were exploring, a storm came on, and not
being able to leave the vault the officers dressed Stunt up in some of
the cerements that had been unrolled from the mummies by way of
amusement, little expecting the fun that it was afterward to produce.
When Joe came in as he has described, we all hid ourselves, and, if
truth must be spoken, he was more than half sprung." Joe grumbled
out an expletive. "Stunt went to him, and we had as fine a piece of
pantomime——"

"Panter what?" uttered Joe, with vehemence, "there 's no such
rope in the top, you lubber ! and arter all you can say I werily believes it wur King Herod ; but, you see, messmates, what with running so hard, and what with losing my canteens, I got dumbfounder-
ed all at once, and then they claps me in limbo for knocking down the
sentry."

"And the officers begged you off," said the sergeant, "on account
of the fun they 'd enjoyed, and you was sent away on board, to keep
you out of further mischief, Joe, and to prevent your going a mummy-
hunting again. As for Corporal Stunt ——"

"Corporal D—n !" exclaimed Joe in a rage, "it 's all gammon
about your Corporal Stunt ; and in regard o' the matter o' that, what
have you got to say in displanation o' the woice ? There I has you
snug enough anyhow ; there was no mistake about the woice," and Joe
chuckled with pleasure at what he deemed unanswerable evidence in
his favour.

"It may be accounted for in the most sensible way imaginable,"
said the sergeant ; "Corporal Stunt was what they call a ventrilo-
quist."

"More gammon !" says Joe ; "and, what 's a wentillerquis, I should like to know; and how came the mummies to muster out of their niches when I woke?"

"We placed them there whilst you were asleep," replied the sergeant, "and, as for Stunt, he was as drunk and drowsy as yourself."

"Ay,—ay, sergeant!" said Joe, affecting to laugh, "it's all very well what you're overhauling upon, but I 'm blessed if you 'll ever make me log that ere down about Corporal Stunt and the wentiller consarn. I ounly wish I had the canteens now."

"Get a musket ready there for'ard!" shouted his lordship from the gangway, "fire athwart the brig's bows."

"They seem to be all asleep aboard, my lord!" said Mr. Nugent. "At all events they don't seem to care much about us."

"You're mistaken, Mr. Nugent," replied his lordship, as he directed his night-glass steadily at the stranger, "she's full of men, and if I am correct in my conjectures, there are many, very many eyes anxiously watching our motions."

"The musket was fired, and the brig came to the wind with her maintopsail to the mast. The frigate ranged up to windward of her, and the sonorous voice of Lord Eustace was heard,

"Brig a-hoy! What brig's that?"

"L'Hirondelle de Toulon," responded the commander of the vessel hailing through his speaking-trumpet. "Vat sal your ship be?"

"His Britannic Majesty's frigate, the Spankaway," answered Lord Eustace: "lower away the cutter, Mr. Nugent, and board her."

The two craft had neared each other so closely, and the moon shone with such clearness and splendour, that every thing was perfectly visible from each other on the decks of both. The brig was full of men, and when Lord Eustace had announced the name of his ship, the sounds had not yet died away upon the waters when out burst a spontaneous cheer from the smaller vessel such as only English throats could give,—it was a truly heart-stirring British demonstration, and there was no mistaking it. The effect was perfectly electric on the man-of-war's men,—the lee gangway was instantly crowded as well as the lee ports, and, as if by a sudden communion of spirit that was irrepressible, the cheer was returned.

There is amongst thorough tars a sort of freemasonry in these things that no language can describe,—it is the secret sign, the mystery that binds the brotherhood together,—felt, but not understood —expressed, yet undefined.

"Where are you from?" shouted his lordship as soon as the cheering had subsided.

"From Genoa, bound to Malta, your honour," answered a voice in clear English: "we 're a Cartel."

"Fortune favours us, Monsieur Capitaine," said his lordship to Citizen Begaud; "the exchange of prisoners can be effected where we are, and I will take it on my own responsibility to dismiss you on the usual terms, if you wish to return to France."

"A thousand thanks, my lord," returned Begaud, with evident satisfaction. "Yet all places are alike to me now. You have heard my narrative, and I hope, if we part, you will not hold me altogether in contempt and abhorrence. My spirits are depressed—my star is dim and descending—my destiny will soon be accomplished."

"You fought your ship bravely, Monsieur," said Lord Eustace,

" and I trust your future career will redeem the past. You have suffered much, and experience is a wise teacher to the human mind. But there is one thing I am desirous of having explained. You say that Robespierre detained you for some time before he gave you a pardon for the Countess—do you think he was aware of her approaching execution ?"

" Aware of it, my lord ?" exclaimed the French Captain, in a tone approaching to a shriek : " Danton, whom you well remember I said I met quitting the bureau, had the death-warrant, with the wretch's signature, in his hand—'twas solely for the purpose of destruction that he detained me—he knew the villain would be speedy—they had planned it between them.".

" All ready with the cutter, my lord," exclaimed Mr. Sinnitt, coming up to the gangway, and saluting his noble captain.

" Board the brig, Mr. Nugent, and bring the master and his papers to the frigate," directed Lord Eustace. " Call the gunner—a rocket and a blue light."

Both orders were obeyed; the signal was readily comprehended by Mr. Seymour, who hove-to in the prize, and in a few minutes Nugent returned from his embassy with the master of the cartel and the officer authorized to effect an exchange. The papers were rigidly examined—there were no less than one hundred and six Englishmen on board the brig, the principal portion of whom had been either wrecked or captured in merchant-men, and were now on their way to Malta for an equal number of French prisoners in return ; the commander-in-chief at Genoa, rightly judging that British humanity would gladly accede to the proposition. There were no officers, but Lord Eustace undertook to liberate Citizen Captain Begaud—the preliminaries were arranged—the Frenchmen, man for man, were transferred to the brig (his lordship throwing in a few hands who earnestly implored his consideration)—the Englishmen were received on board the frigate—necessary documents were signed, and they parted company—the brig making sail for Toulon—the Spankaway rejoining her prize.

" We've made a luckly windfall, Seymour," hailed his lordship when the frigates had closed; " I 've a hundred prime hands for you. Out boats, Mr. Sinnitt, and send the new men away directly—but first of all, let every soul of them come aft." A very few minutes sufficed to execute the command. " My lads," said his lordship, addressing them, " are you willing to serve your country ?—speak the word. I 've. an object in view that will produce a fair share of prize-money—enter for his majesty's service, and you shall have an equal distribution with the rest. Yonder 's your ship, a few hours will probably bring us into action, and I know every man will do his duty."

With but few exceptions, the seamen promptly entered, and were sent away to the Hippolito, where Mr. Seymour was instructed to station them at the guns with all possible despatch.

" Well, here we goes again," said old Savage, as the order was given to bear up and make sail, " it 's infarnally provoking not to be able to discover what the skipper's arter. There 's the Pollytoe running away ahead, and Muster Seymour 's just fancying himself first Lord o' the Admirality."

" Beat to quarters, Mr. Sinnitt," exclaimed his lordship, " and cast loose the guns."

"Well, I'm—— if I can make anything on it, Jack," grumbled the boatswain; "what are we going to engage now—the Flying Dutchman, or Davy Jones?"

"Mayhap a whole shole of Joe's mummies, sir," said Jack Sheavehole, with a respectful demeanour, as he cast loose his gun upon the forecastle, and threw his eye along the sight. Suddenly his gaze was fixed, he then raised his head for a moment, looked eagerly in the same direction, and once more glanced along the gun. "Well, I'm blessed if there aint," says he,—his voice echoed among the canvass as he shouted—"two sail on the starboard bow."

"Who's that hailing?" said the captain, as he walked forward to the bows, with his glass under his arm.

"It's Jack Sheavehole, your honour, my lord," replied the boatswain's mate, his eye still steadily fixed upon the objects.

"If they're what I expect, it will be a hundred guineas for you, my man, and, perhaps something better," said his lordship. "Where are they?"

"Just over the muzzle of the gun, my lord," answered Jack, as a fervent wish escaped him, that his lordship's expectations might be realized; for the hundred guineas, and something better, brought to his remembrance Suke and the youngsters.

Lord Eustace took a steady persevering sight through his night glass, as the men went to their quarters, and the ship was made clear for action; his lordship then ascertained the correct distance of the Hippolito ahead to be about two miles. "Get top-ropes rove, Mr. Savage," said he; "heave taut upon 'em, and see all clear for knocking the fids out of the topmasts."

"Ay ay, my lord," responded the boatswain, as he prepared for immediate obedience, but mumbling to himself, "What the —— will he be at next; rigging the jib-boom out o' the cabin windows, and onshipping the rudder, I suppose. Well, I'm——, if the sarvice arn't going to the devil hand-over-hand; I shouldn't be surprised if we have to take a reef in the mainmast next."

"Mr. Sinnitt," said his lordship, "let them pass a hawser into the cutter,"—the boat had not been hoisted up again,—"take the plug out, and drop her astern."

"D'ye hear that, Joe?" growled the boatswain; "there'll be more stores expended if she breaks adrift, and I'm —— if I can make it out; first of all, we goes in chase o' nothing—now here's a couple o' craft in sight, that mayhap may be enemies' frigates,—he's sinking the cutter to stop our way. Well, we shall all be wiser in time."

The strangers were made out to be two ships, standing in for the land, and whilst they were clearly visible to the Spankaway and the Hippolito, the position the moon was in prevented the strangers from seeing the two frigates. At length, however, they did obtain sight of them, and they immediately hauled to the wind, with their heads off shore.

"There's a gun from the prize, sir," shouted one of the men forward, as the booming report of a heavy piece of ordnance came over the waters.

"Run out the two bow-guns through the foremost ports, and fire blank cartridge," said his lordship. "Where's the gunner?"—Mr. Blueblazes responded, "Ay ay, my lord."—"Draw all the shot on the larboard side," continued Lord Eustace, to the great astonishment of the man of powder, and still greater surprise of the old boatswain.

"Mr. Seymour is making signals, my lord," said the third lieutenant ; "and he 's altered his course towards the strangers."

"Very good, Mr. Nugent," said his lordship; "let them blaze away with the bow-guns, but be careful not to shot them."

The Hippolito kept discharging her stern chasers as she stood towards the strangers, who made all possible sail away, and the Spankaway fired her bow-guns without intermission, as she pursued her prize.

"What an onmarciful waste of powder," said the boatswain to his mate ; "I say, Jack, just shove in a shot to take off the scandal o' the thing."

Whether Jack complied or not, is unknown. The boat astern was cut away, the Spankaway felt relieved, and drew up with the prize ; the strangers retained their position, about three or four miles distant, and thus the chase continued till daylight, no one being able to make out what it all meant.

THE CASTLE BY THE SEA.

FROM UHLAND.

AND didst thou see that castle,
   That castle by the sea?
The rosy-tinctured cloudlets
   Float o'er it bright and free.

'Twould be bending down its shadows
   Into the crystal deep,—
In the sunset's rays all glowing
   'Twould tower with haughty sweep.

"Ay, wot ye well, I saw it—
   That castle by the sea,
And the pale moon standing o'er it,
   And mists hung on its lee."

The wind and ocean's rolling,
   Was their voice fresh and strong?
Came from its halls the echoes
   Of lute and festal song?

"The winds, the waves around it
   In sullen stillness slept,
Forth came a song of wailing,—
   I heard it, and I wept."

The king and his proud ladye,
   Were they pacing that high hall,
With crowns of gold, and girded
   In purple and in pall?

And led they not exulting
   A maid of rarest mould,
Bright as the sun, and beaming
   In tresses all of gold?

"I saw that king and ladye—
   The crown gemmed not their hair,
Dark mourning weeds were on them—
   The maid I saw not there."

E. N.

LEGISLATIVE NOMENCLATURE.

AMONGST THE MOTLEY CHARACTERS AND COMBINATIONS IN THE NEW HOUSE OF COMMONS MAY BE FOUND

A *Duke*, an *Erle*, a *Bannerman*,
  A *Barron*, and a *Knight*;
A *Northland Lord*, a *Denison*,
  With *Manners* most polite.

A *Kirk* and *Chaplin* still remain,
  Tho' the House has lost its *Clerk*;
But a *Parrott*'s there to say amen,
  And a *Fox* and *Woulfe* to bark !

Saint *Andrew*, holy man, is gone,
  Who *Knightley*, *Neeld*, and *Praed*,*
A *Haytor*† of the poor man's joy,
  And Sunday *Baker* trade.

A *Leader*, and a *Crewe* with *Spiers*,
  Conspire against *A'Court*;
But *Dick* declares, and *Darby* swears,
  No-el is meant nor *Hurt*.

They've hunted *Roebuck* from his hold,
  And *Buck*-ingham and *Bruen*;
But a *Sheppard* stays to guard the fold,
  And save the flock from ruin !

There's *Cow*-per, *Bull*-ers, and Knatch-*bull*,
  With *Lamb*-ton, *Hinde*, and *Hogg*;
A brace of *Martins*, *Finch*, and *Hawkes*,
  And *Pusey* in a *Bagge* !

There's *Moles*-worth, *Duck*-worth, *Cod*-rington,
  Three *Roches* and a *Seale*;
A *Rose*, a *Plumptre*, and a *Reid*,
  With *Hawes* and *Lemon Peel*.

A *Bold*-ero, with *Muskett* armed,
  Goes thro' the *Woods* to *Chute*; ‡
He fires some *Rounds*, and then brings down
  A *Heron* and *Wilde Coote* !

Great Dan, with his smooth *Winning-ton*,
  Contrives his *Poyntz* to *Wynn*;
For his supple *tail* has stronger grown,
  Tho', alas ! he's lost his *Finn* !

Two *Baillies* and an Irish *Maher*,§
  And *Burroughes*, *Power*, a *Bewes*; ‖
Two Tory *Woods*, a *Forester*,
  With *Hastie*, *Vigor*, *Hughes* ! ¶

A *Cave*, a *Loch*, a *Hill*, a *Fort*,
  A *Divett*, and a *Trench*;
A *Fleming* and a *Bruges*, *Guest*,
  With *Holland Folkes* and *Ffrench*.

A *Hob*-house, *Wode*-house, *Powers-court*,
  Two *Est-courts* and a *Hall*;
The *Hutt*, alas ! they've undermined,
  And left a *Black-stone*, *Wall* !

* Prayed.   † Hater.   ‡ Shoot.   § Mayor.   ‖ Abuse.   ¶ Hews.

A *Marshall-Law*, with *Power*, *C. Vere*,*
  And *Foley* and *Strange-ways*;
Three *Palmers* on a pilgrimage,
  A *Gally* in a *Hayes!* †

Tho' *North* and *West* are both displaced,
  An *East-hope* has been gained;
While *East-nor*, *East* and *West*-enra,
  Their stations have maintain'd!

Camp-bells we have, and Durham *Bowes*,‡
  With one Northumbrian *Bell*;
From *Stirlingshire* they 've sent *For-bes*,§
  To *Lisburn* for *Mey-nell!* ‖

Tho' *Beau-clerk* and *Beau-mont* are gone,
  We 've *Fellowes*, *Hale* and *Young*,
In *Style* to carry on the *Ball*,
  And dash and *Strutt* a *Long*.

A *Horsman* with *Fre-mantle* trots
  Two *Miles* to *Wynn* a *Pryse*;
Two *Walkers*, *Pryme*, the distance run,
  More confident than *Wyse*.

A *Chapman* with his *Packe* and *Price*,
  A-*Potter* with his *Clay*;
A *Fresh-field*, *Baring*, *Pease*, and *Rice*,
  A thriving *Field-en Hay*.

A *Carter*, *Coopers*, *Turners*, *Smiths*,
  A *Collier* with his *Coles*;
A *Master-Cartwright* with his *Maule*,
  A *Bolling-Green* and *Bowles*.

A *Black*-burn, *Blew*-itt, and *Brown*-rigge,
  And *Black*-ett, *White*, and *Grey*;
With double *Scarlett*, *Orange-Peel*,
  And *Brown* and *Green*-away.

There 's *Crawford*, *Wood*, and *Pattison*,
  And *Barings* passing *Rich*;
With *Money-penny* and a *Grote*,
  And *Grimston* and *Grimsditch*.

There 's *Rum-bold*, *Tancred*, and *Phill-potts*,
  A *Butler* from Kilkenny;
A *Heath-coat*, *Thorn-hill*, and *Broad-wood*,
  With *Mild-may* and *Ma-hony*.

A *Bodkin*, *Sharpe*, Kent *Hodges*, *Blunt*,
  A *Miller* and a *Baker*;
With sinners, saints, and Methodists,
  Socinians, and a *Quaker!*

Staunch Papists, Presbyterians,
  And Churchmen great and small;
With *Mathew*, *Mark*, and *Luke*, and *John*,
  Old *Adam* and *St. Paul!*

                              G. W.

* Severe.   † Haze.   ‡ Beaux.   § For Bess.   ‖ My Nell.

NOBILITY IN DISGUISE.

BY DUDLEY COSTELLO.

" They name ye before me,
    A knell to mine ear ;
    A shudder comes o'er me.——"

BYRON.

ONE of the evils of an increasing population is the difficulty of find-ing names for all the new-comers. As long as the census remained proportionate to the superficies of the country, and every man could entrench himself within the walls of his own domicile, or isolate him-self between his own hedges, the principle of individuality continued unassailed; but when, from a thousand causes, the population became doubled, almost within our recollection, and men were forced to herd together, gregarious by compulsion, we felt that a blow had been struck at personal identity which it would require the utmost inge-nuity to parry.

Amongst the many responsibilities entailed upon parents, not the least, in these prolific times, is that of providing their offspring with names which shall carry them safely through the wear and tear of after-life without encroaching upon the privileges, or sharing in the disgraces, of others. The man, for instance, who *happens* to bear the *not-impossible* name of Smith, and who chooses to christen his son by the not-uncommon one of John, commits an error as fatal as can well be imagined. At school that son is buffeted by mistake, and birched by accident, for the broken windows and invaded orchards: the acts of another John Smith. As he advances towards man's estate, his good reputation is stolen, and a bad one substituted, by the graceless conduct of a namesake. He is dunned for debts he never contracted, rendered liable for hearts he never broke, and imprisoned for assaults he never committed. He is superseded in the affections of his mis-tress by another John Smith, disinherited on his account, and when he dies—for even Smiths must die—no tear is shed to his memory, no record commemorates his decease; like the pebble which is cast into the ocean, a little circle just marks the spot for a moment, and the waves of oblivion roll over it for ever!

The same melancholy fate haply attends the possessors of the names of Green, Brown, Jones, Robinson, Thompson, and others no less familiar. The destiny of one becomes involved in the general lot of all; the multitude can no more distinguish between them than they can separate one sheep from a flock, or one bee from a swarm. The hand of fate is on the unhappy crowd,—" they are the victims of its iron rule;" and victimised to a certainty they would have re-mained, had not a boldly-conceiving individual invented a mode of particularising that which was general, severing the with which bound them in one universal faggot. It was effected in this wise. He con-sidered the name he bore—one of those already alluded to—as being only the type of *man ;* and, spurning at the imbecility or indifference of a godfather, who had thus neutralised his existence at the very outset, he resolved to intercalate certain high-sounding appellations, which of themselves would attract sufficient attention, but, when combined with his own futile denomination, would be sure to strike, from the absurdity of the contrast, or singularity of the juxta-posi-'tion'. Thomas Brown was a name as insignificant as parents or sponsors could make it; but when, in the course of time, it swelled itself into Thomas Claudius Fitzwilliam Carnaby Browne, it was impossible to pass it unregarded. The feat once accomplished, like the broken egg of Columbus, it became of easy performance; and few were the Thompsons, few the Simpsons, and fewer still the Johnsons, who did not claim " the benefit of the act."

A prospective advantage was included also in their calculations. As time wore away, the obnoxious Thomas or John was silently dropped; and then, by a daring *coup-de-maître*, the plebeian sur-name, which had been gradually contracting its powers, was altogether sunk, and the grub became a butterfly of most aristocratic pretensions. This is no vain theory founded on chance occurrences, but a truth which every one will recognise who runs over the list of his acquaintance, or examines the visiting-cards on his mantel-piece. It is as impossible now-a-days to meet with a man content to bear the opprobrium of a single monosyllabic name, as to raise money without security, or induce any one to avoid politics in conversation. The ancient prejudice against the " homo trium literarum" is now wholly removed; and we verily believe that Cavendish Mortimer Pierrepoint, an acknowledged scion of the swell-mob, would find more favour in the eyes of society than plain Benjamin Bunks, a well-known respectable hosier or linendraper, if a question of right were at issue between them.

There are two classes of persons who build up to themselves an altar of vain-glory founded on names of self-assumption. The first are those who, being cast originally in the basest metal, add the pinchbeck of quality to enhance the value of the original plebeian pewter; the second, of " dull and meagre lead," who thereunto conjoin the glare of brass or gloom of iron by the adoption of double names of equal dissonance. Examples are rife everywhere. Mr. and Mrs. Vokins, while their fortune was yet to make, were happy and content " as such;" but, the carriage once set up, the arms *found*, and the visiting-cards printed, her friends are awake to the pleasing consciousness that " Mrs. Ferdinand Vokins" is " at home" every alternate Wednesday during the season.

Mr. Mudge was a plain, simple Glo'stershire squire, shooting partridges on the paternal acres, and called " Young Mr. Mudge," as manhood and whiskers expanded on his native soil. He comes to town, sees the world, and discovers, for the first time, despite the importance which inflates him, that he is nameless. He accordingly borrows from the French, and is straightway transformed into " the interesting Mr. Montmorency Mudge, who plays so divinely on the flute," though his very existence had been a question but a few brief hours before.

The Badgers, though proud of course of their name *as a family name*, have daughters to marry, and sons to provide for: it is of no use to be good unless one appears so; and therefore Mrs. *Howard* Badger's suppers are the best in town, while Mr. Howard Badger is received with smiles at the Treasury.

Plain Boss would have succeeded nowhere, except, perhaps, on a street-door; but Felix Orlando Boss may enter the gayest drawing-room in Christendom, announced by files of intonating footmen.

We are invited to dine, and seek to ascertain the profit and loss of the invitation by inquiries of a fellow *convive* as to the guests who will be there : he is *l'ami de la maison*, and, to give due emphasis to the description, and honour to the Amphitryon, he thus enumerates them. " Oh, you'll have the Mortimer Bullwinkles, Mr. and Mrs. Frederick Cutbush, the Stafford Priddys, Sir Montague Stumps, Mr. Temple Sniggers, the Beauchamp Horrockses, and Mrs. Courtenay Cocking ; nobody else, that I remember." "Won't the Wartons be there ?" "I don't know,—who are they ?—I never heard of them :—what's their *other* name ?"

And so it is : this " other name,"—this *alter ego*—becomes the grand desideratum in description,—the passport to fashion and celebrity.

The anonymous in authorship is no longer regarded, save in the instance of those veterans in literature whose silence is more signifi- cant than the loud-tongued voices of a million aspirants. We need no sign-post to show us the way to London, neither do we seek a name to anticipate their page. But the new candidates for fame are of a different order. The title-page of a work is in their estimation a maiden shield whereon it is their privilege to quarter the names of all their lineage, concentrated in themselves, or pompously appealed to in the names of others. Hence we have, " Rambles in Russia, by Charles Valentine Mowbray Muggins ;" " Thoughts on the Poor- Laws, by Pygmalion Gammage ;" " The Exile ; a poem, by Brownlow Busfield, of the Middle Temple, Barrister-at-Law ;" " Desperation ; a novel, by Grenville Grindle, Esq. ;" " The Veil Withdrawn, or, A Peep behind the Curtain, by the Nieces of the Hon. and Rev. Fitzherbert Fineclark ;" and " Domestic Tyranny, or, The Stony- hearted Step-father, by Lavinia Cecilia Bottomley, only child of the late Captain Roderick Bottomley, of the Bombay Cavalry."

It is no longer our cue to be rendered " illustrious by courtesy ;" we compel the admiration which the niggard world so carefully with- holds, and extort the approbation it would smother. It matters little how raw, how shapeless, how crude, how undigested be the mass when drawn from the quarry of its creation ; its uncouth aspect and angular deformity offer no impediment to the lapidary's skill, but ra- ther enhance its value ; and the more barbarous the name which ignorant parents have transmitted, the wider is the scope afforded to their descendants for rendering the adjunct more brilliant by the contrast.

He who is born Buggins, and changeth not, perisheth unregarded ; his name appears in the Newgate Calendar, and whatever his fate, it is deemed a just one. But he who (though equally degraded in the annals of nomenclature by the repulsive or sneaking appellations of Jaggers, Blatcher, Gullock, or Lumkin,) adds to his patronymic the soft seduction or romantic interest of Albert, Eustace, Stanley, or Fitzmaurice, may appeal to the lord in waiting, or a patroness at Almack's, and kiss the hand of royalty, or bow at the shrine of beauty.

The motto is old and true, which many "gentlemen of coat-ar- mour" do bear, that " Fortune favours the bold ;" the daring specu- lators in the names of others are eminently successful in their ad- venture after greatness. To this category belong the sheriffs and aldermen, the bearers of addresses, and the deputed of corporations ;

these are they who may literally be said to have greatness " thrust upon them."

The Mayor of Norwich, hight Timothy Gamblebuck, urged by the ambitious spiritings of Mrs. G., kneels at his sovereign's feet, and, rewarded by an accolade, returns, in the triumph of knighthood and plenitude of loyalty, " Sir Timotheus Guelph Gamblebuck" by *more* than royal permission.

Mr. Sheriff Hole, presented by a peer, and similarly honoured by the king, marks his sense of his patron's kindness by the insertion of his title before the cavernous epithet, and figures at urban festivals as Sir John Cornwallis Hole, the most aristocratic on the shrieval archives.

Sir Marmaduke Fuggles, Sir Cholmondeley Bilke, Sir Constantine Peregrine Rumball, Sir Temple Gostick, and Sir Peter Sackville Biles, are amongst the many whom female instigation or personal desire have led to illustrate the glory of ancient houses. It is somewhere said in " Pelham " that one's unknown neighbour, or opposite at dinner, must necessarily be a baronet and Sir John ; it is no less true that at the corner of every street, in the avenues of every ball-room, a newly created knight lies in waiting to devour one. A man with a bright blue coat, and, if possible, brighter buttons, with black satin waistcoat and *very* gold chain, with large hands and a face of red portent, cuts in with us at whist ; his antagonists are perpetually appealing to him by his brilliant title. " It is your deal, Sir Vavasour,"—" My ace, Sir Vavasour,"—" Sir Vavasour, two doubles and the rub ;"—till, bewildered by the glories of our feudal partner, we lose the game, and stealthily inquire of some one near, " Who *is* the gentleman opposite ?" " Sir Vavasour Clapshaw " is the whispered reply, recalling the name of one much respected in our youthful days, — a celebrated artist in the cricket-bat line, who has now pitched his wicket within the precincts of aristocracy, and bowls down society with the grandeur of his *préfixe*.

A lady in crimson velvet, with a bird of paradise in her blue and silver " turband," and a marabout boa wreathed round her neck, with long white gloves tightened unto bursting, and serpentine chains clinging unto suffocation, is seated in lofty pride at the *upper* end of the *principal* saloon, and overwhelms by the dignity of her demeanour all who come within the vortex of her " full-blown suffisance."

" Lady—what did you say ? Harcourt, or Harewood,—which ?— I didn't distinctly hear." " Yes, Lady Harcourt." " Why, I thought she was dead." " Oh, yes, the *Countess* is dead ; but this is Lady Harcourt Bumsted : that 's her husband, Sir Julius,—he was knighted last Wednesday."

" There 's honour for you !—grinning honour," as Falstaff has it.

Notabilities like these are nearly as illustrious as the surreptitious knights and dames who, by dint of surpassing impudence, pass current for as good as they. Both classes remind us of the gypsy-herald " *Rouge-Sanglier*," whose colours were as bright, and trappings as gay, as those of the legitimate " *Toison d'Or :*" they have but one fault ; like him, their blazon is false, their arms are wrongly " tricked," metal overlays metal, gold covers brass, and native *gules* gives way to intrusive purple. The glory of our chivalry is often awkwardly eclipsed when it happens that a Frenchman is called upon to designate the new-made knight; he treats his Christian name with as much indifference as he manifests in the spelling of his surname,—a rule he always applies to those of British growth. We know a clever, shrewd, little, antiquarian Frenchman, whom no persuasion can induce to abbreviate a single letter of reference to page, folio, edition, or date; but who, whenever he has occasion to mention a knight or baronet of his acquaintance, invariably omits his *nom de baptême*. How pleasantly it would sound to hear the announcement of "Sir Biddles," "Sir Doody," or "Sir Farwig!" and yet this would be the predicament of these worthies were they ungraced by noble *prænomina*.

The second class whose merits we propose to discuss are the illustrators of the "Binomial Theorem,"—the double-named families,— who, too hideous to walk alone, conjoin ugliness of equal intensity to scare and appal wherever they make their way. It is not sufficient for such as they that their name be Groutage or Gramshaw; they incontinently connect it—if they can—with "a worser," (to use the showman's phrase,) and "double-up" with Rapkin or Titterton. Thus we hear, at our morning concert, Mrs. Rapkin Gramshaw's carriage stopping the way; and a vain and desolate outcry in the Opera colonnade for the chariot of Mrs. Titterton Groutage. It would matter little if we were only doomed to *hear* these names thus generally repeated; but there is a mode of administering them which makes us *feel* them, scorching and searing our inmost heart of hearts! A double name—no matter how base or dissonant—is held to be the most grateful to ears polite, as if the natural consequence of the intermarriage of two great discords must of necessity give birth to harmony.

How often have we writhed under the cruel infliction, when, betrayed by bad weather during a morning call, we have sat through the tedious hour of detaining rain, and listened to the forgotten glories of the races of Slark and Cutbush! It is a rule with *all people*, —no matter how they may be designated *now*, or how utterly their names defy the ingenuity of antiquaries to render their etymology,— to derive their ancestral honours from the time of William the Conqueror! It is true that the bastard Duke had a general letter of licence for the enlistment of all the vagabonds that swarmed in Europe at the period of his expedition; and we know how many ruffians of all classes, from the predatory baron to the pillaging freebooter, thronged to his standard,—and so far there may often be some show of reason in the pretension.

But our claimants for origin among the Conqueror's *noblesse* are not to be expected to dwell on this point with historical minuteness; what they wish to imply when they tell us that "the Smookers and Tites came over with the Conqueror," is, that they were equal in station to the De Albinis and De Warennes, who led their forces to the battle of Hastings, and gave the Conqueror his crown.

"Ours is a very old family indeed," says a thick-headed Devonshire squire, with scarcely wit enough to spell the name he bears,— "we came over with William the Conqueror: the Chubbs are a very old family; the first of the name was William the Conqueror's standard-bearer, Reginald de Chubb. Here's our coat of arms, we've got it on *all* our carriages,—three Chubs proper, in a field vert; the crest a hand and dagger,—*because* he saved the king's life!"

We knew this man's grandfather well, "excellent well,—he was a fishmonger," and sold the chubs he boasts of!

Miss Eleanor Pogson Lillicrap is a very fine young lady indeed; she discourses much on the gentility of Pa's and Ma's family, but chiefly of Ma's.

"The Lillicraps are very ancient,—a very old family in Sussex,—settled there long before Magna Charta; indeed, I believe they came over with the Conqueror. But the Pogsons — Ma's family—are much older,—in fact, descended directly from Alfred."

And this is perfectly true;—Alfred Pogson kept a butcher's shop at Brighton, and was Miss Eleanor's grandfather!

Some persons are not content with one bad name, but write and engrave it in duplicate. There are the Brown Browns, and the Jackson Jacksons, the Cooper Coopers, and the Grimes Grimeses. These families consist of many members, every one of whom is enumerated at the greatest possible length. We once saw the programme of some private theatricals to be enacted one Christmas at the Gamsons',—we beg pardon, the Gamson Gamsons'. It ran as follows,—the play being Romeo and Juliet:

Romeo	Mr. Gamson Gamson.
Mercutio	Mr. John Gamson Gamson.
Benvolio	Mr. Charles Peter Gamson Gamson.
Tybalt	Mr. James Timbury Gamson Gamson.
Capulet	Mr. Philip de Walker Gamson Gamson.
Friar Lawrence	Mr. Wellington Gamson Gamson.
Juliet	Miss Gamson Gamson.
Lady Capulet	Mrs. Gamson Gamson.
Nurse	Miss Horatia Gamson Gamson.
Page	Miss Octavia Juliana Gamson Gamson.

And, had there been more characters to fill up, there would still have been Gamson Gamsons to supply the vacuum.

Double-named people abound in watering-places, and shine in subscription-lists. The Master of the Ceremonies' book faithfully announces the arrival of Mr. and Mrs. Bennett Hoskins Abrahall, and Sir Joseph and Lady Moggridge Shankey. We are told in the provincial records of "fashionable movements" that Mr. Raggs Thimbleby has taken a house for the season on the New Steine at Brighton; and that Mrs. Pilcher Frisby intends to pass the winter at Cheltenham. The Poles are in distress, and require a subscription; who heads the list?—Mr. Munt Spriggins! There is to be a meeting in favour of the Spitalfields weavers; who takes the chair?—Sir Runnacles Faddy! But there would be no end to the list were we to enumerate even a tithe of those who "rush into our head." The proverb which dooms the dog to destruction that bears "an ill name" is reversed in the case of man; affix whatever inharmonious compound you please to the patronymic of a Briton, and you only add to his celebrity: and we are firmly of opinion that the time is not far distant, when, the powers of permutation being exhausted, opprobrious epithets will assume their place in the rank of names, and figure in the annals of fashion; Sir Ruffian Rascal will then walk arm-in-arm with Lord Percy Plantagenet, and the "lovely and accomplished" Miss Mortimer be led to the altar by the wealthy and fashionable Sir Swindle Bully!

ANOTHER ORIGINAL OF "NOT A DRUM WAS HEARD."

Our readers will recollect that in our first number the facetious priest of Water-grass-hill made a notable discovery that the Rev. Mr. Wolfe's celebrated lyric on the burial of Sir John Moore was not original, but a translation from a French poem written to commemorate the loss of a certain Colonel de Beaumanoir, who fell in India while defending Pondicherry against the forces of Coote. Father Prout, it is well known, loves a joke, and we must be cautious how we receive his evidence, more especially as another claim to the original of Mr. Wolfe's lines has been set up on behalf of a German poet. The following verses were found, it is said, in the monastery of Oliva, near Danzig, where it is well known that, during the Swedish war in Germany under Gustavus Adolph, a Swedish general of the name of Thorstenson fell on the ramparts of Danzig, and was buried during the night on the spot. Our readers must determine the question for themselves. Our own mind is thoroughly made up as to this controversy.

> Kein Grabgesang, keine Trommel erscholl
>   Als zum Wall' seine Leiche wir huben;
> Kein Krieger schoss ihm sein Lebewohl
>   Wo wir still unsern Helden begruben.
>
> Wir gruben in stummer Nacht ihn ein
>   Mit Bayonetten in Erd' und in Trümmer,
> Bey des trüben Mondlichts schwankendem Schein
>   Und der matten Lanterne Geflimmer.
>
> Kein unnützer Sarg seine Brust einhegt',
>   Nicht mit Linnen und Tüchern bedecket;
> Er lag, wie ein Krieger sich schlafen legt,
>   Im Soldatenmantel gestrecket.
>
> Gar lange Gebete hielten wir nicht,
>   Wir sprachen kein Wort von Sorgen;
> Wir schauten nur fest auf das todte Gesicht
>   Und dachten mit Schmerz an den Morgen.
>
> Wir dachten, als wir gewühlet sein Bett'
>   Und sein einsames Kissen gezogen,
> Wie Fremdling und Feind über 's Haupt ihm geht,
>   Wenn fern wir über den Wogen.
>
> Wenn sie über der kalten Asche sodann
>   Den entflohenen Geist mögen kränken:
> Er achtet es nicht, wenn er ruhen nur kann
>   In der Gruft wo ihn Schweden versenken.
>
> Unser schweres Geschäft war nur halb gethan,
>   Als die Glocke zum Rückzug ertönte;
> Wir hörten der Feinde Geschosse nahn,
>   Da die ferne Kanone erdröhnte.
>
> Wir legten ihn langsam und traurig hinein,
>   Frisch blutend vom Felde der Ehren;
> Wir liessen, ohn' Grabmal und Leichenstein,
>   Ihn nur mit dem Ruhme gewähren.

INDEX

TO

THE SECOND VOLUME.

END OF THE SECOND VOLUME.

LONDON:
PRINTED BY SAMUEL BENTLEY,
Dorset-Street, Fleet-Street.